Teaching Language in Context

2nd edition

Alice Omaggio Hadley

University of Illinois at Urbana-Champaign

Also available:

Teaching Language in Context - Workbook

by Elizabeth Rieken

0-8384-4068-1

Heinle & Heinle Publishers

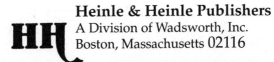

A Division of Wadsworth, Inc.

Boston, Massachusetts 02116

Dedication

To my husband Henry, with my deepest appreciation for his patience, encouragement, and support throughout this project.

Publisher: Stanley J. Galek
Editorial Director: Janet Dracksdorf
Marketing Managers: Elaine Uzan Leary; Cheryl Carlson; Susan Mraz
Production Editor: Pamela Warren
Editorial Production Manager: Elizabeth Holthaus
Manufacturing Coordinator: Jerry Christopher
Cover Design: Hannus Design Associates
Text Design and Electronic Composition and Prepress: PC&F, Inc.
Illustrations: Len Shalansky

Manufactured in the United States of America
ISBN 0-8384-4067-3

Heinle & Heinle Publishers is a division of Wadsworth, Inc.

10 9 8 7 6 5 4 3 2

Table of Contents

Preface

The language teaching profession of the 1990s has been both blessed and challenged by the substantial growth and expansion of knowledge that has taken place in our field in the past few decades. We have been blessed with a renewal of interest in language learning in this country and a greater recognition of its place in the curriculum of the future. We have been revitalized by the excitement generated as we pursue new directions in research and develop more creative ways to enhance learning in the classroom. Yet we are challenged by the many unanswered questions that our research efforts have only begun to address, and by the need to sort through the profusion of developments and ideas in our field and clarify for ourselves our own vision of the learning/teaching process.

Rod Ellis, in his excellent book entitled *Understanding Second Language Acquisition*,[1] argued that language teachers would greatly benefit from attempting to make their own theories of how second language acquisition occurs explicit. This continuing struggle to understand, clarify, and articulate one's beliefs and practices is at the very heart of what it means to be a professional. We as teachers need to be able to choose wisely among the multitude of options that are presented in the professional literature and to know why we think these choices are best. At the same time, all of us need to be willing to be open to new ideas that lead to professional growth and positive change.

This book has been written in an attempt to assist readers interested in classroom language learning in the process of clarifying their own beliefs about language teaching and learning. I have chosen to organize this second edition of *Teaching Language in Context* around the set of hypothesized principles of language teaching that I presented in the first edition—princi-

---

[1]Rod Ellis, *Understanding Second Language Acquisition* (Oxford: Oxford University Press, 1985).

ples derived in part from my own understanding of the concept of "proficiency," as described in the ACTFL Proficiency Guidelines.[2] These principles represent some of my own assumptions about teaching and are offered as one way to look at the issues before us. But the set of hypotheses are not meant to be prescriptive. As Strasheim[3] pointed out in 1976, we have moved out of the period of our professional history that was governed by absolutes. Neither are these hypothesized principles meant to define a particular methodology. Many practitioners reject the idea that one "true way" can be found for all learners, who bring a wide variety of personalities, cognitive styles, and learning preferences to our classrooms. Rather, the principles set forth in the third chapter of this new edition are derived from the theories explored in Chapters 1 and 2 and serve as an organizer for the discussion of theory and practice that unfolds in subsequent chapters.

In Chapter 1, "On Knowing a Language," various theoretical and practical insights into what it means to be competent or proficient in a language are explored. This chapter, new to this edition, extends the discussion of the first edition about the nature of language proficiency, partly in response to the proliferation of ideas about this concept and its meaning since the first edition appeared in 1986. Most of us in the foreign and second language field consider teaching "for communication" or "for proficiency" our ultimate goal. Yet what do these terms mean precisely? In recent years, concepts such as "communicative competence" and "proficiency" have been used to refer to a wide variety of practices and approaches, and undoubtedly their meanings have been overextended and sometimes distorted. These concepts are considered in this first chapter, and various theoretical models of language competence are reviewed and discussed. The *ACTFL Proficiency Guidelines* are described briefly, and oral proficiency level descriptions are summarized. Research about levels of proficiency attained by students in high school and college programs is examined, and some misconceptions about proficiency are also discussed.

Chapter 2, "On Learning a Language," is also new to this edition, expanding on some of the theoretical issues treated in the first edition of *Teaching Language in Context.* It deals with the question of how adult learners *develop* proficiency in a second language. Many new theoretical viewpoints have been advanced in the professional literature in the past two decades, and any approach to language teaching that we ultimately choose should be informed by these developments and the insights they provide. The sample of theoretical positions about the way in which adults acquire a second language has been chosen to reflect a continuum of perspectives

[2]*ACTFL Proficiency Guidelines* (Yonkers, NY: ACTFL, 1986).

[3]Lorraine Strasheim, "What is a Foreign Language Teacher Today?" *Canadian Modern Language Review* 33 (1976):39–48.

from empiricist to rationalist views. Five theoretical viewpoints are reviewed and summarized in the chapter. Because learners are not alike, theoretical models of how learners acquire language should take into account the role that learner differences might play in the process of proficiency development. The last section of the chapter is devoted to this important issue; and learner differences, learning styles, and personality variables that need to be considered when choosing teaching approaches are briefly described and discussed. This topic will also be treated in Chapters 5 through 9 when specific skills, feedback strategies, and testing principles are discussed.

In Chapter 3, a set of hypothesized principles for classroom teaching that are derived from the discussions in Chapters 1 and 2 are presented, and a rationale for each principle is given. The chapter then looks at a variety of methodological approaches, both from a historical perspective and in terms of current practices, analyzing their salient features. Underlying theoretical assumptions are explored, as well as teaching strategies and techniques that typically predominate in each approach.

Chapter 4 presents a review of the research, in both first and second language learning, regarding the role of context in the comprehension and production of discourse. Chapter 5 then offers suggestions for contextualizing listening and reading practice, as well as a rationale for incorporating such activities into classroom instruction. In this second edition, many new activities based on authentic materials have been included. The role of video and computer technology in fostering the development of listening and reading skills is also briefly discussed.

Chapters 6 and 7 provide guidelines for contextualizing practice in speaking and writing, as well as ideas for integrative activities involving listening, speaking, reading, writing, and culture. Creative language-use activities and formats for small-group communicative interaction are also presented. Some ideas for responding to specific learner problems in each of these skill areas are also highlighted.

Chapter 8 treats the teaching of culture, including various models for choosing cultural topics and materials and activities that integrate the teaching of language and culture.

Chapter 9 presents formats for proficiency-oriented classroom testing, as well as a description of oral proficiency testing techniques used in conjunction with the ACTFL and ILR proficiency guidelines (see note at end of Appendix A). Item types for classroom tests of listening, reading, speaking, writing, and integrated skills are presented in contextualized, situational formats, ranging along a continuum from "careful style" activities to those tapping the more informal or unplanned "vernacular style."[4] Additional suggestions are included in this edition for the use of authentic materials in classroom tests and quizzes.

[4]E. Tarone, "On the Variability of Interlanguage Systems." *Applied Linguistics*, 4(1983):143–63.

The final chapter synthesizes the material in the preceding pages by illustrating how daily lesson planning can reflect a proficiency-oriented approach. Practical suggestions for syllabus design, text selection, the teaching of grammar, record keeping, and the elicitation of student feedback for the improvement of instruction are discussed.

The appendices to the second edition include various practical resources for the language teacher. Appendix A includes the most recent ACTFL Proficiency Guidelines for listening, speaking, reading, and writing. The other appendices include additional illustrative material relating to Chapters 7 and 10.

The reader will notice that certain key ideas relating to the development of language proficiency recur throughout the book in cyclical fashion. For example, the concept of contextualized language use is presented in Chapter 1, where models of language competence are discussed. This concept recurs in the discussion of methodology in Chapter 3, is examined from the perspective of the researcher in Chapter 4, recurs in Chapters 5, 6, and 7 and in discussions of practical classroom techniques, appears again in Chapter 8 on teaching culture, and is central to the illustrations of testing procedures in Chapter 9. Important themes, or threads, are thus woven through the chapters to achieve an integrated perspective of language learning and teaching. Such an integrated framework is essential if we are to make reasoned and purposeful choices among the myriad of approaches, strategies, and materials available to us as language teaching professionals.

This book is designed to address the needs and concerns of those whose primary interest is the teaching of second and foreign languages to adult learners in classroom settings. It does not attempt to treat issues relating to language acquisition in children or the acquisition of a second language by learners in informal or natural settings, although it may be possible for the reader to extrapolate some ideas for these situations from some of the chapters. It is designed to be used as a basic or supplementary text in methodology courses for pre- and in-service secondary teachers and university teaching assistants, or as an up-to-date reference and resource for experienced professionals and researchers. The novice teacher or teacher trainee will find practical ideas for teaching language and culture, as well as some background information to help them formulate their own hypotheses about language learning. The experienced practitioner will, hopefully, find some new teaching ideas or gain a new perspective on some familiar techniques or approaches. It is also hoped that this book will stimulate further research and contribute to the theory-building process, a process that must continue as our knowledge about language acquisition and learning grows in the years ahead.

Alice Omaggio Hadley
Urbana, Illinois
January, 1993

Acknowledgments

I would like to express my sincere thanks and appreciation to all those colleagues and friends whose helpful comments, support, and encouragement were invaluable to me in the preparation of this book. Specifically, I would like to thank the following people, who carefully read and reviewed part or all of the manuscript in its various stages: Margaret Azevedo, Stanford University; Diane Birckbichler, Ohio State University; Jeannette Bragger, Penn State University; Cheryl Brown, Brigham Young University; Joan Carson, University of Georgia; Susan Colville-Hall, University of Akron; Kathy Corl, Ohio State University; Eileen Glisan, Indiana University of Pennsylvania; Gail Guntermann, Arizona State University; JoAnn Hammadou, University of Rhode Island; Carol Klee, University of Minnesota; Katherine Kulick, College of William and Mary; Judith Liskin-Gasparro, Middlebury College; Sally Magnan, University of Wisconsin, Madison; Laura Martin, Cleveland State University; Keith Mason, University of Virginia; Genelle Morain, University of Georgia; Betty Myer, Miami University of Ohio; June Phillips, Tennessee Foreign Language Institute; Virginia Scott, Vanderbilt University; Judith Shrum, Virginia Polytechnic Institute and State University; Susan St. Onge, Christopher Newport College; Janet Swaffar, University of Texas, Austin; Robert Terry, University of Richmond; and Barbara Wing, University of New Hampshire.

I would also like to thank Charles H. Heinle and Stanley J. Galek of Heinle & Heinle Publishers for being open to the approach that I wished to take in this book, and for their unconditional support of the project from start to finish. I owe a very special debt of gratitude to Janet Dracksdorf and Pam Warren, whose careful work and unending patience in the editing of the manuscript and the follow-through in galleys and page proofs is appreciated. Special thanks are due also to Kathleen Sands Boehmer who copyedited the manuscript.

A.O.H.

1

On Knowing a Language: Defining and Assessing Proficiency

Introduction

The language teaching profession has recently experienced substantial growth due to the rapid expansion of knowledge that has taken place in our field in the past few decades. There has been an abundance of creative new approaches, materials, teaching ideas, and technological innovations in recent years, and no lack of stimulating, scholarly debate about how best to use them. Never before in our professional history have we had so many choices; never before has the need for professionalism and critical judgment been clearer. The struggle to understand, clarify, and articulate one's beliefs and practices is at the very heart of what it means to be a professional.

This book has been written in an attempt to assist teachers, teacher educators, and students interested in classroom language learning in the process of clarifying their own beliefs about language learning and teaching, both in terms of theoretical issues and practical implications for classroom instruction. Its purpose is, therefore, not to promote a particular theory or methodology; rather, it seeks to review and summarize past and current language acquisition theories, examine various recent trends that have influenced teaching practice, and extract from our rich heritage of resources those elements that seem most relevant to the construction of viable models for teaching.

Consider for a moment the fundamental question: "How can we help students learning a second language in a classroom setting become proficient in that language?" As we explore that question further, at least three subquestions emerge:

1. What does *proficient* mean?
2. How do people become proficient in a language?
3. What characterizes a classroom environment in which opportunities to become proficient are maximized?

With each of these subquestions, a new area of inquiry is opened, raising issues that are equally difficult to resolve. Being proficient implies that one *knows* a language, but to what degree? A given student might *know* a little German, but not enough to really *do* anything with it. The student's knowledge of another foreign language, Spanish, will allow him or her to carry on a simple conversation and handle his or her needs as a tourist. But the student wouldn't say that he or she really knows Spanish. The individual certainly does not claim to be proficient in that language. What does *knowing a language* involve? How proficient can people become in a language other than their own? Is there a difference between the way people learn their native language and the way they learn a second one? What does *learn* mean? Can people become proficient in a second language in a formal classroom environment? Is the age at which a person begins to acquire a language a factor? To what degree or level can a person's competence develop in a second language if he or she begins study as an adult? What are the features of a proficiency-oriented approach to instruction? What curriculum and materials should a teacher choose?

These are only a few of the many questions that challenge us as language teachers. In this and subsequent chapters, some of the answers that have been proposed in recent years to questions such as these are explored. Chapter 1 looks at the issue of language proficiency and how that concept might be defined and understood. Chapter 2 summarizes some of the theoretical approaches to the question of how adults become proficient in a second language. Chapter 3 then proposes a set of hypothesized principles of language teaching that are derived from the issues surrounding the concept of proficiency. These principles serve, in turn, as an organizer for the chapters that follow.

• • • • • • • • • • • *Defining Language Proficiency*

What does it mean to be *proficient* in a language? What does one have to know in terms of grammar, vocabulary, sociolinguistic appropriateness, kinesics, cultural understanding, and the like in order to know a language well enough to use it for some real-world purpose?

We might shed some light on these questions by understanding first what *proficient* means in a more general context. The *American Heritage Dictionary of the English Language* (1978) defines *proficient* as "performing in a given art, skill or branch of learning with expert correctness and facility," and further specifies that the term implies "a high degree of competence through training." Implied in this definition, then, is the idea that *proficiency* refers to a somewhat idealized level of competence and performance, attainable by experts through extensive instruction.

The terms *competence* and *performance*, as used in the dictionary definition, introduce yet another complication, especially for those familiar with the field of languages and linguistics. These two terms, used for centuries by philosophers and scientists to characterize all types of knowledge (Brown 1980), were fundamental to Chomsky's (1965) theory of transformational-generative grammar. In his theory, Chomsky distinguished between an *idealized* native speaker's underlying *competence* (referring to one's implicit or explicit knowledge of the system of the language) and the individual's *performance* (or one's actual production and comprehension of language in specific instances of language use). Because the native speaker's performance is so often imperfect, due to such factors as memory limitations, distractions, errors, hesitations, false starts, repetitions, and pauses, Chomsky believed that actual performance did not properly reflect the underlying knowledge that linguistic theory sought to describe:

> *Linguistic theory is concerned primarily with an ideal speaker-listener, in a completely homogeneous speech community, who knows its language perfectly and is unaffected by such grammatically irrelevant conditions as memory limitations, distractions, shifts of attention and interest, errors (random or characteristic) in applying his knowledge to the language in actual performance (p. 3).*

Thus, Chomsky felt that, for the purposes of developing a linguistic theory, it was important to make the competence-performance distinction. He also believed it was necessary to study and describe language through idealized abstractions rather than through records of natural speech, which was so often flawed.

From Grammatical Competence to Communicative Competence

Chomsky's competence-performance distinction served as the basis for the work of many other researchers interested in the nature of language acquisition. In an influential position paper published in 1980, Michael Canale and Merrill Swain (1980a) reviewed and evaluated the various theoretical perspectives on competence and performance that had been articulated in response to Chomsky's work. According to their review, two of the most notable extensions to Chomsky's theory came from Campbell and Wales (1970) and Hymes (1972). Campbell and Wales accepted Chomsky's methodological distinction between competence and actual performance, but they pointed out that Chomsky's conceptualization of these terms did not include any reference to either the *appropriateness* of an utterance to a particular situation or context or its *sociocultural significance*. For Campbell and Wales, the degree to which a person's production or understanding of the language is appropriate to the context in which it takes place is even more important than its grammaticality. They referred to Chomsky's very restricted view of competence as "grammatical competence," and to their more inclusive view as "communicative competence" (Campbell and Wales 1970, p. 249).

Hymes (1972) also felt that there are rules of language use that are neglected in Chomsky's view of language. Like Campbell and Wales, Hymes espoused a much broader view, in which grammatical competence is but one component of the overall knowledge the native speaker possesses. This broader notion of "communicative competence" incorporated sociolinguistic and contextual competence as well as grammatical competence.

During the 1970s, some linguists and researchers, proceeding from the earlier work previously cited, began to refer to "communicative competence" as a notion that was distinct from "grammatical" or "linguistic" competence. As Canale and Swain (1980a) point out, there was some disagreement in the literature of the 1970s about whether or not the notion of communicative competence included grammatical competence as one of its components.

> *It is common to find the term "communicative competence" used to refer exclusively to knowledge or capability relating to the rules of language use, and the term "grammatical (or linguistic) competence" used to refer to the rules of grammar. . . . It is equally common to find these terms used in the manner in which Hymes (1972) and Campbell and Wales (1970) use them (p. 5).*

Perhaps one of the best-known studies involving the concept of communicative competence in the early 1970s was that done by Savignon (1972) at the University of Illinois. In that study, Savignon sought to compare the effects of various types of practice on communicative skills development. Her definition of communicative competence did incorporate linguistic competence as one of its components: "*Communicative competence may be defined as the ability to function in a truly communicative setting—that is, in a dynamic exchange in which linguistic competence must adapt itself to the total informational input, both linguistic and paralinguistic, of one or more interlocutors*" (p. 8). She went on to point out that successful communication would depend largely on the individual's willingness to take a risk and express himself in the foreign language, and on his resourcefulness in using the vocabulary and structures under his control to make himself understood. According to Savignon, the use of gestures, intonation, and facial expression also contributes to communication, but linguistic accuracy, though of some importance, should be considered as only one of the major constituents of a communicative exchange.

In a later definition of communicative competence, Savignon (1983) outlines the following characteristics:

1. Communicative competence is a dynamic rather than a static concept that depends on the *negotiation of meaning* between two or more persons who share some knowledge of the language. "In this sense, then, communicative competence can be said to be an *interpersonal* rather than an intrapersonal trait" (p. 8).

2. Communicative competence should not be thought of as only an oral phenomenon. It applies to both written and spoken language.

3. Communicative competence is context-specific, in that communication always takes place in a particular context or situation. The communicatively competent language user will know how to make appropriate choices in register and style to fit the particular situation in which communication occurs.

4. It is important to bear in mind the theoretical distinction between *competence* and *performance*. "Competence is what one *knows*. Performance is what one *does*. Only performance is observable, however, and it is only through performance that competence can be developed, maintained, and evaluated" (p. 9).

5. Communicative competence is *relative* and depends on the cooperation of all those involved. "It makes sense, then, to speak of *degrees* of communicative competence" (p. 9).

Savignon's view of the notion of communicative competence emphasizes the negotiative nature of communication. This is certainly an important point, and one that should be kept in mind when assessing any given sample of speech, writing, or receptive skills performance.

Most of the definitions of communicative competence discussed in Canale and Swain's (1980a) review include slightly different components or view the relationship or importance of components to be somewhat different. As mentioned earlier, the role of grammatical competence seems to be the most controversial. Munby (1978) contends that the term "communicative competence" should include the notion of grammatical competence. Failure to include it in the definition might lead one to conclude: (1) that grammatical competence and communicative competence need to be developed separately, usually with attention given first to grammar; and (2) that grammatical competence is not an essential component of communicative competence. Canale and Swain (1980a) maintain that even instructors who agree that grammatical competence is indeed an important part of communicative competence could still prefer to address grammatical competence separately from or prior to the teaching of sociolinguistic rules of language use:

> *Just as Hymes (1972) was able to say that there are rules of grammar that would be useless without rules of language use, so we feel that there are rules of language use that would be useless without rules of grammar (p. 5).*

In order to determine how one might best design communicative approaches to language teaching, Canale and Swain felt it was necessary to clarify further the concept of "communicative competence." Drawing on the work of scholars such as Campbell and Wales (1970), Hymes (1972), Savignon (1972), Charolles (1978), Munby (1978), and Widdowson (1978), they formulated a model of communicative competence that would eventually consist of four major components: (1) grammatical competence, (2) sociolinguistic competence, (3) discourse competence, and (4) strategic competence.

In the Canale and Swain model (1980a; Canale 1983a), *grammatical competence* refers to the degree to which the language user has mastered the linguistic code, including knowledge of vocabulary, rules of pronunciation and spelling, word formation, and sentence structure. Canale and Swain (1980b) maintain that such competence is an essential concern for any communicative approach that is oriented toward the eventual attainment of higher levels of proficiency, in which accuracy and precision of understanding and expression are important goals.

Sociolinguistic competence addresses the extent to which grammatical forms can be used or understood appropriately in various contexts to convey specific communicative functions, such as describing, narrating, persuading, eliciting information, and the like. Such factors as topic, role of the participants, and setting will determine the appropriateness of the attitude conveyed by speakers and their choice of style or register. Brown (1980) uses the term "register" to refer to the many styles available to proficient speakers of a language. Speakers can vary their choice of vocabulary, syntax, pronunciation, intonation, and even nonverbal features to tailor their message for a particular person or social context. Registers range from very informal to very formal styles, and apply to both spoken and written discourse. Brown points out that the skilled use of appropriate registers requires sensitivity to cross-cultural differences, making this type of competence especially difficult to attain (pp. 192–93).

Discourse competence, the third component of the Canale and Swain model, involves the ability to combine ideas to achieve cohesion in form and coherence in thought. A person who has a highly developed degree of discourse competence will know how to use cohesive devices, such as pronouns and grammatical connectors (i.e., conjunctions, adverbs, and transitional phrases), to achieve unity of thought and continuity in a text. The competent language user will also be skilled in expressing and judging the relationships among the different ideas in a text (coherence). (See also Widdowson 1978; Hatch 1978, 1983, 1984, 1992; Brown and Yule 1983; and Larsen-Freeman and Long 1991 for further discussions of the role of discourse factors in language use.)

Strategic competence, the final component of the model, involves the use of verbal and nonverbal communication strategies to compensate for gaps in the language user's knowledge of the code or for breakdown in communication because of performance factors. Canale (1983b) adds that strategic competence can also be used to enhance the rhetorical effectiveness of one's communication (p. 339). This component is qualitatively different from the other three in that it emphasizes the use of effective strategies in negotiating meaning. Students at lower levels of proficiency can benefit from learning effective communication strategies such as paraphrasing through circumlocution or approximations, using gestures, and asking others to repeat or speak more slowly.

Although Canale and Swain refer to their theoretical framework as a model of communicative competence, they acknowledge that the term "communicative competence" itself may be problematic, since there has been so much disagreement and confusion about what it means. Canale (1983a) maintains that "the distinction between communicative competence and actual communication remains poorly understood . . . in the second language field" (p. 4). He prefers the term "actual communication" to the earlier term "communicative performance" used in the 1980 version of the model, since the latter term tends to lead to confusion with Chomsky's competence-performance distinction. Canale stresses, however, that his use of the term "communicative competence" refers to both underlying knowledge about language and communicative language use and skill, or how well an individual can perform with this knowledge base in actual communication situations.

The Canale and Swain model has had a great deal of influence on the thinking of many scholars who are working towards a better understanding of what communicative language proficiency entails. Bachman (1990) has proposed a model for a theoretical framework of "communicative language ability" that incorporates some of the same components identified by Canale and Swain, but arranged and explained in a somewhat different fashion. His framework consists of three major components: (1) language competence, (2) strategic competence, and (3) psychophysiological mechanisms. The first component is made up of various kinds of knowledge that we use in communicating via language, whereas the second and third components include the mental capacities and physical mechanisms by which that knowledge is implemented in communicative language use. Bachman identifies the first component—*language competence*—as "knowledge of language" (p. 85), and relates it to other frameworks of communicative competence such as those described by Hymes (1972), Munby (1978), Canale and Swain (1980), and Canale (1983). The components of language competence are depicted in Illustration 1.1. In Bachman's description of *language competence*, two major types of abilities are included. The first is *organizational competence*, which relates to controlling the formal structure of language (*grammatical competence*) and knowing how to construct discourse (*textual competence*). The second type of ability is called *pragmatic competence*, which relates to the functional use of language (*illocutionary competence*) and knowledge of its appropriateness to the context in which it is used (*sociolinguistic competence*). Each of the four subcomponents of the model is further defined, as shown in Illustration 1.1. *Grammatical competence* includes control of vocabulary, morphology,

Illustration 1.1
Components of
language competence.

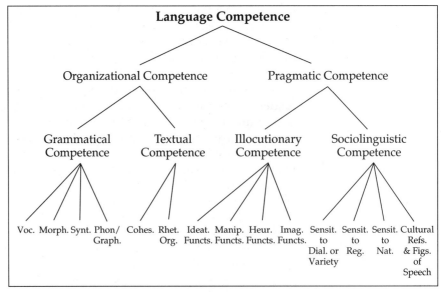

Source: L. Bachman, *Fundamental Considerations in Language Testing.* Oxford: Oxford University Press, 1990, p. 87. Reprinted by permission of the Oxford University Press.

syntax, and phonemic and graphemic elements; *textual competence* includes cohesion and rhetorical organization. *Illocutionary competence* comprises control of functional features of language, such as the ability to express ideas and emotions (*ideational functions*), to get things done (*manipulative functions*), to use language to teach, learn and solve problems (*heuristic functions*), and to be creative (*imaginative functions*). Finally, *sociolinguistic competence* includes such things as sensitivity to dialect and register, naturalness (or native-like use of language) and understanding of cultural referents and figures of speech (Bachman, 1990, pp. 87–98).

Bachman's framework represents a promising alternative for looking at communicative language ability and for addressing the question: "What does it mean to know a language?"

The models of language ability described in this section have been derived from various theoretical perspectives about the nature of language and language use. In the next section, we will examine the development of a model of language ability that arose initially not from a particular theoretical perspective on language competence or performance, but from a series of grass-roots initiatives originating among practitioners.

Communicative Competence and the Notion of Proficiency

In one sense, a focus on proficiency has always driven language learning and teaching. Obviously, no program has ever claimed to be oriented toward "non-proficiency" or incompetence. Yet it is only within the past decade or so that practitioners have begun to use the term "proficiency" in a new light. Prior to the communicative language teaching movement of the 1970s, foreign language proficiency had been defined and conceptualized largely in terms of structural accuracy by many members of the academic community. In the past twenty years, many teachers have come to understand that language proficiency is not a monolithic concept representing an amorphous ideal that students rarely attain; rather it is comprised of a whole range of abilities that must be described in a graduated fashion in order to be meaningful.

With the definitions of "communicative competence" of the 1970s came new insights into the various components of language ability that needed to be developed in order to know a language well enough to use it. Yet most of these early models did not specify *levels* of competence in a way that could help practitioners measure their students' progress or articulate program goals. Across language learners and language programs, the degrees of proficiency needed, desired, or attained can vary considerably, depending on such factors as purpose, motivation for language study, or learning environment. Without a clear understanding of what we mean by "proficiency," communication about goals and outcomes and articulation among programs and settings can be difficult and frustrating. As Higgs and Clifford (1982) indicated, some specification about levels of proficiency and what they mean is needed to help refine the concept for practitioners:

> *A student cannot merely be declared competent in communication. The functions that he is competent to express must be specified. The degree of proficiency required to survive as a tourist is not the same as that required to negotiate treaties. One finds that content areas and language functions needed for discussing abstract ideas differ from those used in telling about one's immediate needs or one's latest European vacation. . . .We must tell [our students] not that they are competent to speak German, but that they are competent to meet routine physical and social obligations in an environment where German is spoken (pp. 60–61).*

The *ACTFL Provisional Proficiency Guidelines*, published in November 1982, were the first attempt by the foreign language teaching profession to define and describe levels of functional competence for the academic context in a comprehensive fashion. The history of the development of these guidelines has been outlined by Liskin-Gasparro (1984), who traces the "quest for proficiency" from its antecedents in the ancient world to the modern conceptualizations of the 1970s (p. 13). It was during this decade that a convergence of events—the establishment of the President's Commission on Foreign Language and International Studies, the work in communicative syllabus design in Europe, the beginning of communicative language teaching movements in the United States, and the work of government agencies to refine the ways in which functional language ability was taught and tested—led to a series of projects that would give birth to a significant new movement in language education (p. 13). Some of the events described in Liskin-Gasparro's comprehensive historical review are highlighted below.

The Move Toward National Standards

Throughout the history of language teaching, instructors and curriculum specialists have attempted to set goals and define outcomes for language learning to foster greater articulation among levels of instruction and improve communication about what was being accomplished. For decades, these goal statements, articulated on the local or state level, had taken the form of long lists of topics to be "covered." Achievement tests were designed by individual teachers to see how well students had learned the designated material. Yet comprehensive lists of content and tests of discrete linguistic features seemed to have limited usefulness in shaping and changing language instruction in any significant way. By the late 1970s, it was becoming increasingly clear that the focus of curricular planning and testing would need to shift from a micro-analysis of what was being *taught* to a macro-analysis of what students could actually do with the language before any real progress could be made (Scebold 1992).

By the end of the decade, it had become increasingly apparent that a widely used, nationally approved procedure for assessing language proficiency was needed. It seemed that the academic community was ready to seek some consensus on defining more clearly than ever before proficiency goals and standards for second language programs. This interest in setting standards reflected the more general concern about excellence in education that was brewing on the national level. The need for standards in the area of foreign languages and international studies was pointed out by Paul Simon (Illinois) and other congressmen, who, together with language professional organizations, urged the establishment of a special presidential commission. This initiative was supported by President Jimmy Carter, and in April 1978 the President's Commission on Foreign Language and International Studies was formed.

In the commission's report published a year later (*Strength through Wisdom*, 1979) it became painfully apparent that this nation was in serious trouble in terms of the foreign language competence of its citizenry. Statements such as "Americans' incompetence in foreign languages is nothing short of scandalous, and it is becoming worse" (p. 12) brought national attention to the need for support of second language education programs in the nation's schools. Equally disturbing were facts reported about the ignorance of high school students in international matters. The commission found, for example, that 40 percent of 12th graders could not locate Egypt on a map!

Among recommendations included in the commission's report was that a "National Criteria and Assessment Program" be established to develop foreign language proficiency tests and to report on, monitor, and assess foreign language teaching in the United States. This recommendation paralleled other similar recommendations that had been made by the MLA-ACLS Language Task Force for the President's Commission in late 1978:

Recommendation 10. Institutions and, where appropriate, state educational systems should be encouraged by the Modern Language Association to adopt *nationally recognized performance or proficiency standards,* and make such standards known widely to students and faculty.

Recommendation 12. The Modern Language Association and the American Council on the Teaching of Foreign Languages should secure funding for the *revision and redevelopment of tests for the measurement of proficiencies in the four language skills in all the most commonly taught and wide-use languages.* Such tests should be developed by committees consisting of both secondary school and college teachers. (Brod 1980, cited in Liskin-Gasparro 1984).

At the same time that the MLA-ACLS task forces were making the above recommendations, the Educational Testing Service (ETS) was approaching the problem of proficiency testing from another perspective. As early as 1970, Protase Woodford of ETS had coined the term *Common Yardstick,* which would be used some ten years later to refer to a project attempting to define language proficiency levels for academic contexts using a scale parallel to the one used by federal government schools since World War II (Liskin-Gasparro 1984). The government scale had been developed in the early 1950s by linguists at one of the major government language schools, the Foreign Service Institute (FSI), in order to describe the speaking abilities of candidates for foreign service positions. It made provision for eleven major ranges of proficiency, beginning with 0 (no functional ability in the language) to 5 (proficiency equivalent to that of an educated native speaker), using "+" designations between levels. (See Illustration 1.2 for a brief description of the scale.)

In addition to the proficiency scale, FSI had developed an interview-based evaluation procedure for assigning a rating. This procedure was also of interest to the *Common Yardstick* project. During the 1970s, ETS cooperated with other organizations in Great Britain and Germany, representatives of the U.S. government, and business and academic groups, to develop and refine the proficiency scales and the interview procedure for academic use (Liskin-Gasparro 1984). The outcome of this project was an adaptation of the government scale, currently known as the ILR (Interagency Language Roundtable) scale, involving an expansion of the lower levels

Illustration 1.2
Relationship of the
ILR Scale to the ACTFL
Scale.

ACTFL Scale	ILR Scale
	5 Native or bilingual proficiency
	4+
	4 Distinguished proficiency
	3+
Superior	3 Professional working proficiency
Advanced High	2+
Advanced	2 Limited working proficiency
Intermediate High	1+
Intermediate Mid	1 Survival proficiency
Intermediate Low	
Novice High	0+
Novice Mid	0 No practical proficiency
Novice Low	

Source: Buck, Byrnes, and Thompson, 1989, p. 2–15. Reprinted by permission of ACTFL.

to allow greater latitude and precision in describing proficiency below ILR Level 2.

The work begun by the *Common Yardstick* project was continued in 1981 by the American Council on the Teaching of Foreign Languages (ACTFL), in consultation with MLA, ETS, and other professional associations, under a grant entitled "A Design for Measuring and Communicating Foreign Language Proficiency." Some of the groundwork for this project had been laid by ACTFL in 1978 when a planning grant was obtained to begin work on the drafting of proficiency standards. This earlier project included a comprehensive literature review, the convening of European and American experts on syllabus design and testing, consultations with various language organizations and publishers, and meetings with practitioners. The 1981 project brought together a large number of scholars who worked together to create both the generic and language-specific proficiency descriptions known as the *ACTFL Provisional Proficiency Guidelines*. The statements they created for speaking, listening, reading, writing, and culture were evaluated by scholars at various universities, critiqued by potential users, and disseminated in November of 1982 in provisional form. Since 1982 they have been reviewed and revised as new insights and knowledge have been incorporated. (See Liskin-Gasparro 1987 for specific details about revisions in the 1986 guidelines. The most recent generic descriptions are provided in Appendix A.)

As one reviews some of the history surrounding these developments, it becomes clear that the proficiency guidelines were essentially the product of a number of grass-roots initiatives. The projects were informed by literature reviews and consultation with scholars who had expertise in various theoretical perspectives of language learning. But rather than emerging from a particular theory of language learning, they came about primarily as a result of the perceived needs of practitioners in both government and academic settings who wanted to make a difference in the way languages were taught and communicate more effectively about the results of that instruction. As Ed Scebold, Executive Director of ACTFL, expressed it, the initiators of the proficiency projects used their many years of experience as teachers, their good sense, and trial and error to make the system come together (Scebold 1992). Yet in spite of the fact that the proficiency descriptions were not initiated from a particular theoretical perspective, they share many of the same components of other theoretically-derived models of communicative language ability, such as the one developed by Canale and Swain, described earlier. The congruence of these various models will become clear as we look at the way in which proficiency is assessed using the *ACTFL Proficiency Guidelines*, to be discussed in the next section.

Assessing Language Proficiency Using the ACTFL Proficiency Guidelines

The *ACTFL Proficiency Guidelines* define and measure language ability in speaking, listening, reading, and writing. Global ratings are assigned by eliciting samples of performance and evaluating those samples using a set of interrelated criteria. It is important to understand that the scale described in Illustration 1.2 is not linear in nature; rather, it is a multidimensional, expanding spiral (Liskin-Gasparro 1987). As one goes up the scale, progressively more language skill is needed to attain the next level. It might be helpful to think of the proficiency levels in terms of an inverted pyramid, such as the one depicted in Illustration 1.3.

One can see that relatively little positive change is needed to progress from the Novice level to Intermediate, but that relatively more change is

Illustration 1.3
Inverted Pyramid
Representing ACTFL
Rating Scale with Major
Ranges and Sublevels.

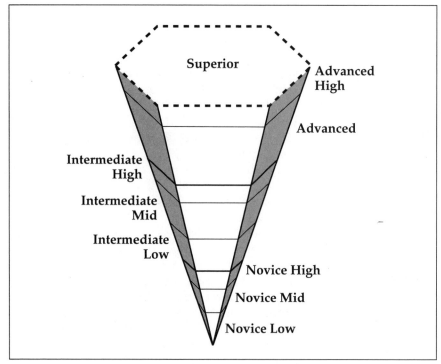

Source: Buck, Byrnes, and Thompson, 1989, p. 2–14. Reprinted by permission of ACTFL.

needed to make the leap from the Intermediate level to Advanced, and so on up the scale. The Superior level of proficiency on the ACTFL scale corresponds to Levels 3, 4, and 5 on the government scale (see Illustration 1.2). As Liskin-Gasparro (1984) points out, the most difficult leap on the ILR scale is from Level 4 to Level 5. Indeed, it is unusual for non-native speakers to attain the latter rating.

Levels of proficiency on the ACTFL scale can be distinguished by considering the five interrelated assessment criteria underlying the proficiency descriptions: **global tasks/functions, context, content, accuracy**, and **text type**. Illustration 1.4 presents the assessment criteria for speaking proficiency as they appear in the 1989 *ACTFL Oral Proficiency Interview Tester Training Manual* (Buck, Byrnes, and Thompson 1989). These criteria are interrelated in that the Oral Proficiency Interview (OPI) is an *integrative* test, "i.e., it addresses a number of abilities simultaneously and looks at them from a global perspective rather than from the point of view of the presence or absence of any given linguistic feature" (p. 3–1). One should therefore not think in terms of discrete points of grammar or discrete tasks or skills when considering a rating of a speech sample. Trained testers are skilled in their ability to use the assessment criteria to assign a global rating based on the overall communicative ability of the speaker.

Global Tasks/ Functions	Context	Content	Accuracy	Text Type
Superior Can discuss extensively by supporting opinions, abstracting and hypothesizing	Most formal and informal settings	Wide range of general interest topics and some special fields of interest and expertise; concrete, abstract and unfamiliar topics	Errors virtually never interfere with communication or disturb the native speaker	Extended discourse
Advanced Can describe and narrate in major time/aspect frames	Most informal and some formal settings	Concrete and factual topics of personal and public interest	Can be understood without difficulty by speakers unaccustomed to nonnative speakers	Paragraph discourse
Intermediate Can maintain simple face-to-face conversation by asking and responding to simple questions	Some informal settings and a limited number of transactional situations	Topics related primarily to self and immediate environment	Can be understood, with some repetition, by speakers accustomed to non-native speakers	Discrete sentences and strings of sentences
Novice Can produce only formulaic utterances, lists and enumerations	Highly predictable common daily settings	Common discrete elements of daily life	May be difficult to understand, even for those accustomed to non-native speakers	Discrete words and phrases

Illustration 1.4
ACTFL Assessment
Criteria: Speaking
Proficiency

Source: Buck, Byrnes, and Thompson, 1989, p. 3–9. Reprinted by permission of ACTFL.

A brief description of each of these criteria, as summarized from the *ACTFL Oral Proficiency Tester Training Manual* is given below:

- **Global tasks/functions** refers to real-world tasks that the speaker can do in the language. At the lowest level of the scale, functions such as naming various objects or using basic greetings are typically within the ability of the persons interviewed. In the Intermediate range, interviewees can handle somewhat more challenging tasks such as describing a person or place simply, or asking for information. Persons rated as Advanced are capable of extended description and narration in different time frames. At the highest ranges of proficiency, interviewees are capable of quite complex tasks, such as developing an argument cogently and persuasively, supporting an opinion, or discussing a hypothetical situation extensively and with sophistication. As one's proficiency increases, the complexity of the language used to accomplish these tasks and the accuracy and precision with which the task can be accomplished also increases.

• **Context** refers to "the circumstances or settings in which a person uses language" (Buck, Byrnes, and Thompson 1989, p. 3-2). At lower levels of proficiency, one can typically handle very predictable situations or contexts "which permit greater use of memorized or learned material because of the predictable, scripted nature of the settings and the concrete nature of interactions firmly based in the present" (p. 3-2). At the higher levels of proficiency, the context of conversation typically demands more of the participant due to the unpredictability of the situation and the need for flexibility in dealing with it. The sophistication of language needed to argue one's point of view in a political discussion or to handle an unexpected problem in the foreign culture typically exceeds that needed to order food in a restaurant or to ask for a night's lodging.

• The **content** dimension of the assessment criteria, referring to topics or themes of conversation, "is the *most variable element* of the OPI" (Buck, Byrnes, and Thompson 1989, p. 3-2). Each oral interview is different, as the topics discussed depend on the interests and background of the person being interviewed. However, the content at the lower levels often centers on autobiographical information and personal experiences and interests, since these types of topics allow the interviewee to stay in "the here-and-now" and deal with concrete rather than abstract content. As one's proficiency increases, the range of topics one can discuss with facility increases. At the higher levels of proficiency, the range of content that the interviewee can discuss comfortably and with facility is as wide as that typically handled in the native language.

The **content** dimension of the assessment criteria should not be thought of as a hierarchical list of topics or themes. The same topic can usually be explored at virtually any level of proficiency. The following example serves to illustrate how a topic such as "the family" might be discussed differently at the various levels on the scale. *Novice* speakers might be able to enumerate the members of their families but say very little else about them. At the *Intermediate* level, speakers might give a brief description of family members or mention some of their activities or interests, whereas speakers at the *Advanced* level can talk about family members in detail, recount events that the family has shared together, or talk about future plans. At the *Superior* level, more abstract topics such as the societal forces that threaten family life, the issues surrounding family planning, or the role of the family in the target culture might be discussed. Thus, it is not the topic or content *per se*, but rather the depth and breadth of the discussion and the precision and sophistication with which it is handled that will differ from one level of proficiency to the next.

- **Accuracy** "refers to the **acceptability, quality and precision of the message** conveyed" (Buck, Byrnes, and Thompson 1989, p. 3-4). Included among the features considered when assessing accuracy are *fluency, grammar, pronunciation, vocabulary, pragmatic competence,* and *sociolinguistic competence.* Many Novice speakers tend to make errors in most or all of these areas, often rendering them incomprehensible to native speakers who are not used to dealing with foreigners. (However, it *is* possible for Novice speakers to be quite accurate, especially when using memorized material, though the amount of language they can use is extremely limited.) Generally, one can characterize speakers at the lower end of the scale as intelligible, but typically the native-speaking conversational partner bears the responsibility of negotiating communication. The OPI Tester Manual clarifies the process by which accuracy is assessed in an interview:

  > In general, **the degree to which the speaker relies on the listener for filling in gaps in the message** due to imperfect control of the language is one way to assess accuracy. As proficiency increases, the responsibility of the interlocutor for negotiating the message decreases. At the same time, the global tasks associated with higher levels of proficiency—describing, narrating, hypothesizing, supporting opinion, and dealing with abstractions—require refined and elaborated use of grammatical, lexical and sociolinguistic rules as well as effective use of cohesive devices to transmit complex messages. Mere intelligibility will not suffice, and most of the responsibility for carrying on the conversation can no longer be placed primarily on the listener (Buck, Byrnes, and Thompson 1989, p. 3-6).

- **Text type** in the set of assessment criteria refers to the structure of the discourse, i.e., "the quantity and organizational aspects of speech" (Buck, Byrnes, and Thompson 1989, p. 3-6). Typically, speakers rated as Novice can produce mainly isolated words or phrases, whereas Intermediate-level speech is characterized by sentence-length discourse. To attain the rating of Advanced, speakers must demonstrate their ability to function in paragraph-length discourse, using appropriate connectors and transitional phrases. Finally, speakers rated Superior can speak extensively in an organized and sequenced fashion.

As more specific characteristics for each level of the ACTFL scale are outlined below, it becomes clear how the components of communicative competence described by Canale (1983a) and others can be measured on a hierarchical scale within the context of these five assessment criteria. Thus, the proficiency guidelines capture much of the current thinking about the nature of communicative competence and represent one way to quantify the various elements of that construct.

For those unfamiliar with the *ACTFL Proficiency Guidelines*, the following shorthand characteristics of each proficiency range in oral skills should prove helpful. They are synthesized from the *ETS Oral Proficiency Testing Manual* (Liskin-Gasparro 1982), the *Oral Proficiency Interview Tester Training Manual* (Buck, Byrnes, and Thompson 1989), and from various ACTFL proficiency workshops.

Novice (ILR Level 0/0+) Individuals performing at the Novice level of proficiency, though perhaps capable of some limited expression in the language, have no real functional ability to communicate with what they know. Typically, their speech is characterized by the use of a few memorized words or phrases, with little or no syntactic variation beyond the scope of the prefabricated, familiar material at their disposal. They can often give short lists of vocabulary and/or answer simple questions relating to highly predictable common daily settings. Questions relating to names of basic objects, names of family members, weather expressions, days of the week, time of day, and the like will often elicit some sample of speech when all other attempts at conversation fail. This is not to say that every speaker rated at the Novice level can say something about these topics, nor that these are the only content areas that such individuals can control. Rather, they are meant to suggest the *type* of speech one can expect to elicit at the lowest levels of oral proficiency.

Speakers rated at the Novice-High (ILR 0+) level on the academic scale have considerably more memorized material within their control and some ability to communicate their own personal messages with that material. However, they are still unable to create with the language; that is, they are generally not able to handle conversational topics with which they are unfamiliar or to paraphrase to express ideas they haven't expressed previously. They are also unable to handle a typical "survival situation" that would be encountered in the target culture, such as finding a room at a hotel, obtaining directions, ordering a simple meal, handling transportation needs, and the like. These skills constitute the minimal or threshold capabilities of the Intermediate range of proficiency.

Intermediate (ILR Level 1/1+) Individuals in the Intermediate range of oral proficiency have the following characteristics:

1. They can create with the language; that is, they can express their own thoughts without relying exclusively on prefabricated or memorized responses to get their meaning across.

2. They are capable of *asking* questions as well as answering them. Whereas Novice-level speakers respond to questions in a "knee-jerk" fashion with one or two words, Intermediate-level speakers answer with longer phrases or full sentences and are capable of holding up their own end of the conversation by making inquiries and offering more elaborate responses.

3. They have at least a minimal level of sociolinguistic competence in that they can handle everyday social encounters (greetings, leave takings, the use of polite formulas, and the like) with some degree of appropriateness.

4. They can handle a simple "survival situation" that one might expect to encounter while traveling or residing for a short time in the target culture. Finding lodging, food, transportation, obtaining directions, and the like present few problems for an Intermediate-level speaker.

5. Their discourse is characterized by simple sentences or phrases, normally limited to present time, with little use of cohesive devices or embedded sentence structure. Intermediate-level speech is usually quite inaccurate, even in basic structures, and vocabulary is quite limited. However, Intermediate-level speakers are intelligible to native speakers who are *used to dealing with foreigners.*

At the Intermediate-High (ILR 1+) level, speakers begin to take on some of the characteristics of the Advanced range of proficiency. However, they are unable to sustain performance at this higher level during the course of the interview and, therefore, do not meet the minimal threshhold characteristics for the Advanced level.

Advanced (ILR Level 2/2+) Speakers in the Advanced range are capable of sustained conversation and can be characterized as follows:

1. They can narrate and describe in major time/aspect frames. In addition, their narrations and descriptions are sustained in longer discourse segments; that is, Advanced-level speakers generally speak in paragraphs rather than in short phrases or sentences.

2. They can talk about a wide range of concrete topics, including autobiographical details, daily routines at home, school, or at the workplace, current events, and the like. They can participate fully in casual conversations, expressing facts, giving instructions, describing places, people, and things, reporting on events, and providing narration about past, present, and future activities.

3. They can "live off of the economy" of the target culture and can handle routine work requirements with facility. Faced with a "survival situation" in which a complication has arisen (such as a

missed plane, an unsatisfactory hotel room, a flat tire, or similar situation in which one must explain one's way out of trouble), Advanced-level speakers can get their message across successfully.

4. They show a greater degree of sociolinguistic competence in their speech, including some sensitivity to register and to the appropriateness of certain expressions in a given context.

5. Their strategic competence is improved. Some ability to paraphrase and to cope in more complicated situations or in unforseen circumstances is one of the hallmarks of speakers in this proficiency range.

6. Their discourse competence is also improved as they continue to use longer and more complex sentence structure to express their meaning. There is growing evidence of the ability to use cohesive devices to unify discourse.

7. Although they still make errors in some basic structures, their control of the grammatical system is much improved over that of Intermediate-level speakers. They still display patterns of errors, however, and their linguistic system tends to break down when they are asked to perform functions that are controlled at the next highest level of proficiency. Nonetheless, Advanced-level speakers are comprehensible to native speakers who are *not used to dealing with foreigners.*

At the Advanced-High level, speakers have many of the characteristics of the Superior range, although they cannot sustain performance at that level.

Superior (ILR Levels 3, 3+, 4, 4+, 5)
The ACTFL scale collapses under one proficiency range all of the government ranges above Level 3. The reason for this will soon become clear. Basically, Superior-level speakers can be characterized as follows:

1. They have, at the very minimum, a "professional" level of proficiency; that is, they can handle a broad range of topics and situations, give supported opinions, hypothesize, provide complicated explanations, describe in detail with a great deal of precision, and can tackle virtually any practical, social, professional, or abstract topic that they can discuss in their native language.

2. Although they may make random errors in grammar, especially in the more complicated structures of the language, speakers at the Superior level rarely make errors that would interfere with comprehension or disturb the native speaker.

3. At the lower end of the Superior range (ILR Level 3), speakers may lack some precision in vocabulary, but they are rarely at a loss to express their meaning through paraphrase or circumlocution. Strategic competence is high at this level, as is discourse competence. Though the Level 3 speaker may be unfamiliar with some

idiomatic expressions and unable to easily shift registers, sociolinguistic competence is continuously developing. Only at Levels 4 and 5, however, would speakers be able to systematically tailor their language to any audience in a totally appropriate fashion. At these higher levels, vocabulary also becomes much more precise, and speakers can choose from a wide range of synonyms in much the same manner as they do in their native language.

As stated previously, the brief descriptions of proficiency levels given here are summary statements, or shorthand characteristics, used to familiarize practitioners with the concepts relating to proficiency testing. Note that the level definitions do *not* specify particular grammatical structures or lexical items that need to be controlled, but outline instead more generalized performance criteria that must be met at each level of proficiency. Performance within the levels of proficiency is not completely uniform; on the contrary, there is often quite a wide variation in the *details* of performance, especially in the intermediate and advanced ranges. The descriptions provided by the *ACTFL Guidelines* (see Appendix A) provide more complete information about the nature of the performance that might be expected within proficiency ranges. For the most complete description and discussion of oral proficiency testing, see Buck, Byrnes, and Thompson (1989).

As was mentioned earlier, the components of language proficiency that underlie the ACTFL descriptions—functions or tasks, grammatical competence, sociolinguistic features, pragmatic competence, discourse competence, organizational abilities—correspond in many respects with those underlying various theoretically derived models of communicative language ability. This is not to say that all of these models are the same. There are some important differences in the way in which the components are arranged and the way in which tests are constructed. (Some of these issues are treated later in this chapter.) But in spite of these differences, there seems to be a basic agreement among the various models about what aspects of knowledge and performance are important in describing language proficiency. As we in the language teaching profession continue to develop our understanding in the years ahead, we can attempt to reach greater consensus as we build on this common ground.

•••••••••••• *Proficiency and Language Acquisition Theory*

As we have already seen, the proficiency guidelines generated through the ACTFL projects were meant to describe levels of competence in listening, speaking, reading, and writing, based largely on many years of observation and testing in both the government context and in the academic community. They were not designed to present a theoretical model of language competence nor to explain how language acquisition might occur. Yet there is a rather strong degree of compatibility between the *global* level descriptions of linguistic and functional features in the oral proficiency guidelines and the overall sequence of development that some language acquisition theorists describe. Ellis (1985), in his comprehensive review of language acquisition theory and research, concludes that four macro-stages of linguistic development are probably universal:

Stage One: Interlanguage forms resemble those of pidgin languages, with more or less standard word order, regardless of the target language. Parts of sentences are omitted, and learners use memorized chunks of discourse in their communication.

Stage Two: Learners begin to use word order that is appropriate to the target language and to include most of the required sentence constituents in their speech. Language production in these first two stages is often quite inaccurate, however, as learners begin to include target-language features in their speech, but not consistently as a native speaker would use them.

Stage Three: Learners begin to use grammatical morphemes systematically and meaningfully.

Stage Four: Learners acquire complex sentence structures such as embedded clauses and relative constructions and use them with greater facility and precision (summary based on pp. 62–63).

Ellis cautions that these four stages are not clear-cut, but tend to blend into one another.

In discussing the functional and/or contextual aspects of language development, Ellis points out that early-stage learners, like children learning their first language, benefit from talking about the here-and-now. They seem to be most successful and accurate when they are presented with tasks that are cognitively simple and that allow for reference to concrete objects or events in the immediate environment (pp. 88–89). As one moves to more advanced stages of language development, one can begin to talk about more "displaced activity" (p. 89), such as events in more distant time frames or abstract situations or topics. If learners are pushed to produce language that is too cognitively complex for their level, however, they may experience a kind of linguistic breakdown. Ellis explains that this is due to the fact that when tasks present difficulties that are not linguistic in nature, they divert learners' attention from form. When this happens, learners cannot focus on those forms that are the most recently acquired and, thus, not fully automatized, leading to more error-ridden speech (p. 89). This phenomenon of linguistic breakdown is often observed in ACTFL oral proficiency interviews during the "probe" phase, when the level of the conversation is deliberately raised to see if the learner can function at the next highest level of proficiency. Ellis's observation supports the notion that linguistic breakdown is a reliable indicator of task difficulty, and serves to identify those aspects of a learner's interlanguage that are still relatively unstable and, thus, not fully acquired.

The central premise of Ellis's view of language acquisition is that there are identifiable global stages of development that all language learners seem to follow. On a micro-level within these broad stages, much variability can be seen. To reconcile the claim that there are universal sequences of general development and that there is variability on the micro-level, Ellis proposes a distinction between the *sequence* of development and the *order* of development in language acquisition (p. 64). The four macro-stages described above relate to *sequence*, whereas the development of specific grammatical or morphosyntactic features of language relate to *order*. The order of linguistic development can vary from learner to learner, depending on such factors as native language background and individual preferences for approaching the learning task (p. 63). Following Hatch (1974), he describes two very different approaches to language acquisition that might affect the order in which discrete linguistic features of the language are acquired within the four broad stages. Learners who are characterized as "data gatherers" emphasize the acquisition of vocabulary and fluency, often at the expense of grammatical accuracy. "Rule formers," on the other hand, are concerned with form and attempt to use the language accurately, sometimes at the expense of fluency. Differences such as these can contribute to different learner performance profiles on a micro-level, even though the students being evaluated are grouped in the same global level of proficiency.

As we consider the observations Ellis makes in evaluating the nature of language acquisition, much of which is based on studies of oral production, we begin to see a kind of intellectual fit between the developmental sequence that has been furnished through the insights and experience of practitioners and the one that research and theory describes. The global levels of oral proficiency (*Novice, Intermediate, Advanced, Superior*) as defined in the *ACTFL Proficiency Guidelines* are compatible, in terms of describing general linguistic development, with the four stages of development that Ellis outlines. Within those various proficiency levels, testing experience has shown that learner language can differ substantially on a micro-level. Thus, the four global level designations of the guidelines seem to be capturing a continuum of development similar to the one that Ellis describes as universal, lending support to their usefulness as an overall organizational framework within which pedagogical choices can be made.

Some Research Findings About Oral Proficiency

What level of proficiency can students expect to reach at the end of a given program of study? What is the average proficiency level of classroom teachers in high school and college programs? How long does it take to reach the Superior level of proficiency in a given language? These and other questions have been addressed in recent years through the use of oral proficiency interviews and other kinds of tests administered in both government and academic settings.

In an early study reported by Carroll (1967), the foreign language proficiency of 2784 college seniors majoring in French, German, Italian, Russian, and Spanish at 203 institutions was measured with a battery of tests. These tests included the MLA Foreign Language Proficiency Tests for Teachers and Advanced Students in all four skills, the Modern Language Aptitude Test, and two questionnaires administered to students and to the foreign language department chairmen, respectively. In an independent study, FSI personnel administered oral interviews to 127 French, Spanish, German, and Russian language teachers participating in NDEA Summer Institutes in 1965. The teachers also took the MLA skills tests at the end of their summer experience. Scores for listening and speaking on the MLA tests were then equated with the FSI ratings in speaking; scores on the reading and writing portions of the MLA battery were equated with the FSI ratings on reading. Carroll reports that the correlations between the FSI and MLA scores were substantial, especially when looking at corresponding skill areas. Based on this independent study, the FSI ratings were estimated for the college seniors who had taken the MLA tests. The study concluded that "the median graduate with a foreign language major can speak and comprehend the language only at about an FSI Speaking rating of "2+". . . ." (p. 134). It is important to bear in mind that the students who were tested were foreign language *majors* at the end of their college program who had concentrated on both language and literature study for at least four years, who may have had additional coursework in high school, and who may have spent some time abroad. The teachers at the NDEA institutes who had actually been tested with both the FSI and MLA measures had mean scores comparable to those of the college seniors, with teachers in French and Spanish averaging an FSI speaking rating of "2+", those in German a "3", and those in Russian a "1+" (p. 145).

In a more informal study undertaken by ETS in 1979, approximately thirty first- and second-year high school students in Spanish were tested using the oral interview. Liskin-Gasparro (1984) reports that "although the students varied considerably in their ability to communicate orally, none of them reached Level 1. Some of them were rated 0+ but most would have rated a 0 on the ILR scale" (p. 27). This study confirmed the need to expand the lower ranges of the ILR scale if they were to be adapted for academic use, especially at the high school level.

Magnan (1986) conducted a study at the University of Wisconsin in which she interviewed forty students of French, randomly selected from course lists in the first through fourth years of college study. The oral interviews were rated independently by two certified testers at ETS. Inter-rater reliability was .72.

Magnan found that students' proficiency increased from first to second year, with first-year students ranging from Novice Mid to Intermediate Mid/High on the scale, and second-year students ranging from Intermediate Low to Advanced. An increase was also seen from second to third years, as the third-year students' ratings ranged from Intermediate Mid/High to Advanced/Advanced High. There was not much difference in scores for the fourth-year students, with French majors ranging from Intermediate Mid to Advanced High at the end of their college course of study. It is not surprising to see such a plateau occurring between third and fourth year, since students in these courses were, for the most part, at the Advanced level of proficiency. Magnan explains that this level of oral proficiency represents a broad range of ability and that the scale may, therefore, not be sensitive to real differences between third and fourth-year levels.

In discussing the overlapping levels observed in her investigation, Magnan points out a very important aspect of the relationship between oral proficiency level and level of study. "Students at the same level of oral proficiency may be enrolled in different levels of study, and students of the same level of study may be at different levels of oral proficiency" (Magnan 1986, p. 430). It is also likely that students who have attained a given level of oral proficiency may be at an entirely different level of proficiency in the other skill modalities. Magnan explains the lack of congruence between course level and attained oral proficiency in terms of the many sources of variation that exist in language classrooms: students differ in abilities, motivation, learning strategies, commitment, and amount of prior language study in high school; and materials, teachers, and methods vary considerably as well. Placement procedures may also be tapping different language skills, as many large institutions do not test oral proficiency because of practical problems in test administration.

In spite of these areas of overlap, Magnan's study does show that oral proficiency increased with time and that students in college course sequences were able to attain the Intermediate level of proficiency after just one year, even if they had had no previous experience with French in high school (p. 432).

In reviewing other studies similar to her own, Magnan found her results to be consistent with what other researchers had learned. Hirsch (1985) had found that students ranged from Novice High to Advanced High in the first two years of language study at Cabrillo College in California; studies by Kaplan (1984) and Cramer and Terrio (1985) reported small numbers of students tested in the third and fourth year at their institutions to be in the same ranges as those in the Wisconsin study—from Intermediate High to Advanced High; Wing and Mayewski (1984) found second-year French students at the University of New Hampshire to be generally in the Intermediate-Mid range, while third-year students typically scored at the Intermediate-High level. They also reported similar results in Spanish, German, and Russian. However, Wing and Mayewski caution that the ratings in their study were given by beginning testers involved in a training project, and that experienced testers lowered the ratings fifty-three percent of the time (p. 23). This tendency of inexperienced testers to inflate ratings was corroborated in a study by Levine, Haus, and Cort (1987). They asked eight high school French and Spanish teachers with an average of 14.5 years of teaching experience but with no proficiency assessment training to read the ACTFL scale descriptions and then predict the rating of four students randomly selected from their classes. When two certified testers then rated thirty of these students, they found that the teachers had consistently overrated pupil performance. The researchers maintain that an oral proficiency familiarization workshop might help teachers become more accurate in their judgments. They cite research by Adams (1978), Shohamy (1983), and Liskin-Gasparro (1984) that provides evidence of the benefits of training. However, they caution that familiarization workshops cannot "put the teachers at the competency level of trained and certified testers" (p. 50).

The need for training in order to become an accurate interviewer and rater is pointed out by Liskin-Gasparro (1987), who says that "there seems to be no shortcut around intensive training workshops that expose the participants to numerous speech samples and engage them in extensive discussion of the relationship between those speech samples and the words of the level descriptions" (p. 25). Therefore, we must be cautious in interpreting studies of oral proficiency levels attained by students when it is not clear whether certified raters/testers were involved in the assessment procedure.

Most studies of college students to date have demonstrated the difficulty of reaching the Superior level of proficiency in an undergraduate program of studies. However, a Canadian study of high school graduates who had significant exposure to French showed that some of those students were able to achieve a Superior level of proficiency (Hamm 1988). One needs to interpret these results with some caution, however, because only one interviewer was used in the study, and it is not specified whether this interviewer was a certified tester. The study compared two groups of Ontario high school graduates. The French core group had been exposed to a daily period of French of approximately one hour from Grade 1 through graduation and had taken a six-week French language course in Quebec in the summer after graduating. The immersion group had taken either an early, middle, or late immersion program followed by twelve or thirteen credits in French in the high school. This group also had traveled to Quebec or a francophone country or had worked in a francophone environment. Results indicated that the median proficiency level of the French core group (with approximately 1,500 hours of instruction) was Intermediate High/Advanced, and that of the immersion group (with between 3,000 and 7,000 hours of exposure) was Advanced/Advanced

Plus. One student in the French core group was rated Superior, whereas six students in the immersion group attained that rating.

Hamm reports, however, that the general level of accuracy of the French core students who had attained the Advanced level was quite good and more consistent than that of their immersion counterparts. She points out that although the results cannot be generalized since the interviewees in her study were self-selected and represented a relatively small sample, the study reveals the effects of different programs on proficiency. In this study, immersion students with 3,000 to 7,000 hours of exposure to French had an advantage in terms of general communicative skills and ease of expression. On the other hand, core French students seemed to be more accurate, even when they had had at least 1,500 fewer hours of instruction. Hamm's Canadian study shows the advantages of having long sequences of language study in terms of building proficiency. It also indicates that the amount of time to reach a given level of competence can vary considerably with different learners and with different learning conditions.

The issue of the time needed to attain significant levels of oral proficiency is one that is of special interest to teachers, administrators, program designers, and students alike. Over a series of several years, FSI collected information for its own programs in training diplomatic personnel in order to determine the interaction of student ability level and the amount of time needed to reach the upper levels of oral proficiency. Illustration 1.5 reveals the results of their study in various languages.

It is important to keep in mind that the data given in Illustration 1.5 were collected in a very special context, that of intensive language training of adults at the Foreign Service Institute. The amount of time to reach a given level of proficiency will undoubtedly vary among students in this type of context as it does in high school or college programs. What this chart does indicate, however, when considered in conjunction with the research reported earlier in this section, is that we must amend our expectations for student attainment of oral proficiency to conform more closely to the realities of language study in formal classroom contexts. If it typically takes 720 hours of instruction under the rather ideal conditions of intensive study at the Foreign Service Institute for an adult with high aptitude to become proficient at the Superior level in French or Spanish, it is difficult to expect students in a four-year high school program or a four-semester college sequence to reach that same level of competence after 200 or 300 hours. On the other hand, we can be very encouraged when we find that students in programs such as the one in Wisconsin reported earlier (Magnan 1986) are able to function after one year at the Intermediate level of proficiency. This represents the ability to use the language creatively to meet one's needs on a daily basis in the target culture and to have conversations in the language about topics of personal interest. The attainment of Advanced and Advanced High ratings by students who had taken three or

Illustration 1.5
Expected Levels of
Speaking Proficiency
in Languages Taught
at the Foreign Service
Institute

Group I: Afrikaans, Danish, Dutch, French, Haitian Creole, Italian, Norwegian, Portuguese, Romanian, Spanish, Swahili, Swedish

Length of Training	Aptitude for Language Learning		
	Minimum	Average	Superior
8 weeks (240 hours)	1	1/1+	1+
16 weeks (480 hours)	1+	2	2+
24 weeks (720 hours)	2	2+	3

Group II: Bulgarian, Dari, Farsi, German, Greek, Hindi, Indonesian, Malay, Urdu

Length of Training	Aptitude for Language Learning		
	Minimum	Average	Superior
16 weeks (480 hours)	1	1/1+	1+/2
24 weeks (720 hours)	1+	2	2+/3
44 weeks (1320 hours)	2/2+	2+/3	3/3+

Group III: Amharic, Bengali, Burmese, Czech, Finnish, Hebrew, Hungarian, Khmer, Lao, Nepali, Pilipino, Polish, Russian, Serbo-Croatian, Sinhala, Thai, Tamil, Turkish, Vietnamese

Length of Training	Aptitude for Language Learning		
	Minimum	Average	Superior
16 weeks (480 hours)	0+	1	1/1+
24 weeks (720 hours)	1+	2	2/2+
44 weeks (1320 hours)	2	2+	3

Group IV: Arabic, Chinese, Japanese, Korean

Length of Training	Aptitude for Language Learning		
	Minimum	Average	Superior
16 weeks (480 hours)	0+	1	1
24 weeks (720 hours)	1	1+	1+
44 weeks (1320 hours)	1+	2	2+
80–92 weeks (2400–2760 hours)	2+	3	3+

Source: Judith E. Liskin-Gasparro. *ETS Oral Proficiency Testing Manual.* Princeton, N.J.: Educational Testing Service, 1982.

four years of course work in the studies reviewed in this section is also very encouraging. However, further studies need to be done to see if such findings can be generalized and supported.

• • • • • • • • • • • • **Issues in Language Proficiency Assessment: Caveats, Clarifications, and New Directions**

As we emphasized earlier in this chapter, the *ACTFL Proficiency Guidelines* and the oral interview procedure represent one possible way to define and measure proficiency. As with any new development in the field, the guidelines have been received with enthusiasm by some members of the profession and viewed with skepticism by others. In recent years, there have been several scholars who have criticized the ILR and ACTFL Guidelines and have questioned the appropriateness of the Oral Proficiency Interview for capturing adequately the construct of communicative language proficiency. This section presents some of the issues that have been raised since the guidelines appeared. The review of literature is not meant to be comprehensive, but represents the broader questions that need to be addressed in future research as well as suggestions that might be incorporated in any further revisions of the guidelines.

Questions Regarding Oral Proficiency Assessment

One of the earlier articles dealing with problems in proficiency assessment was written by Lantolf and Frawley (1985), who questioned the logic and validity of the *ACTFL Proficiency Guidelines* on philosophical grounds, objecting to their analytic approach to testing and the use of the "native-speaker yardstick" (p. 339). They assert that the definitions of proficiency levels are circular and not based on empirical reality. They also question whether the criteria used in oral proficiency testing are the same as those used by native speakers engaged in communication with nonnatives, where conversational partners cooperate in the negotiation of meaning. The authors seem to object to criterion-referenced testing of any type: "At best, criterion-referenced tests measure the extent to which the person performs with reference to analytically derived levels and nothing more" (p. 340).

Lantolf and Frawley also object to the use of "the educated native speaker" as the reference point against which performance is judged. They assert that the native speaker "is not a theoretically interesting construct, since the construct is neither unitary nor reliable" (p. 343). Although the *ACTFL Proficiency Guidelines* no longer use the standard of the "educated native speaker" in the level descriptions, there are still implications in some of the definitions that a prototypical native speaker group exists (Bachman and Savignon 1986). This seems like a valid point that should be considered in any further revisions of the guidelines.

Lantolf and Frawley do not propose, however, any clear alternative to the guidelines or the oral testing procedure that would resolve some of the problems they have identified. Rather, they suggest that the profession "delay any decision to implement guidelines of any nature until research is able to develop a clear understanding of what it means to be a proficient speaker of a language" (p. 344).

Other scholars, such as Bachman and Savignon (1986) and Clark and Lett (1988) disagree with this point of view, recommending instead that a research agenda be designed to address the questions and problems associated with current testing procedures. Bachman and Savignon affirm the usefulness of the development of guidelines and "common metric" tests for a wide range of language abilities, and consider the current guidelines a good starting point. However, they suggest that some further development is needed to capture the full context of language use represented in theoretical frameworks of communicative language proficiency. They assert that in examining definitions of communicative competence and proficiency, they "are struck more by similarities than by differences" (p. 381). Differences seem to relate not to the components of language proficiency identified, but rather to the relative importance accorded to them in the assessment procedures.

One of their objections to the current guidelines is that they include both context and content descriptions in the scale definitions. In their view, this confounds language ability descriptions with test method and can create problems with comparability of test results across different contexts and settings. They propose that the specifications of language abilities be divorced from elicitation procedures and conditions, enabling interviews to be geared to the needs and interests of the particular candidate. This suggestion might be explored further in subsequent revisions of the guidelines. However, it would be useful to conduct research studies to determine whether skilled interviewers currently vary elicitation techniques to correspond to the special needs and interests of candidates in the way that Bachman and Savignon suggest. Tester training emphasizes that the content and context samples given in the guidelines are not meant as checklists of discrete points to be included in every conversation, but rather serve as indicators of the kinds of topics and situations that might be used to elicit a speech sample. Liskin-Gasparro (1987) suggests that inter-interviewer reliability studies be conducted to investigate whether two or more experienced testers elicit comparable speech samples from the same group of speakers, a suggestion that is also made by Shohamy (1987).

Clark and Lett (1988) propose a detailed research plan for looking at issues relating to the reliability and validity of the oral interview and make specific suggestions about ways in which the current guidelines could be refined and improved. In contrast to Lantolf and Frawley's view, Clark and Lett consider the development and use of the ILR scale and testing procedure to be the most significant measurement initiative to have occurred over the last three decades (p. 72). However, they point out that no one test can provide us with more than a small sample of language and cannot represent the full range of language-use situations that one might expect to encounter. The current oral interview procedure, in their view, constitutes a "highly realistic sample of polite, reasonably formal conversation between relative strangers" (p. 56) but does not sample language nearly so well from other sociolinguistic contexts requiring differing styles or registers. They suggest that in order to get a more comprehensive view of a person's language proficiency, a variety of measures is needed that would test language use in different contexts and situations.

Shohamy (1987) reports on a number of research studies that show that different speech styles and functions are tapped with different kinds of oral interactions. She found that performance in an oral interview such as the OPI does not accurately predict performance on another kind of oral task, such as reporting, role-play, or discussion (Shohamy 1983; Shohamy, Reves, and Bejerano 1986). She argues that more than one kind of oral interaction is needed to test oral proficiency in a valid way, and that multiple tasks should be designed to obtain a more representative sample of speech, preferably conducted by different testers.

In regard to the question raised by Lantolf and Frawley about whether the hierarchy of oral proficiency levels inherent in the guidelines has any basis in reality, some preliminary research reported by Dandonoli and Henning (1990) suggests that it does. Statistical analyses performed on oral interviews in both English and French indicate that the difficulty continua associated with the level descriptions were upheld, with few exceptions. A second validity check involved comparing ratings given to speech samples by experienced raters with those given to the same samples by untrained native speakers who were told to rank order the samples using whatever criteria they chose. Ratings of samples in both English and French showed a very high correlation: for English, the correlations ranged from 0.904 to 1.000 with a mean of 0.934; for French, correlations ranged from 0.857 to 1.000 with a mean of 0.929 (p. 20). This high correspondence of ratings by trained testers and untrained native speakers constitutes strong evidence of the face validity of the oral proficiency guidelines for both English and French.

Questions Regarding Proficiency Assessment in Other Skills

Thus far in our discussion of language proficiency, we have concentrated on oral skills and their measurement, since the oral interview procedure developed by the ILR and adapted for academic contexts by ETS and ACTFL has been widely discussed, disseminated, and debated in the past decade among language professionals. Research and critical commentary relative to the guidelines have not been limited to the oral proficiency scales. Dandonoli and Henning (1990) investigated the construct validity of the guidelines in all four skill areas, as well as the Oral Interview procedure itself. Their results provided "strong support for the use of the Guidelines as a foundation for the development of proficiency tests and for the reliability and validity of the Oral Proficiency Interview" (p. 11). Their investigation also uncovered areas where additional research must be done to refine the guidelines and test procedures, especially in listening comprehension (p. 20). The most problematic finding of the study was the relatively low level of validity exhibited by the French listening test. The tests used were developed specifically for the validation study of the guidelines, mainly because the existing proficiency tests in listening and other skill areas had not been developed from the criteria underlying the guidelines and did not span the entire scale (p. 13). Both multiple-choice and open-ended test methods were devised for listening and reading. The low level of construct validity in the French listening test may have been due to either the guidelines themselves or to the tests that were designed for the project (p. 20). The authors stress the need for further research to replicate the study's goals and identify more clearly possible modifications needed in the guidelines or the tests used to measure proficiency in the different skill areas.

Lee and Musumeci (1988) have questioned the validity of the reading proficiency definitions, especially with respect to the issue of text types and the implied developmental progression of reading skills. In terms of the latter issue, the authors have inferred from their reading of the guidelines and the associated literature a developmental progression that would limit the use of a given reading skill (such as skimming, scanning, or making inferences) to a particular proficiency level. This inference, however, is not warranted, as the guidelines do not suggest that learners at any given level of proficiency will use one and only one process as they approach a given reading text. (See Dandonoli 1988; Galloway 1988; and Omaggio Hadley 1988 for various objections to the design of the reading model used in the study.) However, the objections raised by Lee and Musumeci with regard to the current specifications of text types within the level descriptions may have some validity. Research on reading in recent years has indicated a far greater role in comprehension for the reader's own background knowledge as he or she interacts with texts of various types. A study by Allen, Bernhardt, Berry, and Demel (1988) involving high school students in French, Spanish, and German revealed that text type alone was not a significant predictor of reading difficulty, a result that is consistent with Lee and Musumeci's findings. Revised descriptions of the reading proficiency levels may need to include more overt references to the knowledge that readers bring to texts and acknowledge more thoroughly the interactive, schema-based nature of reading.

The Notion of Language Proficiency: Some Further Clarifications

Whether one uses the *ACTFL Proficiency Guidelines* or some other framework for describing language ability, it is important to bear in mind that these descriptions are meant to be used to *describe* and *measure* competence in a language, not to prescribe methods, materials, or approaches to language teaching and learning. As Bachman and Savignon (1986) point out, the terms "proficiency" and "communicative competence" have both been stretched far beyond their original meanings in the professional literature of the past two decades. The term "communicative competence," for example, has been used in so many different ways that "it has become an accretion of meanings, a beneficent chameleon that takes on whatever characteristics the user believes to be 'good' and 'right'" (Bachman and Savignon 1986, p. 381). The same can be said for the term "proficiency," which has suffered much the same fate in recent years. Elsewhere, I have listed some common misconceptions about proficiency that have surfaced in professional discussions in the 1980s (Omaggio Hadley 1988, 1990). It might be helpful at this point to further clarify what "proficiency" is by focusing briefly on what it is *not*.

1. **Proficiency is not a theory of language acquisition.** As seen in the discussions earlier in this chapter, the *ACTFL Proficiency Guidelines* do not outline a theory of language acquisition, nor are they derived from a particular theoretical perspective. Some congruence can be seen between the global stages of development that are inherent in the guidelines for oral proficiency and the overall developmental progression suggested by research and theory, as summarized in Ellis (1985). In addition, there are some parallels between the components of language proficiency inherent in the guideline descriptions and the aspects of language that have been described in various theoretical models of competence and/or performance. This is not to say that the implications about language development in the guidelines are wholly accurate or that the level descriptions are free from problems. We have reviewed some of the criticisms of the current descriptions and have identified problems that need to be resolved as our knowledge continues to develop about language proficiency in all skill areas. The guidelines and associated testing procedures will undoubtedly be modified in the years ahead to correspond to new insights provided by theory and research.

2. **Proficiency is not a method of language teaching.** As we have seen throughout this chapter, proficiency is focused on *measurement*, not method. There are no methodological prescriptions in the guidelines. The descriptions of what learners can *do* in functional terms can have an effect, however, on what methods and procedures we choose to use in our classrooms to help students attain certain goals. Instruction that fosters the growth of proficiency for all learners will need to be flexible in order to accommodate learners' differing needs and preferences. Rather than being prescriptive or restrictive in nature, proficiency-oriented instruction must embrace and reconcile many different approaches and points of view about language learning and teaching. Second and foreign language instruction can derive some direction and focus from a better understanding of the concept of proficiency as an organizing principle (Higgs 1984). Within that general framework, the language learning experience can be enriched by an integration of multiple perspectives that

respond to the differing needs and interests of both students and their teachers. More will be said about ways in which the concept of "proficiency" can affect teaching methodology in Chapter 3.

3. **Proficiency is not a curricular outline or syllabus.** Because the proficiency descriptions are evaluative in nature and because they identify in a global way some stages through which language learners typically pass, they may have some interesting implications for curricular design. However, the guidelines neither provide a curricular outline nor imply that a particular kind of syllabus or sequence of instruction should be followed. The guidelines do not describe incremental or discrete steps in performance, but provide holistic and integrative descriptions. Just as many different methods may lead to the development of language proficiency, many different curricular sequences can be derived from an intelligent and careful examination of the guidelines. As Galloway states, "the roads to proficiency are as many and varied as are the descriptions of the destinations themselves" (Galloway 1987, p. 36).

4. **Proficiency does not imply a preoccupation with grammar or error.** This misconception arises when one confuses the concept of proficiency itself (a way to measure language competence and performance) with various methods and approaches that individuals have advocated for developing proficiency. Because the higher levels of proficiency are characterized by accuracy and precision in the use of language, many practitioners and researchers believe that some attention must be paid to the development of accuracy in formal language teaching programs (see, for example, Canale and Swain 1980; Higgs and Clifford 1982; Long 1983; Lightbown 1985, 1990; Swain 1985; Ellis 1990; Stern 1990.) However, the precise role and value of grammatical instruction and various kinds of error correction and feedback in achieving this goal is the subject of lively debate in the 1990s. More will be said about this issue in Chapter 3.

• • • • • • • • • • • • • *Summary: On Knowing a Language*

In this chapter various definitions and theories of what it means to "know" a language have been examined. We have explored the concepts of competence and performance, studied various definitions of communicative competence, and traced the development of the notion of proficiency, especially as it is described in the *ACTFL Proficiency Guidelines*. The way in which various components of language ability can be integrated in a variety of different frameworks for describing and defining language proficiency has been illustrated. Some common misconceptions surrounding the use of the term "proficiency" have been discussed, most of which have arisen out of an improper extension of the term beyond its intended use for measurement and assessment. Although one can draw implications from the proficiency guidelines for making instructional decisions, "proficiency" is neither a method nor a specific blueprint for designing a curriculum.

In the next chapter, a number of theories about how adults become proficient in a second language will be considered. As we explore various perspectives on the language learning process, we can begin to trace the source of many teaching practices that have been advanced across the years. An understanding of language acquisition theory can thus inform the choices we make among these options and provide important insights into our own current beliefs and practices.

• • • • • • • • • • • • *Activities for Review and Discussion*

1. Write a brief paragraph describing what it means, in your opinion, to "know a language."
2. What components of language ability are common to the definitions of communicative competence, communicative language ability, and proficiency described in this chapter? Describe each of these components briefly.
3. Various theoretical models of language ability include discussions of "grammatical competence." What does this term mean to you?
4. Give a brief description of the global levels of oral proficiency, as defined in the *ACTFL Proficiency Guidelines*. Then decide what level of oral proficiency you would assign to each of the following learner profiles:

   a. Sarah B. knows enough Spanish to speak simply, with some circumlocution, in casual conversations about concrete topics, such as her own background, her family and interests at school, her travels, and various current events. She can express facts, give instructions, describe, and narrate in past, present, and future time. She handles elementary constructions with accuracy most of the time, but still makes patterned errors, especially when trying to express an opinion or support her point of view.

   b. Sam R. has no practical speaking ability in Russian, though he does know a few isolated words and expressions. He can name the days of the week and the months of the year, name a few basic objects and colors, and use a few memorized expressions, such as "Hello," "How are you?" and "Goodbye." However, he really can't use what he knows, even in a very simple conversation. Native speakers have a very difficult time understanding him because of his heavy American accent.

c. Bill R. can converse in both formal and informal situations, resolve problems, deal with unfamiliar topics, describe in detail, and offer supported opinion in his second language, French. He is quite adept at talking about his special field of competence—political science—and is generally able to handle any topic of discussion he can handle in English. He has a slight accent and occasionally makes errors, but they never interfere with communication or disturb native speakers.

d. Gail P. knows enough German to cope with routine, daily situations in a German-speaking environment. She can create with the language, ask and answer questions, and participate in conversations dealing with everyday topics. Most native speakers understand what she is saying, though she is sometimes not comprehensible to people who aren't used to dealing with foreigners because she makes frequent errors in pronunciation and grammar. She can handle requests for services, like renting a room or ordering a meal, though sometimes she has to search for the appropriate words, which makes her speech a little hesitant.

e. Mary Anne T. speaks Chinese well enough to participate fully in casual conversations, especially when the discussion relates to topics such as her family, her work as a missionary, her travel experiences, and current events. She does have some difficulty expressing her point of view in Chinese, and her language tends to break down when the discussion gets too complex. Sometimes she miscommunicates, but most native speakers, including those who have never dealt with Americans, can understand her meaning. In her work in the mission field, which includes social ministry, Mary Anne is good at giving instructions, explaining and describing various health-related procedures, and talking with people about her past travels and her aspirations for the future.

5. Galloway (1987) has stated that the *ACTFL Proficiency Guidelines* are neither a curricular model nor a methodological prescription, but that one might be able to look for *implications* in the descriptions for making instructional decisions. What implications for instruction do you see in the guidelines? What kinds of goals might you set for students at the Novice level in any of the skill modalities (speaking, listening, reading, writing)? How might your goal statements differ for students at the Intermediate level? the Advanced level?

References: Chapter 1

ACTFL Proficiency Guidelines. Hastings-on-Hudson, NY: American Council on the Teaching of Foreign Languages, 1986.

ACTFL *Provisional Proficiency Guidelines.* Hastings-on-Hudson, NY: American Council on the Teaching of Foreign Languages, 1982.

Adams, Marianne L. "Measuring Foreign Language Speaking Proficiency: A Study of Agreement Among Raters." In John L.D. Clark, ed., *Direct Testing of Speaking Proficiency: Theory and Application.* Princeton, NJ: Educational Testing Service, 1978.

Allen, Edward D., Elizabeth B. Bernhardt, Mary Therese Berry, and Marjorie Demel. "Comprehension and Text Genre: An Analysis of Secondary School Foreign Language Readers." *The Modern Language Journal,* 72, ii (1988): 163–72.

Bachman, Lyle F. *Fundamental Considerations in Language Testing.* Oxford: Oxford University Press, 1990.

Bachman, Lyle F. and John L. D. Clark. "The Measurement of Foreign/Second Language Proficiency." *Annals of the American Academy of Political and Social Science* 490 (1987): 20–33.

Bachman, Lyle F. and Sandra J. Savignon. "The Evaluation of Communicative Language Proficiency: A Critique of the ACTFL Oral Interview." *The Modern Language Journal* 70, ii (1986): 380–90.

Brod, Richard I., ed. *Language Study for the 1980s: Reports of the MLA-ACLS Language Task Forces.* New York: Modern Language Association, 1980.

Brown, Gillian, and George Yule. *Discourse Analysis.* Cambridge: Cambridge University Press, 1983.

Brown, H. D. *Principles of Language Learning and Teaching.* Englewood Cliffs, NJ: Prentice Hall, 1980, 1987.

Buck, Kathryn, Heidi Byrnes, and Irene Thompson, eds., *The ACTFL Oral Proficiency Interview Tester Training Manual.* Yonkers, NY: ACTFL, 1989.

Burn, Barbara. "The President's Commission on Foreign Language and International Studies: Its Origin and Work." *The Modern Language Journal* 64 (1980): 7–8.

Campbell, R. and R. Wales. "The Study of Language Acquisition." In J. Lyons, ed., *New Horizons in Linguistics.* Harmondsworth, England: Penguin Books, 1970.

Canale, Michael. "From Communicative Competence to Communicative Language Pedagogy." In J. Richards and Richard Schmidt, eds., *Language and Communication.* London: Longman, 1983a.

_____. "On Some Dimensions of Language Proficiency". In J. W. Oller, Jr., ed., *Issues in Language Testing Research.* Rowley, MA: Newbury House, 1983b.

Canale, Michael and Merrill Swain. "Theoretical Bases of Communicative Approaches to Second Language Teaching and Testing." *Applied Linguistics* 1 (1980a): 1–47.

_____. Introduction to the *Ontario Assessment Instrument Pool/French as a Second Language: Junior and Intermediate Divisions (Grades 6 and 9).* Toronto, Ontario: Ontario Ministry of Education, 1980b.

Carroll, John B. "Foreign Language Proficiency Levels Attained by Language Majors Near Graduation from College." *Foreign Language Annals* 1 (1967): 131–51.

Charolles, M. "Introduction aux problèmes de la cohérence des textes." *Langue française* 38 (1978): 7–41.

Chomsky, Noam. "A Review of B.F. Skinner's *Verbal Behavior*." *Language* 35 (1959): 26–58.

_____. *Aspects of the Theory of Syntax*. Cambridge, MA: M.I.T. Press, 1965.

Clark, John L.D. *Foreign Language Testing: Theory and Practice*. Philadelphia: Center for Curriculum Development, 1972.

Clark, John L.D. and John Lett. "A Research Agenda." Chapter 2 in Pardee Lowe, Jr. and Charles W. Stansfield, eds., *Second Language Proficiency Assessment: Current Issues. CAL/ERIC Language in Education: Theory and Practice, 70.* Englewood Cliffs, NJ: Prentice Hall, 1988.

Cramer, Hazel and Susan Terrio. "Moving from Vocabulary Acquisition to Functional Proficiency: Techniques and Strategies." *French Review* 59 (1985): 198–209.

Dandonoli, Patricia. "MLJ Readers' Forum." *The Modern Language Journal, 72* (1988): 450.

Dandonoli, Patricia and Grant Henning. "An Investigation of the Construct Validity of the ACTFL Proficiency Guidelines and Oral Interview Procedure." *Foreign Language Annals* 23, i (1990): 11–22.

Ellis, Rod. *Understanding Second Language Acquisition*. Oxford: Oxford University Press, 1985.

_____. *Instructed Second Language Acquisition*. Oxford: Basil Blackwell, 1990.

Galloway, Vicki. "From Defining to Developing Proficiency: A Look at the Decisions." Chapter 2 (pp. 25–73) in H. Byrnes and M. Canale, eds., *Defining and Developing Proficiency: Guidelines, Implementations and Concepts*. ACTFL Foreign Language Education Series. Lincolnwood, IL: National Textbook Company, 1987.

_____. "MLJ Readers' Forum." *The Modern Language Journal, 72* (1988): 450–52.

Gass, Susan M. and Carolyn G. Madden, eds. *Input in Second Language Acquisition*. Cambridge, MA: Newbury House, 1985.

Hamm, Christiane. "The ACTFL Oral Proficiency Interview in a Canadian Context: The French Speaking Proficiency of Two Groups of Ontario High-School Graduates." *Foreign Language Annals* 21, vi (1988): 561–67.

Harley, Birgit, Patrick Allen, Jim Cummins, and Merrill Swain, eds., *The Development of Second Language Proficiency*. Cambridge: Cambridge University Press, 1990.

Hatch, Evelyn. "Second Language Learning—Universals." *Working Papers in Bilingualism* 3 (1974): 1–17.

_____. "Discourse Analysis and Second Language Acquisition." In E. Hatch, ed., *Second Language Acquisition: A Book of Readings*. Rowley, MA: Newbury House, 1978.

_____. *Psycholinguistics: A Second Language Perspective*. Rowley, MA: Newbury House, 1983.

_____. "Theoretical Review of Discourse and Interlanguage." In A. Davies, C. Criper, and A. Howatt, eds., *Interlanguage*. Edinburgh: Edinburgh University Press, 1984.

_____. *Discourse and Language Education*. Cambridge: Cambridge University Press, 1992.

Higgs, Theodore V. "Language Teaching and the Quest for the Holy Grail." In T.V. Higgs, ed., *Teaching for Proficiency: The Organizing Principle*. ACTFL Foreign Language Education Series, Vol. 15. Lincolnwood, IL: National Textbook Company, 1984.

_____. "Proficiency Assessment and the Humanities." *ADFL Bulletin* 18, i (1986): 6–8.

Higgs, Theodore V. and Ray Clifford. "The Push toward Communication." Chapter 1 in T. V. Higgs, ed., *Curriculum, Competence, and the Foreign Language Teacher*. ACTFL Foreign Language Education Series, vol. 13. Lincolnwood, IL: National Textbook Company, 1982.

Hirsch, Bette. "A Proficiency-Based French Conversation Course." *French Review* 59 (1985): 210–18.

Hymes, Dell. "On Communicative Competence." In J.B. Pride and J. Holmes, eds., *Sociolinguistics*. Harmondsworth, England: Penguin Books, 1972.

Kaplan, Isabelle. "Oral Proficiency Testing and the Language Proficiency Curriculum: Two Experiments in Curricular Design for Conversation Courses." *Foreign Language Annals* 17 (1984): 491–98.

Krashen, Stephen. *Principles and Practice in Second Language Acquisition*. New York: Pergamon Press, 1982.

Lantolf, James P. and William Frawley. "Oral Proficiency Testing: A Critical Analysis." *The Modern Language Journal* 69 (1985): 337–45.

Larsen-Freeman, Diane and Michael H. Long. *An Introduction to Second Language Acquisition Research*. White Plains, NY: Longman, 1991.

Lee, James F. and Diane Musumeci. "On Hierarchies of Reading Skills and Text Types." *The Modern Language Journal*, 72 (1988): 173–87.

Levine, Martin G., George J. Haus, and Donna Cort. "The Accuracy of Teacher Judgment of the Oral Proficiency of High School Foreign Language Students." *Foreign Language Annals* 20, i (1987): 45–50.

Lightbown, Patsy M. "Can Language Acquisition be Altered by Instruction?" In K. Hyltenstam and M. Pienemann, eds. *Modelling and Assessing Second Language Acquisition*. Clevedon, Avon: Multilingual Matters, 1985.

_____. "Process-Product Research on Second Language Learning in Classrooms." Chapter 6 in Harley, Birgit, Patrick Allen, Jim Cummins, and Merrill Swain, eds., *The Development of Second Language Proficiency*. Cambridge: Cambridge University Press, 1990.

Liskin-Gasparro, Judith E. *ETS Oral Proficiency Testing Manual*. Princeton, NJ: Educational Testing Service, 1982.

_____. "The ACTFL Proficiency Guidelines: A Historical Perspective." In T. V. Higgs, ed., *Teaching for Proficiency: The Organizing Principle*. ACTFL Foreign Language Education Series, vol. 15. Lincolnwood, IL: National Textbook Company, 1984.

_____. "The ACTFL Proficiency Guidelines: An Update." In A. Valdman, ed., *Proceedings of the Symposium on the Evaluation of Foreign Language Proficiency*. Bloomington, IN: Indiana University, 1987.

Long, Michael. "Does Second Language Instruction Make a Difference? A Review of the Research." *TESOL Quarterly* 17 (1983): 359–82.

Lowe, Pardee. *Manual for Language School Oral Interview Workshops*. Washington, DC: Defense Language Institute/Language School Joint Oral Interview Transfer Project, 1982.

Lowe, Pardee and Charles Stansfield, eds. *Second Language Proficiency Assessment: Current Issues. CAL/ERIC Language in Education: Theory and Practice 70.* Englewood Cliffs, NJ: Prentice Hall, 1988.

Magnan, Sally S. "Assessing Speaking Proficiency in the Undergraduate Curriculum: Data from French." *Foreign Language Annals* 19, v (1986): 429–37.

Morris, W., ed. *The American Heritage Dictionary of the English Language.* Boston: Houghton-Mifflin, 1978, 1992.

Munby, J. *Communicative Syllabus Design.* Cambridge: Cambridge University Press, 1978.

OmaggioHadley, Alice. "Proficiency-Based Instruction: Implications for Methodology." *IDEAL* 3 (1988): 25–37.

_____. "MLJ Readers' Forum." *The Modern Language Journal* 72 (1988): 452–54.

_____. "Le concept de compétence fonctionnelle et son impact sur les programmes et l'enseignement des langues étrangères." *Etudes de linguistique appliquée* 77 (1990): 85–96.

Savignon, Sandra J. *Communicative Competence: An Experiment in Foreign Language Teaching.* Philadelphia: Center for Curriculum Development, 1972.

_____. *Communicative Competence: Theory and Practice.* Reading, MA: Addison-Wesley Publishing Company, 1983.

Scebold, C. Edward. Personal communication, 1992.

Shohamy, Elana. "Rater Reliability of the Oral Interview Speaking Test." *Foreign Language Annals* 16 (1983): 219–22.

_____. "Reactions to Lyle Bachman's Paper 'Problems in Examining the Validity of the ACTFL Oral Proficiency Interview'." In A. Valdman, ed., *Proceedings of the Symposium on the Evaluation of Foreign Language Proficiency.* Bloomington, IN: Indiana University, 1987.

Shohamy, Elana, T. Reves, and Y. Bejerano. "Introducing a New Comprehensive Test of Oral Proficiency." *English Language Teaching Journal* 40 (1986): 212–22.

Stern, H. H. "Analysis and Experience as Variables in Second Language Pedagogy." Chapter 7 in Harley, Birgit, Patrick Allen, Jim Cummins, and Merrill Swain, eds., *The Development of Second Language Proficiency.* Cambridge: Cambridge University Press, 1990.

Strength through Wisdom: A Critique of U.S. Capability. A Report to the President from the President's Commission on Foreign Language and International Studies. Washington, DC: U.S. Government Printing Office, 1979. [Reprinted in *The Modern Language Journal* 64 (1980): 9–57.]

Swain, Merrill. "Communicative Competence: Some Roles of Comprehensible Input and Comprehensible Output in its Development." Chapter 14 in S. Gass and C. Madden, eds., 1985.

Widdowson, H.G. *Teaching Language as Communication.* Oxford: Oxford University Press, 1978.

Wing, Barbara and Sandi Mayewski. *Oral Proficiency Testing in College-Level Foreign Language Programs.* Hastings-on-Hudson, NY: ACTFL Materials Center, 1984.

2

On Learning a Language: Some Theoretical Perspectives

•••••••••••• *Introduction*

In Chapter 1, various ways to define and describe language competence were explored, and components of language that were thought to be important in designing models of "communicative competence" and "language proficiency" were identified and considered. We saw that many of the same components (grammatical, lexical, phonological, pragmatic, sociolinguistic, and discourse features) were included in the various models that have been proposed. Although we have not reached complete consensus on the question of what it means to know a language, the profession is in basic agreement about the features of language that are relevant to that question.

This chapter addresses another fundamental question that concerns language researchers and practitioners: How do adults become proficient in a second-language? Consensus about this question may be far more difficult to achieve. Ellis (1985) comments that there has been a great deal of theorizing about second-language acquisition (SLA), especially since the early 1970s, and that "the research literature abounds in approaches, theories, models, laws, and principles" (p. 248). He speculates that perhaps the profession has generated far too many theories, agreeing with Schouten (1979) that "too many models have been built and taken for granted too soon, and this has stifled relevant research" (p. 4, cited in Ellis 1985, p. 248). McLaughlin (1987) observes that "in the present stage of the development of our knowledge, it seems premature to argue for the 'truth' of one theory over another" (p. 6). Practitioners who have been buffeted across the years by pressures to adopt different approaches to teaching, due to the changing winds of theory, might tend to agree with this point of view.

There are those who feel, however, that it is time that the profession work toward developing a macro-theory that will be comprehensive in its power to explain language acquisition. Spolsky (1989) argues for the development of a new general theory of second-language learning, outlining seventy-four separate "conditions" or factors in language learning

Illustration 2.1

Discussion Guide
Theories Of Second-
Language Learning

This discussion guide is designed to help teachers explore their assumptions and beliefs about language learning and teaching. The statements relate to various theoretical viewpoints discussed in this chapter. For each statement, mark to what degree you agree or disagree, using the scale to the right. 1 = Strongly Disagree, 5 = Strongly Agree.

1. One can learn a language only through extensive practice. Explicit knowledge of the rules is not very useful. 5 4 3 2 1

2. Humans have an innate, biological capacity for learning languages and are genetically programmed to learn languages in certain ways. 5 4 3 2 1

3. We can learn a lot about how humans learn from observing animal learning. 5 4 3 2 1

4. Adults learn foreign languages in much the same way as children learn their native language. 5 4 3 2 1

5. Error correction should be minimal in the classroom; it is of some limited use when the goal is formal learning, but of *no* use when the goal is acquisition of communicative ability in the language. 5 4 3 2 1

6. Students should never be required to produce speech in the second language unless they are ready to do so. Speaking fluency will emerge naturally if students are exposed to the language long enough. 5 4 3 2 1

7. When presenting new material to second-language learners, the teacher should be sure that it is organized and sequenced to relate to knowledge they already have. 5 4 3 2 1

8. Adult learners can reach a relatively high level of proficiency in a second language without having a conscious knowledge of its grammar. 5 4 3 2 1

9. Formal classroom instruction is of little use when communication is the goal. 5 4 3 2 1

10. Language learner errors should be corrected as soon as possible so that they do not become established habits. 5 4 3 2 1

11. Teachers should not explain grammar, but should organize learning so that learners can deduce the rules for themselves. 5 4 3 2 1

12. Learning should at all times be meaningful. Rote learning is of very little use in mastering a second language. 5 4 3 2 1

13. Students should have an opportunity to practice new forms and structures in controlled practice activities before being asked to communicate their own meaning using those features. 5 4 3 2 1

14. Language learners acquire the grammatical features of a language in a predictable order when language learning occurs in natural language use situations. 5 4 3 2 1

15. At any given stage of development, learners' language performance is quite variable. Teachers should expect learners to make more errors when they are focused on meaningful communication than when they are focused on form. 5 4 3 2 1

that would need to be integrated into such a comprehensive model. McLaughlin (1987), however, points out that micro-theories, which try to deal with a smaller range of phenomena and are limited in scope may be "intrinsically more satisfactory" (p. 9) although in the final analysis an adequate theory will have to be comprehensive enough to explain a wider range of phenomena. "A satisfactory theory of adult second-language learning must go beyond accounting for how people form relative clauses" (p. 10).

Why do language teachers need to know about theory, especially if it seems unlikely that we can reach agreement about how language learning and acquisition take place? McLaughlin (1987) explains that the function of a theory is to "help us understand and organize the data of experience . . . bring[ing] meaning to what is otherwise chaotic and inscrutable" (p. 7). Ellis (1985) maintains that every teacher already has a theory of language learning, but that many teachers may have never articulated what that theory is (p. 2). The fact, however, that we choose to do certain activities in the classroom and decide not to do others shows that we are working on some underlying assumptions about what is useful in promoting the development of language proficiency. Therefore, before examining some of the theories that have been influential in the field of language teaching over the years, it might be constructive to make a preliminary assessment of some of the assumptions that may underlie our own beliefs about language learning.

Illustration 2.1 presents a set of statements that can serve as a guide for discussion or as an instrument for self-assessment to help teachers clarify and articulate their current beliefs about the way adults develop competence in a second language. The reader may want to complete the survey before going on to the next section.*

Exploring Theories of Language Learning

Recent reviews of language acquisition theory (McLaughlin 1978, 1987; Ellis 1985, 1990; Brown 1987; Larsen-Freeman 1991) have attempted to group various theoretical perspectives along a kind of continuum, ranging from *empiricist* views on one end to *rationalist* or *mentalist* positions on the other, with theories that blend these two perspectives placed somewhere in between. This opposition of viewpoints is not new; Chomsky had made the rationalist/empiricist distinction in discussing linguistic theory in 1965, and Diller (1978) spoke of the existence of a longstanding language teaching controversy between the *rationalists* and the *empiricists* "whose roots can be traced to the beginnings of modern thought" (p. vii). The basic difference

*For a comprehensive survey of foreign language teacher attitudes about a wide range of methodological issues, see R. DeGarcia, S. Reynolds, and S. Savignon, "Foreign Language Attitude Survey," *Canadian Modern Language Review*, vol. 32 (1976): 302–04.

between the two positions seems to lie in the presumed locus of control of the process of language acquisition. The rationalist position assumes that humans have an innate capacity for the development of language, and that we are genetically programmed to develop our linguistic systems in certain ways (Chomsky 1965; McLaughlin 1978, p. 19). Larsen-Freeman (1991) refers to this point of view as a "nativist" or "innateness" position, which is in strong opposition to the "behaviorist" or "environmentalist" perspective. This latter position is characteristic of the empiricists, who maintain that it is the learner's experience that is largely responsible for language learning and is more important than any specific innate capacity (Larsen-Freeman 1991, p. 323.) McLaughlin (1978) characterizes the empiricist viewpoint as one that is skeptical of any explanation of language learning that cannot be observed. Learning is seen as the result of external forces acting on the organism rather than the programmed unfolding of language through internal biological mechanisms. Empiricists, therefore, assume that there is no special species-specific language ability, but that language learning is just one aspect of general learning ability or capacity (pp. 19–20).

The next section provides a sampling of theories representing these different categories or classifications, chosen to reflect some of those perspectives that have had the most influence or potential influence on classroom practice. Because there is such a profusion of competing theoretical viewpoints in the professional literature, this discussion will not be comprehensive. The interested reader would do well to consult additional sources such as Ellis (1985, 1990), Brown (1987), McLaughlin (1987), Spolsky (1989), and Larsen-Freeman and Long (1991) for more detailed treatments of a wide spectrum of theoretical viewpoints.

From Empiricism To Rationalism: A Theoretical Sampler

The various theories of language learning to be discussed in this section have been placed along the continuum in Illustration 2.2, which depicts in graphic form the range of viewpoints referred to in the preceding pages. The placement on the continuum is not meant to be exact or precise, but rather locates theories in a general way in terms of their compatibility with empiricist or rationalist points of view. The characteristics and underlying assumptions of each of these theories will be briefly summarized below. For a more thorough treatment of a particular theory, consult the primary sources in the references.

An Empiricist Perspective: Behaviorism

Since ancient times philosophers have believed that human learning and animal learning might be parallel, if not contiguous (Chastain 1976). Chastain points out that it was the publication of Darwin's *Origin of the Species* in 1859 that made this belief more credible, since Darwin's theory implied that there was indeed a continuity between the human species and the lower animals, and by implication between the human mind and the animal mind. In the late nineteenth and early twentieth centuries, a growing interest in animal

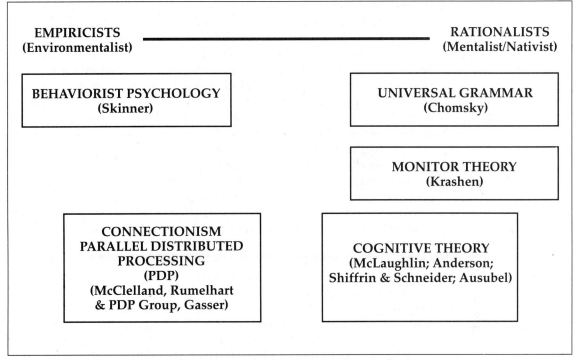

Illustration 2.2 The Rationalist-Empiricist Continuum (Based on McLaughlin 1978, 1987; Brown 1987; Larsen-Freeman 1991; Larsen-Freeman and Long 1991)

behavior led to the growth of experimental psychology and the school of behaviorism. Experimentalists, such as John B. Watson (1878–1958), reacted strongly against the tradition of the times that the province of psychology was the *introspective study* of conscious experience, and maintained that psychological data ought to be limited to that which could be directly observed, as in the other objective sciences (Hilgard 1962). This "scientific" or empiricist approach to psychology caught on, particularly in the 1920s, and soon the psychologist's couch was replaced with laboratory tables on which rested intricate mazes, boxes, and cages. Within the walls of these experimental contraptions, rats, pigeons, and other small animals were learning through "conditioning" to turn to the left or right, peck at disks, and press bars to obtain food. The S-R (stimulus-response) school of psychology grew out of these experiments, and it was this newest form of behaviorism that prevailed in psychology and education into the 1950s.

In S-R psychology, all behavior is viewed as a response to stimuli, whether the behavior is overt (explicit) or covert (implicit). According to the theory, behavior happens in causal, associative chains; all learning is thus characterized as associative learning, or habit formation, brought about by the repeated association of a stimulus with a response (Hilgard

1962). This process of habit formation, or *conditioning,* was thought to be of three basic types: (1) classical conditioning, (2) operant conditioning, and (3) multiple response learning (pp. 253–274).

In *classical conditioning* (best known through experiments done by Pavlov), an association between a conditioned stimulus and a response was repeatedly strengthened through the presentation of that stimulus with another, unconditioned one. In Pavlov's experiments with dogs, the unconditioned stimulus was meat powder and the response was salivation. When Pavlov repeatedly presented the meat powder with the simultaneous ringing of a bell, the dog learned to salivate to the sound of the bell (the conditioned stimulus), even in the absence of the meat.

In *operant conditioning* (also known as *instrumental conditioning*), the response to a stimulus is learned although it is not normally a natural response to that stimulus. A rat pressing a bar in its cage may at first do so randomly. But if the rat discovers that pressing the bar releases a food pellet, it learns to push the bar again for the same reward. The *operant* (the random bar-pushing behavior) becomes conditioned (purposeful behavior) because it produces an effect that is rewarding.

In *multiple-response learning,* the animal learns a whole chain of behaviors and performs them in succession, always in the same order. A rat that runs a maze learns a fixed series of turns through conditioning, rewarded by a food pellet or two for his trouble.

What has all of this to do with language learning? As Chastain (1976) points out, behaviorism took a strong foothold in the thinking of psychologists by the middle of the century, influencing, in turn, the views of the education community:

> *Soon behaviorists concluded that all learning consisted of some form of conditioning. The organism was conditioned to respond in a specific way to a selected stimulus. Complex activities were nothing more than a complex collection of conditioned responses. Since all learning is conditioned and since human learning is similar to learning in animals, the next step was to conclude that human learning could be, and is, conditioned in the same way. The belief was that humans are reinforced by their environment in much the same way as the rat in a maze (p. 105).*

B. F. Skinner (1957), perhaps the best known proponent of S-R psychology, used the term *operant conditioning* to describe verbal learning. In his view, language is characterized as a sophisticated response system that humans acquire through automatic conditioning processes. Some patterns of language are reinforced (rewarded) and others are not. Only those patterns reinforced by the community of language users will persist. In Skinnerian psychology, the human being is likened to a machine with multiple working parts. The mind is thought to be a *tabula rasa* onto which are stamped associations between various stimuli in the environment and responses chosen from outside the organism for reinforcement (Chastain 1976).

Illustration 2.3
Summary: Behaviorist
Theory (Based on
Skinner 1957; Hilgard
1962; Chastain 1976;
Wardhaugh 1976)

Summary: Behaviorist Theory

1. Human learning and animal learning are similar.
2. The child's mind is a *tabula rasa*. There is no innate pre-programming specifically for language learning at birth.
3. Psychological data should be limited to that which is observable.
4. All behavior is viewed as a response to stimuli. Behavior happens in associative chains; in fact, all learning is associative in nature.
5. Conditioning involves the strengthening of associations between a stimulus and a response through reinforcement.
6. Human language is a sophisticated response system acquired through operant conditioning.

Skinner's theory of verbal learning was consistent with the prevailing beliefs of many applied linguists of the 1940s and 1950s who maintained that second-languages should be learned through extensive drill and practice without recourse to rationalistic explanation. In his *Outline Guide for the Practical Study of Foreign Languages* (1942), Bloomfield had argued for an essentially behavioristic approach:

> *The command of a language is not a matter of knowledge: the speakers are quite unable to describe the habits which make up their language. The command of a language is a matter of practice. . . . Language learning is overlearning: anything else is of no use (Bloomfield 1942, p. 12, cited in Chastain 1976, pp. 107–08).*

Illustration 2.3 summarizes the main points of the behaviorist view of language learning. Behaviorist theory, in conjunction with the structuralist views of language that prevailed in the 1940s and 1950s, laid the theoretical foundations for audiolingual language teaching methodology, discussed in more detail in Chapter 3.

Critique: We have seen that behavioristic theories of language learning were based on the assumption that language learning was like any other kind of learning, and, therefore, one could extrapolate heavily from general learning theory and even from animal learning. This viewpoint was seriously challenged by Chomsky (1959) in a very critical review of Skinner's work. Chomsky maintained that language behavior was far more complex than the establishment of S-R connections, and that Skinner's theory could not possibly explain the creativity of children in generating language.

According to McLaughlin (1978), Skinner's 1957 treatise, *Verbal Behavior,* was not supported by research with human subjects. There was, in fact, no real research base ever generated by behaviorists to look at child language use, let alone second-language learning (p. 21). Evidence gleaned from subsequent studies of child language behavior shows that a simple behavioristic perspective does not provide a satisfactory explanation of what has been found: it seems that imitation and reinforcement have a much smaller role to play in child language than Skinner and his colleagues imagined. Parents rarely correct their children's grammatical errors, but respond instead to the message content. If errors are thus positively rewarded (or at least ignored), how then do children eventually eliminate them? Furthermore, children often produce forms that they never heard their parents or other adults say ("I goed," "two foots"). Imitation of adult speech cannot account for the way children produce language: "The child's language is simply too strange" (McLaughlin 1978, p. 22).

With Chomsky's review of Skinner's theory there came a paradigm shift toward the other end of the theoretical continuum. If language development was highly creative, then language learning theories needed to account for the creative processing that was taking place in the human mind. By the mid-1960s, the pendulum was swinging in the direction of the rationalist point of view

Three Rationalist Perspectives of Language Learning

1. Universal Grammar Various reviews of theories of language learning (Chastain 1976; Wardhaugh 1976; McLaughlin 1978, 1987; Ellis 1985, 1990; Brown 1987; Larsen-Freeman 1991) group a variety of perspectives within the "rationalist" camp. Other terms used in association with this perspective are "nativist," "mentalist," and "cognitive." A highly influential nativist viewpoint grew out of Chomsky's work, starting with the publication in 1957 of his book, *Syntactic Structures* and his critique of Skinner in 1959. As we saw earlier, Chomsky had rejected the behaviorist perspective and adopted instead a mentalist viewpoint that was closely related to the basic principles and beliefs of cognitive psychology (Chastain 1976, p. 137). Other theorists, such as Eric Lennenberg (1967) and David McNeill (1966) believed that language was a species-specific, genetically determined capacity and that language learning was therefore governed by biological mechanisms. In 1965, Chomsky had concluded that children were born with some kind of special language processing ability and had proposed the existence of a "language acquisition device" (LAD). A year later, McNeill (1966) characterized this LAD as having various innate linguistic properties. Brown (1987) summarized them as follows: (1) the ability to distinguish speech sounds from other sounds; (2) the ability to organize language into a system of structures; (3) the knowledge of what was possible and what was not possible in any linguistic system; and (4) the ability to construct the simplest possible system based on the linguistic data to which one was exposed.

Chomsky argued further that it must be the case that children were innately programmed to acquire language since they do it so quickly (in just a few years) and with such limited (and less than ideal) input. He also believed that they could not help but construct a certain kind of linguistic system—a particular transformational or generative grammar—any more than they could help the way their visual system perceived solid objects or lines and angles (Chomsky 1965, p. 59). Although a child's experience with language input could have an effect on language learning, the "ultimate form will be a function of those language universals that exist in the human mind" (McLaughlin 1978, p. 24).

Universal Grammar theory posits the existence of a set of basic grammatical elements or "fixed abstract principles" that are common to all natural human languages and that predispose children to organize the input in certain ways (Chomsky 1965). The principles themselves are thought to be innate, a product of the "LAD." They include *substantive* universals, which consist of fixed features of languages like phonemes or syntactic categories like nouns and verbs, as well as *formal* universals, which are more abstract, and which place limits or constraints on the possible rule systems or on the options children have for constructing a grammar (Chomsky 1965, pp. 27–30; Ellis 1985, pp. 192–93).

An example of a substantive universal is the principle that all languages have vowels. Yet each language has a set of vowels selected from all the possible vowels available, resulting in differing phonological characteristics from language to language. Formal universals are statements about what grammatical rules are possible in human languages. Ellis (1985) provides the following example: one might formulate certain principles that place limits on how languages can use word order transformations in order to form questions. All languages must operate within those limited options, yet each language has its own particular "parameters" or "settings" for question formation. The child's task is to discover which of the various options applies in his or her language. This is where environmental input is crucial: the child needs to hear the language spoken in order to select the appropriate options and thus set the parameters correctly (p. 193).

According to Chomsky, the universal principles that children discover constitute their "core grammar," which is congruent with general principles operating across all languages. The "peripheral grammar" consists of rules or features that are not determined by universal grammar, but that might be derived from an older form of the language, borrowed from another language, or that might have arisen accidentally (Ellis 1985, p. 193; McLaughlin 1987, p. 95). Rules of the core grammar might be easier to acquire than the rules of the peripheral grammar, since the latter are thought to be "outside of the child's preprogrammed instructions" (McLaughlin 1987, p. 96).

Chomsky's Universal Grammar theory and associated derivative approaches to the study of linguistic universals are quite complex. Most discussions of the research in this area require some specialized knowledge of theoretical linguistics in order to fully understand the findings. As was mentioned earlier, the discussion of theories in this chapter is meant to be introductory in nature; readers interested in a more detailed treatment

Illustration 2.4
Summary: Universal Grammar Theory (Based on Chomsky 1965; Ellis 1985; McLaughlin 1987; Larsen-Freeman 1991).

Summary: Universal Grammar Theory

1. Language is a species-specific, genetically determined capacity.
2. Language learning is governed by biological mechanisms.
3. The ultimate form of any human language is a function of language universals, a set of fixed abstract principles that are innate.
4. Each language has its own "parameters" whose "settings" are learned on the basis of linguistic data.
5. There is a "core grammar," congruent with universal principles, and a "peripheral grammar," consisting of features that are not part of universal grammar.
6. Core grammar rules are thought to be relatively easier to acquire, in general, than peripheral rules.

should consult the sources cited in this section. For a summary of some of the main premises of Universal Grammar theory that have been presented here, see Illustration 2.4.

Critique:

How does Universal Grammar in child language acquisition affect adult second-language learning? McLaughlin (1987) states that Universal Grammar theory "does not concern itself with second-language acquisition" (p. 91), but that a number of second-language researchers have applied principles of Universal Grammar to this domain in an effort to find sufficiently sophisticated explanations of the very complex characteristics of interlanguages. Some theorists operate on the assumption that the same universals that children use to construct their native language are available to adults; others believe that they are no longer available, and that different cognitive processes must be involved in adult second/foreign language learning (see Larsen-Freeman 1991). The rationalist theories that are discussed in the next two sections represent two different perspectives in this debate.

2. Krashen's Monitor Theory: First and Second-Language Acquisition are Similar

One of the most influential and widely discussed models of language learning/acquisition in recent years is Stephen Krashen's "Monitor Model." The most complete description of the theory (1982) describes five central hypotheses:

1. *The acquisition-learning distinction,* which states that adults have two distinct and independent ways of developing competence in a second language: *acquisition,* which is a subconscious process similar, if not identical, to the way children develop ability in their first language; and *learning,* which refers to conscious knowledge of the rules of grammar of a second language and their application in production.

2. *The natural order hypothesis,* which maintains that acquisition of grammatical structures (primarily morphemes) proceeds in a

predictable order when that acquisition is natural (i.e., not via formal learning).

3. *The monitor hypothesis,* which states that acquisition is the sole initiator of all second-language utterances and is responsible for fluency, while learning (conscious knowledge of rules) can function only as an "editor" or "monitor" for the output. This monitor operates only when there is sufficient time, the focus is on form, and the language user knows the rule being applied.

4. *The input hypothesis,* which maintains that we acquire more language only when we are exposed to "comprehensible input"—language that contains structures that are "a little beyond" our current level of competence ($i + 1$), but which is comprehensible through our use of context, our knowledge of the world, and other extralinguistic cues directed to us. According to this hypothesis, acquirers "go for meaning" first, and, as a result, acquire structure as well. A third part of this hypothesis states that input need not be deliberately planned to contain appropriate structures ($i + 1$): if communication is successful and there is enough of it, $i + 1$ is provided automatically. A final part of the input hypothesis maintains that speaking fluency cannot be taught directly, but rather "emerges" naturally over time. Krashen maintains that although early speech is not grammatically accurate, accuracy will develop over time as the acquirer hears and understands more input.

5. *The affective filter hypothesis* states that comprehensible input can have its effect on acquisition only when affective conditions are optimal: (1) the acquirer is motivated; (2) he has self-confidence and a good self-image; and (3) his level of anxiety is low. When learners are "put on the defensive" (see Stevick 1976), the affective filter is high, and comprehensible input can not "get in." (For a fuller account of these five hypotheses, see Krashen 1982, pp. 9–32).

Krashen suggests that there are certain implications for classroom practice if language instruction is to be consistent with his theory. Among these are:

1. The main function of the classroom may be to provide comprehensible input in an environment conducive to a low affective filter (i.e., high motivation, low anxiety).

2. The classroom is most useful for beginners, who cannot easily utilize the informal environment for input. That is, it is useful for foreign language students who do not have input sources outside of class or those whose competence is so low that they are unable to understand the language of the outside world (pp. 33–37).

3. The requirements for optimal input are that it be (a) comprehensible, (b) interesting and relevant, (c) *not* grammatically sequenced,

(d) provided in sufficient quantity to supply $i + 1$, and (e) delivered in an environment where students are "off the defensive" (p. 127).

4. Error correction should be minimal in the classroom; it is of *some* limited use when the goal is learning, but of *no* use when the goal is acquisition. Error correction raises the affective filter and should, therefore not be used in free conversation or when acquisition is likely to take place (pp. 116–117).

5. Students should never be required to produce speech in the second language unless they are ready to do so. Speaking fluency cannot be taught, but "emerges" naturally in time with enough comprehensible input.

Illustration 2.5 summarizes the main premises of Monitor Theory. A more completely developed model of language teaching using Krashen's theory as a basis is given by Terrell (1977, 1982). His "Natural Approach" is discussed in detail in Chapter 3.

Critique: A number of the hypotheses and assertions in Krashen's theory of second-language acquisition have been challenged in recent years. In an early review of the Monitor Model, Munsell and Carr (1981) questioned the distinction between "learning" and "acquisition" and the notion of "conscious" and "unconscious" rules. The reviewers also seem to object to the underlying nativist assumptions of the model and the implications that language learning is distinct from other kinds of learning. In their view, language skill is much like other kinds of skilled performance:

> *Krashen may not wish to extend Monitor Theory to chess, yet the measured characteristics of the knowledge of skilled chess players bear some striking similarities to the characteristics of linguistic knowledge. . . . Similarly, such disparate areas of skill as sports and mathematics seem to benefit from early emphasis on conscious and systematic learning despite the fact that expert performances in these areas also display a number of characteristics that formally resemble expert performance in language. We cannot imagine trying to learn basketball, monopoly, bridge, or quantum mechanics simply by watching people do them, trying them, and creatively constructing the rules. It is much easier to start with conscious exposition of the rules and build one's skill upon that foundation (pp. 498–99).*

Munsell and Carr imply that Krashen should incorporate language learning theory into a wider context where the nature of human skilled performance in general is explored. This point of view is congruent with the commentary on Monitor Theory made by McLaughlin (1987) who leans toward a more *cognitive* perspective.

McLaughlin's objections to Monitor Theory are summarized in the following five points:

Illustration 2.5
Summary of Monitor
Theory (Based on
Krashen 1982)

Summary: Monitor Theory

1. Adults have two distinct ways to develop competence in a second language: *acquisition,* which is a subconscious process, and *learning,* which is conscious.
2. *Acquisition* is similar to the process by which children acquire their native language. *Learning* involves conscious knowledge of rules.
3. When *acquisition* is natural, the order in which certain grammatical features of the language are acquired is predictable.
4. *Learning* can function only as an "editor" of what is produced, since *acquisition* is the sole initiator of all second-language utterances. Learning can serve as a "monitor" of performance only under certain conditions.
5. We acquire new structures only when we are exposed to "comprehensible input" ($i + 1$). Input does not need to be deliberately structured or planned for the acquirer. If communication is successful, $i + 1$ will happen automatically.
6. For acquisition to take place, the learner must be motivated, have a good self-image, and be free from anxiety.
7. Error correction should be minimized in the classroom, where the main purpose of instruction should be to provide comprehensible input.

---

1. The acquisition-learning distinction is not clearly defined. Therefore, the central claim that Krashen makes that "learning" cannot become "acquisition" cannot be tested.
2. Various studies have shown that the Monitor does not work the way Krashen originally thought it would, and he has had to place more and more restrictions on the conditions under which it would be used effectively. McLaughlin believes that these restrictions make Krashen's conceptualization of "learning" of limited usefulness in explaining a learner's conscious knowledge of grammar.
3. The case for the Natural Order Hypothesis is quite weak due to methodological problems. "If the Natural Order Hypothesis is to be accepted, it must be in a weak form, which postulates that some things are learned before others, but not always" (p. 56).
4. Since no clear definition is given of "comprehensible input," McLaughlin believes the Input Hypothesis is also untestable.
5. The Affective Filter Hypothesis is also questionable, not only because Krashen has not explained how this filter develops, but also because it does not take individual differences among learners into account. McLaughlin states that this hypothesis is incapable of predicting the course of linguistic development with any precision (p. 56).

Although Krashen's theory has been criticized on a variety of points by a number of scholars, it has also had a strong influence on thinking in the field over the past fifteen years. Virtually everyone who talks about language learning in recent years seems compelled to consider whether it is "learning" or "acquisition" that is the focus of attention in one's remarks. Many people feel that the distinction has at least an intuitive appeal and that it represents some psychological reality. In the same way, many practitioners recognize the need to provide learners with "comprehensible input" and find Krashen's recommendation that affective considerations be primary in the classroom very appealing. In many ways, Krashen has articulated in his Monitor Theory hypotheses about language learning that have touched a responsive chord for many practitioners. This is not to say, however, that the criticisms reviewed above should not be considered seriously as one evaluates the merits of Monitor Theory.

As mentioned earlier, some theorists prefer a cognitive view of language learning which recognizes essential differences between the way children and adults process information. Although there may be some similarities between child and adult language learning, Cognitive Theory predicts that adult second-language learning will differ in some important ways from the way in which children acquire their native tongue.

3. Cognitive Theory: First and Second-Language Learning Differ

Larsen-Freeman and Long (1991) categorize various cognitive approaches to language acquisition as "interactionist" views, where both external and internal factors are considered in accounting for language acquisition (p. 266). Although this characterization may be valid, the emphasis on environmental factors seems rather limited when compared to the role assigned to internal or mental processes in descriptions of Cognitive Theory given by Ausubel (1968), Ellis (1985, 1990), and McLaughlin (1987, 1990). For this reason, the theory has been placed toward the rationalist end of the continuum in Illustration 2.2.

We have seen that Universal Grammar theory considers the role of innate linguistic universals in language acquisition and claims that there is a specific *linguistic* capacity that is unique to the human species. Cognitive Theory, by contrast, derives from the field of cognitive psychology and focuses on the role of more *general* cognitive processes involved in language acquisition, such as transfer, simplification, generalization, and restructuring (McLaughlin 1987). Like Universal Grammar, Cognitive Theory is in direct opposition to Behaviorist Theory because, from a cognitive perspective, learning is believed to result from internal mental activity rather than from something imposed from outside the learner (Ellis 1990, p. 7). McLaughlin (1990) characterizes the cognitive approach to second-language acquisition as follows:

1. Cognitive psychology emphasizes *knowing* rather than *responding* and is concerned with studying mental processes involved in the acquisition and use of knowledge. "The focus is not stimulus-response bonds, but mental events" (p. 113).
2. The cognitive approach emphasizes *mental structure* or *organization*. Following Jean Piaget's view that "all living creatures are born with

an invariant tendency to organize experience" (McLaughlin 1990, p. 113), cognitive psychology assumes human knowledge is organized and that anything new that is learned is integrated into this structure.

3. Cognitive Theory, as opposed to Behaviorist Theory, views the learner as one who acts, constructs, and plans rather than simply receives stimuli from the environment. Therefore, a complete understanding of human cognition would require an analysis of strategies used for thinking, understanding, remembering, and producing language.

According to Cognitive Theory, second-language learning is seen as the acquisition of a complex cognitive skill. For a language learner to become proficient, subskills of this complex task must be practiced, automatized, integrated, and organized into internal representations, or rule systems, that are constantly restructured as proficiency develops (McLaughlin 1987, pp. 133–34).

Automization refers to the process of making a skill routine through practice. McLaughlin explains the way this is thought to occur using an information processing model developed by Shiffrin and Schneider (1977). In this model, memory is thought to consist of a large number of "nodes" that become associated with one another and activated in sequence through learning. In *automatic processing,* certain nodes are activated every time a certain input is presented. This activation pattern has been built up through consistent practice so that it becomes a learned response over time. Once such an automatic response is learned, it occurs quite quickly and is difficult to suppress or change (McLaughlin 1987, p. 134).

In *controlled processing,* memory nodes are activated in a given sequence on a temporary basis—that is, the response has not yet been "learned" or automatized. For the response to happen, the learner has to give the process his full attention. It is difficult, therefore, to do "controlled" tasks if there is any distraction or interference (p. 135).

In the Shiffrin and Schneider model, skills are learned (automatized) only after they have first been under controlled processing. "Thus controlled processing can be said to lay down the 'stepping stones' for automatic processing as the learner moves to more and more difficult levels" (Shiffrin and Schneider 1977, cited in McLaughlin 1987, p. 135).

This distinction between controlled and automatic processing can be useful as one considers the various tasks involved in second-language learning. Tarone (1982, 1983) has described a whole range of language "styles" that learners produce when engaged in various kinds of tasks. McLaughlin maintains that these style variations relate in part to the continuum of controlled to automatic processing. According to Tarone (1982, 1983) the *vernacular style,* represented by informal use of the language with little attention to form, is produced when language is being processed automatically. The *careful style*, on the other hand, is elicited when learners engage in heavy monitoring and/or attention to the form of their production. This monitoring represents a more controlled processing of the language needed to accomplish the task. Tasks that demand such monitoring include grammaticality judgments or form-focused production activities of various kinds. Tarone (1982) explains that the learners' interlanguge system should be thought of as a *continuum,* ranging from the vernacular to the careful style, and does not, as Krashen (1982) has claimed, consist of two discrete systems differentiated on the basis of whether or not the attention to form is conscious or subconscious.

The "variability" of learner language is evident when students at different proficiency levels engage in tasks of different types. Teachers may have noticed this phenomenon of variability when their students perform differently while doing a discrete-point grammar task on a test or for an assignment than they do when using the language more naturally or informally in conversation or in free composition. Rather than feeling frustrated and confused by this phenomenon, teachers and students might be encouraged by a view of language learning such as this that accounts for such differences in performance.

While McLaughlin, following Shiffrin and Schneider, contrasts controlled and automatic processing, Ellis (1990) adds Anderson's (1980, 1985) distinction between *declarative* and *procedural* knowledge as another way to look at how information is processed and stored. *Declarative knowledge* is explicit and conscious, and can be articulated by the learner. It involves "knowing that" (e.g., definitions of words, facts, rules). *Procedural knowledge,* on the other hand, is "knowing how" (e.g., how to produce language as one performs linguistically). This type of knowledge might be more or less implicit or explicit, conscious or unconscious, or relatively controlled or relatively automatic in nature. Ellis explains that Anderson's model of learning consists of three stages: (1) the cognitive stage, where learners use conscious declarative knowledge; (2) the associative stage, where they start to proceduralize this knowledge; and (3) the autonomous stage, where language performance becomes more or less automatic and errors disappear (Anderson 1985, pp. 234–35; Ellis 1990, p. 177). All of these models attempt to explain the processes by which learning becomes internalized and eventually "automatic," but each looks at the processes involved in somewhat different ways.

Cognitive Theory further maintains that there is more to developing a complex skill than automatizing the sub-skills of which it is comprised. The learner also has to impose an organizational structure on the new information that is constantly being added to the system. As new information is learned, the organization of the existing information might have to be changed, or "restructured," to accommodate what is new. That is why both *automatization* and *restructuring* are key concepts in this view of language learning (McLaughlin 1987, p. 136).

The idea of the development of internal "structures" or organized cognitive systems and networks is central to views of learning that derive from Cognitive Theory. Cognitive psychologists have tried to explain, from a psycholinguistic viewpoint, how such internal representations of the foreign language develop within the learner's mind. Other cognitive theorists, working from an educational perspective, have sought to describe ways in which teachers can organize instruction so that learning is enhanced. One early proponent of applying general principles of cognitive psychology to educational contexts was David Ausubel (1968), who emphasized the importance of active mental participation by the learner in meaningful learning tasks. Central to his understanding of learning was the concept of "cognitive structure," which he defined as the quantity, clarity, and organization of the learner's present knowledge in a given subject. This knowledge consists of facts, concepts, theories, and raw perceptual data (Ausubel 1968, pp. 127-28) and was thought to be hierarchical in nature. New information could be related to it in superordinate, coordinate, or subordinate relationships (p. 52). Of course, the addition of new information implied a reorganization, or "restructuring," of the system in some way.

Ausubel believed that only two types of learning are relevant to educational contexts: *rote learning* and *meaningful learning* (p. 24). Rote learning is arbitrary and verbatim; that is, the material to be learned is not integrated or "subsumed" into one's "cognitive structure," but is learned as an isolated or discrete piece of information. In this way, the cognitive system is not "restructured," because the new information does not become integrated. Learning lists of vocabulary, especially when there is no connection between the words or context to which they can be related, would be an example of a rote learning task. Vocabulary words or dialogue lines that are memorized rotely but that are not integrated into existing cognitive structure might easily be lost later. Conversely, some rotely learned material might be available for years, but such material can only be reproduced verbatim if it is not integrated into the cognitive network in some way. Rotely learned information cannot be changed or paraphrased unless it is processed meaningfully.

Meaningful learning, on the other hand, is relatable to what one already knows and thus can be easily integrated into one's existing cognitive structure (p. 24). If one knows that in French, descriptive adjectives agree in gender and number with the noun they modify, the new information that possessive adjectives also agree in this way can be easily mastered and retained. In this instance, the concept of adjective agreement might be thought of as the "subsumer," or "anchoring idea" (p. 92), and the possessive adjective agreement rule would be subsumed under it in cognitive structure. Perhaps the same student will study Spanish the following year. The rule that Spanish descriptive adjectives agree with the nouns they modify can then be subsumed via correlation with the French agreement rule.

Ausubel adds, however, that in order for learning to be meaningful, the learner has to have an intention to learn—that is, a willingness to approach the learning task with the intention of relating the new material meaningfully to what is already known (p. 38). A potentially meaningful bit of information might be learned rotely if the learner approaches it as a rote (i.e., verbatim) task and does not relate it to other information he/she already has. In Ausubel's view, learning must be meaningful to be effective and permanent.

How can teachers enhance the meaningfulness of new material for students and increase the chances that it will be anchored to what is already known? Ausubel suggests that the material be organized so that it is more easily relatable to previously learned material. New material should also be sequenced appropriately so that it can be integrated into previous knowledge. He recommends the use of advance organizers, which are introductory materials at a high level of generality presented in advance of the new material to be learned. Organizers might include devices such as pictures depicting the general context for the new material, titles for stories, provision of a verbal description of the general context, or reviews of previously learned concepts, including grammar rules. Such organizers will facilitate the learning process by providing a kind of general anchoring idea to which the new knowledge can be attached—to "bridge the gap between what the learner already knows and what he needs to know before he can successfully learn the task at hand" (p. 148). Ideas such as these underlie "cognitive approaches" to methodology, treated in Chapter 3.

Illustration 2.6 summarizes some of the assumptions underlying Cognitive Theory, as represented by the various perspectives described in this section.

Critique: How does Cognitive Theory hold up under critical scrutiny among the competing theories discussed thus far? McLaughlin's (1987) critique includes several cautionary statements. First, conceiving of language learning as a "complex cognitive skill" is not comprehensive enough. Language learning also involves acquiring a "complex linguistic skill" (p. 150). By itself, cognitive theory is not capable of explaining some of the constraints on the development of language that may result from linguistic universals, for example. McLaughlin believes that Cognitive Theory needs to be linked to linguistic theories of second-language acquisition. If both viewpoints are explored together, a cognitive perspective of language learning might become more powerful. For example, the understanding of "restructuring" in second-language acquisition would be more comprehensive and enriched by research into the linguistic details of the restructuring process (p. 150). Cognitive Theory also does not predict explicitly when certain features of a first language will be transferred to a second language or explain why certain features do not transfer. Linguistic theory may make more specific predictions, thus adding information about language learning that Cognitive Theory alone cannot provide.

Illustration 2.6

Summary: Cognitive Theory (Based on Ausubel 1968; Tarone 1982, 1983; Ellis 1985, 1990; McLaughlin 1987, 1990)

Summary: Cognitive Theory

1. Learning results from internal mental activity. Language learning is a type of general human learning and involves the acquisition of a complex cognitive skill.

2. Subskills involved in the complex task of language learning must be practiced, automatized, and integrated into organized internal representations, or rule systems, in cognitive structure.

3. Internal representations of language are constantly restructured as proficiency develops.

4. Skills are automatized (learned) only after they have first been under "controlled processing." Controlled processing, which requires attention to the task, leads to automatic processing, where attention is not needed to perform the skill (Shiffrin and Schneider 1977; McLaughlin 1987).

5. Some researchers (Tarone 1982, 1983; Ellis 1985) maintain that learners' production is variable, depending on the degree of attention they pay to language form as they carry out various tasks. Informal tasks that demand little active attention elicit the "vernacular style," while tasks that require active attention and monitoring elicit the "careful style."

6. Some cognitive theorists (Anderson 1980; Ellis 1985) distinguish between *declarative* knowledge, which involves "knowing that," and *procedural* knowledge, which involves "knowing how."

7. Ausubel (1968) emphasizes that *meaningful learning,* which is learning that is relatable to what we already know, is preferable to *rote learning,* which is arbitrary and verbatim. Only *meaningful* material can be integrated into existing cognitive structure.

Ellis (1990) adds that although Cognitive Theory is much more convincing than Behaviorism, it is not able to account satisfactorily for the fact that there are quite a number of regularities in the way in which second-language knowledge is acquired in classroom learning (p. 8). Although it is important and appropriate to extrapolate from general Cognitive Theory when looking at classroom language learning, Ellis feels that second-language learning might be different from other kinds of learning (such as learning history or science) in some important ways. This view is congruent, at least in part, with what Universal Grammar theory is saying about language learning being a specialized kind of competence and not just a subset of general human learning. As with most other theories discussed in this chapter, applications from Cognitive Theory must be explored and tested more thoroughly in the years ahead to determine its value in understanding how people become proficient in a second language.

Connectionism: A New Challenge to Rationalist Models of Cognition

The rationalist models described in the last section share a common belief that language is rule-governed behavior and that language learners, therefore, develop complex, internalized rule systems that can be represented symbolically (Gasser 1990). In the past few years, there has been increased interest shown in *connectionist* models of the mind which challenge traditional symbolic models of cognition. Connectionist theorists have attempted to base their models on what is known about the function of the human brain. According to McClelland (1989), the term "connectionist models" was introduced by Feldman (1981) to refer to those models of the mind that describe mental processing by means of connections among very simple processing units. McClelland and other scholars have been interested in determining what kind of processing mechanism the mind really is. Does the human brain process information one step at a time, in a serial or sequential manner, like a conventional computer? Or does it engage in processing information throughout a network of simple processing units that "fire off" simultaneously, in concert? Neuroscience indicates that the human brain consists of "some tens of billions of neurons" (McClelland 1989, p. 8) which are available for processing of human thought and perception. Neurons are thought to be "relatively sluggish, noisy processing devices, compared to today's computers" (p. 8), yet the mind is capable of recognizing objects or perceiving a complex visual scene in an instant. How are these two facts about mental processing reconciled? McClelland and his colleagues argue that interconnected processing units would have to work in a parallel rather than in a serial manner to achieve such rapid results. Therefore, the mind must be a parallel, rather than a sequential, processor of information.

Theoretical models of mental processing that are based on a parallel view are known as parallel distributed processing (PDP) models, neural models, or connectionist models (McClelland 1989, p. 9). Connections between simple processing units are thought to have different strengths or "weights." In connectionist models, *learning* consists of adjusting the strengths of connections so that a given "teaching input" eventually results in a desired "output" (Pinker and Prince 1989). That is, connections are either strengthened or weakened in response to regularities in patterns of input that are presented to the system (Gasser 1990). Thus, the network of connections is "trained" to make certain associations between inputs and outputs. As Rumelhart and McClelland (1986a) explain, *"knowledge is in the connections* rather than in the units themselves" (p. 132).

Thus, connectionist models of the mind do not posit discrete symbols or rules as conceptual or "higher-order" units or sets of units surrounded by a clear boundary; rather, knowledge consists of "fluid patterns of activation across portions of a network" (Gasser 1990, p. 180). Where rationalist models of cognition describe a kind of "central executive" that oversees the general flow of processing, choosing rules or principles to be applied and executing them, connectionist models consider the control of information processing to be distributed among the many parts of the network (Rumelhart and McClelland 1986a, p. 134). As Gasser (1990) explains, there are no rules to be executed. Larsen-Freeman and Long (1991) add that "the networks control what looks like rule-governed behavior, but which is simply a reflection of the connections formed on the basis of the relative strengths of various patterns in the input" (p. 250). This perspective of cognition is thus quite different from that of rationalist theories such as Universal Grammar, Monitor Theory, or Cognitive Theory.

An example of how a connectionist model might work in language acquisition is described by Rumelhart and McClelland (1986b) and summarized as follows by Pinker and Prince (1989). Rumelhart and McClelland demonstrated that their computerized network model, which had not been programmed with any grammatical rules and had no representations of words, verb stems, suffixes, or conjugation patterns within it, could "learn" to use regular and irregular English past-tense verb forms correctly simply by comparing its own version of the past tense forms with the correct versions provided by the "teacher" over an extensive number of trials. The network simply adjusted the strengths of the connections between processing units until the difference between inputs and outputs was sufficiently reduced. The PDP system thus demonstrated rule-like behavior without having any rules. Furthermore, the system exhibited some of the same types of behavior that young children exhibit when learning the verb system of English: first, children use past tense forms (both regular and irregular) correctly; then, as they overgeneralize the -ed ending from regular to irregular verbs, they produce incorrect forms like "goed" or "broked"; finally, they work out the rule system and begin to produce both regular and irregular verb forms correctly. The Rumelhart and McClelland demonstration seems to suggest that associationist theories of language acquisition, such as those the behaviorists espoused in the 1950s, might have some merit (Pinker and Prince 1989, p. 183). However, Pinker and Prince take exception to the Rumelhart-McClelland model and point out some empirical flaws, which, in their view, weaken the case of a connectionist account of language behavior. Some of their arguments are summarized in the *Critique* section, below.

Because connectionist models are so new, it is difficult to characterize a connectionist perspective on linguistics or second-language learning at this point other than in very general and tentative terms. Illustration 2.7 summarizes some of the points made in this discussion. For a more thorough treatment of the theory and the various models that have been developed, see the sources cited in this section.

Critique: Because input and learning through association plays so crucial a role in the development of knowledge in connectionist models, various scholars have placed this theoretical perspective in the empiricist camp (see, for example, Pinker and Prince 1989, Gasser 1990, Larsen-Freeman and Long 1991). Gasser (1990) points out that some scholars have seen it as "a revival of behaviorism dressed up to look like neuroscience" (p. 183). Interestingly, Rumelhart and McClelland (1986a) maintain that PDP

Illustration 2.7

Summary:
Connectionism and
Parallel Distributed
Processing (Based on
Rumelhart and
McClelland 1986a;
McClelland 1989;
Gasser 1990; Larsen-
Freeman 1991).

Summary: Connectionism and Parallel Distributed Processing

1. Connectionist theory assumes no innate endowment or mechanism specifically pre-programmed for language learning.
2. Learning consists of the strengthening of connections between and among simple processing units in complex neural networks.
3. Cognitive processing is assumed to occur in a parallel and distributed fashion throughout the network rather than in a sequential or serial fashion.
4. Knowledge is in the connections rather than in the processing units themselves.
5. The strength of connections is determined by the relative frequency of patterns in the input.
6. There are no "rules" in connectionist systems, although they exhibit regular or "rule-like" behavior.

models are "quite agnostic about issues of nativism versus empiricism" (p. 139). They suggest that connectionist systems can be viewed from either a nativist or an empiricist world view (p. 140). The extreme nativist view would suggest that all the interconnections were genetically predetermined, or "wired in," at birth; the extreme empiricist view would hold that there are no predetermined limits on the way the system's network of interconnections might be constituted. A third possibility would be an interactionist perspective, where the nature of the system might be genetically determined, but where all the connections could be modified as the person interacted with the environment. Rumelhart and McClelland seem to favor this third perspective, and suggest that "there is probably a good deal of genetic specification of neural connection, and there is a good deal of plasticity in the pattern of connectives after birth" (p. 140, note 6). Because many scholars seem to categorize connectionist theory as environmentalist, it has been placed on the left-hand side of the continuum in Illustration 2.2.

As was mentioned earlier, various researchers have identified some problems with PDP models (see, for example, Fodor and Pylyshyn 1988; Lachter and Bever 1988; Pinker and Prince 1989). Pinker and Prince argue that "the fact that a computer model behaves intelligently without rules does not show that humans lack rules, any more than a wind-up mouse shows that real mice lack motor programs" (p. 184). In their view, PDP models of language and cognition are incorrect for several reasons. They claim, for example, that the Rumelhart-McClelland model has nothing corresponding to various formal linguistic notions such as *segment* or *string* (relating to phonemes), or to *stem, affix,* or *root* (relating to word formation), making it difficult for the model to distinguish among similar-sounding words. There is also nothing in the model corresponding to constructs such as *regular rule* or *irregular exception.* The authors claim that the model makes wrong predictions about the kinds of rules that would be easy to learn versus those that would be difficult, adding that the computerized model seems to learn bizarre, non-existent rules for forming the past tense as easily as it learns simple, very common rules. Thus, it does not seem sensitive to psychologically significant differences between regular and irregular verbs.

An additional problem identified by Pinker and Prince relates to the way in which the computerized model begins to make overgeneralization errors in producing past-tense forms. Whereas overgeneralization in the model is triggered by a large influx of regular verb forms into the teaching presentation in stage two, the onset of overgeneralization in children is not associated with changes in the ratio of irregular to regular verb forms in the input. Rather, overgeneralization errors seem to be triggered by some internal changes in the child's language mechanisms, associated with chronological age (p. 190). Pinker and Prince believe that "the Rumelhart-McClelland model is an extremely important contribution to our understanding of human language mechanisms" (p. 192), and that the flaws they see in the model provide further insights into how language acquisition occurs.

While some scholars consider PDP models problematic, others see them as representing an interesting alternative view of cognition that is worthy of further exploration (see, for example, Gasser 1990, who has proposed a connectionist framework for second-language acquisition research.) Whatever the merits and problems of connectionist accounts of learning might be, this new perspective on cognition presents an interesting challenge to the rationalist perspectives that have been dominating our field since the 1960s.

• • • • • • • • • • • ## *The Role of Individual Learner Factors in Second-Language Learning*

Most scholars and practitioners in the field today agree that both the rate and the degree of success of second-language learning is affected by individual learner differences (Ellis 1985, p. 99). Many also believe that learner factors such as age, aptitude, attitude, motivation, personality, cognitive style, and preferred learning strategies need to be considered in any comprehensive theory of second-language acquisition. Ellis (1985) remarks that SLA researchers may acknowledge the importance of such factors in the eventual attainment of advanced levels of proficiency or in approaches to specific tasks, but research on acquisition orders (or the *route* of SLA) has tended to ignore individual differences or minimize their importance (p. 99). The conventional wisdom, it seems, has been that second-language acquisition theories should attempt to explain how "the learner" develops competence, as though learners were a relatively homogeneous lot. This assumption, however, is being challenged as more and more scholars recognize that differences among people might matter a great deal more than we had once thought.

In recent years, various publications have dealt with the importance of individual learner factors in language learning (see, for example, McLaughlin 1983, 1987; Birckbichler 1984; Ellis 1985, 1990; Brown 1987; Wenden and Rubin 1987; O'Malley and Chamot 1989; Stevick 1989; Tarone and Yule 1989; Galloway and Labarca 1990; and Oxford 1990). Studies of learner characteristics have looked at how various kinds of factors might affect "success" with language learning, as well as learners' approaches to different language learning tasks, and students' attitudes toward specific learning environments and situations.

In some of the earlier research on learner characteristics (Naiman, Frohlich, and Stern 1975; Rubin 1975; Stern 1975), investigators were interested in identifying what "good" language learners did or what types of characteristics they had. The intention was to see if some of these characteristics and strategies could be taught to learners who were not so successful. But as Stevick (1989) points out, the search for one definitive set of characteristics that would identify "good" learners from "poor" ones may have begun with a faulty premise. Stevick conducted interviews with a number of language learners who had achieved superior levels of proficiency in a variety of languages. He had hoped to identify how they were alike so that we might "teach their secrets to our students" (p. xi). As he began to analyze his interview data, however, he found that successful learners were even more different from one another than he had expected. It seems that even "good learners" are a rather heterogeneous lot!

Though perhaps disappointing from the point of view of the researcher interested in identifying a formula for "success," Stevick's findings are also quite positive, in that "many of the things [successful learners] were describing fitted well with one or another abstract, theoretical concept in the field" (Stevick 1989, p. xi.) Although no one theoretical model of second-language acquisition was unambiguously supported, each model was confirmed in some ways by the interview data he collected.

Galloway and Labarca (1990) have provided an excellent review of recent literature about the host of learner factors that should be considered in any theoretical or practical discussion of second-language learning. In their introduction, the authors note that educators often feel challenged, if not irritated, by differences, irregularities, or change (p. 111). Dealing with individual differences in the classroom might seem a daunting problem for many teachers, who face multiple classes (with multiple preparations) every day with 20 or 30 students in each class. Yet most everyone agrees, at least in principle, that students must be treated as individual *persons* who have differing needs, styles, and preferences.

What are some of the specific ways in which learners differ? Galloway and Labarca (1990) discuss learner differences in several categories. First, they contend that people sense things differently, responding to the physical environment around them (time of day, degree of comfort, degree of physical activity, amount of light, etc.) in diverse ways. People also tend to learn best through one or a combination of sensory modalities (through the ears, through the eyes, through touch, through movement). It follows that methodological decisions that limit use of a preferred modality will be ill-suited to a significant subset of learners.

For example, if the method prescribes that input to the learners will be primarily auditory in the beginning phases of instruction, learners who depend on visual information may be disadvantaged. Teachers need to consider such modality preferences and use a multi-sensory approach, appealing to all types of learner preferences. "What is called for is not a teaching method, but a teaching repertoire" (Galloway and Labarca 1990, p. 115).

A second way in which learners differ is in their social preferences. Some people prefer learning with others, interacting in small groups or engaging in competitive activities. Others may prefer learning alone and are energized by opportunities to read or do individual projects.

A third variable is the way in which learners tend to process information mentally. Various cognitive style differences have been explored in the literature. The following list is based on summaries given in Abraham (1978) and Claxton and Ralston (1978). The dimensions mentioned here are not mutually exclusive, but represent alternative ways of characterizing cognitive behavior:

Field Independence, first isolated by Witkin and his colleagues to characterize perceptual behavior, involves the degree to which one perceives things analytically or globally. A person with a high degree of field independence tends to perceive individual items as discrete from their backgrounds, whereas a person with a low degree of field independence may take a more global approach to a task and find it difficult to overcome the influence of the surrounding context or "field." The most commonly used test to determine degree of field independence is the *Group Embedded Figures Test,* where the individual tries to find a simple geometric figure embedded in a more complex array of geometric lines (Oltman, Raskin, and Witkin 1971).

Breadth of categorization. This style dimension reflects the individual's tendency to construct broad or narrow categories for items. The broad categorizer tends to make very wide category designations so as to include many items, whereas the narrow categorizer prefers smaller, more exclusive category designations.

Leveling-Sharpening. The leveling-sharpening continuum accounts for how information is assimilated in memory. Levelers tend to blur similar memories, while sharpeners maintain distinctions among the items stored. This dimension is quite similar to that of **preception-reception,** where the person who is preceptive assimilates new information into previously held concepts, and the receptive person tends to take in new information without preconceived notions about how it "fits" into existing categories.

Impulsiveness-Reflectiveness. This style dimension is concerned with the speed with which a person makes decisions. Impulsive individuals make decisions rapidly, whereas reflective individuals prefer to take their time before deciding on an answer or making a choice.

Systematicness. Some people prefer to complete a task using a clear procedure or plan and following it in a linear or systematic fashion. Others prefer to develop their ideas freely and may skip from the part to the whole in an intuitive fashion.

Tolerance of Ambiguity. A person who has a high tolerance of ambiguity can deal with uncertainty fairly comfortably. A person who has a low tolerance may become anxious or frustrated when a task presents unknown elements or seems ambiguous or difficult.

Flexibility-Inflexibility. Persons who can easily find alternative solutions to a problem or can think of a variety of answers to a question are characterized as flexible, whereas individuals who are unwilling to abandon a particular solution to a problem and consider other possibilities, or who tend to think in terms of one "right" answer would be characterized as inflexible on this dimension of cognitive style. (See also Birckbichler 1984, who links this dimension to Guilford's [1967] distinction between *convergent* and *divergent* thinking p. 62.)

Galloway and Labarca (1990) and Oxford (1990), as well as other researchers studying learner factors also point out that people adopt different learning strategies as they approach particular tasks. "Learner strategies are task-specific tactics or techniques, observable or nonobservable, that an individual uses to comprehend, store, retrieve, and use information or to plan, regulate, or assess learning" (Galloway and Labarca 1990, p. 141). Many learners are not aware of the strategies that they use to approach a task and would profit, perhaps, from making them explicit. Hosenfeld (1979) did a fascinating study with a high-school learner named Cindy who became aware, through strategy training, of her own approach to reading in French as well as to the approach of another student she was studying as a model of a successful reader. After eight sessions with the researcher, thinking aloud while she read and talking about her strategy use, Cindy exhibited some new and effective reading strategies that she had not used previously. Readers interested in learning more about the types of strategies learners typically use should consult such sources as Oxford and Ehrman (1989), O'Malley and Chamot (1990), Oxford (1990) and the other sources mentioned above.

The professional literature of the last three decades is replete with information about learner styles, strategies, and personality differences.

Yet how does one accommodate these differences in the second-language classroom? For many practitioners, the very idea of individualizing one's instruction "evokes the defeating image of one-on-one instruction guided by 150 variations on a lesson plan" (Galloway and Labarca 1990, p. 129). Rather than start by trying to identify and meet the needs of all learners in the classroom simultaneously, Galloway and Labarca suggest that we begin by attending to *some* of the needs of *all* of our learners. They advocate "learner-friendly" environments where the teacher makes a concerted effort to arrange instruction so that it is meaningful for learners and fosters their independence. Activities that challenge students to solve problems and take responsibility for their own learning are needed, as is instruction in effective strategy use or application of learned concepts to new settings and situations. The teacher, in their view, needs to fulfill two crucial roles:

> *(1) that of the 'architect', who . . . carefully plans the construction, connection, consolidation, and comfort of classroom experiences; and (2) that of the 'mediator' . . . who guides students to observe, activate prior knowledge, represent information, select strategies, construct meaning, monitor understanding, assess strategy use, organize and extend learning.*
>
> *(Galloway and Labarca 1990, p. 130).*

The authors view the teacher as one who provides structured guidance, yet who knows when to retreat to allow the learners to work on their own. "At least part of the art of interactive teaching involves a process of finding a balance between providing enough support but not imposing too much control" (p. 131). By helping students to become aware of their own strategies and learning preferences, as well as guiding them expertly to become effective and autonomous learners as they approach various learning tasks, teachers can go a long way toward accommodating individual learner needs more effectively.

Summary: On Learning a Language

In this chapter, various models of second-language acquisition have been selected for discussion from among the many theoretical viewpoints that have been advanced in the field in recent years. The highlights of five theoretical perspectives, chosen to represent different points along the rationalist-empiricist continuum, were reviewed and summarized. As teachers consider these and other perspectives on language learning, it is hoped that they may begin to clarify their own beliefs and understand how they relate to language acquisition theory. In the last section of the chapter, the issue of individual learner factors and their role in language learning and instruction was briefly discussed. As we consider the question: "How do adults become proficient in a second-language?", the only certainty is that the question is tremendously complex. Yet the strides that we are making as a profession to answer that question have been encouraging, as research into SLA is flourishing, and the insights we have gained into the nature of the learning process bring promise for the continued improvement of our teaching.

In the next chapter, a set of hypothesized principles of instruction that are derived from concepts in Chapters 1 and 2 will be presented and discussed. We will then consider various approaches to teaching that have been prevalent in the professional literature over the years with a view to understanding their underlying assumptions and essential characteristics. It is hoped that this review of principles, premises, and priorities will enable second-language teachers to articulate more clearly their own convictions about language learning and teaching, and evaluate the many options that are available to them as they plan instruction that is responsive to the needs of their students.

• • • • • • • • • • • • • *Activities for Review and Discussion*

1. Go back to Illustration 2.1 and answer the questions in the Discussion Guide to assess some of your own beliefs about second-language learning theory. Then, in small groups, compare and discuss your answers.

2. For each of the items in the Discussion Guide in Illustration 2.1, identify the theoretical approach in this chapter with which the statement is compatible. (Some statements may be compatible with more than one theory.) Then analyze your own answers to the questionnaire to see if you currently favor one theoretical viewpoint over others. Do you lean towards the empiricist or the rationalist end of the continuum shown in Illustration 2.2?

3. Choose three theoretical approaches described in this chapter and review the main premises associated with each one. (You may want to consult the summary tables at the end of each description.) Then, for each of the three theoretical points of view, make a list of teaching practices that you think would be compatible with that approach. Compare your three lists. Are there practices that would be compatible with all three theories? Are there practices that would be compatible with only one? Explain your answer briefly.

4. Think about the way you approached the learning of a second language, either on your own or in a formal classroom setting. What theoretical approach described in this chapter best characterizes your learning experience? Were there aspects of that learning experience you would like to change if you were to begin the study of a new language? Explain your answer briefly.

5. Many second-language educators believe that learner characteristics play an important role in language learning. How might you

deal with individual differences in your classroom? What are some practical ways in which you might accommodate learner differences in preferred learning style, personality, or strategy use?

•••••••••••• ## REFERENCES

Abraham, Roberta. "The Nature of Cognitive Style and Its Importance to the Foreign Language Teacher." (1978) [ED 168 358].

Anderson, J. *Cognitive Psychology and its Implications.* San Francisco: Freeman, 1980.

_____ *Cognitive Psychology and its Implications,* 2nd ed. New York: Freeman, 1985.

Ausubel, David. *Educational Psychology: A Cognitive View.* New York: Holt, Rinehart, and Winston, 1968, 1978.

Birckbichler, Diane W. "The Challenge of Proficiency: Student Characteristics." Pp. 47-78 in G. A. Jarvis, ed., *The Challenge for Excellence in Foreign Language Education.* Reports of the Northeast Conference on the Teaching of Foreign Languages. Middlebury, VT: Northeast Conference, 1984.

_____, ed. *New Perspectives and New Directions in Foreign Language Education.* The ACTFL Foreign Language Education Series. Lincolnwood, IL: National Textbook Company, 1990.

Bloomfield, Leonard. *Outline Guide for the Practical Study of Foreign Languages.* Baltimore: Linguistic Society of America, 1942.

Born, Warren C., ed. *The Foreign Language Teacher in Today's Classroom Environment.* Reports of the Northeast Conference on the Teaching of Foreign Languages. Middlebury, VT; Northeast Conference, 1979.

Brown, H. Douglas. *Principles of Language Learning and Teaching,* 2nd ed. Englewood Cliffs, NJ: Prentice Hall, 1987.

Chastain, Kenneth. *Developing Second Language Skills: Theory to Practice,* 2nd ed. Chicago: Rand McNally, 1976.

Chomsky, Noam. *Syntactic Structures.* The Hague, The Netherlands: Mouton and Company, 1957.

_____ "A Review of B.F. Skinner's *Verbal Behavior.*" *Language* 35 (1959): 26–58.

_____ *Aspects of the Theory of Syntax.* Cambridge, MA: M. I. T. Press, 1965.

Claxton, Charles S. and Y. Ralston. *Learning Styles: Their Impact on Teaching and Administration.* AAHE-ERIC/Higher Education Research Report No. 10 (1978). [ED 167 065].

Diller, Karl Conrad. *The Language Teaching Controversy.* Rowley, MA: Newbury House, 1978.

Ellis, Rod. *Understanding Second Language Acquisition.* Oxford: Oxford University Press, 1985.

_____ *Instructed Second Language Acquisition.* Oxford: Basil Blackwell, 1990.

Feldman, J. A. "A Connectionist Model of Visual Memory," in G. E. Hinton and J. A. Anderson, eds., *Parallel Models of Associative Memory.* Hillsdale, NJ: Erlbaum, 1981.

Fodor, J. A. and Z. W. Pylyshyn. "Connectionism and Cognitive Architecture: A Critical Analysis." *Cognition* 28 (1988): 3–71.

Galloway, Vicki and Angela Labarca. "From Student to Learner: Style, Process, and Strategy." Chapter 4 in D. Birckbichler, ed., *New Perspectives and New Directions in Foreign Language Education.* The ACTFL Foreign Language Education Series. Lincolnwood, IL: National Textbook Company, 1990.

Gasser, Michael. "Connectionism and Universals of Second Language Acquisition." *Studies in Second Language Acquisition* 12 (1990): 179–99.

Guilford, J. P. *The Nature of Human Intelligence.* New York: McGraw-Hill, 1976.

Hilgard, Ernest R. *Introduction to Psychology,* 3rd ed. New York: Harcourt, Brace and World, Inc., 1962.

Hinton, G. E. and J. A. Anderson, eds. *Parallel Models of Associative Memory.* Hillsdale, NJ: Erlbaum, 1981.

Hosenfeld, Carol. "Cindy: A Learner in Today's Foreign Language Classroom." In W. Born, ed. *The Foreign Language Teacher in Today's Classroom Environment.* Reports of the Northeast Conference on the Teaching of Foreign Languages. Middlebury, VT: Northeast Conference, 1979.

Jarvis, G. A., ed. *The Challenge for Excellence in Foreign Language Education.* Reports of the Northeast Conference on the Teaching of Foreign Languages. Middlebury, VT: Northeast Conference, 1984.

Krashen, Stephen. *Principles and Practice in Second Language Acquisition.* New York: Pergamon Press, 1982.

Lachter, J. and T. Bever. "The Relationship Between Linguistic Structure and Associative Theories of Language Learning: A Constructive Critique of Some Connectionist Learning Models." *Cognition* 28 (1988): 195–247.

Larsen-Freeman, Diane. "Second Language Acquisition Research: Staking Out the Territory." *TESOL Quarterly,* vol. 25, ii (Summer 1991): 315–50.

Larsen-Freeman, Diane and Michael H. Long. *An Introduction to Second Language Acquisition Research.* White Plains, NY: Longman, 1991.

Lennenberg, Eric. *Biological Foundations of Language.* New York: John Wiley, 1967.

McClelland, James L. "Parallel Distributed Processing: Implications for Cognition and Development." Chapter 2 (pp. 8–45) in R. G. M. Morris, ed., *Parallel Distributed Processing: Implications for Psychology and Neurobiology.* Oxford: Clarendon Press, 1989.

_____, D. E. Rumelhart, and the PDP Group, eds. *Parallel Distributed Processing: Explorations in the Microstructure of Cognition. Volume 2: Psychological and Biological Models.* Cambridge, MA: M. I. T. Press, 1986.

McLaughlin, Barry. *Second-Language Acquisition in Childhood.* Hillsdale, NY: Lawrence Erlbaum, 1978.

_____ *Theories of Second-Language Learning.* London: Edward Arnold, 1987.

_____ "Restructuring." *Applied Linguistics* 11, ii (1990): 113–28.

McLaughlin, Barry., T. Rossman, and B. McLeod. "Second-Language Learning: An Information-Processing Perspective." *Language Learning* 33 (1983): 135–58.

McNeill, David. *Developmental Psycholinguistics.* In F. Smith and G. Miller, eds., *The Genesis of Language: A Psycholinguistic Approach.* Cambridge, MA: M. I. T. Press, 1966.

Morris, R. G. M., ed. *Parallel Distributed Processing: Implications for Psychology and Neurobiology.* Oxford: Clarendon Press, 1989.

Munsell, Paul and Thomas Carr. "Monitoring the Monitor: A Review of *Second-Language Acquisition and Second Language Learning.*" *Language Learning* 31 (1981): 493–502.

Naiman, N., Maria Frohlich, and H. H. Stern. *The Good Language Learner.* Toronto: Ontario Institute for Studies in Education, 1975.

Oltman, Philip K., Evelyn Raskin, and Herman A. Witkin. *Group Embedded Figures Test*. Palo Alto, CA: Consulting Psychologists Press, 1971.

O'Malley, J. Michael and Anna Uhl Chamot. *Learning Strategies in Second-Language Acquisition*. Cambridge: Cambridge University Press, 1990.

Oxford, Rebecca L. *Language Learning Strategies: What Every Teacher Should Know*. Rowley, MA: Newbury House, 1990.

Oxford, Rebecca and Madeleine Ehrman. "Psychological Type and Adult Language Learning Strategies: A Pilot Study." *Journal of Psychological Type* 16 (1989): 22–32.

Pinker, S. and A. Prince. "Rules and Connections in Human Language." Chapter 9 (pp. 182–99) in R. G. M. Morris, ed., *Parallel Distributed Processing: Implications for Psychology and Neurobiology*. Oxford: Clarendon Press, 1989.

Rubin, Joan. "What the `Good Language Learner' Can Teach Us." *TESOL Quarterly* 9 (1975): 41–51.

Rumelhart, D. E. and J. L. McClelland. "PDP Models and General Issues in Cognitive Science." Chapter 4 (pp. 110–149) in D. E. Rumelhart, J. L. McClelland, and the PDP Research Group, eds., *Parallel Distributed Processing: Explorations in the Microstructure of Cognition. Volume I: Foundations*. Cambridge, MA: The M. I. T. Press, 1986a.

_____ "On Learning the Past Tenses of English Verbs." Chapter 18 (pp. 216–71) in J. L. McClelland, D. E. Rumelhart, and the PDP Group, eds., *Parallel Distributed Processing: Explorations in the Microstructure of Cognition. Volume 2: Psychological and Biological Models*. Cambridge, MA: M. I. T. Press, 1986b.

Schneider, W. and R. M. Shiffrin. "Controlled and Automatic Processing. I: Detection, Search, and Attention." *Psychological Review* 84 (1977): 1–64.

Schouten, M. "The Missing Data in Second Language Learning Research." *Interlanguage Studies Bulletin,* vol. 4 (1979): 3–14.

Shiffrin, R. M. and W. Schneider. "Controlled and Automatic Human Information Processing. II: Perceptual Learning, Automatic, Attending, and a General Theory." *Psychological Review* 84 (1977): 127–90.

Skinner, B. F. *Verbal Behavior*. New York: Appleton-Century-Crofts, 1957.

Smith, Frank and George Miller, eds. *The Genesis of Language: A Psycholinguistic Approach*. Cambridge, MA: M. I. T. Press, 1966.

Spolsky, Bernard. *Conditions for Second Language Learning*. Oxford: Oxford University Press, 1989.

Stern, H. H. "What Can We Learn from the Good Language Learner?" *The Canadian Modern Language Review* 31 (1975): 304–18.

Stevick, Earl. *Memory, Meaning, and Method: Some Psychological Perspectives on Language Learning*. Rowley, MA: Newbury House, 1976.

_____ *Success With Foreign Languages: Seven Who Achieved it and What Worked for Them*. Englewood Cliffs, NJ: Prentice Hall, 1989.

Tarone, Elaine, "Systematicity and Attention in Interlanguage." *Language Learning* 32 (1982): 69–84.

_____ "On the Variability of Interlanguage Systems." *Applied Linguistics* 4 (1983): 142–63.

_____ and George Yule. *Focus on the Language Learner*. Oxford: Oxford University Press, 1989.

Terrell, Tracy D. "A Natural Approach to Second Language Acquisition and Learning." *Modern Language Journal* 61 (1977): 325–37.

_____ "The Natural Approach to Language Teaching: An Update." *Modern Language Journal* 66 (1982): 121–32.

Wardhaugh, Ronald. *The Contexts of Language.* Rowley, MA: Newbury House, 1976.

Wenden, Anita and Joan Rubin. *Learner Strategies in Language Learning.* Englewood Cliffs, NJ: Prentice Hall, 1987.

3

On Teaching a Language: Principles and Priorities In Methodology

Once, in the throes of the audiolingual revolution, we "knew the truth." Today, I am working with only a set of working hypotheses for myself as a foreign language teacher (Strasheim 1976, p. 42).

For many years, it seemed that the language teaching profession was engaged in a series of "revolutions," most of which had their origins in an attempt to reach some consensus about the best way—"the one true way" (Strasheim, 1976)—to teach a foreign language. Yet despite a few short-lived rallies around a common flag, our professional history has been marked more often by controversy than by consensus. It is true that some of the major shifts in perspective over the years have led to positive and long-lasting change. Yet Grittner (1990) voices concern about the unfortunate recurrence throughout our history of "evangelistic movements that suddenly emerge, capture the attention of many teachers, cause an upheaval in methods and materials, and then—just as suddenly—fade from view" (p. 9). He speaks of these revolutionary movements as "bandwagons" that demand a fervent commitment from their followers to a single theory of teaching and that reject all other methods or approaches as ineffectual and outmoded (p. 10). The common premise behind the search for a unitary approach to learning and teaching seems to be that there exists an ideal method which, once discovered, will unlock the door to language proficiency for all learners and will make the learning process swift and effortless.

Traditionally, language practitioners in search of the "one true way" have grouped themselves along the same empiricist/rationalist continuum that was reviewed in the last chapter, aligning themselves more or less with their counterparts in theoretical linguistics (Chomsky 1965; Diller 1978). For methodologists, the basic distinction between the two ends of the continuum has been one of philosophy. Empiricists believed that language was an oral phenomenon consisting of concrete "signs" that could be described. Empiricist methodologies treated language learning as habit formation through mimicry, memorization, and drilling. Rationalist saw language not as structure, but as rule-governed creativity (Chomsky 1965). Rationalist methodologies emphasized meaningfulness and understanding of psychologically real rules of grammar (Diller 1978).

Swaffar, Arens and Morgan (1982), following Diller, characterize the *rationalist/process* approach as one in which high priority is placed on identifying form as meaningful, using problem-solving strategies. The *empiricist/skills* approach, by contrast, places highest priority on reproduction of correct forms.

This controversy over methodological approaches is not just a phenomenon of the twentieth century. Kelly (1976) has described a gradual evolution of language teaching over 25 centuries that is characterized by frequent shifts in focus, purpose, and practice. Interestingly enough, some of the quarrels of the past have a familiar ring. Kibbee (1987, 1989) cites evidence, for example, of a heated debate dating from the sixteenth century about the way in which oral skills ought to be taught. Claude de Sainliens, in his work entitled *The Frenche Littelton. A most Easie, Perfect, and Absolute way to learne the frenche tongue,* published in 1576, stated that one should not entangle students in rules, but allow them to practice first through dialogue memorization:

> *If the Reader meaneth to learne our tongue within a short space, he must not entangle himselfe at the firste brunte with the rules of the pronunciation set (for a purpose) at the latter ende of this booke, but take in hande these Dialogues: and as the occasion requireth, he shall examine the rules, applying their use unto his purpose . . . (de Sainliens 1576, cited in Kibbee 1987, 1989).*

Jacques Bellot attacks this point of view in his *French Method* of 1588:

> *There bee some holding this opinion, that the most expedient & certaine way to attaine to the knowledge of tongues is to learne them without any observation of rules: But cleane contrary I doe thinke that he which is instructed in any tongue what so ever by the onely roate, is like unto the Byrd in a cage, him and (which is much worse) not understanding that which he sayth, because he is voyde of all foundation of good and certaine doctrine . . . (Bellot 1588, pp. 2–3, cited in Kibbee 1987, 1989).*

Four hundred years later, the essential argument has not greatly changed. By the middle of the twentieth century, theorists and practitioners had transposed the debate to the modern context, where methodologists steeped in cognitive psychology or universal grammar argued with those espousing behaviorism in a vain effort to convince one another that they were right about language teaching. One of the more recent versions of the age-old debate has erupted in the controversy surrounding the overt teaching of grammar and the use of error correction in language instruction. In this instance, "natural" approaches to language learning, where the teaching of grammatical rules and the use of error correction techniques are largely discouraged in the classroom, are opposed to more "cognitive" orientations toward methodology, which maintain that students must understand the basic rule system underlying the new language and receive corrective feedback in order to improve. Many language educators who have witnessed these various versions of the same arguments over the years have become somewhat weary of the debate, and are cautious in their enthusiasm for any new trends that seem like old "bandwagons" in disguise. Some have shunned "revolutions" altogether and have decided instead to adopt an "eclectic" approach (Warriner 1980). And with eclecticism comes a new kind of diversity within the profession, at least on the issue of methodology.

It is not surprising that in the 1980s, many practitioners and foreign language educators still felt the need to reach some sort of consensus about language teaching, but were unsure about how this could be accomplished. The effort to establish uniform goals and standards for language proficiency following the Carter Presidential Commission on Languages and International Studies in 1979 was a manifestation of this need for consensus. As was pointed out in Chapter 1, one result of this effort—the development of the *ACTFL Proficiency Guidelines*—has sparked a great deal of interest within the language teaching community. But rather than searching for consensus about teaching methodology, this project attempted to reach consensus about describing and measuring language abilities, building on the work done previously in language testing by the government language schools. This shift from methodology to measurement questions marks a significant change in direction for the profession. After many years of fruitless searching for the "one true way," we may be realizing at last that the controversy has been raging on the wrong battlefield. Instead of searching for one definitive approach to teaching, we have begun looking for some "organizing principle" (Higgs 1984) that can facilitate communication about the nature of language proficiency, and thus about the development of goals and objectives for language teaching. In this way, our various methods, approaches, materials, and curricula might begin to make collective sense. This "organizing principle" must go beneath and beyond any one approach and relate in some clear way to "those elements of soundness and truth that are to be found in any method that has survived long enough to have received a name" (Stevick 1976, p. 103).

In the first edition of this book, I chose the concept of *proficiency*, as defined in the *ACTFL Proficiency Guidelines*, as the organizing principle for discussing issues related to language teaching. This general concept continues to provide a framework for the second edition. As was emphasized in Chapter 1, it is important to remember that the *Guidelines* are neither a curricular model nor a methodological prescription in and of themselves. However, it is certainly possible to derive various implications from them for instruction (Galloway 1987). Because the *Guidelines* describe language abilities in a hierarchical fashion, they can provide insights for organizing instruction. First, practitioners can use the broad level definitions to evaluate the suitability of their current curricular goals and course objectives for learners in their classrooms. Thus, a teacher whose students are currently at the Novice level in a given skill area will choose objectives, activities, and materials that differ substantially from those they might choose for students at the Advanced level. Secondly, by understanding what *general* kinds of abilities lie at each level of proficiency, teachers can plan to shift the emphasis of instruction as students progress to allow for the development of requisite skills. In this way, the *Guidelines* can serve as an overall frame of reference within which pedagogical choices can be made.

Orienting Instruction Toward Proficiency

If the proficiency level definitions do indeed describe a global developmental progression in language skills, what kinds of implications for instruction might one derive from examining them? The statements below represent my own attempt to identify some guiding principles for organizing and planning instruction in a second language. These principles apply to instruction at all levels of proficiency, from Novice to Superior, and are meant to be flexible enough to relate to varying needs and purposes for study. For example, if students are attempting to learn the language well enough to use it in traveling, exposure to a variety of situations likely to be encountered in the target culture will be necessary. Students will need practice in accomplishing everyday tasks associated with travel, and will benefit from understanding some basic facts about life in the target culture. The ability to get their meaning across will be primary, but students will also profit from some practice with language forms to enhance their comprehensibility, as well as their ability to comprehend others. When the students' ultimate, long-range goal is to develop proficiency at the higher levels on the scale, the same principles will hold, but specific objectives and/or criteria for meeting those objectives might change. In order to be rated "Advanced" in oral proficiency, for example, students will need to be able to use the language in a variety of contexts with considerable flexibility and creativity. They will need to communicate with a reasonable degree of precision and coherence. In order to accomplish diverse tasks related to living and working in the culture, they will have to be able handle a wide range of situations with confidence, showing sensitivity to cultural norms and customs. The five principles given below outline general characteristics of a classroom environment that I believe would be conducive to the achievement of all of these goals. The principles are stated in the form of "hypotheses," since our knowledge base is constantly growing, necessitating revisions and adjustments to accommodate new ideas. Indeed, a few of the hypotheses have been revised somewhat since they first appeared in 1986 in an effort to clarify them and incorporate some of the insights generated recently in the field of language teaching.

Hypothesis 1. *Opportunities must be provided for students to practice using language in a range of contexts likely to be encountered in the target culture.*

Corollary 1. *Students should be encouraged to express their own meaning as early as possible after productive skills have been introduced in the course of instruction.*

Corollary 2. *Opportunities must be provided for active communicative interaction among students.*

Corollary 3. *Creative language practice (as opposed to exclusively manipulative or convergent practice) must be encouraged in the proficiency-oriented classroom.*

Corollary 4. *Authentic language should be used in instruction wherever possible.*

Hypothesis 2. *Opportunities should be provided for students to practice carrying out a range of functions (tasks) likely to be necessary in dealing with others in the target culture.*

Hypothesis 3. *The development of accuracy should be encouraged in proficiency-oriented instruction. As learners produce language, various forms of instruction and evaluative feedback can be useful in facilitating the progression of their skills toward more precise and coherent language use.*

Hypothesis 4. *Instruction should be responsive to the affective as well as the cognitive needs of students, and their different personalities, preferences, and learning styles should be taken into account.*

Hypothesis 5. *Cultural understanding must be promoted in various ways so that students are sensitive to other cultures and prepared to live more harmoniously in the target-language community.*

Each of these principles is explored in more detail in the next section. They are then related to the discussion of specific teaching methodologies. Indeed, most of the methods described in this chapter draw upon principles such as these to varying extents. But before examining the hypotheses in more detail and discussing the way they relate to particular methods, it would be useful to try to clarify the concept of *methodology* itself.

Methodology and Proficiency

Definitions Richards and Rodgers (1986) maintain that there is a fundamental difference between a philosophy of language teaching at the level of theory and principles and a set of procedures derived from them (p. 15). They cite the work of Edward Anthony (1963), who described three hierarchical levels of conceptualization: (1) *approach*, which was defined by a set of theoretical principles; (2) *method*, which was a procedural plan for presenting and teaching the language; and (3) *technique*, which involved strategies for implementing the methodological plan. Westphal (1979) uses a similar conceptualization in defining the terms *syllabus, approach, strategy,* and *method* as follows:

> The syllabus *refers to the subject matter content of a given course or series of courses and the order in which it is presented; the* approach *is, ideally, the theoretical basis or bases which determine the ways in which the syllabus is treated; a* strategy *or* technique *is an individual instructional activity as it occurs in the classroom (p. 120).*

She goes on to explain that a *method* consists of combinations of these three factors, although some combinations are more congruent with course goals than others. For example, it would be rather difficult to expect students to become proficient enough in speaking to function easily in a foreign setting if their teacher used a literary syllabus, a grammar-translation approach, and strategies for learning activities based primarily on translation. However, Westphal believes that "it is quite possible to meet highly 'academic' objectives using a communicative approach to the grammatical syllabus and incorporating many humanistic strategies" (p. 120). The former combination of factors is not congruent with the goal of functional proficiency, at least not in beginning and intermediate sequences of instruction. The latter combination seems more eclectic, in that the instructor "borrows" from communicative approaches the basic theoretical and philosophical perspectives, uses a grammatical syllabus (instead of a functional one, which some communicative approaches would suggest), and treats the subject matter using humanistic techniques that have been suggested in yet another type of approach. These three factors, coupled with the actual text and course materials selected and the teacher's own individual style, could be said to constitute a method.

In a somewhat different definition, Swaffar, Arens, and Morgan (1982) conceive of methodology as a "task hierarchy." They maintain that the differences among major methodologies are to be found in the *priorities* assigned to various tasks rather than to the collection of tasks themselves.

> All major methodologies, whether skill or process-oriented, aspire to the same result: a student who can read, write, speak, understand, translate, and recognize applications of the grammar of the foreign language. Methodological labels assigned to teaching activities, are, in themselves, not informative, because they refer to a pool of classroom practices [that] are universally used (p. 31).

Therefore, it is not *what* activities are used so much as *when* and *how* they are used that distinguishes methods from one another. According to Swaffar and her colleagues, definitions of methods or approaches need to involve a description of (1) the hierarchy, or value structure, of activities, and (2) the position of such activities in the learning sequence.

Stevick (1976) also maintains that methods are best differentiated from one another in terms of factors such as "the place of memorization, or the role of visual aids, or the importance of controlling and sequencing structure and vocabulary, or how the teacher should respond when a student makes a mistake, or the number of times a student should hear a correct model, or whether to give the explanation before or after practice, or not at all, and so forth" (p. 105). The factors that he mentions go beyond the selection of learning tasks to include philosophical and theoretical principles about ways of proceeding. But whether we adopt these points of view or some other, it makes sense to differentiate methods in terms of priorities rather than make binary oppositions between and among them. In assessing the relative value of various factors in any teaching approach, we can begin to assess the degree to which that approach corresponds to the concept of proficiency. The working hypotheses presented earlier will now be explored in more detail.

Methodology and Proficiency: Five Working Hypotheses

Hypothesis 1. *Opportunities must be provided for students to practice using language in a range of contexts likely to be encountered in the target culture.*

A proficiency orientation will give students, from the beginning of instruction, ample opportunities to (1) learn language in context and (2) apply their knowledge to coping with real-life situations. Some of the contexts likely to be included at the Novice and Intermediate levels in general-purpose courses are basic travel and survival needs (food, clothing, hotel accommodations, transportation, and the like), handling daily social encounters appropriately, and coping with school- or work-related situations. Students can also be taught to handle simple question-and-answer situations and discuss or write about concrete topics, such as their own background, family, and interests.

As was pointed out in Chapter 1, the contexts and content areas suggested here are not offered as a prescribed set of topics or themes that must be "covered" in the early stages of language learning, but rather as examples of the kinds of topics and situations that students might be able to handle with some facility. At the lower levels of proficiency, students will probably be most comfortable with very predictable situations that allow them to use some memorized or learned material or to concentrate on autobiographical information or personal experiences and interests. At the higher levels of proficiency, the range of topics and contexts will expand beyond the "here-and-now" and the very familiar to include more abstract or specialized content. An examination of the assessment criteria used in

Illustration 3.1
Context and Content
Features of Major
Proficiency Levels

Context and Content

Superior
 Context: Most formal and informal settings
 Content: Wide range of concrete and abstract general interest topics and some
  special fields of interest and expertise

Advanced
 Context: Most informal and some formal settings
 Content: Concrete and factual topics of personal and general interest

Intermediate
 Context: Some informal settings and a limited number of transactional situations
 Content: Topics mostly related to self and immediate environment

Novice
 Context: Highly predictable common daily settings
 Content: Common discrete aspects of daily life

Source: Buck, Byrnes, and Thompson 1989, p. 3–3. Reprinted by permission of ACTFL.

---

oral proficiency testing reveals this progression of general context and content features for each major proficiency level (see Illustration 3.1). In order to orient instruction towards proficiency goals, teachers may want to consider these same criteria in choosing classroom materials and activities.

The first hypothesis has several corollaries that relate to designing and choosing a proficiency-oriented methodology.

> **Corollary 1.** *Students should be encouraged to express their own meaning as early as possible after productive skills have been introduced in the course of instruction.*

Therefore, methods that emphasize memorization or that severely limit personal expression in the early stages of instruction are not as easily adaptable to proficiency goals as those that encourage more creative language use. Only at the Novice Level do learners work almost exclusively with memorized material. To reach the Intermediate range of proficiency, learners need to be able to create with the language.

> **Corollary 2.** *Opportunities must be provided for active communicative interaction among students.*

The use of small-group and paired communicative activities that allow students to practice language in context for some simulated or real communicative purpose should lead more readily to the development of oral proficiency than instructional formats that are primarily teacher-centered or that focus mainly on language forms and convergent answers. Research by Pica and Doughty (1985) provides empirical support for small-group work involving communicative interaction over exclusively teacher-fronted instructional formats. Using three groups of students from "low-intermediate level ESL classes," the researchers contrasted teacher-fronted and group decision-making activities in terms of the grammaticality of the language produced, the amount of monitoring the learners engaged in, the number of turns each learner took in the interactions, and the overall quantity of language produced by individual students. They found that, on the average, learners involved in small-group work were just as grammatical as they were when involved in teacher-centered activities. There was also more self-monitoring in the groups than in teacher-fronted instruction, although self-correction constituted a relatively small percentage of the discourse. Another interesting finding was that learners who were targeted for observation in small-group activities took significantly more conversational turns than they did in the teacher-centered activities, suggesting that students do get more opportunities for individual practice in small groups. In spite of the benefits provided by the small-group activities, Pica and Doughty do not recommend an abandonment of whole-class instruction. They caution that a "steady diet" of group activities might restrict the amount of grammatical input available to the learner and lead to a "stabilized nontarget variety" of the language (p. 132).

This concern for developing accuracy while maintaining a communicative environment for learning is central to any approach that is oriented toward proficiency goals. Communicative language practice need not be totally unstructured, especially in the early stages of language skills development. Learners will need opportunities to make their own output more comprehensible (see Hypothesis 3 below.) This goal of comprehensibility and greater precision is totally compatible, it seems, with greater involvement by students in the creation of the discourse in the classroom. Gass and Varonis (1985) maintain that active involvement of learners is a necessary aspect of language acquisition, "since it is through involvement that the input becomes 'charged' and 'penetrates' deeply" (p. 150).

Most scholars agree that communicative practice is optimal when it involves exchanges of information in situations where some *information gap* exists, and that language practice that involves totally predictable (and therefore noncommunicative) exchanges is less useful in building proficiency. A judicious balance of activities that work on communicative skills with those that focus on the development of accuracy seems most sensible. (To illustrate how this might be accomplished, sample activities ranging from structured to unstructured practice are provided in Chapters 5, 6, and 7.)

Corollary 3. *Creative language practice (as opposed to exclusively manipulative or convergent practice) must be encouraged in the proficiency-oriented classroom.*

Students who hope to advance in their skills beyond the Novice range must learn to create with the language. They must be encouraged to paraphrase, think divergently (i.e., think of many possible answers), and let their imagination and creative ability function as fully as possible within the limits of their level of linguistic competence. Methods that help students create in the new language by including well-conceived, divergent-production and imaginative tasks should build the flexibility, fluency, and strategic competence needed to achieve higher levels of proficiency while at the same time encouraging the development of linguistic accuracy that is so important at those higher levels.

Corollary 4. *Authentic language should be used in instruction wherever possible.*

The contexts for language practice should be devised, as much as possible, from culturally authentic sources. The use of real or simulated travel documents, hotel registration forms, biographical data sheets, train and plane schedules, authentic restaurant menus, labels, signs, newspapers, and magazines will acquaint the students more directly with real language than will any set of contrived classroom materials used alone. Videotapes of authentic or simulated exchanges between native speakers, radio and television broadcasts, films, songs, and the like have long been advocated by foreign language educators as stimulating pedagogical aids. The proficiency-oriented classroom will incorporate such material frequently and effectively into instruction at all levels.

Just how to make the most effective use of authentic language materials in beginning classes remains somewhat unclear. Krashen (1982) maintains that people acquire language that is directed at their current level of competence, but which includes some structures that are somewhat beyond that level as well. He asserts that language learners/acquirers will understand structures that are beyond them from contextual cues in the message or from extralinguistic cues.

If Krashen's input hypothesis is true, then we might obtain the best results by using simplified versions of authentic materials with Novice- and Intermediate-level students and moving gradually toward incorporating more complete, unedited language samples with Advanced-level learners. We might also consider providing enough extralinguistic cues to render unedited authentic materials comprehensible to Novice- or Intermediate-level students. Whether material is edited or not, it is important to choose input that is appropriate in form and content to the student's current level of proficiency. In addition, the task that students are asked to do with authentic material must be geared to their proficiency level. More will be said about the choice of texts and tasks in Chapter 5.

The use of authentic texts does not imply that we should abandon the use of materials created for instructional purposes. Rather, a blend of the two seems more appropriate. Krashen suggests that "we can teach vocabulary, situational routines, grammar, whatever we like, and as long as we fill it with acquisition opportunities, as long as we keep providing comprehensible input, we are contributing to natural language acquisition" (p. 30). Another factor to consider is that students' proficiency levels in listening and reading may be well in advance of their proficiency levels in speaking and writing. Students who could not handle certain materials well in the productive skills may be quite capable of comprehending them.

It is also important to remember that natural language includes the comprehensible input provided by teachers in everyday exchanges in the instructional setting that are communicative in nature, from giving directions to recounting personal anecdotes in the target language. The proficiency-oriented classroom is one in which such natural acquisition opportunities are exploited as fully as possible.

Hypothesis 2. *Opportunities should be provided for students to practice carrying out a range of functions (tasks) likely to be necessary in dealing with others in the target culture.*

Traditional classroom instructional settings tend to limit the role of the student to that of responder; that is, students are most often asked to answer questions. In teacher-centered approaches, students are very seldom asked to make inquiries, act out simulated survival situations, narrate or describe events, hypothesize, argue, persuade, provide opinion, or carry out many other language functions that are necessary in everyday encounters with others in the target language. In many cases, functional practice of this sort is reserved for advanced conversation courses, many of which the majority of students never take. Proficiency-oriented methodologies should introduce students to a variety of functional tasks that have been carefully sequenced to help them cope with the real-world communication demands they will face. (As well as activities that afford practice in using language functions are presented in Chapter 6.)

Hypothesis 3. *The development of accuracy should be encouraged in proficiency-oriented instruction. As learners produce language, various forms of instruction and evaluative feedback can be useful in facilitating the progression of their skills toward more precise and coherent language use.*

The role of formal instruction and feedback in language acquisition has been the subject of debate in recent years, with some scholars arguing that "grammar instruction" and "error correction" do very little to encourage lasting positive change in learners' production, either in speech or in writing (see, for example, Terrell 1977, 1982; Krashen 1982; VanPatten 1987; Savignon 1988). Other scholars, however, argue that both instruction and feedback can have a positive impact on second language acquisition (see, for example, Long 1983; Swain 1985; Ellis 1985, 1990; Lightbown 1990; Lightbown and Spada 1990; Stern 1990). It seems that some of the debate regarding "error correction" centers on an understanding of the meaning of the term. Ellis (1990) suggests that we adopt Long's (1977) distinction between the terms "feedback" and "correction," where "feedback" refers to the process of giving students information so that they can tell if their production or comprehension of the language is correct, and "correction" refers to the result of feedback, or its effect on learning (Long 1977; Ellis 1990, p. 71).

It might also be useful to distinguish among various forms of corrective feedback, ranging from very direct and immediate correction of errors to more indirect and/or delayed correction strategies. It seems that those who have argued that no error correction should take place in the classroom are, in actuality, advocating indirect correction via more comprehensible input or negotiation of meaning among interlocutors. A clearer understanding of the terms being used by various scholars might reveal more consensus on this issue than has been evident from the literature.

The thrust of this hypothesis is that there is a role for form-focused instruction in a proficiency-oriented approach, used in a judicious blend with communicative language teaching practices. It also implies that a whole continuum of feedback strategies may be useful at different times in second language instruction. If interlanguage consists of variable styles, as Tarone (1983) and Ellis (1985) have suggested, there is a place for "careful style" activities, where attention is given to formal aspects of language, as well as for "vernacular style" activities, where communication of one's meaning is the primary focus. Lightbown (1990), in reviewing some of the recent literature relating to language learning in classrooms, concludes that "we all seem to feel the need to restore form-based instruction and error correction as part of the language teaching/learning context" (p. 90), although she cautions that more research needs to be done to determine the precise benefits of such activities. Lightbown and Spada (1990) point to the benefits of a combination of communicative language teaching and form-focused instruction—a kind of "hybrid" approach that recognizes the contributions of both kinds of teaching to the learning process.

It should be clear from the discussion thus far that "building toward greater precision and coherence" does not imply that students should be expected to produce only correct utterances or that an optimal methodology should provide "wall-to-wall insurance against error" (Stevick 1980, p. 24). Learners obviously do not generally produce correct speech or writing when creating with the language. Research has repeatedly shown that errors can be very useful in determining an individual's current internalized rule system and yield important diagnostic information. If one adopts the hypothesized principles outlined in this chapter, learners will be encouraged to create with the language and express their own meaning from the beginning of instruction. Therefore, errors of all types are to be expected.

Higgs and Clifford (1982) have suggested that we might be able to help students produce more accurate speech if we adopt an "output hypothesis" similar to Krashen's input hypothesis. That is, students might best acquire productive skills when they are encouraged to engage in tasks that are just beyond their current level of competence. To translate this idea into classroom practice, instructors might (1) provide comprehensible input in addition to formal instruction, (2) encourage students to express their own meaning within, or even slightly beyond, the limits of their current level of competence, and (3) consistently provide appropriate feedback (direct or indirect, immediate or delayed, depending on the activity and its purpose). Swain (1985) has proposed a similar hypothesis, in which students are encouraged to produce "comprehensible" or "pushed" output. In studying productive skills of immersion students in Canada, she had found that their grammaticality had fallen far short of native performance (p. 245). This caused her to question Krashen's hypothesis that comprehensible input was the only causal variable in second language acquisition, since the immersion students she was studying had been receiving comprehensible input for seven years. She concluded that input was not enough to promote grammatical development in a second language, and that something in the immersion setting was still lacking: "What then is missing? I would like to suggest that what is missing is output" (p. 248).

Swain argued that one-to-one conversational exchanges certainly provided an excellent opportunity for acquisition to occur, but that the best kinds of exchanges were those in which there had been a communication breakdown—"where the learner has received some negative input—and the learner is pushed to use alternate means to get across his or her message" (p. 248). Although one can succeed in getting across a message using deviant grammatical forms and sociolinguistically inappropriate language, Swain felt that "negotiation of meaning needs to incorporate the notion of being pushed toward the delivery of a message that is not only conveyed, but that is conveyed precisely, coherently and appropriately" (p. 249). She saw this idea of being "pushed" in one's output as parallel to Krashen's "i + 1" description of comprehensible input, and thus called her idea "the comprehensible output hypothesis." More will be said about this hypothesis, as well as the general role of feedback and instruction in language acquisition, in Chapters 6 and 7.

Hypothesis 4. *Instruction should be responsive to the affective as well as the cognitive needs of students, and their different personalities, preferences, and learning styles should be taken into account.*

As we saw in Chapter 2, learners differ from one another in many ways. In order to teach responsively to the individuals in our classes, we need to be aware that there will be important differences in cognitive style, personality, motivation, aptitude, and modality preference among our learners. This hypothesis speaks to the need to vary classroom activities in a way that will address the needs and preferences of as many students as possible, thus contributing to a more comfortable and flexible learning environment. As Galloway and Labarca (1990) state, "what is called for is not a teaching method, but a teaching repertoire" (p. 115). Any "method" that requires strict adherence to a limited number of techniques or strategies will undoubtedly be very poorly suited to at least a subset of learners in the classroom. Instruction that fosters the growth of language proficiency for all learners will need to be flexible, and will be characterized by a kind of principled or "informed eclecticism" (Richards and Rodgers 1986, p. 158) that takes students' preferences and feelings into account.

One of the hallmarks of several recent methodological developments is the greater emphasis on the affective aspects of learning and acquisition (see, for example, the discussions of the Counseling-Learning Approach, the Natural Approach, and Suggestopedia presented later in this chapter.) Scovel (1991) refers to affective factors as "those that deal with the emotional reactions and motivations of the learner" (p. 16), which constitute a subset of factors among the many other learner variables that need to be considered in instruction.

Proponents of humanistic methods believe that learning should be aimed at the deeper levels of understanding and personal meaningfulness to be maximally effective. Such methods emphasize the need to reduce anxiety and tension, which inhibit performance and create resistance to natural language acquisition and to learning. Stevick (1980) emphasizes the close relationship between poor performance and anxiety and tension in the learning environment (due to self-critique as well as criticism by others). This relationship is central to Krashen's (1982) filter hypothesis (see Chapter 2), based on the concept of the affective filter, somewhat akin to a mental block: "With acquirers who do not have self-confidence, where the situation is tense, where (in Stevick's words) they are on the defensive, the filter goes up" (p. 25). When the affective filter goes up, the resultant feelings are conflict, anxiety, aloneness, and a sense of guilt for failing. These feelings are clearly out of harmony with the best conditions for acquisition (Stevick 1980).

Horwitz and Young (1991) compiled a series of papers examining the role of anxiety in language learning. In the introductory chapter, Daly (1991) links the more general construct of "communication apprehension" to problems encountered with oral communication in second language classrooms. "Communication apprehension is the fear or anxiety an individual feels about orally communicating" (p. 3). Daly points out that there are other related constructs, such as writing apprehension and receiver apprehension (associated with listening), which may also be relevant to the problems foreign language learners can experience, but that anxiety about oral communication seems to be most directly related to "language anxiety."

Horwitz, Horwitz, and Cope (1991) point out that, in addition to "communication apprehension," test anxiety and fear of negative evaluation can play a role in the development of foreign language anxiety among classroom learners. In addition, they suggest that foreign language anxiety can arise because of the difficulty of engaging in genuine or authentic communication when one's linguistic skills are limited. "The importance of the disparity between the 'true' self as known to the learner and the more limited self as can be presented at any given moment in the foreign language would seem to distinguish foreign language anxiety from other academic anxieties, such as those associated with mathematics or science" (p. 31).

Brown (1984) maintains that lowered anxiety and inhibition will increase comprehensible input and, therefore, affect acquisition, but he cautions that evidence about the precise role of anxiety in language learning is still quite scanty. He hypothesizes that although too much anxiety may have harmful effects on learning, *too little* anxiety may also cause failure. If a student's affective filter is too low, there may be little motivation to learn. "We do well to note that anxiety can be debilitative but it can also be *facilitative* . . . As teachers we should allow some of the anxiety and tension to remain in our classes lest our students become so 'laid back' that they fail to perceive the input when it comes!" (p. 278).

Scovel (1991) presents various research studies that indicate mixed results about the relationship of anxiety to foreign language learning, with some studies showing that it inhibits performance and other studies showing some anxiety to be facilitative, as Brown (1984) suggests. Clearly, more research is needed to determine the role of emotions such as anxiety in second language learning.

Daly (1991) suggests that anxiety, or "communication apprehension" may be only one of many possible reasons why students are reluctant to talk in classrooms. Other reasons for reticence might be a lack of preparation or motivation, a lack of confidence, or an unwillingness to disclose one's feelings or thoughts (p. 6). This last consideration is especially important for teachers to remember when planning activities that are personalized in nature. We need to be sensitive to the feelings of students, allowing them the flexibility to participate in discussions in ways that do not require sharing of personal information if they prefer not to do so.

Whether or not we agree with the need to include certain types of affective activities in the classroom, most language educators today recognize that students will probably attain a given degree of proficiency more rapidly and will be more motivated to continue in their studies in an environment that is accepting, relaxed, and supportive.

Hypothesis 5. *Cultural understanding must be promoted in various ways so that students are sensitive to other cultures and prepared to live more harmoniously in the target-language community.*

For many years, foreign language educators have been emphasizing the need to incorporate a cultural syllabus into the curriculum and to promote global awareness and cross-cultural understanding. (See, for example, Stern 1981). When language acquisition activities are based on authentic cultural material or embedded in a cultural context, we can begin to attain this important goal. In Chapters 5 through 9, many sample activities are given that attempt to blend the study of language and culture. Specific strategies for teaching cultural understanding and for incorporating cultural content into language lessons are given in Chapter 8.

The Proficiency Orientation of Existing Methodologies: A Preliminary Appraisal

In order to make a preliminary appraisal of the extent to which various existing teaching approaches and methodologies are oriented toward proficiency, it would be useful to determine how many of the hypothesized elements discussed in the previous section are assigned a relatively high priority in a given approach.

There are several problems, however, in any formal comparison of methods in this way. As stated earlier, it is often difficult to clearly define a method to the satisfaction of everyone familiar with it, since there are currently many individual variations and interpretations of each method being used. If, as Westphal (1979) suggested, we consider method as a combination of a given *syllabus*, a philosophical or theoretical *approach*, and a choice of teaching *strategies*, all of which are then "seasoned" with a teacher's personal style, we many find it relatively difficult to characterize any methodology in the abstract. Before the demise of the purest form of audiolingualism in the late 1960s, such a methodological comparison would not have been as difficult, since teachers using the audiolingual method were expected to follow a particular syllabus, use accepted materials and teaching strategies, and subscribe to the underlying theoretical basis on which the methodology was founded. (However, not all teachers followed the method as rigidly as they had been trained to do, even though it was prescriptive down to the smallest detail.) Since the early 1970s many foreign language practitioners have been electing to use selected techniques from a variety of methods in their classrooms or adapting a given method or approach to suit the abilities, needs, and interests of their students. Therefore, each method or approach presented in the following pages may be interpreted or understood somewhat differently by different people.

A second problem associated with a methodological comparison of this kind is that it will almost certainly be subjective to some extent. Those who favor a given method or approach may attribute characteristics to it that others may not associate with it at all. One way to achieve some objectivity in comparing and contrasting methodologies and approaches would be to refer to a commonly accepted set of descriptions such as those provided by Benseler and Schulz (1980) to the President's Commission, or those found in methods texts published in the past twenty years. (See, for example, Rivers 1975, 1981; Chastain 1976, 1988; Allen and Valette 1977; Richards and Rodgers 1986.) Using such descriptions as a guide, one could then make a preliminary appraisal of each method or approach in terms of its proficiency orientation, keeping in mind that variations of any given methodology might alter the appraisal considerably.

The pages that follow describe a variety of methods and approaches that have been used and discussed by second language educators in this century. Because not every method that has been proposed can be treated in detail here, emphasis is placed on those that (1) have had a profound influence on second language teaching in this country or (2) have received significant attention in the recent literature on language teaching. The description of each method is comprised of five parts: (1) the theoretical and/or philosophical premise upon which the method is based, (2) a list of the method's major characteristics, (3) a sample lesson plan or brief description of classroom activities, (4) a preliminary assessment of the proficiency orientation implicit in the method as described, and (5) a discussion of the method's possible drawbacks or commonly perceived shortcomings, particularly in terms of proficiency goals. In relation to the third part of the description, it is important to note that no one day of instruction, however typical, can suffice to illustrate a methodology completely. Every method or approach incorporates a variety of activities that may not be captured in one lesson plan chosen to illustrate it. Even so, the lesson plans outlined in this chapter should give us a fairly good idea of how instruction is generally organized in classrooms using these approaches.

Three "Traditional" Methods

The three methods described in this section constitute the most common ways of approaching foreign language teaching before the 1970s, when rapid developments in second language acquisition research ushered in a profusion of new approaches. These descriptions are based for the most part on characterizations provided by Chastain (1976), Benseler and Schulz (1980), and Rivers (1981).

The Grammar-Translation Method: "Mental Discipline"

Background The grammar-translation approach to language teaching was congruent with the view of faculty psychologists that mental discipline was essential for strengthening the powers of the mind. Originally used to teach Latin and Greek, this method was applied to the teaching of modern languages in the late nineteenth and early twentieth centuries. Its primary purpose was to enable students to "explore the depths of great literature," while helping them understand their native language better through extensive analysis of the grammar of the target language and translation.

Major Characteristics

The grammar-translation method, in its purest form, had the following characteristics:

1. Students first learned the rules of grammar and bilingual lists of vocabulary pertaining to the reading or readings of the lesson. Grammar was learned deductively by means of long and elaborate explanations. All rules were learned with their exceptions and irregularities explained in grammatical terms.
2. Once rules and vocabulary were learned, prescriptions for translating the exercises that followed the grammar explanations were given.
3. Comprehension of the rules and readings was tested via translation (target language to native language and vice versa). Students had learned the language if they could translate the passages well.
4. The native and target languages were constantly compared. The goal of instruction was to convert L1 into L2 and vice versa, using a dictionary if necessary.
5. There were very few opportunities for listening and speaking practice (with the exception of reading passages and sentences aloud), since the method concentrated on reading and translation exercises. Much of the class time was devoted to talking *about* the language; virtually no time was spent talking *in* the language.

A Sample Lesson Plan

The lesson plan that follows is based on a description given by Rivers (1981, pp. 1–2) of a typical grammar-translation class. Before class begins, the students, seated in rows with books open, are about to begin a new section. On the page before them is a *reading selection,* preceded by several columns of *vocabulary* listed with native-language equivalents. The lesson proceeds as follows:

9:00–9:05 Short vocabulary quiz. Students write out the new words as the teacher reads the native-language translation.

9:05–9:15 Various students are asked to read aloud in the target language from the reading selection in the book. After several minutes, the teacher reads a few sentences aloud to the students and then asks them to spend a few minutes reading the rest of the passage silently.

9:15–9:25 Students begin to translate the sentences of the passage into their native language. Occasionally the teacher offers help when students stumble.

9:25–9:40 The core of the lesson now begins with the grammar explanation. On the blackboard, the teacher has placed an outline of the uses of the past tense, examples of which are drawn from the reading passage. The rules are explained in detail in the native language. If students are not familiar with the grammatical terminology used in the explanation, time is taken out to teach it. Students copy the explanations and rules, as well as the examples and various exceptions, into their notebooks.

9:40–9:50 The rest of the lesson is spent on written tasks, such as writing out verb paradigms and filling in the blanks in grammatical exercises. Some time is also spent in translating sentences, usually consisting of nonsequiturs seeded with the grammar point of the lesson, from the native language to the new one. Students who do not complete these tasks before class ends are asked to complete them for homework, as well as to memorize the vocabulary list preceding the reading in the next section of the book.

Proficiency Orientation Very few, if any of the elements hypothesized to contribute to the development of proficiency are present in this sample lesson of the grammar-translation method. Certainly, in terms of oral proficiency, this method has little to offer. There is virtually no sign of spoken language, and the little oral practice that is in evidence consists of reading aloud. There is no personalization or contextualization of the lesson to relate to students' experience, no pair or group interaction for communicative practice, no concern for the teaching of cultural awareness, at least on an everyday level. Affective concerns seem to be nonexistent, as students are clearly in a defensive learning environment where right answers are expected. The only thing that can be said is that there *is* a concern for accuracy, but this concern is so prevalent as to prevent students from creating with the language or venturing to express their own thoughts. It is only while *creating with the language* that students have an opportunity to build toward higher levels of proficiency. In addition, it is during creative language practice that the most informative error-correction feedback can be given, since this type of practice allows students to try out their hypotheses about the target language in a natural way. As Higgs and Clifford (1982) point out, the particular kind of concern for accuracy that characterizes grammar-translation methodology is *not* necessarily conducive to building toward proficiency and may, in fact, be quite counterproductive.

Potential Drawbacks The lack of orientation towards proficiency goals is the most obvious drawback of this method, at least as it is traditionally described. The meticulous detail of the grammar explanations, the long written exercises, the lengthy vocabulary lists, and the academic forms of language presented in the readings render language learning both strenuous and boring. Perhaps a modified form of grammar-translation methodology would be useful at the higher levels of proficiency, where the purpose of instruction is to fine-tune students' control of the target language, especially in terms of learning to use specialized vocabulary or developing competence in written stylistics. The method does not seem appropriate, however, for students at the Novice through Advanced levels, even though that is where it is typically used.

Strasheim (1976) sums up her appraisal of the shortcomings of the grammar-translation approach with the following personal anecdote:

> *It was one day while my third-year class was parsing one of Cicero's lengthier Latin accusations of Catiline that the mental discipline objective proved its real efficacy, for I fell asleep in a class I was teaching. All I can say in my own defense is that the mass of the class had preceded me into the Land of Nod by at least a clause—or two (p. 40).*

The Direct Method: A Rationalist Perspective on Language Learning

Background   The direct method movement, as advocated by educators such as Berlitz and Goun, originated in the nineteenth century. Advocates of this "active" method believed that students learn to understand a language by listening to it in large quantities. They learn to speak by speaking, especially if the speech is associated simultaneously with appropriate action. The methodology was based essentially on the way children learn their native language: language is learned through the *direct* association of words and phrases with objects and actions, without the use of the native language as the intervening variable. Various oral and "natural" methods have evolved since the nineteenth-century version to be described next. (See, for example, Terrell's Natural Approach. This variation is treated in a separate section.)

Major Characteristics   The methodology advocated by Berlitz, among others, had the following characteristics:

1. Language learning should start with the here-and-now, utilizing classroom objects and simple actions. Eventually, when students have learned enough language, lessons move on to include common situations and settings.
2. The direct method lesson often develops around specially constructed pictures depicting life in the country where the target language is spoken. These pictures enable the teacher to *avoid the use of translation,* which is strictly forbidden in the classroom. Definitions of new vocabulary are given via *paraphrases* in the target language, or by miming the action or manipulating objects to get the meaning across.
3. From the beginning of instruction, students hear complete and meaningful sentences in simple discourse, which often takes the form of question-answer exchanges.

4. Correct pronunciation is an important consideration in this approach, and emphasis is placed upon the development of accurate pronunciation from the beginning of instruction. Phonetic notation is often used to achieve this goal.
5. Grammar rules are not explicitly taught; rather, they are assumed to be learned through practice. Students are encouraged to form their own generalizations about grammar through *inductive* methods. When grammar is explicitly taught, it is taught in the target language.
6. Reading goals are also reached via the "direct" understanding of text without the use of dictionaries or translations. (Based on Rivers, 1981, pp. 31–35.)

A Sample Lesson Plan

The following description of a direct method class is based on one given by Rivers (1981, p. 3).

9:00–9:10 The teacher comes into the classroom and immediately begins speaking in the target language, greeting students and asking about classroom objects. Students answer in the target language. The teacher continues to ask questions and occasionally gives commands. As the students obey these orders, they recount in the target language exactly what they are doing and the class then tells the teacher what has happened (using past time in their account of the actions just performed).

9:10–9:25 The lesson develops next around a picture, which the teacher uses to teach the core vocabulary. Various actions and objects are discussed in reference to the activity depicted in the picture. The teacher demonstrates those activities and concepts that are not immediately apparent through mime and waits until the class seems to understand. The students then repeat the new words and phrases and try to form their own sentences in response to the teacher's questions. (This is done with little or no corrective feedback and the students' responses are often quite inaccurate.)

9:25–9:45 Once the vocabulary has been taught and absorbed, the teacher asks the students to *read* a passage on a similar theme aloud from their text. The teacher models the sentences to be read first and the students mimic either in chorus or individually. The passage is *never translated*, but the teacher assures comprehension by asking questions in the target language, to which the students respond, also in the target language. If difficulties arise, the teacher might explain briefly in the target language while the students take notes.

9:45–9:50 The lesson concludes with a song. When the class ends, students leave with a sense of accomplishment, since they have been actively involved all period.

Proficiency Orientation

Various elements of the class just described are congruent with the hypotheses presented earlier in this chapter. Students are certainly engaged in oral language use that is contextualized and, to some extent, personalized. There has been some description and narration in the lesson, although the bulk of the class is spent in responding to teacher questions. The use of culturally oriented pictures makes students aware of some of the everyday situations they might encounter in the target community, and vocabulary is useful for coping in survival situations. The use of paraphrase to explain vocabulary encourages students to learn that skill, which is important in developing proficiency beyond the Novice level. The affective needs of the student are addressed in group activities that allow for individual contributions without hypercorrection. Yet this lack of correction, which characterized the earliest versions of the direct method, often led to early fossilization, a problem discussed below.

Potential Drawbacks

Rivers (1981) makes the following comments about the direct method, as depicted in this sample lesson plan:

> *At its best, the direct method provides an exciting and interesting way of learning a language through activity . . . If care is not taken by the teacher, however, students who are plunged too soon into expressing themselves freely in the new language in a relatively unstructured situation can develop a glib but inaccurate fluency, clothing native-language structures in foreign-language vocabulary. This "school pidgin" is often difficult to eradicate later . . . because it has been accepted and encouraged for so long (p. 33).*

Rivers (1981) argues that, in the purest form of the direct method, insufficient provision was made for systematic practice of structures in a coherent sequence. However, she points out that some modern adaptations of this methodology do use structured practice, grammatical sequences that proceed one step at a time, and grammar explanations, sometimes given in the native language. "To counteract the tendency toward inaccuracy and vagueness" (p. 35), translation is even permitted in some modern versions of the method.

Audiolingual Methodology: An Empiricist Perspective on Language Learning

Background

In Chapter 2, we saw that the theory underlying audiolingual methodology was rooted in two parallel schools of thought in psychology and linguistics. In psychology, the behaviorist and neobehaviorist schools were extremely influential in the 1940s and 1950s. At the same time, the structural, or descriptive, school of linguistics dominated thinking in that field. Chastain (1976) explains that, up until this time, the emphasis had been on historical linguistics, which sought to explain linguistic data through the examination of manuscripts and the documentation of changes in vocabulary and form over time. But as linguists began to concentrate on the study of Indian languages, many of which had no writing systems, the oral form of language became the only data source. From these field studies of Indian languages evolved the school of *structural,* or *descriptive,* linguistics. Language teaching based on this school of thought operated on the following premises:

1. Language is primarily an oral phenomenon. Written language is a secondary representation of speech.
2. Linguistics involves the study of the *recurring patterns* of the language.
3. The major focus of study is phonology and morphology.
4. Language is acquired through the *overlearning* of its patterns.
5. All native languages are learned orally before reading ever occurs. Therefore, second languages should be learned in the "natural order": listening, speaking, reading, and writing.
6. In learning languages, a student should begin with the patterns of the language rather than with deductive learning of grammatical rules (Chastain 1976, p. 110).

The marriage of structural linguistics and behaviorist psychology resulted in a new theory of language learning which described the learning process in terms of conditioning. This theory was translated into practice in the 1940s in the Army Specialized Training Program intensive language courses, first taught at the Defense Language Institute. Later, this same essential methodology was to dominate academic programs in the country in the 1950s and 1960s, thanks mainly to summer institutes, funded by the National Defense Education Act (NDEA), which trained and retrained large numbers of pre- and in-service teachers in the audiolingual method (ALM).

Major Characteristics The audiolingual method, also known as the Aural-Oral, Functional Skills, New Key, or American Method of language teaching, was considered a "scientific" approach to language teaching. Lado (1964), in a book entitled *Language Teaching: A Scientific Approach,* proposed the following "empirical laws of learning" as the basis for audiolingual methodology:

1. *The fundamental law of contiguity* states that when two experiences have occurred together, the return of one will recall or reinstate the other.
2. *The law of exercise* maintains that the more frequently a response is practiced, the better it is learned and the longer it is remembered.
3. *The law of intensity* states that the more intensely a response is practiced, the better it is learned and the longer it will be remembered.
4. *The law of assimilation* states that each new stimulating condition tends to elicit the same response that has been connected with similar stimulating conditions in the past.

5. *The law of effect* maintains that when a response is accompanied or followed by a satisfying state of affairs, that response is reinforced. When a response is accompanied by an annoying state of affairs, it is avoided (Lado 1964, p. 37).

These behaviorist laws underlie the five basic tenets of the audiolingual method, listed in Chastain (1976) and summarized below:

1. The goal of second language teaching is to develop in students the same abilities that native speakers have. Students should, therefore, eventually handle the language at an *unconscious* level.
2. The native language should be banned from the classroom; a "cultural island" should be maintained. Teach L2 without reference to L1.
3. Students learn languages through stimulus-response (S-R) techniques. Students should learn to speak without attention to *how* the language is put together. They should not be given time to think about their answers. Dialogue memorization and pattern drills are the means by which conditioned responses are achieved.
4. Pattern drills are to be taught initially without explanation. Thorough practice should precede any explanation given, and the discussion of grammar should be kept very brief.
5. In developing the "four skills," the natural sequence followed in learning the native language should be maintained.

Rivers (1981) further clarifies the major characteristics of the audiolingual method by listing Moulton's (1961) "five slogans" of the method:

1. Language is speech, not writing.
2. Language is a set of habits.
3. Teach the language and not about the language.
4. A language is what native speakers say, not what someone thinks they ought to say.
5. Languages are different (Rivers 1981, pp. 41–43).

The last statement relates to the fact that structural linguists rejected the notion of a universal grammar that could serve as a framework for the organization of the facts of all languages (Rivers 1981, p. 43). Instead, they used contrastive analysis to select those features of the target language that would be especially troublesome for the learner.

An examination of an audiolingual textbook will yield further insights into the way the method was translated into practice. Every ALM textbook chapter consisted of three basic parts: (1) the dialogue, (2) pattern drills, and (3) application activities. There were very few grammar explanations within the pages of the text: some books had none at all. If grammar was included, it was always presented after the drills. Types of pattern drills included:

1. *Repetition drills,* in which no change was made. Students simply repeated after the teacher's model.

2. *Transformation drills,* in which the students were required to make some minimal change, reinforced afterward by the teacher or the tape recorder. The various types of transformation drills included *person-number substitutions, patterned response drills, singular-plural transformations, tense transformations, directed dialogue, cued response,* and *translation drills.*

Application activities included such things as dialogue adaptations, open-ended response drills, recombined narratives in which the material presented in the dialogues was transformed slightly, guided oral presentations in which students had a chance to use the memorized material for personal expression, and conversation stimulus activities, which resembled semicontrolled role-plays. In all of these activities, students worked mainly with memorized material, repeating it, manipulating it, or transforming it to meet minimal communicative needs.

A Sample Lesson Plan

The following lesson, based on a description given by Rivers (1981, pp. 4–6), is typical of an ALM class day:

9:00–9:15 The class repeats the lines of a new dialogue, following the teacher's model. To illustrate the meaning of the sentences, the teacher makes stick-figure sketches of the people in the dialogue on the board and points to them as the lines are said. First, everyone repeats the lines in chorus. When a pair of sentences has been repeated well in chorus, the teacher divides the class into two groups and the same lines are repeated, with one group responding to the other's line in turn. Next, individual rows of students take a dialogue line and repeat it. Finally, the teacher calls on individuals to repeat the new sentences in front of the class.

9:15–9:40 The teacher moves on to the pattern drilling phase of the lesson, in which structures that were used in the dialogue are now drilled one by one. The class first chorally repeats the drill sentence after the teacher's model. Then they do transformations of the sentence according to the teacher's cues. Transformations may include minimal changes in vocabulary or involve a morphological manipulation of some type. Seven or eight changes of this type are effected by the class in chorus. When the class has had enough practice that they are performing the transformations easily, the teacher asks students to identify what the sentences have in common. The rule, when satisfactorily inducted, is then further drilled through more pattern practice in smaller groups and finally with individual response.

9:40–9:50 A chain drill is used as a final consolidating activity. Students ask one another questions or give one another cues, going down a row from student to student in a chain of stimulus and response. The teacher indicates the homework for the next class session, which consists of listening to lab tapes and practicing more patterns and recorded dialogues, as well as transcribing several times certain words or phrases from the text.

Throughout the entire lesson, the teacher has insisted on absolutely correct forms. Any and all errors have been corrected on the spot, often with a request that other students repeat the correct response in chorus, followed by a repetition from the student who made the error originally. The class has been teacher-centered throughout the 50-minute period; the students' role has been to respond to the teacher's stimulus.

Proficiency Orientation

The ALM approach, when adhered to strictly, tends to force students to perform continuously at the Novice level since they are never asked to say anything they haven't seen before or haven't committed to memory. The methodology does not encourage creation on the part of the learner except in very minimal ways. Not until well into the second year of the course syllabus are students asked to do very much in the way of free expression. However, the method does have some positive aspects that should be mentioned. The use of colloquial, sociolinguistically appropriate language in the dialogues and recombination narratives is a feature that was missing in older methods such as grammar-translation. The focus on oral skills led to good pronunciation and accurate speech, at least when students were asked to give structured responses with which they were familiar. Audiolingual methods have also stressed the teaching of culture and prepare students to deal in some measure with everyday situations in the target language community.

Potential Drawbacks

The enthusiasm with which second language teachers had originally received this revolutionary methodology was dampened within a relatively short time. First, the method did not deliver what it had promised: bilingual speakers at the end of instruction. For one thing, the S-R approach did not account for the variety of learning styles in the language classroom, as some students learn better by seeing the language first or by learning grammatical rules deductively. These options were not provided. Furthermore, both teachers and students found the avoidance of grammar discussions frustrating and time consuming. The continuous repetition required for overlearning and memorization was monotonous and was a considerable physical strain on both teachers and students. Because the method was antimentalistic, students were expected to be satisfied with parroting the cues given by the teacher, even if they did not immediately understand them. Since many students felt the need to know what they were learning and why, this disregard for meaningful learning in favor of rote learning caused considerable dissatisfaction, and even failure for some learners. Even when drills were meaningful, the monotonous repetition eliminated the effects of meaningfulness and contextualization. Strasheim (1976) sums up general dissatisfaction with the purest form of audiolingualism as follows:

> Every student, probably dating from Cain and Abel, has recognized this awful dichotomy between "classroom thinking" and "real-life thinking;" the

successful student, for generations, has been the one who could keep them separate. In the late sixties, however, students were not content to keep the two discretely apart . . . Our "one true way" had had a life of under 10 years (p. 41).

By 1970, many language practitioners were looking for alternatives to ALM, or at least for ways to adapt the approach to suit their students' and their own needs. Today, many teachers continue to use selected audiolingual techniques within an eclectic framework.

Reactions to Audiolingualism: Two Mentalist Perspectives

Background   When second language acquisition theorists of the late 1960s and early 1970s began to reject behaviorist views of language learning in favor of rationalist and mentalist perspectives, applied linguists began to look for approaches to the classroom that were more congruent with the prevailing theories of the times. Ellis (1990) describes two mentalist perspectives on teaching that contrasted quite strongly with one another. One view was based on principles of first-language acquisition and was characterized by an attempt to simulate "natural" learning processes in the classroom. He characterizes this view, described in a series of articles by Newmark (1966) and Newmark and Reibel (1968), as the *cognitive anti-method.* Contrasting strongly with this perspective was the view that grew out of Chomsky's competence-performance distinction and that held that learners must understand and analyze the rules of the language to build their competence. This view, described most thoroughly by Chastain (1976), was called the *cognitive-code method.* Because these two perspectives have had a strong influence on the development of American language teaching methodologies in subsequent years, they will be described briefly below.

The Cognitive Anti-Method

Major Characteristics   Ellis (1990) describes the following major theoretical assumptions underlying the Cognitive Anti-Method, articulated by Newmark (1966) and Newmark and Reibel (1968):

1. "Second language learning is controlled by the learner rather than by the teacher" (Ellis 1990, p. 35). The learner is engaged in problem-solving, using the input as the data from which the system of language is discovered.
2. Learners have an innate ability to learn languages. Their language acquisition capacity is qualitatively like that of a child.
3. One need not pay attention to form in order to acquire a language. Linguistic analysis is not necessary for language learning, and grammatical rules and explanations are not useful in the classroom.

4. Learners do not acquire linguistic features one by one but acquire language globally. There is, therefore, no need to sequence instruction through selection and grading of the input.

5. Errors are inevitable and should be tolerated. Learners will eventually discover and correct their own errors and, therefore, do not have to receive error correction from the teacher.

6. L1 interference will disappear with more exposure to the target language. Contrastive analysis and the overt comparison of L1 with L2 is therefore of little use.

(Based on Ellis 1990, pp. 35-37)

Ellis remarks that the *cognitive anti-method* did not have many adherents, in part because it was "before its time" (p. 38) and in part because it was "too radical" (p. 40). Another problem was that the pedagogical ideas that Newmark and Reibel (1968) proposed were rather fragmentary in nature. Although the authors maintained that the teacher should not interfere with the natural learning process, some of the pedagogical techniques that were used as illustrations in their 1968 article seemed to have behavioristic overtones. For example, Newmark and Reibel suggested that adults would learn a second language most easily and effectively by memorizing dialogues and practicing situational variants of those conversations, "substituting new items from previously learned dialogues corresponding to slight changes [students] wish to introduce into the situation" (p. 153). One of their central concerns was finding ways to "increase the likelihood that the student will imitate the language behavior of his teacher" (p. 153). The use of such terms as "memorization," "substitution," and "imitation" seem somewhat incongruent in an ideological approach that, according to Ellis (1990), was firmly based in Chomsky's "cognitivism" (p. 35).

The most controversial aspect of the cognitive anti-method was the proposal that structural features should not be taught overtly and that language materials need not be ordered grammatically. Many practitioners, as well as scholars, thought this view was too extreme. Diller (1978), for example, considered the idea that grammatical instruction should be abandoned as a rationalist "heresy," and argued instead for a combination of meaningful learning with conscious attention to form using materials graded for difficulty (pp. 90–92).

Some of the ideas advanced by Newmark and Reibel, however, continued to have an appeal for those who believed that classroom language learning was too far removed from real language use. When Krashen introduced his Monitor Theory in the late 1970s, he incorporated some of the same notions that had been proposed in the cognitive anti-method, arguing their merits on somewhat different theoretical grounds. Many practitioners who were looking for more communicative approaches to teaching began to show interest in the *Natural Approach*, which translated

Krashen's theory into practice. A sample lesson plan and evaluation of this approach will be given later in the chapter.

The Cognitive-Code Method

Major Characteristics

A basic assumption underlying cognitive methodology was that meaningful learning was essential to language acquisition, and that conscious knowledge of grammar was important. This viewpoint contrasted strongly with both audiolingualism and the cognitive anti-method described above.

Chastain (1976) has characterized the basic tenets of the cognitive approach as follows:

1. The goal of cognitive teaching is to develop in students the same types of abilities that native speakers have. This is done by helping students attain a minimal control over the rules of the target language so that they can generate their own language to meet a previously unencountered situation in an adequate fashion.

2. In teaching the language, the instructor must move from the *known* to the *unknown*; that is, the student's present knowledge base (cognitive structure) must be determined so that the necessary prerequisites for understanding the new material can be provided. This knowledge base includes not only student's present understanding of the new language, but also their understanding of how their native language works, as well as their general "knowledge of the world." Students must be familiar with the rules of the new language before being asked to apply them to the generation of language. The foundation, or *competence*, must come first. *Performance* will follow once the foundation is laid.

3. Text materials and the teacher must introduce students to situations that will promote the *creative use of the language*. The primary concern is that students have practice going from their underlying understanding of the way the language works to using the language in actual communication of ideas.

4. Because language behavior is constantly innovative and varied, students must be taught to understand the rule system rather than be required to memorize surface strings in rote fashion. Therefore, grammar should be overtly explained and discussed in a cognitive classroom.

5. Learning should always be *meaningful*; that is, students should understand at all times what they are being asked to do. New material should always be organized so that it is relatable to students' existing cognitive structure. Since not all students learn in the same way, the teacher should appeal to all senses and learning styles. (Based on Chastain, 1976, pp. 146–147)

A Sample Lesson Plan The lesson plan that follows is representative of one interpretation of the way in which cognitive teaching is translatable to the classroom context. In this particular interpretation, an effort has been made to combine an essentially *structural syllabus* with a *cognitive approach* using a variety of *communicative and personalized activities and teaching strategies*. Many other interpretations of cognitive teaching are possible, since no one cognitive method really exists.

9:00–9:10 The lesson begins with a presentation of the new vocabulary, which relates to the description of personality. Students look at a series of visuals in the text, which depicts four students engaged in a variety of activities, as the teacher presents the new words, most of which are descriptive adjectives. The teacher explains in the target language how the personality of each of the students in the visuals is different: Paul is a politically aware student; he is *active, involved*, and *enthusiastic* about politics. Georges is a *quiet* student; he is *timid, gentle*, and *agreeable*. Marie-Jeanne is *artistic, somewhat bizarre*, and *nonconformist*. By contrast, her roommate Frédérique is *arrogant, traditional*, and *conservative*. The lesson proceeds as students learn the new vocabulary in context, repeating the new words after the teacher's model, and using them in simple sentences to describe the students depicted in the visuals in response to the teacher's questions.

9:10–9:20 The teacher next explains the way adjectives are formed in French, using the visuals as well as students in the classroom as contextual support. Grammar explanation is done in the native language, although later, when students have more language available to them, the explanations will be done principally in French. This phase of the lesson establishes the *cognitive base* from which the students' language skills can be developed.

9:20–9:35 Students then show their understanding of the principles of adjective agreement by doing a variety of exercises that are both contextualized and personalized. Using a list of adjectives relating to personality provided by the teacher, students try out their skills by describing themselves, their classmates, and famous people. Exercises are controlled to some extent, and students are provided with a model or framework, although they must process what they are saying meaningfully at all times and consciously *select* both word and form. Some of the exercises involve word association, the use of synonyms or antonyms, and hierarchical categories of vocabulary. Students do some exercises first in pairs or small groups. The teacher, after five to seven minutes of this activity, has the class come back to the whole group to share some of the descriptions they have generated.

9:35–9:50 The fourth phase of the lesson plan involves an *application activity* in which self-expression, using the new structure and vocabulary, is promoted. Students, divided into groups of three, are given *conversation cards* (see Chapter 6), two of which have four or five native-language questions using the structures and vocabulary just presented. The third card has appropriate French equivalents of the questions on Cards 1 and 2. The student holding this card "monitors" the questions asked by his two classmates during the conversation, helping out when necessary and ensuring that the questions are formed correctly. Students ask one another questions based on the native-language cues on their cards and respond in a personalized, relatively unconstrained fashion. The teacher circulates among the groups and offers help when needed. At the end of ten minutes, the class comes back to a whole-group format and students offer short resumes of the information obtained in the conversation activity. The teacher asks the students to write a short summary of their conversation in French for the next class day.

Proficiency Orientation

Much of the activity of this class period is proficiency-oriented, since language is being used in context for the whole 50 minutes, students are speaking a large portion of the class time, and conversations and activities in which students create with the language are being used. At the same time, there is a concern for developing accuracy, both through an understanding of the underlying principles of grammar being applied and through the monitoring of responses and the use of corrective feedback. As students' skills progress, more class time will be devoted to communicative and creative activities, and students will be encouraged to express their own meaning without excessive support from the text materials. (See Chapters 5 through 7 for more examples of communicative and functional language practice activities of this type.)

Potential Drawbacks

Care should be taken when using an essentially cognitive approach to avoid spending too much time on the explanation of grammar, especially in the native language. Many teachers are tempted to devote a large portion of the class hour to explanations, operating on the premise that a cognitive orientation to methodology implies that students need a thorough understanding of the grammatical system of the new language. While this may be an ultimate goal for some students, it is not necessary to devote an inordinate amount of time to explanation per se or to expect a thorough understanding of the details of the grammatical system all at once. Rather, a proficiency-oriented approach will promote this basic understanding through the use of contextualized practice activities in which students constantly use the new structures in a personalized way. Also, structures can be taught in a *cyclical* fashion in which they are constantly reentered in new contexts as instruction progresses over time.

Obviously, any approach that is proficiency-oriented will have to devote some time to the teaching of cultural understanding, a factor that is not evident in the lesson plan just cited. As was pointed out earlier, no one day of instruction, however typical, can suffice to illustrate a methodology. It is assumed that most methodologies depicted in this chapter will incorporate activities of various sorts, even though they may not be captured in one lesson plan chosen for the purposes of illustration. The reader should keep this in mind as some of the more recent approaches to language teaching are discussed in the next sections.

A Functional Approach: Communicative Language Teaching

Background Richards and Rodgers (1986) describe Communicative Language Teaching (CLT) as an *approach* rather than a method, since it is defined in rather broad terms and represents a philosophy of teaching that is based on communicative language use. CLT has developed from the writings of British applied linguists such as Wilkins, Widdowson, Brumfit, Candlin, and others, as well as American educators such as Savignon (1983), all of whom emphasize notional-functional concepts and communicative competence, rather than grammatical structures, as central to language teaching (Richards and Rodgers 1986, p. 65). Although the movement first began with a reconceptualization of the teaching syllabus in notional-functional terms, CLT has broadened to encompass a wide range of principles for developing communicative competence. Richards and Rodgers (1986), citing Finocchiaro and Brumfit (1983), outline 22 major distinctive features of this approach. Some of these principles are summarized below.

Major Characteristics

1. Meaning is of primary importance in CLT, and contextualization is a basic principle.
2. Attempts by learners to communicate with the language are encouraged from the beginning of instruction. The new language system will be learned best by struggling to communicate one's own meaning and by negotiation of meaning through interaction with others.
3. Sequencing of materials is determined by the content, function, and/or meaning that will maintain students' interest.
4. Judicious use of the native language is acceptable where feasible, and translation may be used when students find it beneficial or necessary.
5. Activities and strategies for learning are varied according to learner preferences and needs.
6. Communicative competence, with an emphasis on fluency and acceptable language use, is the goal of instruction. "Accuracy is judged not in the abstract, but in context" (p. 92).

(Based on Finocchiaro and Brumfit 1983, pp. 91–93, cited in Richards and Rodgers 1986, p. 67–68.)

Richards and Rodgers state that although CLT does not claim a particular theory of language learning as its basis, there are several theoretical premises that can be deduced from a consideration of the approach:

1. *The communication principle:* Activities that involve communication promote language learning.
2. *The task principle:* Activities that involve the completion of real-world tasks promote learning.
3. *The meaningfulness principle:* Learners must be engaged in meaningful and authentic language use for learning to take place. (Richards and Rodgers 1986, p. 72).

Sample Classroom Activities

Because CLT is a comprehensive approach and not a method, it is difficult to characterize it by any one sample lesson plan. However, the kinds of classroom activities that would be representative of CLT include interactive language games, information sharing activities, task-based activities, social interaction, and functional communication practice (Richards and Rodgers 1986). Savignon (1983) suggests designing the curriculum to include language arts (or language analysis activities), language-for-a-purpose (content-based and immersion) activities, personalized language use, theater arts (including simulations, role-plays, and social interaction games), and language use beyond the classroom (including inviting L2 speakers into the classroom and planning activities that take learners outside the classroom to engage in real-world encounters). She gives many examples of communicative language teaching ideas that can be used to generate a classroom atmosphere conducive to the development of communicative competence in all skill areas. For a more complete treatment of communicative language teaching, consult the sources cited above, as well as Brumfit and Johnson (1979), Littlewood (1981), Finocchiaro and Brumfit (1983), and Yalden (1987).

Proficiency Orientation

Clearly many of the tenets of CLT are congruent with the principles outlined at the beginning of this chapter. Communicative language teaching, like any instruction oriented toward proficiency goals, is not bound to a particular methodology or curricular design, but represents a flexible approach to teaching that is responsive to learner needs and preferences. In many ways, CLT represents a repertoire of teaching ideas rather than a fixed set of methodological procedures, and as such is not easily defined or evaluated. The congruence of any particular version of CLT with proficiency goals will depend on the choices made by the program designers and instructors.

Modern Adaptations of the Direct Method

Although the two approaches to be described next are in some ways quite different from one another, each has evolved to some extent from direct methodology.

Total Physical Response

Background

This approach is based on the belief that listening comprehension should be developed fully, as it is with children learning their native language, before any active oral participation from students is expected. Further, it is based on the belief that skills can be more rapidly assimilated if the teacher appeals to the students' kinesthetic-sensory system. The approach, developed by James J. Asher, utilizes oral commands that students carry out to show their understanding. As with the direct method, the target language is the exclusive language of instruction. Students are exposed to language that is based in the here-and-now and that is easily understood through mime and example.

Major Characteristics

Asher, Kusudo, and de la Torre (1974) summarize three key ideas that underlie the Total Physical Response approach:

1. Understanding of the spoken language must be developed in advance of speaking.
2. Understanding and retention is best achieved through *movement of the students' bodies* in response to commands. The imperative form of the language is a powerful tool because it can be used to manipulate students' behavior and guide them towards understanding through action. Asher et al. state that their research indicates that most of the grammatical structures of the target language and hundreds of vocabulary items can be learned through the skillful use of the imperative by the instructor.
3. *Students should never be forced to speak before they are ready.* As the target language is internalized, speaking will emerge naturally.

Sample Classroom Activities

A few examples of commands students respond to in relatively early training will serve to illustrate this methodology. The activities described are presented in Asher, Kusudo, and de la Torre (1974). The reader may want to read this or other source material for a more complete understanding of the way the method works. (See also Asher 1982.)

Listening Training. Students sit in a semicircle around the instructor. The instructor asks them to be silent, listen to commands in Spanish, and then do exactly what she does. The students are encouraged "to respond rapidly without hesitation and to make a distinct, robust response with their bodies" (p. 27). For example, when the teacher commands students to run by saying ¡*Corran!*, students are to run with gusto. Commands such as "Stand up! Walk! Stop! Turn! Walk! Stop! Turn! Sit down!" are then executed in succession in Spanish. The instructor simultaneously executes the commands as they are given, accompanied by the two students seated beside her. This routine is repeated several times until individual students indicate that they are willing to try it alone without the instructor acting as a model. Each variation of the routine is different to avoid the memorization of a fixed sequence of behaviors.

Next, commands are expanded to full sentences, such as "Walk to the door! Walk to the window! Walk to the table! Touch the table!" As students learn more vocabulary in this way, "surprises and novelty" are introduced, and the instructor begins to use playful, bizarre, and "zany" directives to keep students' interest high. Three samples that Asher et al. (1974) give are the following:

> *When Henry runs to the blackboard and draws a funny picture of Molly, Molly will throw her purse at Henry.*
>
> *Henry, would you prefer to serve a cold drink to Molly, or would you rather have Eugene kick you in the leg?*
>
> *Rosemary, dance with Samuel, and stick your tongue out at Hilda. Hilda, run to Rosemary, hit her on the arm, pull her to her chair and you dance with Samuel (pp. 27–28).*

Production. Asher et al. state that after about ten hours of training in listening, students are "invited but not pressured" to reverse roles with the instructor and give their own commands in Spanish. The instructor then performs in response to the students' commands. After this is successfully done, about 20 percent of all class time will be spent in role-reversal of this type. Later, skits are prepared and performed by students, and still later, problem-solving situations are used. In this latter activity, students are presented with an unexpected difficulty in a typical survival situation or other setting in a Latin country and are expected to talk their way through the situation to a solution.

Reading and Writing. Although there is no formal training in reading and writing in the approach as described by Asher et al., they do state that the instructor spent a few minutes at the end of each class session writing structures or vocabulary on the blackboard for students requesting explanation. Students generally copied the expressions into their notebooks. No English equivalents were given. Most expressions were those already heard during the class session.

Proficiency Orientation

TPR methodology, as described by Asher et al. (1974), is affectively appealing to many students: the atmosphere in the class is warm and accepting, allowing students to try out their skills in creative ways. The focus on listening skills in the early phases of instruction allows students to experience the new language in a low-anxiety environment, and the use of techniques to act out what is understood ensures that comprehension of the language is taking place. It seems that TPR is not really designed to be a comprehensive "method" in and of itself, but represents instead a useful set of teaching ideas and techniques that can be integrated into other methodologies for certain instructional purposes. TPR techniques have been used effectively by many practitioners, and methodologies such as the Natural Approach, to be described next, include them among their instructional strategies.

Potential Drawbacks

If TPR is the only strategy used for language teaching, there may be some substantial limitations on what can be effectively accomplished in terms of proficiency goals. Although "with imagination, almost any aspect of the linguistic code for the target language could be communicated using commands" (Asher et al. 1974, p. 26), the functional use of language as described in the proficiency guidelines and the contexts normally used in the target culture do not seem to be a natural outcome of this methodology. There is also very little emphasis on the development of accuracy in Asher's description of the method.

The Natural Approach

Background Terrell (1977, 1982) based his methodology on Krashen's theory of second language acquisition, discussed in detail in Chapter 2. Terrell's main premise is that "it is possible for students in a classroom situation to learn to communicate in a second language" (1977, p. 325). His definition of communicative competence is interesting in that it resembles the description of Level 1/1+ (Intermediate) proficiency:

> I use this term to mean that a student can understand the essential points of what a native speaker says to him in a real communication situation and can respond in such a way that the native speaker interprets the response with little or no effort and without errors that are so distracting that they interfere drastically with communication. I suggest that the level of competence needed for minimal communication acceptable to native speakers is much lower than that supposed by most teachers. Specifically, I suggest that if we are to raise our expectations for oral competence in communication we must lower our expectations for structural accuracy (1977, p. 326, emphasis added).

From this statement, it seems that the goal of the Natural Approach is set at an Intermediate (survival) proficiency in the second language, at least in oral/aural skills. This will have important implications for classroom practice. According to Higgs and Clifford (1982), "if the goal is to produce students with Level 1 survival skills, then the optimum curriculum mix would be . . . a primary emphasis on the teaching and practice of vocabulary" (p. 73), with little emphasis on structural accuracy. This principle holds true in some respects in the Natural Approach, as we shall see below.

Major Characteristics Terrell (1977) provided the following guidelines for classroom practice in the "Natural Approach":

1. *Distribution of learning and acquisition activities.* If communication is more important than form in beginning and intermediate levels of instruction, then most, if not all, classroom activities should be designed to evoke communication. Terrell suggested that the entire class period be devoted to communication activities. Explanation and practice with linguistic forms should be done outside of class for the most part. "This outside work must be carefully planned and highly structured" (p. 330); explanations must be clear enough

to be understood by students so that classroom time is not wasted in grammatical lectures or manipulative exercises. Terrell suggested that teachers make specific assignments, collect student work, and provide some type of systematic feedback on that written work. However, "the student should realize that the primary responsibility is his for improvement in the quality of his output" (p. 330).

2. *Error correction.* According to Terrell, there is no evidence to show that the correction of speech errors is necessary or even helpful in language acquisition. In fact, such correction is negative in terms of motivation, attitude, embarrassment, and the like, "even when done in the best of situations" (p. 330).

3. *Responses in both L1 and L2.* Terrell suggested that initial classroom instruction involve listening comprehension activities almost exclusively, with responses from students permitted in the native language. "If the student is permitted to concentrate entirely on comprehension by permitting responses in L1, he can rapidly expand his listening comprehension abilities to a wide variety of topics and still be comfortable in the communication process" (p. 331). Listening comprehension will, of course, take the form of "comprehensible input," as Krashen has explained that term. At first, simplified speech or "foreigner talk" is used. This type of speech has the following characteristics:

   a. a slower rate, with clear articulation, diminished contractions, longer pauses, and extra volume
   b. the use of explanations, paraphrases, gestures, and pictures to define new words or concepts
   c. simplification of syntax and the use of redundancy
   d. the use of yes/no questions, tag questions, forced choice (either/or) questions, and questions with a sample answer provided (Terrell 1982, p. 123)

Terrell (1977) summarized the main principles of his method as follows (p. 329):

1. Beginning language instruction should focus on the attainment of immediate communicative competence rather than on grammatical perfection.
2. Instruction needs to be aimed at modification and improvement of the student's developing grammar rather than at building that grammar up one rule at a time.
3. Teachers should afford students the opportunity to *acquire* language rather than force them to *learn* it.
4. Affective rather than cognitive factors are primary in language learning.
5. The key to comprehension and oral production is the acquisition of

vocabulary. "With a large enough vocabulary, the student can comprehend and speak a great deal of L2 *even if his knowledge of structure is for all practical purposes nonexistent!* (p. 333, emphasis added).

Sample Classroom Activities

Three types of activities dominate the classroom lesson in the Natural Approach. All of these activities are highly contextualized and personalized. Terrell (1982) maintained that "a low-anxiety situation can be created by involving the students personally in class activities . . . The goal is that the members of the group become genuinely interested in each others' opinions, feelings, and interests and feel comfortable expressing themselves on the topics of discussion" (p. 124).

The three types of acquisition activities are:

1. *Comprehension (preproduction) activities,* which consist of listening comprehension practice, with no requirement for students to speak in the target language. Comprehension is achieved by contextual guessing, TPR techniques, the use of gestures and visual aids, and data gleaned from personalized student input. One technique that Terrell used in beginning classes is description of students in the class in terms of hair color, clothing, height, and other physical attributes. Students are asked to stand up when described, or questions are asked so that students being described are identified by the others in the class.

The preproduction (comprehension) phase of instruction lasts, according to Terrell, about four to five class hours for university students, but could last several months for younger students.

2. *Early speech production* will occur once students have a recognition vocabulary of about 500 words. Production activities begin with questions requiring only single-word answers or with either/or questions in which the alternatives are provided. This type of production parallels that of young children who first begin to speak in holophrastic (single-word) utterances. Another type of production activity is the sentence-completion response, in which a personalized question is asked and the answer is provided except for one word, which students supply.

3. *Speech emergence* occurs after the early speech production phase and is encouraged through the use of games, humanistic-affective activities, and information and problem-solving activities. During all of these activities, the teacher is careful not to correct errors, as this is potentially harmful to the students' speech development.

As can be seen from this description, the Natural Approach classroom is one in which communication activities, contextualized acquisition opportunities, and humanistic learning techniques dominate.

Proficiency Orientation

There are quite a few elements of the proficiency-oriented classroom in the above description, if one bears in mind that the ultimate goal of instruction is survival-level communication. The students learn language *in context* in personalized activities. There is a very warm, affective atmosphere in class, and opportunities for group communicative practice abound. Students are encouraged to *create with the language* at all times. The obvious missing element, however, is the complete lack of corrective feedback during classroom practice. It is also not clear from Terrell's description how important a role cultural authenticity and cultural learning play in classroom activities; no doubt most opportunities to teach students how to cope in the target culture are exploited in this approach.

Potential Drawbacks

One aspect of Natural Approach methodology that may not be congruent with proficiency goals is the lack of form-focused instruction or corrective feedback in classroom instruction. This issue has been a source of controversy in recent years, with some scholars claiming that explicit instruction in grammar is not helpful in the classroom and that errors should never be corrected during oral activities. It is important to remember, however, that Terrell did suggest that there was a role for corrective feedback in written work, although he maintained that the study of grammatical principles and the correction of errors should be the student's responsibility. In his last writings, however, Terrell (1991) seemed to be amending his point of view on the issue of form-focused instruction. He suggested that explicit instruction in grammar might have some benefits for learners acquiring the language in the classroom, including its use as an advance organizer and as a means of establishing form-meaning relationships in communicative activities. In addition, he hypothesized that learners who are able to monitor their speech may produce more grammatical utterances that they will then "acquire." This acknowledgement of a potentially positive role for explicit grammar instruction marks an important modification in the Natural Approach, as described by Terrell in his earlier work.

Humanistic Approaches to Language Teaching

Since the early 1970s, various approaches to language teaching employing humanistic strategies have been advanced, with names such as *confluent, personal, affective, facilitative, psychological, futuristic,* and *humanistic education*. All of these varieties are based on movements in psychotherapy, such as values clarification and sensitivity training, in which the affective development of the individual is the first concern. Galyean (1976) gives a detailed description of many of these approaches, and the reader may want to read this source for a thorough understanding of the humanistic movement in education. One humanistically oriented methodology that has received some attention in recent years is described in the following section.

Community Language Learning

This approach, alternatively called Community Language Learning (CLL) and Counseling-Learning, stresses the role of the affective domain in promoting cognitive learning. Developed by Charles Curran (1976), it is founded on techniques borrowed from psychological counseling. The basic theoretical premise is that the human individual needs to be understood and aided in the process of fulfilling personal values and goals. This is best done in community with others striving to attain the same goals.

Major Characteristics The first principle of CLL is that the teacher serves as the "knower/counselor" whose role is essentially passive. He or she is there to provide the language necessary for students to express themselves freely and to say whatever it is they want to say. The class is comprised of six to twelve learners seated in a close circle, with one or more teachers who stand outside the circle, ready to help. The techniques used are designed to reduce anxiety in the group to a minimum and to promote the free expression of ideas and feelings. The method provides for five learning stages:

Stage 1. Students make statements aloud in their native language, based on whatever they desire to communicate to the others in the group. The teacher, placing his or her hands on the student's shoulders, translates the utterance softly into the student's ear. The student then repeats the utterance after the teacher's model, recording it on tape. Another student, desiring to make a response, will signal this desire to the teacher, who then comes around the circle and provides a target-language equivalent for this student in the same way. Again, the response is recorded on tape, so that at the end of the conversation the whole dialogue is recorded. This tape-recorded script is used later in the class session as a source of input for the analysis and practice of the language. This process is illustrated in the sample lesson plan given later.

Stage 2. This second stage, known as the "self-assertive stage," differs from the first in that the students try to say what they want to without constant intervention and help from the teacher.

Stage 3. In this "birth stage," students increase their independence from the teacher and speak in the new language without translation, unless another student requests it.

Stage 4. The "adolescent" or "reversal" stage is one in which the learner has become secure enough to welcome corrective feedback from the teacher or other group members.

Stage 5. This "independent" stage is marked by free interaction between students and teacher(s): everyone offers corrections and stylistic improvements in a community spirit. By this time, the trust level is high, and no individual is threatened by this type of feedback from others in the group. At all times, the atmosphere is one of warmth, acceptance, and understanding. (Based on Stevick 1973, reprinted and revised in Curran 1976, pp. 87–100.)

A Sample Lesson Plan

The following lesson has been provided by Earl Stevick, who has a thorough understanding of CLL methodology and has written thoughtful interpretations of it in various books and articles. (See in particular Stevick 1976, 1980, 1990.) This particular lesson is a fictional account, written by Stevick in a personal communication a few years ago. It embodies some CLL principles but is not an example of the standard technique taught by Counseling-Learning Institutes.

9:00–9:10 Students talk among themselves, first about remedies for a headache that one of the members has, then about the "Tylenol Murders." The teacher sits in the circle and takes notes, but does not participate except to give words and phrases on request and, twice, to "fail to understand" a sentence that would have caused trouble for a native speaker unaccustomed to hearing foreigners (i.e., a Level 2 criterion). Fluency varies from halting to fairly good, but all group members seem to be saying what they mean and to be absorbed in the conversation. Errors of grammar are frequent, but with the exceptions already noted, the teacher does not call attention to them.

9:10–9:15 The teacher summarizes the conversation and gives brief answers to two questions about why he or she said something in a particular way.

9:15–9:28 Working from notes, the teacher writes on a flip chart a series of sentences based on the content of the conversation, making sure that each person's contribution is represented in at least one sentence. The teacher then underlines various words or endings and the students collectively give appropriate meanings or grammatical functions.

9:28–9:41 Using cards that the teacher has prepared based on the content of the preceding session, students play "Concentration" as a means of vocabulary review.

9:41–9:50 Using sentences from this and earlier sessions, students work in pairs or groups of three, forming and answering questions. The teacher moves from group to group and monitors the activity, answering questions as they arise.

Proficiency Orientation

Many elements hypothesized to contribute to the building of proficiency are present in this lesson: there is contextualized and personalized learning throughout the class hour; students are creating with the language; there is attention to accuracy without sacrificing affective concerns. In fact, one of the major strengths of the method seems to be the warm, community atmosphere that is created by the procedure and the provision of corrective feedback in this humanizing context. The teacher takes care to help students induce the grammatical system from their own input and isolates important and useful vocabulary that they need to review for active control.

Potential Drawbacks
One area that may need attention in using CLL methodology is that of course content or context. As described, the procedure does not ensure that a variety of contexts necessary for coping in the target culture is included. Since the content is determined by the participants in the group, who may not necessarily know what to expect in encounters in the target culture, some survival skills may be neglected. This problem may be easily remedied, however, if the teacher is willing to encourage or enable students to include such content in the lesson on occasion. For example, the conversation could center around authentic material that students had read or viewed (Stevick 1992).

Another potential drawback is that some students may feel uncomfortable with the apparent lack of structure or sequence in the introduction of grammatical and lexical items. This problem also could be dealt with if the teacher is willing to introduce some control in this regard.

The Silent Way: Learning through Self-Reliance

Background
Introduced by Gattegno (1976), this method can be classified as cognitivist in orientation. In Gattegno's view, the mind is an active agent capable of constructing its own inner criteria for learning. The three key words of the philosophy behind this approach are *independence, autonomy,* and *responsibility:* every learner must work with his or her own inner resources (i.e., existing cognitive structures, experiences, emotions, knowledge of the world) to absorb learning from the environment. The Silent Way assumes that learners work with these resources and *nothing else,* as they are solely responsible for what they learn. The teacher's role is to guide students in the hypothesis-testing process in which they are constantly engaged. (For a thorough discussion of the theories behind Gattegno's approach, see Gattegno 1976; Stevick 1980, 1990; and Richards and Rodgers 1986.)

Major Characteristics
Stevick (1980) outlines five basic principles underlying the Silent Way:

1. Teaching should be subordinated to learning.
2. Learning is not primarily imitation or drill.
3. In learning, the mind equips itself by its own working, trial and error, deliberate experimentations, suspending judgment, and revising conclusions.

4. As it works, the mind draws on everything it has already acquired, *particularly its experience in learning the native language.*

5. If the teacher's activity is to be subordinate to that of the learner, then the teacher must stop trying to interfere and sidetrack that activity (p. 137).

Karambelas (1971) isolated the following techniques and principles in the Silent Way:

1. Repeated modeling of utterances by the teacher is avoided because mimicry is not necessary. In the Silent Way, students may hear a given word only once, if at all. The teacher, as implied by the name of the approach, remains essentially silent.

2. Material is never subjected to rote memorization. Rather, students become familiar with new structures and recognize them through contextualized use and practice.

3. Correction is seldom offered by the teacher, since learners are assumed to have developed their own inner criteria of correctness and are capable of correcting their own errors.

4. Oral work is often followed by writing practice early on in instruction.

5. Whenever possible, the learner is made responsible for his or her own learning.

The method is perhaps best known for its use of colored rods, called Cuisenaire rods, for teaching the basic structures of the language. A set of color-coded phonetic and word charts is also essential to the Silent Way classroom. As in the direct method, the target language is the exclusive language of instruction.

Sample Classroom Activities

Perhaps the best source of sample lesson material is Stevick (1980), who provides a wealth of examples with insightful commentary on the way the lessons work. For purposes of illustration, Stevick gives workshop audiences an "experience" with the method and is careful to point out that it is not a "demonstration." In this experience, six people are invited to sit around a table in the front of the room, in view of the rest of the audience. The instructor first opens a bag of rods (colored sticks of different lengths) and deposits them on the table. The instructor next picks up various rods, examines them, and then finally selects a long one. Motioning to everyone to be silent and listen, he or she pronounces the work *çubuk,* the Turkish word for "rod."

After a few seconds of silence, the instructor motions the six participants to say the word in chorus. After a few choral repetitions, the individuals are asked one by one to pronounce the word as the instructor picks up the same rod. If any one learner's pronunciation is off, making it difficult for a native speaker to understand, the instructor has the student try again by motioning silently. If this second attempt fails, the instructor motions to someone who has said the word correctly to produce it again. Soon everyone can say "rod" appropriately in Turkish.

Then the instructor pushes all of the rods toward one learner and motions for him or her to pick up one, saying *çubuk* in the process. When this student has successfully produced the word, the rods are placed in front of someone else. This process continues until the students deduce that *çubuk* means "rod," and not a particular length of rod.

After teaching *çubuk,* the instructor then introduces the concept of the numbers 1, 2, and 3. He or she does this by setting out six rods, one single one, a group of two, and a group of three. The instructor then makes a show of counting them, to get across the idea that the new words to be introduced are numbers. Motioning again for silence and attention, the instructor pronounces each numeral in the same way that the word for "rod" was introduced. Beginning with the word for "two" (*iki*), students soon learn to say *iki çubuk* when the group of two is indicated. Again, students have multiple opportunities to say the words, picking up or pointing at the rods as they do so to confirm what they are saying.

The lesson continues on this principle of "teach, then test, then get out of the way" (Stevick 1980, p. 56). Students use the new words they have learned to manipulate the rods, either through the silent directions given by the instructor or on their own initiative.

Proficiency Orientation

It is difficult to make an assessment of the proficiency orientation or potential drawbacks of this method without first having extensive experience using it. However, from my own limited experience in observing Silent Way demonstration classes, it does seem that this method is oriented in several ways towards proficiency goals. Because students are responsible for their own learning, they must pay close attention and actively interact with others in the class. Students use the language meaningfully and creatively, within the limitations imposed by the vocabulary and structures of the lesson, as they are invited to construct their own messages early in the learning sequence. The students' attention is constantly being directed to accuracy as they attempt to produce the language, and the students themselves, in cooperation with the teacher, serve as monitors of their own output in a low-anxiety, cooperative atmosphere.

Potential Drawbacks

One of the drawbacks of this method is that learners do not work with authentic, culturally based materials or hear authentic native speech, at least in the early phases of instruction. If students are to develop a functional proficiency in the language, it would seem that they need ample opportunities to hear native speakers using the language in authentic exchanges and to practice using the language to cope with everyday situations they might encounter in the target culture. The place of culture and culture-based language instruction is not clear from the literature about the Silent Way. Richards and Rodgers (1986) explain that manuals for teachers are generally not available and that the Silent Way teacher is responsible for designing and sequencing instruction (p. 107).

Suggestopedia: Tapping Subconscious Resources

Background This method, also known as *Suggestive-Accelerative Learning and Teaching* (SALT), and the *Lozanov Method,* originated in Bulgaria. It was introduced by Georgi Lozanov (1978), a psychotherapist and physician, who believes that relaxation techniques and concentration will help learners tap their subconscious resources and retain greater amounts of vocabulary and structures than they ever thought possible.

Hallmarks of the method include the "suggestive" atmosphere in which it takes place, with soft lights, baroque music, cheerful room decorations, comfortable seating, and dramatic techniques used by the teacher in the presentation of material. All of these features are aimed at totally relaxing students, allowing them to open their minds to learning the language in an unencumbered fashion.

Chastain (1988) describes Suggestopedia as a wholistic method that tries to direct learning to both the left and right hemispheres of the brain. Learning should involve both analysis and synthesis at the same time, using both the conscious and the unconscious mind. Because Lozanov sees anxiety as a hindrance that severely limits learning potential, two teaching principles are proposed to break down the sociopsychological constraints of traditional learning environments. The first principle is that of *infantilization,* which is designed to help students recapture the kind of learning capacities they had as children. The second is that of *pseudopassivity,* which refers to a relaxed physical state of heightened mental activity and concentration (Chastain, 1988, p. 104). The general goal of the method is to enable students to learn language in an atmosphere that is liberated from the restrictive influences that students experience in more traditional classroom settings.

Major Characteristics and Sample Classroom Activities An instructional cycle consists of three parts, summarized below. This characterization is based on Stevick (1980) and Bancroft (1982).

1. First, there is a review of the previously learned material, exclusively in the new language. Games and skits are often used for this purpose. Mechanistic practice is avoided.
2. Next, new material is presented in context through lengthy dialogues, which are introduced in two "concert" phases. Prior to the concert phases, students listen to a guided imagery tape in order to relax. This relaxation aspect is a key element of the method (Bragger 1991). The dialogues (ten of which are used in the first course) represent typical language-use situations in the target culture. The

dialogues are constructed so to have continuity in plot and context throughout the course. Characters in the dialogues are given names that rhyme and have a variety of interesting personalities and professions. In the activation phase (see Phase 3, below), students may adopt the roles of these characters for language-practice activities.

In the active concert, students listen to music as the teacher reads the dialogue lines, usually one at a time. Students follow along in the book, with the target language text on the left side of the page and the English equivalent on the right side. The teacher's voice inflection changes with the music. For example, the first line might be shouted, the second whispered, and the third said in a normal voice. The tone of the presentation does not necessarily correspond with what is being said, but is used simply to provide variety and contrast to increase the "suggestive" quality of the presentation. Students listen to this dialogue while practicing controlled breathing techniques to assure concentration.

During the passive concert, students listen to the reading of the text again, this time with eyes closed. The dialogue is read at a normal rate of speech, accompanied by more baroque music. The two concert phases are designed to allow students to absorb the new material at an *unconscious level.*

3. After both concerts are finished, there is an eight-hour follow-up session on the new material, called the *activation phase.* At this point, students engage in role-plays and practice activities to "activate" the material they have learned in the concerts. When grammatical explanations are needed, they are provided in the native language.

Some American adaptations of Suggestopedia include shorter class periods, larger class sizes, and shortened forms of the active seances (see, for example, Bancroft 1982). Readers interested in more detailed discussion of this method should consult Stevick 1980, Bancroft 1982, and Richards and Rodgers 1986.

Proficiency Orientation

This method seems to have a variety of features that are helpful in the development of language proficiency. The language is initially presented in context through dialogues that are culturally based. Such texts based on everyday life give students models that can be used to develop functional proficiency through role-plays and other interactive language-practice activities. The method also addresses the affective needs of students by providing a relaxed and nonthreatening atmosphere for learning. There also seems to be an interest in the development of accuracy, as explanations are provided for grammatical structures learned and the material is practiced and reviewed in Phases 1 and 3 of the instructional cycle.

Potential Drawbacks One possible drawback with a dialogue-based approach is that the input material seems to be almost exclusively pedagogically prepared. The use of authentic input material, both for reading comprehension and for listening, seems somewhat limited, at least from descriptions of the method in the literature. Perhaps the dialogue material is supplemented at some point with unedited, authentic presentation texts; if not, this might be one way in which the Lozanov method could be adjusted to correspond more closely to proficiency goals.

Chastain (1988) maintains that adapting Suggestopedia to the typical classroom situation "presents huge problems because Lozanov recommends implementation only in its original and complete format, which does not fit the typical classroom schedule" (p. 103). The adaptations mentioned earlier (see Bancroft 1982) have attempted to address this difficulty.

Summary: On Teaching a Language

In this chapter we have seen how principles and priorities in language teaching have shifted and changed over the years, often in response to paradigm shifts in linguistic and learning theory. Historically, methods that adhere to empiricist viewpoints have contrasted sharply with those that derive from a rationalist perspective of human learning. The various methodologies and approaches that have been reviewed in this chapter have experienced differential success and popularity among practitioners. Today, many teachers are adopting an eclectic approach to language learning and teaching, believing that the age-old search for the "one true way" can be futile and frustrating. As we realize that learning is an extremely complex process and that learners are individuals with different personalities, styles, and preferences, we have begun to look for a multiplicity of ways to respond to the challenge of teaching. Eclecticism, however, needs to be principled if instruction is to be effective, and techniques and activities need to be chosen intelligently to relate to specific program objectives (Richards and Rodgers 1986).

This chapter has proposed some general principles that might orient our teaching toward proficiency goals. The hypothesized principles focus on providing instruction that is meaningful, interactive, and responsive to learner needs. In the next chapter, we explore the important role that context plays in fostering this type of learning environment.

Activities for Review and Discussion

1. Give a brief definition for each of the following terms:

    a. Methodology
    b. Syllabus
    c. Approach

    d. Strategy

    e. Eclecticism

    f. Proficiency-oriented instruction

2. What are the five working hypotheses outlined in this chapter? How does each relate to the idea of teaching language in context?

3. In which methods or approaches described in this chapter would the following classroom activities or teaching practices be prevalent or receive a high priority? Explain briefly why these practices are considered beneficial to language study by advocates of the approach you identify.

    a. Frequent use of manipulative pattern drills

    b. Learning of grammar rules with exceptions and irregularities noted

    c. Tape-recorded group conversations, with the teacher acting as a counselor/informant

    d. Musical accompaniment to language-learning activities

    e. Frequent use of commands

    f. Translation of reading passages from native to target language and from target to native language.

    g. Exclusive use of the target language in all phases of instruction

    h. Absence of error correction during class sessions

    i. Heavy emphasis on correct pronunciation

    j. Observance of the "natural order" of listening, speaking, reading, and writing in language teaching activities

    k. Use of colored word charts and Cuisenaire rods in instruction

4. Of the five working hypotheses outlined in this chapter, are there any hypotheses that you don't agree with? Are there any hypotheses that you might want to add to the ones discussed in this chapter?

5. Consider, in light of the five working hypotheses, the teaching approach you currently use, or one that you are familiar with through observation or personal experience. What characteristics of this approach would you consider conducive to the development of proficiency? What characteristics might need modification to make the approach more proficiency-oriented?

• • • • • • • • • • • • *References*

Allen, Edward D., and Rebecca M. Valette. *Classroom Techniques: Foreign Languages and English as a Second Language.* New York: Harcourt Brace Javonovich, 1977.

Anthony, E. M. "Approach, Method, and Technique." *English Language Teaching* 17 (1963): 63–7.

Asher, James. *Learning Another Language through Actions: The Complete Teacher's Guide.* Los Gatos, CA: Sky Oak Productions, 1982.

Asher, James, JoAnne Kusudo, and Rita de la Torre. "Learning a Second Language through Commands: The Second Field Test." *The Modern Language Journal* 58 (1974): 24–32.

Bancroft, W. Jane. "The Lozanov Method and Its American Adaptations." *The Modern Language Journal* 62 (1982): 167–75.

Bellot, James. *The French Method, Wherein is Contained a Perfite Order of Grammar for the French Tongue*. London: Robert Robinson, 1588. Reprinted: Scolar 1970. [Cited in Kibbee 1987.]

Benseler, David P. and Renate A. Schulz. "Methodological Trends in College Foreign Language Instruction." *The Modern Language Journal* 64 (1980): 88–96.

Birckbichler, Diane W., ed. *New Perspectives and New Directions in Foreign Language Education*. The ACTFL Foreign Language Education Series. Lincolnwood, IL: National Textbook Company, 1990.

Bragger, Jeanette. Personal communication, 1991.

Brown, H. Douglas. "The Consensus: Another View." *Foreign Language Annals* 17 (1984): 277–80.

Brumfit, C. J. and K. Johnson, eds. *The Communicative Approach to Language Teaching*. Oxford: Oxford University Press, 1979.

Buck, Kathryn, Heidi Byrnes, and Irene Thompson, eds. *The ACTFL Oral Proficiency Interview Tester Training Manual*. Yonkers, NY: ACTFL, 1989.

Byrnes, H. and M. Canale, eds., *Defining and Developing Proficiency: Guidelines, Implementations and Concepts*. ACTFL Foreign Language Education Series. Lincolnwood, IL: National Textbook Company, 1987.

Chastain, Kenneth. *Developing Second Language Skills: Theory to Practice*, 2nd ed. Chicago: Rand McNally, 1976.

_____ *Developing Second Language Skills: Theory and Practice*, 3rd ed. New York: Harcourt Brace Jovanovich, 1988.

Chomsky, Noam. *Aspects of the Theory of Syntax*. Cambridge, MA: M. I. T. Press, 1965.

Curran, Charles. *Counseling-Learning in Second Languages*. Apple River, IL: Apple River Press, 1976.

Daly, John. "Understanding Communication Apprehension: An Introduction for Language Educators." Chapter 1 (pp. 3–13) in E. Horwitz and D. Young, eds., *Language Anxiety: From Theory and Research to Classroom Implications*. Englewood Cliffs, NJ: Prentice Hall, 1991.

de Sainliens, Claude. *The French Littelton. A most Easie, Perfect, and Absolute way to learne the frenche tongue*. London: Thomas Vautroullier, 1576. [Cited in Kibbee 1987.]

Diller, Karl Conrad. *The Language Teaching Controversy*. Rowley, MA: Newbury House, 1978.

Ellis, Rod. *Understanding Second Language Acquisition*. Oxford: Oxford University Press, 1985.

_____ *Instructed Second Language Acquisition*. Oxford: Basil Blackwell, Ltd., 1990.

Finocchiaro, M. and C. Brumfit. *The Functional-Notional Approach: From Theory to Practice*. New York: Oxford University Press, 1983.

Galloway, Vicki. "From Defining to Developing Proficiency: A Look at the Decisions." Chapter 2 (pp. 25–73) in H. Byrnes and M. Canale, eds., *Defining and Developing Proficiency: Guidelines, Implementations and Concepts*. ACTFL Foreign Language Education Series. Lincolnwood, IL: National Textbook Company, 1987.

Galloway, Vicki and Angela Labarca. "From Student to Learner: Style, Process, and Strategy." Chapter 4 (pp. 111–58) in D. Birckbichler, ed., *New Perspectives and New Directions in Foreign Language Education.* The ACTFL Foreign Language Education Series. Lincolnwood, IL: National Textbook Company, 1990.

Galyean, Beverly. "Humanistic Education: A Mosaic Just Begun." Chapter 7 (pp. 201–44) in G. Jarvis, ed., *An Integrative Approach to Foreign Language Education: The Challenge of Communication.* The ACTFL Foreign Language Education Series, vol. 8. Lincolnwood, IL: National Textbook Company, 1976.

Gass, Susan M. and Carolyn G. Madden. *Input in Second Language Acquisition.* Rowley, MA: Newbury House, 1985.

Gass, Susan M. and E. M. Varonis. "Task Variation and Nonnative/Nonnative Negotiation of Meaning." Chapter 9 (pp. 149–161) in S. Gass, and C. Madden, eds. *Input in Second Language Acquisition.* Rowley, MA: Newbury House, 1985.

Gattegno, Caleb. *The Common Sense of Foreign Language Teaching.* New York: Educational Solutions, 1976.

Grittner, Frank M. "Bandwagons Revisited: A Perspective on Movements in Foreign Language Education. Chapter 1 (pp. 9–43) in D. Birckbichler, ed., *New Perspectives and New Directions in Foreign Language Education.* The ACTFL Foreign Language Education Series. Lincolnwood, IL: National Textbook Company, 1990.

Harley, B. P. Allen, J. Cummins, and M. Swain, eds. *The Development of Second Language Proficiency.* Cambridge: Cambridge University Press, 1990.

Higgs, Theodore V. "Language Teaching and the Quest for the Holy Grail." Introduction (pp. 1–10) in T. V. Higgs, ed., *Teaching For Proficiency, the Organizing Principle.* The ACTFL Foreign Language Education Series. Lincolnwood, IL: National Textbook Company, 1984.

Higgs, Theodore V. and Ray Clifford. "The Push Toward Communication." In T. V. Higgs, ed., *Curriculum, Competence and the Foreign Language Teacher.* ACTFL Foreign Language Education Series, vol. 13. Lincolnwood, IL: National Textbook Company, 1982.

Horwitz, Elaine K., Michael B. Horwitz, and Jo Ann Cope. "Foreign Language Anxiety." Chapter 3 (pp. 27–36) in E. K. Horwitz and D. J. Young, eds. *Language Anxiety: From Theory and Research to Classroom Implications.* Englewood Cliffs, NJ: Prentice Hall, 1991.

Horwitz, Elaine K. and Dolly J. Young, eds. *Language Anxiety: From Theory and Research to Classroom Implications.* Englewood Cliffs, NJ: Prentice Hall, 1991.

Jarvis, Gilbert A., ed. *An Integrative Approach to Foreign Language Education: The Challenge of Communication.* The ACTFL Foreign Language Education Series, vol. 8. Lincolnwood, IL: National Textbook Company, 1976.

Karambelas, James. "Teaching Foreign Languages 'The Silent Way'." *ADFL Bulletin* 3 (1971): 41.

Kelly, L. G. *Twenty-Five Centuries of Language Teaching: 500 BC- 1969.* Rowley, MA: Newbury House, 1976.

Kibbee, Douglas. "Plus ça change . . . 600 Years of French Dialogues." Paper presented at the Annual Meeting of the American Association of Teachers of French. San Francisco, CA, 1987.

_____ "L'Enseignement du français en Angleterre au XVIe siècle." Pp. 54–77 in P. Swiggers and W. Van Hoecke, eds., *La Langue française au XVIe siècle:*

Usage, enseignement, et approches descriptives. Paris: Leuven University Press, 1989.

Krashen, Stephen. *Principles and Practice in Second Language Acquisition.* New York: Pergamon Press, 1982.

Lado, Robert. *Language Teaching.* New York: McGraw-Hill, 1964.

Lightbown, Patsy M. "Process-Product Research on Second Language Learning in Classrooms." Chapter 6 (pp. 82–92) in B. Harley, P. Allen, J. Cummins, and M. Swain, eds. *The Development of Second Language Proficiency.* Cambridge: Cambridge University Press, 1990.

Lightbown, Patsy and Nina Spada. "Focus-on-Form and Corrective Feedback in Communicative Language Teaching: Effects on Second Language Learning." *Studies in Second Language Acquisition* 12, iv (1990): 429–48.

Littlewood, W. *Communicative Language Teaching.* Cambridge: Cambridge University Press, 1981.

Long, Michael. "Teacher Feedback on Learner Error: Mapping Cognitions." In H. Brown, C. Yorio, and R. Crymes, eds., *On TESOL '77.* Washington, DC: TESOL, 1977: 278–94.

_____ "Does Second Language Instruction Make a Difference? A Review of the Research." *TESOL Quarterly* 17 (1983): 359–82.

Lozanov, Georgi. *Suggestology and Outlines of Suggestopedy.* New York: Gordon and Breach, 1978.

Mohrmann, C., A. Sommerfelt, and J. Whatmough, eds., *Trends in European and American Linguistics, 1930–1960.* Utrecht: Spectrum, 1961.

Moulton, W.G. "Linguistics and Language Teaching in the United States: 1940–1960." Pp. 82–109 in C. Mohrmann, A. Sommerfelt, and J. Whatmough, eds., *Trends in European and American Linguistics, 1930–1960.* Utrecht: Spectrum, 1961. [Cited in Rivers 1981.]

Newmark, L. "How Not to Interfere in Language Learning." In E. Najam, ed. *Language Learning: The Individual and the Process,* [Reprinted in Brumfit and Johnson, 1979.] *International Journal of American Linguistics* 32 (1966) Part 2: 77–83.

Newmark, L. and D. Reibel. "Necessity and Sufficiency in Language Learning." *International Review of Applied Linguistics in Language Teaching* 6 (1968): 145–64.

Pica, Teresa and Catherine Doughty. "Input and Interaction in the Communicative Language Classroom: A Comparison of Teacher- Fronted and Group Activities." Chapter 7 (pp. 115–32) in S. Gass and C. Madden, eds., *Input in Second Language Acquisition.* Rowley, MA: Newbury House, 1985.

Phillips, June K., ed. *Building on Experience: Building for Success.* The ACTFL Foreign Language Education Series, vol. 10. Lincolnwood, IL: National Textbook Company, 1979.

Richards, Jack C. and Theodore S. Rodgers. *Approaches and Methods in Language Teaching: A Description and Analysis.* Cambridge: Cambridge University Press, 1986.

Rivers, Wilga M. *A Practical Guide to the Teaching of French.* New York: Oxford University Press, 1975.

_____ *Teaching Foreign Language Skills,* 2nd ed. Chicago: University of Chicago Press, 1981.

Savignon, Sandra J. *Communicative Competence: Theory and Classroom Practice.* Reading, MA: Addison-Wesley, 1983.

Savignon, Sandra J. "In Second Language Acquisition/Foreign Language Learning, Nothing is More Practical than a Good Theory." *IDEAL* 3 (1988): 83–98.

Scovel, Thomas. "The Effect of Affect on Foreign Language Learning: A Review of the Anxiety Research." Chapter 2 (pp. 15–23) in E. Horwitz and D. Young, eds. *Language Anxiety: From Theory and Research to Classroom Implications.* Englewood Cliffs, NJ: Prentice Hall, 1991.

Stern, H. H. "Directions in Foreign Language Curriculum Development." In *Proceedings of the National Conference on Professional Priorities.* Hastings-on-Hudson, NY: ACTFL, 1981.

_____ "Analysis and Experience as Variables in Second Language Pedagogy." Chapter 7 (pp. 93–109) in B. Harley, P. Allen, J. Cummins, and M. Swain, eds., *The Development of Second Language Proficiency.* Cambridge: Cambridge University Press, 1990.

Stevick, Earl W. "Review Article: Counseling-Learning: A Whole- Person Model for Education." Pp. 87–100 in Charles Curran, *Counseling-Learning in Second Languages.* Apple River, IL: Apple River Press, 1976. [Reprinted with modifications from *Language Learning* 23, ii (1973): 259–71.]

_____ *Memory, Meaning and Method: Some Psychological Perspectives on Language Learning.* Rowley, MA: Newbury House, 1976.

_____ *Teaching Languages: A Way and Ways.* Rowley, MA: Newbury House, 1980.

_____ *Humanism in Language Teaching.* Oxford: Oxford University Press, 1990.

_____ Personal communication, 1992.

Strasheim, Lorraine. "What is a Foreign Language Teacher Today?" *Canadian Modern Language Review* 33 (1976): 39–48.

Swaffar, Janet K., Katherine Arens, and Martha Morgan. "Teacher Classroom Practices: Redefining Method as Task Hierarchy." *The Modern Language Journal* 66 (1982): 24–33.

Swain, Merrill. "Communicative Competence: Some Roles of Comprehensible Input and Comprehensible Output in Its Development." Chapter 14 (pp. 235–53) in S. Gass and C. Madden, eds. *Input in Second Language Acquisition.* Rowley, MA: Newbury House, 1985.

Tarone, Elaine. "On the Variability of Interlanguage Systems." *Applied Linguistics* 4 (1983): 142–63.

Terrell, Tracy D. "A Natural Approach to Second Language Acquisition and Learning." *The Modern Language Journal* 61 (1977): 325–37.

_____ "The Natural Approach to Language Teaching: An Update." *The Modern Language Journal* 66 (1982): 121–32.

_____ "The Role of Grammar Instruction in a Communicative Approach." *The Modern Language Journal* 75 (1991): 52–63.

VanPatten, Bill. "On Babies and Bathwater: Input in Foreign Language Learning." *The Modern Language Journal* 71 (1987): 156–64.

Warriner, Helen. "Foreign Language Teaching in the Schools–1979: Focus on Methodology." *The Modern Language Journal* 64 (1980): 81–87.

Westphal, Patricia. "Teaching and Learning: A Key to Success." Pp. 119–56 in J. Phillips, ed., *Building on Experience: Building for Success.* The ACTFL Foreign Language Education Series, vol. 10. Lincolnwood, IL: National Textbook Company, 1979.

Yalden, Janice. *The Communicative Syllabus: Evolution, Design, and Implementation.* Englewood Cliffs, NJ: Prentice Hall, 1987.

4

The Role of Context in Comprehension and Learning

Hypothesis 1. *Opportunities must be provided for students to practice using language in a range of contexts likely to be encountered in the target culture.*

Chapters 1 and 3 presented a rationale for orienting instruction towards proficiency goals, using the interrelated concepts of *content/context, function,* and *accuracy* as organizing threads. This chapter explores the first of these ideas, beginning with the hypothesis that second language programs should provide students with ample opportunities to (1) learn language in context and (2) apply their knowledge to coping with authentic language-use situations.

This first principle is not particularly controversial in nature. Most educators agree today that students must eventually know how to use the language forms they have learned in authentic communication situations. Some would agree that this goal can best be achieved if the forms of language are presented and practiced in communicative contexts, where focus on meaning and content is primary. The idea that language learning should be contextualized is certainly not new in language teaching, at least from a theoretical point of view. Natural language always occurs in context in that any given utterance is embedded in ongoing discourse as well as in some particular circumstance or situation. As Widdowson (1978) has pointed out, "Normal linguistic behavior does not consist of the production of separate sentences but in the use of sentences for the creation of discourse" (p. 22). Therefore, it seems logical to conclude that classroom activities, instructional materials, and testing procedures should be designed to resemble real language in use.

Unfortunately, many of our classrooms today still do not foster the use of "real language," despite the consensus of many in the profession that this is an important and appropriate goal. As Strasheim (1976) remarked, "the awful dichotomy between 'classroom thinking' and 'real-life thinking'" (p. 41) has been a long-standing problem in education. Her criticism of the monotonous drills and endless repetitions characteristic of audiolingual methodology echoed that of a number of other scholars of the late sixties and seventies. Slager (1978) also emphasized the need for context and "sentence connectedness" in language-practice activities. He cites the work of Jespersen, who in 1904 had urged in his text, *How to Teach a Foreign Language,* that "we ought to learn a language through sensible communications" (p. 11). Jespersen saw nearly 90 years ago that "sensible communication" involved a certain connection in the thoughts communicated, implying that language lessons built around random lists of disconnected sentences were unjustifiable. Yet theory is often many years ahead of practice, and some textbooks currently on the market still present language for practice in non sequiturs. Moreover, it is certainly the case that a large portion of classroom tests today continue to use disconnected discrete-point items.

In 1904, Jespersen chose to illustrate the point that noncontextualized practice is a far cry from real language with the following excerpt from a nineteenth-century French reader.

1. My aunt is my mother's friend.
2. My dear friend, you are speaking too rapidly.
3. That is a good book.
4. We are too old.
5. This gentleman is quite sad.
6. The boy has drowned many dogs.

Source: Jespersen (1904), p. 11, also cited in Slager (1978), p. 72.

Jespersen referred to this type of instruction as "mental gymnastics," replete with "sudden and violent leaps from one range of ideas to another" (p. 11). Disconnected exercises of this type soon become boring. He adds that "grown persons, can, of course, put up with a little boredom, if they think they can attain anything by it; but in their heart of hearts they find such things killing, and so they are. . . ." (p. 15).

Contemporary textbooks are certainly much better conceived than the one from which this example is cited. Yet, unfortunately, disconnected and disjointed language practice activities can still be found in modern texts, mostly in sections where manipulation of formal features or language analysis is the focus.

One way to eliminate this kind of artificiality in texts might be to do away with analytic exercises altogether and use only activities that are communicative and open-ended. Yet there are a number of scholars who believe that a program that fosters the development of proficiency should incorporate both analytic and experiential approaches to language learning (see, for example, Allen, Swain, Harley, and Cummins 1990; Stern 1990). Stern explains that an analytic approach is one in which the language is the object of study, and an experiential approach is one in which language is learned through communication, such as in immersion and content-based classrooms. Allen et al. feel that these two types of teaching may be complimentary and ". . . provide essential support for one another in the L2 classroom" (p. 77). Stern assumes that an analytic strategy "of necessity decontextualizes linguistic features" in order to allow for isolation of the forms for analysis (p. 99). He hastens to add, however, that the forms under study should then be recontextualized. Allen et al. express the belief that learners may benefit most if form and function are instructionally linked. "There is no doubt that students need to be given greater opportunities to use the target language. But opportunities alone are not sufficient. Students need to be motivated to use language accurately, appropriately, and coherently" (p. 77). They discuss the need for some focused practice activities, not only involving grammar, but also functional, organizational, and sociolinguistic aspects of the target language. In these kinds of activities, they posit a role for feedback and correction, and state that more research needs to be done to determine how this can be maximally effective.

The thesis of this chapter is that language use in the classroom, whether for analytic or experiential purposes, ought to be contextualized. Even analytical activities and form-focused practice exercises will be improved if they consist of sentences that are connected to one another in a logical sequence or relationship.

The following sample exercises illustrate two ways in which analytic practice (where the focus is on a particular feature of language) can be devised. The first sample is decontextualized and is typical of some of the exercises still found in current texts. The linguistic feature to be practiced is the use of the subjunctive after certain verbs of volition in French.

Sample 1   **Modèle:** Il regarde son livre. (Nous exigeons que)
Nous exigeons qu'il regarde son livre.

1. Tu achètes du pain. (Je veux que)
2. Vous choisissez une robe. (Votre mère souhaite que)
3. Nous votons cette année. (Tu préfères que)
4. Elle lave son chien. (Nous voulons que)

Model: *He's looking at his book. (We insist)*
We insist that he look at his book.

1. *You are buying bread. (I want)*
2. *You are choosing a dress. (Your mother hopes that)*
3. *We are voting this year. (You prefer that)*
4. *She is washing her dog. (We want)*

The second sample illustrates how the same kind of analytic practice activity can be contextualized to conform to the theme of the unit of study, which, in this case, is politics.

Sample 2   *Une discussion politique.* Que peut-on dire à propos du Président, des sénateurs, des députés et de la politique en générale? Suivez le modèle.

Modèle: M. Leclerc/souhaiter/que/partis de gauche/être/plus agressif.
M. Leclerc souhaite que les partis de gauche soient plus agressifs.

1. Mme Leclerc/vouloir/les/députés/supprimer/impôts.
2. M. Lévêque/exiger/sénateurs/obéir/à/la loi.
3. Mlle Deneuve/préférer/Président/parler intelligemment.
4. Les Duval/désirer/Président/prendre/électeurs/au sérieux.
5. Mme d'Aubigny/exiger/sénateurs/devenir/plus honnête.
6. M. Duchamp/vouloir bien/nous/agir/de façon/plus/libéral.
7. Nous/exiger/vous/voter/ce/année.

A *political discussion.* What can one say about the President, senators, representatives, and politics in general? Follow the model.

Model: *Mr. Leclerc / hope / that / leftist parties / be / more / aggressive*
Mr. Leclerc hopes that the leftist parties will be more aggressive.

1. *Madame Leclerc / want / the representatives / eliminate taxes.*
2. *Mr. Lévêque / insist / senators / obey / law.*
3. *Mademoiselle Deneuve / prefer / President / speak / intelligently.*
4. *The Duvals / want / President / take / electorate / seriously.*
5. *Madame d'Aubigny / insist / senators / become / more honest.*
6. *Mr. Duchamp / really / want / we / act / in a more liberal fashion.*
7. *We / insist / you / vote / this / year.*

Source: Muyskens, Omaggio, Chalmers, Imberton, and Almeras, 1982, p. 415. Reprinted by permission of McGraw-Hill.

Samples 1 and 2 are roughly equivalent in difficulty and structure. But while the sentences in the first example would hardly be said in sequence in a real-world situation, the sentences in the second could conceivably be said in summarizing political views, such as those one might express at a town meeting or in a neighborhood discussion. The use of the subjunctive to express volition, preference, and other emotions is also bound to occur naturally in a political context. For these reasons, the second activity is more natural than the first, although it is still highly structured and focused on a particular grammatical point. Note that it is also possible to do both sample activities without processing the sentences meaningfully. Meaningful processing can be assured for Sample 2 by adding a follow-up task in which students are asked to use the models given to create their own statements about politics. For example, students in small groups could complete sentences such as the following:

> *Nous voulons que nos sénateurs . . . .*
> *Nous exigeons que le Président . . . .*
> *etc.*

> [*We want our senators . . . .*
> *We insist that the President . . . .*
> *etc.*]

Students might also rank order their own concerns about politics, using the exercise in Sample 2 as a point of departure. Another follow-up activity might involve devising campaign slogans for various candidates of the students' choice, using subjunctive constructions where appropriate.

Sample activities 1 and 2 could be thought of as "precommunicative" in nature (Littlewood 1981). That is, they focus primarily on forms and are structured to prepare students to use those forms in communicating their own meanings in subsequent language-practice activities. The fundamental difference between noncontextualized and contextualized practice of this type is that the latter links form with meanings that language learners might genuinely want to convey in natural communicative situations. In designing structured, precommunicative practice, thematically coherent exercises are clearly preferable for this reason.

We have seen that the use of analytic or structured practice, focusing on particular formal features of the language, is recommended by scholars such as Stern (1990) and Allen et al. (1990), in conjunction with experiential language learning. In immersion settings, the focused practice is designed to enable students to refine and shape their communicative output to conform to target language norms. The purposes of precommunicative practice activities are somewhat different, since they are designed to be used *before* students engage in more communicative and open-ended exchanges. Their use is consistent with the positions on language acquisition in adults described by various researchers who affirm that focused practice can be beneficial as students' skills are developing. (See, for example, McLaughlin 1978, 1983, 1987; Slager 1978; Seliger 1979; Higgs and Clifford 1982; Long 1983; Swain 1985; and Ellis 1990.) Higgs and Clifford (1982) concluded that if accuracy is one of the goals of instruction, students need to pass through a period of meaningful, yet structured or "monitored" practice, in order to move toward more open-ended communication. For this reason, they argue against approaches that push too soon for unconstrained communication. The cognitive viewpoint expressed by McLaughlin and others that language learning involves the gradual shift from controlled to automatic processing is shared by Littlewood (1980):

> At first, when a learner needs to communicate through the foreign language, he must search consciously for words in most of the situations he encounters. One reason for this is that many of the lower-level processes are not sufficiently automatic to unfold without his conscious control . . . . Gradually, however, if he gains adequate experience, he increases the range of situations in which he can perform without consciously attending to the linguistic medium. He becomes more capable of devoting his conscious decision-making processes to the level of meaning and of letting the lower-level linguistic operations take care of themselves (p. 442).

Littlewood suggests that classroom activities be designed to follow a sequence in which meaning gradually plays a greater role. He characterizes linguistic activities along a continuum that progresses through the following types: (1) primary focus on form, (2) focus on form (plus meaning), (3) focus on meaning (plus form), and (4) primary focus on meaning. Type 1 activities should be kept to an absolute minimum in proficiency-oriented instruction. Contextualized and meaningful exercises (Type 2 activities) constitute "precommunicative" practice, and are also only one small subset of the types of contextualized activities that can be useful in a communicative language learning environment. Open-ended creative and personalized practice, as well as interactive activities, "information-gap" activities (Brumfit and Johnson 1979), role-plays, games, debates, discussions, and other communicative formats (Littlewood's Types 3 and 4) should also be encouraged for the development of oral proficiency. (See the first three corollaries to Hypothesis 1, pp. 80–82.) Content-based instruction and immersion experiences are "experiential" in nature and offer full contextualization of instruction by definition. More will be said about the benefits of this type of learning environment later in this chapter.

Thus far, we have been concentrating on types of activities that would be useful in developing productive skills in the foreign language. Chapters 6 and 7 will provide samples of such activities in various languages for learners at the Novice through Advanced levels in speaking and writing. In the next section of this chapter, some of the research about the role of context and background knowledge in the comprehension process is reviewed. The discussion will be supplemented by practical guidelines for designing listening and reading instruction in Chapter 5.

The Importance of Context and Background Knowledge in the Comprehension Process: Some Theoretical Considerations

The reasons that have been offered thus far for using contextualized language-practice materials have been based largely on the intuitive appeal of such an approach. Most second language educators would agree, at least in theory, with the idea that learning and practicing language in meaningful contexts is more appealing to both students and teachers than learning isolated bits of language through extensive memorization and drilling. Yet the rationale for contextualizing and personalizing classroom activities should not rest solely upon intuition. When one examines various theories of language comprehension and learning, it becomes clear that additional support can be found for the use of authentic or simulated authentic input in listening and reading, as well as meaningful and contextualized materials for encouraging language production.

The Role of Background Knowledge

Many language students have experienced at one time or another the difficulties and frustrations that can arise when attempting to understand a spoken or written text in the foreign language, especially when one is in the earliest stages of language study. What are some of the causes of difficulties in comprehension? Why are some texts more difficult to understand than others? How might language students approach listening or reading tasks differently to enhance comprehension? How can teachers prepare students so that listening and reading materials become more comprehensible to them? Answers to these and other questions can be found as we look at various comprehension theories that have been proposed over the years and examine available research about the comprehension process.

As we saw in Chapter 2, a common thread running through various perspectives on language acquisition is the view that the meaningfulness and familiarity of second language material plays a crucial role as learners begin to develop their second language skills. Beginning in the 1960s, the role of meaningfulness and organization of background knowledge was particularly emphasized by cognitive psychologists. Educators such as Ausubel (1968) believed that learning must be meaningful to be effective and permanent. For material to be meaningful, it must be clearly relatable to existing knowledge that the learner already possesses. Furthermore, this existing knowledge base must be organized in such a way that the new information is easily assimilated, or "attached," to the learner's cognitive structure. Ausubel stressed that teachers need to provide "advance organizers"—devices that activate relevant background knowledge—to facilitate the learning and retention of new material. Twenty-five years after Ausubel first introduced this concept, language teachers (as well as educators in virtually all other disciplines) continue to recognize the value of providing such organizers in instruction.

How does background knowledge impact specifically on second-language acquisition? It might first be helpful to think about the kinds of knowledge learners can bring to comprehension tasks. In the second-language comprehension process, at least three types of background knowledge are potentially activated: (1) *linguistic information,* or one's knowledge of the target language code; (2) *knowledge of the world,* including one's store of concepts and expectations based on prior experience; and (3) *knowledge of discourse structure,* or the understanding of how various kinds or types of discourse (such as conversations, radio broadcasts, literary texts, political speeches, newspaper and magazine stories, and the like) are generally organized. When language practice is limited to the manipulation or processing of linguistic form, only the first type of background knowledge is involved. By contrast, language learning activities that provide relevant context should be helpful in activating students' knowledge of the world and of familiar discourse structure. One might hypothesize that the need for activating knowledge beyond that of the linguistic code is greatest for learners at lower levels of proficiency, whose imperfect control of the language can be a serious hindrance to comprehension.

This hypothesis is supported by research done by Yorio (1971), who isolates the following factors in the reading process:

1. knowledge of the language (the code)
2. ability to predict or guess in order to make correct choices
3. ability to remember the previous cues and
4. ability to make the necessary association between the different cues selected

In reading a second language, however, new and modified elements appear:

1. The reader's knowledge of the foreign language differs from that of the native speaker.
2. The guessing or predicting ability necessary to pick up the correct cues is hindered by the reader's imperfect knowledge of the language.
3. The wrong or uncertain choices of cues make associations more difficult.
4. Memory span in the foreign language is shortened in the early stages of its acquisition because of lack of training and unfamiliarity of the material, thereby making it more difficult to remember cues previously decoded.
5. At all levels and at all times there is interference from the native language (pp. 108–9).

Yorio concludes that second language readers and listeners are at a disadvantage for several reasons: (1) Rather than recalling cues with which they are familiar, they are forced to recall cues that they either do not know at all or know imperfectly. Because of this, readers and listeners will forget those cues much faster than they would cues in their native language. (2) They must simultaneously predict future cues and make associations with past cues, a slow and painful process in the second language for many inexperienced learners. In response to a questionnaire administered by Yorio, 30 students at the English Language Institute reported that they felt they understood what they were reading while in the process of reading it, but easily "lost the thread," forgetting what went on before as they processed the subsequent sentence. Yorio attributes this difficulty to the need to concentrate on a triple process: storage of past cues, prediction of future cues, and associations between the two. "If they try to predict what is coming, they forget the past cues; if they try to concentrate on the past cues, prediction is impaired" (p. 111).

The problems encountered by Yorio's students are familiar to many language teachers, especially those whose students are at the Novice or Intermediate levels of proficiency. Students at these levels often try to process language in a "word-for-word" fashion, drawing only on one kind of background knowledge—their imperfect knowledge of the target-language code. If such students can be encouraged to use other cues to meanings, such as their knowledge of the world and of discourse structure, the process of understanding should be facilitated. Teachers can help students in this process by providing supplementary cues to meaning, drawing on all three types of background knowledge discussed earlier.

The view that individuals utilize various types of background knowledge when attempting to comprehend written and oral texts was proposed by reading theorists writing in the 1970s, such as Smith (1971) and Goodman (1972). Both researchers addressed first-language reading comprehension primarily, although they have had a strong influence on the development of second-language theories about the nature of the listening and reading process (Barnett 1989). Smith (1971) maintained that efficient readers process selected elements of the text rather than use all the visual cues available on the printed page. He described the process of comprehension as the "reduction of uncertainty" (p. 12). Goodman (1972) suggested that reading is a "psycholinguistic guessing game," involving the interaction between thought and language. He argued that "the ability to anticipate that which has not been seen . . . is vital in reading, just as the ability to anticipate what has not yet been heard is vital in listening" (p. 16). Both Smith and Goodman described "top-down" models of reading comprehension, where the reader is thought to begin with higher-order concepts (such as one's general knowledge of a topic or situation) and work down to the actual features of the text (such as words, phrases, morphology, syntax, and rhetorical structure) (Barnett 1989). In their view, readers sample the textual cues, make use of redundancies, and formulate their hypotheses about what the text is going to say, actively using background knowledge to make appropriate predictions about the ongoing discourse. The sampling process also serves to help readers confirm or reject their hypotheses as they process the information in the text.

Kolers (1973) also claimed that skilled readers do not process words as such, but work on the semantic or logical relations of the material, "even to the point of disregarding, in a certain sense, the actual printed text" (p. 46). In his view, readers sample the visual cues to formulate concepts that are relatable to what they already know. Anderson, Reynolds, Schallert, and Goetz (1977) suggested that what one brings *to* a text is actually *more* important than what is *in* the text (p. 369).

As we will see later in this chapter and also in Chapter 5, strictly "top-down" theories of comprehension have been replaced in popularity by more "interactive" models of reading, which suggest that comprehension involves an interactive process between the reader and the text that moves in a cyclical, rather than a linear, fashion between the reader's own mental activities and the textual features. In such models, "text sampling and higher-level decoding and recoding operate simultaneously" (Barnett 1989, p. 13). In these more recent models, the important role of background knowledge is retained, but is tempered by a recognition of the complexity of factors involved and the nonlinear nature of the comprehension process. One such theoretical perspective, which has had a great deal of influence on second-language theory and research, is described in the next section.

Schema Theory: Using Background Knowledge to Enhance the Language-Comprehension Process

The role played by background knowledge in language comprehension is explained and formalized in a theoretical model known as Schema Theory (Carrell and Eisterhold 1983). One of the basic tenets of this theory is that any given text does not carry meaning in and of itself. Rather, it provides *direction* for listeners or readers so that they can construct meaning from their own cognitive structure (previously acquired or background knowledge). The previously acquired knowledge structures accessed in the comprehension process are called *schemata* (the plural of *schema*). Other closely related terms that are similar, but not quite synonymous, are *scripts, plans, goals, frames, expectations,* and *event chains* (Carrell and Eisterhold 1983, p. 556; see also Bartlett 1932; Schank and Abelson 1977; Rumelhart 1980; Minsky 1982).

Rumelhart (1977) defines a schema as an abstract representation of a generic concept for an object, event, or situation. For example, each of us has an abstract representation for the concept *house*, which may be altered considerably depending upon whether one adds adjectives such as *elegant* or *enormous,* as opposed to *ramshackle* or *squalid.* Cultural differences may also alter the abstract representation for a given concept: *house* may have many of the same attributes as *maison,* yet there will undoubtedly be different mental images associated with the two terms because of cultural factors. According to Rumelhart, "misunderstanding" happens when we have found the wrong schema for a given concept or event.

When a schema represents a whole situation (such as going to a movie, repairing a car, going on a picnic, buying groceries, doing laundry, etc.) a chain of stereotypic events or features are called up in an individual's mind in association with the situation. Schank and Abelson (1977) explain this phenomenon using the term *script,* defined as a structure that describes in a predetermined, stereotypic fashion appropriate sequences of events in a particular context. For example, a generic script for the situation "going to a restaurant" might be as follows: one may call for a reservation, depending on the restaurant, get in the car, arrive at the restaurant, sit at a table, order from the menu, eat the meal in a stereotypic sequence, ask for the check, pay the cashier, and leave. Very different scripts might be activated, however, for the situation "going to a three-star restaurant" versus "going to a fast-food restaurant." In the three-star restaurant situation, the stereotypic sequence of actions would include making a reservation, getting dressed up, going to the restaurant, being seated, having a drink, ordering from the menu, having coffee and an elegant dessert, and the like. If one were going instead to a fast-food establishment, an entirely different sequence of events would be activated (Schank and Abelson 1977, pp. 40–50).

Hudson (1982) refers to the selection of a particular form of a schema as *instantiation*, a term used by Anderson et al. (1976). In the case of the "restaurant schema" mentioned above, one instantiation might involve a quick trip to a drive-up window for a hamburger, while another might involve an elegant evening of fine dining at a restaurant downtown. Comprehending someone's story about going to a restaurant depends, in part, on the schema that is instantiated as one listens. The listener would need to construct a correspondence between the schema he or she had activated and the actual information in the message itself. When both sources of information match sufficiently, the message is said to be understood. Comprehension, therefore, is not a matter of simply processing the words of the message, but involves fitting the meaning of the message to the schema that one has in mind. (Hudson 1982; also, Anderson, Prichert, Goetz, Schallert, Stevens, and Trollip 1976; Rumelhart 1980.)

Any one individual's interpretation of a message will be heavily influenced by his or her personal history, interests, preconceived ideas, and cultural background. For second language learners, distortions in comprehension may be due not only to misunderstandings of the linguistic aspects of the message, but also to misreadings of the script or schema due to cultural differences (Carrell 1981a; Johnson 1982; Carrell and Eisterhold, 1983).

As mentioned earlier, schema theorists describe an interactive model of comprehension. They posit two separate but interrelated modes of information processing: *bottom-up processing* and *top-down processing* (Rumelhart 1980). Carrell and Eisterhold (1983) explain the difference between these two operations in terms of the type of information that is used in comprehending the message and the way in which that information enters the system. Schemata are organized hierarchically, with the most abstract or general schemata at the top and the most specific at the bottom. For example, the schema for "restaurant" is rather generic and abstract, subsuming beneath it more specific schemata like "fast-food restaurant," "family restaurant," or "ethnic restaurant." For each of these schemata, there are "slots" that can be filled with specific information and variable details. When a message is interpreted principally by paying attention to the specific details (including the decoding of individual words or other linguistic cues) and the listener or reader attempts to instantiate the best fitting lower-level schema for the incoming data, bottom-up processing is taking place. This type of processing is considered *data-driven,* moving from the parts to the whole concept (Rumelhart 1980). If, on the other hand, the listener/reader begins with a more general higher-order schema, makes predictions based on background knowledge, and then searches the input for information to fit into the "slots," top-down processing is occuring. This latter type of processing is considered to be *conceptually driven,* moving from the whole to the parts (Rumelhart 1980; Carrell and Eisterhold 1983, p. 557).

Schema theorists point out that bottom-up processing and top-down processing occur at the same time. Details are attended to in order to instantiate the appropriate schema while conceptual understanding of a more general nature allows the listener or reader to anticipate and predict. "Bottom-up processing ensures that the listeners/readers will be sensitive to information that is novel or that does not fit their ongoing hypotheses about the content or structure of the text; top-down processing helps the listeners/readers to resolve ambiguities or to select between alternative possible interpretations of the incoming data" (Carrell and Eisterhold 1983, p. 557).

Carrell (1988) maintains that skilled readers (and presumably skilled listeners) constantly shift from one processing mode to the other as they accommodate to the demands of the task, while lower-proficiency readers/listeners tend to rely too much on one or the other mode of processing, resulting in problems with comprehension (pp. 101–102). Lower-proficiency readers/listeners may be too text-bound—relying too heavily on bottom-up decoding of the words and morpho-syntactic features—or conversely too dependent upon their background knowledge, making unwarranted assumptions and missing relevant features of the input. She attributes this unidirectional processing to five possible causes: (1) lack of relevant background knowledge to help readers use top-down processing; (2) failure to activate available schemata; (3) linguistic or reading skill deficiencies; (4) misconceptions about reading, especially in a foreign language; and (5) individual differences in cognitive style (p. 103). The problems alluded to in (4) may include those induced by inefficient approaches to the teaching of reading, where teachers have students read a text in order to answer questions on numerous details that may have little to do with the overall meaning. Test questions that place heavy emphasis on details and fail to encourage inferencing or global processing may promote decoding and one-way (bottom-up) processing, which in turn may result in lack of comprehension of the main ideas. Teachers need to be careful, therefore, to devise questions and activities that encourage the bidirectional processing that skilled readers use.

Carrell and Eisterhold (1983) explain that there are two basic kinds of schemata used in understanding messages: (1) *content schemata* (relating to one's background knowledge and expectations about objects, events and situations) and *formal schemata* (relating to one's knowledge of the rhetorical or discourse structures of different types of texts.) Both types of schemata are important to the comprehension process, as we will see in the next section.

Research on the Role of Context in Comprehension

In recent years, a significant amount of research evidence has been gathered to support the theoretical models of comprehension discussed thus far in this chapter. In this section, a variety of such studies are summarized. Virtually all of them can be said to lend support to Schema Theory in that they deal with the role of advance organizers (Ausubel 1968, 1978), scripts, and other types of contextual support in language comprehension. The sample of studies is not meant to be comprehensive, but shows the breadth of evidence for a schema-based approach to reading and listening.

Some of the practical questions that second language teachers have asked about the teaching of reading and listening comprehension are addressed in the studies reviewed below. The studies have been grouped to correspond to the following questions:

1. Can pictures, drawings, or other visual organizers actually enhance students' comprehension of texts in the second language? If so, what types of help do they provide? What kinds of pictures might be best to use? Are lots of pictures needed, or does one visual aid suffice? Do students at all levels of proficiency benefit in the same way or to the same degree from the use of pictorial aids? How does the presentation of pictures compare to other kinds of prereading activities?
2. What are the effects of non-pictorial prereading or prelistening activities on comprehension of target-language materials? Does going over key vocabulary with students prior to having them read or listen to a passage enhance their comprehension of the text? What is the effect of giving the students a brief outline, summary, or title of the passage on comprehension? How useful are prequestioning techniques in facilitating comprehension?
3. How important is it for students to have some knowledge of the cultural connotations in a passage prior to attempting to read or understand the text? Does a student's cultural background play a role in comprehension?
4. Does the type of text influence the facility with which students comprehend a passage in a foreign language? Are some rhetorical structures easier to understand than others? Does it help students to have a description or preview of the organization of a passage before attempting to read it?

The Role of Visual Organizers

Four studies relating to listening comprehension conducted by Bransford and Johnson (1972) show clearly that relevant contextual knowledge is a prerequisite for comprehending prose passages in the native language (in this case, English). In all four studies, subjects who were supplied with appropriate contextual information (background knowledge) before hearing a passage demonstrated significantly better comprehension ratings and recall scores than did subjects who were not provided with a context or who were provided with a context after hearing the passage. In these particular studies, the test passages were constructed in a way that made them somewhat ambiguous, rendering them more difficult to understand than prose that provided relevant organizational information about the content in the passage itself. Bransford and Johnson note the importance of finding a suitable organization of one's store of previous knowledge (i.e., a suitable advance organizer or schema) when faced with a passage of considerable difficulty:

> If one generally characterizes comprehension as a process requiring appropriate semantic contexts, then the conditions under which existing structures become activated are extremely important. If a passage does not provide sufficient cues about its appropriate semantic context, the subject is in a problem-solving situation in which he must find a suitable organization of his store of previous knowledge (p. 721).

The four experiments reported by Bransford and Johnson lend considerable support to Schema Theory in that they demonstrate that subjects do not simply interpret sentences per se and store meanings verbatim. Rather, they create "semantic products that are a joint function of input information and prior knowledge" (p. 718).

In the first experiment, prior knowledge was provided or not provided to subjects in the form of a visual. The information in the test passage consisted of a paragraph in which the sentences followed rules of English construction and the vocabulary items were straightforward in nature. However, without the prerequisite background knowledge, the passage was considered by the researchers to be difficult to interpret. The test passage is reproduced below:

> If the balloons popped, the sound wouldn't be able to carry since everything would be too far away from the correct floor. A closed window would also prevent the sound from carrying, since most buildings tend to be well insulated. Since the whole operation depends on a steady flow of electricity, a break in the middle of the wire would also cause problems. Of course, the fellow could shout, but the human voice is not loud enough to carry that far. An additional problem is that a string could break on the instrument. Then there could be no accompaniment to the message. It is clear that the best situation would involve less distance. Then there would be fewer potential problems. With face to face contact, the least number of things could go wrong (p. 719).

The prerequisite knowledge that would make this passage comprehensible was provided to subjects in the form of a picture that gave the listener information about the context underlying the passage (see Illustration 4.1). The passage described various events that could happen, given the pictured context as a conceptual base. The experiment consisted of an acquisition phase (during which subjects listened to the passage), followed by two tasks: (1) subjects were asked to rate the comprehensibility of the passage, and (2) subjects were asked to recall the facts in the passage.

Five groups of subjects participated in the experiment:

1. *The No-Context Group:* Subjects simply heard the test passage and were given no pictorial support.
2. *The Context-Before Group:* Subjects saw the appropriate contextual visual before hearing the test passage.
3. *The Context-After Group:* Subjects first heard the test passage and then saw the appropriate picture.
4. *The Partial-Context Group:* Subjects saw a picture before hearing the test passage, but the objects in the picture were rearranged (see Illustration 4.2).
5. *The No-Context (2) Group:* Subjects heard the test passage twice, but were given no contextual support of any type.

The results of the experiment revealed that only the Context-Before Group (Group 2) had a real advantage in comprehending the passage. Both comprehensibility and recall scores were significantly higher for this group: they scored nearly twice as high as any of the other four groups on both measures.

Bransford and Johnson conclude that the comprehension advantage was derived from removing the ambiguity of the passage through appropriate background knowledge. It was very unlikely, in their view, that the prerequisite information was part of the preexperimental knowledge structure of any of the subjects, so only those who had the correct contextual visual before hearing the test passage could activate the appropriate schema for understanding fully the passage content.

The other experiments conducted by Bransford and Johnson relate to the provision of nonpictorial advance organizers and are treated in the next section.

Several studies in second language comprehension have been conducted that are based in some fashion on the Bransford and Johnson research. Omaggio (1979) conducted a study in reading comprehension in French in which a variety of visual contexts were used as advance organizers. She hypothesized that second language learners are often faced with input material (both in listening and reading tasks) that is by nature unfamiliar, difficult, and therefore unpredictable because of the learners' lack of familiarity with the linguistic code. The provision of additional contextual information in the form of a visual should make the comprehension task

Illustration 4.1
Appropriate context picture for experiment I

Illustration 4.2
Partial context picture for experiment I

Source: Adapted from Bransford & Johnson, 1972.

easier by providing an organizational scheme for the passage as a whole (i.e., appropriate background knowledge or schemata would be activated).

The study investigated specifically the effects of selected pictorial contexts on measures of reading comprehension in both introductory college French (with second semester beginning students) and in the native language (English). The effects of two independent variables were explored: (1) pictorial contextual organizers and (2) type of text material. The pictorial context variable consisted of six levels or experimental conditions: (1) no visual organizer was provided; (2) a single-object drawing depicting the title of the story to be read was provided prior to exposure to the text (see Illustration 4.3); (3) a contextual picture was provided prior to reading depicting action from the beginning of the story (Illustration 4.4); (4) a contextual picture depicting action from the middle of the story was provided

Illustration 4.3
Single-object drawing depicting the title of the story

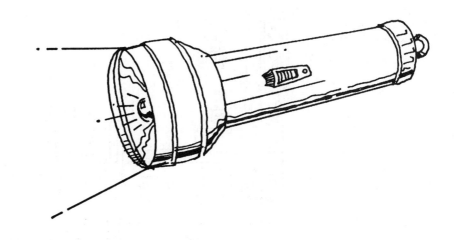

Illustration 4.4
Contextual picture depicting action from the beginning of the story

prior to reading (Illustration 4.5); (5) a contextual picture depicting action from the end of the story was provided prior to reading (Illustration 4.6); and (6) all three contextual visuals were provided simultaneously prior to reading.

The textual variable consisted of three conditions: (1) no text was provided to one group of subjects (i.e., subjects had only the pictures to refer

Illustration 4.5
Contextual picture
depicting action from
the middle of the story

Illustration 4.6
Contextual picture
depicting action from
the end of the story

Note: Pictures have been redrawn from sketches used in the original study.

to in those conditions where pictorial contextual organizers were used); (2)
a 650-word text in French was provided to a second group of subjects; and
(3) the same text was provided in English to a third group of subjects. The

text consisted of a short story, written by Sempé and Goscinny (1967), about a small boy who bought a flashlight with some money his father had given him, played with it continuously, to the general annoyance of his parents, used it until the batteries ran down, and, finally, exchanged it with a friend for a police whistle. The story is appropriate in style and content for adult readers.

Six hundred and sixty-four students participated in the eighteen treatment conditions. Comprehension of the text was measured by asking students to (1) write a resume of the passage content in English and (2) complete a 20-item multiple-choice and true/false test on the text material.

Results of the study showed significantly different effects of the various picture conditions on reading comprehension in the native language (English) and in the target language (French). For subjects reading the text in English, there were no significant differences in scores, regardless of the picture condition under which the text was read. This would suggest that the pictorial contexts had no real effect on reading comprehension in the native language, especially for a text that was cohesive and relatively easy to comprehend. However, for students reading the same text in French, the pictorial contexts used as advance organizers had a significant effect: those subjects who had the picture depicting action from the beginning of the story were at a significant advantage over all the others in the French textual conditions. Comprehension errors were significantly lower, and the number of facts and legitimate inferences recalled from the test passage were significantly higher when this particular pictorial organizer was provided. Data from the control group having this picture, but no text to read, revealed that virtually no relevant information could be gleaned from the visual alone. That is, it was not possible to "read" the picture and score well on the criterion measures. Even the group having all three contextual visuals and no text was unable to produce more than six or seven facts about the story content. These data suggest that the pictures, in and of themselves, did not give the students enough pertinent factual information about the content of the story to affect recall scores or enhance recognition of the events in the story. The advantage of having pictures with the French text must have been due to the fact that they served as an advance organizer or script activator, allowing students to retrieve a relevant schema from their cognitive structure to aid in the comprehension process.

In the case of this text, a possible schema, or script, may have related to a small boy who buys a flashlight, is fascinated with his new toy, plays with it incessantly, generally annoys people with it, and ends up losing it or losing interest in it. As the story is read, this type of generic script is either confirmed, altered, or rejected.

The data in this study revealed that all pictures were not equally effective in enhancing comprehension in the second language. The only picture that was significantly effective in and of itself was the one depicting action from the beginning of the story. The other pictures were relatively ineffective, possibly because of one or more of the following reasons:

1. They provided cues to events occurring late in the story and might therefore have failed to suggest an effective organizational schema to aid comprehension of the facts in the opening paragraphs.
2. They provided too many additional cues to the events of the story all at once and may have been confusing.
3. The single-object visual may have contained too little contextual information to provide an appropriate schema for students reading the story in the second language.

It may be that the best visual context for subjects at relatively low proficiency levels is one that provides enough background knowledge to aid them in finding an appropriate overall schema for comprehending the story, providing cues to the general nature of the passage as a whole without being confusing. For students at higher levels of proficiency, such pictorial aids might be superfluous, as other studies confirm.

In a similar study, Mueller (1980) investigated the effects of a visual organizer on listening comprehension in German. He hypothesized that a visual that provided contextual cues to a listening passage would enhance learner comprehension by providing a schema, or framework, for understanding the text. Specific research questions addressed in the study were:

1. What are the effects of a contextual visual on recall measures in listening comprehension in German?
2. What are the effects of varying the locus of the contextual visual in the sequence of events (i.e., providing the visual before or after hearing the passage)?
3. Do the effects of the visual vary with students' aptitude as measured by prior achievement in German?
4. Are there any significant interaction effects between aptitude and availability of the contextual visual? (pp. 335–36)

Mueller used one criterion variable in measuring the effects of the experimental conditions on comprehension. Subjects were asked to give a free-recall English resume of the passage heard in German. The passage was heard only once. Mueller found that the provision of a contextual visual *before* hearing the passage had the most beneficial effect for German students, especially at the lower proficiency levels. Having a visual after hearing the passage was better than having no visual at all, but not as beneficial as seeing the visual prior to hearing the passage. Mueller concluded that the effects of visual organizers on listening comprehension were inversely proportional to the language proficiency of the students in German. These results support the conclusions reached in the Omaggio study.

Visual Organizers Compared to Other Prereading Activities

In a study involving beginning, intermediate, and advanced ESL students from eight different first-language backgrounds, Hudson (1982) explored the effects of three types of treatments on students' comprehension of reading passages appropriate to their level. Nine passages in all were selected for the experiment, three at each level of proficiency. Each subject was exposed to the following treatment conditions:

1. Subjects read a passage, took a 10-item multiple-choice test, *reread* the passage, and took the test again.
2. In the *pictorial* condition, subjects were given a set of general visuals related to the passage, asked to look them over, given a set of focus questions, and then instructed to write down some of their own predictions about the content of the passage before reading. They took the 10-item comprehension test after finishing the passage.
3. In the *vocabulary* condition, students got a list of vocabulary items that would appear in the reading and discussed definitions for each item. They then read the passage and took the 10-item comprehension test.

Results indicated that, at lower levels of proficiency, the provision of the pictorial context cues (Condition 2, above) greatly aided comprehension of the test passage. While the read/test/reread/retest and vocabulary treatments were less effective at the beginning and intermediate levels than the visual condition, they were as effective or more effective at the advanced level. This result is consistent with those found by Omaggio and Mueller, discussed earlier, who found the visual information significantly facilitative for readers at the lower proficiency levels. Hudson concluded that induced schemata via picture cues can overcome the deficits of the lower-proficiency readers, while more advanced readers are able to bring more nonvisual information to bear on the process of reading comprehension in a second language.

In a second study conducted among Brazilian college students learning English as a foreign language (EFL), Taglieber, Johnson, and Yarbrough (1988) compared the effects of three kinds of prereading activities on reading comprehension. The authors were interested in comparing the ways in which *visual materials, vocabulary learning activities,* and *prequestioning techniques* compared in facilitating comprehension of a variety of texts. In order to generalize beyond one specific kind of passage, 40 sixth-semester EFL students were each given four different genres of reading material: (1) a fairy tale, (2) a legend, (3) a nonfiction article about Thanksgiving, and (4) two short fables. All students experienced all experimental conditions, and thus served as their own controls.

In the *visual condition,* the experimenter presented slides of three drawings taken from the original texts to students before they read the passages. While the students were looking at the pictures, the experimenter encouraged them to process them by describing them, connecting them conceptually, and guessing how the reading passage content might be related to them. In the *vocabulary preteaching condition,* students were given eight words drawn from the text to be read. The words were presented in meaningful sentences, but the sentences were not related to one another (i.e., were not contextualized). In the *prequestioning condition,* students were first given a one-sentence summary of the topic of the passage and then were asked to formulate some questions that came to mind and that might relate to the content of the text. In the *control condition,* students were given no prereading treatment. The findings indicated that all three prereading activities did indeed facilitate comprehension, but that vocabulary teaching was the least effective (and the least well liked by students) of the three.

The researchers concluded that the visual and prequestioning treatments "... appeared to produce a deeper and more active involvement of the subjects prior to reading. Discussion of words in sentences unrelated to each other and unrelated to the upcoming reading may not have been novel or interesting to the students" (p. 466). In addition, the researchers consider prereading activities of the sort used in this experiment as motivational devices. Students in the study indicated that they would appreciate more prereading activities in their foreign language classes. The authors point out the value of such activities in current textbooks, where reading passages are accompanied by pictures and other types of comprehension aids.

In all of the studies discussed in this section, there are clear implications for teaching listening and reading comprehension to language learners at the beginning and intermediate levels of proficiency. It seems that reading and listening passages have to be chosen, first of all, to relate to the learners' own experience so appropriate schemata can be activated. Secondly, prereading and prelistening comprehension aids that activate those schemata need to be provided to enhance comprehension of the text. Practical applications of these principles are illustrated in Chapter 5.

Script Activators and Other Organizers

In the preceding section, evidence was presented about how pictorial contexts of various types can induce appropriate content schemata, aiding in the comprehension process for learners at lower proficiency levels. A variety of studies in both native and second language comprehension have also been done using script activators or other types of advance organizers that are not pictorial in nature.

Titles and Topic Cues

Bransford and Johnson (1972) did a series of three experiments in which subjects listened to an ambiguous passage in their native language (English), with or without the aid of an advance organizer in the form of a title or topic. In each of these experiments, some of the subjects listened to the passage once without being informed of the topic, others were given the topic in the form of a short statement before hearing the passage, and a third group was given the topic after hearing the passage. The test passage was constructed to depict a standard event sequence, or "script," for a common activity:

> *The procedure is actually quite simple. First you arrange things into different groups depending on their makeup. Of course, one pile may be sufficient depending on how much there is to do. If you have to go somewhere else due to lack of facilities, that is the next step; otherwise you are pretty well set. It is important not to overdo any particular endeavor. That is, it is better to do too few things at once than too many. In the short run this may not seem important, but complications from doing too many can easily arise. A mistake can be expensive as well. The manipulation of the appropriate mechanisms should be self-explanatory, and we need not dwell on it here. At first the whole procedure will seem complicated. Soon, however, it will become just another facet of life. It is difficult to foresee any end to the necessity for this task in the immediate future, but one never can tell (p. 722).*

Subjects who received the topic of the passage before hearing it rated it more comprehensible than those who did not receive the topic or who received it after hearing the passage. Recall was also significantly better in the topic-before condition than in the other two conditions. The topic sentence "The paragraph you will hear will be about washing clothes" apparently served as a script activator, or a means of inducing an appropriate schema that greatly facilitated comprehension and recall of the facts of the passage. These results replicate and support the findings of the pictorial context experiment conducted by Bransford and Johnson, discussed earlier (see pp. 138–140).

Schallert (1976) also found that provision of a title influenced comprehension and memory for passages that could be interpreted in two different ways. She found, however, that the effect of the context was greater when students were required to process the text more "deeply" by either rating it for ambiguity or by studying it in order to learn it. When students were asked to look primarily at surface features of the text (e.g., counting four-letter words or counting pronouns), they were less influenced in their recall by the context and recalled less of the passage. Her study showed that meaningful processing is influenced by the provision of a context in the form of a title, but that this is mediated by the type of task the students are asked to do while reading.

Anderson, Reynolds, Schallert, and Goetz (1977) obtained results that showed that the background and interests of the readers greatly influenced their interpretation of ambiguous passages. One test passage could be understood either as the story of a convict trying to escape from prison or a wrestler hoping to break an opponent's hold. A second passage could be interpreted either as an evening among friends playing cards or playing musical instruments. The two passages were read by two groups of subjects: one group consisted of male physical education students and the other of female music students. Results indicated that the interpretation given to the test passages was strongly related to the background interests of the students. The researchers concluded that high-level schemata determine how discourse is understood: ". . . schemata can cause a person to see a message a certain way, without even considering alternative interpretations" (p. 367).

Like the visual organizers discussed in the previous section, familiar scripts can facilitate reading comprehension because they help students to make appropriate predictions and hypotheses about the events that will occur in the story and to correctly interpret unknown vocabulary. Adams (1982) conducted an experiment with second language learners in French in which students read passages about familiar events in a college student's life: playing tennis, grocery shopping, doing laundry, washing dishes, and attending a wedding. For each passage, she deleted a key word and replaced it with a nonsense word. The students' ability to guess the meaning of this nonsense word was manipulated through the use of a script activator—the oral provision of the passage's topic before reading took place. Her results supported the research hypothesis that having the script activator would significantly affect vocabulary scores. Subjects who had the script activator for the passages scored much higher on vocabulary than did those who had no such advance organizer. She concluded that the script activators were most beneficial to second language readers with low proficiency. The higher a student's proficiency level, the less impact the script activators had, since more proficient students could create a context from the linguistic cues in the text itself. These findings are consistent with those reported in the previous section on pictorial aids to comprehension.

Cultural Background Cues

In a study done with ESL readers, Johnson (1982) found that prior cultural background knowledge had a significant effect on reading comprehension scores for a test passage relating to a familiar American custom, Halloween. Students in ESL first experienced some of the most familiar aspects of Halloween. They then read passages in which some of the information was familiar, but other information (relating, for example, to the historical background of the custom and its origins) was unfamiliar. Four groups of students received different amounts and kinds of help with unknown vocabulary in the passage. Subjects were given: (1) no vocabulary list, (2) an opportunity to study the definitions of unfamiliar vocabulary words before reading the passage, (3) the passage with the target words glossed in the passage, and (4) an opportunity to study the vocabulary before reading the passage and definitions of the words glossed in the text.

After reading the passage, students were asked to write resumes of the content in English and to answer true/false questions on the information given. Two weeks later, they were tested on their recall of the vocabulary via a cloze passage. Results showed that students had a greater recall for the familiar material than for the unfamiliar.

Johnson concluded that exposure to meanings of the difficult vocabulary items did not seem to affect comprehension of the passage. However, students in the second group, who studied the target vocabulary before reading the passage (but who did not have glosses available in the text while reading) were at an advantage, since they seemed to recall more propositions from the text, understood more relationships between the ideas of the passage, and wrote more cohesive summaries than did subjects in the fourth group, to whom both a prereading list of vocabulary and in-text glosses were provided. Johnson attributes the problems in the fourth group to the availability of the glossed information in the margins: students were encouraged to process the text word for word, and thus lost the thread of the passage as a whole.

But perhaps Johnson's most important conclusion was that background knowledge helped enhance comprehension more significantly than did knowledge of vocabulary. These results support the findings of Jenkins et al. (1978) that vocabulary training seemed to help students in dealing with single sentences containing target words, but was of virtually no use when comprehension was tested in broader, discourse-length contexts containing the same vocabulary. It seems that "the effects of vocabulary difficulty on reading comprehension are not as clear as the effects of background knowledge" (Johnson 1982, p. 512), a finding that has been replicated in a variety of studies in both native and second languages.

In a study involving listening comprehension, Markham and Latham (1987) found that ESL students' religious background influenced their comprehension of two passages dealing with Christian and Moslem prayer practices. Sixty-five university-level ESL students were involved in the study. Twenty students declared themselves Christian, sixteen were Moslems, and twenty-eight said they were neutral, with virtually no knowledge of either tradition. Listening comprehension scores showed that the Christian students outperformed the others on the passage relating to Christian prayer, and the Moslem students outperformed the others on the passage dealing with the Islamic prayer practices. Students professing a religious preference had higher mean recollection scores on both passages than those who had declared themselves religion-neutral.

In a follow-up to the quantitative study, Markham and Latham taped interviews with six students, two from each religious-preference group. Retrospective data was elicited from these students, whose reports revealed that when an appropriate schema had been activated, students more easily predicted the content of the passage and comprehension was enhanced. For the two students who did not have a religious background congruent with the passages, the texts seemed more difficult and confusing.

Some interesting findings in the qualitative study related to attitudes of the students towards the test passages. One of the Moslem students interviewed objected to the text about Islamic practices because the narrator explained *why* certain prayer rituals were used. He resisted the idea that such practices needed to be justified. He also referred to the narrator of the Moslem passage as a male, even though the voice had been female. The researchers hypothesized that a female narrator for a religious text violated his expectations.

One of the Christian students felt uncomfortable talking about the Moslem passage, revealing certain biases that may have clouded her comprehension. She expressed concern particularly about the role of women in Moslem cultures, and like the Moslem student, remembered the narrator of the Moslem passage as being male. These results suggest that attitudes and emotional reactions as well as knowledge structures may have a role in the instantiation of schemata and ultimately in the comprehension process.

Story Structure and Expectations

Markham and Latham's (1987) qualitative data reveal that cultural expectations can have an effect on the way subjects understand a passage in a second language. In an earlier study, Spiro (1977) showed how one's expectations about the outcome of a story can affect comprehension and recall. Subjects in his study distorted stories with surprise endings (especially after long delays) to make the ending appear more probable. The distortion involved both the addition of elements that were congruent with the subjects' expectations and ongoing hypotheses about the story as well as the deletion of incongruent elements (Rumelhart 1977). These findings indicate that the comprehension process is an active, hypothesis-testing procedure in which the reader constructs his or her own version of the passage from existing schemata and attempts to match that version against the incoming information. When a match cannot be easily achieved, readers either tend to adjust the input to fit their hypotheses, choose a different schema and begin the hypothesis-testing process again, or eventually fail to comprehend. The more different schemata that are required to make sense of a given story, the less comprehensible the story will be (Rumelhart 1977, p. 298).

Research on the effects of *rhetorical* (as opposed to *content*) schemata shows that comprehension also suffers when the *structure* of a story violates the expected norm. For example, most stories involve a problem-solving episode of some type in which (1) something happens to the protagonist, (2) this event sets up a goal to be accomplished, and (3) the remainder of the story is a description of the problem-solving behavior used to accomplish the goal (Rumelhart 1977). Most simple stories, such as fables, tales, and short narratives, use this generic problem-solving motif as their essential rhetorical structure. Violations of this stereotypic structure might cause the reader to fail to comprehend.

Carrell (1981b; 1984b) conducted research on this question in a study involving two groups of university-bound, intermediate-level ESL subjects. One group of subjects read a simple story that was structured in a stereotypic fashion, according to the subjects' expectations. The second group read the same content, but the story structure was deliberately violated. Carrell found that when the content was kept constant but the story's rhetorical structure was violated, second language reading comprehension suffered. Thus, the role of formal (i.e., rhetorical or discourse) schemata in language comprehension is shown to be as important to consider as that of content schemata.

In a study conducted with French university students, Lee and Riley (1990) wanted to find out if giving students an advance organizer that provided cues about the rhetorical structure of a foreign-language text would enhance their comprehension of the passage, measured by a recall task in their native language. Students in the third semester of French were given one of two texts: (1) a passage describing the leisure-time activities of the French and (2) a text about the problem of the pillaging of historical sites and some possible solutions. The first text consisted of a *collection of descriptions* rhetorical organization, while the second was characterized as a *problem/solution* organization. The authors review previous research by Carrell (1984b), who had shown that for ESL students, the more loosely organized structure of *collections of descriptions* was more difficult to recall than the more tightly organized *comparison, causation* and *problem/solution* type of text. Furthermore, Carrell (1985) had also shown that teaching ESL students about the rhetorical structure of a text before reading it improved their comprehension.

Lee and Riley designed their study to include three conditions: (1) no rhetorical framework provided; (2) a minimal framework given before reading, consisting of a one-sentence description of the organization of the passage; and (3) an expanded framework provided before reading, consisting of a somewhat more detailed two-sentence description of the way the text was organized.

Findings indicated that the problem/solution passage was significantly easier to comprehend than the more loosely organized descriptive passage for all students. In general, students who had the expanded framework as an advance organizer remembered significantly more than those who had the minimal framework or no framework. Those who used the framework to organize their resumes also recalled more than those who did not use the framework, and their resumes were more coherent. The authors concluded that providing readers at lower levels of proficiency with advance organizers about the structure of the passage may be an important step in helping them learn how to get the most information from a foreign-language text.

Conclusion: Contextualization and Schema-Based Understanding

It seems clear from many of the studies reported in this chapter that comprehension is an active process where students *interact* with the text, using background knowledge that they bring to the comprehension process as well as the linguistic and rhetorical features of the text itself (Carrell and Eisterhold 1983). When the input provided to language learners is organized and easily relatable to what they already know, the burden of comprehension and learning is eased considerably. Research into schema-based understanding supports the view that learning language in context (i.e., larger discourse frameworks) may be easier than processing language in "bits and pieces" or in isolated sentence frames. "By dealing with related units of information rather than isolated bits, more efficient processing becomes possible." (McLaughlin 1983, p. 138.)

This brings us back to the point at which this chapter began: students need to learn language in logical contexts, either through authentic discourse-length input or through language learning materials that simulate authentic input using sentences that follow in logical sequence. Their reading and listening input, as well as productive practice activities, need to extend beyond the borders of the single sentence to encompass the widest possible contexts in which language is used for communicative purposes. While linguistic science (and pedagogical materials, by analogy) have traditionally centered on the sentence for the purpose of analysis, the field of discourse analysis has increasingly emphasized the importance of *intersentential* relationships in understanding and producing language (Brown 1980).

Brown makes this point very clear in his discussion of the concept of pragmatics:

> *A single sentence can seldom be fully analyzed without considering its context. We use language in stretches of discourse. We string many sentences together in cohesive units such that sentences bear interrelationships. . . . Both the production and comprehension of language are a factor in our ability to perceive and process stretches of discourse, to formulate representations of meaning from not just a single sentence, but referents in both previous sentences and following sentences (p. 189).*

He goes on to point out that without *context*, without the intersentential and suprasentential relationships of discourse, it would be difficult to communicate unambiguously with one another. This applies to written as well as to spoken language: ". . . the same intersentential relations that are created in spoken language hold true as the writer builds a network of ideas or feelings and the reader interprets them" (p. 190). Second language learners must be made aware of the conventions and constraints of discourse in the target language if they are to fully understand and communicate with the speakers of that language. The role of sociocultural factors, such as appropriate style or register of speech to be used in a given situation, needs to be taught overtly at various points along the course of the curriculum. Students also need to learn expressions and structures that will help them speak and write cohesively and coherently so that their discourse competence, an important component of communicative competence, can be developed. Obviously, if second language students are never given an opportunity to use language beyond the sentence level in classroom practice activities, the development of these and other important discourse skills will be neglected.

• • • • • • • • • • • • *Integrating Language and Content: Immersion and Content-Based Instruction*

One way to ensure that language learning occurs in a meaningful context and that language processing goes beyond the level of the isolated sentence is to develop instructional models where language and content are closely intertwined. In recent years, numerous scholars have discussed the merits of *content-based instruction* for the teaching of foreign languages in the United States, especially at the elementary school level (see, for example, De Lorenzo and Gladstein 1984; Genesee 1985; Swain and Lapkin 1989; Snow, Met, and Genesee 1989; Met 1991). Many of the principles of content-based instruction are derived from those used in the design of *immersion* programs, begun in Canada in 1965 and widely used in the teaching of French to Anglophone children in Canadian schools. Adaptations of the immersion model for schools in the United States have served various purposes: (1) as educational, cultural, and linguistic enrichment programs in the elementary grades; (2) as magnet schools to bring about an ethnic and/or racial balance within a school district; and (3) as a means of achieving a kind of two-way bilingualism in communities with large minority populations (Genesee 1985, p. 544). Although the initial purposes for the development of immersion and content-based instruction differed in Canada and the United States, a common goal of such programs is the development of significant levels of language proficiency through experiential learning in subject-matter areas.

Content-based and immersion programs in this country have been limited, for the most part, to the early grades, at least in the teaching of foreign languages to English-speaking children (Genesee 1985). Programs at the secondary school level and at the university level have been developed for the most part to accommodate the needs of limited English proficiency (LEP) learners or to help non-native speakers of English integrate successfully into English-language instructional contexts (see, for example,

Mohan 1986; Cantoni-Harvey 1987; Crandall 1987; Snow and Brinton 1988; Snow, Met, and Genesee 1989). Met (1991) defines content-based foreign language learning as "instruction that uses learning objectives and activities drawn from the elementary school curriculum as a vehicle for teaching foreign language skills" (p. 281). She adds that the foreign language can be the sole language of instruction, or it can be used to augment and supplement instruction in the native language. Included under the rubric of "content-based instruction" are partial and total immersion models as well as programs for language-minority children in the United States, where instruction in their native language is supplemented by content-based instruction in English.

Because current models of content-based foreign language instruction in the United States are derived in large part from Canadian programs, it would be useful to understand what the term "immersion" means in that context. Genesee (1985) defines Canadian immersion programs as those in which the target language is used for teaching regular school subjects. He describes three immersion models that have been used successfully in Canadian schools. The first is called *early immersion*, where the first two, three, or even four grades of schooling are done completely in French, followed by a gradual incorporation of English-language instruction up until sixth grade, when instruction in the two languages is evenly divided. The second model is *delayed immersion*, where students in fourth and fifth grade receive instruction in French, followed by a reintegration into the regular English-language curriculum in subsequent grades. The third model is *late immersion*, beginning with all-French instruction in seventh or eighth grade (usually following one year of "core French," which consists of a daily period of language instruction in an otherwise English-language curriculum; Swain and Lapkin 1989). Programs can be characterized as either *total immersion* or *partial immersion* models, the latter involving approximately 50 percent of the school day in French and the other half in English. Swain and Lapkin (1989) add that at the secondary level, early immersion students can choose to take several subjects in French if they so desire, as can students completing the delayed or late immersion programs after one or more years of French-language instruction in all subjects.

Extensive research has been done on the effects and benefits of immersion programs in Canada (see, for example, Pawley 1985, who lists over 30 research reports). Studies generally show that students develop a relatively high level of functional proficiency in the second language (Swain and Lapkin 1989). While it is true that early immersion learners sometimes show a slight advantage in listening and speaking skills, these differences are not always significant, and early immersion students do not surpass late-immersion students in literacy skills. Swain and Lapkin characterize the adolescent and adult learners as being more efficient, especially in the areas of reading and writing. They posit several possible reasons for this greater efficiency among the older learners: (1) they already know how to read and write in their native language when they begin the immersion experience, and thus can transfer these skills to the new language; (2) they are cognitively more mature than the younger learners, and are thus "better able to abstract, to generalize, and to classify from the beginning of their second language learning experience" and to attend consciously to what they are learning (p. 152). Swain and Lapkin conclude that teachers of adults in second language learning situations should therefore not be discouraged: "Your learners have many cognitive and language learning strategies to draw on, and your task is, in part, to help them to make use of these strategies" (p. 153).

This is not to say that early immersion programs should be abandoned. On the contrary, the success of enrichment programs such as the ones in Culver City, California and Montgomery County, Maryland, as well as magnet school programs such as those in Cincinnati, Milwaukee, and San Diego is well documented, and such American innovations are extremely promising (Genesee 1985). It seems clear that more children should have the opportunity to benefit from early content-based instruction in American schools. But even when such opportunities are not available, the Canadian data suggest that it is possible for older learners to benefit from content-based instruction as well. In some ways, older learners may have some advantages over younger learners.

Swain and Lapkin (1989) point out that the immersion model is not without its problems. The spoken and written French of both early and late-immersion students have fallen short of native-like proficiency, even after 5,000 or more hours of instruction. They attribute this problem to the fact that content has been emphasized at the expense of language skills in most immersion classes:

> "We have learned that grammar should not be taught in isolation from content. But then, neither should content be taught without regard to the language involved. A carefully planned integration of language and content, however, holds considerable promise" (p. 153).

Snow, Met and Genesee (1989) and Met (1991) agree that it is unlikely that desired levels of proficiency in the second language will emerge simply through content-based teaching, and argue for a careful planning of language learning objectives that will be integrated and coordinated with content instruction.

Swain and Lapkin (1989) describe some of the problems that underlie current methodological practice in immersion settings. They base their comments on observations of early immersion classes in Grades 3 and 6 (Swain and Carroll 1987) and in Grade 7 of a late immersion program (Stevens 1976). The observations reveal, first of all, that immersion teachers are primarily content teachers. Because they spend most of their time teaching subject-matter lessons, they tend to dominate the class time, giving students little opportunity to use the second language beyond sentence-length answers to factual questions on the material. Linguistic errors in the classes that were observed were rarely corrected (in Swain and Carroll's study, only 19 percent of the time), but when they were, the correction policy was confusing and inconsistent. Feedback tended to be contradictory in many of the classes. Swain and Lapkin conclude that "such a lack of consistent and non-ambigous feedback surely cannot be an aid to learning" (p. 155). They suggest instead that teachers set aside a regularized time and place for feedback and correction activities, and that these activities be based on their own spoken and written production in the content-based lessons. For example, students could listen to what they said during a social studies lesson on tape, and then work on ways to improve their communication through peer correction and consultation of dictionaries and other resources in order to prepare an error-free version of their discourse. "Throughout this process, students are using language and communicating freely in it. They are clarifying the intent of the learner's spoken utterance or written text. They are learning content *and* they are learning language" (p. 155). The authors suggest that integration of form-focused lessons with the content being taught would greatly improve immersion methodology. The suggestions given by Swain and Lapkin (1989) for improvements in methodological practice have relevance to any second-language classroom setting in which language is taught in context.

In discussing the effectiveness of a content-based instructional program at the college level for ESL students, Snow and Brinton (1988) come to many of the same conclusions about the need to integrate language and content in a coherent fashion. In the "adjunct model" for ESL students at the University of California at Los Angeles, minority-language students take part in a Freshman Summer Program designed to help them adjust to university life and prepare for academic coursework in English. In this program, students enroll concurrently in two linked courses: a language course, such as intermediate-level ESL for academic purposes, and a content course, such as Introduction to Psychology. Key features of this model include the integration of native and non-native English-speaking students in the content course with a "sheltering" of the ESL students in the language course. The assignments in the ESL course are designed to complement and support the learning in the content course. "The focus in the ESL class is on essential modes of academic writing, academic reading, study skills development, and the treatment of presistent structural errors" (p. 557). Instructors from both the content and ESL language courses meet regularly to plan assignments so that the ESL courses can best serve the students' linguistic and academic needs. The authors give an example of a typical written assignment, where students use the content course lecture notes to write definitions of concepts, and from there build paragraphs or write a more extensive definition paper. "In all such assignments, emphasis is placed on both the accuracy of content and on the accuracy and sophistication of the language used to communicate this content" (p. 559).

In all of these content-based instructional settings, then, the collective wisdom seems to be that simply teaching language through content or content through language is not enough. Rather, an integration of form-focused activities and content-based assignments is needed to achieve the best results, regardless of the age or level of proficiency of the students.

• • • • • • • • • • • • • *Summary: The Role of Context in Comprehension and Learning*

In this chapter, the role of context in comprehension and learning has been explored. We have seen both the intuitive appeal of such an approach and the theoretical and research base that exists to support it. While our linguistic and pedagogical traditions have concentrated on the sentence for the purpose of analysis and instruction, it seems clear that language teaching in the years to come must concentrate on the wider contexts of authentic language use and actively teach discourse skills in the classroom.

In the next three chapters, practical suggestions for selecting reading and listening input, as well as for teaching reading, listening, speaking, and writing *in context* are presented within the framework of a proficiency-oriented approach. The ideas offered should help students make rapid progress in the comprehension skills as well as expand and enrich their competence in using language beyond the sentence level, an important step in developing functional proficiency in a second language.

• • • • • • • • • • • • *Activities for Review and Discussion*

1. Define and give several examples of each of the following concepts:
   a. Background knowledge
   b. Advance organizer
   c. Schema

2. Look at the list of practical questions on p. 137. After having read the review of studies in this chapter, what tentative answers might you give to each of these questions? What do we still need to know in order to clarify the issues and find more definitive answers? Discuss with others in your group how teachers might be involved in seeking information that will add to our current knowledge about the role of context in comprehension and learning.

3. Examine your current language textbook and evaluate it in the light of the principles discussed in the chapter. Do the textbook's chapters explore themes that are relevant for learners and based on authentic cultural contexts? To what degree are language exercises

contextualized and/or personalized? To what extent are students encouraged to use language in discourse-length rather than sentence-length frames? Are readings drawn from authentic sources? To what extent are advance organizers provided? Make a list of the strengths and weaknesses of the textbook. What suggestions would you make to the publisher if you were asked to provide input for a revision of the text?

•••••••••••• *References*

Adams, Shirley J. "Scripts and Recognition of Unfamiliar Vocabulary: Enhancing Second Language Reading Skills." *The Modern Language Journal* 66 (1982): 155–59.

Allen, Patrick, Merrill Swain, Birgit Harley, and Jim Cummins. "Aspects of Classroom Treatment: Toward a More Comprehensive View of Second Language Education." Chapter 5 (pp. 57–81) in B. Harley, P. Allen, J. Cummins, and M. Swain, eds., *The Development of Second Language Proficiency.* Cambridge: Cambridge University Press, 1990.

Anderson, R.C., J.W. Prichert, E.T. Goetz, D.L. Schallert, K.V. Stevens, and S.R. Trollip. "Instantiation in General Terms." *Journal of Verbal Learning and Verbal Behavior* 15 (1976): 667–79.

Anderson, R.C., R.E. Reynolds, D.L. Schallert, and T.E. Goetz. "Frameworks for Comprehending Discourse." *American Educational Research Journal* 14 (1977): 367–81.

Ausubel, David. *Educational Psychology: A Cognitive View.* New York: Holt, Rinehart and Winston, 1968. [2nd ed., 1978.]

Bartlett, Frédéric C. *Remembering: A Study in Experimental and Social Psychology.* Cambridge: Cambridge University Press, 1932.

Bransford, John D. and Marcia K. Johnson. "Contextual Prerequisites for Understanding: Some Investigations of Comprehension and Recall." *Journal of Verbal Learning and Verbal Behavior* 11 (1972): 717–26.

Brown, H. Douglas. *Principles of Language Learning and Teaching.* Englewood Cliffs, NJ: Prentice Hall, 1980. [2nd ed., 1988.]

Brumfit, C.J. and K. Johnson. *The Communicative Approach to Language Teaching.* Oxford: Oxford University Press, 1979.

Cantoni-Harvey, Gina. *Content-Area Language Instruction.* Reading, MA: Addison-Wesley Publishing Company, 1987.

Carrell, P.L. "Culture-Specific Schemata in Second-Language Comprehension." In R. Orem and J. Haskell, eds., *Selected Papers from the Ninth Illinois TESOL/BE Annual Convention, the First Midwest TESOL Conference.* Chicago, IL: TESOL/BE, 1981a: 123–32.

_____ "The Role of Schemata in L2 Comprehension." Paper presented at the 15th Annual TESOL Convention. Detroit, MI, March, 1981b. [Cited in Carrell and Eisterhold 1983.]

_____ "Evidence of a Formal Schema in Second Language Comprehension." *Language Learning* 34, ii (1984a): 87–112.

_____ "The Effects of Rhetorical Organization on ESL Readers." *TESOL Quarterly* 18 (1984b): 441–69.

_____ "Facilitating ESL Reading by Teaching Text Structure." *TESOL Quarterly* 19 (1985): 727–52.

_____ "Some Causes of Text-Boundedness and Schema Interference in ESL Reading." Chapter 7 (pp. 101–113) in P. Carrell, J. Devine, and D. Eskey, eds. *Interactive Approaches to Second Language Reading.* Cambridge: Cambridge University Press, 1988.

Carrell, P.L., J. Devine, and D. Eskey, eds. *Interactive Approaches to Second Language Reading.* Cambridge: Cambridge University Press, 1988.

Carrell, P. L. and J. Eisterhold. "Schema Theory and ESL Reading Pedagogy." *TESOL Quarterly* 17 (1983): 553–73.

Coady, James. "A Psycholinguistic Model of the ESL Reader." In R. Mackay, B. Barkman, and R. R. Jordan, eds., *Reading in a Second Language.* Rowley, MA: Newbury House, 1979.

Crandall, JoAnn, ed. *ESL Through Content-Area Instruction.* CAL/ERIC Language in Education: Theory and Practice, no. 67. Englewood Cliffs, NJ: Prentice Hall, 1987.

De Lorenzo, William D., and Lois A. Gladstein. "Immersion Education à l'Américaine: A Descriptive Study of U.S. Immersion Programs." *Foreign Language Annals* 17, i (1984): 35–40.

Ellis, Rod. *Instructed Second Language Acquisition.* Oxford: Basil Blackwell, 1990.

Genesee, Fred. "Second Language Learning Through Immersion: A Review of U.S. Programs." *Review of Educational Research* 55 (Winter, 1985): 541–61.

Goodman, Kenneth S. "Reading: A Psycholinguistic Guessing Game." In L. Harris and C. Smith, eds., *Individualizing Reading Instruction: A Reader.* New York: Holt, Rinehart, and Winston, 1972.

Harley, B., P. Allen, J. Cummins, and M. Swain, eds., *The Development of Second Language Proficiency.* Cambridge: Cambridge University Press, 1990.

Haugeland, John, ed. *Mind Design.* Cambridge, MA: M.I.T. Press, 1982.

Higgs, Theordore V. and Ray Clifford. "The Push toward Communication." In T. Higgs, ed., *Curriculum, Competence, and the Foreign Language Teacher.* ACTFL Foreign Language Education Series, vol. 13. Lincolnwood, IL: National Textbook Company, 1982.

Hudson, Thom. "The Effects of Induced Schemata on the 'Short Circuit' in L2 Reading: Non Decoding Factors in L2 Reading Performance." *Language Learning* 32 (1982): 1–31.

Jenkins, J.R., O. Pano, and J. Schreck. "Vocabulary and Reading Comprehension: Instructional Effects." 1978. [EDRS: ERIC Document #160 999.] [Cited in Johnson 1982.]

Jespersen, Otto. *How to Teach a Foreign Language.* London: George Allen and Unwin, Ltd., 1904.

Johnson, Patricia. "Effects on Reading Comprehension of Building Background Knowledge." *TESOL Quarterly* 16 (1982): 503–16.

Kolers, Paul A. "Three Stages of Reading." In F. Smith, ed., *Psycholinguistics and Reading.* New York: Holt, Rinehart, and Winston, 1973.

Laberge, D. and S.J. Samuels, eds., *Basic Processes in Reading: Perception and Comprehension.* Hillsdale, NJ: Lawrence Erlbaum Associates, 1977.

Lee, James F. and Gail Riley. "The Effect of Prereading, Rhetorically-Oriented Frameworks on the Recall of Two Structurally Different Expository Texts." *Studies in Second Language Acquisition* 12, i (1990): 25–41.

Littlewood, William T. "Form and Meaning in Language Teaching Methodology." *The Modern Language Journal* 64 (1980): 441–45.

_____ *Communicative Language Teaching: An Introduction.* Cambridge University Press, 1981.

Long, Michael. "Does Second Language Instruction Make a Difference? A Review of the Research." *TESOL Quarterly* 17 (1983): 359–82.

Mackay, R., B. Barkman, and R.R. Jordan, eds., *Reading in a Second Language.* Rowley, MA: Newbury House, 1979.

Markham, Paul and Michael Latham. "The Influence of Religion-Specific Background Knowledge on the Listening Comprehension of Adult Second-Language Students." *Language Learning* 37, ii (1987): 157–70.

McLaughlin, Barry. "The Monitor Model: Some Methodological Considerations." *Language Learning* 28 (1978): 309–32.

_____ *Theories of Second Language Learning.* London: Edward Arnold, 1987.

McLaughlin, Barry, T. Rossman, and B. McLeod. "Second Language Learning: an Information-Processing Perspective." *Language Learning* 33 (1983): 135–58.

Met, Myriam. "Learning Language through Content: Learning Content through Language." *Foreign Language Annals* 24 (1991): 281–95.

Minsky, Marvin. "A Framework for Representing Knowledge." In J. Haugeland, ed., *Mind Design.* Cambridge, MA: M.I.T. Press, 1982.

Mohan, Bernard A. *Language and Content.* Reading, MA: Addison-Wesley Publishing Company, 1986.

Mueller, Gunter A. "Visual Contextual Cues and Listening Comprehension: An Experiment." *The Modern Language Journal* 64 (1980): 335–40.

Muyskens, Judith, A. Omaggio, C. Chalmers, C. Imberton, and P. Almeras. *Rendez-vous: An Invitation to French.* New York: Random House, 1982.

Omaggio, Alice C. "Pictures and Second Language Comprehension: Do They Help?" *Foreign Language Annals* 12 (1979): 107–16.

Pawley, Catherine. "How Bilingual are French Immersion Students?" *The Canadian Modern Language Review* 41, v (1985): 865–76.

Rumelhart, David. "Understanding and Summarizing Brief Stories." In D. Laberge and S. Samuels, eds., *Basic Processes in Reading: Perception and Comprehension.* Hillsdale, NJ: Lawrence Erlbaum Associates, 1977.

_____ "Schemata: The Building Blocks of Cognition." Chapter 2 (pp. 33–58) in R. Spiro, B. Bruce, and W. Brewer, eds., *Theoretical Issues in Reading Comprehension.* Hillsdale, NJ: Lawrence Erlbaum Associates, 1980.

Schallert, D.C. "Improving Memory for Prose: The Relationship between Depth of Processing and Context." *Journal of Verbal Learning and Verbal Behavior* 15 (1976): 621–32.

Schank, Roger and Robert Abelson. *Scripts, Plans, Goals, and Understanding: An Inquiry into Human Knowledge Structures.* Hillsdale, NJ: Lawrence Erlbaum Associates, 1977.

Seliger, Herbert W. "On the Nature and Function of Language Rules in Language Teaching." *TESOL Quarterly* 13, (1979): 359–69.

Sempé, R. et J.J. Goscinny, "La Lampe de poche." In *Joachim a des ennuis.* New York: Harcourt, Brace, and World, 1967.

Slager, William R. "Creating Contexts for Language Practice." In E. Joiner and P. Westphal, eds., *Developing Communication Skills.* Rowley, MA: Newbury House, 1978.

Smith, Frank. *Understanding Reading.* New York: Holt, Rinehart, and Winston, 1971.

Snow, Margarite Ann and Donna M. Brinton. "Content-Based Language Instruction: Investigating the Effectiveness of the Adjunct Model." *TESOL Quarterly* 22, iv (1988): 553–74.

Snow, Margarite Ann, Myriam Met, and Fred Genesee. "A Conceptual Framework for the Integration of Language and Content in Second/Foreign Language Instruction." *TESOL Quarterly* 23, ii (1989): 201–17.

Spiro, R.J. "Inferential Reconstruction in Memory for Connected Discourse." In R.C. Anderson, R.J. Spiro, and W.E. Montague, eds., *Schooling and the Acquisition of Knowledge.* Hillsdale, NJ: Lawrence Erlbaum Associates, 1977.

Stern, H. H. "Analysis and Experience as Variables in Second Language Pedagogy." Chapter 7 (pp. 93–109) in B. Harley, P. Allen, J. Cummins, and M. Swain, eds., *The Development of Second Language Proficiency.* Cambridge: Cambridge University Press, 1990.

Stevens, F. "Second Language Learning in an Activity-Centered Program." MA Thesis, Montreal: Department of Educational Technology, Concordia University, 1976. [Cited in Swain and Lapkin 1989.]

Strasheim, Lorraine. "What is a Foreign Language Teacher Today?" *The Canadian Modern Language Review* 33 (1976): 39–48

Swain, Merrill. "Communicative Competence: Some Roles of Comprehensible Input and Comprehensible Output in its Development." Chapter 14 in S. Gass and C. Madden, eds., *Input in Second Language Acquisition.* Cambridge, MA: Newbury House, 1985.

Swain, Merrill and S. Carroll. "The Immersion Observation Study." Part II, pp. 190–341 in B. Harley, P. Allen, J. Cummins, and M. Swain, eds., *The Development of Bilingual Proficiency. Final Report: Classroom Treatment.* Toronto: Modern Language Centre, OISE, 1987. [Cited in Swain and Lapkin 1989.]

Swain, Merrill and Sharon Lapkin. "Canadian Immersion and Adult Second Language Teaching: What's the Connection?" *The Modern Language Journal* 73, ii (1989): 150–59.

Taglieber, Loni K., Linda L. Johnson, and Donald B. Yarbrough. "Effects of Prereading Activities on EFL Reading by Brazilian College Students." *TESOL Quarterly* 22, iii (1988): 455–71.

Widdowson, H.G. *Teaching Language as Communication.* Oxford: Oxford University Press, 1978.

Yorio, Carlos A. "Some Sources of Reading Problems for Foreign Language Learners." *Language Learning* 21 (1971): 107–15.

5

···

A Proficiency-Oriented Approach to Listening and Reading

In the last chapter we saw that comprehension, both in listening and in reading, is an active process involving at least three interrelated factors: (1) the individual's knowledge of the linguistic code, (2) cognitive skills of various types, and (3) the individual's knowledge of the world. We saw how relevant contextual information can play an important role in comprehension, especially at lower levels of proficiency, where extra-linguistic cues and advance organizers can activate appropriate schemata to close the gaps in comprehension caused by an imperfect knowledge of the code.

This chapter explores practical issues relating to the teaching of listening and reading. The questions addressed are the following: Why should these skills be actively taught? How are listening and reading skills similar? How are they different? How can authentic materials be used in teaching comprehension skills in the lower proficiency ranges? What specific strategies can be used for teaching listening and reading, particularly at the Novice, Intermediate, and Advanced proficiency ranges?

·········· ## A Rationale for Teaching Listening and Reading

When audiolingual methodologies became popular in the early 1960s, many second language programs and materials began to place primary emphasis on the development of oral proficiency, a reversal of the trend in the grammar-translation era that emphasized reading as the primary goal of language study. In the years that followed, oral communication continued to receive high priority in many second language classrooms. Yet an increasing number of educators today are recognizing the need to achieve a balance in program goals through the reintroduction of comprehension-based activities and materials into the curriculum.

Attitudes about the importance of comprehension skills in language acquisition have been influenced, in large part, by developments in second language acquisition theory. Certainly Krashen's (1982) views about the need for comprehensible input in language acquisition have sparked interest in comprehension-based methodologies and materials. As we saw in Chapter 2, most recent language acquisition theories recognize the important role that input plays in the development of proficiency in all skill modalities, and an increasing number of scholars and practitioners believe that comprehension processes and strategies need to be taught actively in second language classrooms.

Barnett (1989) maintains that reading has always held an important place in foreign and second language programs, with the possible exception of the period when audiolingual methodology dominated in American classrooms. But she adds that reading is now seen in a different light, namely "as communication, as a mental process, as the reader's active participation in the creation of meaning, as a manipulation of strategies, as a *receptive* rather than as a *passive* skill" (p. 2). She cites Byrnes (1985), who refers to both reading and listening as receptive skills in which readers and listeners actively *"produce understanding"* (Byrnes 1985, p. 78; Barnett 1989, p. 2). As a source of "comprehensible input," reading becomes valued in the communicative classroom, especially when authentic materials can serve the dual purpose of developing reading skills and of fostering cultural insights and understanding. Barnett goes on to list other reasons for including reading skill development as a vital part of the second language curriculum: (1) reading is still essential in the teaching of literature, which remains an important goal in many programs; (2) it is a skill that can be maintained after students complete formal language study; (3) it fosters the development and refinement of literacy skills. Indeed, second language reading research may have a significant impact on our understanding of this larger issue of literacy, which is of national concern.

Although most of the research studies involving the development of foreign language receptive skills have been devoted to understanding the reading process (Lund 1991), there is a very strong interest in the language teaching community today to increase students' listening comprehension skills as well. James (1986) advocates the direct teaching of listening skills for motivational reasons. He cites research by Lowe (1985), who found that, in terms of the ILR Proficiency scale, English-speaking learners performed better in listening comprehension tasks than in speaking activities 47 percent of the time in French, and 76 percent of the time in Spanish, as averaged over all levels of proficiency (p. 37). In Spanish, the listening comprehension advantage tended to be strongest at ILR levels 2 through 4+. At levels 1+ and lower, the listening and speaking scores tended to be equal (p. 37). In French, the offset in listening and speaking began sooner, and the comprehension advantage was measurable at the 0+/1 border (p. 40). However, Lowe cautions that a greater facility in listening than in speaking may not hold across different languages, and there may in fact be a negative offset for some languages (i.e., where listening proves more difficult than speaking). James' (1986) point, in reviewing Lowe's data, is that if there is indeed a comprehension advantage, then introducing more listening activities early into the learning process will be motivating to learners and allow them to experience success.

Long (1986) argues that teaching oral skills is only teaching half of the process of communication, and adds that students gain a sense of confidence with the language when their listening abilities are well developed. Feyton (1991) further comments that the field of language teaching has moved from a "response-oriented paradigm to one of input, or stimulus-oriented learning" (p. 175), and adds that listening should not be thought of as an "activity," but taught directly as a skill in its own right.

Joiner (1986) cites four trends that have brought more attention to the development of listening skills in recent years: (1) *comprehension-based approaches,* which advocate a pre-speaking or "silent period" and which maintain that listening is the foundation skill for all language development; (2) *emphasis on the receptive skills* in general, which has been growing since the early 1980s; (3) the prevalence of *functional-notional approaches* and concepts, with their emphasis on oral communication; and (4) *the development of the ACTFL Proficiency Guidelines,* fostering an interest in the use of authentic materials for listening and reading and emphasizing communicative skill development (pp. 45–46).

Swaffar, Arens, and Byrnes (1991) argue forcefully for the inclusion of more reading, listening, and writing activities in a communicative curriculum to allow students to use their higher-order cognitive skills. Authentic reading and listening materials, as well as writing activities that involve analysis and interaction with texts give adult learners more of an opportunity to engage in challenging tasks appropriate to their level of cognitive maturity.

Rivers (1975) has pointed out another important reason for developing both listening and reading skills, citing research that shows that adults spend 45 percent of their time listening and 11 to 16 percent of their time reading (Rankin 1962, in Rivers 1975, p. 58). She adds that "these data are from a pre-television, pre-talking picture, pre-dictaphone era," which would lead one to believe that in this age of heavy media saturation, the percentages are probably even higher, especially for listening. When we realize that more than three-fifths of all communicative interaction involves comprehension skills, the importance of focusing on effective strategies for enhancing those skills becomes even more apparent.

In the 1960s and 1970s, there seemed to be very few published materials for the systematic teaching of listening and reading, partly because comprehension processes were still not well understood and partly because teachers often assumed that students would somehow develop comprehension skills "naturally" (see Snow and Perkins 1979 on this point with regard to listening). In the past decade, there has been a growing interest in designing materials to teach comprehension more actively, especially through the use of culturally authentic texts, videotaped materials, and computer-assisted instruction that allows for greater interaction between the learner and the text. Teachers need more access to listening and reading materials based on natural disourse along with appropriate comprehension activities that teach the process of comprehension so that skills are transferable to other situations and texts. Publishers of foreign and second language instructional materials are recognizing this need, and there is an increasing number of high-quality texts and ancillaries designed especially for this purpose.

In addition to new and better materials, teachers need ideas for structuring and sequencing instruction so that a classroom plan for teaching listening and reading comprehension can be devised. Effective ways to integrate comprehension and productive skills with the teaching of culture are also needed. Some specific ideas for planning instruction of this type are provided in this and subsequent chapters. First, however, it would be useful to look at some of the similarities and differences in listening and reading tasks, many of which derive from the relationship between speech and writing.

Similarities in Listening and Reading

We have already seen that listening and reading comprehension are both highly complex processes that draw on knowledge of the linguistic code, cognitive processing skills, schema-based understanding, and contextual cues both within and outside the text. Both skills can be characterized as problem-solving activities involving the formation of hypotheses, the drawing of inferences, and the resolution of ambiguities and uncertainties in the input in order to assign meaning. Stevick (1984) refers to the process of assigning meaning as the generation of *images*. An *image* is a set of items (sensory, emotional, temporal, relational, purposive, or verbal in nature) that travel together in memory. When one item comes into consciousness, it tends to bring other items associated with it in the mental image of which it is a part. Stevick maintains that in listening and reading comprehension, images are generated (either accurately or inaccurately) from a small sample of items that were in the original image. That is, even if the comprehender does not recognize or understand all of the items in the input, some of the items that are understood may serve to generate the image well enough to ensure global comprehension. For example, a student listening to a passage or reading a text may get the meaning of unknown words from context or can report the gist of the message, even though he or she may not be able to account for all of the details. The *goal* of both reading and listening comprehension, in Stevick's view, is to generate the intended image from the input and react appropriately. This reaction may be physical, emotional, or intellectual in nature.

Bernhardt and James (1987) use the metaphor of the jigsaw puzzle to describe the comprehension process. The reader/listener begins constructing the puzzle by selecting pieces, very slowly at first, until a hypothesis about the whole picture can be formed. Once this initial hypothesis is made, the image of the whole can guide further selection and interpretation of the parts. Of course, if the initial hypothesis is wrong, problems in comprehension will arise, and the process of building the puzzle can break down or become frustrating, "especially when the puzzle constructor is convinced that some of the pieces are either *missing* or were even cut wrong" (p. 66).

Although the goals and some of the global processes in listening and reading comprehension are often similar, the nature of the input (speech or writing) and the way in which that input is processed are quite different.

Differences between Spoken and Written Discourse

Richards (1983) has outlined several ways in which speech differs from writing. These differences, summarized below, offer us insights into the nature of listening and reading tasks, especially when students are listening to or reading authentic, unedited discourse.

1. The organizational unit of discourse varies in speech and in writing. Written discourse is normally constructed in sentences, whereas the major constituent in the planning and delivery of spoken discourse is the clause.
2. The observance of grammatical conventions also differs in speech and in writing. Whereas written discourse typically consists of well-formed sentences, spoken discourse can often include ungrammatical or reduced forms, dropped words, and sentences without subjects, verbs, auxiliaries, and other parts of speech.
3. In well-written discourse, sentences flow in logical sequence and there is evidence of planning of thought. In spoken conversational discourse, pauses, hesitations, false starts, and corrections make up between 30 and 50 percent of what is said. In addition, speakers tend to use fillers and silent pauses to "buy time" as they plan what they want to say next.
4. Coherence in written discourse is created differently than in speech, since writing tends to be more planned and tightly organized. A written text is usually produced by one person, allowing the discourse to flow logically as the topic is developed. Conversational speech, on the other hand, is generally not planned and therefore not as organized as written discourse. Often there are topic shifts, since the development of the topic of conversation is cooperatively constructed.
5. Because conversations are interactive, relying on both verbal and nonverbal signals, meanings are negotiated between conversational partners. Many things may be left unsaid because both parties

assume some common knowledge. In many types of written discourse, however, the person communicating the message may be addressing it to a wide and essentially anonymous audience and therefore cannot negotiate meaning directly with the reader. Common knowledge cannot always be assumed: more background information may be needed in order to communicate clearly (pp. 224–26).

Stevick (1984) points out that the way in which the communication is organized for delivery also differs in speech and in writing. Whereas spoken language moves along a time axis, written language is visually presented, and its overall duration and organization can be seen at a glance. He hypothesizes that aural comprehension may be more difficult than reading for this reason. Lund (1991) found this to be the case in a study involving beginning and intermediate students of German, where their reading comprehension was superior to their comprehension in listening. This reading advantage appeared to diminish somewhat by the time students reached the third semester, however. Lund concluded that although there may be an initial advantage for listening in the case of children who are learning to read in their native language, the opposite appears to be true for adults engaged in second language learning. "There may be in many situations an initial advantage to readers for unfamiliar and authentic texts, but this conclusion may not hold for noncognate languages or where diverse writing systems are involved" (p. 201).

Lund also found that having a text presented twice, either in reading or listening, significantly benefitted students at all levels in the study. However, the study clearly indicated that for beginning students, reading and rereading resulted in superior comprehension to listening and relistening. This may be due, in part, to the fact that listeners cannot control the pace of presentation of the text, and often appear to be "grasping at words" (p. 201). This relates to what Stevick (1984) calls the "accessibility" of the text, which differs in the two modalities. In reading, one can look back at what was read before and also look ahead to get an idea of what is coming. The listener, however, cannot do this, and any inattention to what is being said at the moment may easily cause him or her to lose an important part of the message, or even all of it.

The contrasts between oral and written language become more complex when one considers the range and variety of text types that can be encountered. In discussing the nature of oral language, Byrnes (1984), following Beile (1980), identifies four basic modes of speech:

1. *Spontaneous free speech*, characterized by the interactiveness and production constraints reviewed above;
2. *Deliberate free speech*, such as that which is characteristic of interviews and discussions;

3. *Oral presentation of a written text,* as in newscasts, more formal commentaries, and lectures; and

4. *Oral presentation of a fixed script,* such as that produced on stage or in a film (p. 319).

Written discourse also has a variety of text types. Grellet (1981) identifies some of the kinds of texts readers might encounter in the target language. A summary of her comprehensive list, regrouped into categories, is given below:

1. **Literary texts,** such as novels, short stories, plays, poems, essays, and the like;

2. **Specialized or technical texts,** such as reports, reviews, textbooks, handbooks, statistical data, diagrams, flow charts, etc.;

3. **Correspondence,** such as personal or business letters, postcards, notes, or telegrams;

4. **Journalistic literature,** such as articles from newspapers and magazines, editorials, headlines, classified ads, weather reports, television listings;

5. **Informational texts,** such as dictionaries, guidebooks, phrase books, phonebooks, timetables, maps, signs, price lists, etc.;

6. **Miscellaneous Realia** of various kinds, such as tickets, menus, recipes, advertisements, etc. (Based on Grellet 1981, pp. 3–4.)

When one considers the variety of text types and modes of speech, it becomes clear that "successful comprehension" will depend on the purposes for which the individual is listening or reading. "Understanding a written [or oral] text means extracting the required information from it as efficiently as possible" (Grellet 1981, p. 3). "Extracting the required information" may mean in one instance that the listener or reader simply scans the input to find some detail of interest, such as listening to a series of sports scores or scanning a television log to find an interesting program. In another situation, certain main ideas and a few supporting details may be required to ensure successful comprehension (such as listening to directions to get to someone's house). In still another situation, the listener or reader might need to get all of the finer details of the message in order to understand it well enough to carry out some specific purpose or function (such as reading a set of directions to build or make something). The design of appropriate comprehension tasks for oral or written discourse, then, becomes a function of text type, the purpose for which the comprehender is listening and reading, and the information and skills the listener/reader brings to the text. Bernhardt and James (1987) add that "the road to effective instruction must lie in acknowledging individual differences in readers *and* texts" (p. 71). The importance of these considerations will become apparent in the next sections, where suggestions for listening and reading activities for various proficiency levels are given.

•••••••••••• *Teaching Listening Comprehension*

Some Processes and Skills Involved in Listening Comprehension

Because very little data exist to enlighten us about the processes involved in second language listening comprehension, it is necessary to turn to native language research for some insights. According to Richards (1983), studies indicate that listeners take in raw speech and hold an image of it in short-term memory. They then try to organize that image into its constituents, identifying both their content and their function or purpose. These constituents are then grouped together to form a coherent message, which is held in long-term memory as a *reconstructed* meaning rather than in its original form (based on Clark and Clark 1977, p. 49). In addition to storing the meaning of the message (its content), listeners also try to determine the speaker's intentions when delivering the message, calling upon their knowledge of the situation, the participants in the communication, and the goals and purposes. This *interactional* view of meaning stresses the role of inference in comprehension. The listener's interpretation of the message constitutes the creative dimension of the listening process (pp. 221–222).

Richards (1983) proposes a tentative model of the listening process involving the following steps:

1. The type of interactional act or speech event is determined (e.g., a lecture, a speech, a conversation, a debate).
2. Scripts (schemata) relevant to the particular situation are retrieved from long-term memory.
3. The goals of the speaker are inferred through references to the actual situational context as well as to the script(s).
4. A literal meaning is determined for the utterance.
5. An intended meaning is assigned to the message.
6. This information (Stevick's *image*) is retained and acted upon, and the actual form of the original message is deleted (p. 223).

Given this model of listening comprehension, Richards proposes a list of 33 microskills that are needed in listening to conversational discourse, and adds 18 more that are used in academic listening (pp. 228–229). These skills range from very discrete tasks, such as discriminating among individual sounds, recognizing syntactic patterns, and identifying key words to more global tasks, such as extracting main ideas and understanding the relationships among the parts of the discourse. Different listening activities can be devised to help learners develop these various microskills at each level of proficiency. Some specific suggestions for designing listening tasks are given in the next section.

Planning Instruction for the Development of Listening Proficiency

How can teachers determine which types of materials and tasks to use for listening instruction for their students? There are some indications in the recent literature on comprehension that may help. First, most scholars agree that at the lowest proficiency levels, listening materials that present very familiar and/or predictable content and that are relevant to students' interests will be best, given that students will be able to use their knowledge of the world to aid them in comprehension when their linguistic skills are deficient. Videotaped materials can be especially useful at the lower ranges of proficiency because of the visual contextual support they provide, as long as students know that they are not expected to understand every word. As teachers design the tasks to be accomplished with various listening materials, they should keep in mind the normal or natural purposes for which someone might listen to a given text. The tasks need to be geared to such purposes but also to the overall level of competence of the students. One can expect, in general, that students will be able to understand the gist and/or a few main ideas in familiar passages at the lower levels of proficiency, and eventually extract more and more precise information of a detailed nature from a given listening text as their proficiency develops. Beginning and intermediate students will need prelistening activities to help them anticipate and predict the relevant content in the passage. Preliminary research indicates that multiple opportunities to listen for a variety of different purposes will also be helpful in increasing students' understanding (Lund 1991).

Lund (1990) describes a plan for designing listening instruction, based partly on Richards (1983) and partly on the *ACTFL Proficiency Guidelines* for listening. He constructs a taxonomic framework for listening comprised of two basic elements: (1) *listener function*, which relates to what the learner attempts to process from the message and (2) *listening response*, which corresponds to the way in which the listener shows comprehension of the message. Illustration 5.1 presents Lund's taxonomy for teaching second language listening. He suggests that this matrix be used to design instruction so that the full range of competencies in listening is practiced. The sample tasks given for purposes of illustration all relate to listening to an authentic text type: radio advertisements.

The six functions, listed across the top of the taxonomic framework, refer to what the listener is trying to attend to in the message. Each function thus represents a potential goal of listening comprehension. Listener function, in Lund's view, is perhaps the most important consideration in designing instruction in listening, since it provides listeners with a purpose for listening, and thus defines how they need to approach the task. The six functions are described briefly below (Lund 1990, pp. 107–109):

Function \ Response	Identification	Orientation	Main Idea Comprehension	Detail Comprehension	Full Comprehension	Replication
Doing			Pantomime the product			
Choosing			Match ads and pictures		Select best ad	
Transferring	List adjectives		Write magazine ad	List the selling points		
Answering		What kind of text?	What goods are advertized?			
Condensing			Write close-caption text			
Extending			Second ad in campaign			
Duplicating			- - - - - - -			Transcribe the text
Modeling			Create own ad			
Conversing			"Talk back" to the ad			

Illustration 5.1
Lund's Function-Response Matrix for Listening (Advertisement Example)

Source: Lund, Randall J. "A Taxonomy for Teaching Second Language Listening." *Foreign Language Annals* 23, ii (1990), p. 111. Reprinted by permission.

1. *identification:* recognition or discrimination of aspects of the message rather than attention to the overall message content. This category might include identification of words, word categories, phonemic distinctions, morphological distinctions, or semantic cues to meaning.
2. *orientation:* identification of important facts about the text, such as the participants, the situation, the general topic, the tone, the text type, and the like. "Orientation is essentially 'tuning in' to or preparing to process the information" (p. 108). Lund considers this function as especially important for Novice listeners, who need advance organizers and/or script activators to enhance comprehension.
3. *main idea comprehension:* understanding of the higher-order ideas in the listening passage. An example drawn from advertisements is understanding what product is being promoted. Lund, following the

ACTFL Guidelines descriptions, states that this function "typically distinguishes the intermediate listener from the novice" (p. 108). His 1991 study of Novice and Intermediate German students indicates that listeners seem to rely more on top-down (schema-based) understanding than they do when they are reading an equivalent text. Listeners seemed to report more main ideas, but also made more erroneous assumptions that were based on the wrong choice of schema (Lund 1991, p. 200).

4. *detail comprehension:* understanding of more specific information. "The amount of detail one can understand typically distinguishes the advanced listener from the intermediate" (p. 108). In his study with first, second, and third-semester German students, Lund (1991) found corroboration for this assertion for both listening and reading. Memory for details in both modalities improved as course level increased. Understanding of detail was also improved with a second listening of the text.

5. *full comprehension:* understanding of both the main ideas and supportive detail. Lund maintains that this level of comprehension is the goal of instruction in listening proficiency. Although one does not need or want to listen to every message with full comprehension, the ability to do so when desired marks a superior level of listening proficiency.

6. *replication:* ability to reproduce the message in either the same modality (through repetition of the content) or in a different modality (such as transcription or dictation). Lund explains that replication does not imply a higher level of proficiency than full comprehension, but represents a different purpose and thus a different way of attending to the message.

These six listener functions are combined with the nine listening responses (listed vertically on the taxonomy) and a particular text to define listening tasks. The nine responses are derived in part from a list of common task types provided by Richards (1983): *matching or distinguishing, transferring, transcribing, scanning, extending, condensing, answering, and predicting* (p. 235). Lund's list of tasks is described briefly as follows:

1. *doing,* which implies a physical response of some sort, such as in TPR methodology;

2. *choosing,* which involves activities such as putting pictures in order or matching a product to an advertisement;

3. *transferring,* which might involve drawing, tracing a route, filling in a graph, or other kinds of transferring of information from one modality to another;

4. *answering*, such as completing a set of questions asking for specific information in the text;
5. *condensing*, involving such activities as preparing an outline, taking notes, or preparing captions for pictures based on the listening passage;
6. *extending*, which implies going beyond the text to create an ending, complete a partial transcript, change the text, or embellish it in some way;
7. *duplicating*, which provides evidence that the function of replication has been accomplished;
8. *modeling*, which involves imitation of features of the text or of the text as a whole; and
9. *conversing*, implying some kind of interaction with the text, either in a face-to-face conversation or in using interactive video programs.

Lund maintains that growth in listening proficiency can be understood in terms of progressing through these listening functions, learning to do new functions with familiar texts or performing lower-level functions with more difficult texts. This suggests that texts should be used recurrently. "Learners can be led to orient themselves to a text, then to process main ideas, then to fill in details. . . . Texts can be reused over greater time spans or in different levels of instruction" (p. 112).

Like the proficiency guidelines descriptions, Lund's taxonomy is not meant to suggest a linear progression, but a cyclical one. "The proficiency guidelines appear as a linear scale only because they identify the highest function that can be performed on the wide and unselected range of texts that can be expected in the target culture" (Lund 1990, p. 112). Lund adds that many of the microskills that Richards (1983) lists can be integrated into the various cells of his taxonomy.

Some scholars discussing the incorporation of listening tasks into the curricular sequence suggest that it is not the *text* that should be graded, but rather the *task* itself (see for example Byrnes 1985; Joiner 1986; Bacon 1989; Lund, 1990). Various techniques that may be appropriate for learners at different levels of proficiency are suggested in Illustration 5.2. Several of the techniques included at the lower two levels (Novice/Intermediate) include extralinguistic support, such as pictures, graphic materials, or physical activity to help students whose listening skills are relatively weak. At the higher levels of proficiency, tasks require the fuller comprehension of the text, including more detail and an understanding of nuances.

Many of these task types are illustrated in the next sections. Before discussing specific techniques, however, we need to consider the type of materials that might be used in the classroom for building listening skills.

Illustration 5.2

Listening tasks

Suggested Tasks for Building Listening Proficiency

Novice/Intermediate
Prelistening activities
Listening for the gist
Listening with visuals
Graphic fill-ins
Matching descriptions to pictures
Dictation and variations (familiar content, simple structures)
Clue searching (listening for cues to meaning, such as key words, syntactic
    features, actor/action/object, etc.)
Distinguishing registers (formal/informal style)
Kinesics/Physical response
Recursive listening (multiple sequenced tasks)
Inferential listening (drawing inferences not presented overtly in the text)
Paraphrase in native language
Completion of native language summary
Comprehension checks (various formats)
Remembering responses of others

Advanced/Superior
Dictation and variations (may include unfamiliar content, more complex structures)
Completing target language summary
Paraphrasing (target language)
Note taking/outlining
Summarizing (Native language/target language)
Recursive listening (multiple tasks)
Inferential listening (drawing inferences, conclusions not presented overtly in the text)
Identifying sociolinguistic factors
Style shifting
Reaction/analysis activities
Creative elaboration activities

Using Authentic Materials for Listening and Reading Instruction

In Chapter 3, it was recommended that authentic materials be used in instruction whenever possible (see, for example, the discussion relating to Corollary 4, p. 82). As Geddes and White (1978) have noted, this move towards authenticity in language instruction reflects the increased interest in recent years in the communicative functions of language. Yet using *only* unedited, nonpedagogical materials in the classroom would seem to create more problems than it would solve, since materials are often difficult to select, obtain, or sequence for learners at lower proficiency levels. Unmodified authentic discourse is often random in respect to vocabulary, structure, functions, content, situation, and length, making some of it impractical for classroom teachers to integrate successfully into the curriculum on a frequent basis (p. 137). Some scholars have suggested that authentic listening materials may be very frustrating for beginners (Ur 1984; Dunkel 1986) and listening to material that is beyond the learner's comprehension can be anxiety-producing (Meyer 1984; Byrnes 1984; Joiner 1986). Other scholars have advocated the use of authentic materials early in instruction, provided that texts are chosen that can be related to the learners' experience, the text length is not too great, and advance organizers, orientation activities, and schema-based prelistening techniques are used (James 1986; Long 1986; Bacon 1989; Lund 1990, among many others.) Appropriate listening strategies also need to be actively taught, especially to low-proficiency learners. In arguing for the use of authentic texts in listening, Bacon (1989) states that while we are "protecting our students from the frustration of extended speech, . . . we might also be denying them the satisfaction of being exposed to and understanding real speech." She adds that real language must be "intelligible, informative, truthful, relevant, and sociolinguistically appropriate" (p. 545).

The term "authentic material" can have a variety of meanings in the literature on listening and reading comprehension. Rogers and Medley (1988) refer to authentic materials as "language samples, either oral or written, that reflect a naturalness of form and an appropriateness of cultural and situational context that would be found in the language as used by native speakers" (p. 468). They group materials into video, audio, and print media resources, and provide a very useful list of resources in French and Spanish that teachers of these languages would do well to consult. Geddes and White (1978) distinguish between two types of authentic discourse: (1) *unmodified authentic discourse,* which refers to language that occurred originally as a genuine act of communication, and (2) *simulated authentic discourse,* which refers to language produced for pedagogical purposes, but which exhibits features that have a high probability of occurrence in genuine acts of communication (p. 137).

As Geddes and White (1978) have pointed out, the difficulties students face when encountering unmodified authentic speech are well known to most teachers: often students tend to panic when they hear native speakers in conversations, radio broadcasts, films, or other natural contexts. Learners typically try to focus their attention equally on every part of the discourse. Because they cannot possibly attend successfully to everything heard with equal intensity, students often give up, even when it would have been possible for them to get the gist or understand a few of the important details. Teachers can help students overcome these problems by using controlled and guided activities for listening such as those illustrated in the next few pages.

"Teacher talk," or "caretaker speech," is another type of listening material that contributes to the acquisition of the language. According to Krashen, Terrell, Ehrman, and Herzog (1984), it tends to consist of a simplified code, characterized by slower, more careful articulation, the more frequent use of known vocabulary items, and attempts to ensure comprehension via restatements, paraphrases, and nonverbal aids to understanding.

Yet "teacher talk" can sound quite authentic since it is generally not planned or scripted. Rather, it flows naturally as the teacher develops a given theme or topic and often involves interactive exchanges with students. These exchanges, when not contrived or overly structured, have the flavor of a real conversation.

"Teacher talk" might also include the recounting of personal anecdotes relating to the instructor's own experiences in the target culture. (Some sample reading activities based on teacher anecdotes are given later in this chapter.) Native-speaker visitors can also provide comprehensible input, especially if they are aware of the level of listening ability of the students and gear their comments to that level. Students might be asked to prepare questions in advance of the visit and thereby have some control over the conversational topics.

A good way to incorporate simulated authentic discourse into the classroom is through the use of semiscripts (Geddes and White 1978). A semiscript is a set of notes or a simple outline that is provided to native speakers for the purpose of generating a monologue or conversation that sounds authentic. The notes might include specific vocabulary or structures that should be incorporated in the speech sample, or simply indicate the general ideas to be mentioned or discussed. The discourse that is created from the semiscript can be recorded on audio or videotape for use in the classroom.

An example of a semiscript for a videotaped conversation in French is given below, followed by the actual unrehearsed dialogue that resulted. This dialogue was transcribed from the sound track and is completely unedited, which gives it its authentic flavor. The videotape, produced at the University of Illinois, consists of a split-screen telephone conversation in which a student calls to rent a room in response to a want ad.

Semiscript

How to Rent an Apartment (*Comment louer un appartement*)

The caller:

1. Telephone call to Madame Rivière (42.57.18.80 in Paris) to inquire about a want ad for a student room.
2. Ask for particulars—location, amenities, etc.
3. Make an appointment to see the apartment.

The landlady:

1. Small apartment with a kitchenette and shower, not far from métro Saint-Maur.
2. Third floor, phone in the corridor.
3. Free to show apartment tomorrow afternoon, about 2:30.

With this semiscript in hand, the two native speakers making the videotape carried out the following unrehearsed conversation in French:

La Propriétaire:	Allô?
L'Etudiante:	Allô. C'est le 42.57.18.80 à Paris?
La Propriétaire:	Oui, certainement.
L'Etudiante:	Je voudrais parler à Madame Rivière.
La Propriétaire:	Oui, c'est elle-même.
L'Etudiante:	Ah, Madame Rivière, c'est au sujet de la petite annonce.
La Propriétaire:	Oh, oui, oui.

L'Etudiante: Euh, vous avez une chambre d'étudiant, n'est-ce pas?
La Propriétaire: Oui, c'est une chambre d'étudiant, oui.
L'Etudiante: Est-ce que je pourrais avoir des détails?
La Propriétaire: Alors, euh, c'est une pièce indépendante. Vous avez un coin cuisine et puis un coin douche.
L'Etudiante: Ah, est-ce que c'est loin du Quartier Latin?
La Propriétaire: Oh, une demi-heure en métro, par là.
L'Etudiante: Oui, c'est quel métro?
La Propriétaire: Métro Saint-Maur.
L'Etudiante: Oui, je connais. Euh, est-ce que c'est à l'étage?
La Propriétaire: Oui, c'est au deuxième étage.
L'Etudiante: Pas d'ascenseur, bien sûr.
La Propriétaire: Ah non.
L'Etudiante: Ah, c'est dommage. Euh, est-ce que vous avez le téléphone?
La Propriétaire: Euh. Pas dans la chambre, non. Euh, si vous voulez l'usage du téléphone, alors ce serait dans le couloir.
L'Etudiante: Oh, c'est ennuyeux ça.
La Propriétaire: Oh, mais c'est très pratique. C'est tout près de votre chambre. Il y a pas de problèmes et il y a pas grand monde chez moi.
L'Etudiante: Bon, enfin, est-ce que je pourrais venir voir cette chambre?
La Propriétaire: Oui, certainement, quand vous voulez.
L'Etudiante: Je suis libre l'après-midi d'habitude.
La Propriétaire: Bon, ben, ça tombe bien parce que le matin je ne suis pas libre et puis, vous pensiez venir demain?
L'Etudiante: Oui, demain après-midi si vous voulez.
La Propriétaire: Bon, parce que, attendez, demain, euh, j'ai quelqu'un à déjeuner, alors, vers deux heures trente.
L'Etudiante: Oui, vers deux heures trente, ça va.
La Propriétaire: Bon, c'est parfait. Est-ce que je peux avoir votre nom?
L'Etudiante: Oui, c'est Mademoiselle Françoise Coulont.
La Propriétaire: Bien, mademoiselle, et bien, je vous attendrai demain alors.
L'Etudiante: D'accord.
La Propriétaire: Au revoir.
L'Etudiante: Au revoir, à demain.

Landlady: Hello?
Student: Hello. Is this 42-57-18-80 in Paris?
Landlady: Yes, certainly.
Student: I'd like to speak to Madame Rivière.
Landlady: Yes, this is she.
Student: Madame Rivière, I'm calling in reference to the ad in the paper.
Landlady: Oh, yes?
Student: Uh, you have a student room, don't you?
Landlady: Yes, it's a student room, uh-huh.
Student: Could I have some information about it?
Landlady: Well, uh, it's a single room. You have a little kitchenette and a shower.
Student: Oh, is it far from the Latin Quarter?
Landlady: Oh, a half-hour by metro, or thereabout.
Student: Uh huh, which metro stop is it?

Landlady: The Saint-Maur stop.
Student: Oh yes, I know where that is. Uh, is it on an upper floor?
Landlady: Yes, it's on the third floor.
Student: No elevator, of course.
Landlady: Oh no.
Student: Oh, that's too bad. Uh, is there a phone?
Landlady: Uh, not in the room. Uh, if you want to use the phone, then you'd use the one in the hallway.
Student: Oh, that's inconvenient . . .
Landlady: Oh, it's no trouble. It's right close to your room. It's not a bother and there aren't a lot of tenants.
Student: All right, so could I come to see the room?
Landlady: Yes, certainly, when you like.
Student: I'm usually free in the afternoon.
Landlady: Good, well, that'll be good because I'm not free in the morning, and so . . . you were thinking of coming tomorrow?
Student: Yes, tomorrow afternoon, if that's OK.
Landlady: Good, because, wait . . . tomorrow, uh, I have someone coming for lunch, so . . . about 2:30?
Student: Yes, about 2:30, that's good.
Landlady: Good, that's perfect. Could I have your name?
Student: Yes, it's Mademoiselle Françoise Coulont.
Landlady: Fine, mademoiselle, well, I'll look for you tomorrow, then.
Student: OK.
Landlady: Goodbye.
Student: Goodbye. I'll see you tomorrow.

Source: The Random House/University of Illinois Video Program in French 1986, pp. 105–106. Reprinted with permission.

Activities using simulated authentic exchanges such as this are explored in the next section, along with other ideas for teaching listening comprehension.

• • • • • • • • • • • • *Sample Formats for Listening Comprehension*

Listening for the Gist   *Sample 1*   (Novice)

Objective   Students listen to a phone conversation and choose the best general description of its content from four options provided in English.

Text   The phone conversation (pp. 176–78) between a student and a landlord about an apartment advertised in the classified section of the paper.

Student Task   Listen to the following phone conversation and choose the best description of its contents.

> **a.** two friends discussing problems one of them is having with her landlord

        b. a woman calling to ask her landlord about making repairs in her new apartment

        c. a woman inquiring about an apartment she is interested in renting

        d. two friends talking about the new apartment one of them has just rented.

Follow-up   Students discuss their choices and their rationale for making them (i.e., words or expressions they heard that gave them cues to meaning, knowledge of the world, etc.) They then listen to the dialogue a second time to confirm or refine their hypothesis, with teacher guidance.

Sample 2   (Novice)

Objective   Students identify products that are being advertised by matching pictures of the products to the passages heard. (See Lund's Taxonomy p. 171)

Text   Various radio commercials are recorded from a target-language station.

Student Task   Drawings of the products (or pictures, if available) are marked with a letter (A, B, C, etc.) and placed in the front of the classroom. Students listen to the recorded advertisements one at a time. As they listen, they try to identify which product is being described by writing down the appropriate letter of the visual that matches the description.

Recursive Listening   In recursive listening activities, students listen to the same text several times, each time with a different listening purpose. In the following samples, pre-listening activities and organizers are illustrated as well as the specific listening tasks themselves.

Sample 1   (Novice/Intermediate)

Objective   Students listen to a passage that includes announcements on board an airplane interspersed with conversation between two passengers. On the first listening, they attempt to distinguish between the formal register of the announcements and the informal register of conversation. On the second listening they will fill out a form with some pertinent flight information.

Prelistening Activities   The teacher orients the students to the passage by telling them that it takes place on an international flight. She explains that the passage includes both formal and informal speech, and asks the students to listen the first time for differences in tone of voice, speech overlap, and delivery. They are instructed to raise their hands each time they hear the register shift.

Passage   VIASA ¡Donde el tiempo pasa volando![9]

         Capitán: Señores pasajeros, a nombre del comandante, quien les habla, Pedro Lange Churión, y de la tripulación de VIASA, Venezolana Internacional de Aviación, donde el tiempo pasa volando quisiéramos darles la bienvenida al vuelo 804 con destino a Nueva York. Vamos a volar a una altura de 20.000 pies y a una velocidad de 900 KM por hora. Aterrizaremos en el aeropuerto Kennedy a la una de la tarde, hora de Nueva York. Los dejo en manos de la tripulación que estará encantada de atenderles en este viaje.

Azafata: Buenos días. ¿Qué desea tomar?
Viajera: Buenos días. Bueno, este, . . . e . . . ¿Qué tiene?
Azafata: De todo . . . depende . . . bebidas, vino, tragos . . .
Viajera: *¿Qué bebidas* tiene?
Azafata: Usted tiene . . . Coca Cola . . . limón . . . jugo de naranja . . .
Viajera: *Ah, bueno,* deme un jugo de naranja, sin hielo.
Azafata: ¿Sin hielo? Está bien. Y para comer . . . ¿Qué prefiere, pollo o . . . o . . . pescado?
Viajera: Este . . . pollo, por favor.
Azafata: Muy bien. ¿Algo más?
Viajera: Eh . . . ¿Qué periódicos tiene?
Azafata: Tenemos *El . . . Tiempo,* eh . . . el *New York Times . . . El Nacional . . .*
Viajera: *El Tiempo, El Tiempo.*
Azafata: *¡El Tiempo!* Bueno. Muy bien. Ahora mismo se lo traigo, señorita.

[bip . . . bip]

Capitán: Señores pasajeros, en este momento estamos a punto de aterrizar. Favor de abrocharse los cinturones de seguridad y de poner el respaldo . . . el respaldo de su asiento en posición vertical.

Azafata: Por favor, suba la mesita, abroche su cinturón. Gracias.

Second Listening Students fill out the form below as they listen to the passage a second time, this time attending to some important details.

COMPREHENSION EXERCISE

"VIASA ¡Donde el tiempo pasa volando!"

You are about to embark on an adventure in flying. Supply the missing information.

Nombre del piloto: _____ Lange-Churión

Nacionalidad de la aerolínea: _____

Número del vuelo:_____

Destino: _____

Altura: _____ pies; Velocidad: _____ KM/hora

Aeropuerto: _____; Hora de llegada: _____

Una bebida que se ofrece: _____

Una comida que se ofrece: _____

Un periódico que se ofrece: _____

Source: Bacon 1989. Passage and exercise reprinted by permission from "Listening for Real in the Foreign Language Classroom," *Foreign Language Annals,* vol. 22, no. 6, 1989, p. 548.

Sample 2 (Novice/Intermediate)

Objective   Students watch a videotaped telephone conversation between a student and a potential landlord who has offered a room for rent. As they watch the video the first time, they listen for vocabulary related to lodging. On the second viewing, they attempt to summarize the phone call by writing down in English all that they understood. On the third viewing, more detailed information is sought to supplement their recall. The overall objective is (1) to be able to summarize the telephone conversation and (2) have a general idea about how to go about renting a student room in Paris.

Prelistening Activity   Before viewing the video, certain relevant vocabulary is elicited through a cloze passage that summarizes the general theme of the passage. The passage, which serves as a script activator, is given below:

Complétez le passage suivant.

Françoise cherche une chambre. Elle regarde _____

dans le journal. Elle veut une chambre près de l'université

parce qu'elle est _____. Elle veut aussi une

chambre près du _____ parce qu'elle n'aime

pas marcher. Un _____ dans la chambre est

une nécessité parce qu'elle aime appeler ses amis. Elle va voir

un petit studio à 3h15 de _____ aujourd'hui.

Le studio est au cinquième étage et il n'y pas d'ascenseur. Alors

elle doit monter à pied.

Passage   The video segment is the one developed from the semiscript found on pp. 176–78.

First Viewing   Students watch the video and jot down any vocabulary they hear that relates to lodging. The vocabulary is then pooled from class members and put on the board.

Second Viewing   Students write an English-language summary of all they remember from the phone conversation. Students' recollections are then pooled, and the class constructs a general summary of the story.

Third Viewing   Students listen and attempt to supplement their original synopsis of the video with more details. They listen for such things as the phone number, details about the room and the location, and information about the appointment made. These supplementary details will depend, of course, on what students were able to extract from the second viewing.

Follow-Up Tasks   The following activities are designed to offer practice with the vocabulary and language functions presented in the video.

i. Guided writing: Use this hypothetical situation as the subject of a short composition:

Vous venez de recevoir une bourse pour étudier à la Sorbonne l'année prochaine. Un de vos professeurs aux Etats-Unis vous donne le nom et l'adresse d'un Monsieur Huret qui travaille à une agence immobilière à Paris. Cette agence propose des appartements à loyer modéré pour étudiants. Ecrivez une lettre à M. Huret. Précisez la sorte de logement que vous cherchez.

ii. Find a copy of a French newspaper like *Le Matin* and ask students to look through the classified ads for their dream house. If no paper is available the instructor can invent a few ads or have students write ads for their present house or apartment or for a house or apartment they would like to rent.

The following models may be useful:

La Grande Motte. Résidence écartée. 6 pièces, vue sur mer. cuisine ultra-moderne, piscine, jardins, terrain de tennis. 8500f Bureau de vente Ezzine Agence Beausoleil 40611 Montpellier

Vieille Maison avec terrasse, au centre de Paris. 4 pièces lumineuses au 7ème étage. 13 rue Levecq 06801 Meudon

Source: Prelistening and follow-up tasks are found in K. Hagen *The Random House/University of Illinois Video Program for French: Instructor's Guide.* Urbana, IL: University of Illinois, 1986. Reprinted with permission.

Sample 3   (Intermediate)

Objective   Students listen to a brief news report about an official order given to inspect aircraft that transport military personnel. They listen first to extract pertinent vocabulary in order to focus on the topic. The second cycle asks students to listen for the basic story line in the news report. A third and fourth hearing focus on supporting details.

Passage   *La secretaria de transporte de los Estados Unidos, E.D., ordenó una intensa inspección de las compañías de aviación con vuelos de alquiler especialmente esas empresas que rentan sus aviones para vuelos militares. Esta es la cuarta inspección ordenada después del accidente de AeroAir en que murieron doscientos cuarenta y ocho soldados.*

First Listening   The instructor tells students that the news report they will hear deals with flying and asks them to write down some words they hear that deal with this topic.

Second Listening   The instructor probes the students' knowledge of the world to see if they can anticipate the general theme of the article. Students are asked to think of a recent airline disaster and see if the news story talks about it.

Third Listening   Students listen for reactions to the events and write down words associated with these reactions.

Illustration 5.3
Drawing of student room for Novice-level listening activity with visuals (Sample 1)

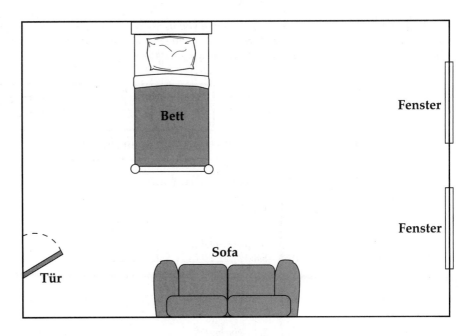

Fourth Listening | More detail is now elicited so that full comprehension of the news report is achieved.

Source: Weissenrieder, Maureen. "Listening to the News in Spanish." *The Modern Language Journal* 71, i (1987): 18–27. Reprinted with permission.

Listening with Visuals | In this kind of activity, students listen to material that corresponds to a visual aid of some kind and either identify a picture being described, identify objects within the picture, follow a map or diagram, or draw a simple sketch.

Sample 1 (Novice)

Objective | Students listen to a passage to identify and draw common objects in a room and show comprehension of expressions of location.

Prelistening Activity | Students activate relevant background knowledge by thinking of vocabulary for objects in their rooms or by identifying common objects in a picture or drawing of a student room.

Passage | A native-speaking exchange student provides a simple sketch of his/her bedroom with most of the furniture missing, but with a few items designated in the sketch and labelled. The student either describes the room on tape or comes to the class as a visitor and provides the description orally.

Student Task | See Illustration 5.3 for a sample sketch (in German). Students complete the sketch as they listen. They may ask the visitor questions for clarification.

Illustration 5.4
Menu (Sample 2)

Gruppenarbeit. Before you listen to the audio texts, look at the menu from the restaurant **Heuändres** in Bad Ditzenbach. Work with your group to answer the questions and complete the tasks.

Gasthaus **HEUÄNDRES** Pension

7341 Bad Dietzenbach • Telefon (07334)5320

Hirnsuppe	3.50
1/2 Hähnchen	
Salate	14.90
Schweinekotelett	
Salate	15.90
Schweinekotelett, gegrillt	
Blumenkohl	
Pommes frites	16.90
Schweinebraten	
Sauerkraut	
Salzkartoffeln	15.90
Rindsbraten	
Reis	
Salate	17.90
Kalbsbraten	
Spätzle	
Salate	16.90
Pfeffersteak	
Reis	
Salate	19.50
Hirschkalbbraten	
Spätzle	
Salate	24.50
Entenviertel	
Blaukraut	
Semmelknödel	18.50

Bedienungsgeld und Mehrwertsteuer sind in den Preisen inbegriffen.

Source: Arendt et al. *Kreise: Erstes Jahr Deutsch im Kontext.* Boston: Heinle & Heinle Publishers, 1992, p.97.

Textarbeit	Text work (*English Translation*)
1. Szene 1: Wer bekommt was? Kreuzen Sie die passende Spalte an.	**1.** Scene 1: Who gets what? Mark the appropriate column.

	Mann	Frau	Kind		Man	Woman	Child
Exportbier				Export Beer			
Wein				Wine			
Cola				Cola			
Suppe				Soup			
Rindsbraten				Roast Beef			
Entenviertel				Duck			
Hähnchen				Chicken			

2. Szene 2: Was bestellt der Mann, was bestellt die Frau? Füllen Sie die Tabelle aus.	**2.** Scene 2: What does the man order, what does the woman order? Fill out the chart.

	Hauptgericht	Beilage	Getränk		Main dish	Side dish	Drink
Frau				Woman			
Mann				Man			

Illustration 5.5
Forms used in German listening activity with visuals (Sample 2)

Source: Arendt et al. 1992, p. 98.

Sample 2 (Novice/Intermediate)

Objective   Students listen to a series of conversations about choosing food from a restaurant menu provided in their textbook. They attempt to understand various aspects of these conversations, including the attitudes of the speakers toward the choice of food, the selections they make, and the prices they pay.

Prelistening   Before listening to the audiotaped conversations, students study the menu in Illustration 5.4 in small groups and answer various questions about the foods. The textbook includes a chart with food groups and students are asked to place the menu items under the appropriate category.

Listening Tasks   Students listen to a series of mini-conversations on audiotape.

1. Students listen to a conversation between two customers discussing the menu. They then answer questions about one of the customer's impressions of the fare.
2. Students listen to two exchanges between a waitress and her customers. They fill out forms, such as the ones in Illustration 5.5, as they listen.

3. Students hear two more conversations between a waitress and her customers to determine what they ate, drank, and paid for the meal. They enter this information onto a form provided in the text.

Source: J. Arendt, C. Baumann, G. Peters, and R. Wakefield. *Kreise: Erstes Jahr Deutsch im Kontext.* Boston: Heinle & Heinle Publishers, 1992, pp. 97–99.

Sample 3 (Intermediate/Advanced)

Objective   Students listen to a weather report presented on an interactive videodisc and attempt to extract enough information to be able to (1) understand the general forecast; (2) distinguish between two weather maps and choose the one that is relevant to the text; and (3) reproduce a simple weather map by moving weather symbols onto the map on the computer screen.

Prelistening   Students review various weather expressions through a series of exercises on the computer screen.

Passage   The following passage is heard as students watch a videotape about preparing for a party. In the scene in which this forecast is heard, two young women are selecting clothing for a party. The radio is on, and the passage represents a portion of the broadcast. For this particular set of activities, students can suppress the dialogue between the two women and listen selectively to the radio program:

> Bonsoir. Sortez vos imperméables ou bien alors restez chez vous car ce weekend sera frisquet et humide. En effet, une vague de pluie traversera la France durant les trois prochains jours, touchant d'abord les régions du Nord-ouest, du Pas-de-Calais et de la Bretagne dans la nuit de vendredi à samedi. Elle atteindra Paris dans la matinée de samedi pour aller ensuite arroser les régions de l'Est jusqu'à Lyons.
>
> Les temperatures baisseront sensiblement par rapport à cette semaine: 10 degrés à Paris demain soir, 8 à Lyons, 6 à Strasbourg, 9 à Lilles. Le Sud sera épargné par cette fraîcheur: il sera 14 à Bordeaux, 16 à Toulouse, 18 à Marseille, le record du jour étant 20 à Ajaccio en Corse.
>
> Sur l'agenda: demain c'est la Sainte Carine, alors bonne fête à toutes les Carines! Le soleil sa lèvera à 6h.39 et se couchera à 7h.29, soit une minute de moins qu'aujourd'hui. Il me reste à vous souhaiter une très bonne soirée à l'écoute de France-Inter. Bonsoir!
>
> Sample 3 Translation:
>
> *Good evening. Get out your umbrellas or else stay at home because this weekend will be chilly and wet. As a matter of fact, a wave of rain will cross France in the next three days, hitting first the northwestern regions, Pas-de-Calais and Brittany between Friday night and Saturday. The rains will reach Paris Saturday morning and then move on to dampen the eastern regions as far as Lyon.*
>
> *Temperatures will be noticeably lower compared to this week: 10 degrees in Paris tomorrow night, 8 in Lyon, 6 in Strasbourg, 9 in Lilles.*

The south will be spared this cold snap: it will be 14 in Bordeaux, 16 in Toulouse, 18 in Marseille, and the day's high will be 20 in Ajaccio in Corsica.

For the datebook: tomorrow is Saint Catherine's day, so happy holiday for all you Catherines! The sun will rise at 6:39 a.m. and will set at 7:29 p.m.—that's one minute earlier than today. All that's left for me to do is to wish you a good evening to all you listeners of France-Inter. Good night!

First Listening   Students choose among multiple-choice options the best synopsis of the weather forecast provided on the screen.

Second Listening   Students see two maps on the computer screen and indicate which map replicates the facts as heard in the weather forecast.

Third Listening   Students use a mouse to move weather symbols onto the map depicted on their screen as they listen to an extended version of the weather report including Friday's and Saturday's forecasts.

Source: Text and ideas for activities excerpted from *Qu'est-ce qu'on attend pour faire la fête!,* an interactive video project of the University of Illinois Language Learning Laboratory, created by Ulric Chung, 1993. Weather report written by Catherine Garnier and Ulric Chung.

Other ways in which visuals or pictures can be used for Novice and Intermediate level listening comprehension include:

1. *Map Activities.* Students are provided with a simple map of a fictitious city, campus, or street with boxes denoting houses, stores, etc. After a prelistening activity in which appropriate vocabulary for place names and prepositions of place have been reviewed, students are given a set of directions. As they listen, they follow the directions by (a) filling in names of places on the map or (b) drawing a pathway on the map according to the directions given.

2. *Ordering or Sequencing Pictures.* Students look at a series of pictures or drawings that are in scrambled sequence. As they listen to a simple set of descriptions of the actions, objects, or people depicted, they indicate the order of the pictures by placing a number next to each one (i.e., 1 next to the picture in the first simple description, 2 next to the second description, and so on). It is best to use descriptions that form continuous discourse. When the pictures, sequenced appropriately, form a simple narrative or dialogue, students hear language in contexts beyond the sentence level and have a better opportunity to develop comprehension skills that will be transferrable to natural settings.

3. *Choosing the Correct Picture from a Description.* In this activity, students are given a set of similar pictures with one or two details differing in each one. For example, the same person can be depicted wearing slightly different clothing in a series of three or

four visuals. As students listen to a passage in which clothing is described, they choose the most appropriate visual to match the information provided.

4. *Drawing Sketches from a Description.* A simple description of objects, people, or actions can be read several times while students attempt to draw what is being described. For the Novice level, the descriptions should involve vocabulary that is very familiar and sentence structure should be quite simple. This same technique can be used in more complex descriptions for the Intermediate or Advanced level, and may also be combined with a production task by having students provide the descriptions from a drawing themselves.

Graphic Fill-Ins   Graphic fill-ins consist of incomplete forms, diagrams, or other graphic material that can be completed as students listen to a passage, either with native-language words or with words or short phrases in the target language. Items might also be circled or underlined to complete the printed form. (See Illustration 5.5 as well as those that follow.)

Sample 1   (Intermediate)

Objective   Students listen to telephone messages and note down the key information so they could then transmit it to a friend.

Directions   Explain that two students, Tom and Kenji, have a telephone-answering machine. When they aren't home it records telephone calls for them.

Instruct students to listen to the messages on the machine. These may be recorded or read by the teacher. Students are asked to characterize the callers by answering questions such as: Are they friends, classmates, parents? What do they call about? Ask students to complete the forms for each message with the important information.

Passages   1. Tom, this is Nancy from your English class. Remember me? I'm calling to find out about this week's assignment. I'm still not feeling well and will probably not be back until Monday. So can you call me at 657-4940 anytime until 11 P.M.? Thanks.

2. I'm Mrs. Henry from the foreign student office returning Kenji Suzuki's call. I'm sorry but we still don't have your transcripts. Sometimes the mail is very slow, so wait a couple of weeks before you fill out another request form. And call me at extension 4745 if you have more questions.

(Additional passages are played in different speech styles and registers, some informal and others more formal.)

Student Task   See Illustration 5.6.

Illustration 5.6

Telephone message form for Intermediate-level graphic fill-in activity (Sample 1)

Listen to the messages on Tom and Kenji's answering machine. Fill out a message slip for each message, using a form such as the one shown. Be sure to note down all the important information on the form for each call. Then decide whether the callers are (1) friends, (2) classmates, (3) parents, or (4) school personnel.

To _____

Date _____ Time _____

WHILE YOU WERE OUT

M _____

of _____

Phone _____

TELEPHONED	PLEASE CALL
CALLED TO SEE YOU	WILL CALL AGAIN
WANTS TO SEE YOU	RUSH

Message _____

_____

_____

_____

_____ Operator

Source: Passages and Illustration 5.6 adapted from J. Tanka and P. Most, *Interactions I: A Listening/Speaking Skills Book.* Random House, 1985. Reprinted by permission of McGraw-Hill.

Sample 2 (Intermediate)

Objective
Students listen to a series of excerpts from letters written by French-speaking penpals. As they listen, students fill in the table given in Illustration 5.7 with biographical details about the letter-writers.

Prelistening
An advance organizer in the form of a one-sentence description of the listening passages and a set of key vocabulary items is given to students, who are told to look at the table they are to fill out in English before they hear the excerpts. The advance organizer, in French, and the graphic fill-in are given in Illustration 5.7.

Passage
Students hear three excerpts from letters with natural-language self-descriptions by two young women and a young man. Three speakers talk about their native countries, describe themselves, and discuss their favorite hobbies and pastimes. One sample passage is given below:

Cher Jean-Pierre,

Notre professeur nous a donné le nom de correspondants français. Nous avons tiré au sort et c'est ton nom que j'ai tiré. Je m'appelle André Delcourt et j'habite à Trois-Rivières dans la province de Québec. Je suis assez grand, blond et musclé. Je

Illustration 5.7
Graphic fill-in
(Sample 2)

Vous allez entendre trois extraits de lettres écrites par des correspondants étrangers. Ecoutez-les et remplissez le tableau ci-dessous. Vous allez entendre deux fois les extraits. Mais d'abord, voici quelques mots utiles.

classe de terminale	*equivalent of senior year in high school*
citoyenne	*citizen*
fana (fanatique)	*fan*
roux	*red-headed*
frisés	*curly*
mouton	*sheep*
tirer au sort	*to draw (a name)*

Prenez quelques secondes pour regarder le tableau suivant.

Maintenant, écoutez le premier extrait, et remplissez le tableau selon ce que vous entendez.

	Native country	Age	Physical description	Hobbies
Mamisoa				
Marie-Louise				
André				

vais fêter mon dix-neuvième anniversaire la semaine prochaine. J'adore les sports. Je fais du hockey sur glace et du ski de fond en hiver et du canoë-kayak en été . . .

(Dear Jean-Pierre,

Our teacher gave us the name of French penpals. We chose names at random and I picked yours. My name is André Delcourt and I live in Trois-Rivières in the Province of Quebec. I'm kind of tall, blond and athletic. I'm going to be nineteen next week. I love sports. I play ice hockey and do cross-country skiing in the winter and canoeing in the summer . . .)

Postlistening
Activity

Students choose a person from the three described and write a letter to that person, describing themselves in a similar manner.

Alternate Activity

If teachers have access to a list of real-life penpals, students can choose to write to one of them instead. An interesting alternative to this listening activity would be based on students' own penpals who have been asked to send a cassette tape describing themselves and their interests. Students could then respond with a cassette of their own in the target language, which they might prepare first in writing and peer-edit with teacher help. This activity adds a written and spoken component to the listening exercise, all of which is potentially rich in cultural information.

Source: Illustration 5.7 and passage are from F. Coulont-Henderson, E. McKee, and A. Omaggio, *Kaléidoscope: Cahier d'exercices oraux et écrits, 2nd. ed.,* New York. Random House, 1988, p. 3–4 (workbook/tapescript). Reprinted by permission of McGraw-Hill.

Comprehension Checks

Teachers have often used comprehension questions of various sorts to test students' understanding of a listening passage. Such questions have often required students to extract somewhat detailed factual information from the passage, regardless of its relative value in enabling the listener to accomplish some communicative purpose. When using comprehension checks such as those described below, teachers should consider (1) the purpose of the listening activity and (2) the type of information that would be needed to accomplish that purpose in an authentic situation. These considerations can then help teachers decide on the quantity and specificity of information required as they design the comprehension task.

A variety of comprehension checks are typically used with listening material, including open-ended questions on the content, true/false questions, multiple-choice alternatives, completions, and summaries. When using comprehension checks, two considerations should be kept in mind to ensure more effective listening strategies on the part of the learners:

1. Consider providing the questions, completions, or other type of comprehension check *before* students hear the passage. This gives students an idea of the passage content, thus serving as an advance organizer and providing a "schema" for comprehension.
2. Have students try to do some of the comprehension exercises *while listening* to the passage rather than after it has been read or played. This helps students focus on relevant features of the discourse as they are being heard rather than requiring them to retrieve a set of facts from memory.

Sample 1 (Novice)
Using Student Compositions

Objective

Students listen for the main ideas and some supporting detail in very simple familiar material produced by other students in composition assignments.

Prelistening Activity | Students have written compositions on very familiar topics for another assignment. Before listening to a sample of these compositions, they review the theme(s) of the compositions briefly.

Directions | Instruct students to take notes (in English or in the target language) on the information they will hear as various compositions are read, noting down as many details as they can.

Student Task | The teacher or the student author of the composition reads the corrected version to classmates. After the first reading, students are asked to share what details they heard with other class members. A second reading may be made for further information if necessary.

Sample 2 (Intermediate)
Completion of an English-Language Summary

Objective | Students listen for the main ideas and some supporting detail in an interview with a French university student about vacations.

Prelistening Activity | In the target language, students talk about their vacation plans or about typical American vacations. They discuss where people typically go, the amount of time and money they spend, and the best vacation spots in their own view or in the view of many Americans. The teacher might begin to point out some of the similarities and differences in the French attitude towards vacations in preparation for the listening passage or he/she may choose instead to allow students to detect these attitudes themselves as part of the comprehension check.

Passage | The listening passage is a recorded interview made in France with a university student. The interview is unrehearsed and unedited, making it an example of unmodified authentic discourse.

Directions | Give students a copy of an incomplete summary of the interview in English, such as the one illustrated below. (The summary could be in French, making the task a listening/writing exercise. This example is a pure listening comprehension check, however, since no production is required in the target language.) Have students complete the summary in their own words, according to the facts in the interview.

Student Task | Complete the passage below in your own words, based on the information in the recorded interview you heard.

1. According to Denis, this year (1983) was an unusual one for French travelers because _____.

2. In theory, French vacationers go to countries such as _____, _____, and _____ because _____.

3. The best vacation spots in France are typically _____ and _____,

although lately there has been more tourism in _____ (etc.)

Source: A. Omaggio, E. McKee, and F. Coulont-Henderson. *Kaléidoscope: Cahier d'exercices oraux et écrits.* Random House, 1984, p. 15. Reprinted with permission of McGraw-Hill.

Listening/Writing Formats

A combination of listening and writing tasks that resembles the real-world skill of note-taking can be used to build comprehension skills at all levels of proficiency. Intergrative formats such as dictations, variations on dictation, and other kinds of gap-filling exercises are especially useful.

One advantage of dictation as an exercise in listening and writing is that it can combine many discrete points of structure and vocabulary in natural language contexts. Teachers may construct their own dictations (for Novice through Advanced levels) or use authentic discourse as the source of the dictated material (Advanced and Superior levels).

Among the listening/writing formats that may be used from the Novice through Superior levels are:

1. *Dictation of Questions in the Target Language.* Students first write down the questions dictated by the teacher. They then write answers in the target language to those questions. Questions should either follow one another in logical sequence or relate to a given theme.
2. *Partial, or Spot, Dictations.* Students fill in gaps on their written copy of a passage.
3. *Dictation of Sentences in Random Order.* All sentences, when re-arranged, form a logical paragraph or conversation. Students first write the dictated material and then rearrange it.
4. *Dictation of Directions for Arriving at a Destination.* Students first write a set of directions dictated by the teacher. They then follow the directions on an accompanying map.
5. *Dictation of a Description.* Students write the dictated material and then, from a set of alternatives, choose the picture that matches the description they have written down.
6. *Full Dictation of a Passage.* Students might be asked to answer comprehension questions on a passage after they have written it down. They might also be asked to circle items of a certain lexical or grammatical category (such as all the verbs in the future tense) to draw their attention to a topic that is being emphasized in a particular lesson.

A note-taking activity that has potential for developing cultural awareness is given below. This activity combines listening, speaking, reading, and writing in an integrative fashion as the students engage in the process of completing its various steps.

Sample (Advanced)

Objective
: Students sharpen their listening skills through a note-taking exercise with a series of associated production tasks in writing and speaking.

Prelistening Activity
: Students are told they will be listening to an interview recorded with an exchange student from the target country. They are asked to fill out a form with the information they hear in the recorded interview, writing in the target language. They are also told that not all of the information requested on the form will be given in the interview. They will therefore have to design appropriate questions to elicit the needed information after they have heard the passage twice.

Text
: The instructor records an interview with an exchange student from the target culture, eliciting information about his or her interests, family life, etc. The instructor then prepares a short form such as the one below. The example is given in English for purposes of illustration, but the form can be in the target language to include writing practice:

Student
: Fill in the information requested on this form as you listen to the interview. You will hear the passage twice. There are some items on your form for which no information is given. After you have filled in all the facts you hear, design appropriate questions to get the rest of the information you need.

Interviewee's name _____

Occupation _____

Home country _____

Town where born _____

Reason for visiting the United States _____

_____

Preferred leisure activities _____

_____

Impressions of this university _____

_____

Similarities noticed between United States and native country _____

_____

_____

Cultural differences noticed _____

_____

_____

Future plans _____

_____

Etc.

Follow-up   If possible, the teacher invites the exchange student to visit the class the next class period and students use their questions to continue the interview.

The suggestions in this chapter for teaching listening comprehension skills, though certainly not exhaustive, represent some of the techniques that are available to teachers who are dealing mostly with students at the Novice, Intermediate, and Advanced levels. It has been stressed that listening comprehension should not be assumed to develop "naturally," without any guidance from the teacher: the processes involved in language comprehension need to be actively taught if students are going to attain optimal levels of proficiency. The same can be said about reading comprehension, discussed next.

Teaching Reading Comprehension

Some Processes and Skills Involved in Reading Comprehension

As we saw in Chapter 4 in the general discussion of comprehension processes, both visual and nonvisual information is involved in comprehension. The reader's preexisting knowledge about the linguistic code as well as his or her knowledge of the world can be as important as the actual words of the text. In fact, it seems that the more nonvisual information the reader possesses, the less visual information is needed (Phillips 1984).

Various models of reading comprehension have been developed in association with first-language reading research, and a few of these were referred to in Chapter 4. A very comprehensive and helpful review of many reading models in both first and second language reading can be found in Barnett (1989). She categorizes these models into three basic types. The first type is comprised of *bottom-up models*, which are essentially "text-driven": the reader begins essentially by trying to decode letters, words, phrases, and sentences and "builds up" comprehension in a somewhat linear fashion from this incoming data. The second type includes *top-down models*, which can be thought of as "reader-driven," where schemata that the reader brings to the text drive comprehension. The third group of models are considered *interactive* in nature. Such models posit an interaction between reader and text: high-level decoding and sampling from the textual features happen simultaneously and in a cyclical fashion. A recent variation on this third type of model in native language reading is Pearson and Tierney's (1984) "composing model" of reading, which "views comprehension as the act of composing a new version of the text for an inner reader" (Barnett 1989, p. 31). Barnett classifies this type of conceptualization as a *reading/writing model,* since it takes into consideration similarities in the reading and writing processes. In many of the native-language reading models described in Barnett's review, it is the reader rather than the text that is primary in the comprehension process.

Swaffar, Arens, and Byrnes (1991) have developed a "procedural model for integrative reading" (pp. 73–91) that synthesizes text and reader-based features. Their model is "procedural" in that it is meant to guide reading behavior rather than predict reader processing. It assumes that there are two parallel sets of interactive top-down and bottom-up processes, with one set relating to the reader and the other relating to the text (p. 74). Thus the message of the text interacts with the perceptions, knowledge background, and skills of the reader. The Swaffar et al. model is designed to deal with the practical issues surrounding second language reading, although it is derived in part from theoretical perspectives in first-language reading.

It is clear that native-language reading models cannot be applied directly to second language reading, especially for adult learners who are already literate in their native language. However, many of the insights from native-language reading research can and have been used to gain an understanding of L2 reading processes. For second language readers, especially in beginning levels, the reading task often becomes a laborious "bottom-up" decoding process, mainly because readers lack knowledge of the code, as well as knowledge of the cultural context of the reading material. Bernhardt (1986) reviews research in second language reading in which bottom-up (text-dependent) models have been applied. She concludes that in general, second language readers become more efficient at gathering information from the text as their proficiency develops (p. 97). This is consistent with Lund's (1991) research on reading in German, reported earlier (see p. 172).

Second language reading research within the framework of top-down or schema-based models was reviewed to some extent in Chapter 4. Bernhardt, in summarizing some of the L2 research done within this framework suggests that comprehension of discourse seems to be influenced more by conceptual factors than by linguistic factors. In a study she conducted with German students reading literary texts, for example, she found that the reader's ability to visualize the passage content and relate to it personally was more important in predicting comprehension than was his or her linguistic competence and conversational proficiency (p. 99). Yet no one model or type of model is sufficient in itself to explain what happens when language learners try to comprehend written texts. Bernhardt argues for an approach that reconciles the strengths of all the different types of models and acknowledges their different insights. "It is clear from all the models that the comprehender is an active participant in the comprehension process who perceives and selects features of text and features of the world at large for processing and for synthesizing" (p. 99).

The importance of considering our students as individuals who approach a text with differing background knowledge, interests, motivations, skills, and strategies becomes clear when one considers the interactive nature of reading. In order to help students become more efficient and successful readers, teachers need to keep such individual factors in mind. They also need to think about both the purposes for which students might be reading and the reading skills, strategies, and processes involved in achieving these purposes.

According to Phillips (1984), reading purposes have often been dichotomized into *reading for information* or *reading for pleasure*. She cautions that the lines between these types of reading are not really rigid, and in fact both objectives can be facets of a single reading assignment. The determination of the purpose(s) for reading a given passage should have implications for the way in which the reading task is designed and comprehension is assessed. For example, when a student is reading for specific information, it makes sense to consider the accuracy with which details are understood as well as the amount of detail reported relating to that information. When students are reading something for pleasure, evidence of comprehension might be assessed differently. In a similar manner, the stages or sequenced steps a reader will go through when approaching a passage will also be a function of the reader's own purposes or objectives. An individual might skim the table of contents of a target-language magazine to get a global view of the type of topics covered, and then read an article of particular interest more intensively.

Phillips (1984) reviews work by Munby (1979) and Grellet (1981) who have analyzed various reader purposes and processes in second language reading.

Munby's (1979) model of reading instruction divides types of reading into two categories, according to purpose: he characterizes reading as being either *intensive* or *extensive*. In *intensive reading*, often for information, students need to understand linguistic as well as semantic detail and pay close attention to the text. Four types of understanding are specified for training in intensive reading: (1) understanding the plain sense, or factual, exact surface meanings in the text, (2) understanding implications, which involves making inferences and being sensitive to emotional tone and figurative language, (3) understanding the relationship of ideas in the reading passage, including intersentential relationships and linkages between paragraphs, and (4) being able to relate the reading material to one's own knowledge and experience (p. 144).

In *extensive reading*, often for pleasure, students need not necessarily comprehend all the details of the text. Rather, speed and skill in getting the gist are the most important criteria for training in this type of reading task. Understanding in a general way the author's intent, getting the main ideas, and reacting to the material personally are also reading goals when reading extensively (Phillips 1984).

Grellet (1981) discusses four main ways that one can read a given text. These are (1) *skimming,* or quickly running one's eyes over the text to get the gist, (2) *scanning,* or quickly searching for some particular piece of information in the text, (3) *extensive reading,* and (4) *intensive reading.* She points out that these different ways to approach reading are not mutually exclusive, but may in fact be done in succession when approaching a given text.

In teaching reading comprehension, we need to design tasks that correspond to all of these purposes and processes in reading. Grellet (1981) proposes that activities designed to check comprehension relate to both the content of the passage and its discourse structure, or organization. Questions or tasks can be designed to clarify the passage's function, its general argumentative organization, its rhetorical structure, the use of cohesive devices, and the understanding of intersentential relationships. To help students understand the *content* of the passage, tasks can relate to understanding the plain facts, the implications, the suppositions, and evaluation of the text (Grellet 1981; Phillips 1984).

Using Authentic Materials

The same rationale for the use of authentic materials relates to reading as well as listening comprehension practice. Reading specialists point out that simplifying texts reduces their natural redundancy, which might actually make them more difficult to read. Authentic written materials should also be presented, if possible, in their original form to allow students to use nonlinguistic cues to interpret meaning (Grellet 1981). Although one needs to select texts for the lowest levels of proficiency that deal with familiar, interesting topics or present cultural information (including realia) in a fairly straightforward fashion, a wide variety of text types can be used, as long as the tasks are geared to the students' capabilities in reading. Some tasks that might be appropriate for different levels of reading proficiency are presented in Illustration 5.8. As in the case of the listening task types presented earlier in the chapter, the difficulty of the task will vary depending on the nature of the text, its level of familiarity and interest, the precision of detail that is necessary in carrying out the task, and the knowledge and competence that the student brings to the reading material. Thus, the lists in Illustration 5.8 should be interpreted as a set of suggestions and not as rigid prescriptions for developing learning activities.

Illustration 5.8
Reading tasks

Suggested Tasks for Building Reading Proficiency

Novice/Intermediate	Advanced/Superior
Anticipation/Prediction activities	Skimming/Scanning
Prereading activities (various)	Comprehension checks (various)
Skimming	Contextual guessing
Gisting	Making inferences
Detecting functions of texts	Extracting specific detail
Scanning	Paraphrasing (target language)
Extracting specific information	Resumé (native or target language)
Contextual guessing	Note-taking/Outlining
Simple cloze (multiple-choice)	Identifying sociolinguistic features
Filling out forms	Understanding idioms
Comprehension checks (various)	Understanding discouse structure
Clue searching	Understanding intentions
Making inferences	Analysis and evaluative activities
Scrambled stories	Creative elaboration
Resumé (native language)	
Passage completion	
Identifying sociolinguistic features	
Identifying discourse structure	
Identifying link words/Referents	

Techniques for Teaching Reading Skills

This section illustrates how various reading comprehension formats can be used with Novice-, Intermediate-, Advanced-, and Superior-level learners. Some activity types are more appropriate to one level of proficiency; many of them, however, can be used at various levels. To adapt a given sample activity format to a particular level of proficiency, a teacher can simply choose an appropriate topic, create task demands that are congruent with reading purposes at that level, and adjust his or her expectations for accuracy in comprehension accordingly.

Any of the activities listed here can be used in isolation, but Phillips (1984) points out that a whole range of practice activities might be used in concert to integrate individual skills so that higher levels of proficiency might be achieved. She has developed a five-stage plan for reading instruction that can be used either in the classroom, in individualized instructional settings, or in computer-adaptive instruction. The five stages she identifies are:

1. *Preteaching/Preparation Stage.* This important first step helps develop skills in anticipation and prediction for the reading of graphic material. Phillips points out that students need to build expectancies for the material that they are about to read. This assertion is supported

by the research reviewed in Chapter 4, where we saw how important advance organizers and contextual cues are in helping readers build and/or retrieve from memory appropriate schemata to help them comprehend. Some activities Phillips recommends for this first stage of reading include:

a. Brainstorming to generate ideas that have a high probability of occurrence in the text
b. Looking at visuals, headlines, titles, charts, or other contextual aids that are provided with the text
c. Predicting or hypothesizing on the basis of the title or first line of a text what significance it might have or what might come next (pp. 289–90).

2. *Skimming/Scanning Stages.* Both of these steps are distinct processes involving, as we saw earlier, getting the gist (skimming) and locating specific information (scanning). Phillips points out that skilled readers do some scanning while attempting to skim a text; however, she feels that practice is needed in each skill for second language students. Some of the practice activities needed for this stage include:

a. Getting the gist of short readings, paragraphs, or other graphic material
b. Identifying topic sentences and main ideas
c. Selecting the best paraphrase from multiple-choice options of the main idea of a text or of the conclusion
d. Matching subtitles with paragraphs
e. Filling in charts or forms with key concepts
f. Creating titles or headlines for passages
g. Making global judgments or reacting in some global fashion to a reading passage (p. 290).

Swaffar (1983) proposes that teachers have students move directly from skimming to scanning with any reading task. First students skim the passage to determine what general category fits the content of the passage (i.e., is it about a problem, people or organizations, events, or ideas?). Then students scan the text more carefully to locate a few of the main ideas relating to this global category.

3. *Decoding/Intensive Reading Stage.* Phillips maintains that this stage is most necessary when students are "learning to read" rather than "reading to learn." Decoding involves guessing from content the meaning of unknown words or phrases and may be needed at the word, intrasentential, intersentential, or discourse level. Readers need to be taught not only how to guess the meaning of content

words, but also how to interpret the force of connectors, determine the relationships among sentences or sentence elements, and the like. Again, the extent of decoding that will go on in this stage will depend on the purpose for reading a given passage. As Phillips states, "In the final analysis, conscious, detailed decoding is not a common goal of reading" (p. 293). Rather, fluency and rapid understanding are the most common objectives in reading, and it is only when comprehension is impeded by unknown words, complex structures, or very unfamiliar concepts that skilled readers resort to decoding.

4. *Comprehension Stage.* In this step, comprehension checks of various sorts are made to determine if students have achieved their reading purpose(s). Phillips feels that reading comprehension exercises should (a) not confound the reading skill with other skills, such as writing, listening, or speaking if they are to be considered pure tests of reading comprehension, and (b) reading comprehension checks should project the reader through several phases of the reading process.

5. *Transferable/Integrating Skills.* In this final stage of teaching reading, Phillips maintains that exercises should be used that help students go beyond the confines of the specific passage to enhance reading skills and effective reading strategies per se. Exercises that encourage contextual guessing, selective reading for main ideas, appropriate dictionary usage, and effective rereading strategies to confirm hypotheses are among those identified as especially helpful in this stage (pp. 294–95).

The next section explores some of the possible formats that address the development of skills for these various stages. Additional samples using these and other task formats can be found in Grellet (1981) and Phillips (1984).

Sample Formats for Reading Comprehension

Anticipation/ Prediction *Sample* (Novice/Intermediate)

Objective Students anticipate the content of personal ads in Spanish and then scan the ads to find information about the various people who wrote them.

Prereading Activity Students are presented with the list below consisting of types of personal information. They mark the items they would expect to find in personal ads:

a. age	**f.** number of credit cards
b. race	**g.** physical description
c. annual income	**h.** astrological sign
d. occupation	**i.** telephone number
e. religion	**j.** marital status

After marking their choices, students look over the text in Illustration 5.9 and try to determine the format of a typical Mexican ad. They then list the types of information they find and match that list to the items they marked above. They then discuss whether or not their expectations were met and what aspects of the ads they did not anticipate.

Text See Illustration 5.9.

Cultural Comment Students read a cultural commentary about Mexican personal ads that explains their typical format and the type of information they might contain. Students can then compare and contrast ads in Mexican and American newspapers and magazines.

Scanning Students then scan the ads in Illustration 5.9 to see if they can find various individuals described, as in the activity below.

Use cognates and other cues to match the advertisers with the descriptions provided in their ads. Fill in the blank in number 6 with the person who fits the extra description.

_____ 1. *Margarita Capdepont*

_____ 2. *M. Esperanza*

_____ 3. *José Alfredo Aguilar*

_____ 4. *Apolonio de la Cruz*

_____ 5. *Octavio Arreola*

_____ 6. _____

a. *wants to share her joys and sorrows with penpals of any age*

b. *a young woman of 17 who wants to trade objects of all kinds*

c. *a 34-year old single man who wants to cultivate a deep relationship with someone kind*

d. *a high-school student (a young girl) who wants penpals from around the world*

e. *a young man of 25 who wants to correspond with women between 16 and 28*

f. *a young man who says he is serious and sentimental and wants to meet a young woman a few years younger than himself.*

Source: Laura Martin, *Entre Líneas,* 2nd ed, Heinle & Heinle, 1991. Illustration 5.9 from page 67. Activity ideas adapted from pages 66–68. Text from Rutas de Parión, no. 599 (6 junio 1983) Editorial Mex-Ameris, S.A.

Skimming/Getting the Gist *Sample 1* (Novice)

Objective Students skim various French documents to identify their function. In this case, the documents are tickets of various kinds.

Text/Task See Illustration 5.10.

Illustration 5.9
Anticipation/Scanning
Activity in Spanish

Club de la Amistad

Por: LEONOR MONTIEL

*¿Te gusta coleccionar postales, llaveros, pósters, etc.
Y también objetos de países lejanos?
Aquí encontrarás los nombres y direcciones de muchos
jóvenes que comparten tu ideal.*

HIDALGO

Apolonio de la Cruz.— 62 B.1, Zimapan, Hgo.— "Tengo 25 años, soy un joven decente, sin vicios ni problemas familiares. Deseo tener correspondencia con damitas de 16 a 28 años con fines amistosos o sentimentales. Prometo contestar y enviar fotografía".

Lucy y amigas.— Argentina No. 102-A, Col. Maestranza 42060, Pachuca, Hgo.— "Somos tres chicas de 14 y 15 años, simpáticas y no mal parecidas. Quisiéramos que nos escribieran chicos de todo el mundo, con fines amistosos o sentimentales. Los esperamos, foto".

M. Esperanza.— Lista de Correos, Progreso de O. Hgo.— "Deseo me escriban chicas y chicos de todo el mundo, para iniciar una linda amistad y poder intercambiar todo tipo de objetos, no importa raza, religión ni nada. Soy una chica estudiante de 17 años".

Yeison Valencia.— Lista de Correos, Villa de Tezontepec, Hgo.— Desea tener correspondencia con chicas del Edo. de Hidalgo con fines amistosos o sentimentales, enviar fotografía. Seriedad".

R.V.T.— Leona Vicario No. 105, Pachuca, Hgo.— "Dama de 48 años, decente, sin hijos, divorciada, de buenos sentimientos. Desea tener correspondencia con caballero de edad apropiada a la suya con fines matrimoniales en corto plazo. Enviar fotografía".

Liliana Jiménez.— Sec. Tollan, Tula de Allende, Hgo.— "Quisiera iniciar una bonita amistad con muchachos y muchachas de todo el mundo, sin importar edad ni nada, podremos hablar de nuestras alegrías y penas e intercambiar todo lo que quieran. Te espero".

Ignacio V.— Estación de Ferrocarriles, Apulco, Hgo.— "Soltero de 42 años, sin vicios, trabajador y responsable. Desea encontrar a damita cariñosa, sincera y hogareña, para formar un hogar estable en corto plazo, e iniciar una vida de felicidad. Foto".

Rosa M. O.— Av. 21 de Marzo, Sur No. 107, Tulancingo, Hgo.— "Odontóloga de 50 años, dulce, cariñosa, de buenas costumbres, sencilla, hogareña y sin problemas. Desea le escriba caballero honesto de cualquier nacionalidad con fines matrimoniales, foto".

CHIAPAS

Margarita Capdepont.— Av. 20 de Nov. No. 36, Palenque, Chis.— "Niña alegre, simpática y de buenos sentimientos, de 15 años, estudiante de secundaria. Quisiera conocer a chicos y chicas de todo el mundo, con fines amistosos, no se arrepentirán".

Ariel Alfaro.— Apdo. Postal No. 365, Tuxtla, Chis.— "Soy un chico Aries de 16 años, estudiante, alegre y simpático. Me gustaría conocer a jóvenes de ambos sexos, de todo el mundo, con fines amistosos y para intercambiar todo lo que quieran".

Tere García.— Lista de Correos, Tuxtla, Chis.— "Deseo me escriban muchachas y muchachos de cualquier lugar del mundo, para intercambiar postales, timbres y fotografías e iniciar una sólida amistad, en la que reine la sencilléz, confianza, etc".

José Alfredo Aguilar.— 2a. Calle Sur Poniente, No. 69, Comitán, Chis.— "Con fines sentimentales deseo conocer a señorita de 18 a 20 años, profesionista, de 1.70 m. de estatura. Soy un caballero profesionista de 23 años. Seriedad y foto".

Octavio Arreola.— 5a. Norte y 2a. Poniente S/N Pijijiapan, Chis.— "Tengo 34 años, soy una persona que se siente muy sola y necesita de gente buena que le quiera, sin pensar en los defectos físicos. Busco amistad sincera, prometo contestarles".

Gabriela Domínguez.— 9a. Pte. Sur No. 543, Tuxtla Gutiérrez, Chis.— "Me gustaría entablar una bonita amistad por correspondencia con jóvenes mexicanos y de todo el mundo, para poder conversar sobre política, literatura, etc. Tengo 16 años".

Illustration 5.10
Matching a text to its
function (Sample 1)

QUELS SONT CES DOCUMENTS? Choose from the descriptions below the one that matches each of the four documents pictured. Place the number of the description next to the letter for each document (A, B, C, or D).

1. A parking ticket with a fine of eight francs.
2. A ticket for full-price admission to a historical site.
3. A permit for parking for a full day in a designated lot.
4. A discount-price ticket to a historic site.
5. A ticket for parking good until 3 P.M.

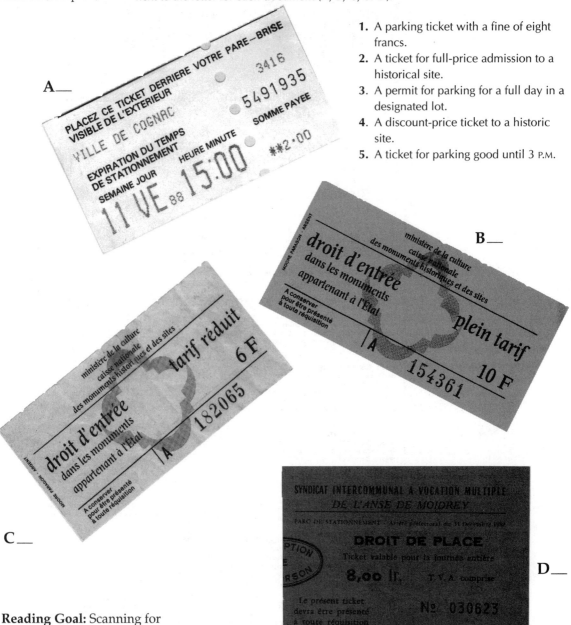

Reading Goal: Scanning for details/Matching text to its function.

Sample 2   (Novice)

Objective   Students match English-language synopses to descriptions of excursions in French to show comprehension of the gist of the text.

Sample 2   (Intermediate)

For intermediate readers, the synopses are in French and students name the excursion, describe and give details about departure/return times, price, day of the week, etc.

Text   See Illustration 5.11.

Student   The Novice level task is given below:

Task   EXCURSIONS EN PROVENCE. Several American students studying in Provence are writing postcards and letters home telling of sights they have seen in the south of France. Match the excerpts from their correspondence to the descriptions in the travel brochure to discover which of the six excursions they took. Place the number next to each excursion in the blank next to the excerpt that matches it.

1. _____ " . . . We spent the whole day touring the ancient cities of the region. It seems so hard to believe that I saw a real Roman arena . . . ."

2. _____ " . . . You'll never believe this, Mom, but I had the best dinner last night—a kind of fish soup that was really delicious!"

3. _____ " . . . and last Thursday we went on this beautiful tour around a nearby mountain, with about six stops along the way to see the sights . . . "

4. _____ " . . . I saw the neatest castle last weekend—built on some cliffs that were kind of a golden color. We saw this rustic little village too . . . ."

Source: Brochure distributed by the Office du Tourisme et Tylène Transports Tourisme, Résidence de Galice D Square Dr. Henri Bianchi 13090 Aix-en-Provence. Illustration by Michel Palmi.

Skimming/Scanning Getting the Main Idea

Sample 1   (Intermediate)

Objective   Students skim and scan descriptions of short stays in the country in France and match them to French-language descriptions of types of trips students want to make.

Text   See Illustration 5.12.

Student Task   SEJOURS A LA CAMPAGNE. Trouvez le séjour qui correspond le mieux aux besoins suivants:

1. _____ Vous voulez rester dans un petit village du terroir limousin et faire des randonnées guidées.

Illustration 5.11
Travel brochure (Sample 2)

EXCURSIONS
TARIFS 87

commentées par chauffeur parlant Français / Anglais.
French and English speaking driver.

1

Tous les mardis :
AVIGNON / LE PONT DU GARD / ARLES

Avignon*, ancienne résidence des papes (Palais Papal, Notre Dame des Doms, le Pont St Bénezet). Le Pont du Gard*, merveille de l'antiquité construit vers l'an 19 avant J.C. Puis l'ancienne capitale romaine d'Arles* : les arènes, le théâtre antique, l'église et le cloître St Trophime.

Départ d'Aix à 8 h
Retour à Aix vers 19 h
PRIX : 180 F / P

*arrêt - visite

2

Tous les mercredis :
LA CAMARGUE / LES BAUX-DE-PROVENCE

Entrée dans la vaste plaine de soleil et de rêve par Arles, porte de la Camargue : L'Etang de

Vaccarès, le Parc Ornithologique de Pont de Gau*, les Saintes-Maries-de-la-Mer*. Continuation de l'excursion vers la chaîne des Alpilles et le site exceptionnel du village des Baux*.

Départ d'Aix à 8 h
Retour à Aix vers 19 h
PRIX : 185 F / P

3

Tous les jeudis :
LES CONTRASTES DE STE VICTOIRE

Circuit périphérique de la montagne Ste Victoire (sites pittoresques, nombreux arrêts).

Départ d'Aix à 11 h
Retour à Aix vers 18 h
PRIX : 160 F / P

Recommandés

4

Tous les samedis :
CASSIS : son port, ses calanques LES CHAINES DE PROVENCE

Merveilleux petit port de pêche, Cassis vous attend*. Visite des calanques en bateau : temps libre pour baignade, shopping, déjeuner.
Continuation de l'excursion vers Gémenos et entrée dans le Massif de la Ste Baume. Par une route sauvage franchissant le Col de l'Espigoulier* (728 m), points de vue sur : le Pic de Bertagne, la chaîne de St Cyr, Marseille, la chaîne de l'Etoile, la Montagne Ste Victoire.

Départ d'Aix à 10 h
Retour à Aix vers 18 h
PRIX : 160 F / P
Visite des calanques INCLUSE.

* arrêt - visite

5

Tous les samedis soirs :
DINER BOUILLABAISSE A CASSIS

Dégustation du plus célèbre des plats Provençaux dans un restaurant du port de Cassis.

Départ d'Aix à 20 h
Retour à Aix vers 0 h 30
PRIX : 250 F / P

Bouillabaisse, dessert, café et vin inclus.

6

Tous les dimanches :
ROUSSILLON/GORDES LE VILLAGE DES BORIES

Après avoir traversé les villages de Rognes et Cadenet bref, arrêt au château de Lourmarin* (visite extérieure), par la combe de Lourmarin et Apt, continuation vers Roussillon*. Ses falaises d'ocre aux nuances variées donnent à ce village et à ses alentours un aspect fort original. L'excursion se poursuivra vers Gordes* dont le château renaissance abrite le Musée Vasarély* et se terminera par la visite du curieux village des Bories* aux constructions rustiques de pierre sèche.

Départ d'Aix à 9 h 30
Retour à Aix vers 18 h
PRIX : 170 F / P

Recommandés

* arrêt - visite

Illustration 5.12   Vacations in the country (Sample 1)

SÉJOUR PÉDESTRE

BELLEGARDE-EN-MARCHE, carte K4.
Séjour pédestre 1 semaine en Haute Marche et Combraille.
Du 7 juillet au 1er septembre, sauf semaine du 15 août.
Randonnées en étoile, à la découverte du pays. Un accompagnateur, M. Guy Couturier, de Bellegarde, vous fera découvrir des chemins presque oubliés dont d'anciennes voies gallo-romaines; accès par train direct Paris-Auzances.
Hébergement : rustique, dans une vieille maison; feu de cheminée, veillées . . .
Prix, par personne, en pension complète :
Du samedi 11 h 30 au samedi 16 h. 800 F
Informations et réservation :
M. Guy Couturier,
23190 Bellegarde-en-Marche,
tél. (55) 67.68.79.

BERSAC-SUR-RIVALIER, carte F3.
Week-end pédestre.
Petites vacances scolaires et week-ends.
Randonnées accompagnées par un jeune berger.
Hébergement : en maison familiale de vacances.
Prix, par personne, en pension complète :
Du vendredi 18 h au dimanche 18 h : 110 F
Journée supplémentaire .... 55 F
Informations et réservation :
Vacances en Limousin,
Bersac-sur-Rivalier,
87370 Saint-Sulpice-Laurière,
tél. (55) 71.43.69.

CUSSAC, carte C5.
Week-end ou 1 semaine à pied au pays des Feuillardiers.
Ouvert toute l'année.
Séjour dans un petit village caractéristique de ce terroir limousin : Fayollas, situé à 2 km du bourg de Cussac. Le propriétaire du gîte se propose de vous guider par les chemins du pays des feuillardiers pour vous en faire découvrir la vie et les traditions.
Hébergement : gîte pour 4 personnes; séjour avec coin cuisine et cheminée; 2 chambres, 1 lit 2 places, 2 lits simples, avec draps et couverture; salle d'eau; wc, chauffage.
Prix, forfait-gîte pour 4 personnes, repas non compris.
1 semaine,
Du samedi 16 h au samedi 10 h : 500 F
Week-end sauf juillet et août,
Du vendredi 18 h au dimanche 18 h : 167 F
Informations et réservation :

SR 23–87. Service de réservation Loisirs-Accueil Creuse, Haute-Vienne en Limousin, n° 87-7904. C.C.I., 16, place Jourdan, 87000 Limoges, tél. (55) 34.70.11.

SAINT-GENIEZ-Ô-MERLE, carte J9.
Week-end « découverte de la Xaintrie ».
Toute l'année sauf juillet et août.
Accueil de groupes de 12 à 32 personnes, avec accompagnement.
A travers la Xaintrie, pays fait de croupes vallonnées, inséré entre les gorges profondes de la Maronne et de la Dordogne, 35 km de sentiers vous feront apprécier cette région si paisible, pleine de charme et de nuances, découvrir ses précieux vestiges d'un passé riche d'histoire, le mur vitrifié de Sermus, l'église du Vieux Bourg, la Croix Percée de Rouzeyrol et les prestigieuses tours et ruines de Merle.
Hébergement : capacité totale 32 personnes; bungalows au lieu-dit « Moulin de Lacombe », gîte d'étape ; repas et petits déjeuners en auberge rurale, un repas gastronomique composé exclusivement de spécialités régionales.
Prix, par personne en pension complète :
Week-end du samedi 8 h au dimanche 20 h .... 230 F
Journée supplémentaire .... 80 F
Informations et réservation :
Mairie de Saint-Geniez-Ô-Merle, service du tourisme,
19220 Saint-Privat, tél. (55) 28.21.86.

SÉJOUR BICYCLETTE

COMPREIGNAC, carte E4.
1 semaine le Haut-Limousin à vélo.
Toute l'année.
Circuit du lac de Saint-Pardoux à la Basse-Marche par les étangs, et les monts de Blond; itinéraire au profil vallonné mais sans difficulté majeure, alternant une journée de transfert d'hébergement et une journée de libre randonnée autour du gîte. Sans accompagnement, bicyclettes et documentation fournies au départ.
Hébergement : en gîtes-chambres d'hôte à la ferme ou au village ; déjeuner libre.
Prix, par personne en demi-pension :
1 semaine, du samedi 18 h au samedi 10 h :
Vélo compris .... 560 F
Sans location de vélo .... 500 F
Informations et réservation :
SR 23-87   Service de réservation.
Loisirs Accueil, Creuse, Haute-Vienne en Limousin, n° 87-3901,
C.C.I., 16, place Jourdan, 87000 Limoges, tél. (55) 34.70.11.

CAMPS, carte l10.
Séjour cyclo 1 semaine.
Toute l'année.
Entre les vallées de la Cère et de la Dordogne, à proximité des ruines de Merle : itinéraires et circuits établis suivant les possibilités de chacun; bicyclettes fournies.
Hébergement : en hôtel-restaurant, 5 chambres ou en camping à quelques pas du plan d'eau.
Prix, en pension complète :
1 semaine, du samedi ou dimanche 18 h, au samedi ou dimanche 18 h :
Hôtel, 2 personnes,
Chambre double .... 750 F
Hôtel, 1 personne...........................1050 F
Camping, 1 personne .... 550 F
Informations et réservation :
M. et Mme Solignac,
le bourg de Camps, 19430 Mercœur,
tél. (55) 28.51.83.

DUN-LE-PALESTEL, carte H2.
Week-end ou 1 semaine, séjour vélo et carriole
Ouvert toute l'année sauf 3e semaine d'octobre.
Séjours composant des promenades autour de Dun-le-Palestel, en vélo et en carriole et la possibilité de pratiquer le tennis et la pêche. Mise à disposition du vélo pendant toute la semaine.
Hébergement : en hôtel 1 étoile, dans le bourg, chambres individuelles ou doubles dans cette maison rustique.
Prix, en pension complète :
1 semaine, du lundi 18 h au dimanche 18 h :
1 personne .... 999 F
2 personnes ....1665 F
Week-end, du vendredi 18 h au dimanche 18 h :
1 personne .... 333 F
2 personnes .... 555 F
Informations et réservation :
SR 23-87   Service de réservation
Loisirs-Accueil, Creuse, Hte-Vienne en Limousin, n° LF 23-8,
C.C.I., 16, place Jourdan, 87000 Limoges, tél. (55) 34.70.11.

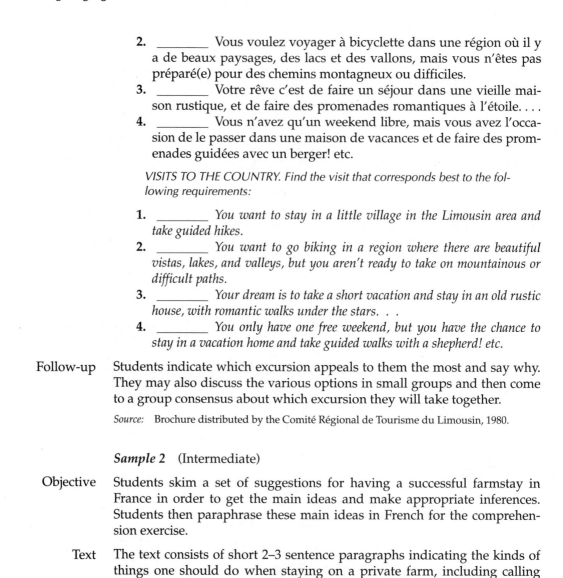

2. _____ Vous voulez voyager à bicyclette dans une région où il y a de beaux paysages, des lacs et des vallons, mais vous n'êtes pas préparé(e) pour des chemins montagneux ou difficiles.

3. _____ Votre rêve c'est de faire un séjour dans une vieille maison rustique, et de faire des promenades romantiques à l'étoile. . . .

4. _____ Vous n'avez qu'un weekend libre, mais vous avez l'occasion de le passer dans une maison de vacances et de faire des promenades guidées avec un berger! etc.

VISITS TO THE COUNTRY. Find the visit that corresponds best to the following requirements:

1. _____ *You want to stay in a little village in the Limousin area and take guided hikes.*

2. _____ *You want to go biking in a region where there are beautiful vistas, lakes, and valleys, but you aren't ready to take on mountainous or difficult paths.*

3. _____ *Your dream is to take a short vacation and stay in an old rustic house, with romantic walks under the stars. . .*

4. _____ *You only have one free weekend, but you have the chance to stay in a vacation home and take guided walks with a shepherd! etc.*

Follow-up   Students indicate which excursion appeals to them the most and say why. They may also discuss the various options in small groups and then come to a group consensus about which excursion they will take together.

Source: Brochure distributed by the Comité Régional de Tourisme du Limousin, 1980.

Sample 2   (Intermediate)

Objective   Students skim a set of suggestions for having a successful farmstay in France in order to get the main ideas and make appropriate inferences. Students then paraphrase these main ideas in French for the comprehension exercise.

Text   The text consists of short 2–3 sentence paragraphs indicating the kinds of things one should do when staying on a private farm, including calling ahead, respecting the schedule and property of the hosts, offering to help with small chores, making your own bed, etc.

Task   Students complete the activity below to show comprehension of the main points of the text.

QUELQUES CONSEILS POUR UN SEJOUR PROFITABLE DANS UNE CHAMBRE D'HOTE EN FRANCE. Lisez le texte suivant qui vous donne de bons conseils pour profiter des vacances à la campagne. Puis choisissez les deux conseils les plus importants pour chaque catégorie ci-dessous et réécrivez-les en utilisant vos propres mots.

Pour choisir la meilleure ferme:

1. _____

2. _____

Pour faire une réservation:

1. _____

2. _____

Pour vous intégrer à la vie de la ferme:

1. _____

2. _____

Pour obtenir le meilleur prix:

1. _____

2. _____

SOME ADVICE FOR A PROFITABLE STAY IN A BED & BREAKFAST IN FRANCE. Read the following text which gives you good advice about how to profit from a farmstay in the country. Then choose the two most important pieces of advice for each of the categories below and write them in your own words in French.

To choose the best farm:

1. _____

2. _____

To make a reservation:

1. _____

2. _____

To integrate into the life of the farm:

1. _____

2. _____

To get the best price:

1. _____

2. _____

Source: Original activity based on a text from M. Smith, *Vacances et Weekends à la ferme*. Paris: Editions Balland, 1988.

Sample 3   (Intermediate)

Objective   Students read for the main ideas in a text that gives advice about what NOT to do on a farmstay in France.

Text   The text is similar to the one in Sample 2, but this time advises travellers about what not to do during a visit to a farm in France. See Illustration 5.13.

Student Task   Students complete the following activity that asks them to match the letter of the paragraph in the text to a paraphrase of the main idea expressed. The example is given in English, but can also be done in French since the ideas are paraphrased.

> *WHAT YOU SHOULD AVOID IF YOU SPEND YOUR VACATION IN A BED AND BREAKFAST. Here are a few pieces of advice for you if you want to stay with farmers during your vacation in France. Find the letter of the paragraph in the text that corresponds to each of the ideas below:*
>
> 1. _____ *It's a bad idea to arrive at a farm without having made a reservation in advance.*
> 2. _____ *Farmers get up very early in the morning. So don't spend the whole evening chatting.*
> 3. _____ *A stay at a farm is not the same thing as a stay in a hotel in town.*
> 4. _____ *There are "false" farms that you should avoid because they are too commercialized.*
> 5. _____ *There are some subjects of discussion that you should avoid if you want to enjoy your stay with your hosts.*
> 6. _____ *It's a good idea to ask permission from your hosts before you go off exploring the property.*

Follow-up   Students complete the following task with the same text above, but this time try to infer how certain problems arose because the visitors did NOT read the advice in the text.

> PROBLEMES DE LOGEMENT. The travellers cited below apparently experienced some problems last summer because they did not read the bed-and-breakfast guidebook. Match the problems cited with the letter corresponding to the paragraph of the text that they *should* have read.
>
> 1. _____ "We really didn't have much luck getting a reservation for a farm vacation last summer. We were in France for the first two weeks of August and we could hardly find a place to stay!"
> 2. _____ "I don't know why the farmer at our last *chambre d'hôte* wouldn't let little Jenny ride on the tractor. I thought that's what farmstays were all about!"

Illustration 5.13
Advice for travellers. Getting the main idea (Sample 3)

A ne pas faire

A **N'attendez pas des** agriculteurs qu'ils vous offrent les mêmes services qu'un hôtel. Vous êtes, avant tout, chez des particuliers qui ne sont en rien des professionnels du tourisme. Ils souhaitent vous accueillir en amis et vous faire partager tous les bienfaits de la campagne.

B **Ne troublez pas** la vie de la ferme. Il faut éviter de marcher dans les cultures, de détériorer les arbres fruitiers, d'effrayer les animaux, de gaspiller les récoltes (par exemple en arrachant une grappe de raisin pour n'en manger qu'un seul grain). Evitez de pincer les fruits pour voir s'ils sont mûrs, d'ouvrir les barrières des prés, sans les refermer derrière vous.

C **N'essayez pas** de vouloir conduire, à tout prix, le tracteur. Dans la plupart des fermes, cela vous sera refusé en raison des problèmes d'assurances et des risques que cela comporte.

D **N'arrivez pas** à l'improviste, sinon vous risquez de trouver les chambres occupées par d'autres personnes.

E **Ne discutez pas** trop politique. C'est un terrain épineux qui risque fort de gâcher vos vacances.

F **Ne retenez pas** trop tard les agriculteurs, le soir à la veillée, car le lendemain matin, pendant que vous sommeillerez tranquillement au fond de votre lit de grand-mère, ils seront depuis longtemps au travail dans les champs ou à l'étable.

G **Ne soyez pas** trop envahissant lors d'un long séjour. Pensez que les agriculteurs, eux aussi, ont besoin de mener leur vie sans être trop dérangés.

H **N'allez pas systématiquement** dans une ferme pendant les jours de fêtes ou durant les mois de juillet et d'août. Sachez que, hors saison ainsi que pendant les jours de semaine, vous profiterez mieux de l'hospitalité des agriculteurs.

I **Ne restez pas** plus d'une journée (pas plus d'une heure si possible) dans ces fermes trop commerciales qui commencent malheureusement à fleurir dans certaines régions de France. Elles portent préjudice aux vrais agriculteurs dont la seule ambition est de vous faire partager et de vous faire découvrir leur vie. Alors, évitez les « fermes restaurants » ou « fermes hôtels » ou autres établissements douteux avec parking, salles pour banquets, grands panneaux publicitaires, bars, dancing, etc. Si vous tombez dans le piège d'une de ces fausses fermes dépourvues de caractère et de simplicité, écrivez-nous pour nous le signaler.

3. _____ "I was sure we could get a room at that last farm without calling ahead. It seemed so out of the way and this is the off-season. . ."

4. _____ "I wonder why no one made the bed this morning. Do you suppose we're supposed to make it ourselves?"

Source Text from M. Smith, *Vacances et Weekends à la ferme*. Paris: Balland, 1988.

Scanning/Extracting Specific Information

Sample 1 (Intermediate)

Objective
: Students scan a set of descriptions of four farms in order to identify which one corresponds to the particulars given in the exercise. Details relate to the kinds of information important in making a decision about choosing lodging.

Text
: See Illustration 5.14.

Student Task
: Students answer the questions below by choosing the letter corresponding to the farm being described.

> **a.** Les Berzellières
> **b.** Les Chaliers
> **c.** La Butte
> **d.** Le Tôt
> **e.** None of the above.

> **1.** _____ Which farm is the most expensive for two people staying one night and having only breakfast?
>
> **2.** _____ Which farm does not offer an evening meal?
>
> **3.** _____ Which farm does not allow dogs?
>
> **4.** _____ Where would you stay if you wanted to see race horses?
>
> **5.** _____ Which farm is closest to Mont-Saint-Michel?
>
> **6.** _____ Which farm is the largest?

Follow-up
: Students in small groups decide which farm appeals to them the most. They may then be asked to compose a letter in French asking for a reservation. Teachers will need to supply students with an appropriate format and formulae for correspondence for this task.

Source: Text from M. Smith, *Vacances et Weekends à la ferme.* Paris: Balland, 1988.

Sample 2 (Novice/Intermediate)

Objective
: Students scan restaurant ads in order to extract important details to complete a given task or set of tasks.

Text
: See Illustration 5.15.

Student Task
: Students complete the comprehension tasks given in the following set of activities in German. Novice level students can complete the activities in English; Intermediate level students can do the comprehension task in German.

Illustration 5.14

Extracting specific information (Sample 1)

LA FERME

Camille et Jeanne vivent dans une maison typique. Ils élèvent un troupeau de vaches laitières sur 15 ha de bocage.

LES DISTRACTIONS

Tennis à 2 km. Piscine à 3 km. L'abbaye d'Hambye n'est pas loin ainsi que Villedieu-les-Poêles. Centre équestre à 4 km et pêche à 3 km.

LES CHAMBRES

Deux chambres à l'étage avec lavabo. Salle d'eau et w.c. communs. Chauffage électrique.

LES REPAS

Petit déjeuner. Repas du soir pris à la table familiale, devant la grande cheminée. Cidre tiré du fût et poulet fermier.

LES PRIX

Environ 94 F la nuit pour deux personnes avec le petit déjeuner. 110 F par jour et par personne en demi-pension.

Adresse
Camille ANDRÉ
« Les Berzellières »,
Route de l'Abbaye,
50410 PERCY
Tél. 33.61.23.75

LA FERME

Une belle propriété de 36 ha où les Duguépéroux élèvent des bovins et des chevaux de course. Ils possèdent aussi un camping à la ferme et un gîte rural.

LES DISTRACTIONS

Le Mont-Saint-Michel est à 10 km. Les ports de Cancale et de Saint-Malo à 35 km. Pêche, chasse et équitation aux alentours.

LES CHAMBRES

Trois chambres dont deux dans un gîte rural, idéal pour une famille. Salle de bains et w.c. communs. Chauffage central.

LES REPAS

Petit déjeuner. Vente de cidre et de calvados fermiers.

LES PRIX

130 F la nuit pour un couple avec le petit déjeuner.

Adresse
Adolphe DUGUÉPÉROUX
« Les Chaliers », Macey
50170 PONTORSON
Tél. 33.60.01.27

Illustration 5.14
Continued

LA FERME

Confortable et accueillante, la maison des Trincot, qui élèvent des bovins sur 20 ha, est à 500 m de la route Avranches-Rennes.

LES DISTRACTIONS

Pêche à proximité. Tennis à 1 km. Piscine et équitation à 16 km. Le Mont-Saint-Michel est à 11 km. Cancale et Saint-Malo à 38 km.

LES CHAMBRES

Deux chambres, chacune avec lavabo. Salle de bains et w.c. communs. Chauffage électrique.

LES REPAS

Petit déjeuner. Repas du soir possible.

LES PRIX

118 F la nuit pour un couple, petit déjeuner compris. 90 F par jour et par personne en demi-pension.

LA FERME

Janine s'occupe d'un élevage de vaches laitières et de jeunes bovins. Elle cultive aussi des carottes. La propriété couvre une vingtaine d'hectares.

LES DISTRACTIONS

La plage est à 2 km : école de voile, club équestre et tennis.

LES CHAMBRES

Cinq chambres avec lavabo aménagées dans les combles. Salles d'eau et w.c. communs. Chauffage électrique. Les chiens ne sont pas acceptés.

LES REPAS

Petit déjeuner. Repas du soir pour dépanner.

LES PRIX

118 F la nuit pour deux personnes, petit déjeuner compris.

Adresse
François TRINCOT
« La Butte », Vessey
50170 PONTORSON
Tél. 33.60.20.32

Adresse
Janine GIRARD
« Le Tôt », Annoville
50660 QUETTREVILLE
Tél. 33.47.50.99

Illustration 5.15 Scanning restaurant ads (Sample 2)

GAZINO + RESTAURANT

Türkische Spezialitäten

Spezialküche mit Koch aus der Türkei.

Edle türkische Landweine mehr als 100 verschiedene Gerichte

Geöffnet von 10.00 – 1.00 Uhr
Fr + Sa + Feiertage bis 3.00 Uhr
Kein Ruhetag, durchgehend warme Küche

Jeden Abend Bauchtanz und Life-Musik
8 München 21, Eisenheimerstraße 61
Tel. 5 70 62 85 u. 5 70 63 18

NEUERÖFFNUNG   **NEUERÖFFNUNG**

— La Toscana —

Pizzeria   Ristorante

Ein Lokal für die ganze Familie

Die Familie Rossi wünscht ihren neuen und alten Gästen
ein herzliches Willkommen.
Wir bieten Ihnen in unserem neuen Lokal
eine gemütliche Atmosphäre.
Täglich neue Spezialitäten zu günstigen Preisen.
Unser kaltes Buffet gibt Ihnen die Möglichkeit, selbst einen feinen
Teller zusammenzustellen zum Preis von DM 7.50.
Pizza ab DM 6.– für 1 Pers., ab DM 10.50 für 2 Pers.,
Fleischgerichte ab DM 11.50.
Große Auswahl italienischer Weine, speziell aus der Toscana.
Jedes Gericht und Getränke auch zum Mitnehmen.
Öffnungszeiten:
11–14.30 Uhr • 17.30 bis 24.00 Uhr. Kein Ruhetag.
Agnes-Bernauer-Str. 21 • München-Laim • ☎ 5 70 41 10

Agnes Bernauer-Stuben

Pächter: Kurt Völkl

Neben unseren bekannt guten bayrischen Spezialitäten haben wir
ab 15. Juni was Neues

Essen vom heißen Stein

Es wird serviert mit pikanten Saucen und franz. Weißbrot

Friedenheimer Straße 27 – 8000 MÜNCHEN 21
Telefon 0 89/57 59 26

Restaurant **SLAWONIEN** im Bürgerbräu

In unserem schönen Biergarten unter alten Kastanien haben Sie für
ein gemütliches Zusammensein viel Platz, ca. 160 Plätze gedeckte
Tische, ca. 100 Plätze für Brotzeitmitbringer.

● Löwenbräu Bierausschank frisch vom Faß.

● Bayrische Brotzeitschmankerl.

● Kroatische/internationale Küche.

LÖWENBRÄU   ● Nebenzimmer für Festlichkeiten.

Die Familie PRKA, seit über einem Jahr Ihre Wirtsleute, freuen sich auf Ihren Besuch.

Agricolastr. 16, 8 München 21, Tel. 0 89/56 49 06

● **Der Treff** ●
für Feinschmecker!

Griechisches
Spezialitäten-Restaurant

ATHEN

Pilsner Urquell

vom Faß
täglich geöffnet
von 12–14.30/
17.30–24, Sa.
17.30–24 Uhr,
durchgehend
warme Küche
**Bei schönem
Wetter
servieren wir
für SIE
auf unserer
Gartenterrasse**
Parkplatz
vor dem
Haus
U 4+5 Westendstr.,
2 Min. zu uns
Westendstr. 223
Nähe
Zulassungsstelle
☎ 57 78 86

Luitpold Hof

Königlich Bayrisch

Wiedereröffnung seit 31. Mai 89

In den alten Räumen des Hahnhofes entstand ein komplett neu eingerichtetes

bayrisches Spezialitäten-Restaurant

Hier ist der Gast noch König.

Das außergewöhnliche Restaurant für jedes Alter.
Zum Ausschank gibt es bei uns alle Kaltenberg Biere – König Ludwig frisch vom Faß.
Gemütliche Atmosphäre!
Preiswerte Menüs zum Mittagstisch.
Werktags Menü I 8,80, Menü II 12,80
Für Familienfeiern stehen Ihnen schöne Nebenräume zur Verfügung.
Tel. Platzreservierungen sind möglich.
Jetzt neu ganztägig geöffnet von 10.00 – 1.00 nachts
Einen angenehmen Aufenthalt wünschen Ihnen die Wirtsleute Familie Märkl
Agnes-Bernauer-Straße 51, 8000 München-Laim **Telefon 0 89/56 20 87**

✦✦✦✦✦✦✦✦✦✦✦✦✦✦✦✦✦✦✦✦✦✦✦

Gaststätte Zwickl

Altaubing, Marzellgasse 1, Telefon 8 71 25 41
● **Gemütliche Atmosphäre**
● **Gutbayrische Küche**
● **Nebenzimmer** geeignet für Familien- und Betriebsfeiern.

**Kleiner, gemütlicher
Biergarten**

Auf Ihren Besuch freuen sich die Wirtsleut!
Familie Gröll

✦✦✦✦✦✦✦✦✦✦✦✦✦✦✦✦✦✦✦✦✦✦✦

1. Students scan the restaurant ads to complete a table giving the name, type of food, hours, phone number, and attractions of each restaurant listed.
2. A list of criteria is given for various situations and students find a restaurant that matches those criteria (for example, one is looking for a place that can accommodate a large group, serves a certain kind of food, or is open at certain hours).

Source: Text and activities from J. Arendt, C. Baumann, G. Peters and R. Wakefield, *Kreise: Erstes Jahr Deutsch im Kontext.* Boston: Heinle & Heinle, 1992, pp. 111–12.

Intensive Reading/Guessing from Context

Sample 1 (Novice/Intermediate/Advanced)

Objective

Students learn to guess at the meaning of unknown words by using contextual cues in the passage.

Student Task

Students read a short passage and underline any words or expressions they do not know. The whole class then considers each unknown word and tries to see how much they can guess about it. For Novice-level readers, the text can be another student's composition, a pedagogically prepared text with recombined material and a few new words, a set of signs or simple labels, etc. For Intermediate and Advanced readers, texts can be taken from authentic sources, such as journalistic literature or short stories.

Reading Strategies

Teachers can help students become better contextual guessers by teaching them to approach unknown words or expressions with specific strategies, such as:

a. Figuring out what part of speech the word must be, using the surrounding context or the morphology as cues
b. Seeing if the word is used elsewhere in the context or if a contrast or analogy is implied that can help derive meaning
c. Using one's knowledge of the world or of the specific context of the reading to deduce possible meanings for the word

Source: Grellet 1981, p. 42.

Sample 2 (Intermediate/Advanced)

Objective

Students guess the meaning of an unknown word that is repeated several times within a paragraph by using contextual guessing strategies.

Student Task

In the travel brochure excerpt below, guess the meaning of the word "gîte" from its context. Explain your rationale for the guess you make.

SÉJOUR PÉDESTRE
CUSSAC, carte C5.
Week-end ou 1 semaine à pied au pays des Feuillardiers.
Ouvert toute l'année
Séjour dans un petit village caractéristique de ce terroir limousin :
Fayollas, situé à 2 km du bourg de Cussac. Le propriétaire du gîte se pro-
pose de vous guider par les chemins du pays des feuillardiers pour vous
en faire découvrir la vie et les traditions.
Hébergement : gîte pour 4 personnes; séjour avec coin cuisine et chem-
inée; 2 chambres, 1 lit 2 places, 2 lits simples, avec draps et couverture;
salle d'eau; wc, chauffage.
Prix, forfait-gîte pour 4 personnes, repas non compris.
1 semaine,
Du samedi 16 h au samedi 10 h : 500 F
Week-end sauf juillet et août,
Du vendredi 18 h au dimanche 18 h : 167 F
Informations et réservation :
SR 23-87. Service de réservation Loisirs-Accueil Creuse, Haute-Vienne
en Limousin, n° 87-7904. C.C.I., 16, place Jourdan, 87000 Limoges, tél.
(55) 34.70.11.

Source: Comité Régional de Tourisme du Limousin, 1980. Technique adapted from Grellet 1981.

Intensive Reading/ Understanding Discourse Structure

Sample   (Intermediate)

Objective   Students show understanding of the main structure of a passage.

Task   Students complete a schematic diagram that shows the main idea, supporting ideas, and details in relationship to one another within the text
they are reading.

Passage   See Illustrations 5.16 and 5.17.

Intensive Reading/ Understanding Link Words and Referents

Sample 1   (Intermediate)

Objective   Students develop skill in understanding the relationship between pronouns and referents in a text.

Student Task   Students read a short anecdote in Spanish. They then are given a few sentences extracted from the reading in which pronouns are used. From a set
of multiple-choice alternatives, they identify the appropriate referent for
the pronouns.

Illustration 5.16
Correctly completed
Intermediate-level
reading activity—
intensive reading/
understanding
discourse structure
(German)

Schematic Activity
Lesen Sie den folgenden Paragraphen und füllen Sie das Diagramm aus!

In Deutschland wächst die Anzahl von Schnellimbißgaststätten. McDonalds's, Wendy's und Kentucky Fried Chicken haben Kettenrestaurants in vielen Städten des Landes. Natürlich mangelt es nicht an traditionelleren Imbißstätten, wo man schnell essen und ein Bier trinken kann. Hier hat man die Wahl unter Imbißstuben, wo man sich hinsetzen kann, dem Stehimbiß einer italienischen Pizzeria oder einem Würstchenstand an der Straßenecke.

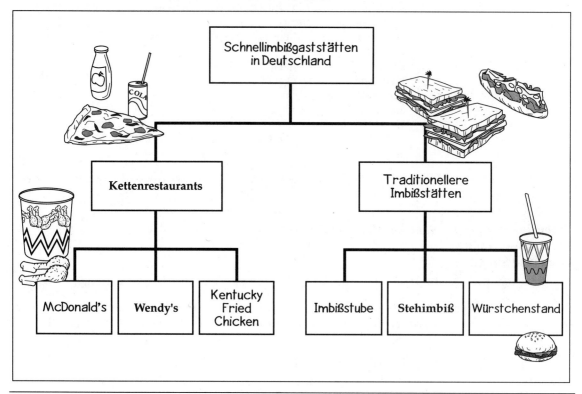

Source: Adapted from *Basic Instructor Training Workshop,* Defense Language Institute

Passage   Les voy a contar lo que nos pasó una vez cuando éramos niños. Estábamos de vacaciones en Santa Cruz, y a mi papá se le ocurrió llevarnos a un restaurante muy elegante. A mi hermanito le sirvieron todos los platos, igual que a los demás, pero él comía muy lentamente. El mesero trató de quitarle el plato, . . . y ¡mi hermanito lo atacó con el tenedor!

Translation:
    I'm going to tell you what happened to us once when we were children. We were on vacation in Santa Cruz, and my father got it into his head to take us to a

Illustration 5.17
Correctly completed
Intermediate-level
reading activity—
intensive reading/
understanding
discourse structure
(English)

Schematic Activity
Read the passage and fill out the following diagram.

There is a growing number of fast-food restaurants in Germany. McDonalds's, Wendy's and Kentucky Fried Chicken have franchises in cities all over the country. Of course, there is no lack of more traditional establishments where you can get a quick bite to eat and a beer to wash it down with. These establishments range from snack bars where you can sit down, to the take-out window of an Italian restaurant selling pizza, to a lunch wagon on the street.

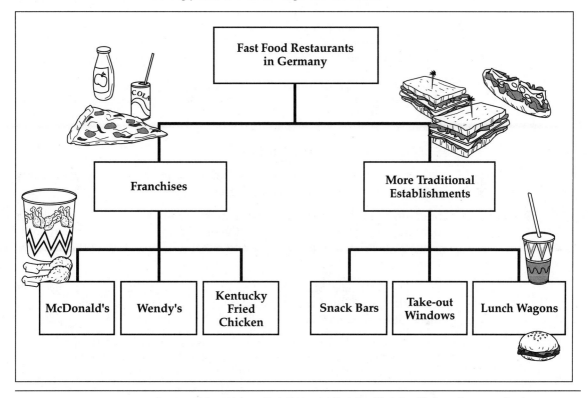

Source: Adapted from *Basic Instructor Training Workshop,* Defense Language Institute

very elegant restaurant. They served all the courses to my little brother, just like the rest of us, but he ate very slowly. The waiter tried to take his plate, . . . and my brother attacked him with his fork!

Task

1. *Les* voy a contar lo que nos pasó una vez cuando éramos niños. *"Les"* refers to...

   a. you (the readers)
   b. the children
   c. the story

2. Estabámos de vacaciones en Santa Cruz, y a mi papá se *le* ocurrió llevarnos a un restaurante muy elegante.
"*le*" refers to . . .

a. the vacation
b. Santa Cruz
c. my father

3. El mesero trató de quitar*le* el plato, . . .
"*le*" refers to . . .

a. the waiter
b. my brother
c. the plate   etc.

Source: Reading passage adapted from *¡Imagínate!*, 2nd ed. by Kenneth Chaistain and Gail Guntermann, Heinle & Heinle, 1991. Idea adapted from Grellet 1981.

Sample 2 (Intermediate/Advanced)

Objective Students learn to recognize and use connectors in narration by substituting synonyms for italicized words in a brief story.

Student Task Students read a passage in which there are temporal expressions in italics that indicate the order of events in the narrative. They then find a synonymous expression in the list below and substitute it for each of the italicized words.

Passage This anecdote has been provided by Gail Guntermann, Arizona State University, and illustrates how a teacher's own story can serve as source material for a personalized and thus "authentic" text.

> . . . *Aquel domingo* mi amiga y yo fuimos en taxi al Panecillo, una colina que queda en el centro de Quito, para desde allí tomar fotos de la ciudad colonial localizada al fondo de dicha colina. *Luego* decidimos bajar a pie, por las escalinatas y sendas de la pendiente. *Después de un rato* nos empezaron a temblar las piernas y nos sentimos un poco débiles. *Mientras* caminábamos por un sitio en construcción, yo no miraba por donde iba, y *de pronto* metí el pie en un agujero, di una vuelta y me caí, oyendo el sonido "¡Crac! ¡Crac! ¡Crac!" *Al principio* pensé que sólo había dislocado el tobillo, pero *mucho más tarde,* en el hospital, me di cuenta de que me había roto tres huesos . . .
>
> Sinónimos posibles: primero, después, enseguida, antes, cuando, a medida que, poco después, en cuanto, tan pronto como, por último, de repente, aquella mañana, entonces, mucho después.
>
> . . . *That Sunday my friend and I went in a taxi to the Panecillo, a hill that is in the center of Quito, to take pictures of the colonial city located at the foot of that hill. Then we decided to climb back down on foot,*

by the stairways and paths of the steep hillside. After a while our legs began to tremble and we felt a little weak. While we were walking through a construction site, I wasn't watching where I was going, and suddenly I stuck my foot in a hole, pivoted around, and fell, hearing the sound of "Crack! Crack! Crack!" At first I thought that I had only dislocated my ankle, but much later, in the hospital, I realized that I had broken three bones . . .

Possible synonyms: first, then, right away, before, when, while, a little later, as soon as, in the end, suddenly, that morning, then, much later.

Source: Anecdote by Gail Guntermann. Idea adapted from Grellet 1981.

Transferable Skills: Teaching Reading Strategies   Hosenfeld, Arnold, Kirchofer, Laciura, and Wilson (1981) suggest a sequence of seven steps to help students develop successful reading strategies when approaching any text.

Diagnosis

1. *Teach students to self-report while reading.* Hosenfeld et al. describe the self-report procedure as one in which students are encouraged to "think aloud" as they try to attach meaning to a second language text. (For an extensive description of this procedure, see Hosenfeld 1979). As students report their thinking processes, the teacher has an opportunity to diagnose reading difficulties and identify specific reading strategies.

2. *Identify students' reading strategies.* Using a checklist of successful reading strategies (such as contextual guessing, the identification of grammatical categories of words, the recognition of cognates, the use of cues from illustrations and glosses, and the like), the teacher records whether a given individual's use of such strategies is satisfactory, unsatisfactory, or nonexistent. This checklist then serves as a diagnostic tool in helping students improve their reading techniques.

Creation of Class Climate

3. *Help students to understand the concept of strategy and to recognize that some strategies are successful, some unsuccessful, and others only moderately successful.* In this step, Hosenfeld et al. suggest that teachers help students compare and contrast the various problem-solving strategies that they are using and identify those strategies that are most successful. One possibility is to ask several students to think aloud as they read a short paragraph. Class members then discuss the strategies used by these students and their effectiveness in understanding the discourse.

Introduction

4. *Help students to identify successful strategies used when reading in their native language.* Beginning with a cloze passage in the native language or with a passage containing nonsense words, students talk about ways in which they can identify the missing words or the

meaning of the nonwords in the passage. Students' guessing strategies can be listed on the board for further discussion.

5. *Help students identify successful strategies for reading text in the second language.* Using a similar type of activity to that described in Step 4, the teacher helps students identify decoding and word-solving strategies in the second language that parallel those they used in their native language.

6. *Provide instruction and practice for specific reading strategies.* Instruction in contextual guessing and other successful reading strategies can be given with a variety of short texts so that students can see their wide applicability across reading tasks. Students can talk about their problem-solving strategies with several types of practice texts: they might work together on a series of cloze passages, use texts with new vocabulary that has been italicized but not glossed, or simply underline any words, expressions, or sentences in a passage that they do not understand and share those problems with other class members. Students who have resolved those problems can explain how they arrived at their conclusions; several students can share problem-solving strategies that worked so that the group can see the variety of techniques available to achieve comprehension.

7. *Repeat Step 2: Identify students' reading strategies.* In this final step in the reading sequence, Hosenfeld et al. suggest that strategies be recorded again on the checklist and matched against those used before the reading instruction sequence began. However, they caution against using this comparison as a basis for assigning a grade in reading, since the interview procedure and the checklist are meant as diagnostic, rather then evaluative, tools for the improvement of reading strategies.

The exercises and teaching suggestions offered in this section are only a few of the many possible reading comprehension and development activities that can be used in a proficiency-oriented approach. For many more ideas and innovative formats for teaching reading in a second language, see (Hosenfeld 1979), Hosenfeld et al. (1981), Grellet (1981), and Phillips (1984).

• • • • • • • • • • • • • ## Summary: A proficiency-oriented Approach to Listening and Reading

In this chapter we have explored various ways to teach more actively the receptive skills of listening and reading. We have seen that both of these skills, though similar in some ways, involve somewhat different processes. In addition, the structures and types of discourse involved in listening and reading are quite different in nature. Comprehension is not a static concept to be assessed in the same fashion at all times; rather, we should think of comprehension in terms of the purpose of the listening or reading activity, the type of text or input that is being processed, and the characteristics of the readers themselves.

The classroom plan for reading instruction provided by Phillips (1984) and summarized in this chapter can be adapted for listening instruction as well (see, for example, Glisan 1988). Swaffer, Arens, and Byrnes (1991) have also developed a pragmatic approach to reading instruction for students whose skills are somewhat more advanced. Teachers using such plans should find that proficiency goals in listening and reading will be reached more easily and more rapidly by second language students, and that the valuable skills students learn in their language classes will transfer to other areas of the curriculum. Such skills should also be of value in learning to speak and write more clearly and coherently—skills that are addressed in the next two chapters.

• • • • • • • • • • • • *Activities for Review and Discussion*

1. As a foreign or second language learner, what difficulties did you experience with listening and reading comprehension? What strategies did you use that you think would be helpful for your students? What strategies did you use that you would not recommend?
2. Imagine that you would like to create a monologue or dialogue on a given theme to provide listening practice for students in your class. You want the text to sound as authentic and unrehearsed as possible. You have access to videotaping facilities and have located several native speakers who are willing to play the roles you designate. Design a semiscript that will provide direction for them as they record the scene.
3. Design a listening activity that includes a visual aid or a graphic of some kind.
4. Using Lund's Function-Response Matrix for Listening on p. 171, describe briefly five or more activities you could do with the same listening material. Choose the listening material from an authentic source, your own textbook materials, or create a passage of your own.
5. Review the five stages of reading that Phillips has identified. Then, using a reading passages from your textbook, supplementary reader, or an authentic source, explain how you would design activities that correspond to each of these reading stages.
6. In your view, what considerations are important in choosing "authentic materials" for either listening or reading comprehension? What potential problems might there be in using certain texts

(for example, negative stereotypes, images or language that might
be offensive, etc.)? What type of cultural lessons would you incorporate when using the authentic texts you chose in the activities
above?

• • • • • • • • • • • • *References*

Arendt, J., C. Baumann, G. Peters, and R. Wakefield. *Kreise: Erstes Jahr Deutsch im Kontext.* Boston: Heinle & Heinle Publishers, 1992.

Bacon, Susan. "Listening for Real in the Foreign Language Classroom," *Foreign Language Annals* 22, vi (1989): 543–51.

Barnett, Marva A. *More than Meets the Eye: Foreign Language Reading.* Language in Education: Theory and Practice, no. 73. CAL/ERIC Series on Languages and Linguistics. Englewood Cliffs, NJ: Prentice Hall, Inc., 1989.

Basic Instructor Training Workshop. (Workshop materials prepared by the Defense Language Institute Foreign Language Center.) Monterey, CA: Defense Language Institute.

Beile, Werner. "Methodische Überlegungen zur Entwicklung der Hörverstehens-fähigkeit." *Zielsprache Deutsch* 2 (1980): 7–15. [Cited in Byrnes, 1984.]

Bernhardt, Elizabeth. "Reading in the Foreign Language." Pp. 93–115 in B. Wing, ed., *Listening, Reading, and Writing: Analysis and Application.* Reports of the Northeast Conference on the Teaching of Foreign Languages. Middlebury, VT: Northeast Conference, 1986.

Bernhardt, Elizabeth and Charles James. "The Teaching and Testing of Comprehension in Foreign Language Learning." Chapter 5 (pp. 65–81) in D. Birckbichler, ed., *Proficiency, Policy and Professionalism in Foreign Language Education.* Report of the Central States Conference on the Teaching of Foreign Languages. Lincolnwood, IL: National Textbook Company, 1987.

Birckbichler, Diane W., ed. *Proficiency, Policy and Professionalism in Foreign Language Education.* Report of the Central States Conference on the Teaching of Foreign Languages. Lincolnwood, IL: National Textbook Company, 1987.

Born, Warren, ed. *The Foreign Language Learner in Today's Classroom Environment.* Reports of the Northeast Conference on the Teaching of Foreign Languages. Middlebury, VT: Northeast Conference, 1979.

Byrnes, Heidi. "The Role of Listening Comprehension: A Theoretical Base." *Foreign Language Annals* 17 (1984): 317–34.

_____. "Teaching toward Proficiency: The Receptive Skills." Pp. 77–107 in Alice C. Omaggio, ed., *Proficiency, Curriculum, Articulation: The Ties that Bind.* Reports of the Northeast Conference on the Teaching of Foreign Languages. Middlebury, VT: Northeast Conference, 1985.

Chung, Ulric. Personal communication, 1992.

Clark, Herbert H. and Eve V. Clark. *Psychology and Language.* New York: Harcourt Brace Jovanovich, 1977.

Coulont-Henderson, Françoise, Elaine McKee, and Alice Omaggio. *Kaléidoscope: Cahier d'exercices oraux et écrits,* 2nd ed. New York: Random House, 1988.

Dunkel, Patricia A. "Developing Listening Fluency in L2: Theoretical Perspectives and Pedagogical Considerations." *The Modern Language Journal* 70, ii (1986): 99–106.

Feyton, Carine M. "The Power of Listening Ability: An Overlooked Dimension in Language Acquisition." *The Modern Language Journal* 75, ii (1991): 173–80.

Geddes, Marion and Ron White. "The Use of Semi-scripted Simulated Authentic Speech in Listening Comprehension." *Audiovisual Language Journal* 16, iii (1978): 137–45.

Glissan, Eileen W. "A Plan for Teaching Listening Comprehension: Adaptation of an Instructional Reading Model." *Foreign Language Annals* 21 (1988): 9–16.

Grellet, Françoise. *Developing Reading Skills.* Cambridge: Cambridge University Press, 1981.

Guntermann, Gail. Personal communication, 1992.

Hagen, Kirk. *The Random House/University of Illinois Video Program for French: Instructor's Guide.* Urbana, IL: University of Illinois, 1986.

Hosenfeld, Carol. "Cindy: A Learner in Today's Foreign Language Classroom." In W. Born, ed., *The Foreign Language Learner in Today's Classroom Environment.* Reports of the Northeast Conference on the Teaching of Foreign Languages. Middlebury, VT: Northeast Conference, 1979.

Hosenfeld, Carol, V. Arnold, J. Kirchofer, J. Laciura, and L. Wilson. "Second Language Reading: A Curricular Sequence for Teaching Reading Strategies." *Foreign Language Annals* 14 (1981): 415–22.

James, Charles, ed. *Foreign Language Proficiency in the Classroom and Beyond.* The ACTFL Foreign Language Education Series. Lincolnwood, IL: National Textbook Company, 1985.

_____. "Listening and Learning: Protocols and Processes." Pp. 38–48 in B. Snyder, ed., *Second Language Acquisition: Preparing for Tomorrow.* Reports of the Central States Conference on the Teaching of Foreign Languages. Lincolnwood, IL: National Textbook Company, 1986.

Joiner, Elizabeth. "Listening in the Foreign Language." Pp. 43–70 in B. Wing, ed., *Listening, Reading, Writing: Analysis and Application.* Reports of the Northeast Conference on the Teaching of Foreign Languages. Middlebury, VT: Northeast Conference, 1986.

Krashen, Stephen D. *Principles and Practice in Second Language Acquisition:* Oxford: Pergamon Press, 1982.

Krashen, Stephen, Tracy Terrell, Madeline Ehrman, and Martha Herzog. "A Theoretical Basis for Teaching the Receptive Skills." *Foreign Language Annals* 17, iv (1984): 261–75.

Long, Donna R. "Listening: What's Really Going on in the Classroom?" Chapter 5 (pp. 28–37) in B. Snyder, ed., *Second Language Acquisition: Preparing for Tomorrow.* Lincolnwood, IL: National Textbook Company, 1986.

Lowe, Pardee, Jr. "The ILR Proficiency Scale as a Synthesizing Research Principle: The View from the Mountain." Pp. 9–53 in C. James, ed., *Foreign Language Proficiency in the Classroom and Beyond.* The ACTFL Foreign Language Education Series. Lincolnwood, IL: National Textbook Company, 1985.

Lund, Randall J. "A Taxonomy for Teaching Second Language Listening." *Foreign Language Annals* 23, ii (1990): 105–15.

_____. "A Comparison of Second Language Listening and Reading Comprehension." *The Modern Language Journal* 75, ii (1991): 196–204.

Mackay, R., B. Barkman, and R. R. Jordan, eds., *Reading in a Second Language: Hypotheses, Organization, and Practice*. Rowley, MA: Newbury House, 1979.

Martin, Laura. *Entre Líneas: A Strategy for Developing Reading Skills, 2nd ed.* Boston: Heinle & Heinle, 1991.

Meyer, Renée. "Listen, my children, and you shall hear..." *Foreign Language Annals* 17, iv (1984): 343–44.

Montiel, Leonor, "Club de la Amistad". *Rutas de Pasión* no. 599 (June 6, 1983). Editorial Mex-Ameris, S.A.

Morley, Joan. *Listening and Language Learning in ESL: Developing Self-Study Activities for Listening Comprehension*. Language in Education: Theory and Practice. CAL/ERIC Series on Languages and Linguistics. Orlando, FL: Harcourt Brace Jovanovich, Inc., 1984.

Munby, John. *Communicative Syllabus Design*. Cambridge: Cambridge University Press, 1978.

_____. "Teaching Intensive Reading Skills," pp. 142–58 in R. Mackay, B. Barkman, and R.R. Jordan, eds., *Reading in a Second Language: Hypotheses, Organization, and Practice*. Rowley, MA: Newbury House, 1979.

Muyskens, Judith, A. Omaggio, C. Chalmers, C. Imberton, and P. Almeras, *Rendez-vous*. New York: Random House, 1982.

Omaggio, Alice C. *Proficiency-Oriented Classroom Testing*. Language in Education: Theory and Practice. CAL/ERIC Series on Languages and Linguistics, no. 53. Washington, DC: Center for Applied Linguistics, 1983.

_____, ed. *Proficiency, Curriculum, Articulation: The Ties that Bind*. Reports of the Northeast Conference on the Teaching of Foreign Languages. Middlebury, VT: Northeast Conference, 1985.

Omaggio, A., E. McKee, and F. Coulont-Henderson. *Kaléidoscope: Cahier d'exercices oraux et écrits*. New York: Random House, 1984.

Pearson, P.D. and R. Tierney, "On Becoming a Thoughtful Reader: Learning to Read like a Writer." In A. Purves and O. Niles, eds., *Becoming a Reader in a Complex Society*. Chicago: Chicago University Press, 1984.

Phillips, June K. "Practical Implications of Recent Research in Reading." *Foreign Language Annals* 17, iv (1984): 285–96.

Purves, A. and O. Niles, eds., *Becoming a Reader in a Complex Society*. Chicago: Chicago University Press, 1984.

Rankin, P.T. "Listening Ability: Its Importance, Measurement, and Development." *Chicago Schools Journal* 12 pp. 177–79, quoted in D. Spearritt, *Listening Comprehension—A Factorial Analysis* (Melbourne: Australian Council for Educational Research, 1962), p. 2. [Cited in Rivers 1975, p. 58.]

Richards, Jack C. "Listening Comprehension: Approach, Design, Procedure." *TESOL Quarterly* 17 (1983): 219–40.

Rivers, Wilga M. *A Practical Guide to the Teaching of French*. Oxford: Oxford University Press, 1975.

Rogers, Carmen V. and Frank W. Medley, Jr. "Language With a Purpose: Using Authentic Materials in the Foreign Language Classroom." *Foreign Language Annals* 21, v (1988): 467–88.

Smith, Michel. *Vacances et week-ends à la ferme*. Paris: Balland, 1988.

Snow, Becky G. and Kyle Perkins. "The Teaching of Listening Comprehension and Communication Activities." *TESOL Quarterly* 13 (1979): 51–63.

Snyder Barbara, ed. *Second Language Acquisition: Preparing for Tomorrow.* Reports of the Central State Conference on the Teaching of Foreign Languages. Lincolnwood, IL: National Textbook Company, 1986.

Stevick, Earl. "Similarities and Differences between Oral and Written Comprehension: An Imagist View." *Foreign Language Annals* 17 (1984): 281–83.

Swaffar, Janet K. *Reading: The Cognitive Process Approach.* Paper presented at the Northeast Regional Conference on Strengthening the Humanities through Foreign Language and Literacy Studies. Philadelphia, PA, 1983. [Cited in Phillips 1984.]

Swaffer, Janet K., Katherine M. Arens, and Heidi Byrnes. *Reading for Meaning: An Integrated Approach to Language Learning.* Englewood Cliffs, NJ: Prentice Hall, 1991.

Tanka, Judy and Paul Most. *Interactions I: A Listening/Speaking Skills Book.* San Francisco: Random House, 1985.

Ur, Penny. *Teaching Listening Comprehension.* Cambridge: Cambridge University Press, 1984.

Weissenrieder, Maureen. "Listening to the News in Spanish." *The Modern Language Journal* 71, i (1987): 18–27.

Wing, Barbara, ed. *Listening, Reading, and Writing: Analysis and Application.* Reports of the Northeast Conference on the Teaching of Foreign Languages. Middlebury VT: Northeast Conference, 1986.

6
Developing Oral Proficiency

In recent years, much of the discussion relating to proficiency-oriented instruction and testing has focused on the development of oral skills. The emphasis on speaking proficiency can be attributed to a variety of factors, many of which are traceable to the widespread popularity of audiolingual methodologies in the 1960s and the communicative competence movement that began in the 1970s. Yet the legacy of our past is not the only impetus for a continued interest in oral proficiency. Many language students consider speaking ability one of their primary goals of study, either because they would derive some personal satisfaction from being able to speak a second language or because they feel it would be useful in pursuing other interests or career goals. It is clear that oral proficiency in a second language can be an important asset for anyone seeking employment in business and industry in the 1990s and the decades ahead.

As we saw in the last chapter, this emphasis on oral proficiency does not and should not mean that other skill areas ought to be neglected in the language curriculum. However, because the ability to function adequately in speaking continues to be an important goal for many second language learners, it is incumbent upon us as language teachers to identify some effective strategies for teaching oral skills in the classroom that will maximize opportunities for the development of useful levels of proficiency.

Our discussion of strategies for teaching the productive skills, whether orally or in writing, begins with an exploration into the nature of *interlanguage* (Selinker 1972)—also called *language-learner language* (Corder 1978)—and how it is thought to develop. The language produced by our students differs in important ways from both child and adult native language use. The first section of this chapter considers several viewpoints of the nature of interlanguage and its development. The second part of the chapter then presents strategies for teaching oral skills, with sample activities illustrating how students can engage in oral production in meaningful and personalized contexts. In the last section of the chapter, ways in which both native speakers and teachers tend to respond to language-learner language are explored, and a range of feedback strategies is suggested to facilitate students' progress toward more precise and coherent language use.

The Nature of Interlanguage

At any given stage of proficiency, the oral and written language competence of non-native speakers, though different from that of native speakers, can be characterized as a coherent system governed by some set of internalized rules. These "rules" should not be confused with the pedagogical rules that one finds in textbooks; many times the learners' rules differ from those that they may have been taught. Often learners are unable to explicitly state the rules by which they are operating. (The same can be said of many native speakers, who know how to use their first language expertly but are unable to explicitly state the rules that govern their language use.)

Seliger (1988) reviews various ways in which non-native rule systems have been described in the literature. Corder (1967) refers to language-learner language as "transitional competence," implying that learner systems are constantly changing. Nemser (1971) refers to the developing grammar as an "approximative system," focusing on the incompleteness of the system as it moves progressively along a kind of continuum between the learner's native language and native competence in the second language. Selinker (1972) characterizes the learner's developing system as "interlanguage," describing it as an intermediate system located somewhere between the learner's native language and the target language, but governed by its own unique and coherent internalized rule system that rarely becomes totally congruent with the system of the second language. Selinker refers to this incongruence between the interlanguage and the target language as "fossilization." He suggests that certain items, rules, or subsystems that are not fully congruent with the target language can become a permanent part of the learner's interlanguage, resistant to further instruction or explanation (Selinker 1974, pp. 118-19).

Corder (1978) and Selinker both think of interlanguage as a continuum, but Corder suggests that there may be various types of continua that can explain how language-learner language develops. If one adopts the continuum suggested by Selinker, for example, one would conceive of the learner progressively adjusting the native language system so that it gradually approximates the system of the target language. Such a view of interlanguage can be called a *progressive restructuring,* and the continuum implied can be called a *restructuring continuum* (Corder 1978, p. 75). This type of conceptualization seems to account for the fact that interlanguage, particularly in its earliest developmental stages, frequently manifests various characteristics of the learner's native language. However, not all learners show consistent evidence of transfer from the native language, and certainly not to the same degree across learners. Corder believes that because this is true, and because the interlanguage is typically simpler, overall, than adult native speech in the language being acquired, one could conceptualize a second type of continuum, called a *recreational*, or *developmental continuum*. Like child language, the system becomes more complex as the language is acquired. However, the child begins with no knowledge of the language, whereas the adult second language learner begins with cognitive structures already intact, in conjunction with comprehensive knowledge of a first language system (Corder 1978, p. 75).

Corder suggests that both continua might actually work in consort and are not necessarily mutually exclusive. It is possible, for example, that learners might follow a restructuring continuum (i.e., going from the native language to the target language) when acquiring the phonological system, but progress along a developmental continuum (i.e., moving from simple to more complex forms and structures) when learning the syntactic system. A second possibility is that learners in a natural setting follow a developmental continuum, while students in formal classroom settings progress along a restructuring continuum. This point of view is compatible, to some extent, with Krashen's (1982) acquisition/learning distinction (see Chapter 2). A third possibility is that both restructuring and developmental processes are operating together in language learning, and that there is a great deal of variability in the way the interlanguages of different individuals develop (Corder 1978, p. 79).

Ellis (1985) emphasizes the notion of variability in his conceptualization of interlanguage and maintains that language learners have a number of competing rules at any given stage of development, with one rule prevailing in one context and another in a different context. In his view, a learner's "competence" is therefore not homogeneous, but heterogenous. Basing his theory partly on Tarone's (1983) work, he suggests that learners have several "styles" from which they select in order to carry out specific tasks (p. 75), and that therefore their performance is quite variable. Illustration 6.1 depicts the sources of variability that can affect linguistic performance, according to Ellis' model of competence.

In Ellis' model of interlanguage competence, variability can be *systematic* or *non-systematic*. *Systematic* variability, in turn, can be subdivided into *individual* variability (due to learner characteristics) or *contextual* variability (due either to the linguistic context or the situational context in which the language is being used) (p. 75). *Non-systematic* variability, on the other hand, can be further subdivided into *free variability* (where competing forms or rules operate in free variation with one another) or *performance variability* (due to the learner's emotional or physical condition, which can provoke slips or hesitations) (pp. 75-76). Although all language use,

Illustration 6.1

Types of variability in interlanguage.

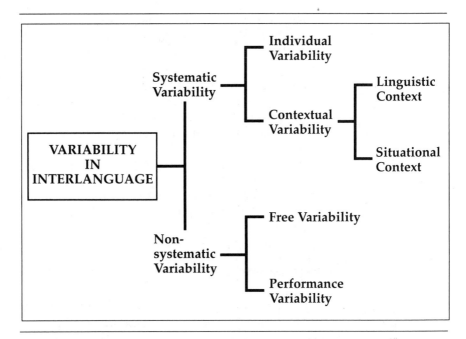

Source: Ellis, Rod. *Understanding Second Language Acquisition.* Oxford: Oxford University Press, 1985, p. 76. Reprinted by permission of Oxford University Press.

including that of native speakers, is thought to be variable, Ellis maintains that language-learner language is even more variable (p. 81).

One source of *contextual variability* is the type of task the learner is engaged in doing. In Chapter 2, we saw that Tarone (1983) suggests that tasks that demand very little active attention, such as "natural" conversation among proficient speakers, elicit the *vernacular style,* while tasks that are heavily monitored, such as making grammaticality judgments or filling in blanks with grammatical forms, elicit a very *careful style* (Tarone 1983, p. 152). This task effect may account for the fact that second language students often perform differently while doing a focused activity than when using the language in conversation or free composition.

A source of variability attributable to *linguistic context* is the level of complexity of the language the learner is attempting to use (Ellis 1985, p. 83). Learners may vary in the forms they use in simple constructions vs. those that they use when sentence structure is more complex. This might, in part, explain why learners' language seems to "break down" when they attempt to communicate more complex ideas in the "probe" phase of oral interviews, or when they attempt to express complex ideas in compositions that require a higher level of proficiency than they currently can control. The type of linguistic features present in language-learner language may be a function of both the nature of the task itself and task difficulty (Ellis 1985). Thus a variable competence view of interlanguage would predict that learners engaged in simple tasks and attending to form would perform most accurately. Indeed, Ellis (1982) found that second language learners in a study he conducted performed most accurately on tasks that were cognitively simple (involving concrete situations in the present time frame) and attributed this to the fact that there was more opportunity for learners to attend to form in such situations (Ellis 1985, p. 89).

Perhaps one of the most interesting hypotheses that Ellis proposes is the idea that "careful style" tasks can have an impact on the development of more accurate usage over time in the "vernacular style." The vernacular style is thought to be the most stable style, since it contains the forms of the interlanguage that the learner has most fully automatized. The careful style, on the other hand, has more interlanguage forms than the vernacular style, since it includes those forms that have not yet become fully automatic and that occur in free variation with more automatic forms. Ellis, following Terone 1983 suggests that new forms that are initially part of learners' careful style could eventually spread to their vernacular style. "Development does not consist of sudden jumps, but of the gradual extension of regularities from formal to progressively informal styles on the one hand, and from simple to increasingly complex linguistic contexts on the other" (p. 94). He adds that, although it might be said that one can communicate effectively with very little grammatical accuracy, learners who would like to conform more completely to sociolinguistic norms of the target culture might benefit from practicing careful style forms in an effort to make accurate usage more automatic. "Whereas vernacular forms are instantaneously available, careful forms are not. However, as the careful forms are used, they are practiced with the result that they become more automatic, require less attention, and so are available for use in interlanguage style nearer the vernacular end of the continuum" (p. 95). As second language proficiency develops, competing forms in the interlanguage that have been used in free variation are sorted out as the learner figures out what forms are used in what contexts. Any forms that are redundant are eventually eliminated. This "mapping" of forms to functions is a slow process involving a constant reorganization of the interlanguage system (pp. 95-96).

One might hypothesize on the basis of these observations that a variety of tasks should be used in the second language classroom, ranging from careful style activities where learners practice using language in planned discourse that is cognitively simple to vernacular style activities, where more complex communicative tasks involving less monitoring are undertaken. A balance of practice with tasks drawn from the whole continuum of styles might lead to more proficient performance in terms of accuracy and fluency.

In the next section, ways to plan oral practice activities so that a balance such as that suggested above might be achieved are described and illustrated. The section begins with a framework for planning instruction that is derived from the oral proficiency descriptions provided by the *ACTFL Proficiency Guidelines.*

Planning Instruction for the Development of Oral Proficiency

Appropriate teaching strategies are likely to vary, depending on students' current level(s) of proficiency and the level envisioned as an instructional goal. In order to provide optimal speaking practice in a given class, we need to determine, at least in some global fashion, what range of levels is likely to be attainable in the course of instruction. The term *range* is used here because it is unrealistic to expect that all students in a given course will be at the same level of oral proficiency at the end of instruction. Determining an expected range of proficiency upon completion of a course might best be accomplished experientially through a preliminary assessment of students' oral proficiency at the beginning and end of the course using the interview procedure described in Chapter 9. After several semesters of testing, an expected range of proficiency should be relatively easy to identify. One can then begin to reorient instruction toward carefully defined goals, derived in part from appropriate level descriptions. Classroom activities can be selected to correspond to current levels of proficiency and to those in the next highest range so that opportunities for progress along the scale can be maximized.

What types of goals are appropriate for students at the Novice, Intermediate, and Advanced levels of speaking proficiency? What kinds of classroom activities are optimal at each of these levels? A variety of curricular plans for instruction in oral skills could be derived from an examination of the *ACTFL Proficiency Guidelines.* As was pointed out in earlier chapters, it is important to bear in mind that the guidelines are *not* a set of goal statements in and of themselves, but are rather descriptions of typical competencies (as well as patterns of weakness) that language users are expected to have at each of the levels of proficiency. As Heilenman and Kaplan (1985), Higgs (1986), and Galloway (1987) have observed, the guidelines are meant to be evaluative in nature and should not be used directly and verbatim as course objectives.

The proficiency descriptions can be useful, however, in the goal-refinement process when planning curricula. Each group of individuals responsible for designing a local curriculum will need to consider what the guidelines imply for their own situation. Although different curricular plans might be roughly similar, no two groups of classroom teachers or curriculum planners are likely to come up with identical goal statements,

Level: Novice
Skill: Speaking

Content
Common topics depicting aspects of daily life such as . . .
 home, work or school environment
 simple facts about self or others
 time of day, dates, weather, seasons
 greetings, leave-takings

Context
Highly predictable everyday situations

Functions
Can use limited memorized material in simple statements or questions such as in . . .
 naming/identifying objects, people, places
 using formulaic expressions

Techniques
Personalized questions
Personalized completions
Personalized agree/disagree
Sentence builders
Word associations
Group puzzles
Surveys and polls
Conversation cards
Forced choice
Slash sentences
Directed dialogue
Logical conclusions

Accuracy
Generally intelligible when using memorized or highly familiar material. May be difficult to understand, even for speakers used to dealing with non-native speakers.

Discourse Structure
One- or two-word answers
Lists or enumerations

Illustration 6.2
Novice-Level Curricular Planning Guide for Speaking

Source: Adapted from DLI Task Force on Curriculum Policy and Planning, June, 1984.

especially since local conditions and the interests and needs of individual groups of students differ.

Illustrations 6.2 through 6.5 represent one type of planning guide for oral proficiency that has been derived from an examination of the *ACTFL Proficiency Guidelines*. This particular planning guide is an adaptation of one that was developed at the Defense Language Institute in Monterey, California during the summer of 1984. The original plan was conceptualized by a team of experts from both the government and academic communities and was designed for military personnel who are engaged in language study at DLI.[1] The plan presented here has been adapted to an academic context and updated to include statements about content, context, function, accuracy, and discourse structure that are based on the most recent oral proficiency tester manual (Buck, Byrnes, and Thompson 1989). A list of teaching strategies that might be appropriate for students within a given level or range of levels of proficiency is also included in the guide.

Level: Intermediate
Skill: Speaking

Content

Everyday survival topics such as . . .
Personal/biographical information
Restaurant/foods
Asking/giving directions
Activities/hobbies
Transportation
Talking on phone
Lodging/living quarters
Money matters
Health matters
Post office
Numbers 1–1000
Customs
Shopping/making purchases

Courtesy/social requirements such as. . .
Greetings/introductions
Making appointments
Making meeting arrangements
Accepting/refusing invitations
Polite, formulaic expressions

Context

Informal situations
Transactional settings of everyday life

Functions

Can create with the language
Can make up own sentences not limited to very familiar or memorized material
Can participate in short conversations
Can ask and answer questions
Can get into, through, and out of a simple survival situation
Can transfer current learned material to new situations/contexts

Techniques

Personalized questions
Personalized completions
Personalized true/false
Sentence builders
Dialogue/story adaptation
Create a story with visuals
Chain stories
Describing objects/processes
Surveys and polls
Conversation cards
Paired interviews
Social interaction activities
Group consensus/problem solving
Story telling
Forced choice
Role plays
Slash sentences
Elaboration
Giving definitions
Guided description/narration
Asking related questions
Logical questions

Accuracy

Comprehensible to native speakers used to dealing with target-language learners
Some accuracy in basic structures
Minimal sociolinguistic knowledge in evidence
Very basic vocabulary related to content areas listed

Discourse Structure

Uses short sentences
Simple question forms
Formulaic expressions
Strings of sentences

Illustration 6.3
Intermediate-Level
Curricular Planning
Guide for Speaking

Source: Adapted from DLI Task Force on Curriculum Policy and Planning, June, 1984.

Level: Advanced
Skill: Speaking

Content

Content widens to include numerous topics, generally of a factual nature, such as. . .

Current events
Press, media
Politics
Economics
Education
Leisure, travel, vacations
Cultural and moral issues
History
Customs and mores

Context

Most informal settings
Some formal situations

Functions

Can narrate and describe in present, past, future time
Can fully participate in casual conversations
Can give instructions, simple reports
Can deal with complications in such situations as one might encounter in living in the target culture
   Complaints, emergency situations, talking one's way out of trouble, etc.
Can make simple comparisons

Techniques

Personalized questions
Personalized true/false
Personalized completions
Dialogue/story adaptation
Chain stories
Group picture stories
Descriptions of objects/processes
Surveys/polls
Conversation cards
Paired interviews
Guided narrations
Forced choice
Debates
Group consensus/problem
  solving
Role plays
Elaboration
Giving definitions
Guided descriptions
Reactions to opinion questions
Situations with complications

Accuracy

Comprehensible to native speakers not used to dealing with foreigners
Sometimes miscommunicates, though good general vocabulary, with some circumlocution
Accent intelligible
Elementary grammar/syntax quite accurate
Patterns of error in more complex structures

Discourse Structure

Able to speak in paragraphs rather than in short sentences

Illustration 6.4
Advanced-Level
Curricular Planning
Guide for Speaking

Source: Adapted from DLI Task Force on Curriculum Policy and Planning, June, 1984.

Level: Superior
Skill: Speaking

Content

Can handle most practical, social, abstract, and professional topics
Special fields of competence
Particular fields of interest

Context

Most formal and informal settings and situations

Functions

Can hypothesize
Can support opinions, persuade
Can describe in detail
Can narrate in detail with precision

Techniques

Agree/disagree
Personalized questions
Surveys/polls
Persuasion
Group consensus/problem solving
Elaboration
Paraphrasing/creative language use
Sociolinguistic competence-build-
   ing activities—functional/notional
   practice
Description of objects and process-
   es (detailed)
Paired interviews
Debates
Levels of speech (style shifting)
Role plays with complications
Simultaneous interpretation
Vocabulary extension (brainstorm-
   ing, vocabulary building in cate-
   gories to develop precision,
   synonyms and near-synonyms,
   study of idioms)

Accuracy

All the language forms are controlled relatively well
Occasional (unpatterned) errors in
common structures
Some patterns of error in more
complex structures
Errors rarely disturb the native
speaker or interfere with comprehension
Vocabulary broad, though not
always idiomatic or precise

Discourse Structure

Extended discourse

Illustration 6.5
Superior-Level Curricular
Planning Guide for
Speaking

Source: Adapted from DLI Task Force on Curriculum Policy and Planning, June, 1984.

This planning guide is presented for purposes of illustrating how one might design instruction with an orientation toward oral proficiency. Practitioners wishing to adapt this model for a particular language may want to further refine and specify course goals within the generic framework it provides. Using a plan such as this one, an instructor can choose and sequence various oral practice activities and teaching strategies for developing speaking skills in the second language classroom.

Sample Formats for Oral Practice

The activities described in this chapter are organized according to the first two working hypotheses, presented in Chapter 3, for designing a framework for instruction that is oriented toward proficiency goals:

> **Hypothesis 1.** *Opportunities must be provided for students to practice using language in a range of contexts likely to be encountered in the target culture.*

> **Hypothesis 2.** *Opportunities should be provided for students to practice carrying out a range of functions (tasks) likely to be necessary in dealing with others in the target culture.*

Activities are further classified according to (1) the proficiency level(s) for which the oral practice formats seem best suited and (2) the structural and functional goals of the activity being illustrated.

Oral practice can and should be used in an integrated fashion with practice in other skill areas. Many of the samples given in the following pages include suggestions for integrating reading, listening, and writing practice with oral practice, either through pre-speaking or follow-up activities. The integration of cultural content is also an important consideration when planning oral practice, and can be done through the choice of content as well as choice of formats, such as in role plays, games, and conversational activities. These activity types have the added benefit of fostering cooperative learning and small-group interaction, both of which can be especially conducive to the development of oral proficiency.

The first group of sample activities in this section illustrates precommunicative practice (Littlewood 1981) that is meaningful and personalized, but that allows students to focus on formal features of the code. These activities are grouped under the discussion of the first corollary to Hypothesis 1. More open-ended and task-based activities are then presented in the discussion associated with Corollaries 2 and 3. Finally, particular attention is given to practicing specific language functions in the discussion associated with Hypothesis 2 (see pp. 263-66).

> **Corollary 1.** *Students should be encouraged to express their own meaning as early as possible after productive skills have been introduced in the course of instruction.*

Most of the activity types in this first section allow students to engage in practicing new features of the language (vocabulary, grammatical forms, pragmatic formulae, etc.) in order to develop some confidence and facility in using them. Formal practice activities have had a place in a variety of approaches to language teaching, although the rationale for their use and the way they were designed has varied considerably. In behavioristic orientations popular in the 1960s, for example, structured "drills" were designed to enable students to form new language "habits." Most of these drills revolved around morphological or syntactic features and were usually not contextualized or meaningful. When cognitive theory became popular in the 1970s, "pattern drills" were replaced with structured but *meaningful* practice activities. These meaningful and communicative exercises represented a way for students to practice subskills involved in the complex process of language learning so that they might become integrated eventually into their internal representations or "cognitive structure." It was thought that through extensive practice, subskills would eventually become "automatized."

Gatbonton and Segalowitz (1988), arguing from an information-processing perspective of language acquisition, suggest that fluency in oral skills can be promoted by means of "creative automatization." Following Shiffrin and Schneider (1977), they also maintain that the development of automaticity requires "a great deal of practice" (p. 474). Language use becomes automatic when the speaker does not need to focus attention on producing forms and thus divert his or her attention away from the meaningful communication task at hand. Gatbonton and Segalowitz suggest that students practice a basic repertoire of expressions or phrases that are commonly needed in many communicative situations, and that such practice be incorporated within communicative activities where repetition of such phrases would occur naturally.

If one adopts the view that learner language is variable (Tarone 1983; Ellis 1985), one might think of meaningful structured practice as consisting of "careful style" activities, as opposed to more open-ended tasks that involve the use of the "vernacular style." As was mentioned earlier in the discussion of interlanguage, Ellis (1985) suggests that "careful style" tasks can have an impact on the development of more accurate usage over time when learners engage in creative language use, as new forms that are initially practiced in learners' careful style eventually spread to their vernacular style. The notion of "automaticity" underlies this perspective on language acquisition as well.

One other aspect of focused practice that should be considered when planning instruction at the Novice or Intermediate level is its affective value. Some students are most comfortable with structured learning environments because of either personality variables or cognitive style preferences. Formal practice activities may be most suitable for students who have a low tolerance of ambiguity or who are reluctant to take risks, especially when they are just beginning language study. The linguistic support of "precommunicative" practice allows such students to practice oral skills within a controlled framework and thus build confidence.

Sample 1   (Novice)

Context Discussing food preferences and eating habits

Function Expressing preferences, choosing foods

Grammatical Feature The use of the partitive article in affirmative sentences and the use of *de* alone in negative sentences in French.

Student Task Students talk together about what they choose to eat for breakfast, lunch, and dinner, using simple sentence frames. They also say what they do not normally eat for these meals. The "?" for each of the columns of choices invites students to mention foods that are not listed, thus encouraging them to go beyond the confines of the exercise.

A table! Qu'est-ce que vous prenez, en général, à chaque repas?

Modèle: Je prends . . . /Je ne prends pas . . .

Au petit déjeuner . . .	Au déjeuner . . .	Au dîner . . .
du bacon	du poisson	de la soupe
des oeufs	des huîtres	un hamburger
des croissants	du poulet	des frites
du café au lait	de la pizza	du fromage
du thé	des spaghetti	du riz
des céréales	de la viande	du veau
du jus d'orange	des légumes	de la dinde
de la confiture	un fruit	de la salade
?	?	?

Come to the table! What do you eat, generally, for each meal?

Model: *I eat . . . /I don't eat . . .*

For breakfast . . .	For lunch . . .	For dinner . . .
bacon	*fish*	*soup*
eggs	*oysters*	*a hamburger*
crescent rolls	*chicken*	*fries*
coffee with cream	*pizza*	*cheese*
tea	*spaghetti*	*rice*
cereal	*meat*	*veal*
orange juice	*vegetables*	*turkey*
jam	*fruit*	*salad*
?	*?*	*?*

Variation To encourage students to recall new vocabulary, pictures of food can be used instead of the lists above. This requires recall of gender as well as vocabulary, and thus makes the activity somewhat more challenging.

Follow-up (Writing) Students can take notes on the preferences of their peers in the group or compare responses, seeing who likes the same kinds of foods or who has different tastes. Students might also choose foods based on particular roles they are assuming: a vegetarian, a person who wants to gain weight, a person on a reducing diet, etc.

Source: Sample exercise from J. Muyskens, A. Omaggio Hadley, and C. Convert-Chalmers, *Rendez-vous, 3rd ed.* New York: McGraw-Hill Publishing Co., 1990, p. 151. Reprinted by permission of McGraw-Hill.

Sample 2 (Intermediate)

Context Discussing daily schedules, personal events

Function Recounting events; narration in the past

Grammar Topic Practicing the *passato prossimo* (a past tense in Italian)

Student Task Simonetta e Graziella sono compagne di camera. Graziella passa il week-end con la famiglia e quando ritorna, domanda all'amica: Che hai fatto questo week-end? Simonetta risponde con una lunga lista.

Esempio: Ascoltare dei dischi
Ho ascoltato dei dischi.

1. visitare un museo
2. pranzare con un amico
3. fare delle compere al centro
4. scrivere agli zii di Chicago
5. leggere una rivista
6. studiare la lezione d'italiano

Simonetta and Graziella are roommates. Graziella spent the weekend with her family, and when she returned, she asked her friend what she had done this past weekend. Simonetta answered with a long list.

Example: *To listen to some records*
I listened to some records.

1. *to visit a museum*
2. *to dine with a friend*
3. *to shop downtown*
4. *to write to my aunt and uncle in Chicago*
5. *to read a magazine*
6. *to study the Italian lesson*

Source: Adapted from Lazzarino, 1980, pp. 93–94. Reprinted by permission of McGraw-Hill.

Follow-up (Listening/Speaking/Reading/Writing) Students in groups of three make a list of activities they did during the past week. One member of the group takes notes. When groups have finished, they report back the activities they listed, comparing their responses with other groups in the class. Students might be asked to decide which group reported the most interesting activities, which was the least ambitious, or which was the most physically active.

Sample 3 (Intermediate)

Context   Social conventions and rules of behavior

Function   Giving advice

Student Task   *L'hôte (l'hôtesse) parfait(e)!* Voici une liste de choses à faire ou à éviter si vous invitez quelqu'un à passer le week-end chez vous. Quels sont vos conseils pour l'hôte ou l'hôtesse parfait(e)? Présentez vos idées à l'impératif, affirmatif ou négatif, selon votre opinion.

1. oublier de faire le lit
2. mettre votre chien de garde dans la salle de bains
3. faire cuire les plats préférés de vos invités
4. acheter de jolies fleurs pour la chambre de vos ami(e)s
5. parler du bon vieux temps
6. être de mauvaise humeur
etc.

The Perfect Host (Hostess). Here is a list of things to do or to avoid doing if you invite someone to stay at your house for the weekend. What is your advice for the perfect host or hostess? Put your ideas in the affirmative or negative imperative form, according to your opinion.

1. *to forget to make the bed*
2. *to put your guard dog in the bathroom*
3. *to make your guests' favorite foods*
4. *to buy pretty flowers for the guests' room*
5. *to talk about the good old days*
6. *to be in a bad mood*
etc.

Follow-up   (Listening/Writing/Reading/Culture) Students in small groups make their own lists of things to do and not to do in various contexts: when getting together for an informal party; when meeting with a professor for an appointment after class; when going for the first time to dinner at the home of a new acquaintance, etc. The teacher has previously solicited similar lists from native speakers (colleagues, friends, exchange students) for the same contexts in the target culture. Students compare their own lists to those prepared by native speakers and note any similarities and differences in the "rules of conduct" listed.

These activities represent a few of the possible formats for precommunicative and/or structured contextualized oral practice. Other generic exercise types suitable for Novice and Intermediate students are illustrated next.

Word Association   Students are asked to think of any related words they can give in response to a stimulus word. This type of exercise is excellent for encouraging the learning of vocabulary in meaningful clusters, as well as for helping students improve their memory for new vocabulary and ultimately increase their fluency and flexibility.

Sample (Novice)

Context   Campus life

Function   Descriptions

Student Task   Students think about associations they have with various locations on their campus. They think of as many words as they can for the following places:

1. the library
2. their favorite campus bar or restaurant
3. the classroom
4. the sports arena etc.

Follow-up   (Cultural enrichment) The teacher obtains word associations from a native speaker or several native speakers for these same concepts. Students compare their own lists of words with those of the native speaker(s) and discuss similarities and differences. (See also Kramsch 1983 and Seelye 1984 for ideas for teaching the connotation of words and concepts.)

Forced Choice   Otherwise known as either/or questions, this type of exercise allows students who are not quite ready for open-ended exercises to choose appropriate structures in the question to provide their own answer. Such a format can easily be personalized as well as meaningful.

Sample (Novice)

Context   Leisure-time activities

Function   Discussing preferences, pastimes

Student Task   A set of forced-choice questions relating to preferences in leisure-time activities is asked, either in a whole-class instructional format or in smaller groups. If students are placed in groups of two or three, one student may be asked to formulate the questions from cues or to read them from cards while the others answer.

1. Preferisce guardare la televisione o leggere?
2. Preferisce passare le serate con gli amici o in famiglia?
3. Preferisce stare zitto o parlare quando ci sono molte persone?
etc.

1. Do you prefer to watch television or read?
2. Do you prefer to spend the evening with your friends or with your family?
3. Do you prefer to keep quiet or talk when there are a lot of people?
etc.

Logical Conclusions   In this type of exercise, students read a short statement or series of statements and decide whether or not an additional sentence follows logically. If it does, students state that the series is logical. If the second sentence is a non sequitur, however, students must change it to make it follow from the first.

Sample (Novice)

Context	Weekend activities
Grammatical/Lexical Focus	Expressions with *faire*
Function	Describing daily activities
Student Task	Students react to the sentences by (a) deciding whether or not they form a logical sequence and (b) creating a new sequence if necessary.

1. Je n'ai plus de vêtements dans l'armoire! Je dois faire la vaisselle!
2. Nos placards sont vides et il n'y a rien dans le frigo. Nous devons faire le marché!
3. J'ai besoin d'exercice. Allons faire le linge.
etc.

1. *I don't have any more clothes in the closet. I need to do the dishes!*
2. *Our cupboards are bare and there's nothing in the refrigerator. We need to go shopping!*
3. *I need some exercise. Let's go do the laundry.*
etc.

Like the forced-choice activity explained earlier, this format permits students who are not quite ready for more open-ended exercises to use the structure provided in the model sentences, enabling them to practice making sequences of statements rather than one-sentence utterances. The format allows for some creativity on the part of the student, yet limits the need for such creativity to structures and vocabulary that the Novice can handle.

Logical Questions This type of exercise encourages students to think of logical questions that would elicit a particular response. The sample format provided here enables students to practice orally the Intermediate-level function of requesting information from others. Because of the unusual format in this particular sample, questions to be formulated are somewhat complicated and might be best saved for students in the higher portions of the Intermediate range.

Sample (Intermediate)

Context	Health, fitness
Function	Asking for information, getting clarification
Grammar Topic	Interrogative sentences
Student Task	*Une émission interrompue.* Un soir d'orage, vous écoutez une émission médicale à la radio. Mais il y a beaucoup de parasites sur l'antenne et vous n'entendez pas tous les mots. Voici quelques extraits de l'émission. Quelles questions doit-on poser pour savoir ce que l'animateur de radio a dit?

Modèle: Lors de notre dernière émission, /////// nous a conseillé de faire plus de marché à pied.

Vous dites: *Qui* nous a conseillé de faire plus de marché à pied?

(*Qui est-ce qui* nous a conseillé de faire plus de marché à pied?)

1. Pour rester en forme, on doit ///////.

2. Pour éviter les problèmes digestifs, /////// est hautement recommandé.

3. Pour échapper aux agressions du monde moderne, nous vous conseillons de consulter à Paris ///////, un grand spécialiste du stress.

4. La nuit, quand on ne peut pas dormir, on peut toujours compter sur ///////. Ça détend tout de suite.

5. Si on suit un régime trop longtemps, on aura besoin de ///////.
Etc.

An Interrupted Program. One stormy night, you're listening to a medical program on the radio. But there's a lot of static and you don't hear all the words. Here are some extracts from the program. What questions do you have to ask to find out what the radio announcer said?

Model: *During our last program, / / / / / / advised us to do more walking.*
You say: Who advised us to do more walking?

1. *To stay in shape, you have to / / / / / /.*

2. *To avoid digestive problems, / / / / / / is highly recommended.*

3. *To escape from the pressures of the modern world, we advise you to consult in Paris / / / / / /, a great stress specialist.*

4. *At night, when you can't sleep, you can always count on / / / / / /. It relaxes you right away.*

5. *If you stay on a diet too long, you'll need / / / / / /.*
etc.

Source: Omaggio et al., 1984, p. 145. Reprinted with permission of McGraw-Hill.

Definitions Students are asked to provide a definition or description of a term for which they are unlikely to know the foreign language equivalent. This activity encourages the development of paraphrasing skills, which are essential at the Intermediate and Advanced levels, as well as the creative use of language to get meaning across in spite of gaps in knowledge (strategic competence).

Sample (Intermediate/Advanced)

Context Health and Fitness

Function Paraphrasing, giving definitions

Student Task Imagine that you are out with a group of German friends who do not speak English. Suddenly, because of all of the new foods that you have sampled, you are not feeling very well. In addition to feeling uncomfortable, you seem to have twisted your foot! You need to express the following ideas in German, but you don't have access to a dictionary. How do you explain what you mean? Using only German, give paraphrases (definitions) for the following ideas:

1. feeling light-headed
2. a splitting headache
3. a cold sweat
4. heartburn
5. a mild sprain

Notice that the context of this activity promotes the use of vocabulary related to health matters, affording some practice in coping in a survival situation appropriate to the Intermediate range. Once the terms in the activity have been learned or satisfactorily paraphrased, students can role-play situations suggested by the scenario or variations on the same theme.

Visually Aided Exercises Students describe a drawing, answer questions, or recount some narrative using a visual stimulus in their text or drawn from some other source. Exercises of this type require recall of target-language vocabulary while encouraging open-ended, creative language use and developing descriptive and narrative functions that are needed to progress to the Advanced level.

Sample (Intermediate)

Context   Eating customs

Function   Simple narration in the present.

Student Task   Students recount the eating habits of Monsieur Duchêne, being sure to mention the time of day for each phase of the narration. This activity can be adapted for narration in the past or future simply by asking students to tell the story as a habitual past action, as a particular set of actions that happened yesterday, or as actions that will happen tomorrow. One possible set of narrative statements is provided in the present tense in Illustration 6.6.

Personalized questions In this most familiar format for personalization, students answer questions directed to them as individuals, using the vocabulary and structures they have been learning and practicing in other exercises. Questions are normally open-ended, but enough guidance is provided to help shy or reluctant students to express their point of view in the second language. Personalized questions can be addressed to individuals within a whole-class instructional format or used by students in pairs or small groups to interview one another. If the latter format is used, a follow-up activity, either oral or written, is useful, especially if answers given are reported back in the form of a personalized summary. Follow-up activities are

Pour Monsieur Duchêne, vivre c'est manger!

A huit heures, M. Duchêne prend son petit déjeuner.

A dix heures et demie, il mange un sandwich.

A midi, il déjeune.

A une heure et quart, il fait la sieste.

A quatre heures moins le quart, il prend le thé.

A six heures vingt, il prend un apéritif et des hors-d'oeuvre.

A huit heures moins vingt, il dîne.

A minuit, M. Duchêne mange encore. Il a de la chance. . . il est somnambule!

For Mr. Duchêne, to live is to eat!
At 8 o'clock, M. Duchêne has breakfast. At 10:30, he has a sandwich. At noon, he has lunch. At 1:15, he takes a nap. At 3:45, he has tea. At 6:20, he has an aperitif and appetizers. At 7:40, he has dinner. At midnight, M. Duchêne is still eating. He's lucky . . . he's a sleepwalker!

Illustration 6.6
Intermediate-level visually aided exercise with possible responses in the present tense

Source: Muyskens et al., 1982 pp. 181–182. Reprinted with permission of McGraw-Hill.

useful for several reasons: (1) they encourage students working in small groups to be task-oriented; (2) they show students that their answers are of interest to others and are worth remembering; (3) they allow students to transform answers to the third person, helping them to develop the ability to narrate or report facts, feelings, or preferences—language functions that are featured at the Intermediate level and beyond.

Sample (Novice)

Context	Personality preferences
Function	Simple description
Grammar Topic	Adjectives and adjective agreement
Student Task	Students interview one another using the questions below in order to find out one another's preferences in friends or a potential mate. Questions are in the form of an either/or choice, making the task appropriate for Novice-level learners since much of the structure is provided for them as they formulate an answer.

1. Hast du lieber Männer und Frauen, die schüchtern oder kontaktfreudig sind?
2. Sind deine Freunde mehr an Sport oder Musik interessiert?
3. Hast du lieber Leute, die idealistisch oder realistisch sind?
4. Interessierst du dich mehr für Männer und Frauen, die praktisch oder phantasievoll sind?
etc.

1. *Do you prefer men/women who are shy or outgoing?*
2. *Are your friends more interested in sports or music?*
3. *Do you like people who are idealistic or realistic?*
4. *Are you interested more in men/women who are practical or imaginative?*
etc.

Follow-up 1	(Writing and Listening) Students write a brief description of themselves on a note card using simple sentences and incorporating various descriptive adjectives. The instructor reads various descriptions aloud and students guess who is being described.
Follow-up 2	(Writing and Reading) Another alternative is to put the descriptions into a classified ad format, using numbers rather than names to identify the individuals described if students prefer their descriptions to be anonymous. Students can then scan the "ads" for those who best match their preferences as stated in the previous exercise.
Personalized Completions	In this type of format, students complete a series of sentences or an incomplete paragraph according to their own situation or point of view.

Sample (Advanced)

Context	Energy issues
Function	Discussing consequences, hypotheses about the future
Grammar Topic	Conditional sentences
Student Task	Students at the Advanced range practice the Superior-level function of hypothesizing and supporting opinion relating to energy issues in the following activity in French.

"Si, par hasard . . . " Imaginez que les événements suivants doivent arriver un de ces jours, ou que l'on discute ce qu'on aurait fait s'ils étaient arrivés à un certain moment dans le passé. Complétez les phrases suivantes selon vos propres opinions. Puis, comparez vos réponses à celles de vos camarades.

1. S'il y a un accident sérieux à la centrale nucléaire de ma région . . .
2. Si l'énergie solaire devenait très populaire . . .
3. Si toutes les réserves de charbon dans le monde étaient tout à coup épuisées . . .
4. Si tout le monde fait construire une maison chauffée à l'atome . . .
5. Si on n'avait jamais fait attention aux dangers de la pollution . . .
etc.

"If, by chance . . . " Imagine that the following events are to happen one of these days, or that you're discussing what you would have done if they had happened in the past. Complete the following sentences according to your own opinion. Then compare your answers to those of your classmates.

1. *If there is a serious accident at the nuclear power plant in my area . . .*
2. *If solar energy became very popular . . .*
3. *If all the coal reserves in the world were suddenly depleted . . .*
4. *If everyone has a nuclear-heated home built . . .*
5. *If we had never paid attention to the dangers of pollution . . .*
etc.

Source: Omaggio et al. 1984, p. 270. Reprinted with permission of McGraw-Hill.

Sentence Builders   By using elements of sentences provided in columns, students make their own statements, choosing whichever elements they wish to use in order to express personal meaning. As Birckbichler (1982) points out, the guidance and structure inherent in sentence-builder activities make them especially useful for Novice learners. Students can feel successful at expressing quite a number of ideas and original statements within a very limited grammatical and lexical corpus.

The following two sample sentence-builder activities are designed to help students practice various polite expressions and functional vocabulary associated with making a phone call. The question marks in each column of the sentence builder invite students to make up their own material for the activity.

Sample 1   (Intermediate)

Context   Making a phone call in a strange city using a public telephone

Functions   Excusing oneself politely, making explanations, asking questions

Student Task   See Illustration 6.7.

Illustration 6.7
Intermediate-level
functional sentence-
builder activity

Imagine you are in a strange city/foreign city and you have to make a telephone call. Use any of the following fragments to compose a question which you would like to ask a passerby.

Polite Excuse	Explanation	Question
Excuse me.	I have to make a phone	Where is the nearest
Excuse me, sir.	call.	phone?
Excuse me, madam.	I forgot to make an impor-	Where is the phone?
Could you help me,	tant phone call.	From where can I call?
please?	I must call my wife.	Where can I make a
May I ask you a question,	I must call my husband.	phone call?
please?	I have to call my boss	Is there a telephone booth
?	right away.	nearby?
	?	?

Source: *Active Lab,* Defense Language Institute, p. 24

Sample 2 (Intermediate)

Context — Taking a phone message

Functions — Making polite apologies, giving explanations

Student Task — See Illustration 6.8

Follow-up — Students compare messages taken or relay their messages to a third student.

In using activities such as those described here and in the following sections, it is important to remember that sequencing activities for practice is almost as important as designing contextualized practice in the first place. It is best to integrate the whole sequence of lesson materials into a single theme, context, or general situation, at least in designing one class day's work or unit of study, instead of jumping from one content or topic to another. The latter practice is the norm in many language classes in which course materials are not contextually or thematically organized.

Corollary 2 *Opportunities must be provided for active communicative interaction among students.*

The use of small-group and paired communicative practice has several advantages in building oral proficiency. First, such practice allows students much more class time for the development of oral skills since everyone produces language during group work, whereas only one student at a time can speak or interact with the teacher in a large-group instructional format. Secondly, working with peers takes some of the pressure off students, who often feel intimidated by the need to perform in front of the whole class. Small-group activities can serve to lower the affective filter, hypothesized by Krashen (1982) to affect acquisition significantly. A third reason for using group activities is that they can increase the quality of

Illustration 6.8
Intermediate-level
functional sentence-
builder activity
(Sample 2)

You receive a pressing telephone call from a client, but your boss is temporarily out of the office. Take a message. Use any of the following fragments in your communication with your phone partner.

Polite Apology	**Explanation**	**Offer to take a Message**
Oh, I'm sorry . . .	He/she's at a meeting.	Could I help you?
I'm sorry . . .	He/she's sick today.	Could I take a message?
I'm afraid . . .	He/she's out of the office right now.	Is there any message?
Sorry, but . . .	He/she's out of town until . . .	Perhaps I could help?
?	He/she's on vacation till . . .	Miss _____ is handling his/her business calls.
	?	Would you like to speak to her?
		?

Source: Active Lab, Defense Language Institute, p. 25

communication by creating information gaps that require effective, naturalistic communication while focusing on the development of certain language functions at the same time. A few examples of small-group activities are given below, divided into three categories: (1) group puzzles, (2) group decision making, and (3) social interaction (mingling).

Group Puzzle   *Sample*   (Intermediate)

Objective   To produce and synthesize multiple clues in the second language in order to solve a problem

Context   Discussing family relationships

Functions   Identifying people and relationships, sharing biographical information, making inquiries about family members and biographical facts

Grammatical Features   Interrogative forms and expressions, possessive adjectives in Spanish

Student Task   Each student in a group of five receives a drawing of a family tree, Illustration 6.9, showing the place of origin of each family member and including a blank space for the name, age, and occupation of each person. No other information is provided on the tree diagram. Each student then receives a biographical information card that describes himself as well as other family members in some detail. Students must share the information on their cards with others in the group by introducing themselves and responding to any questions they might be asked. Group members should answer "No sé" or "Se me olvidó" if asked for information that is not on their cards.

A sample biographical card is given below. Information on the card can be given in English or Spanish, depending on whether the teacher wants students to recall or simply recognize the target language vocabulary for family relationships.

ESTELLE GONZALES
Age: 67 years
Husband: Jaime Gonzales, age 69
Residence: Madrid
Profession: Retired with husband
One daughter, Mariana, who lives in Toledo
Two sons

As students share the information on their cards, they gradually fill in the family tree. A completed tree is given in Spanish in Illustration 6.10. (To create remaining cards, simply divide the family tree information and place it on cards such as the one illustrated above.)

Source: Adapted from Omaggio, 1982.

Calendar Activity *Sample* (Novice to Intermediate)

Objective To discuss activities during a given month and find a date open for everyone in order to plan a party.

Context Everyday activities

Functions Discussing dates, extending invitations, accepting and refusing invitations

Student Task Each student in a group of three has a calendar in French in which the days of a given month are displayed, as in Illustration 6.11. For nine specific dates on each of the three calendars, activities of various sorts are noted. Each calendar has different activities and all the dates for the activities are different so that only three dates are "free" for everyone.

Students consult their calendars and try to find a date when everyone is free to plan a party. Exchanges among the students take the following form:

Student 1: Tu es libre vendredi le 15 septembre?
Student 2: Oui, je suis libre ce jour-là.
Student 3: Ah non, dommage! J'ai quelque chose à faire. Je vais manger chez un ami à 8 heures ce soir-là. Mais je n'ai rien à faire vendredi le 22 septembre. Et toi? etc.

Student 1: Are you free on Friday, September 15?
Student 2: Yes, I'm free that day.
Student 3: Oh no, too bad! I'm busy. I'm having dinner at a friend's house at 8 p.m. that night. But I'm not busy on Friday the 22nd. What about you? etc.

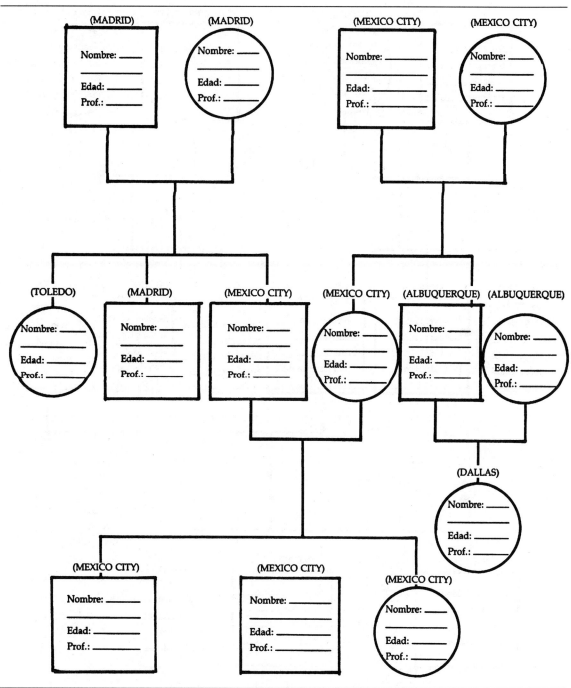

Illustration 6.9 Student Diagram for Group Puzzle, Sample 1

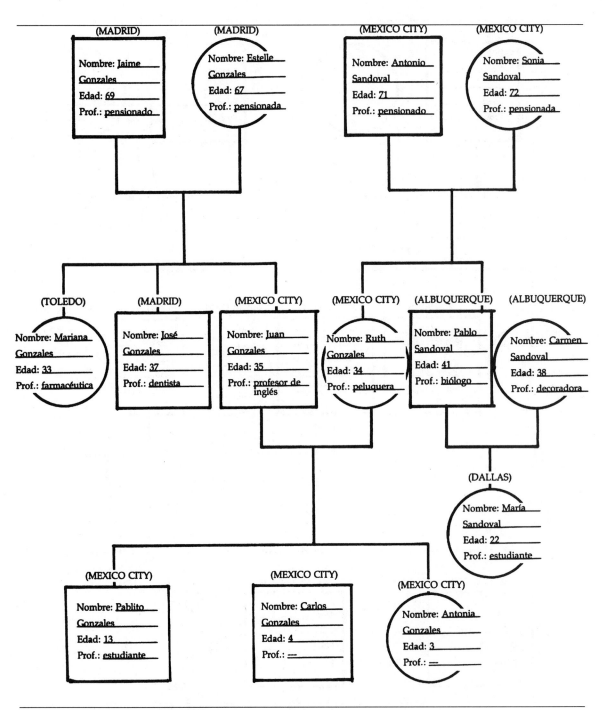

Illustration 6.10   Completed Diagram for Group Puzzle, Sample 1

			SEPTEMBRE			
L	M	M	J	V	S	D
				1 *dîner chez maman 8h*	2 *travailler au MacDo*	3
4 *étudier avec michel 7h30*	5 *à la bibliothèque*	6 *travailler 6h30-10h30*	7	8	9	10
11	12	13 *travailler 6h30-10h30*	14	15	16	17
18	19 *examen de chimie demain!*	20	21	22	23 *anniversaire de Pierre soirée chez Natalie*	24
25	26	27	28	29 *à Lyon pour le week-end*	30	

Illustration 6.11   Calendar Activity, Student 1

Follow-up   When students have found a free date, they plan a party, making a list of guests, plan foods, etc. If students discover a free date immediately, the teacher may ask them to continue searching for an alternate date so that they may get additional practice using the expressions involved in the dialogue.

Variation   Ur (1988) suggests a similar activity for ESL in which pairs of students compare a week's schedule of activities and try to find a time to meet. Schedules are in the form of a 7-day diary, with 2-hour slots to be filled in, from 7 a.m. to 11 p.m., Monday through Sunday. This activity is especially useful for practicing telling time of day and using the future expression "going to." Consult this source for sample diaries, full directions, and suggestions for further variations.

Group Decision Making

Sample (Advanced)
Group Picture Story

Objective
To create an original story by synthesizing the contributions of all group members

Functions
Telling and listening to stories, recounting events, hypothesizing

Grammatical Features
Interrogative words and expressions, descriptive adjectives, past tenses

Student Task
The teacher chooses from magazines several pictures that depict people in odd situations or show several people in some type of conversation. The more "interesting" the situation (or the more ambiguous), the better. The teacher mounts the pictures on construction paper and affixes a sheet of lined paper to the back.

The teacher then distributes the pictures to groups of three to five students, one picture to a group. The students look at the picture and brainstorm for a few minutes to create as many possible questions as the picture can provoke. A group leader may be chosen to write down the questions on the lined sheet, or the picture and writing task can be passed from student to student as each thinks of a question to ask.

Once the groups have had a chance to generate their set of questions, the teacher collects them (as well as the pictures to which they are attached) and redistributes them, each one to a different group. Group members then read the questions associated with their new picture and agree on a story that will answer all of the questions asked. They must recount their story in the past, making sure that the narrative is coherent and complete enough to answer all the questions. A group leader can be responsible for writing the story down as it unfolds, sharing it later with the rest of the class.

Source: Omaggio, 1982.

Social Interaction

Sample (Intermediate)
Biographical Bingo

Objective
To use the foreign language to locate persons with certain attributes in order to solve a problem

Context
Biographical information

Functions
Inquiring about personal preferences and biographical facts

Grammatical Feature
Interrogative words and expressions

Student Task
Students receive a sheet such as the one in Illustration 6.12 on which are listed various personal attributes and biographical facts. Students must circulate (as they would at a party), asking one another questions to find out who has the attributes described in each of the squares of the grid.

Biographical Bingo				
has brother studying Italian	can name Italian fashion designer	parent has travelled to Italy	can prepare an antipasto	has read an Italian novel
likes tortellini	knows a second foreign language	has an Italian cookbook	knows an Italian family	has an Italian sweater
family has Italian car	lives near non-English-speaking family	has brother or sister who speaks another language	has travelled to Europe	wants to visit Italy
has bought Italian chocolate	has a relative who can speak Italian fluently	can name 2 Italian politicians	has relative who has lived in Italy	has seen an Italian opera
has relative with Italian name	has been to Toronto	can name an Italian composer	has an imported camera	has eaten Italian pastry

Illustration 6.12   Student game sheet for "Biographical Bingo". [Idea adapted from Otero and Webb, 1981]

When a student has located someone who has one of the attributes, he must ask that person to sign the square on his description sheet. Students must ask at least one follow-up question relating to that fact or attribute and jot down the additional information next to the signature. When a student has obtained five different signatures in adjacent boxes forming a straight line (as in bingo), he or she wins the game. Students not speaking the target language during the course of play are disqualified from the competition.

Source: Adapted from Otero and Webb, 1981

Other Small Group and Paired Activities

These games and group activities provide a small sampling of formats that increase opportunities for communicative interaction among students in the classroom. Many good suggestions for creating activities for group practice are available in the literature of the last twenty years. Two other activities that have been particularly popular among classroom teachers are (1) interviews and conversation cards and (2) situational role-plays.

Interviews and Conversation Cards (Novice through Superior): In this type of activity, students usually interview one another in pairs: one student asks questions provided either in the text or by the teacher (through indirect translation cues or directed dialogue) while the second student answers according to his or her own thoughts or preferences. Students then can exchange roles, with the second student asking questions and the first answering them. Teachers often have students take brief notes on their partners' responses, or invite several students to report back interesting answers at the end of the interview process.

Bonin and Birckbichler (1975) introduced the concept of the *conversation card*—structured interview cards that can help promote conversation among beginning and intermediate students. Their ideas have led to a variety of adaptations that have proved extremely useful in achieving a blend of communication with a concern for accuracy. The format is extremely flexible: one can use cards with target language questions of a very simple nature for Novice-level learners; one can provide native-language question cues for Intermediate learners and above, including questions on virtually any topic in any time frame; or one can adapt the personalized questions discussed earlier in this section for practice at the Advanced or Superior levels, incorporating controversial topics and issues that require students to support and defend their opinions.

The interview cards in the following sample illustrate how three students can be involved in a conversation that is self-monitoring. The students holding Cards 1 and 2 ask each other questions according to the cues on their cards, as well as any additional follow-up questions they can think of that will keep the conversation flowing. The student holding Card 3 is responsible for checking the accuracy of the questions asked, as well as for helping group members when they are unable to formulate their questions. This third student, therefore, serves as a group monitor and may also be asked to record his or her classmates' answers for a report-back phase later in the class hour. By making students responsible for helping their peers ask accurate questions, the goal of developing greater precision and coherence in speaking can be fostered in an informal atmosphere where communication is also taking place.

Sample   (Intermediate)

Context   Planning vacations and travel

Functions   Asking questions, discussing future plans and goals

Student Task   The questions below are in English, requiring students who are native speakers of English to formulate the questions in their own words in the target language, which is German in this example.

Card 1: Ask your partner . . .

> where he/she plans to go this summer
>
> how long he/she will stay
>
> whether he/she will travel by car, plane, or train
>
> who he/she will travel with

Card 2: Ask your partner . . .

> whether he/she plans to travel one day to a German-speaking country
>
> what country or countries he/she prefers to visit
>
> what cities he/she would like to see
>
> how long he/she would like to stay in Germany

Card 3: Help your classmates ask their interview questions by using the cues below. Be careful to correct your partners when necessary, but be flexible and accept any correct form of the questions. Take notes on the answers you hear so you can report back the discussion to the rest of the class.

Student 1:

1. Wohin möchtest du diesen Sommer reisen?
2. Wie lange bleibst du dort?
3. Reist du mit dem Auto, dem Flugzeug oder dem Zug?
4. Mit wem reist du?

Student 2:

1. Reist du eines Tages in ein deutschsprachiges Land?
2. Welches Land oder welche Länder möchtest du lieber besuchen?
3. Welche Städte möchtest du sehen?
4. Wie lange möchtest du in Deutschland bleiben?

During this interview activity, students should be encouraged to seek help from the teacher, who is circulating among the groups working simultaneously on their cards, whenever they need additional vocabulary or have questions about the acceptability of either questions or responses. This particular interview technique can be used very successfully at all levels of instruction.

Situational Role-Plays   Some excellent ideas for using role plays are found in a variety of sources, including Zelson (1978), Kramsch (1981), Bragger (1985), Hahn and Michaelas (1986), and numerous recent language textbooks (see, for example, the extensive use of role-play suggestions in Higgs, Liskin-Gasparro, and Medley 1989). In role-plays, a situation is presented to a small group of students who may prepare their parts, if necessary, and then act them out for the rest of the class or record them on videotape for playback later. Role-plays might easily be based on videotaped exchanges between native speakers in common survival situations, such as those described in Chapter 5, with students adapting the dialogue they have observed to their own situations or purposes.

Role-plays can be used effectively at virtually any proficiency level. For students at the Novice level, highly structured role-play cards can be designed, with vocabulary hints or partial dialogues supplied, based either on material already presented in class or on the simplest of survival or courtesy situations. Intermediate-level learners can practice role-plays designed around common situations one might encounter in traveling or living in a foreign culture. At higher levels of oral proficiency, the role-play can introduce a conflict situation in which someone must persuade someone else to act in a certain way, or talk his or her way out of trouble, or lodge a complaint. Zelson (1978) gives the following example:

> Your family and another family have gone on vacation together and rented a cottage. As might be expected, your friendship has been subjected to somewhat of a strain after two weeks of togetherness. At last it is over. Complain to and about each other: i.e., eating habits, housework, children, etc. (p. 52)

Other good examples of conflict situations can be found in Kramsch (1981) and the materials prepared by ACTFL following the Haverford Institute in 1983 (See *Applications of Oral Proficiency Testing to Foreign Language Instruction*, 1985). Two examples from this latter source, suitable for high school students, are:

> You are the parent of a 15-year-old girl. She has been asked to a party by a boy you don't like. Tell your daughter why you don't like the boy and why she can't go to the party. (p. 22)

> It is the night of the senior prom and as you arrive to pick up your date (with flowers in hand to match her dress), you see her sneaking out the back door with a guy she used to date. Her mother (who always liked you better than the old boyfriend) notices at the same time and calls out to her. Pick up the action there as Date, Girl, Old Boyfriend, Mother (p. 23).

Role-plays such as these can be derived from lesson themes and structured around a few communicative functions and/or structural features, or they can be more open-ended. To succeed in helping students build proficiency, teachers should be careful to present role-play situations that are at an appropriate level of difficulty for students.

Corollary 3. *Creative language practice (as opposed to exclusively manipulative or convergent practice) must be encouraged in the proficiency-oriented classroom.*

One of the hallmarks of language users in the Intermediate range and beyond is that they can create with the language. In order to develop this ability, students must have opportunities to learn to paraphrase, think divergently, and let their imaginations and creativity function as fully as possible. Birckbichler (1982) has compiled an extremely valuable set of suggestions for creative language practice. Basing her definition of creativity on Guilford's (1959) Structure-of-Intellect Model, she proposes four types of divergent-production factors that relate to the development of creativity in language use. These factors are (1) *fluency,* or the ability to produce a large number of ideas in a given period of time, (2) *flexibility,* or the ability to produce a diversity of ideas belonging to different classes, (3) *elaboration,* or the ability to add to or to embellish a given idea or set of ideas, and (4) *originality,* or the ability to produce uncommon, unconventional, or clever ideas. Drawing on sources from various fields of research on creativity, Birckbichler presents 64 classroom-activity formats related to these four factors. Some ideas that are suitable for several proficiency ranges are presented below.

Fluency   *Sample*   (Intermediate)
Making Up Questions
Students are asked to generate as many questions as possible that they might use in an interview. They may be given a few stimulus questions first and then asked to develop in a brainstorming session some follow-up questions for each one of the original questions. For example:

> *Two foreign exchange students are going to visit your class tomorrow. Individually, or with another student, prepare a list of questions that you would like to ask your visitors. You might include items about their impressions of life in the United States, what schools are like in their country, what they like to do on weekends, etc. (Derived from Birckbichler, 1982, p. 26)*

Flexibility   *Sample*   (Advanced)
Change the Story
Students listen to or read a short story in the target language and are asked to create a new story by changing it in some way. They may tell the story from the point of view of one of the characters, change the time frame to that of another era, imagine a different ending, etc. In doing this, students have an opportunity to be creative with the language while practicing the Advanced-level function of narration in the past.

Elaboration

Sample (Advanced)
Cue Insertion

This activity, based on an original composition written by the student, can be done orally or in writing. If the activity is done in writing, students can be asked to present their new compositions to the class orally during the next class period. The activity requires that students expand each sentence of their original composition by adding more information whenever they see an asterisk.

The following example in English illustrates this technique. The teacher asks a student to use relative clauses to elaborate on a fictitious story he wrote about his vacation. She encourages him to use his imagination, adding details that are serious, funny, mysterious, or sinister, according to his own wishes. The student reworks the composition at home, and presents it to the class orally during the next period.

Make the story you wrote more interesting by adding a relative clause each time you see an asterisk. For example, you wrote: "I spent my vacation in a hotel." Embellish this by adding a clause, such as the following: "I spent my vacation in a hotel that was really mysterious! (. . . whose inhabitants were old; . . . where famous people had stayed; . . . that my brother had recommended; . . . where ghosts had been seen!)"

Student's original composition with cues inserted:

I spent my vacation in a hotel*. The hotel is located on a little street*. The concierge* was really quiet. He only talked to his wife*. Their garden* was very tranquil and looked out on the street. I often sat on a bench* and looked at the people* . . . . (etc.)

Source: Adapted from Omaggio, 1981, p. 56

Originality

Sample (Intermediate/Advanced)
Inventing Machines

Using a sentence-builder format, students develop creative and unusual questions, which others then answer or use as a basis for creating a group story. In the sample activity that Birckbichler (1982) cites from Debyser and Laitenberger (1976), various people, objects, and places appear in numbered lists in three columns. People in Column 1 include such character types as a general, a dancer, or a plumber; the list of objects in Column 2 comprises such items as a sack of sugar, a hammer, or a hard-boiled egg; places included in Column 3 range from a refrigerator or a toolbox to a violin case. The questions created are in the form: "Why did the . . . put a/an . . . in his/her/the . . . ?"

Students can either create their own questions by combining elements from the three columns or draw three numbers to determine their question. For example, a given number combination would generate the question:

"Why did the president put a kilo of sugar in the tool box?" Students working in pairs or small groups can create a reasonable explanation or short narrative to answer this unusual query. Birckbichler warns that teachers must use such "verbal play" activities with some caution, and only on occasion. "Some students may find playing with language to be an interesting and challenging aspect to second language learning, whereas others who tend to view language solely as an expression of reality will be frustrated by verbal play activities" (p. 74).

Many creative writing and guided description activities can be used to encourage autonomous expression in the target language. Students can be asked to generate a context from a list of words, a picture or series of pictures that may or may not be related to one another, or from a group of random objects. In an activity called "Geshicten aus dem Sack" (*Stories out of a bag*), Schmidt (1977) suggests that a paper bag be filled with unrelated objects, which students select one at a time for the purpose of generating a group story, incorporating each of the objects drawn out of the bag into the plot as the story unfolds. Rivers et al. (1976) suggest an activity called "Gossip," in which students are given a sheet of paper containing a series of questions with space after each for writing answers. Each student answers one question. He or she then hides the answer by folding the paper back and passes the sheet on to the next student. After the last question has been answered, the story, which is often quite amusing, is read to the class. These and other similar formats have been used by classroom teachers to help students create with the language in a structured, yet open-ended way and are excellent for developing oral skills beyond the Novice level.

> **Hypothesis 2.** *Opportunities should be provided for students to practice carrying out a range of functions (tasks) likely to be necessary in dealing with others in the target culture.*

As we saw in Chapter 3, students need to be able to carry out a variety of language functions or tasks in order to develop proficiency beyond the Novice level. The term *function*, as it has been used in the proficiency descriptions, refers to a set of generic, global tasks that language users must be able to perform at a given level of proficiency, such as obtaining information or expressing one's point of view. In addition to these basic tasks, one can list many more specific language functions that students might learn to carry out in the target language. "*Functions*," in this sense, "refer to the hundreds of purposes for which people communicate, either orally or in writing" (Guntermann and Phillips 1982, p. 5). In order to help teachers identify functions for active practice, Guntermann and Phillips list some common purposes of language use in all four skill modalities. In speaking and listening, for example, they list such functions as *socializing, establishing and maintaining relationships, influencing others' actions, talking one's way out of trouble,* and the like. For each of these main functions, they provide an inventory of related sub-functions. Similar functional inventories can be found elsewhere in the literature (see, specifically, van Ek 1975; Wilkins 1976; and Kramsch 1981, who outlines applications of discourse analysis to the second language classroom.)

The focus on functional language use in syllabus design can be traced back to 1971, when a team of experts, commissioned by the Council of Europe, began the work of compiling comprehensive catalogues of language functions to be used as resource documents in designing language courses (Johnson 1982). Wilkins (1976), a member of the Council of Europe's team of experts, developed a categorization system for specifying the communicative needs of adults taking language courses for specific work-related purposes. He identified six basic categories of communicative functions, under which many other sub-functions are subsumed (Wilkins 1976): (1) judgment and evaluation (including such sub-functions as approving, disapproving, or blaming), (2) suasion (such as in suggesting, urging, or advising), (3) argument (as in informing, agreeing, asserting, or denying), (4) inquiry and exposition (such as in making comparisons and contrasts, defining, or explaining), (5) emotion (as in expressing feelings such as love or hate), and (6) emotional relations (including greetings, expressing one's sympathy or gratitude, and the like). Wilkins' system continues to have a significant impact on the design of functional syllabuses today, and an increasing number of foreign language textbooks are incorporating functional features and practice activities within a grammatical or cultural framework. Some recent texts use a framework of functional features as the primary organizer, particularly at the Intermediate and Advanced levels where conversational skills are the focus of study.

An example of an activity that is focused primarily on functional language practice is given below. It is taken from a text that is centered around language functions and conversational strategies, presented in audio-taped native-speaker interchanges. In this particular Spanish text, students listen to native-speaker conversations and learn various communication strategies, which they then practice in small-group activities, such as the one below:

Sample (Intermediate)

Context	Health care; a visit to the doctor
Functions	Giving advice; responding to advice; giving one's opinion
Student Task	After hearing a conversation between a doctor and a patient in Spanish, students study various expressions given in the text for giving and receiving medical advice. They then engage in the role-play activity depicted in Illustration 6.13.

As seen in Illustration 6.13, students are directed to play the roles of a doctor and a patient. To prepare for playing the doctor's role, students

Illustration 6.13
Functional Practice
Activity in Spanish

Expresiones útiles para responder a los consejos

Está bien, pero será difícil.	*That's O.K., but it will be difficult.*
¿Crees que . . . ?	*Do you think . . . ?*
¿De veras?	*Really?*
¿De verdad?	*Really?*
Ah, no puedo.	*Oh, I can't.*
Ah, no quiero . . .	*Oh, I don't want . . .*
Porque no me gusta . . .	*Because I don't like to . . .*
Estoy preocupado(a).	*I'm worried.*
No había pensado en eso.	*I had not thought about that.*
Te agradezco los consejos.	*I appreciate your advice.*
(No) Lo haré.	*I will (not) do it.*

El (La) paciente y el (la) médico(a). Con un(a) compañero(a) de clase, hagan el papel de un(a) paciente y el de un(a) médico(a).

1. El papel del (de la) médico(a)

   a. ¿Cómo es el (la) médico(a)? ¿simpático(a)? ¿antipático(a)? ¿paciente? ¿impaciente?
   b. ¿Cómo saluda a los pacientes?
   c. ¿Cómo los trata?
   ch. Prepara una lista de preguntas para averiguar qué problema(s) tiene el (la) paciente.
   d. Prepara una lista de recomendaciones.

2. El papel del (de la) paciente

   a. ¿Cómo eres tú? ¿Qué tipo de persona eres?
   b. ¿Estás dispuesto(a) a seguir las recomendaciones del (de la) médico(a)?

3. Prepara una descripción de tu problema o enfermedad.

4. Piensa en las preguntas más comunes que un(a) médico(a) le hace a un(a) paciente. También, piensa en una enfermedad (imaginaria, claro) y en algunas expresiones para describirla. Leugo, en grupos de dos, hagan el papel de médico(a) y de paciente. Los dos deben alternarse en los dos papeles. Fíjense en las recomendaciones del (de la) médico(a) y en la actitud del (de la) paciente al oírlas.

5. Haz el papel de médico(a) y explica a los otros estudiantes

   a. el problema del (de la) paciente
   b. tus recomendaciones para su mejoría.

Source: Chastain and Guntermann 1991, p. 139.

begin by imagining what the doctor is like and how he/she would act, preparing a list of possible questions to ask the patient. To prepare for playing the patient's role, students are asked to think of what the patient is like, whether he/she will be willing to follow the doctor's directions, and what the nature of the imaginary illness is.

Once these preparations have been made, students take turns playing the roles of doctor and patient in groups of two. As a follow-up activity, individual students are asked to play the role of the doctor and explain to others in the class what the patient's problem is and how it will be treated.

Source: K. Chastain and G. Guntermann, *¡Imagínate!*, 2nd ed. Heinle & Heinle, 1991.

Students can practice *writing* by imagining that they are (1) the patient, writing in his/her journal about the "ordeal" at the doctor's office that day or (2) the doctor, writing in his/her notebook some comments about the patient, his/her illness, attitude, cure, etc.

Functional practice activities such as the one in this sample not only help students learn to carry out various real-world tasks, but also provide them with conversational strategies that are appropriate to the culture of the language they are studying. Such activities contribute to the development of discourse competence, sociolinguistic competence, and strategic competence, all of which are important factors to include in a well designed program for teaching oral communication skills.

Responding to the Learner

When learners engage in language production activities such as those illustrated in this chapter, they are bound to produce errors of various kinds as they struggle to get their meaning across. This is especially true in communicative and open-ended activities, where activity formats are not heavily structured and monitoring of formal features is not as likely to be central to the task. There is no question that a great many of the errors committed by second language learners are systematic. But where do such errors come from? What processes in language learning might be potential sources for production errors in speaking or in writing? What kinds of strategies do learners use in producing language when the ideas they want to communicate require proficiency beyond their current level of competence? How do native speakers react to language-learner language? How can teachers respond to help students develop more precise and coherent language use? These questions form the basis for the discussion in the last part of this chapter. Various answers that have been proposed in the literature in recent years are presented and illustrated in the next sections.

Some Sources of Error in Interlanguage

Selinker (1974) identifies five processes that he believes to be central to second language learning and acquisition, each of which can force non-native items, rules, and subsystems to appear and possibly remain indefinitely in the interlanguage systems of language learners. These five processes are: *language transfer*, or interference from the mother tongue, *transfer-of-training*, or errors due to the nature of the language-learning materials and approaches themselves, *strategies of second language learning,* or errors due to the learner's own approach to the material to be learned, *strategies of second language communication,* or errors due to the way in which the learner attempts to communicate with native speakers in natural language-use situations, and *overgeneralization of target language rules,* or errors due to the way in which the learner restructures and reorganizes linguistic material.

Interference. Errors that can be attributed to language transfer (interference from the native language) can be found at the level of pronunciation, morphology, syntax, vocabulary, or meaning (Richards 1974.) Transfer errors in vocabulary and the encoding of meaning can occur when learners use strategies such as literal translation or language switch (the use of a native-language term without translation) to solve their communication problems (Tarone 1978). An example of an interference error often committed by English-speaking students of French is the use of the expression *"avoir un bon temps"* to mean "to have a good time." The use of a word-for-word literal translation strategy in this case results in an awkward phrase that is not only incorrect, but may also be incomprehensible to native speakers.

Transfer-of-Training. Selinker maintains that some errors may be due to the nature of the learning materials or procedures used in formal second language learning. He cites the example of Serbo-Croatian speakers who learned English from a textbook in which the third-person singular was almost always presented in the masculine form. The interesting fact is that Serbo-Croatian has the same gender distinction as English. Yet, because the learners practiced only the *he* form in textbook drills and exercises, they never really learned to include *she* in their interlanguage repertoire.

Overgeneralization of Target Language Material. Errors derived from overgeneralization result when a previously available strategy or rule is used in new situations where that rule does not apply. For example, students of French often use the auxiliary verb *avoir* exclusively when forming the *passé composé* instead of conjugating certain verbs with the auxiliary *être*. Many ESL students do not add an *-s* to the third-person singular verb form in the present tense, overgeneralizing the use of the form without *-s* in the remaining persons. Overgeneralization is one of the strategies used in reorganizing linguistic material and is sometimes a valuable acquisition tool, but when rules are misapplied and never later refined, this strategy can be an important source of persistent error in interlanguage.

Strategies of Second Language Learning. Language-learning strategies are attempts to develop competence in the language and may include such procedures as the use of formal rules, rote memorization, deliberate rehearsal, contextual guessing, looking for recurring patterns, imitating formulaic routines, seeking opportunities to obtain comprehensible input, appealing for assistance from native speakers or teachers, and the like. Tarone (1980) distinguishes language-learning strategies from language-use strategies, such as communication and production strategies. Production strategies represent attempts to use one's interlanguage system efficiently and clearly, with a minimum of effort, and might include such things as simplification and discourse planning. Communication strategies are quite different from learning strategies and parallel to some extent Selinker's next category, strategies of communication.

Strategies of Second Language Communication. When learners attempt to negotiate meanings with native speakers in authentic language-use situations, they may frequently find themselves at a loss for words due to their imperfect knowledge of the target language. Errors can result from heavy communication demands made on their interlanguage, demands that force them to use strategies like approximation, word coinage, circumlocution, translation, language switch, appeals for assistance, and mime, or else to abandon their message altogether or choose to avoid the topic. Illustration 6.14 presents a typology of these communication strategies with some further definitions of the terms, as given by Tarone (1978, 1980).

It is important to recognize that many of the communication strategies depicted in Illustration 6.14 can be extremely valuable in the language acquisition process and can contribute to the development of the learner's strategic competence, discussed in Chapter 1. The use of paraphrasing strategies, such as approximation and circumlocution, as well as mime or appeals for assistance can often provide learners with new expressions, structures, and vocabulary that they then successfully add to their linguistic repertoire. Teachers need to help learners develop their strategic competence through classroom activities that focus on using circumlocution, definitions, and other paraphrasing techniques that lead to successful communication of meaning. Expressions in the target language such as "I don't understand," "Could you please repeat that?" or "Could you speak more slowly?" can also be taught overtly so that students can appeal for assistance when it is needed. Problems may arise, however, when learners are consistently faced with communication situations that far outstrip their current level of proficiency, leading to over-reliance on compensatory strategies and the use of incomprehensible forms in an attempt to get their message across.

Selinker (1974) uses the term *fossilization* to refer to the permanent retention of non-native interlanguage forms in the learners' developing linguistic system. Selinker and Lamendella (1979) make a distinction between *fossilization* and *stabilization;* in the latter case, non-native items, structures, or subsystems in the interlanguage grammar are not permanent, but may eventually "destabilize" or change toward the target-language norm. If, however, such items remain in the interlanguage, even when the learner's motivation, persistence, ability, and opportunity to learn are optimal, then fossilization may have indeed occurred. Selinker and Lamendella suggest that fossilization is more likely to occur if learners see no reason to improve their interim grammar and decide that it is adequate to serve their needs. Swain's (1985) "pushed output" hypothesis,

Illustration 6.14
A Typology of
Communication
Strategies

Paraphrase

Approximation	Use of a single target language vocabulary item or structure, which the learner knows is not correct, but which shares enough semantic features in common with the desired item to satisfy the speaker (e.g., "pipe" for "waterpipe").
Word coinage	The learner makes up a new word in order to communicate a desired concept (e.g., "airball" for "balloon").
Circumlocution	The learner describes the characteristics or elements of the object or action instead of using the appropriate TL structure ("She is, uh, smoking something. I don't know what's its name. That's, uh, Persian, and we use in Turkey, a lot of").

Transfer

Literal translation	The learner translates word for word from the native language (e.g., "He invites him to drink" for "They toast one another").
Language switch	The learner uses the NL term without bothering to translate (e.g., "balon" for "balloon" or "tirtil" for "caterpillar").
Appeal for assistance	The learner asks for the correct term or structure (e.g., "What is this?").
Mime	The learner uses nonverbal strategies in place of a meaning structure (e.g., clapping one's hands to illustrate applause).

Avoidance

Topic avoidance	Occurs when the learner simply does not talk about concepts for which the vocabulary or other meaning structure is not known.
Message abandonment	Occurs when the learner begins to talk about a concept but is unable to continue due to lack of meaning structure, and stops in mid-utterance.

Source: Tarone 1978, 1980, p. 429.

which was discussed in Chapter 3, is consistent with this viewpoint. She suggests that learners sometimes need to receive negative feedback when they use language imprecisely or incoherently and be encouraged to find more appropriate ways to express their meaning. Classroom activities that challenge learners to move just beyond their current level of competence and that give them feedback about the degree of precision and coherence in their target-language use can provide an optimal balance among proficiency goals as students' skills develop.

How should teachers respond to language-learner language in order to provide helpful feedback without stifling creativity? Which errors should be selected for correction and/or feedback? We may gain some insight into these questions by considering first the way native speakers react to learners' errors, both orally and in writing. The next section presents a summary of results of some studies that have been conducted on this question in a variety of language communities.

Attitudes Toward Interlanguage: Native-Speaker Reaction Studies

There has been a good deal of interest among scholars interested in interlanguage in documenting the reactions of native speakers to the language use of non-natives in an effort to understand what constitutes successful and unsuccessful communication. Although linguistic considerations have been central to many of the studies, affective reactions to learners themselves have also been subject to inquiry.

One important variable to be considered in assessing the results of a given research effort is the nature of the interlanguage sample used to elicit reactions. The speech samples and/or writing samples provided to native-speaker judges essentially define interlanguage operationally for that study. In the studies examined here, the samples have ranged from artificially created sentence pairs, presented out of context, to audiovisual tapes of connected discourse, obtained in naturalistic interview situations. Given that the samples vary considerably, the studies are not directly comparable, and results cannot be as clearly interpreted, therefore, as one might like.

Ludwig (1982) has synthesized the results of twelve native-speaker reaction studies, exploring the themes of comprehensibility, irritation, and acceptability that characterize most of them.

Five of the twelve studies concentrate on the *comprehensibility* of interlanguage—that is, the degree to which the interlocutor understands what has been written or said. In three of these studies (Guntermann 1978; Chastain 1980; Piazza 1980), the sample consisted of artificially created sentences that illustrated what learners might say, rather than authentic discourse. Ludwig points out that one advantage to using constructed samples is that the researcher has maximum control over the linguistic factors that are hypothesized to affect comprehensibility. An obvious disadvantage is that such samples do not represent or replicate real communicative language use and are presented out of context. A particular feature pinpointed in a sentence pair might seem incomprehensible in the absence of contextual support; however, that same feature might be quite a bit more comprehensible if it were embedded in authentic discourse. The results of such studies, therefore, should be interpreted with caution. (See, however, Ngame 1992, below.)

In the three studies in Ludwig's review using artificially created sentences, results revealed a marked degree of sensitivity to verb forms and tense usage, both in terms of *comprehensibility* and *irritation*, the latter term representing the effect the interlanguage message had on the native speaker's perception of the communication.Degrees of irritation can range from unconcerned, undistracted, or aware of the error, to constant preoccupation with the form, and, in the most extreme case, to loss of the message altogether. Although comprehensibility and irritation are linked in these and similar studies, an error that causes irritation does not always interfere with comprehension. Generally, however, the studies reveal that higher comprehensibility is linked with lower irritation, as one would expect (Ludwig 1982).

In a study conducted by Politzer (1978) with German teenagers as informants, a series of sentence pairs was presented and the German students were asked to indicate which item in each pair represented the most serious violation of language rules. The study found that vocabulary errors were considered most serious in 77 percent of the sentence pairs where vocabulary problems were present, that grammatical errors were indicated as serious in sentences where they occurred 50 to 55 percent of the time, and that in 36 percent of the pairings with other error types, phonological errors were indicated.

In Chastain's 1980 study, sentences were constructed from a list of the most frequent and most serious errors perceived by teaching assistants in their Spanish classes at the University of Virginia. Forty-eight native speakers in Madrid evaluated the sentence pairs, 90 percent of which were comprehensible to them. Yet 50 percent or more of the evaluators said that half of the errors, though comprehensible, were unacceptable to them, even though they did not, for the most part, affect the message content. The fact remains, however, that half of the errors deemed serious and stigmatizing to the teachers were considered acceptable by the native-speaker informants, showing a relatively high degree of error tolerance, at least among the population sampled.

In Ensz's 1982 study of French attitudes toward speech errors of American students, an interesting compromise was reached between artificially constructed speech samples and authentic discourse. The technique used in the experiment presented language samples in the context of a passage, but the passage was constructed to meet the needs of the experiment. Three passages were developed, each with five different versions corresponding to error type. In the first version of each passage, pronunciation was quite good, but the vocabulary and grammatical structure was weak. In the second version, pronunciation and grammar were particularly good, but vocabulary was weak. The third version of the passages was characterized by good control of grammatical features, but weaknesses in pronunciation and vocabulary. In the fourth version, grammar and vocabulary usage was good, but pronunciation was poor. The final version of the passages was the most native-like, with some weaknesses in pronunciation only. These pronunciation problems were not as serious, however, as those in the fourth version.

Ensz asked native speakers of French to react to the passages in terms of error tolerance and attitude toward the speakers heard. The sampled population included raters from all age groups and occupations—shopkeepers, salespeople, professionals, teachers, housewives, mothers, and students. Results indicated that the French listeners, irrespective of sex, age, occupation, or home region in France, found grammatical errors to be the least tolerable of the three error types emphasized in the study. The 250 respondants preferred the fifth version of the passages over all the others, followed by the second version, where only vocabulary errors prevailed. The least preferred samples were those in which pronunciation was good, but where vocabulary and grammar errors were prevalent. Ensz concluded that "while an American accent and some anglicisms may be moderately tolerable, American speakers of French should be most concerned that they speak with the greatest possible grammatical accuracy" (pp. 137-38). The fact that raters expressed a significant intolerance for error shows that French-speaking communities may be especially sensitive to accuracy—perhaps more so than are other language groups.

Ngame (1992) conducted a study comparing the reactions of native speakers of two very different language groups to Intermediate-level language samples drawn from ACTFL oral proficiency interviews. He asked 40 native speakers of Swahili and French to listen to 10 samples of learner language in their respective languages and rate them on a seven-point scale according to the comprehensibility and acceptability of the language heard. He also had the native speakers rate the grammatical accuracy, fluency, vocabulary usage, and pronunciation of each of the 10 samples of Intermediate-level speech. Another aspect of the experimental design was the inclusion of 50 single sentences, drawn from the interviews and presented in random order, to ascertain whether the presence or absence of a surrounding meaningful context affected the ratings. Ngame found that contextualization of the samples had no significant effect on ratings, and that the two native-speaker groups rated the speech samples in a very *parallel* fashion. The most interesting finding was that on all measures, the Swahili native speakers were significantly more lenient in their ratings than the French native speakers. For both native-speaker groups, comprehensibility was rated higher than acceptability and the four linguistic measures. Fluency and pronunciation were rated lowest, followed by lexical and syntactic measures, which were rated somewhat more favorably. None of the measures in the oral proficiency samples in French received a mean rating as high as 4 on the 7-point scale. The Swahili speakers gave mean ratings between 4 and 5 on vocabulary and grammatical measures and a mean of 5.62 on the comprehensibility of the contextualized sample, compared to 3.91 in French. Ngame concluded that linguistic and cultural backgrounds have an important impact on native-speaker perception of nonnative speech. He also found that the oral performance of Intermediate-level learners in both languages was considered intelligible despite linguistic errors.

Several native-speaker reaction studies, like those of Ensz and Ngame, have used fuller discourse in presenting samples of interlanguage to informants: Chastain's 1981 study used excerpts from student compositions; Galloway (1980) used interviews and short monologues; and Albrechtsen, Henriksen, and Faerch (1980) presented listeners with spoken interviews on tape. Ludwig (1982) includes these last three studies in her review. The summaries below are based, in part, on points she has highlighted in comparing results from these studies.

In Chastain's study using student compositions, the most frequent response from native speakers was that the written language samples were quite comprehensible (only 10 percent of the errors were considered incomprehensible), but that they were unacceptable. Overall, errors in form were slightly less comprehensible and less acceptable than semantic errors in verb phrases, yet the reverse was true in noun phrases. Generally, however, Chastain reports that native speakers react more negatively to form errors than to word errors, at least in written communications. The study supports the hypothesis that, in Spanish, there is a hierarchy of error gravity from a communicative point of view, with semantic errors in noun phrases most serious, followed by form errors in verb phrases, semantic errors in verb phrases, and form errors in noun phrases (p. 293).

In Galloway's study, videotaped interviews were used as samples to be judged by native Spanish speakers. She found that when learners made a visible effort to communicate, the native speakers responded most favorably to the interlanguage sample. However, she cautions that this attitude of acceptance might well be limited to speakers who are at the beginning stages of language study (Novice and Intermediate), and that tolerance may wane with interlanguage users who have clearly had more exposure to the language. Galloway, as well as Ervin (1977) in Russian, also explored the differences between native and non-native speakers' judgments. Both researchers found that the ratings of second language speakers' performance did not differ significantly between the two groups of judges. In Galloway's results, there was a trend for the native speaker who was *not* a teacher to be most accepting, whereas nonnative teachers were least accepting of inaccurate speech and reacted more negatively to slowness of delivery than did native speakers. Ervin found, on the other hand, that the native-speaking teachers of Russian were the most critical of all the judges, regardless of the proficiency level of the sample, and that nonnative teachers were the most accepting, especially of students in the lower proficiency ranges. Schairer (1992) found support for Galloway's results in a study comparing native-speaking Spanish teachers' reactions with those of native Spanish speakers who were not teachers. She found that the teachers were generally more strict in their judgments than were non-teachers, and that the native speakers who knew no English were more lenient in evaluating the comprehensibility of the samples than were raters who spoke English (p. 311).

The study by Albrechtsen, Henriksen, and Faerch (1980) assessed a wide range of native-speaker reactions to stretches of discourse produced by Danish learners of English, obtained in oral interviews that paralleled in many ways the ACTFL/ETS Oral Proficiency Interview. Native speakers reacted to the speech samples using fourteen bipolar adjective scales (a type of semantic differential), and factor analyses were performed on the data to isolate four separate criteria: personality, content, language (an accuracy criterion), and comprehension. The results on the language and comprehension factors were later compared with results obtained from an objective analysis of the samples in terms of performance features. Highly significant correlations were obtained between the subjective judgments made by the native speakers on the language criterion (using the bipolar adjective measure) and the actual data on the performance features of the interview samples. However, the only performance feature that correlated significantly with the subjective judgment of comprehensibility was the use of communication strategies (see Illustration 6.14). The more communication strategies used by the second language learners in this study, the less comprehensible their discourse was judged to be.

The Albrechtsen et al. results seem to indicate that extensive use of strategies such as message abandonment, approximation, word coinage, circumlocution, literal translation, language switch, appeals for assistance, self-correction, and false starts reveals that the learner is having a great deal of difficulty encoding a message and is being pushed beyond his or her level of competence by the communicative demands of the situation. When this happened in this particular study, the native speakers tended to judge the interlanguage more harshly. The samples that received the most positive evaluations were those in which there were few lexical and syntactic errors and few communication strategies. Samples containing many errors, syntactic and lexical, and a large number of communication strategies were judged most severely, while positive evaluations were obtained for interlanguage samples that contained a fair number of syntactic and lexical errors, as long as there were also few instances of communication strategies used. This finding is intriguing and suggests that further study is warranted to evaluate the effects of the use of communication strategies on native speaker reactions to nonnative speech. Albrechtsen et al. conclude from the analysis of their results that "all errors are equally irritating" (p. 394) and that it is fruitless to search for a hierarchy of error gravity based on typology alone. "Whether an error impairs the intelligibility of the interlanguage or not is perhaps not primarily a function of its inherent qualities, but of the context in which it occurs" (p. 393).

One can reach certain general conclusions, however, about the gravity of errors in more global terms. In general, texts rated most negatively were characterized by lack of contextual support for errors in content words, extensive use of restructurings and self-corrections, and incorrect use of conjunctions and pronouns, resulting in illogical and incoherent discourse.

Texts rated most positively, on the other hand, generally included contextual support for errors in content words, choice of semantically related words when substitution strategies were used, and correct use of connectors, such as conjunctions and pronouns. One implication for teaching might be that teachers need to pay more attention to suprasentential elements of discourse—a finding that supports the ideas presented in earlier chapters about teaching language in context and using fuller discourse as a basis for language practice activities.

One other study reveals that native-speaker attitudes toward an interlanguage speech sample, in terms of grammaticality, may be distinguishable from attitudes towards the speaker of the target language himself. Gynan (1984) used a questionnaire in soliciting native-speaker reactions to speech samples in which three types of questions were featured: (1) the natives were asked to agree or disagree with statements about the formal aspects of the sample; (2) they were to indicate whether or not they liked the speech they heard; and (3) they were asked to indicate their socio-affective response to the person speaking.

Analyses of these data showed that attitudes toward *speech* are measurably different from attitudes toward the *person speaking*. Gynan thus distinguishes two ideas that have been confused, in his view, in other native-speaker reaction studies: irritation and acceptability. In his view, *irritation* is an affective language attitude (i.e., an attitude about the speaker), whereas *acceptability* is an evaluative attitude toward the speech sample itself. Gynan feels that native speakers may not be willing to state that they are annoyed, bothered, or irritated by interlanguage, but that they may be quite willing to state that the interlanguage is less accurate or less comprehensible than the native language.

In Gynan's study, five samples of Spanish were elicited by asking the speakers to describe a series of photographs. Speakers ranged from native to nonnative speakers whose language included: (1) a typical standard Mexican variety, (2) a Northern Mexican variety, (3) fluent Spanish spoken by a native speaker of English, (4) an intermediate learner's Spanish, and (5) a beginning learner's Spanish. Native speakers were chosen from a variety of backgrounds. The results showed that mean affect scores for all the samples were noticeably higher than mean language scores and that the most variance in attitude was attributable to the region from which the judges came. The rater characteristics in this study, in general, made very little difference in terms of attitudes toward the interlanguage itself; rather, differences in rater characteristics did have a significant effect on the socio-affective attitudes towards the speakers of the interlanguage.

In general, the last two language users in this study received negative evaluations and negative judgments of work potential, showing that they were not yet at the threshold of communicative proficiency needed to satisfy practical demands when living off the economy. The better of these two students was in his fourth semester of language study and had been receiving a grade of B in his courses. This finding has interesting implications for classroom teachers and lends support to the hypothesis that some type of error correction or feedback is warranted in the beginning levels of instruction.

Error Correction Strategies for the Classroom

In Chapter 3, a rationale for providing students with corrective feedback was presented in the discussion associated with Hypothesis 3, reproduced below:

> **Hypothesis 3.** *The development of accuracy should be encouraged in proficiency-oriented instruction. As learners produce language, various forms of instruction and evaluative feedback can be useful in facilitating the progression of their skills toward more precise and coherent language use.*

Throughout this chapter, as well as in Chapters 5 and 7, a whole range of instructional formats and strategies that can be used to help learners develop their language skills has been illustrated. The formats that are presented range along a kind of continuum from those that focus on formal features of the target language to those that invite students to use the language in task-based, more creative ways. This section examines the types of evaluative feedback that can be useful in responding to learner language as students engage in speaking activities of various types. (Feedback and correction strategies useful in responding to student writing are presented and discussed in Chapter 7.)

Many scholars and practitioners agree that the type of feedback one provides to students should vary according to the purposes of the activity in which they are engaged. When learners are focused on mastery of particular features of the language, they will probably profit most from fairly direct and immediate feedback on the correctness of their responses. If, on the other hand, they are attempting to communicate ideas in an open-ended or creative task, the most beneficial feedback may be a positive response to the message that is being conveyed and further input from the teacher or their classmates that is meaningful and communicative in nature. Any corrective feedback that is needed can be reserved for a later time, or provided indirectly in substantive responses. Teachers need to develop a whole range of feedback mechanisms and determine when and how to use them to foster optimal growth in proficiency.

How can one determine what feedback strategies are most useful for students involved in particular kinds of practice activities? The answers are certainly not simple. As was pointed out in Chapter 2, learners differ widely in terms of their personality characteristics, learning styles, and learning preferences. What works for one student may not work well for another. Furthermore, students at a relatively low level of oral proficiency may need different kinds of feedback than students whose proficiency is higher. A few examples from studies on the effects of feedback illustrate the complex nature of the issues involved in responding to learner needs and preferences. In the context of oral work, Cathcart and Olsen (1976) found that students felt the need to be corrected and preferred consistent corrective feedback. Courchêne (1980) reports similar results in a study with ESL students. On the other hand, Walker (1973) reports that students believe frequent correction destroys their confidence and prefer to be allowed to communicate freely without constant intervention from the teacher. A complicating factor in studies such as these is the fact that the exact nature of the "feedback" or "correction" provided and the conditions under which students were corrected can differ considerably from study to study, yielding conflicting results. The assumption that all learners receive corrective feedback in the same way and with the same degree of enthusiasm is also problematic. As we examine various feedback strategies below, we need to keep in mind that they may work differentially with different learners and should therefore not be used in a rigid or prescriptive fashion.

Walz (1982) has provided a useful review of issues related to error correction and gives practical suggestions for responding to students' errors. He presents various opinions that have been voiced in the literature about which errors should be corrected by teachers and which can be safely ignored. Allwright (1975) has argued that errors that interfere with meaning and comprehension are clearly more important than those that do not, an opinion shared by many other scholars. Burt and Kiparsky (1974) have suggested that teachers distinguish between *local* errors, or those that do not go beyond the clause or sentence level, and *global* errors, or those that interfere with comprehension by causing confusion in the relationships between and among the major parts of the discourse. Examples of local errors include lack of agreements, misused or missing articles, or verb-phrase errors that do not impede comprehension. Global errors include the misuse or absence of logical connectors, the lack of proper tense sequences, the misuse of pronouns, and errors involving other features of language that create cohesive and coherent discourse across sentences. Burt and Kiparsky contend that global errors should be corrected and that local errors that do not interfere with comprehension should usually be left alone. Again, the wisdom of this policy will depend on the *purpose* of the activity in which the student is engaged. If students are concentrating on mastery of some formal feature of the language, they will benefit from knowing if they have gotten it right, even if the error is "local." A lack of feedback in this instance might be confusing to learners who are expecting to have their hypotheses confirmed or rejected by the teacher or a group monitor. If, on the other hand, the student is communicating a message without focusing on its form, the immediate and invasive correction of his or her speech may be annoying, disruptive, or discouraging, especially if the error being pinpointed does not impede comprehension.

Hendrickson (1979) suggests that a hierarchy be established for oral errors based on the students' current level of proficiency. He proposes that global errors be corrected for elementary students and that frequent local and global errors be targeted for intermediate students. Advanced students should be alerted to any errors that have a stigmatizing effect on native speakers.

Cohen (1975) suggests a comprehensive system for error selection, including four areas of analysis:

1. *Basic Information about the Error.* One needs to consider what was said versus what was meant.
2. *Importance of the Correction.* The most important errors can be determined using the following criteria:

   a. Intelligibility
   b. High frequency
   c. High generality of rules
   d. Stigmatizing or irritating effects
   e. Number of students affected
   f. Pedagogical focus

3. *Ease of Correction.*
4. *Characteristics of Students.* Correction may depend on individual differences, such as each student's past history, current state of mind, and affective considerations.

Ervin (1981, cited in Magnan, 1982) suggests that an error-correction hierarchy might be based on error severity, determined by the intersection of three factors: (1) effect, or degree of stigmatization, (2) comprehensibility, and (3) source of error in the student's competence or performance grammar. He proposes a three-dimensional model, shown in Illustration 6.15.

The highest priority for correction would be given to errors that stigmatize, cause a lack of comprehension, and originate in the learner's competence grammar; the lowest priority would be given to errors that are generally tolerated by native speakers, do not interfere with comprehension, and are due to performance errors.

Walz (1982), in summarizing these various correction schemes, suggests one of his own. He posits four basic criteria for selecting errors to be corrected:

1. *Comprehensibility.* Above all, choose errors that interfere with understanding first.
2. *Frequency.* More frequent errors should be corrected consistently, while isolated slips can be left alone.
3. *Pedagogical Focus.* It is best to correct errors that reflect misunderstanding or incomplete acquisition of material that is the focus of

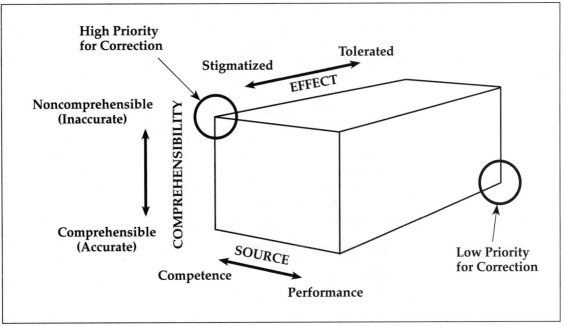

Illustration 6.15
Ervin's Model for Error
Severity

Source: Ervin, 1985 (Personal Communication).

current classroom practice. If such errors are left uncorrected, students who notice the mistake might become confused about their own understanding of the concept being covered.

4. *Individual Student Concerns.* Walz suggests that all good teachers get to know students well enough to be able to sense their reactions to various correction techniques. More capable, secure students will profit more from the correction of minor errors than will students who feel less capable. These latter students might profit most from the correction of major mistakes only.

Correction and feedback strategies may differ not only in terms of the learner's capabilities or level of performance, the task at hand, and the focus of the activity, but also in terms of the modality in which the task is accomplished (i.e., oral vs. written production). Written errors may reflect different processing strategies than oral errors, and thus require different treatment. In addition, feedback given on written work is usually more private than that given during oral activities, and thus might be more extensive. For these and other reasons already mentioned, error-correction policies need to be flexible. However, a certain consistency in the teacher's response to student work is also desirable if students are to derive maximum benefit from the feedback they receive.

It may also be helpful for teachers to discuss with students the feedback policy they use and their rationale for choosing it. As was mentioned above, Walz (1982) suggests that teachers can often sense their students' reactions to feedback and adjust their responses according to perceived learner capabilities. Teachers might consider going one step further and asking students directly about their own preferences for feedback, both for oral and written practice. Student desires can then be taken into account as teachers consider how they are going to respond to students' language use.

Most practitioners recognize that error correction must be done in a positive manner to be most effective. Teachers should correct gently, and with respect, especially in oral work that is being done in front of others.

Another consideration in providing feedback relates to *who* does the correcting. Students are often capable of self-correction and can also help correct one another. Some ideas for peer correction, as well as self-correction with teacher guidance, are given in the next section.

Some Procedures for Giving Feedback During Oral Practice Activities

Walz (1982) classifies error-correction procedures into three basic categories: (1) self-correction with the teacher's help, (2) peer correction, and (3) teacher correction. There are many specific techniques within these categories that teachers can use to provide corrective feedback to students. The following suggestions are appropriate for activities where a focus on accuracy and formal correctness is desired. This would be the case, for example, if particular linguistic features are being practiced orally in structured exercises.

1. *Self-Correction with Teacher Helping*

    a. *Pinpointing.* The teacher localizes the error without providing the correct form by repeating the student's response up to the point at which the error is made, hesitating, and exaggerating the last word slightly with a rising intonation:

    S: Je vais aller *à le** supermarché.

    T: Je vais aller . . .

    S: Je vais aller au supermarché.

    b. *Cuing.* Instead of supplying the correct answer, the teacher provides some options for the incorrect or missing element, as in an oral multiple choice:

    T: When is your next class?

    S: My next class is . . . uh . . . (student hesitates over time expression)

T: At one o'clock? two o'clock? two thirty? . . .

S: My class is at three o'clock.

c. *Providing your own answer.* The teacher cues the student by providing his or her own answer to the question, thereby supplying a model:

T: Where did you go on your vacation?

S: I . . . uh . . . (student hesitates over the verb form)

T: I went to Colorado and Utah this summer. What about you?

S: Oh! I went to Florida with my friends.

d. *Repetition of an answer, with correction.* Without making an overt correction, the teacher repeats the student's response, subtly correcting the mistake. This technique is somewhat indirect: some students will pick up the cue, while others may not notice.

T: Avez-vous des disques de musique classique?

S: Non, je n'ai pas *des** disques.

T: Oh, tu n'as pas de disques. As-tu des cassettes?

S: Non, je n'ai pas de cassettes.

e. *Rephrasing a question, after a formally correct, but inappropriate response to the original formulation has been given:*

T: When are you leaving for vacation?

S: I am going to Florida.

T: Oh, that sounds like fun! But when are you leaving? Monday, Tuesday, . . . ?

S: I'm leaving on Sunday.

2. *Peer Correction.*

a. *Student monitors.* When monitoring devices are used in small-group work (such as "corrector's cards" in structured conversation and interview activities that provide cues to the correct form of questions and/or answers), students are able to provide feedback for their peers. For an example of a student monitoring card, see the sample activity using conversation cards on p. 259

b. *Group monitoring with checklists.* Students might also enjoy recording their own speech or conversations in small groups on occasion, following this with a group correction activity where closer attention can be paid to form and/or content. A checklist can be provided by the teacher for this group work that cues students about the types of features to look for in the speech sample. For example, if students in a small group are conversing about past events, the teacher can provide the group with a list of questions to ask themselves as they listen more closely to what they said. Questions could relate to grammatical features (forms of the past tense[s], for example), discourse features (the use of connectors, appropriate strategies for turn-taking, and the like), or vocabulary (the use of a variety of words and expressions studied). Students can be asked to present their own corrections for the teacher's reactions and then re-record their conversation, incorporating the changes they have identified (A similar idea, proposed by Swain and Lapkin (1989) was discussed in chapter 4, p. 156.).

3. *Teacher Correction.*

   a. *Direct correction of errors.* Teachers can choose to correct students' responses directly by modeling the appropriate form of the utterance that the student attempted to make, preserving as much of what was said as possible, and drawing the students' attention to the change. It may be followed by a request for the student or the whole class to repeat the corrected response. This technique may be most defensible when students are engaged in doing structured exercises and the teacher wants to maintain a fairly rapid pace. However, direct and immediate correction may not be as beneficial to learners as more indirect techniques that invite the learner to self-correct with teacher help.

   b. *Indirect correction.* This technique involves the repetition of a student response with a correction made, but without drawing the student's attention to the change or requiring a repetition of the corrected material. Note that the technique outlined in 1.d, above, involves indirect correction through the teacher's *response* to the learner rather than by repetition of what the learner said, and includes an invitation to the student to give another response of a similar type. This strategy not only gives the student a chance to process the feedback given by the teacher, but also informs the teacher about whether or not that feedback was heard and could be used by the learner. The strategy in 1.d also has a more "conversational" feel to it than a direct correction where no further interchange with the student takes place.

As was mentioned earlier, the feedback strategies outlined above are most appropriate when the focus of the oral activity is at least partially on formal accuracy of the response. Teachers might respond to students differently in more open-ended, communicative exchanges when the focus is primarily on the meanings being expressed. In such cases, the feedback should be positive and substantive, as the teacher expresses interest in the student's ideas and follows up with additional questions or comments. An example in English below serves to illustrate this strategy:

> T: Could you tell me something about your family?
> S: I have two *brother** and one sister.
> T: Oh, there are four children in your family too. I have three brothers. What are your brothers like? (etc.)

In this exchange, the student's answer is valued for what it is, and no specific attention is drawn to the error made since it does not interfere with comprehension. The teacher's response provides the positive message that the student has been understood and that it is interesting to engage him or her in further conversation. Responding to the message rather than to its form can, in this case, be motivating to learners who are struggling to communicate with minimal proficiency in the new language. Note, however, that in the teacher's response, an indirect correction of the plural *brothers* has been given through further conversation with the student. Thus it is possible that communicative exchanges between teachers and students that are not focused on correction *per se* can still provide corrective feedback incidentally as the conversation continues.

Summary: Developing Oral Proficiency

In this chapter, we have considered the nature of language-learner language and explored ways to help students develop their proficiency in speaking. As we have seen throughout this chapter, a proficiency-based approach to oral skill development should provide not only a wide variety of instructional techniques and activity formats, but also a balanced approach to feedback and correction strategies geared to the purposes of the activities chosen for practice. Communicative activities should be encouraged from the beginning of instruction, but there is reason to believe that such activities should be carefully planned so that they are within the range of the students' competence. Activities that require students to communicate their own meaning, yet are easy enough to avoid over-reliance on communication strategies, seem to hold the most promise in a proficiency-oriented approach. Attention to accuracy does not imply a classroom environment where grammar rules reign supreme and correction is rigidly imposed. Rather, the proficiency-oriented classroom is one in which students have ample opportunities to use language creatively and to obtain appropriate feedback with which they can progressively build and refine their interlanguage to approximate the target language norm. This feedback is provided in an atmosphere characterized by acceptance of error as a necessary condition for linguistic growth, an atmosphere in which the teacher is seen as a valuable resource in the language-learning process.

The ideas presented in this chapter represent only a small sampling of those that have been suggested in the professional literature in recent years. The reader is encouraged to explore some of the sources in the references at the end of the chapter for more ideas for activities and creative practice formats.[2]

Notes:

1. The DLI Task Force on Curriculum Policy and Planning (June 1984) included the following consultants and DLI staff members: Mahmood Taba Tabai (DLI, Chair); Sabine Atwell (DLI); Diane Birckbichler (Ohio State University); Maj. Lloyd Brimball (DLI); Benjamin De La Selva (DLI); Gerard Ervin (Ohio State University); Nabil Faltas (DLI); Jerry Larson (Brigham Young University); John Lett (DLI); David Olney (DLI); Alice Omaggio (University of Illinois at Urbana-Champaign); Frank Synn (DLI); and Galal Walker (Ohio State University). This task force developed a plan for curriculum and materials development based largely on the ILR Proficiency Scale, from which the academic ACTFL/ETS scale was derived. The curricular plans provided in this chapter are derived from, but not identical to, those created by the DLI Task Force.

2. Sections of this chapter are revised and expanded from material that appeared in a chapter written for the ACTFL Foreign Language Education Series entitled "The Proficiency-Oriented Classroom." See Omaggio 1984 in the references to this chapter for the full bibliographic citation.

• • • • • • • • • • • • *Activities for Review and Discussion*

1. Define briefly each of the following terms:

   a. Interlanguage
   b. Fossilization
   c. Variability
   d. Overgeneralization
   e. Interference
   f. Performance error
   g. Communication strategies
   h. Feedback

2. Discuss briefly the five processes central to language acquisition identified by Selinker. Give one or two concrete examples of each of these processes, drawing from your own language-acquisition experience or that of your students, if applicable. If possible, get a

sample (oral or written) of language-learner language and identify the possible source(s) of error in that sample.

3. The following terms refer to categories of activities or exercises that can be used to practice oral skills. For each term, give a brief definition and an appropriate sample exercise or activity format.

   a. Precommunicative practice
   b. Forced-choice questions
   c. Logical conclusions
   d. Visually-aided exercises
   e. Personalized completions
   f. Sentence-builders
   g. Elaboration activities
   h. Conversation cards
   i. Situational role-plays
   j. Functional practice activities

4. List some of the advantages of using small-group or paired activities for building oral skills. Then list some potential problems or disadvantages in using this type of instructional format. How can such problems be handled or avoided? What are some important considerations to bear in mind when planning small-group work?

5. Examine various language textbooks and evaluate them in terms of their potential for fostering the development of oral skills. Begin your evaluation by listing various criteria that you would consider important in textbook materials that are proficiency-oriented. Then compare several texts on the basis of your list of criteria.

6. Review the group puzzles, group decision-making activities, and social interaction games that accompany the discussion of Corollary 2 (pp. 250–263). Using these activities as a guide, design a simple communication game that could be used with beginning or intermediate students. Be sure to state your objective(s), the context used, the function(s) practiced, and any grammatical features or lexical items highlighted in the activity.

7. Based on your understanding of the information given in this chapter, discuss the role of feedback in language acquisition.

8. What conclusion have you drawn about the effect of errors on native speakers' reactions to interlanguage? List at least five statements summarizing your conclusions, based on your reading of this chapter.

9. Should students' oral errors be corrected in the language-learning process? If not, why not? If so, what criteria would you use for error correction? Discuss whether or not your criteria would vary, depending on the type of language activity in which students are involved (e.g., communicative versus manipulative practice, etc.).

•••••••••••• *References*

Active Lab: Student Interaction with the Media. Course offered by the Division of Faculty and Staff Development, Defense Language Institute, Presidio of Monterey, CA, n.d.

"Applications of Oral Proficiency Testing to Foreign Language Instruction." Hastings-on-Hudson, NY: ACTFL, 1985 (ERIC Document Reproduction Service no. ED 280 309).

Albrechtsen, D., B. Henriksen, and C. Faerch. "Native Speaker Reactions to Learners' Spoken Interlanguage." *Language Learning* 30 (1980): 365–96.

Allwright, R.L. "Problems in the Study of the Language Teacher's Treatment of Learner Error." In M.K. Burt and H.C. Dulay, eds., *On TESOL '75: New Directions in Second Language Learning, Teaching, and Bilingual Education.* Washington, DC. TESOL, 1975.

Birckbichler, Diane W. *Creative Activities for the Second Language Classroom.* Language in Education: Theory and Practice Series, no. 48. Washington, DC: Center for Applied Linguistics, 1982.

Bonin, Thérèse and D. Birckbichler. "Real Communication through Conversation Cards." *The Modern Language Journal* 59 (1975): 22–25.

Bragger, Jeannette D. "The Development of Oral Proficiency." In A. Omaggio, ed., *Proficiency, Curriculum, Articulation: The Ties That Bind.* Middlebury, VT: Northeast Conference, 1985.

Buck, Kathryn, Heidi Byrnes, and Irene Thompson, eds. *The ACTFL Oral Proficiency Interview Tester Training Manual.* Yonkers, NY: ACTFL, 1989.

Burt, Marina and C. Kiparsky. "Global and Local Mistakes." In J. Schumann and N. Stenson, eds., *New Frontiers in Second Language Learning.* Rowley, MA: Newbury House, 1974.

Cathcart, Ruth L. and Judy E.W. Olsen. "Teachers' and Students' Preferences for Correction of Classroom Conversation Errors." In. J.F. Fanselow and R. H. Crymes, eds., *On TESOL '76.* Washington, DC: TESOL (1976): 41–53.

Chastain, Kenneth. "Native Speaker Reaction to Instructor-Identified Student Second Language Errors." *The Modern Language Journal* 64 (1980): 210–15.

_____. "Native Speaker Evaluation of Student Composition Errors." *The Modern Language Journal* 65 (1981): 288–94.

Chastain, Kenneth and Gail Guntermann. *¡Imagínate! Managing Conversations in Spanish,* 2nd ed. Boston: Heinle & Heinle, 1991.

Cohen, Andrew. "Error Correction and the Training of Language Teachers." *The Modern Language Journal* 59 (1975): 414–21.

Corder, S.P. "The Significance of Learners' Errors." *International Review of Applied Linguistics* 5, iv (1967): 161–70.

_____. "Language-Learner Language." In J.C. Richards, ed., *Understanding Second and Foreign Language Learning: Issues and Approaches.* Rowley, MA: Newbury House, 1978.

Courchêne, Robert. "The Error Analysis Hypothesis, the Contrastive Analysis Hypothesis, and the Correction of Error in the Second Language Classroom." *TESL Talk* 11 (1980).

Debyser, Francis and H. Laitenberger. "Le Crocodile et le moulin à vent." *Le Français dans le monde* 123 (1976): 14–19.

Ellis, Rod. "Discourse Processes in Classroom Second Language Development."

Ph.D. Thesis, University of London, 1982. [Cited in Ellis, 1985.]

_____. *Understanding Second Language Acquisition*. Oxford: Oxford University Press, 1985.

Ensz, Kathleen. "French Attitudes toward Speech Errors." *The Modern Language Journal* 66 (1982): 133–39.

Ervin, G. "A Study of the Use and Acceptability of Target-Language Communication Strategies Employed by American Students of Russian." Ph.D. Dissertation, The Ohio State University, 1977. [Cited in Ludwig, 1982.]

_____. Preconference Workshop for College Teachers of Foreign Languages, Wisconsin Association of Foreign Language Teachers' Conference, Madison, WI, October 1981. [Cited in Magnan, 1982.]

_____. Personal Communication, 1985.

Galloway, Vicki. "Perceptions of the Communicative Efforts of American Students of Spanish." *The Modern Language Journal* 64 (1980): 428–33.

_____. "From Defining to Developing Proficiency: A Look at the Decisions." Chapter 2 (pp. 25–73) in H. Byrnes and M. Canale, eds., *Defining and Developing Proficiency: Guidelines, Implementations and Concepts*. ACTFL Foreign Language Education Series. Lincolnwood, IL: National Textbook Company, 1987.

Gatbonton, Elizabeth and Norman Segalowitz, "Creative Automatization: Principles for Promoting Fluency Within a Communicative Framework." *TESOL Quarterly* 22, iii (1988): 473–92.

Geddes, Marion and Ron White. "The Use of Semi-Scripted Simulated Authentic Speech in Listening Comprehension." *Audiovisual Language Journal* 16, iii (1978): 137–45.

Guilford, J.P. "Three Faces of Intellect." *American Psychologist* 14 (1959): 469–79.

Guntermann, Gail. "A Study of the Frequency and Communicative Effects of Errors in Spanish." *The Modern Language Journal* 62 (1978): 249–53.

Guntermann, Gail, and J.K. Phillips. *Functional-Notional Concepts: Adapting the Foreign Language Textbook*. Language in Education: Theory and Practice Series, no. 44. Washington, DC: Center for Applied Linguistics, 1982.

Gynan, Shaw N. "Attitudes toward Interlanguage: What is the Object of Study?" *The Modern Language Journal* 68 (1984): 315–21.

Hahn, Sidney and Joyce Michaelis. "Classroom Activities: Oral Proficiency in Action," Chapter 7 (pp. 68–81) in Barbara Snyder, ed., *Second Language Aquisition: Preparing for Tomorrow*. Report of the Central States Conference on the Teaching of Foreign Languages. Lincolnwood, IL: National Textbook Company, 1986.

Heilenman, Laura K. and Isabelle Kaplan. "Proficiency in Practice: The Foreign Language Curriculum." In Charles James, ed., *Foreign Language Proficiency in the Classroom and Beyond*. ACTFL Foreign Language Education Series, vol. 16. Lincolnwood, IL: National Textbook Company, 1985.

Hendrickson, James M. "Evaluating Spontaneous Communication Through Systematic Error Analysis." *Foreign Language Annals* 12 (1979): 357–64.

Higgs, Theodore V. "Proficiency Assessment and the Humanities." *ADFL Bulletin* 18, i (1986): 6–8.

Higgs, Theodore V., Judith E. Liskin-Gasparro, and Frank W. Medley, Jr., *Entradas: El español por etapas*. Boston: Heinle & Heinle Publishers, 1989.

Johnson, Keith. *Communicative Syllabus Design and Methodology*. Oxford: Pergamon Press, 1982.

Kramsch, Claire J. *Discourse Analysis and Second Language Teaching.* Language in Education: Theory and Practice Series, no. 37. Washington, DC: Center for Applied Linguistics, 1981.

_____. "Culture and Constructs: Communicating Attitudes and Values in the Foreign Language Classroom." *Foreign Language Annals* 16, vi (1983): 437–48.

Krashen, Stephen. *Principles and Practice in Second Language Acquisition.* New York: Pergamon Press, 1982.

Lazzarino, Graziana. *Prego! An Invitation to Italian.* New York: Random House, 1980.

Littlewood, William. *Communicative Language Teaching: An Introduction.* Cambridge: Cambridge University Press, 1981

Ludwig, Jeannette. "Native Speaker Judgements of Second Language Learners' Efforts at Communication: A Review." *The Modern Language Journal* 66 (1982): 274–83.

Magnan, Sally S. "Native Speaker Reaction as a Criterion for Error Correction." In A. Garfinkle, ed., *ESL and the Foreign Language Teacher.* Report of the Central States Conference on the Teaching of Foreign Languages. Lincolnwood, IL: National Textbook Company, 1982.

Muyskens, Judith A., A. Omaggio, C. Chalmers, C. Imberton, and P. Almeras. *Rendez-vous: An Invitation to French.* New York: Random House, 1982.

Muyskens, Judith A., A. Omaggio Hadley, and C. Convert-Chalmers. *Rendez-vous: An Invitation to French,* 3rd ed. San Francisco: McGraw-Hill, 1990.

Nemser, W. "Approximative Systems of Foreign Language Learners." *International Review of Applied Linguistics* 9, ii (1971): 115–23.

Ngame, Matuku. "A Comparison of French and Kiswahili Native-Speaker Reactions to Nonnative Speech." Ph.D. Dissertation, University of Illinois at Urbana-Champaign, 1992.

Omaggio, Alice C. *Helping Learners Succeed: Activities for the Foreign Language Classroom.* Language in Education: Theory and Practice Series, no. 36. Washington, DC: Center for Applied Linguistics, 1981.

_____. "Using Games and Simulations for the Development of Functional Proficiency in a Second Language." *Canadian Modern Language Review* 38 (1982): 517–46.

_____. "The Proficiency-Oriented Classroom." In T.V. Higgs, ed., *Teaching for Proficiency, the Organizing Principle.* ACTFL Foreign Language Education Series, vol. 15. Lincolnwood, IL: National Textbook Company, 1984.

Omaggio, Alice C., J. Chamberlain, F. Chevillot, and L. Harbour. *Kaléidoscope.* New York: Random House, 1984.

Otero, George and Farren Webb. "Global Education and International Studies." Workshop presented at Southern Illinois University, Carbondale, IL, March 5, 1981.

Piazza, L.G. "French Tolerance for Grammatical Errors Made By Americans." *The Modern Language Journal* 64 (1980): 422–27.

Politzer, R.L. "Errors of English Speakers of German as Perceived and Evaluated by German Natives." *The Modern Language Journal* 62 (1978): 253–61.

Richards, Jack C. "Error Analysis and Second Language Strategies." Pp. 32–53 in J. H. Schumann and N. Stenson, eds., *New Frontiers in Second Language Learning.* Rowley, MA: Newbury House, 1974.

Rivers, Wilga M., M.M. Azevedo, W.H. Heflin, Jr. and R. Hyman-Opler. *A Practical*

Guide to the Teaching of Spanish, New York: Oxford University Press, 1976.

Schairer, Karen E. "Native Speaker Reaction to Non-Native Speech." *The Modern Language Journal* 76, iii (1992): 309–19.

Schmidt, Elizabeth. *Let's Play Games in German*. Lincolnwood, IL: National Textbook Company, 1977.

John H. and Nancy Stenson, eds., *New Frontiers in Second Language* ~wley, MA: Newbury House, 1974.

~~ching Culture: Strategies for Intercultural Communication. .tional Textbook Company, 1984.

cholinguistic Issues in Second Language Acquisition." .5–40) in Leslie M. Beebe, ed., *Issues in Second Language .iple Perspectives*. Rowley, MA: Newbury House, 1988.

.terlanguage." *International Review of Applied Linguistics* 10, iii

guage." In J. Schumann and N. Stenson, eds., *New Frontiers in guage Learning*. Rowley, MA: Newbury House, 1974.

.n T. Lamendella. "The Role of Extrinsic Feedback in Interlanguage ation." *Language Learning* 29 (1979): 363–75.

. and W. Schneider. "Controlled and Automatic Human Information .ssing: II. Perceptual Learning, Automatic Attending and a General .ory." *Psychological Review* 84 (1977): 127–90.

, Merrill. "Communicative Competence: Some Roles of Comprehensible .nput and Comprehensible Output in Its Development." Chapter 14 (pp. 235–53) in Susan M. Gass and Carolyn S. Madden, eds. *Input in Second Language Acquisition*. Rowley, MA: Newbury House, 1985.

Swain, Merrill and Sharon Lapkin. "Canadian Immersion and Adult Second Language Teaching: What's the Connection?" *The Modern Language Journal* 73, ii (1989): 150-59.

Tarone, Elaine. "Conscious Communication Strategies in Interlanguage: A Progress Report." In H. Brown, C. Yorio, and R. Crymes, eds. *On TESOL '77: Teaching and Learning ESL*. Washington, DC: TESOL, 1978.

_____. "Communicative Strategies, Foreigner Talk, and Repair in Interlanguage." *Language Learning* 30 (1980): 417–31.

_____. "On the Variability of Interlanguage Systems." *Applied Linguistics* 4 (1983): 143–63.

Ur, Penny. *Grammar Practice Activities: A Practical Guide for Teachers*. Cambridge: Cambridge University Press, 1988.

Van Ek, J.A. *The Threshold Level in a European Unit/Credit System for Modern Language Learning for Adults*. Strasbourg: Council of Europe, 1975. (Republished in 1980 by Pergamon Press as *Threshold Level English*.)

Walker, John L. "Opinions of University Students About Language Teaching." *Foreign Language Annals* 7 (1973): 102–5.

Walz, Joel C. *Error Correction Techniques for the Foreign Language Classroom*. Language in Education: Theory and Practice Series, no. 50. Washington, DC: Center for Applied Linguistics, 1982.

Wilkins, D.A. *Notional Syllabuses*. Oxford: Oxford University Press, 1976.

Zelson, Sidney. "Skill-Using, Self-Expression and Communication Exercises in Three Dimensions." In E. Joiner and P. Westphal, eds., *Developing Communication Skills*. Rowley, MA: Newbury House, 1978.

7

Becoming Proficient in Writing

If learning to write in a second language were simply a matter of knowing how to "write things down" in the new code, then teaching writing would be a relatively easy task. A few minutes in each class period could be devoted to dictation, transcription, or manipulative written exercises, and a few guided compositions could be assigned for homework during the course of the semester, after which we could all rest easy because we had cleverly managed to work the fourth skill into our crowded curriculum with a minimum of effort.

Unfortunately, learning to write—even in one's native language—is not simply a matter of "writing things down." The fact that it took 45 minutes to compose the preceding paragraph, and that it is taking even longer to write this one, attests to the truth of the statement that writing is more than the mere transcription of speech. Most people who have attempted to put pen to paper to communicate ideas would agree that expressing oneself clearly in writing can be a slow and painful process. Rivers (1975) makes this point in her discussion of the differences between speech and writing:

> Many who know how to "write things down" in their native language avoid expressing themselves in writing almost completely, even in personal letters. To write so that one is really communicating a message, isolated in place and time, is an art which requires consciously directed effort and deliberate choice of language. The old saying, "If you can say it, you can write it," is simplistic in its concept of the communicative aspect of writing (p. 237).

In order to capture the complexity of the writing process, various scholars have suggested the use of more precise terminology to clarify the distinction between the mechanical aspects of writing and the more sophisticated processes involved in written communication. For example, Bizzell (1986) distinguishes between *composing*, which refers to all the processes that lead to the writing of something—reflection about the topic, gathering of information, taking of notes, working on a series of drafts, revising—and *writing*, which refers specifically to the transcription of the material itself. In her view, then, *writing* is subsumed under *composing*. Dvorak (1986), on the other hand, subsumes both *transcription* (focusing on form) and *composition* (focusing on effective development and communication of ideas) under the more generic term *writing*, which she uses to refer to "all the various activities that involve transferring thought to paper" (p. 145).

Perhaps *writing* might best be viewed as a continuum of activities that range from the more mechanical or formal aspects of "writing down" on the one end to the more complex act of composing on the other. This seems most sensible in the context of second and foreign language learning, where beginning language students must first struggle with the transcription of speech before they can engage in more complex forms of written expression. This is particularly true in languages where the writing system itself poses a difficult challenge, such as in Japanese, Chinese, Arabic, Russian or Hebrew for English-speaking learners. But even when the same basic alphabet is used in the new language, "writing down" can be a difficult task for the Novice or Intermediate student.

Magnan (1985) suggests that in secondary schools and in lower-level college classrooms, we might expect students at first to write down or transcribe in the second language something they might say. In that way, writing might be considered primarily as a support skill for speaking. Gradually, however, we can help students shape their written production in the direction of the conventions of proficient writers, teaching the cognitive processes of organization, elaboration, comparison and contrast, explanation, generalization, and the like.

The distinction between writing as a support skill and writing as a communicative art parallels, to some extent, Rivers' (1975) distinction between skill-getting and skill-using activities. In Rivers' schema, skill-getting emphasizes the understanding of the way the language operates while skill-using emphasizes the use of the code for expressive writing and purposeful communication. Written practice in the skill-getting phase includes two categories of activities: (1) *writing down*, or exercises involving copying or reproduction of learned material, concentrating on the conventions of spelling, punctuation, grammatical agreements, and the like, and (2) *writing in the language*, in which students engage in a variety of grammar-practice activities of a controlled nature in order to reinforce their growing knowledge of the linguistic system. Because these two categories of activities focus on writing as a support skill, and do not constitute creative or expressive writing, Rivers describes a second set of activities under skill-using that take students beyond linguistic manipulation. Such activities are designed to develop flexibility and creative language use and include (1) *flexibility measures*, in which students begin writing within a framework (including transformation exercises, sentence-combining practice, expansions, embellishments, idea frames, and similar activities), and (2) *expressive writing*, which includes guided and free

Level: Novice
Skill: Writing

Content

General topics such as . . .

Basic classroom objects
Colors
Numbers
Clothing
Names
Dates
Nationality
Biographical information
Weather/seasons
Family members

Functions

Can copy and transcribe very simple material in familiar contexts
Can list, identify, label
Can supply simple biographical information on forms
Can write very simple paragraphs using memorized or extremely familiar material

Techniques

Simple description with visuals
Paragraph completion
Cloze passages
Sentence builders
Dictations and variations
Filling in forms
Cinquain poetry
Dialogue journals

Accuracy

Material may be characterized by frequent misspellings and inaccuracies, especially when writer ventures beyond very familiar material

Discourse Structure

Lists
Enumerations
Filling out forms
Simple sentences with little coordination or cohesiveness

Illustration 7.1
Novice-level Curricular
Planning Guide
for Writing

Source: Adapted from DLI Task Force on Curriculum and Policy Planning, June 1984.

compositions that fulfill the normal purposes for which we write in the real world. These "normal purposes" include such things as practical concerns (note-taking for study purposes, letter writing, getting and giving information) and creative writing for entertainment and self-expression.

Rivers points out that the most difficult task for the teacher is to know how to effectively bridge the gap between skill-getting and skill-using activities. Perhaps one solution is to minimize the use of writing practice activities that are manipulative or impersonal in nature and choose instead activities that are contextualized, meaningful, and personalized, even when students are focusing primarily on form. Another possibility is to include various kinds of creative writing activities, such as journal writing or *cinquain* poetry (see pp. 300–02), in beginning courses to encourage students to express their own meaning within the limits of their developing competence. As was suggested in the last chapter, a blend of diverse tasks that elicit performance ranging from the "careful style" to the "vernacular style" (Tarone 1983) may be most beneficial for the development of spoken or written proficiency at all levels (see pp. 231–32). Activities that span a range of writing purposes, from writing as a support skill to writing as creative self-expression, are illustrated in the next sections of this chapter.

Level: Intermediate
Skill: Writing

Content

Everyday topics such as . . .

Personal biographical information
Activities, hobbies
Preferences
Daily routine
Lodging
Health matters
Travel and transportation
School/work experiences
Everyday events

Functions

Can create statements and questions well enough to meet practical needs and some limited social demands
Can write . . .
  Short messages
  Paragraphs
  Notes/letters
  Short compositions
  Can take simple notes

Techniques

Descriptions with visuals
Paragraph completion
Cloze passages
Dictations and variations
Graphic fill-ins
Slash sentences
Telegraphic cues
Partial translation
Sentence combining
Elaboration
Guided descriptions and narrations
Composition based on interview
Dialogue journals
Daily journals and diaries
Guided and free composition

Accuracy

Comprehensible to native speakers used to dealing with the writing of nonnatives
Good control of basic constructions, although errors may still be patterned
Frequent errors when venturing beyond simple structures and vocabulary
Generally able to write in present time using everyday, common vocabulary
May have limited dictionary skills

Discourse Structure

Simple sentences with some coordination
Beginnings of paragraphing and organization of ideas
Very limited in use of cohesive elements of discourse

Illustration 7.2
Intermediate-level
Curricular Planning
Guide for Writing

Source: Adapted from DLI Task Force on Curriculum and Policy Planning, June, 1984.

• • • • • • • • • • • • **A Curricular Planning Guide for Teaching Writing**

As in the previous chapter dealing with speaking, the perusal of classroom activities for writing begins with a sample set of guidelines for planning curricula. These guidelines are presented as one way one might organize instruction with the ACTFL proficiency descriptions in mind.

Most of the activities to be described in this chapter attempt to combine writing purposes to some extent: writing is directed in some fashion in the lower ranges of proficiency to support that which is learned in class (i.e., grammatical structures, vocabulary, discourse features), yet assignments

Level: Advanced
Skill: Writing

Content

Topics widen to include . . .

Many familiar and everyday topics
Current events
Factual and concrete topics relat-
ing to personal interests

Context

Academic writing
Personal correspondence
Creative writing (personal journals,
anecdotes, etc.)

Functions

Can write social and more formal
correspondence, discourse of
several paragraphs, cohesive
summaries, resumes with some
detail, description and narration
Can take notes
Can explain point of view simply
Can do some paraphrasing

Techniques

Detailed descriptions and
narrations
Dictations and variations
Partial or full translation
Sentence combining
Elaboration
Peer editing
Process-oriented composing tasks
Pastiches
Journals

Accuracy

Comprehensible to native speakers
not used to dealing with writing
of nonnatives
Sufficient vocabulary for self-
expression with good control of
basic morphology and elementary constructions
Controls language well enough to
narrate and describe in some
detail in past, present, and future
time
May still have quite a few errors in
basic constructions but generally
not patterned, except in more
complicated structures

Discourse Structure

Style obviously foreign yet joins
sentences in relatively cohesive
paragraphs

Illustration 7.3
Advanced-level
Curricular Planning
Guide for Writing

Source: Adapted from DLI Task Force on Curriculum and Policy Planning, June, 1984.

and exercises present language in the context of full discourse so that students learn how to write for communicative purposes. As students' competence increases, writing assignments become less structured, less teacher-directed, and more creative in nature. Students are encouraged to use the language independently to inform, narrate, describe, question, persuade, express feelings and attitudes, discuss ideas, and support points of view. Writing instruction can be designed to help students understand writing as discourse with specific rhetorical strategies and qualities that can vary according to the writer's purpose, and even according to the writer's cultural background (Kaplan, 1966; 1988). Various conventions of written language that distinguishes it in style and tone from spoken discourse can be learned and practiced. Second language writing instruction that is carefully planned can help students learn more about the composing process itself, a recursive, problem-solving activity that has the potential to affect students' writing and thinking skills in their native language, thus extending the benefits of language study well beyond the limits of the second language classroom.

Level: Superior
Skill: Writing

Content
A wide range of practical, social, and professional topics
Specialized fields of interest

Context
Academic writing
Professional contexts
Formal correspondence
Creative writing

Functions
Can use written language effectively for formal and informal exchanges
Can hypothesize and conjecture
Can write all types of correspondence and short research papers
Can support point of view, defend hypotheses

Techniques
Prose style analyses
Peer editing
Process-oriented composing tasks
Pastiches
Translations (native language to foreign language and vice versa)
Extensive note-taking
Full transcription

Accuracy
Good control of a full range of structures
Wide vocabulary
No patterns of errors
Style may still be foreign
May not yet tailor writing effectively to different audiences or styles

Discourse Structure
Discourse competence includes use of complex and compound sentences, coherent paragraphing

Illustration 7.4
Superior-level
Curricular Planning
Guide for Writing

Source: Adapted from DLI Task Force on Curriculum and Policy Planning, June, 1984.

The remainder of this chapter is divided into two main sections. The first section presents activities that are most appropriate for students at the Novice and Intermediate levels of writing proficiency. It includes a blend of guided and open-ended writing practice formats, beginning with strategies for teaching writing as a *support skill*, where the focus is primarily on the mastery of formal features of the written language. Activities designed to bridge the gap to free expression are also included in this section. The second section of the chapter discusses approaches to writing primarily for expressive communication. Research about the composing process from both first language and second language perspectives is reviewed, and various approaches to teaching writing are described. Following this review of the literature, creative writing activities for both the Intermediate and Advanced levels are illustrated, and practical suggestions for responding to student writing are given.

• • • • • • • • • • • • • *Approaches to Teaching Writing at the Lower Levels of Proficiency*

Let us turn now to an examination of several writing activities, beginning with those most appropriate to the Novice level.

Techniques for Teaching Writing as a Support Skill

In almost all of the following activities, writing is not practiced in isolation; rather, skills are practiced in an interdependent fashion. For example, a transcribing activity, such as dictation or note-taking, will involve listening and/or reading comprehension. An activity in which students fill out a form or schedule will involve the ability to read the document to be completed. Obviously, simultaneous use of several skills is common in natural and authentic communication, and it makes sense to practice various skills in concert in the second language classroom to approximate this type of authenticity.

Secondly, although the activity samples in this section are chosen to illustrate how writing can be used to *support* the learning of formal aspects of the new language, there is some concern as well for structuring these tasks so that students can begin to write in discourse-length frames for communicative purposes. Thus there is a planned overlap in these early writing activities between form and function so that the gap between skill-getting and skill-using can be bridged more effectively as students' writing skills progress.

Novice-level Activities

Simple Description with Visuals

Sample 1
Listing

Content
Objects in a room

Functions
Identifying and listing

Student Task
Students are given a picture such as the one in Illustration 7.5, but with the labels removed. They are asked to name the numbered objects in the classroom, beginning their written description with the phrase *Dans la salle de classe, il y a. . . .* (In the classroom, there is. . .)

Source: Picture taken from Rochester et al, 1983, p. 10. Reprinted by permission of McGraw-Hill. A very similar idea is found in Magnan 1985, p. 125.

Sample 2
Completing a Descriptive Paragraph

Content
Objects in student's dormitory room

Functions
Naming and listing within discourse framework

Student Task
Using a picture or line drawing of a student's dormitory room, such as the one in Illustration 7.6, ESL students complete the following description by naming objects in the picture that fit the context of the paragraph.

Illustration 7.5
Visual for use in listing objects in a room

Dans la salle de classe

Source: Rochester, M., J. Muyskens, A. Omaggio, and C. Chalmers. *Bonjour, ça va?* New York: Random House, 1983. Reproduced by permission of McGraw-Hill, Inc.

Passage | Sook-Hee is a student at an American university. She lives in a very nice dormitory room. In her room, there is a _____, a _____, and a _____. There are also several _____. There are no _____, but Sook-Hee does have some _____. She wants to get a _____ for her wall and a _____ for the desk this afternoon when she goes shopping.

Source: Idea from Magnan 1985, p. 125

Sample 3
Completing a Descriptive Paragraph: Function Words

Content | Same as in *Sample 2*

Functions | Describing the physical relationship of objects to one another

Grammatical Feature | Prepositions and locative expressions

Student Task | ESL students are given a picture like the one in Illustration 7.6. They complete the description by supplying the prepositions and locative expressions required by the context.

Passage | Sook-Hee is a student at an American university. This is a picture of her room. Her bed is _____ the window. _____ the bed and the window is a small chest of drawers. There is a bookcase _____ her bed on the

Illustration 7.6
Visual for use in listing objects in student's dormitory room

_____. She has a radio that is _____ the bookcase, and she puts her books _____ the bookcase _____ three shelves. _____ the room she has a very nice desk where she prepares her work for school . . . etc.

Sample 4
Writing a Short Description from Questions

Content   Objects in a student's dormitory room

Functions   Writing a simple description using memorized material

Student Task   Looking at the picture of Sook-Hee's room (see Illustration 7.6), students use the following questions as a guide for writing a short description of the room.

1. Where does Sook-Hee live?
2. Does she have a nice room? What kinds of things does she have in her room?
3. What color is Sook-Hee's room? What color are the walls? the curtains? the bedspread?
4. What does Sook-Hee need for her room?
5. What do you like in Sook-Hee's room? What don't you like?
6. Do you have a room like Sook-Hee's? Describe your room in a few sentences in your second paragraph.

Source: Idea from Magnan 1985, p.125.

Sentence-Builders

Sample
Description of Daily Routine

Content — Typical day in a student's life

Functions — Telling time, describing activities

Student Task — Students are asked to write a composition about their daily routine, using the elements in the sentence-builder as their guide.

I	II	III	IV
Por la mañana	yo	mirar	el radio
A las *X*	nosotros	escuchar	la televisión
Por la tarde	compañero de cuarto	ir	clase de francés
Por la noche	la profesora	estudiar	(nombre de un curso)
		hacer	preguntas unos discos
?	?	?	?

The question mark at the bottom of each column of the sentence builder invites students to add their own ideas to those provided in the list. Students who wish to venture beyond the structure of the activity are, of course, encouraged to do so.

Source: Magnan (1985, p. 126) presents a similar example in English.

Dictation and Variations

Many of the ideas for dictation presented in Chapter 5 (see p. 193) are usable with students at the Novice level. Though the dictation activity can be based on familiar material, it is best to use some recombination or novel approach to that material so that students are stimulated to use both their listening and writing skills. Dictated passages of at least a paragraph in length are best, since this presents language in a discourse-length context. Partial dictations or variations on dictation should also be contextualized. (For an excellent source of ideas on using dictation at various levels of proficiency, see Davis and Rinvolucri 1988.)

Filling in Forms

Sample 1
A Restaurant Menu

Content — Foods

Functions — Naming and listing

Student Task — Students are provided with the incomplete menu in Illustration 7.7. They are told that they have just opened a restaurant and that it is up to them to

Illustration 7.7
Form for use in completing a restaurant menu

Source: Adapted from Terry 1985.

decide what dishes they would like to offer. Categories of foods (appetizers, fish, meat, dessert, and drinks) are given, but no specific foods are named. Students are also asked to make up a name for their restaurant.

Sample 2
Personal Information and Preferences

Content	Autobiographical information, likes and dislikes
Functions	Listing, simple description
Student Task	Students are given the computer-dating form pictured in Illustration 7.8. They are told to fill out the form, giving as true a picture of themselves as possible.

Cinquain Poetry

Content	Varied
Functions	Creating poetry within a simple framework

Illustration 7.8
Form for use in listing
personal information

ORDENA-PAR
Calle Real 15
Madrid 07563

Nombre _____

Apellidos _____

Domicilio _____

_____

_____

Teléfono _____ Fecha de nacimiento _____

Profesión _____

Busco _____

_____

_____

Soy _____

_____

_____

_____

Me gusta _____

_____

_____

_____

Pegar aquí
una foto
reciente

Source: Adapted from Terry 1985.

Student Task   Students, either individually, in small groups, or as a whole class, create
simple poems within a very structured framework, using vocabulary they
have learned and any supplied by the teacher, as requested. A *cinquain*
poem consists of five lines, constructed according to the following scheme:

Line 1: States a subject in one word (usually a noun).

Line 2: Describes the subject in two words (often a noun and an adjective or two adjectives).

Line 3: Describes an action about the subject in three words (often three infinitives or a three-word sentence).

Line 4: Expresses an emotion about the subject in four words.

Line 5: Restates the subject in another single word that reflects what has already been said (usually a noun).

Sample Poems in English, French, and Spanish

Tree
Green branches
Growing, living, reaching
Your shade protects me
Peace

Chien
Optimiste perpetuel
Attend son maître
Il entend des pas . . .
Joie!

Casa
Hogar sencillo
Necesita pintura, reparos
Llena de tantos recuerdos
Refugio

Source: The format for *cinquain* poetry is from Allen and Valette 1977, 321–22.

Intermediate-level Activities: Preparing for Advanced-level Writing

The activity types suggested in this section can serve as a kind of "bridge" between the structured writing activities of the previous section and those that are designed for writing on a more advanced level, to be described in the second half of this chapter. According to the proficiency descriptions in Appendix A, students in the Intermediate range in writing are generally able to create with the language in very familiar contexts, using simple vocabulary, limited narration and description in present time, and very basic grammatical structures. Free and guided composition topics for learners in this range should be chosen to coincide with their present level of proficiency or to help them build skills for the next highest level.

The first few activities in this section emphasize focused written practice. In order to move toward the Advanced level, students will need practice in using both past and future time in more extended narration and description. Therefore, activities that are designed to encourage the use of past and future tenses in both structured practice and guided composition are appropriate for students presently at the Intermediate level.

There are also suggestions in this section for guided writing activities that proceed in stages, with each task adding something new to the written text as students learn to refine and elaborate upon their previous drafts. The use of the microcomputer and sample activities from a computer-assisted instructional program for writing in French are also illustrated.

Slash Sentences   *Sample*   (Intermediate)

Context   Summer leisure activities

Function   Simple narration in the present

Student Task   This activity directs students to write a short narrative from the sentence cues given. The story is about the LeBlanc's summer activities.

Un été à la campagne. Faites des phrases complètes selon le modèle.

Modèle: Les LeBlanc/passer/l'été/à la campagne
Les LeBlanc passent l'été à la campagne.

1. le matin/tout/famille/se réveiller/vers/8 heures
2. M. LeBlanc/descendre/la cuisine/préparer/café
3. Son/femme/faire/petit déjeuner/puis/sortir/dans/le jardin
4. M. LeBlanc/et/son/fils/aller/à la pêche
5. Natalie/se promener/dans/collines/près de/maison . . . etc.

A Summer in the Country. Make complete sentences according to the model.

Model: The LeBlancs/to spend/summer in the country.
The LeBlancs spend the summer in the country.

1. *In the morning/all/family/to get up/around/8 o'clock*
2. *Mr. LeBlanc/to go downstairs/the kitchen/to prepare/coffee*
3. *His/wife/to make/breakfast/then/to go outside/in/the garden*
4. *Mr. LeBlanc/and/his/son/to go/fishing*
5. *Natalie/to take a walk/in/hills/near/house. . . . etc*

Follow-up Task   (Preparing for Advanced level)
Students are now directed to write the paragraph in the past, talking about the way this family used to spend summer vacations. They are asked to embellish the story, adding details about the surroundings, the weather, and specific activities. In French, this story would be written in the imperfect tense. The exercise thus focuses on practicing past-tense narration and adding some elaborative detail, thus preparing students for writing at the Advanced level.

Variation   Students write a narration about their own family's summer activities, using this exercise as a prewriting stimulus activity.

Telegraphic Sentences	*Sample* (Intermediate; Preparing for Advanced level)
Context	Current events
Function	Reporting facts of a story
Purpose	Like slash sentences, telegraphic sentences provide the essential elements to be incorporated into a story, but the format of the stimulus material looks more like a set of notes than a grammatical exercise, thus more closely simulating an authentic task. Students are encouraged to embellish the story as they like. As an Intermediate-level task, students are asked to describe the events using the present tense, as if they were eyewitnesses reporting the action as it happens. As a preparation for Advanced-level writing, students narrate the events as a reporter would, using appropriate past tenses as they tell the story presented in the telegraphic cues.
Student Task	You are a journalist who has just interviewed a witness to a UFO incident. The notes you made during the interview are given below. Write out your report in as much detail as you can, recounting the events in the past. (Notes can be in the target language or English, depending on how much structure and vocabulary the teacher wishes to provide to guide the writing task.)
Notes	Henry Stewart, in field working, about 10 A.M., June 13. Hears strange noise, looks up. Sees blinding light. Distinguishes three objects. Gets frightened. Drops everything and runs for farmhouse. Calls wife to come see. Objects disappear as quickly as they came. Wife doesn't believe story.

Partial Translation	*Sample* (Intermediate)
Context	A visit to Spain as an exchange student
Function	Writing a thank-you letter
Purpose	This activity encourages students to use recently learned vocabulary and grammatical structures in a context that is appropriate to the Intermediate level—writing a letter to family and friends. The activity is structured to focus on discrete points of grammar, but the end-product of the writing task can serve as a model for letter writing in a subsequent activity.
Student Task	Patrick has just returned from studying abroad in Granada, Spain, and is writing a thank-you letter to the family with whom he stayed. Complete the letter in Spanish, using the translation below it as a guide to the missing words.

Santa Fe, 10 de julio de 1992

Queridos Sr. y Sra. Álvarez,

_____ que salé de Granada y los extraño. Mi estancia en su casa _____ y les agradezco con todo el corazón su hospitalidad. _____ mucho en España y _____ mis estudios de español en mi escuela y _____ en la universidad. _____ a mis amigos de mi escuela de Granada y de mi familia española.

Mil gracias y _____ que Uds. puedan visitar la ciudad de Santa Fe _____ . Mis padres quisieran conocerlos.

Un abrazo,
Patrick

Dear Mr. and Mrs. Álvarez,

I left Granada two weeks ago and I miss you. My stay in your house was unforgettable and I thank you with all my heart for your hospitality. I learned a lot in Spain and I'm going to continue my studies in Spanish in my school, and afterwards at the university. I'm going to talk to my friends at school about my school in Granada and my Spanish family.

Many thanks, and I hope that you can visit the city of Santa Fe some day. My parents would like to meet you.

Hugs,
Patrick

Source: Text adapted from Gutiérrez and Rosser 1992, p. 164.

Sentence Combining

Context

Function

Purpose

Sample (Preparing for Advanced level)

Story in a film

Narrating a story

To help students link simple propositions into more complex sentences. In sentence-combining activities, a set of simple sentences or propositions are consolidated through the embedding of words, phrases, and clauses so that the meaning of the whole set is conveyed in one sentence. For example, the following set of simple propositions is combined below:

1. The man is tall.
2. The man has dark hair.
3. The man is standing by the counter.
4. The man looks suspicious.

Combination: The tall, dark-haired man standing by the counter looks suspicious.

Exercises in sentence combining can be used at the sentence, paragraph, or composition level. In the following example, students produce a story several paragraphs in length. An authentic prose paragraph describing the events in an Italian film, *Baratro*, is broken down into simple propositions. Students then try to combine those propositions into more complex sentences and compare their combinations to the original. This technique can be used to teach principles of sentence and paragraph construction and to help students recognize the importance of connectors, qualifiers, and other discourse features.

Student Task   In the following exercise, the clusters of sentences are related. Combine each cluster into a single sentence, varying the length and structure of each of your sentences to avoid monotony.

1. Il film era a colori.
2. Era la storia di miliardari.
3. Abitayano in una villa.

4. La villa era bianca.
5. La villa era su una spiaggia.
6. La spiaggia era solitaria.

7. L'uomo seguiva la trama del film.
8. La donna non seguiva la trama del film.
9. Ognuno pensava ai casi propri.
Etc.

Original Description of Film

Il film era a colori ed era intitolato *Baratro.* Dei miliardari in una villa molto bianca su una spiaggia solitaria, bevevano bibite, nuotavano, prendevano il sole, e si contendevano un patrimonio. L'uomo e la donna non seguivano la trama, e pensavano ciascuno ai casi propri...

Source: Trivelli 1983, pp. 238-39. See also Cooper 1980; Cooper, Morain, and Kalivoda 1980, and Johnson 1982, for extensive examples of sentence-combining activities in several languages.

Paragraph Completion   *Sample*   (Intermediate)

Context   Personal appearance

Function   Description

Purpose   This task is designed to aid writers at the Intermediate level in improving their ability to describe someone in detail.

Student Task   Students writing in French use their imagination to complete the description of the person in the photograph given in Illustration 7.9.

Illustration 7.9
Photograph for use in writing a personal description

Paragraph M. Duval était un _____ homme _____ aux cheveux _____ et _____ . Il avait les yeux _____ et portait une barbe _____ et _____ . C'était un homme très _____ qui pensait beaucoup (à) _____ . Ce matin-là, il avait l'air _____ parce qu'il _____ . . . .

Mr. Duval was a _____ , _____ man with _____ , _____ hair. He had _____ eyes and wore a _____ , _____ beard. He was a very _____ man who thought a lot about _____ . That morning, he seemed _____ because he _____ . . . .

Source: Idea for activity format from Raimes, 1978.

Guided Compositions: A Bridge to Free Expression

The activity suggestions below have some of the characteristics of an approach to writing instruction that Hillocks (1986) calls "the environmental mode" (p. 122) and that Applebee (1986) refers to as "a structured process" orientation to composition (p. 105). In this approach, specific tasks are organized by the teacher to help students engage in the composing process and practice certain aspects of writing that are important to the task at hand. Other aspects of this approach might include the use of model texts and small-group interaction as students work to improve their compositions, using evaluative checklists or other tools provided by the teacher (Hillocks 1986). The suggestions given here show how composition tasks can be guided through the use of prewriting and semi-structured writing activities for the Intermediate-level writers who are preparing to engage more fully in the composing process.

Multiple Tasks Based on a Picture

Raimes (1983) suggests developing a sequence of writing tasks around a single picture, such as a wedding photo, with each task selected to move students to a slightly higher level of difficulty as they add vocabulary, structural sophistication, and/or organizational skills. In the series of tasks given below, the picture in Illustration 7.9 is used as a point of departure and a stimulus for creativity.

Task 1: *Prewriting* (Intermediate)

Students in small groups look at the picture and write as many words and expressions that come to mind. They may be asked to think of vocabulary that will be useful in describing the person or objects in the picture, but also write down words associated with those items to form semantic networks. In addition, students can write down words and expressions depicting feelings that the picture evokes. Groups might then be asked to share their lists with others in the class, or the teacher might make a master list on the board.

Task 2: *Prewriting* (Intermediate)

An alternate task (or one done subsequent to Task 1, above) involves small groups writing down questions that the picture evokes in their minds. Each group then shares their list of questions with the rest of the class to provide a further stimulus for writing.

Task 3: *Description* (Intermediate)

Using the vocabulary generated from Task 1, above, students write a brief composition describing the photograph in as much detail as they can.

Students then share their descriptions with one or two other students in the class. The group can be asked to pool their descriptions to write a second, more complete draft describing the photograph.

Task 4: *Narration* (Intermediate)

Using the question sets generated from Task 2, individual or small groups of students write a narration about the man in the picture, answering the questions given to them by another group in the class. Stories can then be read aloud and compared, or shared by exchanging them with stories written by classmates.

Task 5: *Narration in the Past* (Preparing for Advanced level)

Students are asked to imagine that the man in the photograph is thinking about the first time he visited Paris as a young man. In small groups, they develop a list of possible events, places visited, and persons he might have met in his travels. After discussing various possibilities, students create a story, individually or in small groups, and recount the events in the past, with as much imaginative detail as possible.

Elaboration	*Sample* (Intermediate)
Context	A trip to Paris
Functions	Narration and description
Purpose	Students learn to write fuller descriptions and narrations through the use of cues supplied by the teacher on their first draft. For example, the teacher might take a student's composition and insert an asterisk at every point in the narration where an elaboration could be made. Elaborations might include the addition of adjectives, adverbs, relative clauses, or whole sentences. A more complex cuing system consists of a series of notes, such as in the example below.
Student Task	The student has written an imaginary description of the trip to Paris described in Task 5, above. The teacher asks the student to rewrite the opening paragraph in the second draft as follows: Using the cues in the paragraph below, write a new paragraph that is more detailed and interesting than the original.

Mon premier voyage à Paris était très intéressant[a]. Je suis allé avec mon camarade de chambre[b]. Nous avons loué une voiture[c], mais il était très difficile de conduire à Paris[d]. . . .

My first trip to Paris was very interesting[a]. I went with my roommate[b]. We rented a car[c], but it was very difficult to drive in Paris[d]. . . .

Notes: (These can be in French or English. English is used here for purposes of illustration.)

a. Add a few details about when you took this trip. Also, try to find another word to substitute for the adjective you used here—"interesting" doesn't give us much information.

b. Describe your roommate in a sentence or two. Why did you want to go with him?

c. Add some adjectives to your description of the car.

d. Instead of telling the reader that it was difficult to drive in Paris, try describing the traffic, the parking, or other situations that made driving so hard, and let the reader *conclude* that it was difficult from your description.

Note how the teacher's cues in the sample above relate primarily to the content and style of the student's story rather than to mechanics or grammar. By providing substantive comments of this type, the teacher encourages students to revise in a way that will enhance their creative expression.

Guided Composition Based on Oral Interview

Sample
(Preparing for Advanced level)

Context | Varied topics relating to personal life and preferences

Functions | Narration and description in past, present, and future time

Purpose | To encourage students to practice skills needed at the Advanced level, both orally and in writing.

Student Task | Students are asked to interview a partner by choosing one topic from each of several categories, such as those listed below. They are told to take notes on what their partners say. As a follow-up to the oral interview, they are asked to write a unified composition of at least three paragraphs, telling either (1) what they learned about the person they interviewed or (2) what they would say about themselves on these topics. In the first instance, the composition would consist of a description narrated in the third person; in the second, the composition would be autobiographical. Students are reminded that they should include narration in past, present, and future time.

Topics | **Present**

- Talk about yourself and your family (i.e., where you're from, where your family lives, who the people in your family are, etc.).

- Talk about why you are at this university and why you are taking this course.

- Talk about what you like and dislike about life at this university.
- Talk about things that bore you (interest you, make you happy/angry) and why.

Past

- Describe a recent Christmas (summer/spring) vacation.
- Describe what your life was like last year.
- Talk about a memorable event in your life.

Future

- Describe your career goals and plans.
- Talk about what you'd like to do with the French (Spanish, German, Italian, other language) you know now.
- Talk about your plans for the end of the semester.
- Describe your plans for the coming weekend.

Guided and Free Composition: Writing Letters and Notes

Intermediate level

From writers at the Intermediate level, teachers might expect short essays of two or three paragraphs on themes with which they are familiar. Most appropriate for these students are topics that elicit personal information and simple statements about preferences, concrete experiences, and the like, such as:

1. Imagine you are on vacation at your favorite resort. Write a postcard or short letter explaining what you are doing, what you like about the place, who you are meeting, and similar details.
2. You are writing a letter home to your parents about college life. Give them a description of your typical day at school. Include a short paragraph about your roommate (your favorite teacher/your least favorite class/your dorm room/the food at school) and tell what you like/dislike about that person (situation).
3. Your roommate is a messy person who leaves books, clothes, food, and other possessions all over his or her side of the room. Write a note explaining how you feel about this, and ask your roommate to "clean up his or her act."
4. Write a description of (a) a good friend, (b) a member of your family, (c) a teacher you like/dislike, or (d) your roommate. Give as many details about the person's appearance, personality, and habits as you can.
5. Your best friend at another school has a new roommate who comes from France (Spain, Germany, Italy, country where target language

Illustration 7.10

Composition topic for Intermediate-level students preparing for the Advanced level (Topic 1)

Una tarjeta de Navidad. In order to impress me with the wealth of knowledge you have gained in 101, shortly before you leave campus you send me a Christmas card—written entirely in Spanish. You include a note of at least *five* sentences telling me what you, your family, and your friends *are going to do* during vacation.

Source: Terry 1985.

is spoken). Write a letter to your friend, including a list of questions you would like him or her to ask this exchange student about life in his or her country.

Preparing for Advanced level

Here are a few topics that indicate the type of composition that might be assigned when learners are in the Intermediate range but need to develop skills to progress to the Advanced level:

1. Write a Christmas card to your teacher telling him or her what you plan to do over vacation. (See Illustration 7.10, an exercise suggested by Terry 1985.)
2. Write a page in your personal diary describing your activities over the last semester. (See Illustration 7.11, another exercise suggested by Terry 1985.)
3. You are planning on getting married (getting a new job, moving to another town) and anticipate some major changes in your life. Describe what will be different after you get married (get the new job, move) and how you think you will feel about these changes.

Illustration 7.11
Composition topic for
Intermediate-level
students preparing for
the Advanced level
(Topic 2)

Cher Journal Intime (Dear Diary). In your personal diary (which you keep under lock and key in your sock drawer), you make your last entry for 199__. Write *eight* sentences telling *what you did* (i.e., in the *passé composé*) during this last semester. Be sure to include several memorable occasions and activities.

mardi, le 31 décembre	199__

Source: Terry 1985.

4. You just had a very eventful (fabulous/horrible/exciting/unusual) weekend, and you can't wait to write to your penpal in France (Spain, Germany, Italy, country where target language is spoken) to tell him or her all about it. Recount the events of your weekend in as much detail as possible.

For more ideas on teaching and evaluating writing at this level, see Terry (1989).

Dialogue Journals (Novice through Advanced levels)

One form of free composition that seems particularly appropriate for beginning and intermediate students is the *dialogue journal* (Staton 1983; Peyton and Reed 1990). These journals provide a way for students and teachers to carry on a written conversation with one another and can continue for any length of time during the course of a semester or year. Students obtain a bound composition book or notebook and write on a daily or weekly basis about topics of interest to them, using the full range of functions (questions, promises, apologies, complaints) that might be used in a face-to-face conversation. The teacher then reads the journal entries and responds substantively and personally to them. Because writing at the Novice and Intermediate levels often consists of writing down what students would say orally, this type of journal might be appealing as an alternative or adjunct to structured compositions assigned by the teacher on a periodic basis.

Peyton and Reed (1990) have written an informative handbook incorporating many examples of dialogue journals and the techniques that instructors can use to supplement other types of writing instruction. The authors present some caveats, however, that need to be taken into consideration when using a journal writing approach. One concern that some teachers and/or students have voiced is that the journals are not corrected for structural errors. Research evidence on the effectiveness of error correction in second language writing is conflicting, as is research on the attitudes of students toward correction of their work. However, studies by Cathcart and Olsen (1976), Leki (1986; 1990; 1991), Jones (1988) and Fathman and Whalley (1990) have revealed that many ESL students want all of their errors corrected on both written and oral work. Jones (1988) researched this issue in reference to dialogue journals specifically, and found that almost all of the adult ESL students in his study at the beginning level and almost half of the more advanced students wanted correction in their journals. Peyton and Reed (1990) recognize the importance of responding to this concern, and suggest that teachers talk to students about the purposes of the journal as opposed to the purposes of other writing tasks where corrective feedback is given more systematically. As an activity that falls on the "vernacular style" end of the continuum of writing tasks, dialogue journals can provide students with an opportunity to develop fluency without constantly worrying about form. Nevertheless, teachers might want to go over journals with students who express a desire to be corrected, scheduling conferences with them or negotiating with them that certain kinds of errors will be corrected during a given time period. Leki (1991) adds that ". . . we do well at least to become aware of students' perceptions of their needs and their sense of what helps them progress." (p. 210). Perhaps the best solution is to offer students options and teach them different perspectives or strategies for approaching a writing task, but ultimately respect their right to choose the kind of feedback they believe will enhance their learning most effectively and try to provide it for them.

Writing and the Computer

One relatively recent development in writing instruction is the use of computers and computer-assisted instructional programs in teaching foreign and second language composition. The computer can be an especially useful tool in courses where students have advanced enough in their skills to be able to engage more fully in the composing process, to be described in more detail in the next section.

Smith (1990) describes an experiment in which fourth-semester Spanish students were given opportunities to use two types of computer-based writing tools for the writing component of the course: (1) a computer conferencing system and (2) a word-processing program. The computer conferencing system enabled students to engage in discussions and collaborative writing activities with others in the course. Each new message that was added to a particular discussion became automatically available to all participants, who could consider it and comment upon it as they wished. Smith reports that students using this system engaged in lively debates and creative self-expression, devoting an average of three hours per week for computer-mediated conversational writing. These students paid more attention to meaning than to accuracy, since the computer conferencing format was not used for editing or revision in this study. The second group of students, who used a word-processing program (WordPerfect) as a composition tool, worked primarily on composing and rewriting compositions with a view to producing more accurate writing samples. Students in this group averaged 90 minutes per week on computer-assisted composition work, with some students working in pairs, brainstorming, or peer editing one another's work. A third group of students in the study had no computer-assisted writing opportunities, but did write compositions at home.

Smith compared the groups' achievement on a variety of measures at the end of the semester and found that the computer users improved significantly in their ability to read and express oral and written ideas (pp. 80–81). The students in the control condition improved in their general accuracy in written composition, as did those who were using the word-processing tool for composition. However, the control group did not develop the same level of expressive skills in writing as did those who had worked with the computer. Smith concludes that a combination of activities stressing *both* creative conversational writing (as in the computer conferencing condition) and attention to form (as in the word-processing condition) are necessary to promote the development of writing proficiency.

Greenia (1992) describes intermediate and advanced Spanish composition classes in which students work almost exclusively on the computer, using a standard word-processing program such as WordPerfect or Microsoft Word. He estimates that students using computer-based instruction can produce three to seven times more writing in a semester than can those working without the aid of a computer, multiplying their opportunities to improve through daily assignments of various types. Greenia provides useful and comprehensive guidelines for setting up a writing course of this type. The teacher responds to student work turned in on a diskette, which holds a variety of files including course information and syllabus, a working space for ongoing assignments, a storage space for completed work, a file containing models of writing, another file for practical exercises, a file for a private dialogue journal, and a directory for an open class bulletin board. In this computer-assisted instructional setting, students and teacher work together as a writing community, with students responding to one another's work in a cooperative learning environment.

Tolliver (1992) uses electronic mail to provide informal writing practice for her undergraduate Spanish composition class. Students are asked to participate in e-mail discussions with other students in the course and are evaluated informally as part of their homework grade. Grades for e-mail assignments are based on the students' active participation and on the comprehensibility of their Spanish. Students may respond to discussion topics posted by the teacher or other students, or initiate topics themselves.

Another innovative way to use the computer in writing instruction beginning at a relatively early level of instruction is through a specially designed software program such as *système-D: Writing Assistant for French*, developed by Noblitt and Pet (Windows version) and Noblitt, Solá, and Pet (DOS version). The authors of this program see it as an additional resource for students at the Novice through Advanced level in writing rather than as a replacement for other methods of teaching writing. Scott and Terry (1992) describe *système-D* as a tool that can help students bridge the gap between "skill-getting" and "skill-using" (Rivers 1975). The program provides various kinds of resources, with special directories for vocabulary, grammar, functional expressions and discourse frameworks. The bilingual dictionary gives students access to French/English vocabulary, but also offers examples of how words are used in sentences, conjugations of verbs, and grammar notes associated with the dictionary entries. A three-part index, comprised of grammar references, a list of functional expressions, and a topical vocabulary index, provides students with some of the key information they need to express themselves more fully and appropriately as they write. The teacher's guide authored by Scott and Terry (1992) includes specific guided writing tasks at different proficiency levels, planned to enable students to move toward autonomous writing. The *système-D* program also can be used as an evaluative tool to track students' strategies and processes as they compose at the screen, providing teachers with data that can help them analyze the individual students' writing problems as well as identify their strengths. For example, the software allows teachers to determine how often students ask for dictionary or grammar help, how often they look at examples of words used in a context, or how they engage in paraphrasing strategies. Some of the research done on foreign-language writing using *système-D* is reported later in this chapter.

A sample task—writing a letter—is illustrated below for students whose writing proficiency is currently at the Intermediate level. This task is taken from the *système-D Teacher's Guide* (Scott and Terry 1992) and is the second of three letter-writing tasks that have been graded and structured in stages to elicit progressively more complex discourse. In the sample below, the italicized cues refer to specific index items provided by the software that students can consult on-screen when composing their letters.

Sample   (Stage 2—Intermediate)

Context   You are writing to your French pen pal with whom you have been corresponding regularly.

Tasks

1. Use the appropriate letter format.
Phrases: Writing a letter (informal)

2. Talk about and describe your best friend.
Phrases: Describing people
Grammar: Nouns after *c'est, il est;* Possessive adjectives (6 groups)

3. Tell what you did during your last vacation.
Grammar: **Passé composé;** Verbs with auxiliary *avoir* or *être;* Agreement of past participle; Prepositions with geographical places.
Vocabulary: Traveling; Means of transportation

4. Tell what the weather was like during your vacation.
Phrases: Describing weather
Grammar: **Imparfait**

5. Ask five questions.
Grammar: Interrogative adjective **quel;** Interrogative adverbs; Interrogative pronouns *que, quoi;* Interrogative pronoun **qui**

6. End your letter with the appropriate closing.

Source: Scott and Terry 1992, p. 31.

In this example, as well as in the other writing tasks suggested by Scott and Terry, students receive a good deal of structure and direction for their assignments. Some students or teachers might find this specificity somewhat limiting. Scott and Terry acknowledge this possibility in their instructor's guide. "While most students are grateful for the explicit directions provided in the task-oriented exercises, it is important to note that some students feel that the tasks limit their creativity. The best response to this legitimate criticism is to allow time for free creative expression either with or without *système-D*, but only after they have had sufficient practice with task-oriented exercises" (p. 42). The authors clearly believe that designing tasks that are explicitly structured in this way is helpful to students whose writing proficiency in the language is at a relatively early stage, and that some guided practice is therefore necessary before encouraging students to engage in free writing. This approach seems congruent with the "comprehensible output hypothesis" described in Chapter 3, in which it was suggested that tasks should be designed to help students practice language at their current level of competence or just a little beyond it to encourage greater accuracy of expression (Higgs and Clifford 1982). Swain's (1985) version of this hypothesis would encourage students to achieve greater precision of expression through "pushed output," where students' written or oral production would be reworked until it approached native-like form. With a program like *système-D*, there seems to be a concern for helping students develop accuracy of expression as well as communicative facility through the provision of grammar and vocabulary resources of various sorts. However, the authors caution that students' compositions will not be error-free when they use this program, and that students will need to engage in self-monitoring and receive additional help with improving their written work as they would with a more conventional writing program. Some of the possible ways to respond to students' written work are treated later in this chapter.

● ● ● ● ● ● ● ● ● ● ● ● ● *Expressive Writing at the Intermediate and Advanced Levels: Approaches to Teaching the Composing Process*

This section begins with a brief review of research about native-language and second language writing at the Intermediate to Advanced level, followed by a summary of the kinds of approaches to the teaching of writing as creative communication that have been suggested by various scholars in recent years. Some examples of Advanced-level writing activities are then given, followed by suggestions for responding to student writing through various feedback and evaluation strategies.

What Do We Know About Writing? Insights from First Language Research

Because the preponderance of writing research to date has been done with students writing in their native language, second and foreign-language teachers have had to rely primarily on insights from first language studies. Although there may be many commonalities between first and second language writing, the differences should also be recognized. Kroll (1990) suggests that writing in a second language is more complex, given that the problems native speakers have with composing are compounded in the foreign language context by difficulties with the new code. She also points out that direct transfer of literacy skills from the native to the foreign language cannot be assumed. "In fact, while a background in first language writing may help inform the explorations of second language writing teachers and researchers, it should not be presumed that the act of writing in one's first language is the same as the act of writing in one's second language. For example, first and second language learners may not approach a writing task in the same way nor attend to feedback in the same way" (p. 2). As we have seen in the first part of this chapter, it is possible that, even *within* the context of second language writing, Novice and Intermediate writers may approach tasks and use feedback far differently than do Advanced writers, with whom most of the research in second language writing has been done. Therefore, it makes sense to be cautious in our interpretation of this research when applying the results to our second language classrooms, especially at the lower levels.

With these caveats in mind, what can we learn from studies conducted with native language writers? Let us begin with a description of what good writers do as they engage in the composing process.

Characteristics of Good Writers

Most scholars agree that good writing in any language involves knowledge of the conventions of written discourse in that culture as well as the abilities to choose from near synonyms the precise word that conveys one's meaning, select from a variety of syntactic structures those that transmit one's message most precisely, and adopt a style that will have the most positive rhetorical effect. Obviously, such expertise will not develop merely from practice exercises in grammar and vocabulary at the sentence level. For many years, instruction in rhetoric had emphasized writing at the paragraph level and beyond, and instruction in composition typically provided students with exercises in the development of outlines and plans, the creation of paragraphs with topic sentences, the inclusion of supporting detail, techniques in comparison and contrast, and strategies for smooth transitions. According to Emig (1971), many of the composition texts used before 1970 basically described the writing process as linear in nature, proceeding from the development of an outline to the writing of a first draft, followed by a revision and a final draft. In most of these manuals, writing was seen as "a tidy, accretive affair that proceeds by elaborating a fully pre-conceived and formulated plan" (p. 22). Yet in interviews she had conducted in the 1960s with established writers, Emig found evidence that contradicted many of the precepts of the composition texts. For one thing, experienced writers reported that they proceeded differently in different genres or types of writing. No one ever seemed to outline before writing poetry, and the novelists and short-story writers in her sample seldom made outlines, or at least not elaborate ones. They also said that they did not engage in a linear process of planning, writing, and revision, but rather in a more recursive and integrated process that was not sequenced or fixed. For these expert writers, the "stages" of writing of the composition manuals were not a reality, at least not in a chronological sense.

In a landmark study of the composing process of high school students, Emig (1971) found that the twelve seniors she interviewed, most of whom had been identified as "good" writers by their teachers, did not typically follow the process that the composition manuals were suggesting. Most of them did have a kind of plan for the writing in mind before beginning to write, although it usually wasn't down on paper. The prewriting, planning, and reformulation processes among the students in her sample also varied depending on whether the composition was a "school-sponsored" topic or a topic of their own choosing. Emig's study further revealed that student writing was evaluated most often on criteria that emphasized "the accidents rather than the essences of discourse—that is, spelling, punctuation, penmanship, the length rather than thematic development, rhetorical and syntactic sophistication, and fulfillment of intent" (p. 93). Emig concluded that "much of the teaching of composition in American high schools is essentially a neurotic activity" (p. 99), and certainly not modeled on what good writers typically do.

Krashen (1984) reviewed research on the composing process in the native language and concludes that good writers differ from poor writers in at least three ways:

1. *Planning.* Good writers seem to plan more than poor writers do. This does not necessarily mean that they use an outline in the prewriting stage, but they do show some evidence of planning or organizing before they sit down to write the first draft. They also tend to take more time before beginning to write, whereas less proficient writers report that they prefer to begin to write "just by beginning." Good writers tend to have flexible plans and do not feel compelled to stick to their original ideas if they see a reason for changing the course of their thinking while in the process of composing.

2. *Rescanning.* Good writers stop rather frequently to reread what they have already written before continuing to compose. Krashen found that students in one study who were in regular composition classes tended to pause nearly twice as often during writing and to rescan their work three times as often as remedial students did. He maintains that rescanning helps good writers maintain a sense of the whole composition and that by rereading, planning what to write next, and then rescanning to see if the plan fits, writers invariably end up with better products.

3. *Revising.* Good writers tend to revise more than poor writers do, and they revise somewhat differently. Whereas poor writers tend to pay attention more often to surface form in their revisions, good writers make more changes in content and try to find the line of their argument in the finished draft in order to see if revisions are necessary (pp. 17–18).

Krashen adds that highly proficient writers often write *recursively*—that is, many use a nonlinear approach to the composing process. While writing a draft, for example, proficient writers may interrupt their writing because they have made some discovery that sends them back to reformulate their original idea. Less experienced writers, on the other hand, often feel that they are *not allowed* to do this and try to follow some fixed set of rules they learned in composition class instead. While the good writer understands that composition is a "messy process that leads to clarity" (Shaughnessy 1977, p. 79), the poor writer often does not have a clear idea of the value of revision.

One additional characteristic of proficient writers is their awareness of their audience and their concern for the reader's point of view. Whereas poor writers are "tied to the topic and writer-centered" (Krashen 1984, p. 18), proficient writers are reader-centered and avoid the use of ambiguous referents, words with special meanings of which the reader may be unaware, and the disorganized exposition of ideas that characterize the work of poor writers. Krashen believes that a high degree of writing competence can be achieved through extensive reading, although he bases this hypothesis on evidence that is drawn exclusively from research on native-language writers.

Hillocks (1986) reviewed nearly 2,000 articles on the teaching of writing and compared results of over 500 empirical studies of native-language writing practices. His description of the characteristics of better writers vs. weak writers coincides in many ways with the summary provided by Krashen. Yet Hillocks cautions us not to jump to premature conclusions about how writing should be taught. "The obvious question is one of cause and effect. Are good writers good because they plan more or are more concerned with content, organization, and even audience? Or do good writers devote more attention and energy to planning and content because they have mastered mechanics and need not be preoccupied by such matters?" (p. 28). Hillocks suggests that the hypothesis that instruction should concentrate on planning, organization, or content and abandon attention to mechanics has not been tested thoroughly to date, and that extrapolations from research on good writers to designs for writing instruction may thus be premature.

Applebee (1986) agrees that prescriptions for teaching writing drawn from descriptions of what experts do can lead to inadequate solutions for novice writers. In his view, these kinds of easy, direct applications lie at the heart of process-oriented approaches. He warns that such approaches can become trivialized or reduced to a new formula of lockstep procedures if they are thought of in a generic fashion. Applebee suggests reconceptualizing process instruction so as to link process with product and with a particular writing purpose. In this way, different strategies that writers use to achieve a given purpose can be taught at different times: some writing tasks would require only "the routine production of a first and final draft" (p. 106), while others would require more complex problem-solving strategies. Progress in writing would thus involve the gradual development of a wider repertoire of writing strategies for an ever-broadening range of situations.

Research on the Composing Process: First Language Studies

In reviewing a wide variety of studies done on the composing process of native language writers, Hillocks (1986) identified various findings that are of potential interest to teachers. Some of his conclusions are summarized below:

1. **Teaching Grammar in Isolation.** None of the studies reviewed supported the notion that teaching grammatical concepts in isolation had any positive effect on writing among native speakers. Hillocks

speculates that this might be so because grammatical instruction in sentence-level frames only touches the surface of discourse and does not address the other aspects of the composing process that are measured in empirical studies.

2. **Sentence-Combining Practice.** Research shows positive results for sentence-combining practice, although the effects of this practice might slowly disappear if the practice is not reinforced. Hillocks suggests that sentence-combining practice is well received by students because it builds confidence, stresses positive aspects of writing, and emphasizes the learning of new skills. Monroe (1975) and Cooper (1977, 1981) also found that sentence-combining yielded positive results in foreign language writing instruction. (For a sample of sentence-combining practice in a foreign language, see pp. 305–06.)

3. **Using Models of Good Writing.** Research on the use of models of good writing in writing instruction yields mixed results, with some studies showing benefits and others showing no significant differences between groups. However, Hillocks maintains that the use of models, especially "to illustrate a single characteristic of effective writing, such as the use of concrete detail" can be beneficial at all grade levels (p. 155).

4. **Using Criteria/Checklists for Peer Evaluation.** Strong positive effects have been found in studies where students used a set of criteria or a checklist of questions supplied by their teachers when engaging in peer editing and review of compositions. "As a group, these studies indicate rather clearly that engaging young writers actively in the use of criteria, applied to their own or to others' writing, results not only in more effective revisions, but in superior first drafts" (p. 160).

5. **Free Writing Practice.** The research reviewed, much of which was done with young children, showed very few positive effects for the use of free writing activities as the main focus of instruction, although they might be useful in generating ideas for subsequent writing in a different mode (p. 231).

6. **Teacher Comments.** Most of the studies reviewed showed no significant effects of teacher comments of any kind on the quality of writing, although positive feedback seemed to be preferred in some studies to negative feedback or no feedback. These results seem more conclusive than results in second language studies, which tend to be more contradictory. (Second language studies on feedback effects will be reviewed in the next section.)

Hillocks concludes from these results that some combination of treatments (studying examples of writing, using checklists in peer evaluation and correction, and engaging in revision) seems to be indicated if we hope to improve writing instruction in the native language. However, it is difficult to know exactly what combinations will work with what students until more research is done. In addition, Hillocks makes it clear that much of the research he reviewed was faulty in its design, and nearly 80% of the 500 studies he examined could not be considered in his meta-analysis because of lack of control of important variables (p. 110). It is thus wise for teachers to exercise caution in extrapolating from research studies on writing and keep their limitations in mind. This is especially true when extrapolating from native language research studies in designing foreign and second language instructional programs.

Research on Writing in the Second Language

The amount of research done in second language contexts on writing processes is limited at this time, and much of it relates to the composing processes of advanced learners of ESL. Writing research involving foreign language classroom learners is generally focused on feedback strategies, although some studies have looked at other issues. This section will summarize briefly some of the findings in foreign and second language writing.

Research on the Composing Process: Second Language Studies

Krapels (1990) has reviewed process research in second languages, and reports that studies to date have investigated the composing processes of only about 100 subjects in ESL. In her survey of these studies, she found that there were several commonalities in their designs: (1) studies were either strongly guided by or based on studies in the native language; (2) studies typically involved very small numbers of subjects (typically 4–6 learners); (3) subjects were typically female, advanced in their proficiency, undergraduate ESL learners whose native language was either Spanish or Chinese; and (4) students were seldom chosen randomly, and sometimes were in the researcher's own classes.

Krapels reports contradictory and inconclusive findings with regard to the applicability of native language research results to the second or foreign language context. Some studies indicated that L1 and L2 processes were similar, while others suggested that they were different. The use of the native language in composing in the foreign language varied across studies. Several researchers found that the use of the L1 varied according to the topic, with topics that are rooted in the native language culture engaging more L1 use than topics that focused on the target culture (see, for example, Friedlander, 1990). Krapels cites Silva (1988), who reviewed college-level writing process research between 1982 and 1987 and maintains that one of the greatest problems in second language writing research lies in the interpretation of findings by the researchers or by those who consult their studies. He points out that while some researchers have been modest and tentative in their conclusions, others have made rather bold assertions based on too little evidence, generalizing unjustifiably from very small samples to the larger population of learners, suggesting premature implications, or making "sweeping claims that go way beyond findings in support of a particular popular approach or orientation to writing instruction" (Silva 1988, p. 6, cited in Krapels 1990, p. 50). Krapels agrees with Silva that second and foreign language researchers should begin to look for some of the *differences* between L1 and L2 writing rather than concentrating on the similarities (p. 52).

In the foreign language context, far fewer studies on the composing process *per se* have been done. A pilot study by Bland, Noblitt, Armington, and Gay (1990) used the computer software *système-D* with 10 volunteer subjects in first and second-year college French and tracked their use of resources on the system as they wrote various composition assignments. The researchers found in the query logs of these students three kinds of requests for help: (1) *token matching,* where the students try to find a direct translation of a morphologically complex word or a phrase from English to French, without making any adjustments to the word or phrase; (2) *type matching,* where the students ask for the base forms of words they are looking for in the dictionary (such as infinitives or singular nouns) or ask for a grammatical concept (such as "negation" or "adjective"); and (3) *relexicalization,* which represents an attempt to construct meaning through synonyms, paraphrases, or structurally different expressions. The authors maintain that this third strategy shows a willingness on the part of students to depart from the native language and begin to construct meaning in the new language. They suggest that their findings "confirm the value of assessing facility in circumlocution to distinguish between elementary and intermediate level students" (p. 447). Follow-up interviews suggested that most of the students did not yet understand the value of paraphrasing as a strategy in helping them express their own thoughts in the second language, and the authors recommend that such strategies should be actively taught as a part of writing instruction. Because students' query behavior in this study was somewhat heterogeneous, showing the use of competing strategies and hypotheses about how the language works, the authors felt that more research into this aspect of composing behavior would give us further insight into "the nonlinear progression that characterizes much of the language learning process" (p. 449). This study illustrates clearly that learners typically will resort to the use of their native language when composing in the foreign language, especially at the lower levels of proficiency.

Friedlander (1990) investigated the effects of advanced writers using their native language on the quality of their writing in English as a second language. He cites studies by Chelala (1981), Lay (1982), and Johnson (1985) that corroborate his own findings that students can profit from using their native language while composing on topics in a foreign language in certain instances. The use of the native language can help students retrieve more information on certain kinds of topics and thus enhance the quality of their final compositions. Friedlander's 28 Chinese subjects profited differentially, however, from using Chinese depending on the topic of the composition: they wrote more on topics related to Chinese experiences when they used their native language to plan their writing, but profited more from using English to plan compositions relating to experiences rooted in English-speaking culture. In other words, when the language used for beginning the composing process was matched to the language in which the topic was experienced, the results were superior in terms of content, quality of the plan, and quality of the resulting essay. Friedlander argues against forcing students who are at an advanced level in the second language to plan compositions or engage in parts of the composing process in the target language when this might add to the burden and constraints they are under already. However, he suggests that ESL students at lower levels should be encouraged to do everything in English, since they need as much practice as possible, and their use of their native language would perhaps not be best for them. If developing *linguistic* skills is not the main point of the writing, but refining skills already developed is the goal, then use of the native language in certain aspects of the composing process may be advantageous.

Research on Evaluation and Feedback: Second Language Studies

Opinions about how and when to evaluate student written work vary widely. For example, some researchers, scholars, and practitioners recommend that we respond primarily to content and not to form. Others suggest that we respond to both form and content, with some scholars recommending that response to form be reserved to the final draft and others preferring to respond to formal features throughout the process. There seems to be a general consensus that involving students in their own correction is helpful, and that a combination of teacher, peer, and self-evaluation might yield the most successful results.

Empirical studies on the effects of feedback and evaluation in second and foreign language writing have yielded contradictory results. Studies that seem to indicate that corrective feedback on form was not helpful include those by Semke (1984), Zamel (1985), and Cohen (1987). In Semke's study, German students who were given no corrective feedback on form and were graded solely on amount of communication responded more favorably to that type of treatment than did students who were graded on accuracy alone and had obtained some kind of corrective feedback from the teacher. However, it is possible that the effects of grading and feedback strategy were confounded in this study, since the group of students who received no corrective feedback were rewarded for quantity only and the others who received corrective feedback were rewarded only for accuracy. Students in the no-feedback condition were also directed to write twice as much for an A as students in the other groups. Thus, the effects of feedback *per se*, divorced from the other variables present in the study, are not entirely clear.

Zamel's (1985) study revealed that teachers' feedback on advanced ESL compositions was often inconsistent and contradictory, and that that might render error correction ineffective. Cohen (1987) studied various students' responses to feedback on their compositions, and found that teachers' comments were often confusing, vague, and inconsistent, and that most comments focused exclusively on form. In addition, most of the students in his study were never asked to write a second draft after receiving the teachers' input. He recommends that teachers focus more on process in their comments and use multi-draft assignments. Students also should be taught how to use feedback to enhance their writing skills.

Studies by Lalande (1982), Fathman and Whalley (1985; 1990), and Rieken (1991) have shown beneficial results from teachers' corrective feedback on compositions of second and foreign language learners. Lalande (1982) compared the effects of self-correction versus teacher-correction on compositions in fourth-quarter college German classes. The students in the control group were corrected by their teachers and asked to rewrite their compositions. Students in the experimental group received error codes and charts indicating where they had committed errors and were asked to self-correct using these aids. Self-correction in this second condition was done in class, with students engaged in problem-solving using the codes, their texts, and teacher or peer assistance if necessary. The self-correcting group had statistically fewer errors at the end of the experimental period than did the control group, who received teacher corrections and rewrote their work. Lalande concludes that the combination of awareness of one's errors and rewriting with problem-solving techniques was significantly beneficial for developing writing skills in German. (See Appendix B for samples of the error codes and charts used in Lalande's study, along with a similar error coding system for French.)

Fathman and Whalley (1990) found that when teachers underlined grammatical errors in their students' texts, students made fewer grammatical errors in rewriting their compositions than when no such feedback was provided. Their study also indicated that grammatical and content feedback can beneficially be provided at the same time without overburdening the students. The 72 ESL students in their study rewrote their compositions in class in response to four feedback conditions: (1) no feedback, (2) grammatical feedback (where errors were underlined), (3) content feedback, and (4) both grammar and content feedback. There was a significant reduction in grammatical errors for students receiving grammatical feedback (conditions 2 and 4). Most of the students who received only content feedback improved their content scores, but 35% of them made more grammar errors in their revisions. When students received *both* grammar and content feedback, they all improved on grammar significantly, and 77% also improved on content. The authors concluded that grammar and content feedback, whether given alone or in concert, positively affect rewriting, and that grammatical feedback had more effect on correction of errors than content feedback had on the improvement of the content of the students' second draft.

Rieken's (1991) study investigated the possibility that there might be an interaction between feedback type and cognitive style. She looked at the effects of three different levels of feedback on the writing of high school students of French who differed in the cognitive-style dimension of field independence. She examined the effects of (1) no corrective feedback, (2) indirect correction through substantive comments in which corrections were embedded, and (3) direct correction of errors on students frequency and accuracy of use of the *passé composé*. All students received positive evaluative comments on their compositions and were directed to rewrite them. She found that students who had explicit corrections were significantly more accurate in their use of the *passé composé* when accuracy was calculated on the number of different verbs used, but that there were no significant differences among groups on frequency of use of the past tense. She also found no differences among groups on a post-treatment cloze test except among students with low field-independence (FI). Low FI students who had had direct correction performed more accurately on the cloze test than low FI students in the other feedback conditions. The results suggest that various correction strategies may be differentially effective, depending on the student's cognitive style.

Rieken also found a significant teacher effect, a dimension that is ignored in many empirical studies. It may be that the teacher's attitude toward correction, the way in which they offer it to students, and students' own feelings about the teacher in general are significant factors in the effectiveness of correction strategies.

Another factor that may affect writing performance is whether or not the work is evaluated for a grade. Chastain (1990) examined the effects of grading compositions on the quality of student writing. His study examined the compositions of 14 advanced undergraduate Spanish students, most of whom were majors in their third or fourth year and who were characterized by the researcher as having "good" language skills and high motivation. The course emphasized process over product, and students were expected to write second drafts before turning in compositions for a grade. Compositions in this experiment were written in clusters of three, the first two of which were ungraded and the third one graded. Near the end of the semester, Chastain examined one ungraded and one graded composition for each of the 14 students in the class. He found that students wrote significantly more for the graded composition than for the ungraded and used significantly longer and more complex sentences. However, he found no significant differences in the two compositions in terms of errors, content or organizational grades. Chastain notes that the percentage of error to total words was very low (less than 5% for the whole class) and that students "did study some of the grammar that confounds advanced as well as beginning students" (p. 11). He adds that most of the students were products of grammar-based classes. It is possible that these learners may have been well prepared for a class that emphasized process writing through early concentration on more structured or focused tasks. However, it is difficult to conclude from the study itself what might have led to the relatively low level of error among these motivated students.

As one considers the results of these studies, it seems that the effects of feedback and grading on student writing are quite variable. The effectiveness of feedback may depend, in part, on the level of motivation of students, their current level of proficiency, their cognitive style, the clarity of the feedback given, the way feedback is used, and the attitudes of students toward their teacher and the class. The studies reviewed do seem to indicate that teacher feedback is sometimes confusing, inconsistent, and contradictory, and that feedback that is exclusively focused on form is discouraging to many students. These findings can be useful to teachers as they consider their own feedback strategies and evaluate various ways to respond to student work.

Approaches to Teaching Writing as Creative Communication

Kroll (1990) notes that there seems to have been a paradigm shift among many scholars in native language writing instruction away from a focus on writing as *product* toward a focus on *process*. This same shift has been called for by scholars in foreign language instruction as well. (See, for example, Dvorak 1986 and Barnett 1989). Some researchers (for example, Raimes 1983; Kaplan 1988; Silva 1990) urge a balanced approach that takes both process and product into account. This section summarizes briefly some of the possible approaches to writing instruction that have been advocated by scholars in both native and second language contexts.

Hillocks (1986) identifies four "modes" of writing instruction in native language composition. They include:

1. *The Presentational Mode*, with clear and specific objectives, teacher-centered discussions of writing principles, and assignments involving imitation and analysis of models of writing;
2. *The Natural Process Mode*, which encourages free writing, including the use of daily journals, emphasizes positive feedback from peers and the teacher, fosters cooperative learning with a low level of structure in assignments, and is nondirectional about the qualities of writing to be developed;
3. *The Environmental Mode*, emphasizing clear and specific objectives and group work on particular processes important to some aspect of composing (such as increasing the use of detail in a description). In this approach, principles are taught by the teacher not through lectures or presentations, but through concrete examples and models. Students work together on specific problems, provide one another with peer evaluation, and use teacher-provided checklists, structured questions, or other specific criteria to respond to their

own and others' work. This approach is similar to what Applebee (1986) has called a "structured process mode."

4. *The Individualized Mode,* where students are instructed through tutorials or programmed materials and the instruction is geared specifically to student needs (Hillocks 1986, pp. 116–126).

For ESL classes, Raimes (1983) recommends an eclectic approach to writing and asserts that there is no one answer to the question of how writing should be taught. Rather, "there are as many answers as there are teachers and teaching styles, or learners and learning styles" (p. 5). She reviews six different writing approaches, which are described briefly below. Some of these approaches have also been prevalent in foreign language classes:

1. *The Controlled-to-Free Approach,* which stresses accuracy over fluency or originality and is essentially based in ALM teaching practice. In this approach, students write variations first on sentences, then on paragraphs, then on very controlled compositions, and finally work on free composition when their skills are at an advanced level.
2. *The Free-Writing Approach,* which encourages vast amounts of fluency-based writing with little correction;
3. *The Paragraph-Pattern Approach,* which stresses organization over fluency or accuracy and provides model paragraphs for students to copy, analyze, or imitate;
4. *The Grammar-Syntax-Organization Approach,* which works simultaneously on various formal features as students write to carry out specific writing functions;
5. *The Communicative Approach,* stressing purpose and audience and encouraging interaction among students and the teacher, with less emphasis on form and correctness; and
6. *The Process Approach,* emphasizing the writing process over product, with adequate time provided to develop a piece of writing, a recognition of the recursiveness of the process, and the encouragement of exploration of topics through writing (pp. 7–10).

Raimes points out that there is a degree of overlap in all of these approaches, and advocates an eclecticism that is responsive to learner needs as their skills develop.

Silva (1990) describes what he considers the four most influential approaches in ESL writing from the period 1945 to 1990 as follows:

1. *Controlled Composition,* similar to the "Controlled-to-Free" approach described by Raimes (1983), above;
2. *Current-Traditional Rhetoric,* which is product-oriented, focusing on proper mechanics and usage as well as rhetorical organization and style. This approach tends to focus on paragraph construction (topic sentences, the use of supportive detail, cause-effect or

comparison/contrast patterns) and on essay development (writing introduction, body, and conclusion). It also explores various kinds of expository writing styles. Silva says that although this approach has been "under attack" for a number of years, it is still quite dominant in ESL classrooms (p. 15).

3. *The Process Approach,* reacting against prescriptive techniques and characterized by prewriting activities, multiple drafts, and peer-editing, with final editing for form reserved for the final draft; and

4. *English for Academic Purposes,* where students are taught to write for an academic audience (Silva 1990, pp. 12–17).

As we consider these various methodological approaches to the teaching of writing, it seems that the choice of method will be determined in part by the level of the students, the situation in which they are learning (native language, second language, or foreign language contexts), the goals of instruction, and the needs and preferences of the students. What kinds of skills do students currently have, and what skills do they need to develop? If students are at a relatively low level of writing proficiency, they may need to have the support of a structured approach, such as "controlled composition," a "paragraph-pattern approach," or a "structured process mode" that emphasizes defined objectives and provides clear feedback and evaluative criteria. An eclectic approach, integrating assignments where self-expression through journaling or free writing is encouraged with tasks that are more structured might also be a good option for students in the Intermediate ranges of proficiency. For students who are relatively advanced and who want to improve their expressive or rhetorical skills, a "communicative" approach, stressing such factors as purpose and audience, or an "academic purpose" course, emphasizing writing for a particular kind of audience, might be a good choice. In the final analysis, it is the teacher working with particular students who will need to determine which approach is best. As in any discussion of methodological trends, we are limited in our perspective if we search for just "one true way." Silva (1990) urges teachers to avoid methodological bandwagons and make a professional and reasoned evaluation of the various approaches, preserving the insights that are useful from all of them. This represents both the privilege and the challenge of the classroom teacher of the 1990s, who is left with more questions than answers, given the present state of our knowledge in this domain.

Advanced-level Activities: Preparing for Superior-level Writing

Students who are currently writing at the Advanced level in the second language are generally able to write reasonably accurate, coherent discourse dealing with both concrete and abstract topics. They can narrate events in past, present, and future time and, at the Advanced-High level, are often able to support a point of view relatively coherently. Obviously, students whose writing is at this level will still need to work on improving their grammatical accuracy, their choice of vocabulary, and their rhetorical skills and can profit from a variety of structured practice activities that refine their control of the language in these domains.

However, in addition to developing expertise in the use of advanced features of the language through structured or semistructured language-practice activities, students at this level of competence need to learn more about the composing process itself. The activities suggested in this section are, for the most part, semiguided and free composition tasks that involve rather extensive work on the improvement of discourse skills as well as practice in the composing process. This can be achieved in several ways:

1. Attention can be focused in the prewriting and writing stages on the type of rhetorical structure and organization appropriate to the writing task, and students can create original compositions using extensive guidelines and/or models that exemplify those features.
2. Students can engage in peer-editing activities that sensitize them to rhetorical, organizational, lexical, and grammatical features of their own writing and help them improve their compositions through rewriting activities.
3. Writers can learn to analyze the writing style of experts in the target language and attempt to create original compositions using elements of that style.

According to Jacobs, Zingraf, Wormuth, Hartfiel, and Hughey (1981), the overall aim of composition practice at the Advanced level should be the development of authentic discourse processing skills. The primary focus of such writing practice "should not be the word, the phrase, or the sentence, but the larger elements and processes that must be integrated and synthesized for effective written communication" (p. v). The authors suggest various criteria that should be used in designing composition tasks and tests at this level, and provide the evaluative checklist given in Illustration 7.12.

When designing writing practice at the Advanced level, it is important to include various aspects of the composing process in the instructional sequence. Cooper (1975) identifies the following subprocesses that may be involved in composing:

1. Prewriting gestation, which can last for minutes or for much longer periods of time
2. Planning (with or without written notes or outlines)
3. Getting started
4. Making ongoing decisions about every aspect of writing, from vocabulary choice to syntax, style, and organization
5. Reviewing, rereading, and anticipating what will come next
6. Reformulating and adjusting parts of the manuscript as it evolves
7. Stopping
8. Contemplating the finished draft
9. Revising, as necessary (p. 113).

Illustration 7.12

Checklist for preparing
the writing task

Does the task:

[ ] require writers to *compose* a piece of connected discourse?

[ ] establish a clear purpose for communicating, especially by indicating the intended reader and a context for the task?

[ ] motivate writers to communicate their knowledge and perception of the topic?

[ ] reflect the kind of writing students will normally be expected to do in their academic programs or the real world?

[ ] provide a subject that will interest students of this age, sex, educational level, field of study, and cultural background?

[ ] present a topic about which these students will have knowledge?

[ ] appear to be the right level of difficulty for students of this proficiency range?

[ ] provide a topic that is free of hidden elements of bias?

[ ] present a clearly defined task that cannot easily be misinterpreted?

[ ] provide a topic that is broad enough for every writer to approach from some angle?

[ ] use as few words as possible, and definitions if necessary?

[ ] give clear and concise instructions that indicate also the time allowed for writing and the approximate number of words or length of composition expected?

[ ] present a writable and readable topic, pretested with students similar to the test group?

[ ] include as many modes of discourse as are appropriate to the purpose of the test and to the actual writing needs of the students?

[ ] provide at least two writing occasions, in order to produce an adequate sample of a student's ability?

[ ] require all students to write on the same topic, unless skill at choosing a topic is a part of the abilities being tested?

[ ] allow enough writing time for a reasonable performance?

[ ] provide ruled paper for writing?

[ ] use a coding system for identifying writers so that authorship will be anonymous during the evaluation?

[ ] Is the writing task appropriate to the specific purpose(s) of this test?

Source: Jacobs et al. 1981, p. 22.

The various steps of the composing process need to be taught, discussed, and practiced more overtly than has typically been the case in many foreign language programs, especially when students are at the Intermediate or Advanced level of writing proficiency. In response to this need, a number of process-oriented writing texts have appeared within the past ten years that are designed for language learners at the second-year college level and beyond. For example, Valdés, Dvorak, and Hannum (1984; 1989) have developed a text for advanced Spanish students that leads them through various steps or stages as they engage in creative and expressive writing, concentrating on organization, style, and the development of greater precision in grammar and vocabulary in the process. In the Valdés et al. text students practice various types of writing, including description, narration, and exposition, using rhetorical techniques such as definition, classification, comparison and contrast, and argumentation. The typical writing lesson involves three phases:

1. *Prewriting.* (See Cooper's Step 1, above.) A brief discussion of the type of writing to be attempted by students is followed by a writing model, an analysis of the model's organization and style, a consideration of the reader's and writer's purpose, and a series of exercises that focus on both organizational devices and topics appropriate to that writing function.

2. *Composing.* Students complete the actual writing assignment by following specific guidelines or steps. In some cases, they are asked to write preliminary outlines or answer a series of questions within an organizational framework; in others they are given instructions to follow as they write. (See Cooper's Steps 2 and 3.) Attention is focused throughout this phase on organizational and mechanical considerations (as in Steps 4 through 6).

3. *Revision.* This last phase of the process includes revision of the organizational and stylistic features of the composition and revision of grammar. Checklists with specific questions for reviewing the work are provided, along with directions for rewriting and exercises for grammatical practice. (See Steps 6 through 9.)

This process is illustrated in outline form in the following lesson drawn from Valdés et al. (1984). The topic of the writing lesson is narration.

I. *Etapa uno: Antes de redactar (Step One: Before Writing)*

A. A definition and explanation of the function *narration* is given first in Spanish. Then students learn how narration can be given from a variety of perspectives (third person, first person) and sample texts are provided. Some useful vocabulary relating to chronological details is listed.

B. Students then look at several models of writing taken from authentic sources. Each model is analyzed in terms of the perspective, organization, theme, tone, and stylistic devices used.

C. Exercises in distinguishing narration from other types of discourse and in recognizing the salient features of narrative texts are provided next. One such exercise asks students to identify the parts of the narration in a sample text.

A subsequent exercise asks students to work in small groups to develop a narration on a personal theme, using the one in the above exercise as a model. The directions for the group task are:

Hable cada uno de Uds. de un episodio que haya experimentado en su propia vida. Utilicen el siguiente cuadro para organizar una breve presentación personal.

Tema: El día que _____
(algo pasó)

Detalles que pueden incluirse

Situación: ¿Qué día era?
¿Donde estaba Ud.?
¿Por qué recuerda Ud. el incidente (el día)?
¿Qué estaba haciendo Ud.?
¿Con quién estaba Ud.?

Complicación: ¿Qué occurió primero (después)?
¿Por qué occurió?
¿Por qué fue este un suceso poco comun?

¿Resolución/Desenlace: ¿Qué pasó como resultado de la complicación?
¿Qué efecto tuvo lo ocurrido en Ud.?
¿Qué cambió como resultado de la acción?

(Valdés et al 1984, p. 25. Reprinted by permission of McGraw-Hill.)

Each one of you will talk about an event you have experienced in your own lives. Use the following chart to organize a brief personal presentation.

Theme: The day that _____
(something happened)

Details you can include:

Situation: What day was it?
Where were you?
Why do you remember the incident?
What were you doing?
Who were you with?

Problem: What happened first (afterwards)?
Why did it happen?
Why was this an unusual event?

Resolution/Outcome: What happened as a result of the problem?
What effect did the event have on you?
What changed as a result of the action?

II. *Etapa dos: La redacción (Step Two: Writing the Draft)*
Students begin writing their own composition by following a set of steps outlined in the text.

III. *Etapa tres: La revisión (Step Three: Revision)*

A. In this phase, review of structure and organization, students use a set of questions to review the composition. Among the questions are:
¿Cuenta mi narración algo que sucedió?
¿Qué parte de mi narración contiene la situación?
¿Qué parte de mi narración contiene la complicación?
¿Qué parte de mi narración contiene el desenlace?
¿Mantuve la misma perspectiva a través de toda la narración?
¿Mantuve el mismo tono?
¿Capta la narración la impresión que dejó en mi el incidente?
¿Contribuyen todos los detalles que incluí a dejar esa impresión?
¿Puede seguirse cronológicamente la narración?
¿Utilicé el vocabulario que indica cronología?
¿Qué estrategías utilicé para despertar el interés del lector?

III. Step Three: Revision

A. In this phase, review of structure . . .
Does my narrative tell about an event that happened?
What section of the narrative explains the situation?
What section of the narrative explains the problem?
What section of the narrative contains the outcome?
Did I keep the same perspective throughout the narrative?
Did I maintain the same tone?
Does the narrative convey how I was affected by the incident?
Do all of the details I included help convey my feelings?
Can the narrative be followed in chronological sequence?
Did I use vocabulary items that convey this chronology?
What strategies did I use to capture the reader's interest?

B. In this second phase, review of grammatical features, students are directed to look at their compositions from the point of view of tenses used, reviewing grammatical principles learned in conjunction with the writing lesson. Exercises in choosing preterite versus imperfect tenses in a variety of narrative texts, as well as grammar explanations and review materials on the use of the past tenses in narration, are provided here for those students who need them.

C. In the third phase, review of grammar features studied in previous chapters, students examine their written work once again, this time looking for features of grammar that were learned in previous lessons.

D. In this phase, review of spelling, students check over the composition for spelling and punctuation errors of any type.

E. In the last phase, writing of the final version, students use the information gleaned in Phases A through D to write a final draft that incorporates all necessary corrections and changes.

Source: Valdés et al. 1984, pp. 19–33. Reprinted by permission of McGraw-Hill.

This approach can serve as a good model for the teaching of composition in any language, especially when students are already writing at the Advanced level.

Prose Style Analysis and Pastiche

A procedure suggested by Gaudiani (1981) encourages students to study various styles of writing and make analyses of stylistic elements used by a variety of authors in the target language. She asks students to write style analyses in English, after which they write a composition on a theme of their choice, imitating the style of the author under study.

When students are ready to begin the prose style analysis phase of their training in composition, Gaudiani has them read the excerpt that will be used for the pastiche. They discuss style and organization and notice grammatical and lexical features that the author has chosen to create certain effects. Then working in small groups, students try to write a sample of prose in a fashion that resembles the model. Later students do a second prose style analysis on a new text and write a pastiche individually as their next composition assignment.

The following example in French is designed to help intermediate to advanced composition students to analyze literary prose and incorporate some of the strategies the author uses in their own writing. In this case, students work with a short passage from *L'Etranger* by Albert Camus in which he describes the scene at a nursing home where the leading character's mother has just died. The description of the residents is both impersonal and yet photographic in its detail. Camus uses sound, light, and movement to capture the mood of the residents, and the use of adjectives is especially artful in this particular description.

Before reading the passage, students can be asked to engage in various activities that elicit their own ideas and images around the theme of the text to be studied. For example, students in small groups can discuss their experiences with the elderly and/or with nursing home environments, generating a list of descriptive words and images that come to mind. They might also list words or phrases that express their feelings about these experiences or about the living conditions of many elderly people in their own culture. Anticipation activities can also be designed to help students predict how the author might deal with the scene in the passage to be read.

After reading the passage, students engage in a series of activities that help them analyze the style of the author. The sample "Analyse du texte" provided below asks students to react to the author's perspective as he surveys the scene at the nursing home and notice the stylistic use of images. Students extract words and expressions from the text that relate to sounds, light, and movement both in the physical surroundings and in the descriptions of the people themselves. Students then find examples of the impersonality of the description and react to the lack of compassion on the part of the principal character in the novel.

Sample Prose analysis activity of an extract from Camus' *L'Etranger*

Analyse du texte

1. Après avoir lu ce passage, quelle est l'impression principale que vous avez de l'asile et de ses résidents? [*After having read the passage, what is the principal impression that you have of the nursing home and of its residents?*]

   a. C'est un endroit bien triste sans espoir. [*It's a very sad, hopeless place.*]
   b. C'est un environnement bizarre et effrayant. [*It's a strange and frightening environment.*]
   c. C'est une communauté où les résidents expriment leur affection les uns pour les autres. [*It's a community where the residents express their affection for one another.*]
   d. _____?

2. Comment Meursault voit-il l'asile et ses résidents? [*How does Meursault (the principal character of the novel) see the nursing home and its residents?*]

   a. comme un observateur très sympathique [*as a very sympathetic observer*]
   b. comme un étranger—aliéné sans compréhension [*as a stranger, alienated and uncomprehending*]
   c. comme un jeune homme qui ne s'intéresse pas vraiment à un groupe de vieillards [*like a young man who is not very interested in a group of old people*]
   d. _____?

3. En faisant son portrait de l'asile, Camus utilise beaucoup d'images frappantes: le jeu de la lumière, les descriptions assez détaillées des vieux, les sons, les mouvements. Analysez ces aspects de la

	LA SALLE (*THE ROOM*)	**LES VIEUX** (*THE ELDERLY*)
SONS (*SOUNDS*)		
LUMIÈRE (*LIGHT*)		
MOUVEMENTS (*MOVEMENTS*)		

description ci-dessous en mettant des mots ou des expressions du texte dans le schéma: [*In creating his portrait of the nursing home, Camus uses a lot of striking images: the play of the light, rather detailed descriptions of the old people, sounds, and movements. Analyze these aspects of the description below by placing words and expressions from the text in the boxes of the graph.*]

4. Donnez quelques détails qui montrent que Meursault a de la difficulté à voir ou à entendre les vieux dans la salle: [*Give a few details that show that Meursault has problems seeing or hearing the old people in the room.*]

5. Donnez quelques détails qui montrent que Meursault les voit comme des objets plutôt que des êtres humains: [*Give a few details that show that Meursault sees them as objects rather than as people.*]

6. Comment Meursault réagit-il en ce qui concerne ses émotions? Citez des exemples du texte: [*How does Meursault react emotionally? Give some examples from the text.*]

7. Meursault comprend-il les émotions des vieux dans la salle? Expliquez votre réponse. [*Does Meursault understand the emotions of the old people in the room? Explain your response.*]

After analyzing the excerpt, students are asked to write a description of a different scene in the same style, or change the description written by Camus to one in which the author takes a different point of view of the same scene (for example, a more compassionate view). This task can be done cooperatively in groups or by individuals working alone. Follow-up activities include peer editing of the work produced, as described in the next section.

Refining the Written Draft

Peer Editing   Gaudiani (1981) has written an excellent monograph in which she proposes various ideas for teaching composition at the Advanced level. One of the procedures she suggests is the "class editing process," in which students help one another improve their drafts through a series of "passes."

Each week in the composition class, a small group of students provide for all the others in the class a mimeographed copy of their first draft of the assigned theme. The compositions are typed triple-spaced to enable everyone ample room for written comments. The steps in the class editing procedure are:

1. *Comprehension of Meaning*. Students listen as one of the people who has prepared a mimeographed composition reads it aloud. Class members ask for clarification of any words or expressions they do not understand during this first pass.
2. *Correction of Grammar*. The teacher reads each sentence of the composition and asks the author and the others in the class to provide any needed grammatical corrections.
3. *Analysis of Prose Style*. After the composition has been corrected in the second pass, the class reads it once again silently, after which they comment on the style. When problems relating to sentence length, repetition of words, lack of precision in vocabulary or expression, etc. are discovered, the teacher asks for solutions from class members.
4. *Analysis of Organization*. Students read the composition a fourth time, looking now for such things as paragraphing, the use of topic sentences, and summaries. Suggestions are made on the basis of this fourth pass through the draft.
5. *Overview/Synthesis*. Finally, the class offers general comments on the effectiveness of the composition as a whole in communicating a message (p. 14).

Birckbichler (1985) has suggested that the class editing process may be most effective if students in a composition class work on anonymous writing samples provided from outside their own group, thus eliminating any reluctance to critique the samples for fear of hurting someone's feelings. She suggests using samples from a similar class in a previous year, or from another class offered the same semester. (In either case, it is important to obtain permission from students whose work is being evaluated to use it for peer editing purposes.) In Birckbichler's experience, students said a lot more and got much more out of the class editing procedure when working with anonymous compositions than they did when judging the work of their peers within the same class.

Birckbichler also points out that peer editing activities need a clear focus so that students know exactly what they should be concentrating on in any given part of the process. She suggests that specific questions might be designed by the teacher to guide discussion in each of the steps of the class editing procedure outlined above.

Self-editing Using Teacher-developed Guidelines

Barnett (1989) outlines a self-editing approach to writing that requires advanced students to write two drafts before turning in their compositions for a grade, followed if necessary by a third draft that is written after they receive substantive feedback on form and content, style, organization and the like. She suggests collecting students' notes used in the planning of their first draft, as well as the first draft itself when grading the second draft. The guidelines for writing and self-editing that she provides to students are quite comprehensive, including advice about getting started, strategies for taking notes and using them to develop and organize one's ideas, and procedures for writing successive drafts and evaluating one's writing. The approach encourages students to focus on meaning during the writing of their first draft and correct the form later. One of the strengths of this method is that it does not neglect attention to form, but rather makes it one of several concerns involved in the composing process. In Barnett's approach, teacher comments on the multiple drafts incorporate various aspects of feedback. In response to the first draft, most comments relate to the content and include requests for clarification of ideas and suggestions for reorganization. One or two general comments about form are also included, and positive feedback is given to encourage the student by pointing out strengths. (See Illustration 7.13.) In the response to the second draft, the teacher underlines all remaining errors, highlights a few for focused attention and correction, points out a few places where the student still needs to improve organization, and assigns a dual grade based on form (50%) and content (50%). (See Illustration 7.14.) Barnett maintains that this kind of approach to feedback on compositions yields far more satisfying results for both teacher and students than does an approach based on morphological or syntactic repairs alone.

Evaluation and Grading of Student Writing

Teacher response to students' written compositions has typically taken two forms: (1) corrective feedback on the microlevel and (2) an overall evaluation in the form of a grade. We have just seen how various kinds of qualitative feedback can be given to students through teacher commentary, peer editing, and self editing using guidelines, codes, or checklists. The second type of response—evaluation of the work on a macrolevel—can be given using a variety of scoring schemes and objective techniques. Perkins (1983) has outlined the assumptions, procedures, and consequences of using three principal types of scoring in the evaluation of compositions: (1) holistic scoring, (2) analytical scoring, and (3) primary trait scoring.

> 1. *Holistic Scoring.* When one is attempting to assess the overall proficiency level of a given written sample, holistic scoring has the

Sample Student First Draft with Teacher Comments

[handwritten: Très clair!]

La Presse Libre et Formidable *[handwritten: ← Pourquoi formidable?]*

Aujourd'hui, la presse libre est important aux Etats-Unis et en France parce que ce donne les gens une occasion pour exprimer leurs opinions. Dans une démocratie, il faut donner une voix à les gens, et *[handwritten: qui?]* ils ont besoin de les faits et les opinions d'autres. Si la presse n'était pas libre, les gens devraient croire les faits et les *[handwritten: Oui, d'accord.]* opinions du gouvernement. Ainsi, un peu de gens pouvrait contrôler beaucoup de gens, et ce ne serait pas une démocratie.

[handwritten left margin: ATTN aux formes des mots: à + les = ? etc.]

Dans une démocratie, les gens doivent avoir la protection aussi. Il faut avoir les limitations avec la presse. La presse ne peut pas exprimer les faits faux, spécialement *[handwritten: ceux (ch.8)]* les qui peuvent endommager quelqu'un. Ce n'est pas une probleme avec les journaux respectables, mais c'est une autre probleme. Les journaux forment souvent les opinions, et les gens oublient que toutes les opinions ne sont pas toujours représenté. Les gens doivent lire les journaux avec objectivité et décider quelle position qu'ils vont prendre.

[handwritten left margin: C'est une bonne transition, mais c'est une nouvelle idée. Révisez l'introduction, et mettez-y cette idée.]

[handwritten left margin: ATTN au genre et aux accords]

[handwritten right margin: A quelle sorte de protection faites-vous référence?]

[handwritten right margin: Quel autre problème? Voudriez-vous dire que c'est un problème avec les journaux moins respectables?]

[handwritten right margin: Oui, je comprends.]

[handwritten bottom: Alors, quel est votre argument principal? Mettez-le dans votre conclusion, avec un résumé de vos arguments.]

Illustration 7.13   *Source:* Barnett 1989, p. 41.

Sample Student Second Draft with Teacher Comments
[NOTE: Circled errors are explained on a separate sheet and should be
eliminated from future compositions.]

La Presse Libre et Formidable

La presse libre est important dans une société
démocratique parce que cela donne (les) gens une occasion pour exprimer leurs opinions. Il faut informer
les gens de tous les faits parce que les gens ont une
voix dans le gouvernement. Si la presse n'était pas
libre, les gens devraient croire seulement les faits
et les opinions dont le gouvernement veut d'exprimer.
Ainsi, (un peu de) gens pourrait contrôler beaucoup de
gens, et ce ne serait pas une démocratie.

Personne dans une démocratie ne veut être contrôlé
par (un peu de) gens, mais la presse peut contrôler les
gens aussi. Les gens de la presse contrôle] quelles
informations vont] dans la journal chaque jour. Bien
sûr, les journaux respectablés ne rapportent pas les
faits faux, mais elles forment souvent les opinions,
et les gens oublient que toutes les opinions ne sont
pas toujours représenté. Beaucoup de gens lisent une
seule journal et acceptant les opinions de cette
journal. Les gens doivent lire les journaux avec
objectivité et décider quelle position qu'ils vont
prendre. Parce que nous avons la liberté de la
presse, nous devons pas permettre (les) gens de la
presse abuser de cette liberté et nous contrôler
comme un gouvernement absolu.

C'est mieux expliqué, mais il y a toujours ici une nouvelle idée dont vous n'avez pas parlé dans l'introduction.

les informations qui palaissent

Il faut avoir une conclusion qui résume tout ce que vous avez dit. Voyez-vous que les idées du premier paragraphe se sont perdues?

B+
B+

Illustration 7.14   *Source:* Barnett 1989, p. 42.

highest validity. In this type of scoring procedure, one or more readers assigns a single grade (or rating) to a text based on an overall impression. The criteria involved in producing this impression might include some of the following:

a. The clarity with which the thesis is stated, developed, and supported
b. The effectiveness with which an issue has been raised, treated, and resolved
c. The sufficiency of the support and development of the thesis for the reader
d. The degree to which the writer has accommodated the needs of the intended audience
e. The degree of grammatical and lexical cohesion and overall coherence of the piece
f. The effective use of rhetorical devices
etc. (Perkins 1983, pp. 652–653).

Generally, holistic evaluation is done quickly and impressionistically. A guided procedure may be used for sorting a set of papers or ranking them against one another. Papers can be scored holistically for prominence of certain features considered to be important for the type of writing assigned. The evaluation can be in the form of a letter or number grade, or, in the case of proficiency testing, a rating such as those used in the ACTFL Guidelines.

One of the main drawbacks of holistic scoring methods, according to Perkins, is that they can be highly subjective. Fatigue factors, previous acquaintance with the student, and shifting standards from one paper to the next can lead to unreliable scoring. This type of subjectivity is most obvious when compositions are rated by more than one person. If judges assign different weights to the scoring criteria, it is difficult to obtain reliable scores. Until everyone agrees on what constitutes good writing, consensus among judges might be hard to reach.

One way to avoid the problem of subjectivity is to insist on rater competence and training. If specified criteria are to focus the readers' attention, if some common standard is applied, and if multiple samples of writing are elicited, the chances of success in using a holistic scheme are increased. The ACTFL Guidelines for all skills, including writing, will probably undergo some substantial changes in the years ahead. However, guidelines such as these, when used with appropriate training, may eventually serve as a common metric for holistic scoring in tests of writing proficiency.

2. *Analytical Scoring.* This technique involves the separation of the various features of a composition into components for scoring purposes. One advantage of scoring features separately, especially in classroom instruction, is that more precise diagnostic feedback can be provided to the student. Because the teacher's criteria are more

Illustration 7.15

Composition scoring scheme and sample grades (Gaudiani 1981)

(1) Grammar/vocabulary:
   A = fluent with moments of elegance, few errors
   B = comprehensible, some errors
   C = substantial and significant errors
   D = one or more blocks to communication
   F = unintelligible

(2) Stylistic technique:
   A = skilled use of syntax in terms of content, variation in syntax
   B = clear, appropriate, and sophisticated syntax
   C = errors, but attempts at sophistication and appropriateness
   D = errors and/or inappropriate syntax
   F = garbled syntax

(3) Organization:
   A = well-organized paragraphs, use of clear topic and summary sentences, convincing, easy to follow
   B = good evidence of structuring of paragraphs (perhaps an unwieldy use of patterns of organization)
   C = some attempts at organization, but few topic, development, summary sequences
   D = hard to follow, organization undermines intelligibility
   F = no evidence of planning in structure of paragraphs

(4) Content:
   A = significant, interesting, appropriate, well thought out, appropriate to assignment
   B = generally good work, but facts may be unsupported, or repetitions or clichés may be apparent
   C = careless development of data relevant to content
   D = no effort to make content significant to composition
   F = incoherent or wildly inappropriate content

focused, grading tends to be more reliable as well. Two different analytic scoring schemes are provided in Illustrations 7.15 and 7.16, representing suggestions by Gaudiani (1981) and Jacobs et al. (1981).

Perkins (1983) points out that analytic scoring techniques may have several disadvantages:

   a. A text is more than the sum of its parts, and analytic scoring may isolate the features of the writing from their overall context.
   b. The highest score on any given feature may represent a standard that is too much to expect from writers at a given level of proficiency.
   c. Scoring weights ought to be adjusted, to reflect the type of discourse, since scales with equal weights are not sensitive to variations in purpose, writer's role, or conception of the audience.
   d. The procedure is relatively time consuming (p. 657).

Teachers using analytic scoring techniques may want to keep these caveats in mind and adjust their grading procedures accordingly.

A well written but poorly organized composition will be graded, for instance, as follows:

Grammar/Vocabulary	B = 3
Style	A = 4
Organization	C = 2
Content	B = 3

$$12 \div 4 = 3 \text{ or } B$$

Or, a student who writes unsophisticated syntax in perfect Spanish with little thought about organization or content may receive a poor grade despite "perfect" grammar.

Grammar/Vocabulary	A = 4
Style	D = 1
Organization	D = 1
Content	F = 0

$$6 \div 4 = 1.5 \text{ or } D+$$

On the other hand, students who try hard to write sophisticated sentences, use logical connectives, and organize a well thought out content intelligently may make more grammar/vocabulary errors.

Grammar/Vocabulary	C = 2
Style	B = 3
Organization	B = 3
Content	A = 4

$$12 \div 4 = 3 \text{ or } B$$

Source: Gaudiani 1981, pp. 20–21.

3. *Primary Trait Scoring.* In this type of evaluation scheme, scores are assigned holistically based on a certain feature of the writing that is being emphasized, such as the organization or structure of the piece, the vocabulary, or the tone. The teacher needs to decide to what extent the writing sample exhibits certain characteristics (primary traits) that are essential to accomplishing a given writing purpose. For example, if a student's essay was designed to persuade others to adopt his point of view on an issue, the grade might be based on the number of reasons given in the support of his argument, the elaboration of those reasons, the authorities to whom he appealed, and other features of the discourse related to the function of persuasion. An obvious advantage of this type of scoring is that it focuses on the purpose of the writing task directly; a disadvantage is that it ignores other aspects of writing that are important in the composing process. In addition, this type of scoring can be time consuming and subjective (Perkins 1983, pp. 658–661).

ESL COMPOSITION PROFILE

STUDENT *Sample II b*   DATE   TOPIC *Marriage —argument*

	SCORE	LEVEL	CRITERIA	COMMENTS
CONTENT	19	30-27	**EXCELLENT TO VERY GOOD:** knowledgeable • substantive • thorough development of thesis • relevant to assigned topic	*Topic sentences are*
		26-22	**GOOD TO AVERAGE:** some knowledge of subject • adequate range • limited development of thesis • mostly relevant to topic, but lacks detail	*suitable, need to be*
		21-17	**FAIR TO POOR:** limited knowledge of subject • little substance • inadequate development of topic	*supported with more detail. For what reasons*
		16-13	**VERY POOR:** does not show knowledge of subject • non-substantive • not pertinent • OR not enough to evaluate	*do people marry? Are they*
ORGANIZATION	14	20-18	**EXCELLENT TO VERY GOOD:** fluent expression • ideas clearly stated/supported • succinct • well-organized • logical sequencing • cohesive	*the same in each country?*
		17-14	**GOOD TO AVERAGE:** somewhat choppy • loosely organized but main ideas stand out • limited support • logical but incomplete sequencing	
		13-10	**FAIR TO POOR:** non-fluent • ideas confused or disconnected • lacks logical sequencing and development	
		9-7	**VERY POOR:** does not communicate • no organization • OR not enough to evaluate	
VOCABULARY	16	20-18	**EXCELLENT TO VERY GOOD:** sophisticated range • effective word/idiom choice and usage • word form mastery • appropriate register	*Shift from formal*
		17-14	**GOOD TO AVERAGE:** adequate range • occasional errors of word/idiom form, choice, usage *but meaning not obscured*	*to informal is a bit abrupt.*
		13-10	**FAIR TO POOR:** limited range • frequent errors of word/idiom form, choice, usage • *meaning confused or obscured*	
		9-7	**VERY POOR:** essentially translation • little knowledge of English vocabulary, idioms, word form • OR not enough to evaluate	
LANGUAGE USE	16	25-22	**EXCELLENT TO VERY GOOD:** effective complex constructions • few errors of agreement, tense, number, word order/function, articles, pronouns, prepositions	*Review use of compound sentences,*
		21-18	**GOOD TO AVERAGE:** effective but simple constructions • minor problems in complex constructions • several errors of agreement, tense, number, word order/function, articles, pronouns, prepositions *but meaning seldom obscured*	*introductory dependent clauses, use of modifiers.*
		17-11	**FAIR TO POOR:** major problems in simple/complex constructions • frequent errors of negation, agreement, tense, number, word order/function, articles, pronouns, prepositions and/or fragments, run-ons, deletions • *meaning confused or obscured*	
		10-5	**VERY POOR:** virtually no mastery of sentence construction rules • dominated by errors • does not communicate • OR not enough to evaluate	
MECHANICS	4	5	**EXCELLENT TO VERY GOOD:** demonstrates mastery of conventions • few errors of spelling, punctuation, capitalization, paragraphing	*Review —use of comma and semi-colon.*
		4	**GOOD TO AVERAGE:** occasional errors of spelling, punctuation, capitalization, paragraphing *but meaning not obscured*	
		3	**FAIR TO POOR:** frequent errors of spelling, punctuation, capitalization, paragraphing • poor handwriting • *meaning confused or obscured*	
		2	**VERY POOR:** no mastery of conventions • dominated by errors of spelling, punctuation, capitalization, paragraphing • handwriting illegible • OR not enough to evaluate	

TOTAL SCORE   READER   COMMENTS *Good analogy in the conclusion. Topic could be developed more completely — provide detailed illustrations — can you compare attitudes toward marriage in different countries, at different ages?*

69

◀ Illustration 7.16
Response to a student
composition using ESL
Profile (Jacobs et al.
1981)

Illustration 7.16 ▶
Response to a student
composition using ESL
Profile (continued)

Suggestions:

Needs to work on:

① *specific content — provide illustrations, examples, comparisons to prove major points. Begin by clearly stating your topic sentences — then prove them.*

② *look at word form: are you using the word correctly? — adj., adv., noun, verb, etc.? Choose words carefully to provide more precise meaning. Work on using a thesaurus and dictionary together to solve these problems.*

③ *language use — review use of compound sentences, introductory dependent clauses, use of modifiers, avoiding fragments and tense agreement.*

④ *Punctuation — study: use of comma, semi-colon*

Source: J. B. Hughey, D. R. Wormuth, V. F. Hartfiel, and H. L. Jacobs. *Teaching ESL Composition: Principles and Techniques*. Rowley, MA: Newbury House 1983, pp. 213–14.

Perkins' discussion of these three types of scoring procedures is very helpful for classroom teachers who are looking for more objective measures of written performance, and the reader is encouraged to consult this source for a more detailed discussion. In choosing an evaluative tool, classroom teachers will need to weigh the advantages and disadvantages of each to arrive at a procedure that is objective, fair, and efficient, especially if the teaching of composition receives a higher priority in language classrooms in the coming years.

Summary: Becoming Proficient in Writing

In this chapter, a variety of approaches to the teaching of writing in the second language classroom has been suggested. Ways in which writing can be introduced early in the curriculum as a support skill have been balanced with suggestions for teaching the composing process that leads to effective written communication.

It is important to consider ways to integrate writing with practice in listening, speaking, and reading so that language skills are not artificially separated. An integrative approach provides students with opportunities to use the language they are learning in authentic communication while solidifying control of various aspects of the new language through writing as a support skill. Even when writing activities are used simply as a pedagogical aid, they can be structured in ways that help students learn to produce cohesive and coherent discourse. At every level of proficiency, written practice can also provide diagnostic feedback that will help learners improve their linguistic accuracy. Writing activities can also be used effectively to support and enhance cultural instruction, a topic that is treated in more detail in the next chapter.

Activities for Review and Discussion

1. Compare briefly some of the similarities and differences between speech and writing. Give a rationale for teaching writing as a separate skill in the foreign language classroom. Discuss the difference between writing as a support skill and writing as a creative activity, and the place of each in the foreign language curriculum.

2. If possible, examine samples of student writing in the language you teach (or are planning to teach). Discuss what level of proficiency each of your samples illustrates, giving your rationale. (See the workbook accompanying this text for writing samples in various languages.)

3. Design at least one original writing activity that would be appropriate for each of the following levels of proficiency: (a) Novice, (b) Intermediate, and (c) Advanced. You may use activity formats suggested in this chapter as models, or create formats of your own.

4. Design at least one activity that will help students write more cohesive and coherent discourse. Include a statement of your objective(s), the context to be used, the function(s) and/or grammar topics to be emphasized, and clear directions for the student plus any accompanying stimulus materials (such as visuals, charts, presentation texts, key words, or other organizers).

5. Imagine that you are teaching a class in conversation and composition at the Intermediate level. Using the ideas presented in this chapter as your point of departure, discuss how you would lead your students through the composing process. State (a) how you would determine course goals and objectives for writing, (b) how you would select topics for composition, (c) your methods of providing feedback, (d) the types of feedback you would provide, and (e) your grading procedures.

•••••••••••• *References*

ACTFL Proficiency Guidelines. Hastings-on-Hudson, NY: American Council on the Teaching of Foreign Languages, 1986.

Allen, Edward and Rebecca Valette. *Modern Language Classroom Techniques, 2nd ed.* New York: Harcourt Brace Jovanovich, 1977.

Allen, Patrick, Merrill Swain, Birgit Harley, and Jim Cummins. "Aspects of Classroom Treatment: Toward a More Comprehensive View of Second Language Education." Chapter 5 (pp. 57–81) in B. Harley, P. Allen, J. Cummins, and M. Swain, eds., *The Development of Second Language Proficiency.* Cambridge: Cambridge University Press, 1990.

Applebee, Arthur N. "Problems in Process Approaches: Toward a Reconceptualization of Process Instruction." Chapter 6 (pp. 95–113) in A. Petrosky and D. Bartholomae, eds., *The Teaching of Writing.* Eighty-Fifth Yearbook of the National Society for the Study of Education, Part II. Chicago: University of Chicago Press, 1986.

Barnett, Marva A. "Writing as Process." *The French Review,* 63, i (1989): 31–44.

Birckbichler, Diane W. Personal communication, 1985.

Bizzell, Patricia. "Composing Processes: An Overview." Chapter 4 (pp. 49–70) in A. Petrosky and D. Bartholomae, eds., *The Teaching of Writing.* Eighty-Fifth Yearbook of the National Society for the Study of Education, Part II. Chicago: University of Chicago Press, 1986.

Bland, Susan K., James Noblitt, Susan Armington, and Geri Gay. "The Naive Lexical Hypothesis: Evidence from Computer-Assisted Language Learning." *The Modern Language Journal* 74, iv (1990): 440–50.

Camus, Albert. *L'Etranger.* Germaine Brée and Carlos Lynes, Jr., eds. New York: Appleton-Century-Crofts, 1955.

Cathcart, Ruth L. and Judy E. W. Olsen. "Teachers' and Students' Preferences for Correction of Classroom Conversation Error." In J. F. Fanselow and R. H. Crymes, eds., *On TESOL '76.* Washington, DC: TESOL, 1976.

Chastain, Kenneth. "Characteristics of Graded and Ungraded Compositions." *The Modern Language Journal* 74, i (1990): 10–14.

Chelala, S. "The Composing Process of Two Spanish-Speakers and the Coherence of Their Texts: A Case Study." Ph.D Dissertation, New York University, 1981. [Cited in Friedlander, 1990.]

Cohen, Andrew D. "Student Processing of Feedback on Their Compositions." Chapter 5 in A. Wenden and J. Rubin, eds., *Learner Strategies in Language Learning.* Englewood Cliffs, NJ: Prentice Hall, 1987.

Cooper, C. R. "Measuring Growth in Writing." *English Journal* 64 (1975): 111–20.

Cooper, Thomas. "A Strategy for Teaching Writing." *The Modern Language Journal* 61 (1977): 251–56.

_____. "A Study of Sentence-Combining Techniques for Developing Written and Oral Fluency in French." *The French Review* 53 (1980): 411–23.

_____. "Sentence Combining: An Experiment in Teaching Writing." *The Modern Language Journal* 65 (1981): 158–65.

Cooper, Thomas, Genelle Morain, and Theodore Kalivoda. *Sentence Combining in Second Language Instruction.* Language in Education: Theory and Practice Series, no. 31. Washington, DC: Center for Applied Linguistics, 1980.

Davis, Paul and Mario Rinvolucri. *Dictation: New Methods, New Possibilities*. Cambridge: Cambridge University Press, 1988.

DLI Task Force on Curriculum and Policy Planning. Monterey, CA: June, 1984.

Dvorak, Trisha. "Writing in the Foreign Language." Pp. 145–67 in B. Wing, ed., *Listening, Reading, Writing: Analysis and Application*. Reports of the Northeast Conference on the Teaching of Foreign Languages. Middlebury, VT: Northeast Conference, 1986.

Emig, Janet. Pilot study and Questionnaire, 1964. [Cited in Emig 1971.]

_____. *The Composing Process of Twelfth Graders*. NCTE Research Report No. 13. Urbana, IL: National Council of Teachers of English, 1971.

Fathman, Ann K. and Elizabeth Whalley. "Teacher Treatment of Error and Student Writing Accuracy." Paper presented at the 19th Annual TESOL Convention, New York, March, 1985. [Cited in Fathman and Whalley 1990.]

_____. "Teacher Response to Student Writing: Focus on Form versus Content." Chapter 11 (pp. 178–190) in B. Kroll, ed., *Second Language Writing: Research Insights for the Classroom*. Cambridge: Cambridge University Press, 1990.

Friedlander, Alexander. "Composing in English: Effects of a First Language in Writing in English as a Second Language." Chapter 7 (pp. 109–25) in B. Kroll, ed., *Second Language Writing: Research Insights for the Classroom*. Cambridge: Cambridge University Press, 1990.

Gaudiani, Claire. *Teaching Composition in the Foreign Language Curriculum*. Language in Education: Theory and Practice Series, no. 43. Washington, DC: Center for Applied Linguistics, 1981.

Greenia, George D. "Computers and Teaching Composition in a Foreign Language." *Foreign Language Annals* 25, i (1992): 33–46.

Grittner, Frank M. "Bandwagons Revisited: A Perspective on Movements in Foreign Language Education." Chapter 1 (pp. 9–43) in D. Birckbichler, ed., *New Perspectives and New Directions in Foreign Language Education*. The ACTFL Foreign Language Education Series. Lincolnwood, IL: National Textbook Company, 1990.

Gutiérrez, John and Harry Rosser. *¡Ya verás! Segundo nivel*. Boston: Heinle & Heinle Publishers, 1992.

Hendrickson, James M. "The Treatment of Error in Written Work." *The Modern Language Journal* 64 (1980): 216–21.

Higgs, Theodore V. and Ray T. Clifford. "The Push Toward Communication." In T. Higgs, ed., *Curriculum, Competence, and the Foreign Language Teacher*. ACTFL Foreign Language Education Series, vol. 13. Lincolnwood, IL: National Textbook Company, 1982.

Hillocks, George. *Research on Written Composition: New Directions for Teaching*. Urbana, IL: ERIC Clearinghouse on Reading and Communication Skills and the National Conference on Research in English, 1986.

Hughey, Jane B., Deanna R. Wormuth, V. Faye Hartfiel, and Holly L. Jacobs. *Teaching ESL Composition: Principles and Techniques*. Rowley, MA: Newbury House Publishers, Inc., 1983.

Jacobs, Holly L., S. Zingraf, D. Wormuth, V. Hartfiel, and J. Hughey. *Testing ESL Composition: A Practical Approach*. Rowley, MA: Newbury House , 1981.

Johnson, C. "The Composing Processes of Six ESL Students." Ph.D Dissertation, Illinois State University, 1985. [Cited in Friedlander 1990.]

Johnson, P. "Sentence Combining: A Summary and Bibliography." *ERIC/CLL News Bulletin* 5 (March 1982): 3–4.

Jones, P. "Knowing Opportunities: Some Possible Benefits and Limitations of Dialogue Journals in Adult Second Language Instruction." Masters' Thesis, School for International Training, Brattleboro, VT, 1988. [Cited in Peyton and Reed 1990.]

Kaplan, Robert B. "Cultural Thought Patterns in Intercultural Education." *Language Learning*, 16 (1966): 1–20.

_____. "Contrastive Rhetoric and Second Language Learning: Notes Toward a Theory of Contrastive Rhetoric." Chapter 11 (pp. 275–304) in A. Purves, ed., *Writing Across Languages and Cultures: Issues in Contrastive Rhetoric*. Written Communication Annual: An International Survey of Research and Theory, vol. 2. Newbury Park, CA: Sage Publications, 1988.

Krapels, Alexandra R. "An Overview of Second Language Writing Process Research." Chapter 3 (pp. 37–56) in B. Kroll, ed., *Second Language Writing: Research Insights for the Classroom*. Cambridge: Cambridge University Press, 1990.

Krashen, Stephen D. *Writing, Research, Theory and Applications*. Oxford: Pergamon Press, 1984.

Kroll, Barbara, ed. *Second Language Writing: Research Insights for the Classroom*. Cambridge: Cambridge University Press, 1990.

_____. "Introduction." Pp. 1–5 in B. Kroll, ed., *Second Language Writing: Research Insights for the Classroom*. Cambridge: Cambridge University Press, 1990.

Lalande, John. "Reducing Composition Errors: An Experiment." *The Modern Language Journal* 66 (1982): 140–49.

Lay, N. "Composing Processes of Adult ESL Learners: A Case Study." *TESOL Quarterly* 16 (1982): 406.

Leki, Ilona. "ESL Student Preferences in Written Error Correction." Paper presented at the Southeast Regional TESOL Conference, Atlanta, GA, October, 1986. [Cited in Leki 1990.]

_____. "Coaching from the Margins: Issues in Written Response." Pp. 57–68 in B. Kroll, ed., *Second Language Writing: Research Insights for the Classroom*. Cambridge: Cambridge University Press, 1990.

_____. "The Preferences of ESL Students for Error Correction in College-Level Writing Classes." *Foreign Language Annals* 24, iii (1991): 203–18.

Magnan, Sally S. "Teaching and Testing Proficiency in Writing: Skills to Transcend the Second-Language Classroom." In A. Omaggio, ed., *Proficiency, Curriculum, Articulation: The Ties that Bind*. Reports of the Northeast Conference on the Teaching of Foreign Languages. Middlebury, VT: Northeast Conference, 1985.

Monroe, James. "Measuring and Enhancing Syntactic Fluency in French." *The French Review* 48, vi (1975): 1023–31.

Noblitt, James S. and Willem J. A. Pet. *système-D: Writing Assistant for French*. Windows Version. Boston, MA: Heinle & Heinle Publishers, 1993.

Noblitt, James S., Donald Solá, and Willem J. A. Pet. *système-D: Writing Assistant for French*. DOS Version. Boston, MA: Heinle & Heinle Publishers, 1993.

Perkins, Kyle. "On the Use of Composition Scoring Techniques, Objective Measures, and Objective Tests to Evaluate ESL Writing Ability." *TESOL Quarterly* 17 (1983): 651–71.

Peyton, Joy Kreeft and Leslee Reed. *Dialogue Journal Writing with Nonnative English Speakers: A Handbook for Teachers*. Alexandria, VA: TESOL, 1990.

Raimes, Ann. *Focus on Composition*. New York: Oxford University Press, 1978.

_____. *Techniques in Teaching Writing*. Oxford: Oxford University Press, 1983.

Rieken, Elizabeth. "The Effect of Feedback on the Frequency and Accuracy of Use of the *Passé Composé* by Field-Independent and Field-Dependent Students of Beginning French." Ph.D Dissertation, University of Illinois at Urbana-Champaign, 1991.

Rivers, Wilga M. *A Practical Guide to the Teaching of French.* New York: Oxford University Press, 1975.

Rochester, M., J. Muyskens, A. Omaggio, and C. Chalmers. *Bonjour, ça va?* New York: Random House, 1983.

Scott, Virginia M. and Robert M. Terry. *systéme-D: Writing Assistant for French. Teacher's Guide.* Boston: Heinle & Heinle Publishers, 1992.

Semke, Harriet D. "Effects of the Red Pen." *Foreign Language Annals* 17, iii (1984) 195–202.

Shaughnessy, M. *Errors and Expectations.* New York: Oxford University Press, 1977.

Silva, Tony. "Research on the Composing Processes of College-Level ESL Writers: A Critical Review." Paper presented at the 39th Annual CCCC Convention, St. Louis, MO: March, 1988. [Cited in Krapels 1990.]

_____. "Second Language Composition Instruction: Developments, Issues, and Directions in ESL." Chapter 1 (pp. 11–23) in B. Kroll, ed., *Second Language Writing: Research Insights for the Classroom.* Cambridge: Cambridge University Press, 1990.

Smith, Karen L. "Collaborative and Interactive Writing for Increasing Communication Skills." *Hispania* 73, i (1990): 77–87.

Staton, J. "Dialogue Journals: A New Tool for Teaching Communication." *ERIC/CLL News Bulletin* 6 (March 1983): 1–2, 6.

Swain, Merrill. "Communicative Competence: Some Roles of Comprehensible Input and Comprehensible Output in Its Development." Chapter 14 (pp. 235–53) in S. Gass and C. Madden, eds., *Input in Second Language Acquisition.* Rowley, MA: Newbury House, 1985.

Tarone, Elaine. "On the Variability of Interlanguage Systems." *Applied Linguistics* 4 (1983): 142–63.

Terry, Robert M. Personal communication, 1985.

_____. "Teaching and Evaluating Writing as a Communicative Skill." *Foreign Language Annals* 22, i (1989): 43–54.

Tolliver, Joyce. Personal communication, 1992.

Trivelli, R. J. "Sentence Combining in Italian." *Canadian Modern Language Review* 39 (1983): 237–42.

Valdés, G., T. Dvorak, and T. Hannum. *Composición: Proceso y síntesis.* New York: Random House, 1984. [Second edition, 1989.]

Zamel, Vivian. "Responding to Student Writing." *TESOL Quarterly* 19 (1985): 79–101.

8
Teaching for Cultural Understanding

"The Land of the Monolingual"

Paul Simon, in his provocative book *The Tongue-Tied American* (1980), recounts the story of a Georgia school board member who approached Genelle Morain of the University of Georgia with the question: "Why should a student who will never leave Macon, Georgia, study a foreign language?" Her reply to that challenge was succinct but profound: "That's *why* he should study another language."

The school board member's question echoes the sentiments of many Americans across the years who have considered the study of other languages and cultures inconsequential or superfluous in their children's "basic" education. It is no secret that the American foreign language teacher has had to fight long and hard to maintain a place for languages in the curriculum, if only as an elective subject. Indeed, an examination of enrollment trends in public high schools during the past 100 years reveals the fragility of America's commitment to language study. Draper (1991) presents data that show a dramatic drop in enrollments in foreign languages beginning just after the turn of the century. She reports that in 1905, nearly 90% of all high school students were studying a modern foreign language or Latin. As enrollments in Latin began to decline after 1905, interest in modern foreign languages increased until 1915, when the trend toward modern language study was suddenly reversed. Total foreign language enrollments underwent a long and steady decline during the first half of the century, bottoming out around the end of World War II, when fewer than 15% of high school students were engaged in modern language study. Interest in languages picked up somewhat after World War II, and the number of students studying modern and classical languages increased by about 10% between 1948 and 1965. Enrollments in modern languages reached a plateau of about 27% of the student population in American high schools by the mid-1960s. However, the numbers began to decline once more after 1965 and throughout the 1970s, dipping to just over 20% of the high school population by the early 1980s (Draper 1991).

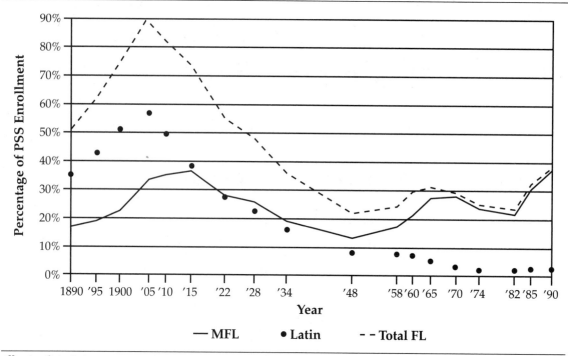

Illustration 8.1
Foreign Language
Enrollments in Public
High Schools,
1890–1990

Source: Draper 1991, p.1.

It is encouraging to note that this declining enrollment trend has been reversing again in recent years as Americans become more aware of the value of second language competence and cross-cultural understanding in a global economy. An increasing number of businesses are recognizing that investment in learning about other languages and cultures can bring significant economic and technological advantages. As our nation's population becomes increasingly diverse, more and more parents, educators, and students have come to recognize the importance of valuing multiculturalism in American society as well as in the world beyond our borders. In response to these and other social, economic, and political changes in the last few decades, many colleges and universities have begun strengthening or reinstating foreign language requirements. The Modern Language Association completed its latest enrollment survey in August 1991, revealing that college enrollments in foreign languages in the fall of 1990 were the highest ever recorded. Nearly 1.2 million students were taking coursework in languages other than English, representing an increase of 30% since the low point of enrollments recorded in 1980 (Brod and Huber 1992).

The encouraging trend at the university level is matched by analogous increases in enrollments at the secondary school level. The latest enrollment survey conducted by the American Council on the Teaching of

Foreign Languages shows that more than 5 million students in the nation's secondary schools are enrolled in foreign language courses, representing more than 29% of the total junior high and high school student population, and over 38% of the nation's high school students. This represents an increase of one-half million students since the last survey taken in 1985. Draper reports that one must go back to 1928 to find higher total foreign language enrollments, when just under half of the nation's high school students were studying a modern language or Latin (p. 1). Draper adds that perhaps the most noteworthy finding of the survey is that the enrollments in modern foreign languages were higher in 1990 than ever before. Nearly 37% of all students in grades 9–12 were studying a modern foreign language, surpassing the previous record of 35.9% in 1915 (p. 2).

Draper (1991) points out that while the increased enrollment figures are encouraging, "the news is not all good" (p. 3). The ACTFL survey found that fewer than 20% of the foreign language students in high school go beyond the second level of study, which means that only about 6% of all high school students have studied more than two years of a foreign language before graduation. Draper concludes that "few students are continuing study for the amount of time needed to gain a working knowledge of the language. . . . To obtain higher levels of proficiency requires much longer sequences of study than are currently being undertaken by the majority of students" (Draper 1991, p. 3). Thus, in spite of the gains in enrollments in foreign languages over the past ten years, there are still more battles to be fought as we strive to meet our educational goals in the areas of language and culture.

This view is expressed in a recent essay by Senator Paul Simon, writing for the 1990 ACTFL Priorities Conference. Looking back over the decade following the publication of *The Tongue-Tied American* (1980), Simon asserts that there have indeed been "a series of small victories," some of them greater than he had expected (Simon 1991, p. 13). "But we have a substantial distance to go. And not much time to get there if we are to serve this nation effectively, if these United States are to be readied for more active economic competition with the rest of the world. And more important, that progress must be achieved if the world's most powerful nation militarily is to contribute to a world of peace and justice" (Simon 1991, p. 13). Simon reminds us that, as far as commitment to language and cultural studies is concerned, the United States still lags far behind other nations. "Visiting recently in Botswana, it struck me that in this nation which we consider a developing nation, the average fourth-grader has had more foreign language study (four years of it) than has the average college graduate in the U.S." (p. 14).

American students' inadequate knowledge of the world is reflected not only in their lack of foreign language skills, but also in their general ignorance of basic information about other nations and peoples. ACTFL (1988) reports that in a recent Gallup survey of 10,800 adults in nine countries, conducted at the request of the National Geographic Society, Americans ranked below adults in Sweden, West Germany, Japan, France, and Canada in their knowledge of world geography. The report reveals that young Americans, aged 18–24, were the worst of all the groups surveyed in all nine countries, scoring lower than their elders and lower than a similar group of young Americans surveyed in 1947. The extent of our global illiteracy is shocking: 75% of the Americans in the study could not locate the Persian Gulf on a map of the world, despite its prominence in the news in recent years. Forty-five percent of the American respondants couldn't find Central America, and 14% couldn't even locate the United States! This lack of geographic knowledge has been attributed to the virtual elimination of geography as a school subject since the 1950s. The National Geographic Society has responded by distributing materials to some 35,000 public, private, and parochial schools and offering workshops and handbooks on the teaching of geography to teachers, with help from the U.S. Department of Education ("America's Ignorance . . ." 1988, p. 1). Studies such as this indicate that, in spite of the progress reported in the preceding pages regarding gains in enrollments in language study, we are still fundamentally a nation of monolinguals, where linguistic isolation coincides with cultural isolation (Simon 1980).

The need for a strong commitment to the development of cultural understanding within the language program is clear in the light of recent developments both nationally and internationally. Reports of "ethnic cleansing" in Eastern Europe, evidence of "hate crimes" against various ethnic or social groups, and continued strife among warring factions throughout the world reveal the crying need for understanding and mutual acceptance among the world's peoples. The valuing of ethnic and cultural diversity must continue to be a high priority in education as our students learn to live in an increasingly interdependent world. There is no question that the successful integration of culture and language teaching can contribute significantly to general humanistic knowledge, that language ability and cultural sensitivity can play a vital role in the security, defense, and economic well-being of this country, and that global understanding ought to be a mandatory component of basic education (Galloway 1985b; Lafayette and Strasheim 1981; Strasheim 1981).

As we have seen, many states, colleges, and universities have supported this point of view in recent years by reinstating language requirements as part of their students' general education. But how do American students react to such requirements? A number of recent surveys of college and university students have shown a generally positive attitude toward required language study, especially if the cultural component is sufficiently emphasized (see, for example, Ely 1986; Morello 1988; Bacon and Finneman 1990; and Roberts 1992). Among the primary reasons for studying Spanish listed by students at a university in northern California were an interest in

Hispanic culture, literature, and history, and a general interest in learning about peoples of other cultures in order to gain a better understanding of the world (Ely 1986). Morello (1988) found that more than half of the students surveyed at the University of Rhode Island agreed or strongly agreed with the statement that the language requirement was a worthwhile experience, and most said that they were primarily interested in developing oral/aural skills and in learning about the culture of the country (p. 437). Spanish students surveyed by Bacon and Finneman (1990) expressed an interest in communicating with native speakers, using the language in their travels, and learning about Hispanic culture. Students also felt that Spanish might help them in their careers, and that learning a language was important as part of a well-rounded education. Roberts (1992) surveyed over 700 entering university freshmen in Michigan using an essay format. The students, divided among 15 majors, were given a choice of topics dealing with either the importance of studying a foreign language or, alternatively, the importance of studying either computer language or sign language in college. Nearly 78% of the students chose to write about foreign language study. All of these students said that they thought language study was valuable, a finding that supports Morello's earlier results. Roberts found that the most commonly cited argument for studying a foreign language (mentioned by over 80% of the students) was that there were benefits from learning about another culture. She adds that most students tended to define culture in conjunction with a particular world view, or total way of life, and felt that language study would help reduce ethnocentrism: "Arguments were made for a better understanding of both global and domestic cultural diversity through foreign language study" (p. 278).

The studies cited above clearly indicate that students want their language courses to emphasize cultural understanding as well as linguistic concerns. Thus teachers and students alike seem to be saying that the study of culture, both as a topic in its own right and as it is embedded in language use, is an important aspect of language teaching that is oriented toward communicative proficiency. Yet even though the teaching of culture has been advocated for many years by foreign language professionals, cultural teaching has remained insubstantial and sporadic in most language classrooms (Stern 1981; Lafayette 1988). Why is this so? Some possible reasons are explored in the next section.

Problems in the Teaching of Culture

There are several reasons why many language courses today still do not include the systematic study of culture. First, the study of culture involves time that many teachers do not feel they can spare in an already over-crowded curriculum (Galloway 1985a). Often teachers content themselves with the thought that students will be exposed to cultural materials *later*, after they have mastered the basic grammar and vocabulary of the language. Unfortunately, "later" never seems to come for most students (Seelye 1984). Furthermore, an approach that envisions the teaching of language and culture in a serial fashion misses the important point that the two are intertwined.

Secondly, many teachers are afraid to teach culture because they fear that they don't know enough about it. Seelye (1984) maintains that even if teachers' own knowledge is quite limited, their proper role is not to impart facts, but to help students attain the skills that are necessary to make sense out of the facts they themselves discover in their study of the target culture. In his view, the objectives that are to be achieved in cross-cultural understanding involve processes rather than facts. "Facts are cheap. They are also meaningless until interpreted within a problem-solving context" (p. 3). Indeed, a "facts only" approach to culture for which the only goal is to amass bits of information is destined to be ineffective for several reasons:

1. "Facts" are in a constant state of flux, especially when they relate to current life-style. Specific data may not hold true across time, location, and social strata (Jarvis 1977; Galloway 1985a).
2. An "information-only" approach to culture may actually *establish* stereotypes rather than diminish them, since such an approach provides no means of accounting for cultural variation (Crawford-Lange and Lange 1984).
3. Amassing facts leaves students unprepared when they face cultural situations not previously studied. If no problem-solving contextually based approach to culture has been used, the students have acquired no tools for processing new phenomena in a way that will facilitate understanding (Crawford-Lange and Lange 1984). Cognitive knowledge alone seems to have little effect on an individual's ability to cope with or adjust to different patterns of behavior (Galloway 1985b).

A third reason that some teachers neglect the teaching of culture is that it involves dealing with student attitudes—"a somewhat threatening, hazy, and unquantifiable area" (Galloway 1985a). Mantle-Bromley (1992) notes that when teaching for cross-cultural understanding in her beginning college Spanish class, she became aware of how little her students understood the notion that their ways of behaving, reacting, thinking, and feeling were bound by their own culture. As Nostrand (1989) expresses it, understanding the variability of cultural concepts "must involve the difficult, relativistic insight that cultures differ in respect to the grid through which reality is perceived" (p. 190). Students often approach target-culture phenomena assuming that the new patterns of behavior can be understood within the framework of their own native culture. When cultural phenomena differ from what they expect, students often react negatively, characterizing the target culture as "strange" or "weird." Mantle-Bromley compares the assumption of equivalence between cultural systems to a similar assumption of equivalence between linguistic systems, an assumption that Bland, Noblitt, Armington, and Gay (1990) have called the "naïve lexical hypothesis." According to Bland et al., many beginning language students seem to assume that for every word in the native language there is an exact equivalent in the target language. This notion is similar to what Higgs (1979) had earlier called the "Lexical Analog Hypothesis," which holds that "the foreign language is the same as the native language, except that it uses different words" (Higgs 1979, p. 338). Students working under such an assumption typically believe that, in order to master the target language, one simply substitutes foreign language words for native language words, using the same syntactic patterns and word orders of the L1. Mantle-Bromley suggest that "teachers . . . not only need to help students revise their *linguistic* patterns, they likewise need to help students revise their *cultural* patterns" (p. 117). She cautions that as this process of acculturation and adjustment occurs, some students may feel that they have to lose their own identity in order to accept and use new behaviors.

Galloway (1992) stresses the importance of recognizing the pervasive influence of culture on one's attitudes, emotions, beliefs, and values, and the concomitant dangers of projecting one's native frame of reference on that of the culture being studied:

> *Cultures are powerful human creations, affording their members a shared identity, a cohesive framework for selecting, constructing, and interpreting perceptions, and for assigning value and meaning in consistent fashion. The complex systems of thought and behavior that people create and perpetuate in and for association are subtle and profound, so elementally forged as to be endowed by their bearers with the attributes of universal truth: Things that fit into this cultural framework are given the labels "human nature," "instinct," "common sense," "logic." Things that don't fit are **different,** and therefore either illogical, immoral, nonsensical, or the result of a naive and inferior stage of development of "human nature" (p. 88).*

Galloway asserts that to understand another culture, one must construct "a new frame of reference in terms of the people who created it" (p. 89). She explains that the process of constructing an appropriate frame of reference is complicated by the fact that cultures have both *functions* (meanings, purposes, needs) and *forms* (manifestations, realizations, operations) that vary widely, not only across cultures, but also within the subcultures of a society (p. 90). A function such as the need for shelter or community may be universal, but the ways in which that need is defined, prioritized, and met in different societies can be extremely diverse: A family dwelling in Ghana differs in significant ways from one in Ohio; the affiliative tendencies in Hispanic culture override the drive toward personal advancement and individualistic self-focusing that is prevalent in the United States (Ortuño 1991). As students are introduced to the target culture, they need to learn to expect differences, and eventually to understand and appreciate their logic and meaning. Galloway points out that any assumptions of cross-cultural similarity should be made with caution, as cultures may not share the same form/function relationships. She warns that the most "ominous potential for interpretational error arise[s] precisely from that which looks familiar" (p. 92), and that facile comparisons that view the target culture through the native-culture lens should be avoided.

In order to help students construct a new frame of reference based in the target culture, Galloway recommends that students begin with an understanding of their own frame of reference, and then, with teacher guidance, explore the target culture through authentic texts and materials. More will be said about the use of authentic materials for fostering cultural understanding later in this chapter.

As we consider the various difficulties that are inherent in teaching culture, the reluctance that some teachers feel in approaching this aspect of foreign language instruction becomes quite understandable. Even if one is committed to accept the challenges of teaching for cross-cultural understanding, one must still grapple with the problem of deciding what aspects of culture to teach. While it is certainly true that the teaching of culture must go beyond the presentation of facts alone, it is also true that cultural instruction is not fact-free! Many instructors feel the need for some sort of organizing scheme that would help them select appropriate cultural content. Without such a scheme, the teaching of culture can become a kind of "trivial pursuit" of isolated bits of information. Galloway (1985b) illustrates the possible results in her characterization of four common approaches to teaching culture:

1. **The Frankenstein Approach:** *A taco from here, a flamenco dancer from there, a gaucho from here, a bullfight from there.*
2. **The 4-F Approach:** *Folk dances, festivals, fairs, and food.*
3. **The Tour Guide Approach:** *The identification of monuments, rivers, and cities.*
4. **The "By-the-Way" Approach:** *Sporadic lectures or bits of behavior selected indiscriminantly to emphasize sharp differences.*

Crawford-Lange and Lange (1984) propose that teachers may not have been adequately trained in the teaching of culture and, therefore, do not have strategies for integrating culture study with language, or for creating a viable framework for organizing instruction around cultural themes. The development of such a framework depends in part on one's definition of *culture*. Stern (1981) believed that the problem of definition has been the source of much of our difficulty in designing quality instruction:

> *The area of what constitutes culture is poorly defined, and courses offered in universities on culture or civilization generally lack a foundation in theory and research. As long as there is such a lack of adequate research it is very difficult to develop a cultural syllabus of quality. Some improvisation is inevitable, and only gradual improvement, as the data base grows, can be expected (p. 16).*

Stern does acknowledge the substantial work of several individuals in the past three decades who have proposed definitions, models, and inventories for the teaching of culture. These frameworks can serve as useful resources for curriculum planners, materials writers, and classroom teachers as they plan cultural instruction. Some of the proposed models are discussed in the next section.

• • • • • • • • • • • • *Definitions, Models, Inventories, and Frameworks: Capturing the Essence of "Culture"*

Brooks (1975) has said that of the several meanings of culture, two are of major importance for us: culture as *everything* in human life and culture as the *best* in human life (p. 20). Prior to the 1960s, the latter definition took precedence in most classrooms. The primary reason for second language study was to permit access to the great literary masterpieces of the target culture and thereby to its "civilization" (Allen 1985). Brooks (1971) referred to this relatively elitist conceptualization as "Olympian culture," or "culture MLA," understood to mean the great music, literature, and art of the country. Seelye (1984) maintains that approaching culture through an elitist perspective has two weaknesses:

> *First, culture is not primarily a laundry list of factors, and second, it is not solely concerned with art, literature, music, history, and geography. Elitism—restricting the study in a given area to the academically gifted and disciplined, while divorcing the cultural content from those aspects of life that concern most people most of the time—is responsible for much of the boredom current in too many social studies and language programs today (p. 8).*

Seelye defines *culture* as a broad concept that embraces all aspects of human life, "from folktales to carved whales" (p. 26). It encompasses everything that people learn to do. This definition includes, therefore, not only "Olympian culture," but also what Brooks has called "Hearthstone culture," or "culture BBV" (beliefs, behavior, and values) (Brooks 1975, p. 21). This anthropological approach to the study of culture includes the patterns of everyday life, the "do's" and "don'ts" of personal behavior, and all the points of interaction between the individual and the society. Brooks maintains that the first, most basic, and all-pervasive element of hearthstone culture is control of the native language, "a group possession and an individual possession as unique and as deeply attached to the personality as the fingers are to the hand or the arms to the body" (1971, p. 57).

With the advent of ALM in the 1960s, hearthstone culture (also called "little-c" culture) began to be emphasized over formal (or "big-C") culture. Many foreign language educators felt that knowing the language, as well as the patterns of everyday life, was a *prerequisite* to appreciating the fine arts and literature (Seelye 1984). Because "communication" goals were beginning to be emphasized, it was only natural that cultural goals should shift from a focus on formal aspects of a civilization to an emphasis on anthropological or sociological concerns. In order to capture the concept of this type of culture and relate it to instruction, complex schemes for analyzing culture were developed in the late 1960s and early 1970s. Allen (1985) presents a comprehensive review of several of these theoretical models and inventories, beginning with Brooks' (1968) five-part definition of culture:

Culture 1: Biological growth

Culture 2: Personal refinement

Culture 3: Literature and the fine arts

Culture 4: Patterns for living

Culture 5: The sum total of a way of life (p. 210)

Brooks felt that language teachers should emphasize Culture 4 in their classrooms first. He further defined it as:

> *the individual's role in the unending kaleidoscope of life situations of every kind and the rules and models for attitude and conduct in them. By reference to these models, every human being, from infancy onward, . . . associates with those around him, and relates to the social order to which he is attached (Brooks 1968, p. 210, cited in Allen 1985).*

Once students have been introduced to Culture 4, some of the aspects relating to Cultures 3 and 5 can be added as the learners' competence increases.

In order to develop a profile, or map, of a culture, Brooks (1968) then identified ten points around which culture study could be based. These were (1) symbolism, (2) value, (3) authority, (4) order, (5) ceremony, (6) love, (7) honor, (8) humor, (9) beauty, and (10) spirit (p. 213). He suggested that language study might be planned in several phases. In Phase I, students would learn the language, plus Culture 4; in Phase II, they would continue studying the language and Culture 4, but begin to add some of Cultures 3 and 5; in Phase III, there would be more in-depth study of language, plus a systematic study of culture through the ten-point profile.

Nostrand (1967), Nostrand and Nostrand (1971) and Seelye (1984) have taken a slightly different view of the curricular problem: for them, defining and identifying key aspects of culture was not sufficient. Goals and objectives had to be set that related not only to descriptive or analytical knowledge of facts, but also to procedural knowledge that would enable students to observe and analyze cultural elements and patterns. Howard and Frances Nostrand (1971) listed nine objectives, or types of understandings, that should be developed in language students as the result of instruction in culture. Allen (1985), following Lafayette and Schulz (1975) lists them in a somewhat abbreviated fashion as follows:

Students should have the ability to . . .

1. React appropriately in a social situation
2. Describe, or ascribe to the proper part of the population, a pattern in the culture or social behavior
3. Recognize a pattern when it is illustrated
4. "Explain" a pattern
5. Predict how a pattern is likely to apply in a given situation
6. Describe or manifest an attitude important for making oneself acceptable in the foreign society
7. Evaluate the form of a statement concerning a culture pattern
8. Describe or demonstrate defensible methods of analyzing a sociocultural whole
9. Identify basic human purposes that make significant the understanding that is being taught (Allen 1985; Lafayette and Schulz 1975)

Seelye (1984) then modified Nostrand's goals into seven goals of cultural instruction:

1. *The Sense, or Functionality, of Culturally Conditioned Behavior. The student should demonstrate an understanding that people act the way they do because they are using options the society allows for satisfying basic physical and psychological needs.*
2. *Interaction of Language and Social Variables. The student should demonstrate an understanding that such social variables as age, sex, social class, and place of residence affect the way people speak and behave.*
3. *Conventional Behavior in Common Situations. The student should indicate an understanding of the role convention plays in shaping behavior by demonstrating how people act in common mundane and crisis situations in the target culture.*
4. *Cultural Connotations of Words and Phrases. The student should indicate an awareness that culturally conditioned images are associated with even the most common target words and phrases.*
5. *Evaluating Statements about a Society. The student should demonstrate the ability to evaluate the relative strength of a generality concerning the target culture in terms of the amount of evidence substantiating the statement.*

6. Researching Another Culture. The student should show that s/he has developed the skills needed to locate and organize information about the target culture from the library, the mass media, people, and personal observation.

7. Attitudes toward Other Cultures. The student should demonstrate intellectual curiosity about the target culture and empathy toward its people (pp. 48–58).

Allen (1985) points out that several issues were still left unresolved when these goals were generated. First, how were teachers to classify or order the various components or elements of which culture is composed? And second, how were these goals and the accompanying classification system to be translated into classroom practice, with a coherent curricular sequence and specific techniques for achieving them?

Nostrand (1967) addressed the first of these issues when he proposed an inventory for analyzing and describing a culture which he called the Emergent Model. In this structured inventory, he tried to interrelate phenomena to describe a sociocultural system, using the main "themes" of the culture as the "handle" by which the system can be grasped.

> *A sociocultural system, and any of its variant lifestyles, is a whole whose parts color one another. This is why a value, a custom, or a word has no one-to-one correspondence in another culture. It is why the cross-cultural contrasting of discrete elements leaves the student with his private belief that only his view really makes sense—unless he learns to feel the "fittingness" of the detail as perceived by the bearer of the other culture (Nostrand 1974, p. 273).*

Nostrand explains that "theme"in this system is not just any "topic," or even a "value." Rather it is "an emotionally charged concern, which motivates or strongly influences the culture bearer's conduct in a wide variety of situations" (p. 277). In Nostrand's view, for example, French culture can be characterized in terms of twelve themes: individualism, intellectuality, the art of living, realism, common sense, friendship, love, family, justice, liberty, patriotism, and traditionalism. The main themes of a culture are explored within the headings of the Emergent Model.

That model, which has appeared in modified form in various publications since 1967, consists of the following headings and subheadings:

I. The culture

   A. Main themes

   B. Ethos or national character

   C. Assumptions about reality

   D. Verifiable knowledge

   E. Art forms

    F. Language

    G. Paralanguage and kinesics

II. The society and its institutions

    A. Family

    B. Religious

    C. Economic-occupational

    D. Political and judicial

    E. Educational

    F. Intellectual-aesthetic

    G. Recreational

    H. Communication

    I. Stratification and mobility

    J. Social proprieties

    K. Status of groupings by age and sex

    L. Status of ethnic and religious minorities

    M. Interpersonal and intergroup conflicts

III. Conflicts

    A. Conflict and conflict resolution

    B. Defense and adjustment mechanisms

IV. The ecology

    A. Attitudes toward nature

    B. Exploitation of nature

    C. Use of natural products

    D. Technology

    E. Settlement and territorial organization

    F. Transportation and travel

V. The individual

VI. The cross-cultural environment

    A. Attitudes toward other cultures

    B. Attitudes toward international and supranational organizations. (Based on Nostrand and Nostrand 1971; cited in revised form in Seelye 1984, pp. 41–42)

There is no doubt that the definitions, goal statements, and inventories cited above have been helpful in clarifying the important themes and topics that need to be integrated into classroom instruction and materials. Yet bridges between these theoretical models and the classroom have been difficult to construct. Lafayette (1988) maintains that culture is still the weakest component of our curricula, partly because cultural material receives uneven treatment in textbooks and partly because many teachers lack significant first-hand knowledge of the culture and/or appropriate techniques for teaching it. He suggests that what is needed is a simple, direct approach to teaching culture that exploits existing content and practice. Although Lafayette acknowledges that a focus on "facts" has been criticized by various scholars, he believes that students should be knowledgeable about a "basic repertoire of information necessary for the comprehension of most cultural concepts" (p. 49). He provides a set of 13 goal statements that he groups into five categories. The goal statements are presented below in a somewhat modified form, incorporating the category designations he describes:

Group I: Knowledge of formal or "high" culture: Students will be able to recognize/explain . . .

1. major geographical monuments
2. major historical events
3. major institutions
4. major artistic accomplishments

Group II: Knowledge of everyday or "popular" culture: Students will be able to recognize/explain . . .

5. "active" cultural patterns, consisting of functions or tasks related to everyday living (such as eating, shopping, travel, obtaining lodging, etc.)
6. "passive" everyday cultural patterns (consisting of underlying realities, such as social stratification, work, marriage, etc.)
Students will be able to . . .
7. act appropriately in common everyday situations
8. use appropriate common gestures

Group III: Affective objectives: Students will be able to . . .

9. value different peoples and societies

Group IV: Multicultural objectives: Students will be able to recognize/explain the culture of . . .

10. target language-related ethnic groups in the United States

11. non-European peoples speaking the target language (Canada, Africa, South America, etc.)

Group V: Process objectives: Students will be able to . . .

12. evaluate the validity of statements about culture
13. develop skills needed to locate and organize information about culture (Based on Lafayette 1988, pp. 49–50).

By incorporating factual, affective, and process objectives into his list, Lafayette has provided a useful synthesis of goals for classroom instruction in culture.

Achieving Balance and Avoiding Bias: Two Considerations in Developing a Cultural Syllabus

Lalande (1985a) has emphasized the need for a balanced perspective of culture when designing curricula, suggesting that presenting only popular culture to the exclusion of "high" culture can shortchange students intellectually (p. 71). Although he would not recommend trying to achieve an exact equilibrium in terms of time and materials to both "high" and "popular" culture, Lalande does suggest that students should be exposed to various aspects of the target culture's intellectual achievements—both artistic and scientific—even in early phases of instruction. He also recommends that cultural information in textbooks be balanced in terms of gender-related issues, the socio-economic classes depicted, and representations of both rural and urban life styles.

Patrikis (1988) recognizes the dangers of ethnocentrism and bias in the presentation of cultural material, and warns about several "sins of commission" that can occur in discussions of culture. The first of these is *stereotyping*, which consists of exaggerating some aspect or characteristic of a culture or its people. Patrikis affirms that we must "learn to distinguish between *types* (common traits) and *stereotypes* (fixed images), to teach our students to identify types and to recognize the limitations of the types" (p. 18). The second "sin" is that of *triviality*, which consists of "reducing the dizzying variety of cultural elements to the silly, the out-of-date, or the quaint" (p. 18), thus presenting "tokens" of a culture divorced from the meaning of their context. The third "sin" is that of *political bias*, which can result either consciously or unconsciously when we select elements of the culture to feature or include while ignoring others. Patrikis gives the example of portraying the lives of women in a culture exclusively from the viewpoint of committed feminists, or, alternatively, from the point of view of opponents to this perspective. Related to this problem is the fourth "sin" of "*dangerous incompleteness*" (p. 20), which consists of leaving a whole subculture or other crucial part of a culture out of the discussion. A course on the Middle East that focuses only on Islamic culture, for example, leaves out consideration of Jews, Christians, members of the Bahai faith, and other minorities who are part of that cultural reality (p. 20).

Patrikis recognizes that objectivity is not an easy goal to achieve:

> *For good or for bad, we all have biases. We see things in terms of what we know. Education, however, can turn a bias into a perspective that opens the eyes and allows understanding rather than into a blinder that restricts vision and ensures ignorance. Perhaps it is not possible to be fully and absolutely objective, but awareness of the problem can lead us to a kind of practical objectivity (p. 16).*

Becoming aware of our own biases and helping students to recognize theirs are thus important first steps in teaching for cultural understanding in our classrooms.

We have reviewed thus far in this section a variety of models for organizing specific cultural phenomena that might serve as a basis for developing a cultural syllabus, as well as various caveats about the need for balance and fairness in the selection of topics and materials. Most scholars have emphasized the importance of including process objectives in any instructional plan, recognizing that "the study of culture and the teaching of culture are acts of inquiry" (Patrikis 1988, p. 17).

Exploring Behaviors and Values: Models for Building Cross-Cultural Understanding

Galloway (1984) has proposed the development of a framework for building cultural understanding based primarily on *process* skills, but incorporating within this framework both factual and sociolinguistic content. She suggests organizing instruction around four primary categories of understanding:

1. *Convention.* The goal of this type of instruction is to help students recognize and understand how people in a given culture typically behave in common, everyday situations (Seelye's Goal 3). Galloway identifies two types of conventions: (1) *context determined* conventions, which include extralinguistic behaviors that are characteristic in a given situation, and (2) *function-determined* conventions, relating to sociolinguistic formulae or conventional utterances that are used to perform tasks in the context. An example of two "convention clusters," or thematic groupings of cultural concepts, is given in Illustration 8.2. In each of these clusters, the outer circle represents extralinguistic information or behaviors that are relevant to the context and the inner circles represent culturally appropriate linguistic utterances.

Illustration 8.2
Convention Clusters

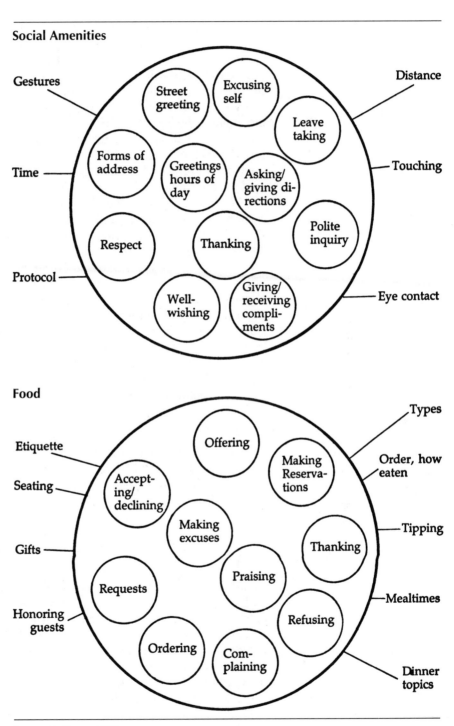

Social Amenities

Food

If one is teaching about the topic of social amenities, for example, a convention cluster could be designed that would consist of both customary behaviors associated with socializing (such as observing appropriate protocol, touching, social distance, concept of time, and the like) and conventional linguistic expressions that would occur in everyday social contexts (such as greetings and leave-takings, making polite requests, or giving and receiving compliments). If one were teaching about foods, the second convention cluster provides a set of possible cultural objectives that include both informational (or behavioral) and linguistic goals. Teachers might focus on such context-determined factors as mealtimes, types of foods, conventions of etiquette, and the like, as well as on appropriate expressions associated with accepting and declining invitations, making reservations at a restaurant, ordering a meal, praising the chef or complaining about the service. In using convention clusters such as these, there is a dual focus on understanding cultural behavior and linguistic considerations in an integrated fashion.

2. *Connotation.* The category of connotation deals with the many culturally significant meanings that are associated with words (Seelye's Goal 4). As students examine their own networks of associations, they can begin to discover that the underlying meanings of words are determined by their cultural frame of reference. Galloway (1985b) explains, for example, how certain words evoke a whole cluster of feelings and images for her that would not be appropriate in other cultures.

> *As a North American, the word "time" makes me nervous. To me it is concrete, real, touchable, linear, made up of uniform segments: seconds, minutes, hours. At the symbolic level, it represents pressure, stress, deadlines, schedules, lists, agenda, responsibility, action. I am hooked into the ethic of lateness, of productivity, of doing. Similarly, because I value and depend on technology, because I fear death, and because both exist across cultures, the former in degrees, the latter as an absolute, I am tempted to conclude that the same meanings are attached to the word universally. Likewise with images I attach to such concepts as beauty, food, family, ancestors, and so on.*

3. *Conditioning.* A third category of cultural understanding has to do with the fact that people act in a manner consistent with their cultural frame of reference, and that all people respond in culturally conditioned ways to basic human needs (Seelye's Goal 1). Students need to learn how to interpret behaviors that are different from their own without making judgments based on their own standards. If students begin to expect cultural differences as natural and inevitable and realize that there are indeed a variety of possible responses to the universal need for food, shelter, social contact, and the like, they may begin to view the other culture more empathically.

4. *Comprehension.* This category of cultural understanding includes such skills as analysis, hypothesis formation, and tolerance of ambiguity (Seelye's Goals 5 and 6). According to Galloway, comprehension goals can best be achieved by paying attention to the source of one's information, examining one's stereotypes, avoiding overgeneralizations, and learning about ways to resolve conflicts through experience-based simulations.

Galloway points out that her four-part treatment of culture is not hierarchically arranged. All four of these skills in cultural understanding need to be developed from the beginning through the more advanced levels of proficiency. She suggests, however, that one might derive insights about levels of cultural understanding from Hanvey's (1979) scheme for measuring cross-cultural awareness. His scheme consists of four stages, which Galloway has depicted in a slightly revised form, as shown in Illustration 8.3:

Level I: Information about the culture may consist of superficial or visible traits, such as isolated facts or stereotypes. The individual very likely sees the culture as odd, bizarre, and exotic. Ideas are often expressed in terms of what the culture lacks. Culture bearers may be considered rude, ignorant, or unrefined at this stage of understanding.

Level II: Learners at this stage focus on expanded knowledge about the culture in terms of both significant and subtle traits that contrast with those of their own culture. The learners might find the culture bearers' behavior irrational, frustrating, irritating, or nonsensical.

Level III: At this stage, the individual begins to accept the culture at an intellectual level, and thus the culture becomes believable because it can be explained. The individual can see things in terms of the target culture's frame of reference.

Level IV: This level, the level of empathy, is achieved through living in and through the culture. The individual begins to see the culture from the viewpoint of the insider, and thus is able to know how the culture bearer feels (Hanvey 1979; described in Galloway 1985a).

Hanvey concludes that achieving Level IV would be an ideal goal, but Level III may be more achievable. In any case, the levels represent stages of understanding or awareness that can fluctuate quite a bit, and the resultant instability of these levels should be kept in mind by anyone wishing to derive a workable sequence of instruction from them.

Ortuño (1991) proposes using a modification of the Kluckhohn model, designed by Kluckhohn and Strodtbeck (1961) to analyze a particular culture's value system, as a framework for analyzing one's own cultural values as well as for making cross-cultural comparisons. She has used an adaptation of this model to teach the cultural component of both elementary language courses and in third- and fourth-semester Spanish literature

Illustration 8.3
Hanvey's levels of
cultural awareness
(cited in Galloway
1985a)

Levels of Cultural Awareness			
Level	**Data**	**Mode**	**Interpretation**
I	Superficial stereotypes	Tourism text	Exotic, bizarre
II	Significant and subtle contrasts	Culture conflicts	Unbelievable, irrational
III	Significant and subtle contrasts	Intellectual analysis	Believable
IV	Awareness as insider	Cultural immersion	Believable from subjective familiarity

courses. The Kluckhohn model is predicated on the assumptions that (1) there is a finite number of common problems that humans face in all societies; (2) solutions to these problems vary, though not randomly; and (3) all alternatives to solutions are universally available, but differentially preferred (Kluckhohn and Strodtbeck 1961, cited in Ortuño 1991, p. 450.) Kluckhohn grouped universal human problems into five basic concerns:

1. *What is man's assessment of innate human nature? (Perception of Self and Others)?*
2. *What is man's relation to nature? (World View)?*
3. *What is the temporal focus of life? (Temporal Orientation)?*
4. *What is the group's principal mode of activity? (Forms of Activity)?*
5. *What is the modality of the group's relationships to others? (Social Relations)? (Ortuño 1991, p. 450)*

Kluckhohn postulated a range of variations that occur across cultures for each of these value orientations. Consider, for example, the first common concern: man's assessment of human nature. One might consider basic human nature to be evil, neutral, a mixture of good and evil, or basically good. One might also believe that human nature is immutable, or, conversely, that people are capable of changing. Cultures vary in their basic beliefs about the nature of humankind: Ortuño maintains, for example, that Americans tend to believe in the basic goodness of all people and are optimistic about progress and even in the ultimate perfectibility of mankind. She acknowledges, however, that plotting a culture's general orientation is subjective and requires some flexibility. She points out that many American anthropologists today assert that man is a mixture of good and evil, while the Puritans believed that man was basically evil (p. 457). Each of these variations within and across cultures has important consequences in shaping the beliefs and behaviors of the individuals who are part of that cultural orientation.

In terms of the second common concern identified by Kluckhohn—man's relation to nature—some cultures view man as subjugated to nature, others see the relationship as one of harmonious coexistence, and still others consider man to be master over nature. The third concern listed—the temporal orientation of cultures—varies from a primary focus on the past and its traditions, to living in the present, to focusing on the future (an orientation toward goals). Cultures also differ in the way one's personal value is determined ("Forms of Activity"). For some societies, one's essential "being" is all-important, while for others, inner development (or "becoming") is stressed. Still another way of viewing one's personal value or worth is by observing what one "does" or "achieves." Kluckhohn's last category looks at group relationships within a society. In some cultures, relationships are defined by means of dominant-subordinate or authoritarian relationships, while in others, the group is seen as a working whole making collective decisions. A third variation views the individual as autonomous and emphasizes egalitarian relationships (Ortuño 1991, pp. 450–51).

Ortuño presents the five value orientations identified by Kluckhohn with their range of variations in a chart form, and illustrates how students can use this framework for understanding their own culture as well as comparing it to that of the target culture. She discusses how American value orientations contrast rather strikingly with those of the Chinese, Japanese, American Indian, Arab, and Hispanic cultures, among others, and suggests ways in which students can be taught to recognize and appreciate these differences. She cautions, however, that teachers need to remind students that although one can make some generalizations about cultural patterning, one must not forget that "a wide range of acceptance of intracultural variants is built into each individual system as well" (p. 457), variants that provide societies with potential sources for change. This point is balanced, however, with Kohl's (1984) observation that societies tend to adhere to their "traditional values," and Ortuño recommends that teachers focus on dominant value orientations within a culture (p. 457). This recommendation contrasts somewhat with that of Patrikis (1988), who prefers to widen the focus to include subcultures as well. The decision about what to include in cultural lessons must ultimately rest with the teacher, who must balance the various viewpoints presented in this section with the practical realities of his or her instructional situation.

Although the language teaching profession may not have yet identified one definitive framework for designing curricula in which language and culture are integrated, we have over the years identified some very useful strategies for teaching culture through language and language through culture. Some ideas for doing this have already been presented in

Chapters 5, 6, and 7, particularly in activities that use authentic texts (including video and audio materials) as a point of departure for comprehension and production activities. Additional instructional strategies and teaching suggestions are presented in the next section.

Strategies for Teaching Culture

Some General Considerations

In designing activities for cultural instruction, it is important to consider the purpose for the activity, as well as its usefulness in teaching language and culture in an integrative fashion. Seelye (1984) believes that every cultural activity teachers use should be related somehow to one or more of the seven goals of cultural instruction that he has outlined (see pp. 363–64). Lafayette (1978, 1988) feels that the most basic issue in cross-cultural education is the degree to which the study of language and culture are integrated. He makes several suggestions for achieving this type of integration:

1. Cultural lessons and activities need to be planned as carefully as language activities and integrated into lesson plans.
2. Present cultural topics in conjunction with related thematic units and closely related grammatical content whenever possible. Use cultural contexts for language-practice activities, including those that focus on particular grammatical forms.
3. Use a variety of techniques for teaching culture that involve speaking, listening, reading, and writing skills. Do not limit cultural instruction to lecture or anecdotal formats.
4. Make good use of textbook illustrations and photos. Use probing questions to help students describe and analyze the cultural significance of photos and realia.
5. Use cultural information when teaching vocabulary. Teach students about the connotative meaning of new words. Group vocabulary into culture-related clusters.
6. Use small-group techniques, such as discussions, brainstorming, and role-plays for cultural instruction.
7. Avoid a "facts only" approach by including experiential and process learning wherever possible.
8. Use the target language whenever possible to teach cultural content.
9. Test cultural understanding as carefully as language is tested (Summary based on Lafayette 1978, 1988).

Crawford-Lange and Lange (1984) suggest a set of questions that teachers might ask themselves in determining the value of a given cultural activity. The questions, listed below, represent minimum criteria for achieving the integration of language and culture study.

Does the process (activity) . . .

1. *Make the learning of culture a requirement?*
2. *Integrate language learning and culture learning?*
3. *Allow for the identification of a spectrum of proficiency levels?*
4. *Address the affective as well as the cognitive domain?*
5. *Consider culture as a changing variable rather than a static entity?*
6. *Provide students with the skill to re-form perceptions of culture?*
7. *Provide students with the ability to interact successfully in novel cultural situations?*
8. *Exemplify that participants in the culture are the authors of the culture?*
9. *Relate to the native culture?*
10. *Relieve the teacher of the burden of being the cultural authority? (p. 146)*

The activities illustrated in the next sections represent formats that can be used to teach culture in a purposeful, integrative fashion in the second language classroom. In the absence of a well-defined assessment model for culture at the present time, activities might best be organized in terms of instructional goal statements. Seelye's scheme of seven goals of cultural instruction seems to be among the simpler ones suggested, yet it also appears relatively comprehensive. Therefore, his scheme has been selected as a point of reference for the strategies that follow.

The Lecture

Perhaps the most common technique that has been used by classroom teachers is the lecture. This strategy can be effective if teachers are careful to (1) keep it brief, (2) enliven it with visuals, realia, and accounts of personal experience, (3) focus on some specific aspect of cultural experience, (4) have students take notes, and (5) use follow-up techniques in which students use the target language actively, either in order to ask questions or to practice the new vocabulary, structures, or situations in the lecture in a cultural context.

Sample: *Presentation of food vocabulary*

Goals   Conventional behavior in common situations (Goal III); cultural connotation of words and phrases (Goal IV).

Procedure   The teacher gives a brief presentation about French markets, using a slide presentation showing various open-air markets, as well as scenes from shop window displays and in supermarkets. As each slide is shown, the teacher names various foods depicted while students take notes. Brief commentaries about the teacher's own preferences in foods and descriptions of items not common to American culture are made throughout the minilecture. After the students have had a chance to note down important vocabulary, the teacher uses various follow-up activities: questions about their preferences in foods for different meals; role-plays in which students make shopping lists and talk about what they would buy in what stores, and the like.

Source: Burnett 1985.

Native Informants

Native informants can be valuable resources to the classroom teacher, both as sources of current information about the target culture and as linguistic models for students. Universities with exchange programs often have several teaching assistants from the target culture, many of whom are the same age or a little older than the students studying the language. Native informants might also be identified within the community if exchange students are not available.

Native speakers might be invited to come to the classroom for an informal discussion with students on a specific topic, or they might be asked to participate in an audio- or videotaped interview or situational role-play (described in the next sections). Galloway (1981) gives the following tips for ensuring a successful classroom visitation by a native-speaking informant.

Previsitation

1. Make the identification of native informants within the local community a class project. Compile a directory of resource persons and update it frequently.
2. Find out what type of honorarium, if any, should be offered to resource persons. Offer to provide transportation to and from school on the day of the visit.
3. Meet with the native speaker before class and provide, if possible, some questions that students have prepared to guide the discussion.
4. Provide students with a detailed map of the country and allow them to study it, noting especially the city and/or region from which the native speaker comes.

During Visitation

1. Encourage students, whenever possible, to ask questions in the target language. This is facilitated if you have had them create questions in advance and have gone over the questions with them. If students are unable to ask a question in the target language, you might consider allowing them to ask their questions in English, but encourage the native speaker to answer them simply in the second language.

2. Have students ask appropriate questions by explaining to them the types of topics that are considered taboo or improper.

3. Don't expect a formal presentation by the native speaker. An informal dialogue usually works best.

4. If the native speaker permits, record the interview on audio- or videotape for future use.

Postvisitation

1. Express your appreciation in writing to both the native informant and any contact group that helped you identify him or her. You might want to ask the class to draft a letter of thanks in the target language.

2. Have students react to the interview in a written assignment, either in English or in the target language, relating their thoughts and reactions to the experience (pp. 91–92).

Audiotaped Interviews

Information about the target culture may be easily obtained by means of an informal interview with a native speaker. Several examples of taped interviews done in French by teaching assistants at the University of Illinois, with accompanying prelistening and postlistening activities, are provided here to illustrate how a variety of cultural goals can be achieved through this activity format. Each of the interview activities centers on a city or country in the Francophone world. The interviewer is an American teacher with a near-native command of French, and the interviewees are residents of the French-speaking countries represented.

Interview 1: Paris

Goals

Evaluating statements about a society (Goal V); researching another culture (Goal VI).

Prelistening Activity

Students discuss their preconceived ideas about Paris in a brainstorming activity. The teacher then shows some slides of Paris and elicits reactions. Comparisons are made between American cities and Paris, based on students' impressions and experiences. This activity is done in French, if the level of proficiency in speaking warrants it. Otherwise, the discussion may be done in the native language.

Interview

Students listen to a taped interview between an American interviewer and two French women who live or work in Paris. The content of the interview consists of facts, impressions, and personal anecdotes relating to the informants' experiences in Paris, as well as their own feelings about life in that city.

Postlistening
Activities

1. Students first answer questions in French on the content of the interview. Sample questions include:

- Give three adjectives that the women used in describing Paris.
- Among the activities available in Paris, which ones do you prefer?
- Describe a typical American tourist from the perspective of the women interviewed. Does that image surprise you? Explain.
- Have your ideas about Paris changed as a result of hearing this interview? In what way?

2. Students then do the following grammatical exercise, based on the interview itself. In this particular exercise, the students must choose between the *passé composé* and the *imparfait,* as these tenses were used by the native speakers in the interview.

Catherine: Bien, je crois qu'il faut tout d'abord dire que je _____ à Paris et que je _____ toute ma vie à Paris, donc, je connais assez mal les autres villes en ce sens que je _____ ailleurs qu'à Paris. (*Verbes:* naître, passer, ne pas vivre)

Jocelyne: Je suis provinciale. Je _____ à Dijon, mais je _____ donc deux ans à Paris, je _____ à Paris et je trouve que Paris, c'est une très belle ville. Mais il y a toujours trop de circulation, et en plus, comme je _____, je _____ entre le centre de Paris et la banlieue, je _____ le métro le soir et ça je _____. (*Verbes:* naître, habiter, travailler, se promener, prendre, ne pas aimer)

3. After completing this exercise, students listen to the taped passage again to check their responses. A discussion follows about the choice of tense in each instance.

4. Finally, students examine the layout of Paris by looking at city, metro, and bus maps brought in by the teacher. Students in groups of two or three choose two monuments, museums, or places of interest in Paris and are assigned a small research project in which they (1) describe the attractions of their selected sites, and (2) describe how to get there by metro, bus, or on foot from a selected location. Groups can present the descriptions of their imaginary visit during the next class meeting.

Source: Burnett and Thompson 1985.

Interview 2: *Montpellier*

Goal Researching another culture (Goal VI).

Prelistening Activity Students are asked to find out two facts about Montpellier for the following class day, when they will be listening to an interview with a native speaker from that city. Before listening to the interview, students pool their facts in French, locating Montpellier on a map.

Interview   The content of the interview includes a discussion about politics and government, as well as music, leisure activities, and school-related topics. Information specific to Montpellier and the surrounding region is also included.

Postlistening   1. Students answer a set of questions about the content of the interview
Activities   in French. Included are questions requiring inferences about the target culture, as well as questions comparing attitudes towards the topics covered from the French and the American points of view.
2. A vocabulary builder activity is used next, in which students come up with synonyms for new words used in the interview.
3. After listening to the interview again, students work in groups of four or five to research topics related to the content in the interview. Students present their information to the class during the next session. The questions and the presentations are done in French, when possible. Among the possible topics are:

- The current government in France: Students find out the overall structure of the French political system and make a diagram of the branches of government.
- French education: Students outline similarities and differences between the American and French educational system, pointing out the positive and negative features of each, in their way.
- Vacations: Students choose two cities in the south of France where they might like to spend a vacation. They explain their choice of cities and describe what activities they might do there. They write short travel ads for each city to persuade other class members to visit them.

Source: Burnett and Thompson 1985.

Interview 3: La Côte d'Ivoire

Goals   The sense, or functionality of culturally conditioned behavior (Goal I); evaluating statements about a society (Goal V); attitudes toward other cultures (Goal VII).

Prelistening Activity   Students discuss their preconceived ideas about the Ivory Coast, telling what they know about the country and giving their impressions of African life in that country. They then see a series of slides (obtained from the African Studies program on campus) giving a contemporary portrait of the land, the people, the economy, and the arts. A map of Africa is examined to locate the Ivory Coast in West Africa.

Interview   A native African student from the Ivory Coast is interviewed about his country. Topics covered include religion, the educational system, music, and government.

Postlistening   1. Students answer a series of general questions on the topics covered
Activities   in the interview. Their opinions about these issues are solicited. They are asked to tell how, if at all, their preconceived notions about the Ivory Coast have changed. They are invited to react, specifically, to the issue of language learning that was brought up in this interview. Samba, the interviewee, speaks eight languages. Students are asked to talk about language study in the United States in light of this fact. Discussion is conducted in French as much as possible.
2. As a vocabulary-building activity, students are given sentences from the interview with new words underlined. They guess the meaning of the words from context and discuss the strategies they used to interpret their meaning.
3. Students are divided into two groups, each of which is split into two smaller teams. The teams debate the following topics:

- Group I: One-half of the group defends an elitist school system while the other half criticizes it.
- Group II: One-half of the group represents a group of missionaries, bent on converting the natives of the Ivory Coast. The other half of the group defends the practice of their African religion and traditions.

Source: Burnett and Thompson 1985.

Videotaped Interviews/Observational Dialogues

Videotaped interviews and situational role-plays are excellent for providing natural, authentic linguistic exchanges that include paralinguistic information as well. They can be used to demonstrate not only conventional language in a variety of survival situations, but also certain conventional gestures and other cultural features, such as appropriate social distance, eye contact, and the like. They are usually best when prepared without a complete script, although partial scripts might be helpful (see Chapter 5). When students watch the videotaped materials, they should be asked to note certain behaviors and conventional linguistic expressions on an observation instrument of some type. Preview and follow-up activities should be planned to help students get the most out of the activity.

In institutions where both videotaping facilities and native speakers are available, locally produced materials can provide a rich resource for both listening comprehension and cultural learning. Videotapes that depict "survival situations," such as those typically used in oral interviews, are particularly useful in beginning and intermediate language classes. At the University of Illinois, for example, native-speaking French teaching assistants working from semi-scripts acted out various scenarios, which were later transcribed and used to develop a variety of classroom activities. Some of the scenes that were taped included greetings and leave-takings, extending and accepting invitations, ordering meals in restaurants, getting rooms at a hotel, asking someone for directions, as well as many other everyday encounters that related to the themes in the course texts. A sample videotaped conversation relating to calling about a room for rent was given in Chapter 5 (see pages 176–78). The following sample relates to a sequence of scenes that depicted inviting a guest for dinner.

Sample: *Social Amenities, Invitations to Dinner*

Goals
Interaction of language and social variables (Goal II); conventional behavior in common situations (Goal III).

Prelistening Activities

1. Students are asked to talk about the way in which Americans greet one another, discussing common expressions in both formal and informal style as well as paralinguistic features of that behavior. They also talk about French greetings and explain or demonstrate how that behavior differs from our own. They are then told to watch for these features on the videotape, noting down conventional expressions heard and gestures observed.

2. Students next talk about various ways in which invitations are extended, accepted, and refused in American culture, both formally and informally. Their knowledge about French customs is elicited and they are asked to watch for and note down the appropriate behaviors they will see on the tape.

3. Finally, students are asked to talk about appropriate behavior when they arrive at the home of a friend as an invited dinner guest, both in the United States and in France. They are asked to observe the social amenities associated with this situation on the videotape, noting down common expressions, paralinguistic behavior, and other features they might see.

4. A fourth activity involves observing the way the French table is set for a dinner party. Students are to note cultural differences in the table setting and important vocabulary associated with the items used.

Viewing the Videotape
Students watch the videotape sequence in which invitations are extended, accepted, and refused in both formal and informal styles. The last tape in the sequence involves the arrival of a dinner guest and the setting of the table. Students take notes as they watch the tape, according to the instructions in the prelistening activities. The videotaped sequence is played twice.

Postlistening
Activities

1. Students talk about the issues raised in the prelistening phase, discussing their notes and pooling their information and impressions.
2. Similarities and differences in behavior in French and American settings are listed on the board.
3. Students draw from memory (or arrange objects brought in by the teacher) to show how the table is set in France.

Another technique is to exchange videotapes (or audiotapes) with a school in the target culture. Students in both the American and the foreign classrooms make tapes in their respective native languages, talking about issues of common interest. The tapes are then exchanged, and each class has an authentic language sample to listen to and answer—a technologically advanced variation on the pen pal, which, of course, is an excellent way to provide language students with culturally authentic material in written form.

Videotaped materials that have been filmed in the target culture are also available from a number of publishers. Rosser (1992) has developed a videotaped program presenting six cultural themes illustrated with images and commentary from various countries in the Spanish-speaking world. This particular program is especially exemplary in that much of the commentary and information given is provided by interviews with native speakers themselves, whose viewpoints can be heard from their own frame of reference. For example, one of the scenes in the videotape presents a Mexican classroom where school children are learning about the gradual loss of Mexican territory to the United States. By listening to this lesson in history and geography from a Mexican perspective, unfiltered through a United States frame of reference, American students can begin to understand how historical events may be differentially interpreted in another culture.

A rich resource of authentic foreign language video materials that can be useful in cultural instruction is provided by the Project for International Communication Studies (PICS), developed at the University of Iowa (Altman 1989). The project, now supported by a consortium of universities, acquires and distributes international video materials, and also serves as a clearinghouse for the development and exchange of ideas for using these materials in the classroom. There has also been an increase in the number of multimedia projects involving computers and video in recent years. Such interactive programs hold a great deal of promise for enriching language and cultural instruction. Teachers interested in learning about many of these multimedia projects might begin by consulting ACTFL's two-volume series on media and technology in foreign language education, edited by Smith (1987, 1989), as well as attending some of the technology fairs that are scheduled in conjunction with major foreign language conferences.

Using Readings and Realia for Cross-Cultural Understanding

As was pointed out earlier in this chapter, students often approach target-cultural phenomena from within their own native-language cultural framework. This is certainly understandable if we adopt a schema-based view of comprehension, whether it be of written or oral texts or of culturally conditioned behavior. Just as students bring their own network of associations and background knowledge to the comprehension of a text, they bring these same elements to the task of understanding another culture. Nostrand (1967, 1974, 1989), Kramsch (1983), Galloway (1984, 1985a, 1985b, 1992), Seelye (1984), Byrnes (1991), and Mantle-Bromley (1992) are among the long list of scholars who have emphasized the importance of helping students recognize and understand the cultural schemata associated with the phenomena they encounter.

Byrnes (1991) suggests that second language instruction "inherently is in danger of trivializing the impact of culture, of tending to emphasize universals, of building on a sense of all humans being alike, of playing to the 'global village' syndrome" (p. 207). She finds it difficult to simulate the appropriate second-culture framework in a classroom where students are surrounded by their native culture, as in the teaching of foreign languages in the United States. For this reason, she prefers to use texts as a vehicle for gaining cross-cultural understanding. Since students will undoubtedly try to interpret target-language texts through the use of their native-language cultural schemata, there is a danger that they will miss the way that the materials represent the reality of the foreign cultural context. Byrnes suggests two ways to alleviate this problem. First, teachers should begin with L2 texts about the target culture that are not too far removed from the reality of the native culture or from the learners' own cultural experiences. Secondly, learners might begin by working with foreign language texts that deal with some familiar aspect of their own native culture. In treating a given theme or topic, Byrnes suggests the following progression of activities: (1) reading about an aspect of the student's own culture in the native language; (2) reading about that same phenomenon, but this time in the target language and from the perspective of the target culture; (3) reading about the same theme or topic in the target culture in the student's native language; (4) reading about the target culture in the target language. By reading a variety of texts on the same topic from different cultural perspectives, students can begin to discern how the cultural phenomenon itself may differ in the two contexts, as well as how attitudes about the phenomenon may differ. Such an intensive look at some circumscribed topics contrasts with the kind of "smorgasbord" approach that is used in many classrooms today. But Byrnes suggests that "an exemplary in-depth treatment of a few topics, broadly related to each other, is likely to yield a greater harvest for the development of cross-cultural competence than a wide casting of the nets" (p. 213). This use of discovery procedures, in her view, should be the core of a program in which cross-cultural competence is the goal. Given that this approach requires students to read unedited authentic texts with attention to detail, it is probably most appropriate for students who are at an Advanced level of proficiency in reading.

Moorjani and Field (1988) caution against an approach to the teaching of culture that does not take into account both the native culture of the students and the target culture, as represented in authentic texts. They cite the work of Tedlock (1983), an anthropologist who maintains that it is futile to try to present another culture strictly on its own terms, without reference to one's own culture. "In other words, the study of a second culture can only be a contrastive process, a dialogue between two ways of living and viewing the world" (Moorjani and Field 1988, p. 26). The authors believe that students should not be expected to understand a second culture by inducing its characteristics through authentic materials alone. "In fact, one infrequently discussed liability of authentic materials is that they assume no intercultural dialogue and can only be effective (as far as the teaching of culture is concerned) with the help of an interculturally sophisticated instructor" (p. 26). Although one might argue about the level of "sophistication" needed by teachers using authentic materials in their classes, the point that students need some kind of guidance as they read and interpret authentic materials is well taken.

Galloway (1992) outlines a four-stage approach to a *cultural reading* of authentic materials, an approach that leads students through the process of guided exploration and discovery. In Stage I *(Thinking)*, students engage in various pre-reading tasks that help them make their own C1 frame of reference more explicit, activating background knowledge and discussing their own beliefs about a topic that they will be encountering in the authentic target-language text. Stage II *(Looking)* involves tasks that help learners orient themselves to the authentic text, such as getting the gist or its global meaning, looking at its organization, structure, genre, and/or intentionality or purpose, and attempting to confirm various expectations or predictions that were elicited in Stage I. This stage of encounter with the text can also serve to help learners recognize what is already familiar, guess from context, and develop a sense of their own ability to deal with the material at some level. In Stage III *(Learning)*, students examine various cross-cultural contrasts and form or test hypotheses about the target culture, identifying areas that need further research. At this stage, students might also work more intensively with the text, searching for details, discussing word connotations, and finding evidence to support their developing ideas about the culture. The last stage in this recursive reading process *(Integrating)* involves reflection on what was read, with a view to integrating the knowledge gained with other related information from readings on the same or similar topics so that a cohesive framework for understanding the culture can begin to form. Galloway suggests that this is a good opportunity to engage students in writing tasks, encouraging them to react to the material personally and/or reflect on what they have learned. She provides many other specific teaching suggestions for all four stages of this process approach to cultural reading. Teachers who would like to use authentic materials in the classroom would do well to consult this source.

In the next pages, a few ideas are presented for activating native-culture schemata in preparation for making cross-cultural comparisons when reading target-language texts. The first sample activity relates to customs and practices associated with extending invitations to one's home for dinner.

Sample 1: *"Devine qui vient dîner?" ("Guess Who's Coming to Dinner?")*

Goals: The sense, or functionality, of culturally conditioned behavior (Goal I); the cultural connotation of words and phrases (Goal IV); researching another culture (Goal VI).

Directions: Students read a text which has been extracted from a guide to etiquette written for people who are known as "BCBG" ("Bon Chic Bon Genre") in France. The introduction to the reading explains that a "BCBG" is someone who belongs to the upper middle class by birth and who follows a certain code of behavior sanctioned by that group. Students are also told that the tone of the text is ironic.

Prereading: Students are given two topics to discuss relating to customs associated with inviting a guest for dinner in the United States. The topics deal with the significance of friendly dinner invitations in American culture and with the kind of atmosphere that is usually created at such gatherings.

Reading Activity: Students fill out the chart in Illustration 8.4. The chart lists in French typical American cultural phenomena associated with dinner invitations and invites the students to fill out the contrasting customs that would be true in the French context, according to the reading.

Postreading Activities: The text presents various comprehension questions and activities that help students further probe the cultural realities revealed in the reading, as well as discuss their own experiences with meal-time situations in the native culture.

Source: Brière, Harlow, and Muyskens 1989, pp. 24–26.

Sample 2: *L'Aide Sociale en France*

Goals: The sense, or functionality, of culturally conditioned behavior (Goal I); cultural connotations of words and phrases (Goal IV); researching another culture (Goal VI).

LECTURE 1　Devine que vient dîner?

Avant la lecture

Sujets à discuter

1. Si un Américain invite quelqu'un à dîner chez lui, quelle en est la signification? Est-il possible de refuser une telle invitation?

2. Aux Etats-Unis est-ce qu'on sort toujours le cristal, la porcelaine et l'argenterie *(silverware)* quand on invite à dîner? De quelles manières est-ce qu'on sert un repas dans une maison américaine? (Pensez, par exemple, aux barbecues.)

Stratégies de lecture

Trouvez les détails. Parcourez rapidement la lecture. Dans le contexte d'une invitation à dîner, trouvez les coutumes françaises qui font contraste avec chacune des coutumes américaines décrites ci-dessous.

Aux Etats-Unis . . .	**En France . . .**
1. Si les invitations sont pour 8h30 du soir, la plupart des invités arrivent à 8h30 ou un peu plus tard. Les amis les plus intimes arrivent souvent en premier.	1.
2. Après le dîner, on passe de la salle à manger au salon ou dans la salle de séjour pour continuer à discuter.	2.
3. On sert souvent du café quand il se fait tard.	3.
4. Après avoir raccompagné la jeune fille qui gardait les enfants, on gare la voiture tout près de son appartement ou de sa maison.	4.

Illustration 8.4
"Guess Who's Coming to Dinner?" Comparing Social Customs in the United States and France

Source: Brière, Harlow, and Muyskens 1989, pp. 24–26.

Directions: Students read a passage about social programs in France. The activity consists of filling out the chart shown in Illustration 8.5 on pages 388–89, which is based on the material in the reading. Like the activity in Sample 1, above, students are invited to complete the chart by writing in the information about France that contrasts with aspects of the same phenomenon in the United States.

Source: Activity designed by Cook 1985, based on a reading in Brière, Frommer, and Woshinsky 1982, pp. 121–124.

READING 1   Guess Who's Coming to Dinner?

Before Reading

Subjects for Discussion

1. If an American invites someone to dinner at his/her house, what does that mean? Is it possible to refuse such an invitation?
2. In the United States, does one always get out the crystal, china, and silverware when one has people over for dinner? What ways does one serve dinner in an American home? (Think, for example, about barbecues.)

Reading Strategies

Find the details. Skim the reading quickly. In the context of a dinner invitation, find the French customs that contrast with each of the American customs described below.

In the United States . . .	In France . . .
1. If the invitations are for 8:30 p.m., most guests arrive at 8:30 or a little later. Often, closest friends arrive first.	1.
2. After dinner, people move from the dining room to the living room to continue the conversation.	2.
3. Often one serves coffee when it gets late.	3.
4. After having taken the babysitter home, one parks the car close to one's apartment or house.	4.

The two samples above are appropriate for students at the Intermediate level of proficiency in reading and are based on materials found in cultural readers. Teachers can develop similar activities using authentic materials drawn from various sources. Lalande (1979) suggests ways in which students themselves can collect authentic materials through correspondence with various businesses and institutions in the foreign culture. A sample letter to a German Chamber of Commerce appropriate for students in a first-year German program is given in Illustration 8.6 on page 390. Lalande allows students to choose their own letter destination and content, maintaining that freedom of choice is a vital ingredient in generating student enthusiasm and motivation for the letter-writing project. He gives several examples of the types of documents students in his German class solicited

---

Quelles sont les responsabilités d'un état envers ces citoyens?

La Question	En France	Aux Etats-Unis
1. Selon la tradition, qui s'occupe de la population?	**1.**	**1.** On compte sur la liberté et l'initiative de l'individu.
2. Qui paie la majorité des dépenses pour l'éducation et les soins médicaux?	**2.**	**2.** L'individu.
3. Comment le gouvernement paie-t-il les programmes sociaux?	**3.**	**3.** On paie les programmes sociaux avec les impôts sur le revenu.
4. Qu'est-ce que c'est que la Sécurité sociale?	**4.**	**4.** C'est un programme qui paie les pensions de retraite.
5. Laquelle est moins élevée grâce aux lois ou à l'aide sociale: la mortalité infantile ou la mortalité au travail?	**5.**	**5.** La mortalité au travail est moins élevée.
6. Est-ce que l'aide sociale indique le rôle important que la famille joue dans la société?	**6.**	**6.** Non, pas vraiment.

Maintenant, écrivez un résumé de cet article. _____

_____

_____

_____

_____

_____

Illustration 8.5
Comparing Social
Programs in the United
States and France

Source: Cook 1985, based on a passage in Brière et al. 1982, pp. 121–24.

and obtained. One student was interested in learning about how to maintain some headphones he had bought that were manufactured in Austria. After asking for information from the company in a letter, the student received a booklet and various instructions for preventive maintenance of his equipment. Another student, who was majoring in journalism, wrote to the editor of a leading German newspaper, inquiring about a variety of topics and policy issues, and in particular asking about freedom of the press in Germany. He received a personal two-page letter from the editor, along with a photocopy of relevant sections of the German constitution relating to guarantees of freedom of the press (p. 18). Lalande reports that students are enthusiastic about the responses they receive, and pleased with their own ability to communicate successfully in a genuine encounter with German-speaking correspondents.

What are the responsibilities of a government towards its citizens?		
Question	**In France**	**In the United States**
1. According to tradition, who takes care of the population?	1.	1. One counts on the freedom and initiative of the individual.
2. Who pays the majority of expenses for education and health care?	2.	2. The individual.
3. How does the government pay for social programs?	3.	3. Social programs are paid for by income taxes.
4. What is Social Security?	4.	4. It's a program that pays retirement pensions.
5. Which is lower, thanks to laws or to assistance programs: infant mortality or job-related deaths?	5.	5. Job-related deaths are lower.
6. Does social assistance indicate the important role that the family plays in the society?	6.	6. No, not really.

Now, write a resumé of this article. _____

_____

_____

_____

_____

_____

_____

Di Donato suggests a related activity that has students write letters to people chosen at random from German phone directories, asking about German customs relating to holidays like Christmas and Easter (Di Donato, cited in Lalande 1985b). These activities have produced many interesting texts for students to read and enjoy, and have even led to further correspondence in some cases. Needless to say, the potential for cultural learning inherent in this type of project is substantial.

Lalande (1985b), Scanlan (1986), Berwald (1988) and García (1991) are among the many scholars and practitioners who have suggested using various forms of realia to help students learn about aspects of daily life in the target culture. An activity for German students provided by Lalande (1993) has students analyze the contents of a German newspaper (see Illustration 8.7, p. 391). After examining the various parts of the paper, students discuss their findings and share their impressions about how this

Illustration 8.6

Example of Letter to Chamber of Commerce —appropriate for students in a first-year German program

---

Champaign, d.11. Januar 1993

Verkehrsamt Graz
Herrengasse 16
A-8010 Graz
Austria

Sehr geehrte Damen und Herren!

Ich lerne Deutsch an der Universität Illinois. Meine Freunde und ich kommen vielleicht im Sommer nach Graz. Was gibt es in Graz zu sehen? Bitte schicken Sie uns Informationen über Ihre Stadt. Vielen Dank.

Mit freundlichem Gruß

Ihr

John Rosenberger

English translation of above letter:
Dear Madam or Sir:

I'm studying German at the University of Illinois. My friends and I might come to Graz this summer. What is there to see in Graz? Please send us some information about your city. Thank you very much.

Sincerely,

Source: Lalande 1993.

particular paper compares to papers in the United States. A follow-up activity involves scanning the entertainment pages and answering questions about the movies that are depicted (see Illustration 8.8, p. 392). This activity can be linked to discussions about dating practices or the influence of foreign films on stereotypes in both German and American culture.

García (1991) has developed a unit for her second-year Spanish course around "Rituals in Hispanic Culture," using authentic materials drawn from newspapers. She uses birth, marriage, and death notices from both American and Hispanic newspaper sources to help students understand the underlying sociocultural context of these documents. Students begin by uncovering their own cultural schemata surrounding these events by reading announcements in their native language. As they look at the announcements, they are directed to focus on key words, content, and structures used. García has her students discuss this material in Spanish, answering various questions that have relevance to the focus of the cultural lesson. For a set of birth announcements, for example, students answer questions in Spanish about the English-language material and then fill out a grid with category designations such as the name of the parents, the name of the

Illustration 8.7
Analyzing a German
newspaper

Search Object	Comments (e.g., is it there? If so, where & what is it like?)
Table of Contents	
Weather Forecast/Map	
Sports	
Editorials	
Classified Ads	
Obituaries	
Movie/Theater Guides	
Radio/TV Guides	
Political Cartoons	
Cartoons	
Letters to the Editor	
Business Section	
Culture Section	
Crossword Puzzle	
Jokes/Humor	
Shape of Paper	
Cost	

Advertisements
—for food
—for drink
—for anything American
—for anything Japanese
—for anything really unusual

Any English words?

Now sum up: which things were similar and dissimilar between this paper and a comparable American newspaper? To which American newspaper might this one best be compared?

Source: Lalande 1993.

child, and the place the child was born. They then look at a similar set of announcements drawn from a Spanish-language newspaper and complete a similar grid, as well as a family tree inferred from the information given. One cultural feature that becomes salient in this activity is the system of Spanish surnames. As students encounter difficulty with this, the teacher gives a brief explanation to allow them to proceed with the task.

Illustration 8.8
Analyzing Movie
Listings

Im Kino—In Deutschland

1. Gibt es Filme, die Sie schon gesehen haben? Welche?

2. Am Wochenende wollen Sie mit Ihrem kleinen Bruder oder mit Ihrer kleinen Schwester ins Kino. Welche drei Filme kommen vielleicht in Frage?

   a) _____ b) _____

   c) _____

3. Sie sind mit einem Freund nach Deutschland geflogen. Am Flughafen haben Sie von Avis ein Auto gemietet. Jetzt wollen Sie mit Ihrem Freund zu einem *drive-in theater*. Wie heißt so was auf deutsch? Schreiben Sie unten den Namen des Filmes (aber nicht von einem amerikanischen Film), der dort gezeigt wird.

   drive-in theater = _____

   der Filmtitel = _____

   die englische Übersetzung des Filmes = _____

4. Geben Sie die Namen von drei amerikanischen Filmen, die Sie noch nicht erwähnt haben.

   a) _____ b) _____

   c) _____

5. Lesen Sie was gerade im *Mathäser Filmpalast* läuft (in der Spalte ganz links). Wie früh kann man am Samstag oder am Sonntag ins Kino? _____ Wie heißt der Film? _____ Welcher Film läuft da schon länger als alle anderen? _____ Welches ist das Mindestalter für Kinder, die den Film *Ghostbusters* sehen wollen? _____

6. Gibt es *film matinees*? _____ Bitte erklären Sie Ihre Antwort.

7. In welcher Stadt Deutschlands sind diese Filme und Kinos wohl zu finden? _____

8. In welchem Kino kann man Bette Midler's *Divine Madness* sehen? _____ Und wo ist das Kino? _____ Und wie ist seine Telefonnummer? _____ Um wie viel Uhr wird der Film gezeigt? _____ Und in welcher Sprache? _____

9. Was meinen Sie? Wie alt oder neu ist dieses Kinoprogramm? _____ Bitte erklären Sie Ihre Antwort.

10. Was halten Sie von der Filmauswahl an diesem Wochenende? Warum?

11. Welchen Film würden Sie mit Ihrem Date gern anschauen? _____ Und nicht anschauen? _____ Bitte erklären Sie beide Antworten.

12. Was für Unterschiede und Ähnlichkeiten gibt es beim Kinogehen und in den Kinoprogrammen zwischen den USA und Deutschland?

(Andere mögliche Gesprächsthemen: Kosten, Erfrischungen im Kino, *dating*, der Einfluß ausländischer Filme auf Stereotypen)

Source: Lalande 1993.

At the Movies—In Germany

1. Are there some movies which you have already seen? If so, which ones?

2. Over the weekend you would like to take your younger brother(s) and/or sister(s) to the movies. Find three movies which you could take them to see.

a) _____   b) _____

c) _____

3. You've flown with a friend to Germany. At the airport you rent a car from Avis. A week later you want to visit a drive-in theater. What are they called in German? Write below the name of a non-American film being shown at the drive-in.

drive-in theater = _____

German film title = _____

English translation of above film title = _____

4. Give the names of three American-made movies which you have not already used.

a) _____   b) _____

c) _____

5. Look at the movie listings for the *Mathäser Filmpalast* (far left column). Which one will be the first or earliest to be shown on Saturday or Sunday? _____ At what time? _____ Which of the films has been running for the longest consecutive period at that theater? _____ What is the youngest recommended age for viewing "Ghostbusters" as indicated in the movie ad? _____

6. Are there any film matinees to go to? _____ Please explain.

7. In which German city are these movie theaters probably located? _____

8. In which theater can you see Bette Midler's "Divine Madness"? _____ Where is the theater located? _____ And its telephone number? _____ (Why do you suppose German movie theaters include their telephone numbers in their ads?) What time will the movie be shown? _____ And in what language? _____

9. How old or recent do you think this movie listing is? _____ Please explain.

10. What do you think of the movie selection/variety on this weekend? Why?

11. Which movie might you like to go to with your date? _____ And which one would you definitely not like to go to with your date? _____ Please explain both of your answers.

12. What are some of the similarities and differences between movie-going in Germany and in the USA? And between newspaper movie guides/listings?

(Possible follow-up activities/discussion on: ticket prices, refreshments, dating, influence of foreign films on cultural stereotypes)

Source: Lalande 1993.

Once these activities have been completed, students discuss differences and similarities between the two cultures. Students consider the fact, for example, that Spanish birth announcements mention the name of the hospital first, whereas announcements in United States newspapers usually reserve this information for last. Students are invited to speculate on reasons for differences such as these, and complete a post-reading assignment outlining similarities and differences for homework. A second task she suggests involves writing their own Spanish-language birth announcement in the manner appropriate to the culture, using a set of information given by the teacher.

García recommends the use of a variety of grids such as those described here to help students take pertinent notes and analyze what they discover from their reading. (Interested readers should consult this source, which presents a wealth of ideas for creating charts and activity formats.) She points out several advantages to using authentic materials in this way:

1. Students are encouraged to think about their own culture and customs and how those customs reflect the values of the society in which they live.
2. Students begin to see how the values and way of life in other societies are manifested in their customs and behaviors.
3. The act of doing comparisons and contrasts and the accompanying analysis activities help students learn to understand and accept different ways of handling basic human needs and see them as valid.

Understanding Culturally Conditioned Behavior: Some Common Teaching Techniques

A number of time-honored teaching ideas have been grouped under this category to illustrate some specific formats for cultural instruction designed to sensitize students to contrasts and commonalities in conventional behavior in the home and target culture. The majority of these ideas were introduced in the 1960s and 1970s, and many are still popular with classroom teachers today. For a number of sample activities using these formats, see Seelye (1984), as well as the other sources provided below.

Culture Capsules A culture capsule is a short description, usually one or two paragraphs in length, of one minimal difference between an American and a target-culture custom, accompanied by illustrative photos, slides, or realia. The technique was developed by Darrel Taylor, a foreign language teacher, and John Sorensen, an anthropologist (see Taylor and Sorensen 1961; Seelye 1984). The technique can be used for independent study, in small groups or with the full class. And culture capsules may be written by students or teachers, or purchased commercially (see, for example, Miller and Loiseau 1974).

To construct a culture capsule, Lett (1977) suggests the following steps:

1. Select a topic of cultural contrast, coordinating it with topics being treated in the textbook.
2. List differences and similarities between target culture and home culture customs in relation to this point of contrast.
3. Define student learning objectives.
4. Organize and outline specific content.
5. Write the capsule in language that will be comprehensible to the students who will use it (i.e., at an appropriate level of proficiency).
6. Check the accuracy of the content and language of the capsule with a native speaker and/or other colleagues.
7. Rewrite as necessary.
8. Prepare or collect appropriate multimedia aids (visuals, slides, clippings, realia, etc.)

The teacher may wish to record the capsule on tape for students to listen to as a group or independently, or the capsule may be read aloud, either by the teacher or by a student. The students might also read the capsule in class or as a homework assignment, or follow along with a printed script as the capsule is presented orally. Another alternative is to have students form small groups, with each person in the group responsible for reading part of the narrative to the others. Such an activity affords good practice in listening comprehension and speaking skills.

Among the follow-up activities Lett suggests are those below:

1. Students perform role-plays based on the capsule, with situations and/or scripts provided by the teacher.
2. Groups of students write role-plays based on the information in the capsule.
3. Individuals or groups write new capsules on closely related topics, creating a "culture cluster" (discussed in the next major section).
4. Individuals or groups research and report on related topics of special interest suggested by the capsule.
5. The content of the capsule is integrated into language-learning activities, such as listening and reading comprehension exercises, communicative oral exercises, and written follow-up activities (dictation, rewriting, short compositions, resumes, and the like).

Culture Clusters   Culture clusters, developed by Meade and Morain (1973), consist of about three illustrated culture capsules that develop related topics plus one 30-minute simulation that integrates the information in the capsules and dramatizes it through a skit or situational role-play (Seelye 1984). The development of the culture cluster might best be approached by selecting a central theme and working backwards to arrive at three or four components that might lend themselves to culture capsules. The videotaped sequence of greetings, invitations, and arrival at the host's house for dinner described earlier (see pp. 381–82) could be easily converted into a culture cluster by supplementing each segment of the tape with a culture-capsule narrative description of (1) greeting behavior, (2) extending invitations, (3) setting the table and (4) arriving at a host's home for dinner and appropriate guest etiquette. The videotape would serve as part of the multimedia presentation, and in the follow-up activity, students could simulate what they have observed and learned.

Culture Assimilators

According to Seelye (1984), the culture assimilator was first envisioned as a programmed, out-of-class technique that would help individuals adjust to a new culture. Developed by social psychologists (Fiedler, Mitchell, and Triandis 1971), a culture assimilator might consist of as many as 75 to 100 "critical incidents" or episodes that take place between an American and a member of the target culture in which some type of conflict or misinterpretation develops. The source of conflict or puzzlement on the part of the American is the lack of an appropriate cultural framework for understanding the incident.

Lett (1977) describes three basic parts to each episode:

1. A critical incident occurs, illustrating some kind of miscommunication between an American and a member of the target culture. This incident may be presented as a dialogue or in narrative form.
2. Students are then presented with four possible explanations of the source of the conflict in multiple-choice form.
3. As students make a choice of explanation, they are directed to a paragraph that provides them with feedback about whether or not their choice was correct. Feedback paragraphs may provide additional cultural information to further clarify the cultural point around which the critical incident has been designed. Distractors (incorrect choices) are designed to be attractive to students who are operating under false stereotypic perceptions or ethnocentric interpretations of the situation.

Culture Minidramas

A minidrama can be constructed from three to five episodes in which a cultural conflict or miscommunication occurs, as in the culture assimilator, above. As each episode is experienced, students attempt to explain what the source of the miscommunication is through class discussion, led by the teacher. After each episode in the series, more cultural information is given, but not enough to identify the precise cause of the problem, which becomes apparent only in the last scene. Seelye (1984) explains that the function of this technique is to lead students to experience the vagueness of much cross-cultural communication due to differing assumptions in the two cultures about the connotation of words or about everyday events and practices. Students see how they might easily jump to false conclusions about the people in the target culture because they are reacting on the basis of their own ethnocentric biases and perceptions (pp. 105–06).

Deriving Cultural Connotations

In the activities that follow, students learn to associate culturally representative images with words and phrases they are learning in the new language (Goal IV). Techniques include the use of visual support materials as well as word-association activities.

Sample 1: Word Association

Students learn to examine their own connotations for words and see that they are not only idiosyncratic, but also culturally bound to some extent. The teacher gives a stimulus word related to a theme in the textbook and asks students to list as many associated words as possible. For the word *house*, for example, students might associate words like *large, split-level, brick, windows, home, lawn, garage,* and so forth.

Students can work individually to generate the lists and then be put into groups to rank-order the words according to their frequency on group members' lists.

The teacher can demonstrate how these images are culture-bound by obtaining similar data from speakers of the target language prior to this activity and presenting that data to students after they have reported their own results. Discussions about the similarities and differences in word-association chains will reveal how words cannot simply be translated from one language to the other, but must be situated in their own cultural context to be fully comprehended.

A slide presentation of houses in the target culture may be used to lend visual support to this activity.

Sample 2: Semantic Mapping

Semantic mapping is a technique that was originally developed by Johnson and Pearson (1978) to teach vocabulary to children learning to read in their native language. It consists of creating a graphic arrangement of associated word clusters around a key word, idea, or concept. Hague (1987) proposes various strategies for using this technique in teaching foreign language vocabulary. To create a semantic map, she outlines six steps: (1) write the foreign language word or concept on the blackboard or put it on a transparency; (2) ask class members to think of as many related words as they can; (3) write the words suggested by the class in categorical clusters, arranged around the original word; (4) have students provide category names for the clusters; (5) discuss the words and their relationships on the semantic map that has been created; (6) revise the map, if necessary, after the group has discussed the various meanings and nuances of the vocabulary that has been elicited.

Hague presents a sample semantic map that can be used in a cultural presentation about "La Corrida de Toros" ("The Bullfight") (see Illustration 8.9). Again, it might be useful to ask a group of native Spanish speakers to create a similar map independently, using the same process outlined above. After American students have created and discussed their own maps, they can then study the map created by the native speakers and discuss any differences in the connotations revealed in the two versions. This same process can be used in creating semantic maps associated with any theme, value, institution, abstract concept, cultural event (such as holidays), or culturally conditioned behavior. Teachers who have access to a group of native-speaking colleagues or students might want to plan for this type of cultural instruction by choosing significant concepts that are related to textbook chapters in courses they are teaching and elicit a series of semantic maps. Maps could be placed in drop files for each cultural unit and collected over a number of semesters. Once enough maps are collected, thematic units associated with new vocabulary can be developed around the cultural connotation of words.

Sample 3: *Practicing Common Vocabulary in Cultural Contexts: A Cross-Cultural Presentation of Foods*

Spinelli and Siskin (1992) maintain that many current textbooks have provided useful vocabulary presentations by grouping new words into semantic clusters, but that cross-cultural differences between seemingly equivalent vocabulary items need to be made more obvious. One of the many examples they give is food vocabulary, which is often presented in semantic groupings (such as drinks, meats, vegetables, fruits, etc.) in language textbooks. However, Spinelli and Siskin argue that there is frequently no mention made of the cultural significance of these foods or drinks or the contexts in which they are normally consumed. Lafayette (1988) agrees, suggesting, for example, that food vocabulary be presented in clusters associated with particular meals.

Some recent textbook presentations do go beyond the simple denotation of vocabulary items to include connotative meanings and depict cultural realities more overtly than in the past. For example, Muyskens, Omaggio Hadley, and Chalmers (1990) present food items in their first-year text through drawings depicting foods placed on a table to depict particular meals throughout the day, as well as tables set appropriately according to the conventions of the target culture. There are also several drawings and photos of holiday meals that are culturally representative, and specialty items are featured in cultural readings that relate the significance of certain dishes to traditional holiday celebrations. Foods in a subsequent chapter are regrouped by depicting them in drawings and photographs of the windows of different specialty stores where they are sold, in open-air markets, and in authentic menus from a variety of restaurants. In this way, students

Illustration 8.9
Semantic map based on
the concept of the
bullfight

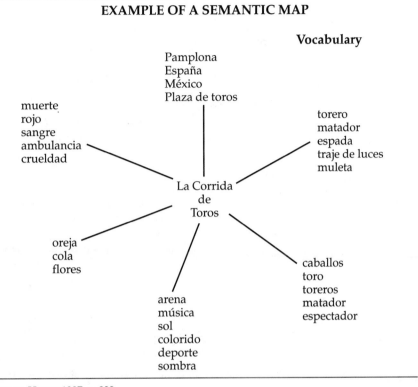

EXAMPLE OF A SEMANTIC MAP

Vocabulary

Pamplona
España
México
Plaza de toros

muerte
rojo
sangre
ambulancia
crueldad

torero
matador
espada
traje de luces
muleta

La Corrida
de
Toros

oreja
cola
flores

caballos
toro
toreros
matador
espectador

arena
música
sol
colorido
deporte
sombra

Source: Hague 1987, p. 222.

become acquainted with the various cultural connotations of foods while
engaging in both focused and open-ended language practice activities in
different skill areas.

Spinelli and Siskin (1992) give the example of a food presentation
based on an authentic Spanish-language document, instructing people in
the art of eating a taco. Using a document such as this allows food vocabulary to be presented within both a functional and cultural framework that
is interesting to students. The authors also suggest that teachers use charts
and graphs to help students analyze when certain foods and drinks are
conventionally consumed in the target culture, or complete sentences that
show knowledge of various customs associated with foods, gifts, etiquette,
and the like. In summarizing their criteria for teaching vocabulary, Spinelli
and Siskin recommend that teachers present vocabulary and have students
practice it (1) within culturally-authentic semantic groupings; (2) in ways
that allow students to see differences between the native and target culture; (3) through the use of visuals where native-culture/target-culture referents differ; and (4) in ways that will reinforce appropriate conventional
target-culture behavior (p. 313).

Sample 4: *Collages*

Seelye (1984) suggests that students select a word that intrigues them and compile images of that word from magazine and newspaper clippings or from their own photography. For example, a student selecting the word *mujer* (woman) illustrates through a collection of magazine photos how social class, age, and Indian and African backgrounds affect the appearance of women in Latin America (p. 55). Students exploring the abstract notion of *beauty* might compile two different collages, one representing United States culture and one representing the foreign culture.

Hypothesis Refinement

Jorstad (1981) describes a seven-step process that enables students to refine their initial perceptions of an aspect of the target culture through research skills. The activity can be related to Seelye's Goals V and VI (evaluating statements about a society and researching another culture). The following example has been adapted to illustrate the process:

Step 1: Students perceive an aspect of the culture through learning materials, teacher presentation, or other source.

Example: Based on films and advertisements they have seen, students notice that German teenagers seem to be riding bikes, motorcycles, and other two-wheeled vehicles more often than driving cars.

Step 2: Students make a statement about the culture as a result of this perception.

Example: "German teenagers seem to use bikes, cycles, and motorbikes more than they use cars."

Step 3: Students seek multiple sources of information about the statement, such as newspapers, movies, slides, books, as well as other media, realia, and native speaker informants.

Example: Students see many ads, textbook pictures, magazines, articles, etc. showing young people on two-wheeled vehicles. A news item about the expense of gasoline in Europe states that gas in Germany costs three to four times as much as it does in the United States. Students' pen pals and acquaintances tell them that a family generally has one car, and young people take the bus, ride bikes, or walk to get around.

Step 4: Students question and compare their sources, examining them for potential limitations, such as publication date, intended audience, and purpose. They describe, analyze, and report their findings.

Step 5: Students modify the statement in Step 2 and continue to seek additional information that can refine the statement further.

Step 6: Students examine a related feature of their own culture using the same process.

Step 7: Students compare their refined statements about their own and the target culture, describing similarities and differences they have found.

In doing these activities, students should use the target language as much as possible—in discussions, in searching through target-language sources, and in making the statements, refined hypotheses, and comparisons between the home and target cultures.

Artifact Study   Artifact study is designed to help students discern the cultural significance of certain unfamiliar objects from the target culture (Galloway 1985a). The activity involves giving descriptions and forming hypotheses about the function of the unknown object (Goal VII). If possible, the teacher brings in the article in question, or obtains pictures of it. Once the article is displayed for all to see, students form small groups and answer such questions as the following, suggested by Galloway:

1. What are the physical qualities of the object? Give as complete a description as possible.
2. How was it made, by hand or by machine?
3. What is its purpose?
4. Is it supposed to be decorative?
5. What role does it play in the culture? What is its social meaning, if any? (Does it have associations with status, wealth, power, prestige?)
6. What facts can be determined about the culture from this object?
7. If this object were yours, what would you do with it?
Etc.

Group discussions should take place in the target language whenever possible. After a suitable amount of time for discussion, the groups report their answers to the questions and compare responses. The teacher then gives a brief explanation of the artifact and its use in the society, and students examine how closely their own hypotheses conform to this explanation. Students determine to what extent their own cultural biases played a role in the formation of their hypotheses about the unknown object.

Decreasing   Activities of this type help students understand the dangers of making
Stereotypic   unwarranted generalizations about the people of another culture and help
Perceptions   sensitize them to the variability within cultures that such generalizations can never capture. Stereotypes are most harmful if they create barriers to understanding and prevent the development of empathy. They are especially unfair if the behavior of one individual from the target culture is generalized to all of its people, a phenomenon that happens very often in tourist encounters. How many Americans have returned from a whirlwind tour of Paris to say that the city was beautiful, but "the people were

nasty?" How many Americans have the strong impression that all Spanish-speaking peoples eat tacos and hot foods, go to bullfights, and take abundant naps? These and other stereotypic impressions can be subjected to scrutiny through well-designed classroom activities.

Heusinkveld (1985) proposes that the foreign language classroom can provide an excellent forum for discussing and understanding cultural stereotypes. She maintains that a "facts" approach, which has been commonly used in the study of culture, often emphasizes rote memorization rather than the development of greater sensitivity to cultural phenomena and understanding of deeper cultural values. She proposes a series of practical classroom activities that will sharpen students' awareness of their own cultural background, followed by activities that enable students to compare and contrast their native cultural context to that of the target country.

The first priority in Heusinkveld's approach is to have students realize how much their own priorities, likes, and dislikes are shaped by their culture. Her classroom activities, thus, first concentrate on heightening students' awareness of American cultural patterns. One activity, for example, asks students to design a short course for foreigners on American culture. In deciding what to include in such a course, students begin to see what is important to them. Heusinkveld provides a list of some 80 American cultural phenomena to help students begin categorizing their culture. They select 15 to 20 topics from this list, discussing and comparing their choices in the target language.

After examining such aspects of surface culture, or external manifestations of underlying values, students then try to discover what those underlying values are. For example, in examining the role of fast-food restaurants in American society, students begin to see how much Americans tend to value convenience, efficiency, and cleanliness. By contrast, they may notice from examining the eating habits of Hispanic or French people that they tend to value family unity, family interaction, a leisurely pace at mealtimes, and the enjoyment of a well-prepared meal.

Heusinkveld also suggests that, once values of both the home and target cultures have been discovered, students can begin to argue *against* United States practices and *for* the practices of the other culture. They thus begin to discover how stereotypes originate. For example, they begin to see how foreigners might easily view our culture as a plastic society obsessed with time and cleanliness, unconcerned about the "finer things" in life. Heusinkveld presents other interesting strategies for heightening cultural awareness through classroom visitors, values activities, and the use of photographs, advertisements, and periodicals from the foreign culture to teach students to observe and interpret cultural differences more effectively.

Mantle-Bromley (1992) suggests that teachers use various attitude-readiness lessons to increase students' self-awareness, look at their own culturally conditioned behavior more closely, recognize the pluralism that exists in every culture, and recognize the riskiness of overgeneralization, which easily leads to stereotypic thinking. One activity that she advocates involves putting an object that can be dismantled into its various pieces into a bag and letting students try to guess the whole from the parts. As students try to guess what the object is from handling the smaller pieces, they can begin to understand how difficult it is to understand another culture by approaching it in a piece-meal fashion (p. 123).

In order to understand stereotypic perceptions, Mantle-Bromley suggests that teachers have students collect items that reinforce stereotypes in our own culture, such as advertisements. Students can discuss how well (or how poorly) advertisements represent the people of the culture and thus can begin to understand how stereotypes originate, how they persist, and why they are so difficult to dispel. Another suggestion she makes is to have students read target-language articles that present counter-examples to specific stereotypes, having students note those things that support or don't support a commonly-held view. An activity that can be useful in underlining the problem of stereotyping might best begin with a target-language article about an American phenomenon, since students will probably be most sensitive to stereotypes about their own culture.

Using Proverbs in Teaching Cultural Understanding

Richmond (1987) points out that in many cultures, particularly in Africa, proverbs are a significant part of everyday cultural expression. In sub-Sahara Africa, for example, proverbs are used in court disputes, political discourse, education—literally in every facet of daily life. Because proverbs are so pervasive in these cultures, they can provide significant insights into the way of life of the people. "African proverbs do carry culture-specific messages which must be understood if the language learner is to interact positively with members of the society" (Richmond 1987, p. 214). Richmond points out that in some sub-Saharan cultures, mastery of proverbs is expected among conversational partners, and indeed needs to be considered in judging proficiency levels in these languages. "Here, the concept of proficiency is tied not so much to the structure of the language, but to the appropriate use of the proverb in culturally-specific situations" (p. 215).

Merely collecting proverbs to present to students is not sufficient. According to Richmond, proverbs need to be categorized so that the concepts contained in them can be related accurately to seemingly similar concepts in the students' native language. "It is important to compare the target language proverbs to those found in the native language of the learner, not only to ascertain if similar values are extant across cultures, but also to avoid misinterpretation by the learner, who may see a false resemblance to one found in the native language" (p. 214). Richmond has developed a "Model of Cross-Cultural Proverb Relationships," identifying and analyzing five categories of proverbs. In his category definitions, he gives examples of proverbs from the Mandinka culture of The Gambia, in West Africa:

Category 1—Target language proverb similar in meaning and expression to native-language proverb.

> English: Grass won't grow on a busy street.
>
> Mandinka: Grass will never grow on the street.

Category 2—Target language proverb similar in meaning to native language proverb, but different in expression.

> English: There's no use crying over spilled milk.
>
> Mandinka: When water falls on the ground you can't pick it up.

Category 3—Target language proverb similar in expression to native language proverb, but different in meaning.

> English: Don't lock the barn door after the horse has run away. (alludes to preventative measures)
>
> Mandinka: It is no use to beat the snake's tracks after the snake has gone. (alludes to missed opportunities or inappropriate timing)

Category 4—Proverb not found in native language, but meaning is comprehensible to outsider of target culture.

> English: (No equivalent proverb)
>
> Mandinka: An old man can see farther sitting down than a child can see standing up.

Category 5—Proverb not found in native language; meaning incomprehensible to outsider of target culture.

> English: (No equivalent proverb)
>
> Mandinka: The sword will neither stand on its tip nor lie flat. (indicating a refusal of several options relating to a request) (From Richmond 1987, p. 214)

Richmond's model is useful in that it points out the dangers of presenting cultural material, such as proverbs, in a way that implies that the underlying ideas and allusions are necessarily equivalent. This point further emphasizes one of the principles with which this chapter began: significant cross-cultural understanding can begin to happen only when students become aware that their own view of the world is culturally bound, and that the viewpoint of those in another culture cannot be fully understood until one begins to appreciate the different cultural framework through which they perceive the world.

Humor as a Component of Culture: Exploring Cross-Cultural Differences

Various language educators have advocated the use of cartoons and other forms of humor in language teaching (see, for example, Mollica 1976; Brown 1977; Morain 1991). As we saw earlier in this chapter, Brooks (1968) included humor among the ten basic themes around which culture study should be based. But as Morain (1991) suggests, humor is one of the neglected areas in the foreign language curriculum, perhaps in part because a foreign culture's humor is sometimes difficult to understand. "My students know that people in other cultures eat different foods, speak different languages, and get married, harried, and buried in different ways. But one of the hardest things for them to grasp is that people in other cultures laugh in the special ways their cultures have taught them to laugh" (p. 397).

Morain (1991) describes a study in which the reactions of American and international students were sought to American cartoons appearing in *The New Yorker* in 1990. A content analysis of all the cartoons published that year was done first to identify the kinds of scripts they contained. Morain explains that it is the juxtaposition of two different scripts or frames (types of schemata) that creates the humor, usually by overlapping opposite or incongruous situations (p. 398). She discovered that there were five general areas of culture with which one must be familiar in order to understand the cartoons that were analyzed: (1) *the social world* (including domestic interactions, popular cultural situations and scenes, social expectations associated with stereotypic character types, and the entertainment world); (2) *the working world* (business, government, the professions, as well as miscellaneous jobs of all kinds); (3) *the language world* (including puns, word plays, slang, folk sayings, body language); (4) *the intellectual world* (history, art, music, science, philosophy, religion, etc.); and (5) *any other world* (including visual gags and fantasy).

Morain selected 12 cartoons and assembled them into packets that were presented to both American and international students at the University of Georgia. Findings indicated that American and international students differed in what they found to be humorous in the cartoons. The two groups agreed more on the cartoons that they thought were *not* funny than on those they found humorous. In addition, international students tended to mark a cartoon funny, even when they didn't understand it. Perhaps the most important finding of the study was that a knowledge of the cultural referents in the scripts of the cartoons was essential for understanding and appreciating the humor.

Morain discovered that the international students found humor to be hard to understand, and most said they experienced a sense of isolation and even alienation from the target culture group when humor passed by them (p. 407). She makes several suggestions for incorporating the study of humor into the foreign language curriculum. Teachers should try to (1) provide students with authentic examples of cartoons, jokes, puns, and other forms of humor across all levels of the curriculum; (2) enrich the cultural component of the curriculum by including childhood experiences, which can supply missing cultural referents; (3) teach students about the conventions of humor in the target culture; (4) help students explore the scripts/frames of cartoons and jokes so that they are better equipped to analyze humor; and (5) give students opportunities to share humor from the target culture with one another (pp. 407–08). Giving students a chance to experience the humor of the target culture will not only be a motivating factor in their study of language, but will also benefit them in terms of their sense of integration into the social life of the people with whom they are trying to communicate.

Summary: Teaching for Cultural Understanding

The activities for teaching culture presented in this section are meant to provide a sampling of ideas for the classroom teacher and are not meant to be exhaustive. They represent some of the most common approaches to the teaching of culture that have been proposed since the early 1970s and that have been tried and tested by classroom teachers. Selection of instructional ideas from among these techniques and activity samples should be guided by the level of cultural awareness and sophistication of the students, as well as by their level of linguistic proficiency, especially in the case of those activities that draw on textual materials. Teachers might want to examine their current course texts carefully to see how various themes and pervasive elements of culture are treated and then design activities that can supplement what has already been provided. The theoretical frameworks and inventories in the first part of the chapter can be useful in doing such a thematic analysis of a textbook, and can certainly be worthwhile for teachers or curriculum committees that are engaged in the process of selecting new materials.

As our understanding of cultural proficiency grows, we will no doubt discover some new ways to infuse cultural goals into a proficiency-oriented curriculum. The problem of how to teach culture in a way that truly integrates this important subject matter with language study is one that should receive high priority in the next decade.

Note: A special debt of gratitude is owed to Dr. Vicki Galloway for sharing many of her ideas on the teaching of culture with me. Her valuable input and her careful reading of this chapter are greatly appreciated.

Activities for Review and Discussion

1. Imagine that you were asked to speak to your local board of education in defense of a high school language program that is being eliminated due to budgetary constraints. How would you argue for retention of that program? If you include cultural learning as one of

the important outcomes of language study, how would you argue that a language course is better than a social studies course in this regard? You may want to draw on some of the points made in the beginning of this chapter as you develop your argument.

2. What are some of the difficulties that language teachers encounter when attempting to teach culture? Do you personally have any reservations about teaching culture? What might language teachers and teacher training candidates do to increase their competence in teaching cultural understanding?

3. Review the various definitions, models, and frameworks for teaching culture that are presented in this chapter. Which one(s) do you prefer? What topics would you choose to emphasize or elaborate on in conjunction with the textbook you are currently using? Explain the rationale for your choice.

4. Which of the strategies for teaching culture described in this chapter do you consider most useful for the language classroom? Why do you think these particular strategies might work for you?

5. In a small group, compare your answers to questions 3 and 4 above. Using criteria that the group agrees upon, design an instrument for evaluating the cultural content and learning activities of language textbooks. Your evaluation instrument might take the form of a set of questions, a checklist of features, or both. You may want to include some of the following ideas in your evaluation criteria: (a) the significance and/or relevance of the cultural topics presented, (b) the types of cultural learning goals included in the program, (c) the value of the cultural learning activities accompanying the material, and (d) the integration of cultural learning with language learning.

6. Using the evaluation instrument generated in question 5, examine and critique your current language textbook (or textbooks provided by your instructor). If the textbook seems deficient in its presentation of culture, discuss how it could be changed.

7. Using one of the models provided in this chapter, design a cultural activity for a particular chapter in the language textbook you are using or in a textbook provided by your instructor.

• • • • • • • • • • • • *References*

Allen, Wendy W. "Toward Cultural Proficiency." In A. Omaggio, ed., *Proficiency, Articulation, Curriculum: The Ties that Bind*. Reports of the Northeast Conference on the Teaching of Foreign Languages. Middlebury, VT: Northeast Conference, 1985.

Altman, Rick. "PICS: The Project for International Communication Studies." Pp. 185–92 in W. F. Smith, ed., *Modern Technology in Foreign Language Education: Applications and Projects*. The ACTFL Foreign Language Education Series. Lincolnwood, IL: National Textbook Company, 1989.

"America's Ignorance of Geography Revealed." *ACTFL Public Awareness Network Newsletter* 7, v (September 1988): 1.

Bacon, Susan M. and Michael D. Finnemann. "A Study of the Attitudes, Motives, and Strategies of University Foreign Language Students and Their Disposition to Authentic Oral and Written Input." *The Modern Language Journal* 74, iv (1990): 459–73.

Berwald, Jean-Pierre. "Mass Media and Authentic Documents: Language in Cultural Context." Pp. 89–102 in A. J. Singerman, ed., *Toward a New Integration of Language and Culture.* Reports of the Northeast Conference on the Teaching of Foreign Languages. Middlebury, VT: Northeast Conference, 1988.

Bland, Susan K., James S. Noblitt, Susan Armington, and Geri Gay. "The Naive Lexical Hypothesis: Evidence from Computer-Assisted Language Learning." *The Modern Language Journal* 74, iv (1990): 440–50.

Brière, Eloise, Judith Frommer, and Barbara R. Woshinsky. *Rendez-vous: La France et la francophonie.* New York: Random House, 1982.

Brière, Jean-François, Linda L. Harlow, and Judith A. Muyskens. *Bravo! Culture et litterature.* Boston: Heinle & Heinle Publishers, Inc., 1989.

Brod, Richard and Bettina J. Huber. "Foreign Language Enrollments in United States Institutions of Higher Education, Fall 1990." *ADFL Bulletin* 23, iii (1992): 6–10.

Brooks, Nelson. "Teaching Culture in the Foreign Language Classroom." *Foreign Language Annals* 1 (1968): 204–17.

_____. "A Guest Editorial: Culture—A New Frontier." *Foreign Language Annals* 5 (1971): 54–61.

_____. "The Analysis of Language and Familiar Cultures." In R. C. Lafayette, ed., *The Cultural Revolution.* Reports of the Central States Conference on Foreign Language Education. Lincolnwood, IL: National Textbook Company, 1975.

Brown, James W. "Comics in the Foreign Language Classroom: Pedagogical Perspectives." *Foreign Language Annals* 10 (1977): 18–25.

Burnett, Joanne. Personal communication, 1985.

Burnett, Joanne and Barbara Thompson. Personal communication, 1985.

Byrnes, Heidi. "Reflections on the Development of Cross-Cultural Communicative Competence in the Foreign Language Classroom." Chapter 3 (pp. 205–18) in B. Freed, ed., *Foreign Language Acquisition Research and the Classroom.* Lexington, MA: D.C. Heath and Company, 1991.

Cook, Kathleen. Personal communication, 1985.

Crawford-Lange, Linda, and Dale Lange. "Doing the Unthinkable in the Second-Language Classroom." In T. Higgs, ed., *Teaching for Proficiency, The Organizing Principle.* ACTFL Foreign Language Education Series, vol. 15. Lincolnwood, IL: National Textbook Company, 1984.

Di Donato, Robert. Personal communication cited in Lalande, 1985b.

Draper, Jamie B. *Foreign Language Enrollments in Public Secondary Schools, Fall 1989 and Fall 1990.* U.S. Department of Education, International Research and Studies Program, Grant #P017A00043. Yonkers, NY: ACTFL, 1991.

Ely, Christopher M. "Language Learning Motivation: A Descriptive and Causal Analysis." *The Modern Language Journal* 70, i (1986): 28–35.

Fiedler, Fred E., Terence Mitchell, and Harry C. Triandis. "The Culture Assimilator: An Approach to Cross-Cultural Training." *Journal of Applied Psychology* 55 (1971): 95–102.

Galloway, Vicki B. *Communicating in a Cultural Context: The Global Perspective.* Proceedings of the 1981 Summer Cross-Cultural Workshop for Foreign Language Teachers. Columbia, SC: South Carolina State Department of Education, 1981.

———. "Communicating in a Cultural Context." *ACTFL Master Lecture Series.* Monterey, CA: Defense Language Institute, 1984.

———. "Communicating in a Cultural Context." Workshop given at the Northeast Conference Winter Workshop, Wakefield, MA, 1985a.

———. "A Design for the Improvement of the Teaching of Culture in Foreign Language Classrooms." ACTFL project proposal, 1985b.

———. "Toward a Cultural Reading of Authentic Texts." Pp. 87–121 in H. Byrnes, ed., *Languages for a Multicultural World in Transition.* Reports of the Northeast Conference on the Teaching of Foreign Languages. Lincolnwood, IL: National Textbook Company, 1992.

García, Carmen. "Using Authentic Reading Texts to Discover Underlying Socio-cultural Information." *Foreign Language Annals* 24, vi (1991): 515–26.

Hague, Sally A. "Vocabulary Instruction: What L2 can Learn from L1." *Foreign Language Annals* 20, iii (1987): 217–25.

Hall, Edward T. *The Silent Language.* New York: Doubleday, 1959.

Hanvey, Robert. "Cross-Cultural Awareness." In E. C. Smith and L. F. Luce, eds., *Toward Internationalism: Readings in Cross-Cultural Communication.* Rowley, MA: Newbury House, 1979.

Heusinkveld, Paula R. "The Foreign Language Classroom: A Forum for Under-standing Cultural Stereotypes." *Foreign Language Annals* 18 (1985): 321–25.

Higgs, Theodore V. "Some Pre-Methodological Considerations in Foreign Language Teaching." *The Modern Language Journal* 63, vii (1979): 335–42.

Jarvis, Donald K. "Making Cross-Cultural Connections." In J. K. Phillips, ed., *The Language Connection: From the Classroom to the World.* ACTFL Foreign Language Education Series, vol. 9. Lincolnwood, IL: National Textbook Company, 1977.

Johnson, Dale and P. David Pearson. *Teaching Reading Vocabulary.* New York: Holt, Rinehart, and Winston, 1978.

Jorstad, Helen. "Inservice Teacher Education: Content and Process." In *Proceedings of the National Conference on Professional Priorities.* Hastings-on-Hudson, NY: ACTFL, 1981.

Kluckhohn, Florence R. and Fred I. Strodtbeck. *Variations in Value Orientations.* Evanston, IL: Row, Peterson, 1961; rpt. Westport, CT; Greenwood, 1976. [cited in Ortuño, 1991]

Kohls, L. Robert. *Survival Kit for Overseas Living.* 2nd ed. Yarmouth, ME: Intercultural, 1984. [cited in Ortuño, 1991]

Kramsch, Claire J. "Culture and Constructs: Communicating Attitudes and Values in the Foreign Language Classroom." *Foreign Language Annals* 16, vi (1983): 437–48.

Lafayette, Robert. *Teaching Culture: Strategies and Techniques.* Language in Education: Theory and Practice Series, no. 11. Washington, DC: Center for Applied Linguistics, 1978.

———. "Integrating the Teaching of Culture into the Foreign Language Classroom." Pp. 47–62 in A. J. Singerman, ed., *Toward a New Integration of Language and Culture.* Reports of the The Northeast Conference on the Teaching of Foreign Languages. Middlebury, VT: Northeast Conference, 1988.

Lafayette, Robert and Renate Schulz. "Evaluating Cultural Learnings." In R. C. Lafayette, ed., *The Cultural Revolution in Foreign Languages: A Guide for Building the Modern Curriculum.* Lincolnwood, IL: National Textbook Company, 1975.

Lafayette, Robert and L. Strasheim. "Foreign Language Curricula and Materials for the Twenty-First Century." In *Proceedings of the National Conference on Professional Priorities.* Hastings-on-Hudson, NY: ACTFL, 1981.

Lalande, John. "The Quasi-Business Letter: Passport to Foreign Culture." *The Modern Language Journal* 63 (1979): 17–20.

_____. "Teaching German Culture in the German Language Classroom: Toward Achieving a Balanced Perspective." *Schatzkammer* 11, ii (1985a): 70–80.

_____. "Making a Connection: Telephone Books, Culture and Language Instruction." *Die Unterrichtspraxis* 18 (1985b): 313–18.

_____. Personal communication, 1993.

Lett, John. "Basic Mechanisms for Presenting Culture." Workshop handout, presented at Indiana State University, March 1977.

Mantle-Bromley, Corinne. "Preparing Students for Meaningful Culture Learning." *Foreign Language Annals* 25, ii (1992): 117–27.

Meade, B. and G. Morain. "The Culture Cluster." *Foreign Language Annals* 6 (1973): 331–38.

Miller, J. D. and M. Loiseau. *USA—France: Culture Capsules.* Rowley, MA: Newbury House, 1974.

Mollica, Anthony. "Cartoons in the Language Classroom." *Canadian Modern Language Review* 32 (1976): 424–44.

Moorjani, Angela and Thomas T. Field. "Semiotic and Scoiolinguistic Paths to Understanding Culture." Pp. 25–45 in A. J. Singerman, ed., *Toward a New Integration of Language and Culture.* Reports of the Northeast Conference on the Teaching of Foreign Languages. Middlebury, VT: Northeast Conference, 1988.

Morain, Genelle G. "X-raying the International Funny Bone: A Study Exploring Differences in the Perception of Humor Across Cultures." Pp. 397–408 in J. A. Alatis, ed., *Linguistics and Language Pedagogy: The State of the Art.* Georgetown University Round Table on Languages and Linguistics 1991. Washington, DC: Georgetown University Press, 1991.

Morello, Joseph. "Attitudes of Students of French Toward Required Language Study." *Foreign Language Annals* 21, v (1988): 435–42.

Muyskens, Judith, Alice Omaggio, Claudine Chalmers, Claudette Imberton, and Paul Amaras. *Rendez-vous.* New York: Random House, 1982, 1986.

Muyskens, Judith, Alice Omaggio Hadley, and Claudine Chalmers. *Rendez-vous,* 3rd ed. New York: McGraw-Hill, 1990.

Nostrand, Howard L. *Background Data for the Teaching of French. Part A: La culture et la société françaises au XXe siècle.* Seattle: University of Washington, 1967.

_____. "Empathy for a Second Culture: Motivations and Techniques." In G. A. Jarvis, ed., *Responding to New Realities.* ACTFL Foreign Language Education Series, vol. 5. Lincolnwood, IL: National Textbook Company, 1974.

_____. "The Beginning Teacher's Cultural Competence: Goal and Strategy." *Foreign Language Annals* 22, ii (1989): 189–93.

Nostrand, Howard L. and Frances Nostrand. "Culture-Wide Values and Assumptions as Essential Content for Levels I to III." In C. J. and P. Castle, eds., *French Language Education: The Teaching of Culture in the Classroom.* Springfield, IL: Illinois Title III, NDEA, 1971.

Ortuño, Marian M. "Cross-Cultural Awareness in the Foreign Language Class: The Kluckhohn Model." *The Modern Language Journal* 75, iv (1991): 449–59.

Patrikis, Peter. "Language and Culture at the Crossroads." Pp. 13–24 in A. J. Singerman, ed., *Toward a New Integration of Language and Culture*. Reports of the Northeast Conference on the Teaching of Foreign Languages. Middlebury, VT: Northeast Conference, 1988.

Richmond, Edmun B. "Utilizing Proverbs as a Focal Point to Cultural Awareness and Communicative Competence: Illustrations from Africa." *Foreign Language Annals* 20, iii (1987): 213–16.

Roberts, Linda P. "Attitudes of Entering University Freshmen toward Foreign Language Study: A Descriptive Analysis." *The Modern Language Journal* 76, iii (1992): 275–83.

Rosser, Harry. *Mosaico Cultural: Images from Spanish Speaking Cultures*. (video) Heinle & Heinle Publishers, 1992.

Scanlan, Timothy. "Looking up French Language and Culture in the Paris *Pages Jaunes*." *The French Review* 59 (1986): 355–88.

Seelye, H. Ned. *Teaching Culture: Strategies for Intercultural Communication*. Lincolnwood, IL: National Textbook Company, 1974, 1984.

Singerman, Alan J., ed. *Toward a New Integration of Language and Culture*. Reports of the Northeast Conference on the Teaching of Foreign Languages. Middlebury, VT: Northeast Conference, 1988.

Simon, Paul. *The Tongue-Tied American*. New York: Continuum, 1980.

_____. "Priority: Public Relations. A Decade of Change to a Decade of Challenge." *Foreign Language Annals* 24, i (1991): 13–18.

Smith, William Flint, ed. *Modern Media in Foreign Language Education: Theory and Implementation*. The ACTFL Foreign Language Education Series. Lincolnwood, IL: National Textbook Company, 1987.

_____. *Modern Technology in Foreign Language Education: Applications and Projects*. The ACTFL Foreign Language Education Series. Lincolnwood, IL: National Textbook Company, 1989.

Spinelli, Emily and H. Jay Siskin. "Selecting, Presenting, and Practicing Vocabulary in a Culturally-Authentic Context." *Foreign Language Annals* 25, iv (1992): 305–15.

Stern, H. H. "Directions in Foreign Language Curriculum Development." In *Proceedings of the National Conference on Professional Priorities*. Hastings-on-Hudson, NY: ACTFL, 1981.

_____. "Toward a Multidimensional Foreign Language Curriculum." In R. Mead, ed., *Foreign Languages: Key Links in the Chain of Learning*. Reports of the Northeast Conference on the Teaching of Foreign Languages. Middlebury, VT: Northeast Conference, 1983.

Strasheim, Lorraine. "Establishing a Professional Agenda for Integrating Culture into K-12 Foreign Languages: An Editorial." *The Modern Language Journal* 65 (1981): 67–69.

Taylor, H. D. and J. Sorenson. "Culture Capsules." *The Modern Language Journal* 45 (1961): 350–54.

Tedlock, D. *The Spoken Word and the Work of Interpretation*. Philadelphia, University of Pennsylvania Press, 1983. [Cited in Moorjani and Field, 1988.]

9

Classroom Testing

Introduction

The language teaching profession has made enormous strides in the past fifteen years in developing better proficiency tests that will allow us to measure our students' general communicative competence, especially in oral skills. During the 1980s alone, over 2,000 language teachers in both commonly and uncommonly taught languages have obtained training in administering oral tests and rating student speech samples using the ACTFL Oral Proficiency Interview (Stansfield and Kenyon 1992). In the mid-1980s, ACTFL undertook a project to develop prototypes of computer-adaptive tests of reading and listening proficiency (Dandonoli 1987), and a few universities are currently using a full battery of proficiency tests based on the *ACTFL Proficiency Guidelines* for entrance and/or graduation requirements (see, for example, Freed 1984, 1987; Barnes, Klee, and Wakefield 1991).

Dandonoli (1987) points out that proficiency tests are appropriate for measuring general progress in the acquisition of language skills, although they should not be used *per se* as classroom achievement tests because they are not meant to sample from a particular course syllabus. The distinction between *proficiency* tests and *achievement* tests relates, in part, to the domain of material being tested and the testing purpose. *Proficiency tests* are used to measure an individual's general competence in a second language, independent of any particular curriculum or course of study. *Achievement tests,* on the other hand, are used to evaluate students' acquisition of certain specified course content, generally for diagnostic purposes. Strictly speaking, a valid achievement test will only test material that has been "covered" during the course of instruction (Clark 1972). This is not to say, however, that there can be no relationship between proficiency testing and classroom achievement testing. Classroom tests can be designed so that they reflect proficiency goals, presenting language in context and requiring students to use the language beyond the sentence level to carry out realistic tasks. When properly constructed, classroom tests can thus sample course material in a manner that is consistent with the principles of

412 •

proficiency testing, while limiting the domain of content to be tested to the material that has been indicated on the course syllabus. Dandonoli maintains that while general proficiency tests should not be used in lieu of classroom tests for the purposes of assigning course grades, they can be quite appropriately used for entrance or graduation requirements, "providing the requirements are stated appropriately and relate to the curriculum content instructional goals" (p. 78).

Although the first attempts to move from a language requirement based on "seat time" to one based on proficiency have met with some problems, there is little question that such a move makes very good sense. The impact of this type of policy change has been multifaceted. Freed (1984) reports on the effects of instituting a proficiency-based language requirement in various language departments at the University of Pennsylvania, beginning in the fall of 1981. The change from a time-based requirement to one based on proficiency, as measured by a battery of exit tests in all skill areas, has had a strong impact on the faculty, teaching assistants (including their training and attitudes), curriculum (methods and materials), and students (test results, attitudes, and motivation). In general, the effects have been very positive, leading to a greater focus on functional language proficiency, better articulation between and among classes, more innovative and diversified teaching strategies and materials, and more involvement of faculty from upper-level courses in the beginning language program. Freed also reports some negative effects, particularly in terms of an increased work load for teaching staff (especially in scheduling, administering, and scoring exams and in managing the details of the testing program); also, some students reported that they experienced considerable anxiety about the exit tests, although in retrospect most students stated that they found the idea of taking the exam far worse than the experience itself (p. 224). Barnes, Klee, and Wakefield (1991) report a decided change in students' attitudes and motivation in the classroom as the result of proficiency-based requirements at the University of Minnesota. Specifically, they are seeing an increased interest in completing more language study in high school in order to place into second-year college courses and an increase in the efforts students are making in their language classes at the university. This latter trend is a direct result of a proficiency-based graduation requirement, since students realize that they will have to demonstrate a certain level of functional language ability in order to pass the Graduation Proficiency Test: "It is no longer adequate to slide by with a low C and a minimum of effort; students are very conscious of the fact that passing the courses is no longer sufficient to complete their degree requirements" (Barnes, Klee, and Wakefield 1991, p. 64).

There is no doubt that the focus on proficiency has had a strong effect on classroom instruction and materials development in the past decade.

Classroom goals in all skill areas are increasingly articulated in communicative and functional terms. Foreign language textbooks are including more communicative activities, authentic materials, and culturally based lesson content than ever before. Yet how are classroom testing practices changing in response to this focus on proficiency? The fact that students can pass language courses, presumably by performing satisfactorily on classroom achievement tests, and still not pass a graduation proficiency test indicates that there might be an incongruence between the stated goals of the course and the ways in which those goals are typically assessed.

Magnan (1991) maintains that classroom tests today are still largely focused on discrete points of grammar and mastery of isolated components of knowledge and skill. Despite the fact that the profession has been advocating communicative language teaching practices for over twenty years, many teachers' testing practices have remained fairly constant, if only for expediency's sake. She attributes the lack of discourse-driven, functional language testing to three main causes: "(1) students or teachers may prefer more familiar discrete-point testing (Bacon and Finneman 1990), as it may seem more straightforward and hence more accessible and objective; (2) teachers may find it difficult and time-consuming to design and grade discourse-based and functional tests; and (3) the profession has not yet developed a widely accepted, practical model of what communicative testing should entail" (p. 136).

This conservative stance in language testing results in an ever-widening gap between the description of course goals—often in terms of proficiency statements—and their measurement. Such a gap can quite easily counterbalance the effects of curricular innovations because students interpret the underlying goals of instruction by looking at the classroom tests they take. As Valette pointed out in 1978, "the content of the tests and the method by which grades are assigned reflects more accurately than any lengthy statement of aims and purposes the real objectives of instruction" (p. 90).

Illustration 9.1 provides a sample excerpt from a decontextualized, discrete-point test that is representative of the type of traditional classroom achievement tests that can still be found in many classrooms today. Of the five-part criteria used in proficiency testing—global tasks/functions, context, content, accuracy, and type of discourse—only one (accuracy) is represented to any extent on this exam. Functional considerations are clearly absent, as students are required to fill in blanks with pieces of discourse for no other purpose than to prove that they know how they work. Items are presented in single-sentence frames, out of context, rendering the content of the test virtually meaningless. There is no evidence of a concern for sociolinguistic considerations, and in the absence of continuous discourse beyond the sentence level, no opportunity to test discourse competence in any fashion whatsoever.

Illustration 9.1

Typical grammar test items

A. Fill in the blanks with the preposition *à* or *de* where necessary. (10 points)
   1. Je ne regrette pas _____ être étudiant à cette université.
   2. Il n'a pas commencé _____ apprendre un métier.
   3. Mon prof m'a conseillé _____ venir en classe tous les jours.
   4. Je déteste _____ l'été parce qu'il fait trop chaud.
   Etc.

B. Complete the translations. (6 points)
   1. _____, on exprime ses opinions. *By voting, one expresses one's opinion.*
   2. Hier, ils ont acheté _____. *Yesterday, they bought an interesting book.*
   3. Mon père nous a raconté _____. *My father told us a shocking story.*
   4. _____ est un droit. *Voting is a right.*

C. Fill in the blanks with the correct form of the subjunctive of the verb indicated. (25 points)
   1. Il faut qu'ils _____ me voir.
      (venir)
   2. Il est possible que je _____ à la maison ce soir.
      (être)
   3. Il est possible que nous _____ de l'argent.
      (avoir)
   Etc.

D. Substitutions. Replace the underlined words with the words in parentheses and make all necessary changes (20 points)
   1. D'habitude, je me levais à 7 heures. (hier)
   2. Vous recevez de jolis cadeaux. (tu)
   Etc.

A. 1. I do not regret _____ being a student at this university.
   2. He has not begun _____ learn a trade.
   3. My professor advised me _____ come to class every day.
   4. I hate _____ summer because it's too hot.

C. 1. It's necessary that they _____ see me. (to come)
   2. It is possible that I _____ at home this evening. (to be)
   3. It is possible that we _____ some money. (to have)

D. 1. Usually, I got up at 7:00. (yesterday)
   2. You receive pretty gifts. (you, familiar form)

Source: Omaggio 1983.

One might argue that the *individual* test sentences do have meaningful content. Yet research by Hosenfeld (1976) has revealed that students do not even have to process the meaning of the individual sentences on the test to do the tasks that are required of them. Many students have learned to "short-circuit" grammatical exercises of this type, a fact that contributes further to the impression that success on language tests involves learning a few grammatical "tricks" rather than processing language for some authentic purpose. In the case of the test items in Illustration 9.1, students would have engaged in much the same processing had the teacher asked them to do the following:

Part A: Indicate what preposition, *à* or *de*, is used after the following verbs:

1. regretter _____   3. conseiller _____

2. commencer _____   4. détester _____

Part B: Translate the following expressions:

1. by voting
2. an interesting book
3. a shocking story
4. voting

Part C: Give the subjunctive for the following verbs:

1. venir (ils)
2. être (je)
3. avoir (nous)
Etc.

This version of the exam is far easier to create than the one in Illustration 9.1, since the teacher has no need to invent sentences in which to embed the discrete points of grammar and vocabulary that are really being tested. Yet such a test hardly represents real language use and even further widens the gap between course goals and testing procedures in the classroom.

In this chapter, alternative formats for classroom achievement testing will be suggested based on many of the previously discussed principles for designing language-practice activities. These formats are suggested as a possible starting point for revising classroom tests to reflect language proficiency goals more directly. One basic principle to be observed throughout the discussion is that classroom tests, like general proficiency tests, should focus not only on the accuracy of the learners' language, but also on language use in context for particular purposes. This can best be achieved by presenting test items in discourse-length frames that resemble natural language. Only then will success on course-specific achievement tests relate in any direct way to improvement in absolute proficiency.

The item formats to be discussed in the next sections are, therefore, proficiency-oriented, yet they still retain some of the characteristics of achievement tests. Because classroom tests are constructed to elicit those aspects of language that have been the object of recent study in class, they tend to be more *limited in scope* than are proficiency tests. By providing the teacher and students with feedback about the mastery of specific material learned during the course of instruction, they constitute *formative evaluation*—a type of evaluation that enables teachers to alter instruction in progress to better address the needs of the learners. Proficiency tests, on the other hand, are *summative evaluation* measures in that they characterize the language abilities of individuals at a given point in time without regard to a specific course of instruction. Clearly, both types of measures are useful in providing feedback to second language learners, and the classroom teacher needs to be aware of the characteristics of both kinds of tests and the situations for which they are most appropriate.

The Case for Hybrid Classroom Tests

In order to revise our traditional classroom tests to make them more oriented towards communicative goals, it is not enough to simply add a few "global" or "communicative" items to the basic instrument represented in Illustration 9.1. Nor can we satisfy our testing needs by periodically administering a few proficiency-type tests in speaking, listening, reading, or writing and somehow averaging those results into a final course grade. An additive approach such as this may only serve to reconfirm the students' hypothesis that learning the vocabulary, phonology, morphology, and syntax of the language is one thing and learning to communicate with those features is quite another.

In this chapter, a hybrid approach to test design is suggested in which specific lexical, grammatical, sociolinguistic, and discourse features being treated in a curricular sequence are tested *as they operate in naturalistic contexts*. This means that there is little place for single-sentence items on course exams or quizzes. Rather, language use must be tested beyond the level of the sentence, a point that Wesche (1981) considers essential in communicative language testing:

> Language testing which does not take into account propositional and illocutionary development beyond the sentence level, as well as the interaction between language behavior and real-world phenomena, is at best getting at only a part of communicative competence. Small wonder that we often find that a student's success at second-language classroom exercises and tests appears to bear little relationship to his or her ability to use the language effectively in a real-world situation (pp. 552–53).

Because natural language *always* occurs in both a discourse context and an extralinguistic, situational context, it makes sense, just in terms of face validity, to give tests that embed the second language features to be tested in situational formats. In addition, students are more motivated when language-learning materials seem relevant to their communicative needs and interests and resemble authentic language use. Shohamy (1982) found that students had a favorable attitude toward oral interviews, for example, for this reason.

Working on the premise that contextualized testing is both preferable and necessary in a proficiency-oriented approach, it is clear that alternatives must be found for the single-sentence formats typically used on achievement tests. Teachers still need to be concerned, however, that their test instruments enable them to analyze students' performance in terms of specific course objectives; that is, the specific grammar, vocabulary, and cultural items treated in a given unit of study need to be *elicited* directly on the test instrument in order to provide diagnostic information on mastery of the material. A test instrument that elicits strictly open-ended responses to questions may not provide the type of targeted feedback teachers need in this regard. The skill, then, to be mastered in designing achievement tests is to create an examination that will require students both to show how well they can use specified features of the language, and to demonstrate that they understand how such features function within naturalistic discourse.

The hybrid test attempts to do this by "artfully combining grammar and context, structure and situation" (Slager 1978, p. 74). A blend of open-ended, or divergent, responses with specific, convergent items seems preferable when testing a given unit of material. Some sections of the test, for example, can focus on discrete points of grammar, vocabulary, discourse or pragmatic features while other sections allow students to respond more freely, using whatever language they know to complete the task. In the light of the insights of Tarone (1983) and Ellis (1985, 1990) regarding the variable competence of learners, such a blend of testing strategies is further supported. If, for example, it is true that student performance varies depending on the degree of attention paid to form and the nature of the language task in which students are engaged, a testing program that elicits samples of students' work using a variety of formats and task requirements will be more revealing, as well as more representative of their true underlying competence.

In addition to administering proficiency-based achievement tests and quizzes of a formal nature, teachers can broaden the range of assessment procedures to include collections of students' work in portfolios (Shohamy 1991; Magnan 1991), samples of oral performance taken during classroom communicative activities, exposés on various topics, including cultural information, and videotaped or audiotaped role-plays or skits. In this way, teachers can determine how well students have synthesized a wide range of material at various junctures along the course of instruction. It also makes sense for teachers to schedule an oral interview or other summative measure at the end of a given course or course sequence to determine the students' overall level of competence. The information gleaned from such summative tests can be of use in program evaluation and in improving articulation, both horizontally and vertically, i.e., between and among curricular offerings.

The following section presents some of the characteristics of test items and formats for classroom quizzes and tests, which constitute the focus of this chapter. The remaining sections of the chapter present samples of testing formats derived from the activity types discussed in Chapters 5 through 8, as well as ways to facilitate the test creation process.

Characteristics of Test Items and Item Types

A classification of test items along the two dimensions depicted in Illustration 9.2 enables us to make useful comparisons and contrasts when considering the characteristics of traditional achievement test items and those to be proposed in the following pages.

The vertical axis represents a continuum relating to the naturalness or authenticity of the language used on the test. Items that would fall along the upper portion of the continuum would consist of drill-like, "textbook" language that bears little resemblance to genuine language use; those items falling along the lower portion would be excerpted from natural discourse or would approximate authentic communicative exchanges. If one considers the typical achievement test in Illustration 9.1, for example, the series of single-sentence frames that show no logical relationship to one another represent a rather stilted, "textbook" approach to language use and would therefore fall close to the upper end of the vertical axis. If, on the other hand, the test items had been derived from natural discourse, with each sentence following the others in a logical progression, they would have fallen within the lower portions of the continuum.

The horizontal axis in Illustration 9.2 represents the degree of specificity of the test items, ranging from those on the left that require the most convergent, or discrete-point, answers to those on the right that require more global comprehension and/or divergent responses. A few examples should serve to clarify this distinction. Suppose the teacher wanted to test the students' control of past-tense narration in the second language. One of the discrete features necessary in narration might be past-tense verb forms; another feature that might be tested could be the use of adverbial connectors, time expressions, and the like. The teacher might construct several test-item formats to determine how well students can handle the function of narration, ranging from formats in which specific linguistic or lexical features are elicited to those in which free response is encouraged. If, for example, a cloze passage were constructed in which specific parts of speech, such as verbs in the past tense, were deleted, and students were asked to fill in the gaps of the passage using a set of vocabulary cues, then the item format would fall along the left-hand portion of the horizontal axis. If, on the other hand, the teacher asked students to write a brief paragraph recounting what they did last weekend, reminding them to use

Illustration 9.2
Schema for assessing
characteristics of
test items

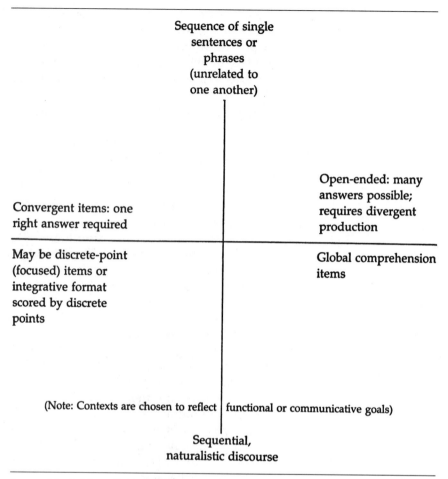

Sequence of single
sentences or
phrases
(unrelated to
one another)

Open-ended: many
answers possible;
requires divergent
production

Convergent items: one
right answer required

May be discrete-point
(focused) items or
integrative format
scored by discrete
points

Global comprehension
items

(Note: Contexts are chosen to reflect functional or communicative goals)

Sequential,
naturalistic discourse

Source: Adapted from Omaggio 1983.

appropriate past tenses in their narration, the item format would fall along
the right-hand portion of the continuum. Note that the latter testing format, although global in nature, could be *scored* in either a global fashion or
in a discrete-point fashion; that is, points could be awarded for the comprehensibility and quality of the communication in a general sense, or they
could be awarded for particular features of the message (such as the
appropriate use of tense and the correct forms of the verbs). A scoring
scheme that awards credit for both the general comprehensibility of the
answer and specific discrete features is another viable option.

It is probably best to construct classroom tests that include items
from various points along the horizontal axis, since this represents a
blend of communicative and linguistic concerns. All of the test items,

however, should fall within the lower ranges of the vertical axis if the test is to represent natural language use. The bottom two quadrants of the schema, then, are the province of proficiency-oriented classroom testing. Contexts for test items should be chosen to reflect the themes of the lessons or units under study, as well as a variety of functional and communicative purposes.

Consider again the traditional test items in Illustration 9.1. It is clear that virtually all of the sample items are enclosed within the upper left-hand quadrant of the schema represented in Illustration 9.2. If the whole test could thus be characterized, it would not reflect real language use to any extent. Students are not asked to synthesize the bits and pieces of language they have been learning for any real-world purpose, and the testing program, therefore, misses the mark entirely, regardless of what the programmatic goals statements might be.

In the next three sections, various formats for testing listening, reading, and writing skills, both separately and in an integrative fashion, are illustrated, along with suggestions for grading these kinds of items.

Listening Comprehension Formats

The diagram in Illustration 9.3 shows how a variety of listening comprehension formats might fall along the horizontal axis of the schema presented earlier for test-item classification. These are only a few of the formats that could be developed using the basic listening comprehension activity types described for Novice, Intermediate, Advanced, and Superior levels in Chapter 5 (see pp. 170–95).

The teacher, in designing the listening portion of a unit exam, might want to include items from several points along the continuum. For learners who are in the Novice and/or Intermediate ranges, for example, a short passage might be read describing a visual of some type and students might be asked to identify various pictured items as they hear them mentioned. This section can be scored in a discrete-point fashion, with points awarded for each item correctly identified. A more global, integrative listening passage might require students to listen to a set of directions and follow a map, tracing a route with their pencils as the directions are given. If there is not enough time to do both kinds of items, the teacher may want to use one type on one exam and switch to the other type for the next exam. Another alternative would be to give students a test that includes one pure listening comprehension section and one section in which listening is combined with another skill (such as writing) in a mixed format.

The next section examines some sample test items for listening comprehension, arranged from the most discrete-point types to the most global formats.

Illustration 9.3
Positions of
sample listening
comprehension
formats on the
assessment schema

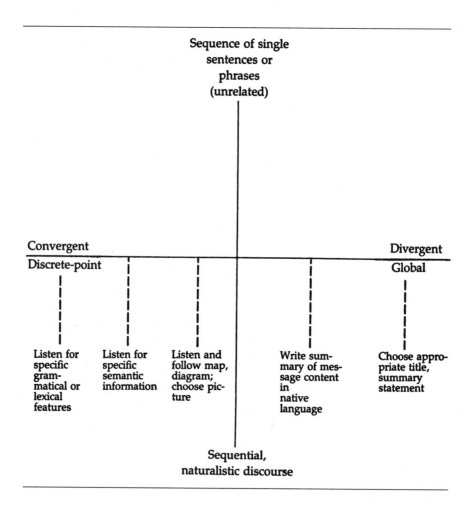

Sequence of single
sentences or
phrases
(unrelated)

Convergent

Discrete-point

Divergent

Global

| Listen for specific grammatical or lexical features | Listen for specific semantic information | Listen and follow map, diagram; choose picture | Write summary of message content in native language | Choose appropriate title, summary statement |

Sequential,
naturalistic discourse

Listening for Specific Grammatical or Lexical Features

In this type of listening item, a passage is read and students are required to listen for specific lexical or grammatical features embedded in the selection. Students might be asked, for example, to listen for cues to tense, gender, or number. If the embedded cues are lexical, they might be asked to listen for numbers, colors, objects in a room, parts of the body, foods, or items in some other lexical category.

In presenting the listening items, the short passage or conversational exchange is read or played on tape once. For Novice or Intermediate listeners, the sentences might then be read more slowly a second time, one by one, with pauses inserted to allow time for writing answers.

Although the following tasks require listening for discrete features of the discourse, the fact that students are hearing a passage in context means that the results might be somewhat less diagnostic than if the passage were not contextualized. This is due to the fact that natural language is redundant and thus often provides multiple cues to meaning. If students are listening for cues to tense, for example, they might well use nonmorphological information, such as time words or overall situational constraints in the passage that would not be available in a single-sentence format. However, the contextualized format has the advantage of encouraging students to derive meaning from all of the available cues, both contextual and structural—a skill that is of great value in processing natural language outside of the classroom context.

Sample 1 (Novice)
Listening for numbers

Context A radio sports broadcast

Function Listening for specific information

Student Task Students listen to a simulated sports broadcast in which the starting line-up of a women's basketball game is being announced. As they listen, they place the number of the player next to her name.

El equipo argentino de baloncesto. The next broadcast is a championship game between the Mexican and the Argentine National Women's Basketball teams. As you hear the starting line-up for the Argentine team, write down the number (numeral 1, 2, etc.) of each player so you can keep track of the points each makes throughout the game. There will be no "instant replay" of the line-up, but you will hear each number twice within the announcement. (5 points)

_____ Margarita López	_____ Elsa Statzner
_____ Silvia Murphy	_____ Ana Paredes
_____ Beatriz Olivencia	

Passage Ahora, les presentamos al Equipo Femenino de Baloncesto de Argentina. Aquí tenemos el número 5, Beatriz Olivencia. Beatriz Olivencia, el número 5 es de Mendoza. De Buenos Aires viene el número 10, Ana Paredes, número 10, Ana Paredes de Buenos Aires. También de la capital viene Silvia Murphy, número 13, número 13 Silvia Murphy de la capital, Buenos Aires. Y de Córdoba viene el número 20, Elsa Statzner, La Srta. Statzner, el número 20. Y de Barriloche viene la fantástica Margarita López, número 35. Sí señores, la famosísima Margarita López, el número 35.

Translation Now let's bring out the Women's Basketball Team from Argentina. Here we have number 5, Beatrice Olivencia. Beatrice Olivencia, number 5, is from Mendoza. From Buenos Aires comes number 10, Ana Paredes, number 10, Ana Paredes from Buenos Aires. Also from the capital comes Silvia

Murphy, number 13. Number 13, Silvia Murphy from the capital, Buenos Aires. And from Córdoba comes number 20, Elsa Statzner, Ms. Statzner, number 20. And from Barriloche comes the fantastic Margarita López, number 35. Yes, fans, the famous Margarita López, number 35.

Source: McMillen Villar and Meuser Blincow 1993.

Sample 2 (Novice)
Recognizing vocabulary in context

Context   Advertising

Function   Recognizing relevant items in a radio advertisement

Student Task   Students imagine that their host family in Guadalajara has decided to buy a larger house and has made a list of items they need to buy to furnish it. As they listen to the test passage, students are directed to check off the items mentioned in the ad that are on the family's list.

todo en venta

_____	una alfombra
_____	una cafetera
_____	una cama
_____	un estante
_____	una lavadora
_____	un lavaplatos
_____	unos sillónes
_____	un sofá

¡QUÉ OFERTAS!

Passage   Liquidación de muebles este fin de semana. Vendemos todo a la mitad del precio, ¡y menos! Tenemos camas, armarios, y cómodas. Hay juegos de muebles de dormitorio para niños, para niñas y para adultos. Sí, tenemos juegos de dormitorio para toda la familia desde un millón de pesos. Para su sala tenemos 150 sofás, y 200 sillónes de todos los colores y gustos.

Cómpre una mesa para el comedor, y otra para la cocina. Con una visita a Muebles San Miguel, se puede decorar toda la casa. Vendemos alfombras, lámparas, y todo tipo de cuadros a precios imposibles de creer. Visítenos en Muebles San Miguel este fin de semana en la Plaza Tapatía.

Translation   Furniture sale this weekend! We're selling everything at half price, and less! We have beds, armoires, and dressers. There are bedroom sets for boys, for girls and for adults. Yes, we have bedroom sets for the whole family from $300. For your living room, 150 sofas and 200 easy chairs in all colors and styles. Buy a table for the dining room, and another for the kitchen. With one visit to San Miguel Furniture you can decorate your whole house. We're selling area rugs, lamps and all kinds of paintings at hard-to-believe prices. Visit us at San Miguel Furniture this weekend in Tapatía Plaza.

una alfombra = area rug
una cafetera = coffee maker
una cama = bed
un estante = book shelf
una lavadora = washing machine
un lavaplatos = dishwasher
unos sillónes = easy chairs
un sofá = sofa

Source: McMillen Villar and Meuser Blincow 1993.

Sample 3 (Intermediate)
Listening for cues to tense

Context   End-of-semester activities

Function   Understanding simple narration of events

Student Task   Students listen to a series of statements about the end-of-semester activities of several students. Some of the students have finished certain tasks; others are planning to do things that still need to be done. Students are asked to indicate on their test papers whether the activity described constitutes something the student (1) will do or (2) has done already.

Example: As you listen to the activities of various students at the end of the semester, indicate whether the activity is something they *will do* or something they *have already done*:

	WILL DO	HAVE DONE
1.	[ ]	[ ]
2.	[ ]	[ ]
3.	[ ]	[ ]
4.	[ ]	[ ]
5.	[ ]	[ ]

Passage
1. Jean-Michel vient de passer l'après-midi à la bibliothèque.
2. Son camarade Etienne étudiera la plupart du week-end chez ses parents.
3. Margarite a déjà passé son examen de chimie à l'amphithéâtre.
4. Karim et Salima feront leurs exposés le dernier jour de classe.
5. Suzanne compte partir samedi matin après son examen de maths.

1. *Jean-Michel has just spent the afternoon at the library.*
2. *His friend Etienne will study most of the weekend at his parents' house.*
3. *Margarite already took her chemistry exam in the amphitheater.*
4. *Karim and Salima will present their exposés the last day of class.*
5. *Suzanne is planning on leaving Saturday morning after her math exam.*

Source: Adapted from Terry 1985.

Listening for Specific Semantic Information

In this type of listening item, students extract specific semantic information from a passage. The information requested can consist of details or may involve a synthesis of several cues or the drawing of inferences.

Sample (Intermediate)
Recording semantic detail

Context Student housing

Function Extracting relevant information from a description

Student Task A passage is read in which a student is describing an apartment she has just rented, including information about location, price, number and size of rooms, utilities, etc. Students are told to listen to the passage and fill in the information on the chart below, based on the passage content.

1. Location _____
2. Rent/month _____
3. Number and type of rooms _____
4. Name of roommate _____
5. Furnishings (check one):
   [ ] furnished   [ ] unfurnished
6. Utilities (check one):
   [ ] included   [ ] not included
7. Phone number of landlord _____

Passage Ich bin so glücklich, Mutter, weil meine Wohnung in einer schönen Straße liegt sehr nah zu den Geschäften und nur zwei Blocks von den

Park entfernt. Und sie kostet nur DM 640 im Monat! Anna wird sie mit mir teilen. Dafür können wir die Miete und andere Kosten teilen. Wir haben zwei Schlafzimmer, eine kleine Küche und ein kleines Wohnzimmer, aber es ist sehr hell. Ich habe sie gern. Anna bringt ihre eigenen Möbel, und ich habe ein Bett, ein Tisch und alles, und so können wir nächsten Dienstag einziehen. Wenn du mich anrufen willst, sollst du die Hauswirtin anrufen. Ihre Nummer ist 428985.

Monika is describing her new apartment to her mother on the phone. Listen to the following excerpts from her conversation. As you listen, fill in the chart on your test copy.

I am so lucky, Mom, because the apartment is on a pretty street right near the shops and only two blocks from the park. And it only costs $400 per month! Anna is going to share it with me. That way we can both divide the rent and the utilities. We have two bedrooms and a little kitchen, and a very small living room, but there's lots of light. I really like it! Anna is bringing her own furniture, and I have my bed and desk and everything, so we're ready to move in next Tuesday. If you want to call me then, just call the landlord. Her number is 428985.

Source: Activity format adapted from Omaggio 1983, p. 15.

Listening and Following a Map or Diagram, or Choosing or Completing a Picture

In listening items of this type, students are required to synthesize a series of cues in order to complete a task. They might be asked, for example, to follow a set of directions with a pencilled line on a map. Another map activity might involve filling in the names of stores or other buildings according to a descriptive passage read to them. A set of names might be entered onto a diagram of a family tree, or a room plan might be completed according to a description of the objects in it. Students might be asked to select from a series of similar pictures the one that is described most accurately in detail, or, alternatively, they might be asked to draw a simple sketch from a description. For other ideas of listening activities of this type, see Chapter 5 (pp.183–91).

Comprehension Questions

Classroom teachers and test developers have used conventional formats such as true/false, multiple choice, and completion questions to assess listening comprehension for years. All of us have taken this type of test, so there is little need to elaborate on this technique here. A few comments, however, seem warranted about the use of such questions. If these formats are to be used to test pure listening comprehension, answers should be elicited in the students' native language in order to avoid mixing skills. Questions written on the students' test copies should also be in the native language, unless the teacher wishes to combine reading and listening comprehension in this section of the test. Ideas for mixed-skills formats will be treated later in this chapter for those teachers wishing to test several modalities at once.

When designing comprehension questions for listening passages, teachers should keep in mind the *purposes* for which one might normally be listening to the type of material chosen. For example, when people listen to a news broadcast, they often pay attention to the main ideas of most of the stories and might only listen carefully to details if the story is of special interest to them. Although some instructors may feel that they haven't really tested comprehension unless they create questions relating to all the details of the passage, this kind of comprehensive testing of the facts may not always be the best way to develop listening competence. A more useful comprehension check in the case of the news broadcast example might involve asking a question or two about the global meaning or main ideas of a particular story, and asking detail questions only about those points that would be relatively salient or likely to be retained by native listeners. If, on the other hand, students were listening to a weather report in order to make a decision about what clothes to wear, it might be appropriate to design questions about the details, since they would constitute the most important aspect of the message for the specified listening purpose.

Writing a Summary of a Message in the Native Language

Formats in which students are asked to write, in the native language, a summary of the facts and/or inferences they were able to understand and retain from a listening passage allow somewhat more freedom in answering, and thus tend to fall along the right-hand portion of the horizontal axis depicted in Illustration 9.3. Because students can select whatever information they want to, these kinds of items may be somewhat difficult to grade. It is clear, however, that grading must be done in some objective fashion.

Bernhardt and James (1987) recommend the use of summaries, or "immediate recall protocols" in both listening and reading comprehension and suggest scoring such protocols using a list of the "idea units" (Bernhardt 1983) of which the passage is composed. Because the ideas of a text are hierarchically arranged, with some more central to comprehension and meaning than others, Bernhardt and James propose differential point values for the various facts and inferences in the passage, with a greater number of points for main ideas or statements that show global comprehension and fewer points for minor details or specific facts.

Alternative scoring procedures that are somewhat less complex can also be used when rating student summaries on classroom tests. One option is to award points strictly on the basis of the number of legitimate facts and inferences recorded by the student, deducting points for wrong information and setting a limit on the total number of possible points that can be earned. Another option is to ask students to write down at least X number of facts and/or inferences gleaned from the passage and to award points for any information that legitimately represents the text, regardless of the nature of the particular facts recorded. This second idea may present the least scoring difficulty and allows the greatest flexibility to the students. It also has the advantage of rewarding students for *whatever* information they got from the passage, rather than penalizing them for something they missed that the teacher considered important.

Global Classification and Gisting

On the extreme right-hand portion of Illustration 9.3 are items that require students to report the gist of a listening passage or classify it globally in some way. Possibilities include asking students to give a title to a passage or to choose from multiple-choice options the best paraphrase of the main idea or the best summary statement. A variety of formats for global-classification items can be derived from the global listening comprehension activities suggested in Chapter 5.

• • • • • • • • • • • *Reading Comprehension Formats*

The formats suggested for listening comprehension in the previous section can be quite easily adapted for testing reading comprehension. Illustration 9.4 shows the way in which various item types fall along the schema's horizontal axis, ranging from convergent or discrete-point formats to those that are more global in nature. The section that follows presents a few ideas to illustrate the range of formats one might use in testing reading skills. This small sample of ideas can be supplemented by consulting Chapter 5.

Reading for Precise Information

Sample 1   (Intermediate)
Circling discrete items within a text

Context   A letter from an exchange student to his parents

Function   Understanding cohesive features of discourse (object pronouns)

Student Task   Students have on their test papers the text of a letter written by an exchange student to his parents describing his impressions of the United

Illustration 9.4
Positions of sample
reading comprehension
formats on the
assessment schema

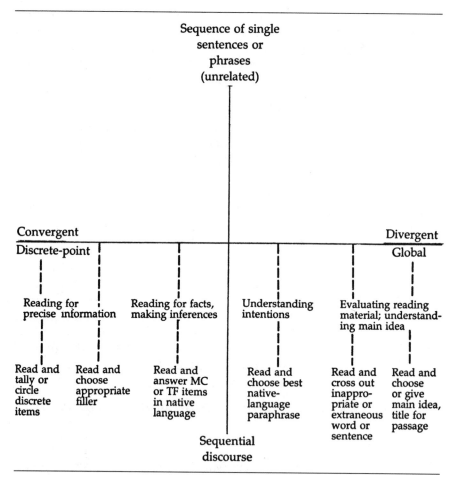

Sequence of single
sentences or
phrases
(unrelated)

Convergent

Divergent

Discrete-point

Global

Reading for
precise information

Reading for facts,
making inferences

Understanding
intentions

Evaluating reading
material; understand-
ing main idea

Read and
tally or
circle
discrete
items

Read and
choose
appropriate
filler

Read and
answer MC
or TF items
in native
language

Read and
choose best
native-
language
paraphrase

Read and
cross out
inappro-
priate or
extraneous
word or
sentence

Read and
choose
or give
main idea,
title for
passage

Sequential
discourse

States. (See Illustration 9.5.) The letter contains eight object pronouns, which students are to find and circle. They are then asked to draw an arrow to the noun, noun phrase, or whole idea represented by each of the object pronouns, underlining that noun or phrase, as in the example in Illustration 9.5.

Points can be awarded for (1) locating the pronoun and (2) identifying the referent correctly.

Sample 2 (Novice)
Filling in charts through semantic matching

Context   Household tasks

Function   Understanding simple descriptions; word associations

Illustration 9.5
Student copy with correct responses for Sample 1—circling discrete items within a text

Mio caro papà e mia cara mamma,

Sono arrivato a New York ieri sera verso le otto. La mia famiglia americana mi ha accolto all'aereoporto Kennedy—i signori Rochester ed i loro tre figli. Voglio (loro) tanto bene. Sono veramente simpatici! I ragazzi si chiamano Bob e Ted. Ho subito detto (loro) che anch'io ho due fratelli. La loro figlia si chiama Anne. Io (la) trovo molto dinamica ed entusiasta, e già (le) parlo molto spesso in inglese.

Dopo il mio arrivo siamo andati a New York a pranzo. È una città incredibile—è quasi impossibile descriverla. Ci sono molti grattacieli, raggruppati insieme, proprio come nelle foto che abbiamo viste. Quasi ci si fa male al collo nel guardarli. I signori Rochester mi hanno spiegato che la gente di New York può riconoscere molto facilmente i turisti perche questi stanno sempre ad ammirare i grandi edifici. Ho detto (loro) che la stessa cosa succede da noi. Sono certo che trarrò profitto dal mio soggiorno qui negli Stati Uniti, e che me (ne) ricorderò sempre. Vi scriverò la settimana prossima. Rispondetemi subito, d'accordo?

Un forte abbraccio,

Marco

Source: Idea for format from Grellet 1981.

Student Task Students supply the names of the parts of an apartment associated with the activities described in the chart.

El apartamento. Your friend Luis has finally found an apartment which he will share with Pierre Legault, a student from Quebec. Both are very busy since Luis has a job and Pierre is studying, so they decide to draw up a chore schedule. **Fill in the chart with the names of the parts of the apartment listing each part only once. (6 points)**

CUARTO	RESPONSABILIDAD	NOMBRE
_____	lavar los platos y limpiar el horno	*Pierre*
_____	servir la comida para cenas especiales	*Pierre*
_____	limpiar la ducha y el lavabo	*Luis*
_____	tender las camas y pasar la aspiradora	*Pierre*
_____	sacudir los meubles (¡y no te olvides encima del piano!)	*Luis*
_____	cuidar las plantas fuera *(outside)* de la ventana o la puerta	*Luis*

Source: McMillen Villar and Meuser Blincow 1993.

Sample 3 (Novice/Intermediate)
Reading for specific details

Context   Invitations to parties/social functions

Function   Reading for information about a party

Student Task   Students read the handwritten invitation in Illustration 9.6 (Invitation A) and answer questions such as the following:

You have received an invitation to a party! Answer the questions below, based on the information given:

1. What is the occasion for the party?
2. Where is it being held?
3. What is the date and time of the party?
4. What two things does the invitation ask you to do?
(Note that the comprehension questions are designed to elicit the kinds of details that would be important to retain in order to properly respond to the invitation.)

Source: Illustration 9.6 is from Gutiérrez and Rosser 1992, pp. 232–33.

Querida amiga,

Eduardo y Carmelita salen para los Estados
Unidos dentro de quince días. Para darles
una despedida y desearles un buen viaje,
estoy organizando una pequeña fiesta en
mi casa... el viernes, 4 de septiembre,
a las 20:30.

    Cuento contigo. Contéstame cuanto antes.
Y sobre todo... ¡no les digas nada a nuestros
invitados de honor! La fiesta será una
sorpresa para ellos.

             Afectuosamente,

             Mercedes

A

Estimada señorita:
   En la ocasión de la quinceañera de nuestra
hija Marisol, la familia está organizando una
fiesta en nuestra casa, Calle Sur Nº 112, el
sábado 17 de julio a las 21:00.
   Nos daría mucho gusto tenerles a usted y a
su hermano Carlos entre nosotros esa noche
para la celebración.
   Tenga la bondad de responder tan pronto
como le sea posible.
   Sin más por ahora, reciba los mejores deseos de,

          Teresa Camacho Del Valle

B

El señor y la señora Rafael Bolaños de la Garza

invitan cordialmente a Rosario Vega Arroyo a disfrutar de

la celebración del segundo aniversario de su boda que

ofrecerán en su residencia el sábado 17 de febrero

a las 20:00

R.S.V.P.

Calle Jardín 87   Tel. 28 03 94

C

Illustration 9.6
Invitations to parties

Source: Gutiérrez and Rosser 1992, pp. 232–33.

Reading for Sociocultural/Pragmatic Cues to Meaning

Sample   (Novice/Intermediate)
Making stylistic distinctions

Context   Invitations to social events

Functions   Understanding conventional expressions; detecting formal vs. informal style

Student Task   Students examine the three invitations to social functions given in Illustration 9.6. They then answer the following questions:

1. Rank the invitations in terms of formality, from least formal to most formal. In one or two sentences, explain why you ranked them as you did.
2. What is the occasion for each of the invitations?
   Invitation A: _____
   Invitation B: _____
   Invitation C: _____
3. For each of the following expressions or ideas in English, give the Spanish equivalent or near equivalent, as represented in the invitations indicated:
   "Dear" _____ (Invitation A)
   _____ (Invitation B)

   Please come . . ." _____ (Invitation A)
   _____ (Invitation B)

   "RSVP" _____ (Invitation A)
   _____ (Invitation B)
   _____ (Invitation C)

   "Yours truly" _____ (Invitation A)
   _____ (Invitation B)

Source: Adapted from Gutiérrez and Rosser 1992, pp. 233-34.

Reading and Choosing the Best Paraphrase

In this type of format, students are given several options and asked to choose the best paraphrase of the main idea of a passage, paragraph, or series of paragraphs. Multiple-choice options can be in either the native language (for testing pure reading comprehension) or the target language. In the latter case, comprehension of the multiple-choice options is also necessary for answering correctly. Another possibility is to ask students to provide a paraphrase of a segment of discourse, in either the native or the target language. In the following example, given four options in the target language, students choose the best paraphrase of the main idea in the test paragraph.

Sample   (Intermediate)
Choosing the best paraphrase of the main idea

Context   Greetings and Leave-takings

Function   Understanding intentions

Student Task   Students read the paragraph in Illustration 9.7 and then choose the best paraphrase of the main idea.

Passage   "Liens culturels: Arrivées et départs"

Choisissez la phrase qui représente le mieux l'idée centrale du passage:

1. Les Français sont, en général, plus affectueux que les Américains.
2. La façon dont les gens se saluent est bien ancrée dans leurs traditions culturelles.
3. Les hommes et les femmes en France suivent des coutumes différentes en se saluant.
4. La tradition exige que les Français s'embrassent quand ils se rencontrent, même s'ils ne se connaissent pas.

Choose the sentence that best represents the main idea of the passage:

1. *The French are generally more affectionate than Americans.*
2. *The manner in which people greet one another is firmly anchored in their cultural traditions.*
3. *Men and women in France follow different customs in greeting one another.*
4. *Tradition demands that French people kiss when they meet one another, even if they don't know each other.*

Source: Text in Illustration 9.7 is from Muyskens, Harlow, and Vialet 1989, p. 7.

When writing multiple-choice items of this type, care must be taken to design the distractors (wrong answers) so that each one is plausible to students who have only partially understood the passage. Note, in the above example, how elements of the passage have been worked into the distractors and how each might make sense to the student who has not synthesized all of the information. Distractor 1 attracts students who infer too much from the passage or who may be prone to form stereotypic impressions of the other culture. The second alternative, which is the correct answer, captures the main idea of the passage in paraphrase form. The second distractor (response #3) is implied in the passage, but does not represent the main idea. The third distractor (#4) is wrong factually, but may be attractive because it combines various elements that were in the passage, albeit incorrectly.

Test writers need considerable practice in writing integrative comprehension items of this type, and any items they write should be tested first on

Liens culturels
Arrivées et départs

Les Français ont une manière particulière de marquer l'existence des autres. Cela se manifeste par ce que l'on pourrait appeler un sens approfondi des arrivées et des départs. Lorsque les Français voient des amis pour la première fois de la journée, ils leur serrent la main ou ils les embrassent. En les quittant, ils leur donnent à nouveau une poignée de main ou ils les embrassent.

La coutume de s'embrasser est la norme entre amis et membres de la même famille. Les hommes se serrent plus souvent la main. La tradition exige *(demands)* souvent trois baisers *(kisses)*. Quelquefois c'est quatre baisers ou deux seulement. C'est une question de région. Le plus souvent on commence par la joue *(cheek)* droite. Que ferait un Américain en retrouvant un groupe d'amis qu'il voit pour la première fois de la journée?

Illustration 9.7
Greetings and Leave-takings

Source: Muyskens, Harlow and Vialet 1989, p. 7

colleagues and/or native speakers so that potential areas of difficulty are eliminated. It is also useful to have someone read the items without looking at the passage, as inexperienced test writers sometimes produce items that have unintentional extraneous cues, allowing the test-taker to choose the correct answer without having read or understood the passage itself.

Writing and Mixed-Skills Formats

The diagram in Illustration 9.8 shows how a variety of writing and mixed-skills formats fall along the horizontal axis of the test classification schema, ranging from the most convergent, or controlled, writing exercises on the left to the most open-ended on the right. The following samples, all of which require written responses in the target language, illustrate the range of formats a teacher might use on a classroom test. These sample items can be supplemented by using some of the ideas for teaching writing presented in Chapter 7.

Sentence Cues

Items of this type consist of "telegraphic" sentences or informal notes: students combine the sentence elements provided into complete and meaningful discourse, adding necessary function words and making necessary changes. To contextualize this type of format, sentences in the section should be logically linked to one another to form a paragraph, or all the sentences should be related thematically in some way.

Illustration 9.8

Positions of sample
writing and mixed-
skills formats on the
assessment schema

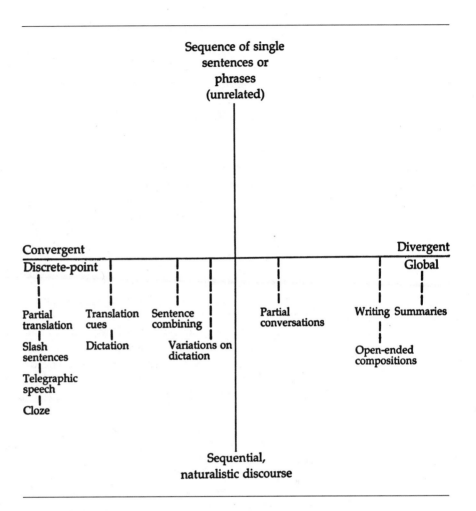

Sample 1 (Novice/Intermediate)
Slash sentences

Context   Impressions of life in an American town

Function   Description, giving opinions

Student Task   Karin is a student from France studying in the United States. She's telling
you her impressions of the campus and the town you live in. Here are the
elements of the statements she makes. Make complete, correct sentences to
reconstruct what she said.

    1. Je/aimer/beaucoup/université/campus/et/ville.
    2. Les étudiants/ici/être/sympathique/mais/pas/sérieux.
    3. Ils/passer/trop/temps/à/bars.

4. Ville/être/petit/mais/charmant.
5. Il/y/avoir/bon/magasins/et/beaucoup/théâtres.
6. Je/aller/cinéma/parce que/je/adorer/films/américain.

1. I/to love/very much/university/campus/and/town.
2. The students/here/to be/nice/but/not/serious.
3. They/to spend/too much/time/in/bars.
4. Town/to be/small/but/charming.
5. There are/good/stores/and/many/theaters.
6. I/to go/movies/because/I/to adore/American/films.

A variety of discrete elements recently learned in class have been embedded into this set of sentences. For example, students show their mastery of present-tense verb forms, including the irregular verbs *avoir* and *être*, as well as the use of adjectives and certain impersonal constructions as they complete the task. This type of integrative format allows the teacher to combine a variety of discrete points of vocabulary and/or grammar into one exercise and thus avoid setting aside a whole section of a test for a single grammatical topic. This latter procedure is quite prevalent in more traditional achievement tests.

The slash sentence format, above, has the advantage of helping students whose proficiency in writing is quite limited to create fuller discourse from very structured sets of cues. The disadvantage, however, is that the format is rather stilted and the stimulus for writing does not resemble natural language use. In the sample below, the cues for writing take the form of simple notes that are expanded by the student into fuller discourse. The "notes" format resembles authentic language use a little more closely, yet retains the advantages of structuring the writing activity to elicit certain features that the teacher would like to test.

Note that Sample 2, below, tests the same essential features and content as were tested in Sample 1. However, the format allows for greater flexibility in testing purpose. For example, if the notes are given to the student in the native language, the writing task is an indirect translation activity and the student must recall necessary vocabulary as part of the test item. If the notes are given in the target language, as below, they provide key vocabulary and a framework for the written paragraph, which changes the nature of the task and lowers the difficulty level considerably. Choice of native or target-language stimuli will thus depend on the testing purpose and the proficiency level of the students who are being tested.

Sample 2 (Intermediate)
Creating full discourse from notes

Context   Impressions of life in an American town

Function	Description, giving opinions
Student Task	(10 pts.) Vous venez d'interviewer Karin, une étudiante d'échange de Nancy, au sujet de ses impressions des Etats-Unis. En utilisant les notes ci-dessous, écrivez un résumé de ce qu'elle a dit. Ajoutez tous les mots nécessaires pour créer un bon paragraphe intéressant.

- aime beaucoup l'université, campus, ville
- trouve étudiants sympathiques
- étudiants pas trop sérieux, trop de temps—bars
- ville—petite, charmante, bons magasins, beaucoup de théâtres
- cinéma souvent, voir films

Student Response   Je viens de parler avec Karin, une étudiante de Nancy. Elle dit qu'elle

aime beaucoup l'université, le campus, et la ville. Elle trouve les étudiants ici très sympathiques. Elle pense que les étudiants ne sont pas trop sérieux parce qu'ils passent trop de temps aux bars. Karin trouve la ville un peu petite, mais charmante. Il y a beaucoup de bons magasins et beaucoup de théâtres. Elle va souvent au cinéma parce qu'elle adore voir les films.

(10 pts.) You have just interviewed Karin, an exchange student from Nancy, about her impressions of the United States. Using the notes below, write a resume of what she said. Add any necessary words to make a good, interesting paragraph.

- *likes the university, campus, town very much*
- *thinks students nice*
- *students not too serious, too much time—bars*
- *town—small, quaint, good stores, lots of theaters*
- *movies often, see films*

Student Response   *I just spoke with Karin, a student from Nancy. She says that she*

likes the university, the campus, and our town very much. She thinks the students here are nice. She thinks the students are not too serious, since they spend too much time in bars. Karin thinks the town is a little small, but charming. There are a lot of good stores and lots of theaters. She often goes to movies because she loves to watch films.

Scoring   An item such as this might be graded using discrete-point or component scoring. For discrete point scoring, teachers might deduct 1/2 points for errors in targeted features such as verbs, adjective agreements, prepositions of place, and/or connectors up to a total of 10 points maximum. For component scoring, teachers might award points for comprehensibility, grammaticality, and ease of expression (i.e., the flow of the discourse), distributed among the 10 points as the teacher sees fit. In either case, it is important to write out criteria for scoring very clearly, especially if more than one teacher will administer and score the test.

Contextualized Partial Translation (Reading and Writing)

In partial translation, elements of discourse are deleted from a short story or dialogue, and students attempt to restore these elements using a native-language version of the text as their guide. This format is an adaptation of a cloze task, but the ambiguity of possible fillers is eliminated through the use of the parallel translation. Like straight translation, this format elicits specific features of the language in a controlled fashion and therefore has high diagnostic power. Partial translation has the further advantage of allowing the teacher to focus on particular parts of the discourse and is generally less time consuming than full translation because less of the text needs to be produced by the student.

In the sample that follows, a dialogue at a restaurant has been constructed, where students restore the text on the left using the native-language cues given on the right. Items to be restored include grammatical and vocabulary features that have been targeted in the unit being studied, as well as pragmatic features such as culturally appropriate conventional phrases used in ordering a meal.

Sample (Novice)
Partial translation using parallel native-language text

Context
Two people eating in a restaurant

Functions
Ordering foods, asking and answering questions about the menu

Student Task
Students complete the dialogue on the left using the native-language text given on the right.

Janine: _____ ! Où est le _____ ?

I'm hungry. Where's the waiter?

Marie: Le voilà. Il arrive avec les _____ .

There he is. He's coming with the menus.

Le serveur: Bonsoir, mesdemoiselles. _____ ce soir?

Good evening, ladies. Would you like an apéritif this evening?

Marie: Pas moi. Et toi, Janine? Qu'est-ce _____ ?

Not me. What about you, Janine? What are you having?

Janine: Moi, je voudrais _____ un _____ .

I'd like to order an appetizer.

Le serveur: Et qu'est-ce que _____ ce soir? Le pâté est _____ . (etc.)

And what are you having tonight? The pâté is excellent. (etc.)

Cloze Adaptation

Another way to provide cues to cloze deletions is to list possibilities in a box next to the paragraphs of a dialogue or story. If cues are provided in alphabetical or random order, students must read the surrounding discourse to know which word fits the context and to produce the correct form. The sample item below is given in English and shows how verbs in the past tense can be elicited through this kind of format.

Sample 1 (Intermediate)
Verb deletions

Context Writing in a travel journal

Function Narrating in the past

Student Task Marisa is writing in her journal about her day in the city of Chicago. Complete the journal entry using the cues to the right. Be sure to use appropriate past tenses.

Friday, November 24

Today _____ the first day I ever

_____ in a city like Chicago. I really

_____ walking by the lake, but the

weather _____ cold by the middle of

the morning and it _____ to rain.

I _____ for a warm place to go to

get out of the harsh weather and I _____

to go into the Museum of Natural History.

What a wonderful place! I _____ for

hours until I _____ hungry, when I

_____ a nice little cafeteria. . . . etc.

to be
to begin
to like
to spend
to turn

to decide
to find
to get
to look
to wander

Sample 2 (Novice)
Personalized cloze passage

Context Writing a letter to a pen-pal

Function Simple description

Student Task Students complete the following letter as they wish, using the cues given below the blanks to guide them.

Firenze, l'otto febbraio

Caro Marco,

Ho letto il tuo anuncio nella rivista *Ciao!* cercando corrispondente. Ho

_____ e sto studiando _____ , _____ , e _____ a _____ .
(age)   (subject)   (subject)   (subject)   (place)

Quando non studio, mi piace _____. I miei sport favoriti sono

(activity)

_____ e _____. Cose ti piace fare?

(name of sport)   (name of sport)

    Dovrei descrivermi: sono _____ , _____ , e _____. Ho i

(adj.)   (adj.)   (adj.)

capelli _____ e gli occhi _____. Miei amici dicono che sono

(color)   (color)

_____ , ma io credo di essere _____.

(adj.)   (adj.)

    Nella tua lettera, dimmi per piacere qualcose su di te.

Tuo amico/a,

_____

Town, Date

Dear Mark,

    I am responding to your request for a pen-pal that I read in Ciao! *I am*

_____ *and I am presently studying* _____ , _____ *and* _____

(age)   (subject)   (subject)   (subject)

at _____. *When I am not studying, I like to* _____. *My favorite sports*

(place)   (activity)

are _____ *and* _____. *What do you like to do?*

(name of sport)   (name of sport)

    I should describe myself to you: I am _____ , _____ , *and*

(adj.)   (adj.)

_____. *I have* _____ *hair and* _____ *eyes. My friends say that I am*

(adj.)   (color)   (color)

_____ , *but I think that I am* _____.

(adj.)   (adj.)

    In your letter, please tell me all about you.

Your friend,

Discourse Transformation

In order to test discourse competence in conjunction with grammatical competence, teachers can design test items in which students are asked to transform the discourse in some way. For example, students might be asked to modify a test passage by replacing any repeated nouns with pronouns, to show that they know both the form and the function of these cohesive elements. Another test item might ask students to elaborate on a passage by adding adverbial elements, relative clauses, connectors and link words, or other detail that would make the discourse flow more easily. In the following sample, the discourse is transformed by changing the time element: the original passage is in present time, whereas the transformed passage is in the past.

Sample (Intermediate)
Discourse transformation

Context   Vacation and travel

Function   Writing letters, recounting events

Student Task   Dominique et Marie-France sont en vacances aux Etats-Unis. Dominique écrit une lettre à leur amie Odile. Mais elle oublie de la mettre à la poste. Retournée en France, elle doit récrire la lettre au passé. Récrivez la lettre au passé pour elle.

Chère Odile,

   Nous passons la première semaine de nos vacances à Los Angeles. Moi, je trouve la ville de Los Angeles très intéressante, mais je crois que Marie-France ne l'aime pas. Les musées et les restaurants sont excellents, mais après une semaine dans une grande ville, elle a envie d'aller à la plage. Alors, nous faisons de l'autostop parce que, comme ça, on voit le paysage et on peut faire la connaissance d'Américains très sympas.

   Nous pensons faire du camping une semaine, mais une jeune Américaine nous invite à rester chez elle. Elle nous sert des repas délicieux et nous buvons beaucoup de bon vin californien. Elle pose beaucoup de questions sur la France et les Français. Elle ne nous croit pas quand nous lui disons que le Français moyen a quatre semaines de vacances payées. A ce moment-là, le jeune Américaine veut devenir française!

Grosses bises,

Dear Odile,

   We are spending the first week of our vacation in Los Angeles. I think the city of Los Angeles is really interesting, but I think that Marie-France doesn't like it. The museums and restaurants are excellent, but after a week in a big city, she wants to go to the beach. So we are hitchhiking because, that way, you see the countryside and you can meet some very nice Americans.

   We were thinking about going camping for one week, but a young American has invited us to stay at her house. She serves delicious meals and we drink lots of good California wine. She asks a lot of questions about France and the French people. She doesn't believe us when we tell her that the average French person has four weeks of paid vacation. When she hears that, our American friend wants to become French!

Hugs and kisses,

In order to save writing time, the teacher may want to provide a partial text on the student's test paper below the original, leaving spaces for the verbs and/or other discourse features that might change as the text is transformed to the past.

Partial Conversations (Reading and Writing)

A somewhat more creative and open-ended format is one in which students supply the other half of a conversation based on the half that they see. This format is especially useful for testing question formation, as in the following example.

Sample (Novice)
Partial conversation

Context   Courses and schooling

Function   Asking for information

Student Task   *Ein Interview.* Brigitte, a German student, is studying at the University of X and meets Mark, an American student who is studying German. She begins to ask him about himself and his studies. Below are Mark's answers. Write an appropriate question for each answer you see.

Brigitte: _____ ?
Mark: Ich heiße Mark.
Brigitte: _____ ?
Mark: Dieses Semester belege ich zwei Kurse: Deutsch und Architektur.
Brigitte: _____ ?
Mark: Weil ich nächstes Jahr in Deutschland Architektur studieren will.
Brigitte: _____ ?
Mark: In einer Wohnung in Schwabing, in der Nähe von der Technischen Hochschule.
Brigitte: _____ ?
Mark: Ich fahre im Oktober nach München.

Brigitte: _____ ?
Mark: *My name is Mark.*
Brigitte: _____ ?
Mark: *I'm taking two courses this semester: German and architecture.*
Brigitte: _____ ?
Mark: *Because I'm going to study architecture in Germany next year.*
Brigitte: _____ ?
Mark: *In an apartment in Schwabing, close to the school of architecture.*
Brigitte: _____ ?
Mark: *I'm going to Munich in October.*

Open-Ended Completions (Reading and Writing)

The example below shows one way in which completion exercises, in which students must supply a logical ending for a set of partial statements, can be related to a short reading passage. At the same time, personal reactions to that passage can be elicited.

Sample   (Intermediate)
Open-ended completion

Context   Clubs and social activities

Function   Expressing opinions and points of view

Student Task: *Une société secrète.* Voici une série de pratiques d'une société secrète sur le campus. Comment réagissez-vous à ces pratiques? Complétez les phrases sous la liste en choisissant une pratique de la société. Choisissez une pratique différente pour chaque opinion que vous complétez.

Les Pratiques de la Société Secrète

A. Chaque membre de la société sait le mot secret.

B. Les femmes doivent porter un chapeau pendant les réunions.

C. Nous dormons pendant les présentations du président.

D. Nous choisissons nos membres dans l'annuaire.

E. Tout le monde prend les réunions au sérieux.

F. Le président de la société a 70 ans.

G. Les membres vont à toutes les réunions.

1. Il est curieux que . . .
2. Il est naturel que . . .
3. Je suis étonné(e) que . . .
4. Mon ami doute que . . .
5. Je suis furieux(-se) que . . .
6. Il est dommage que . . .
7. Il est bon que . . .

A Secret Society. Here is a series of practices of a secret society on campus. How do you react to these practices? Complete the sentences under the list of practices, choosing a different practice for each sentence you complete.

The Practices of the Secret Society

A. Every member of the society knows the secret word.

B. Women have to wear hats during the meetings.

C. We sleep during the president's speeches.

D. *We choose our members from the phone book.*

E. *Everyone takes the meetings seriously.*

F. *The president of the society is 70 years old.*

G. *Members go to all the meetings.*

1. *It is curious that . . .*
2. *It's natural that . . .*
3. *I'm surprised that . . .*
4. *My friend doubts that . . .*
5. *I'm angry that . . .*
6. *It's a shame that . . .*
7. *It's good that . . .*

The test item formats that have been illustrated thus far have been constructed to elicit specific structural and lexical elements in a fairly controlled fashion in order to assess students' mastery of certain features of language. Magnan (1991) expresses several reservations, however, about the extensive use of dialogue or paragraph frames in which grammatical features are embedded on classroom tests. First, if the items are not well constructed there is a danger that students will not need to read the surrounding context in order to perform the task. This can be avoided by constructing the paragraph or dialogue so that students must supply missing elements by making both a semantic and a structural choice among possible options. For example, if a story has been constructed in which verbs in the past tense have been deleted, teachers should not provide cues by simply indicating a verb in infinitive form beneath each blank. In an item constructed in this way, students would only need to look for the subject and conjugate the verb. There would be no need to read the surrounding story, and the contextualization of the passage would not serve any real function. If, on the other hand, the cues are provided in random order in a box to the right of the passage, as in the first sample cloze adaptation on page 442, students must read the surrounding discourse in order to determine (1) what semantic choice among the options is appropriate and (2) what form the verb should take.

A second limitation of paragraph frames is that they can lack naturalness and authenticity. Certainly this is the case for many Novice-level items, since students' ability to produce original discourse is extremely limited. One way to alleviate this problem is to construct passages that are more personalized in nature, such as the second sample cloze adaptation on page 443. Magnan (1991) suggests that one might personalize an item such as the partial conversation illustrated on page 445 by adding a set of personalized questions following the fictitious conversation, related to the topic. For example, the following personalized questions could be added as a second task following the German conversation between Mark and Brigitte:

1. Was ist dein Lieblingskurs dieses Semester?
2. Gib zwei Gründen, warum du Deutsch studierst.
3. Was tust du ger, wenn du nicht studierst?

1. What is your favorite course this semester?
2. Give two reasons why you are studying German.
3. What do you like to do to relax from your studies?

Care must be taken, however, that the follow-up task does not provide the same structures that are being elicited in the primary task, as the validity of the items would then be compromised.

As was pointed out at the beginning of this chapter, test items need to sample students' competencies through the use of a blend of focused and open-ended tasks, allowing teachers to elicit specific features of language for diagnostic purposes as well as allowing students to create their own discourse in order to communicate personal meaning. This is true for tests designed for learners at every level of proficiency, including the Novice level. Later in this chapter, a form for evaluating test items on a variety of dimensions is given. Use of a form such as this can help teachers achieve an appropriate balance of focused and open-ended activities.

The two remaining sample writing formats in this section represent a move toward the more creative, open-ended portion of the continuum depicted in Illustration 9.8. As students develop in their productive skills, the portion of the test that provides opportunities for open-ended and personalized response might be increased to allow for more creative communication. (See also Chapter 7 for open-ended writing tasks that can be used for testing purposes.)

Responding to a Target-Language Text (Reading/Writing)

One way to combine reading and writing skills in a realistic communicative task is to provide students with a target-language text to which they then write a response. In the first sample below, students are asked to write a letter in response to one received from a French pen-pal.

Sample 1
Responding to a letter

Context   Personal letter

Function   Describing oneself, sharing interests, asking for information

Student Task   Students read the brief letter provided on their test copies and then respond as they like, answering the questions posed in the letter. Students are directed to ask several questions of their own to obtain more information from their correspondent.

Illustration 9.9

Letter from a French pen-pal (Sample 1)

---

mardi 24 novembre 1992

Cher(e) _____,

Mon prof de géographie vient de me donner ton adresse et je m'empresse de t'écrire.

Je m'appelle Marie-Aline Poilrat, j'ai 17 ans et j'habite à Hendaye au Pays Basque. Je suis en classe de Terminale au Lycée de Saint-Jean-de-Luz. Je fais des langues. Et toi, en quoi te spécialises-tu?

A Hendaye, pendant la saison, il y a trois fois plus de touristes que d'habitants. Tu devrais voir les embouteillages! Notre maison ne donne pas sur la plage, mais on y est vite en voiture. La plage est à deux kilomètres.

Mon père travaille pour l'Administration des Douanes et ma mère est infirmière à domicile. J'ai un frère Mathieu; il a 14 ans et on ne s'entend pas très bien. Il est nul! Il est toujours en train de se plaindre!

Ma meilleure copine s'appelle Sylvie. Le mercredi après-midi, on joue aux jeux vidéos. C'est super-génial! Nous aimons aussi la piscine et le tennis. Est-ce que tu fais partie d'un club sportif? Quelles sortes de choses est-ce qu'on fait pour s'amuser chez toi? Est-ce que tu habites une grosse ville? Vas-tu souvent à la plage?

Tu dis que tu recherches une correspondante qui aime la musique. Tu tombes bien! Je joue de la guitare depuis 5 ans. J'aimerais bien pouvoir jouer les airs qu'on entend à la radio, surtout les chansons de Patrice Bruel. Je l'adore! Il est super-mignon! Qui est-ce que tu aimes comme chanteur, toi? Réponds-moi vite et dans ta prochaine lettre raconte-moi un peu ta vie. Envoie aussi une photo récente si tu en as une.

A bientôt te lire.

Ton amie
Marie-Aline

Source: Coulont-Henderson 1992.

Text of Letter   See Illustration 9.9.

Scoring   A variety of scoring options can be used to score open-ended compositions of this type (see, for example, the suggestions given in Chapter 7, as well as Terry 1992). A suggestion for holistic scoring is given below:

9-10 points: Letter is well written, answers all questions posed, asks appropriate questions, is well organized, and shows excellent control of linguistic features.

7-8 points: Letter is reasonably well written, answers questions posed, asks appropriate questions, shows good control of linguistic features, with some patterned errors.

5-6 points: Letter is somewhat disorganized, fails to ask or answer questions as directed, shows fair control of linguistic features, with some major errors in common structures.

0-4 points: Letter is poorly written, student fails to follow directions and/or shows poor control of many linguistic features.

Illustration 9.9
Translation

Tuesday, November 24, 1992

Dear _____ ,

My geography teacher just gave me your address and I hurried to write to you.

My name is Marie-Aline Poilrat, I'm 17 and I live in Hendaye in the Basque country. I'm a senior in the Lycée de Saint-Jean-de-Luz. I'm majoring in languages. What about you? What is your major?

In Hendaye, during the summer, there are three times as many tourists as there are residents. You should see the traffic jams! Our house isn't on the beach, but you can get there quickly by car. The beach is two kilometers away.

My father works for the Customs Service and my mother is a home-care nurse. I have a brother Matthew; he's 14 and we don't get along that well. He's worthless! He's always complaining!

My best friend's name is Sylvie. Wednesday afternoons, we play video games. It's really great! We also like swimming and tennis. Do you belong to a sports club? What kinds of things do you do to have fun where you live? Do you live in a big city? Do you often go to the beach?

You said that you're looking for a pen-pal who likes music. You're in luck! I have been playing the guitar for 5 years. I'd like to be able to play the songs on the radio, especially the songs by Patrice Bruel. I love him! He's super! What singers do you like? Answer quickly and in your next letter tell me a little about your life. Send a recent photo too if you have one.

Hope to hear from you soon!

Your friend,
Marie-Aline

Another way to assign points for this item is to use a componential scoring scheme. For example, points can be awarded for comprehensibility, accuracy, organization, fluency, and/or style, with each component receiving a certain proportion of the total point value.

Source: Letter in Illustration 9.9 provided by Françoise Coulont-Henderson 1992. Idea for format from Terry 1985.

Sample 2
Responding to a short cultural reading

Context   Greeting and leave-taking behavior

Function   Writing about cultural conventions and customs, making comparisons

Student Task   Students are asked to read the text about French greeting behavior in Illustration 9.7 (p. 436). They then write a similar paragraph explaining greeting and leave-taking behavior in their own culture, including several points of comparison and contrast with French customs.

Scoring   Points can be awarded for both writing performance and for the cultural comparisons and contrasts students identify in their response.

Guidelines for Creating Contextualized Paper-and-Pencil Tests

Many teachers may see the value of contextualized achievement tests but feel that they do not have the time or the expertise to create such exams on a regular basis. Although creating test items such as those in the previous sections may seem at first glance to be a much more difficult task than creating conventional items, teachers will find that the process becomes much easier with practice. Because the contextualized test integrates so many linguistic and lexical features in a few well-chosen passages, its creation is actually much simpler than when the instrument consists of unrelated items. Experience with graduate students at the University of Illinois has shown that (1) teaching assistants in French have learned within a short period of time how to write good test items, using the models given to them in their methods course, and (2) no one who has helped in the creation of contextualized tests wants to return to conventional testing methods. Students have also reported that they like these tests better: they find them more interesting and relevant, and have felt challenged to use "real" language on the exams.

A few guidelines should help the teacher who would like to try to write quizzes and tests after the models presented in this chapter. When the steps below are followed, preparation of classroom tests should be relatively easy and should not take an inordinate amount of time. Perhaps the best plan is to begin with a short quiz or unit exam rather than a long test.

Step 1. Take an inventory of the material to be covered on the test or quiz planned for the unit or lesson. List the major grammatical features, new vocabulary, discourse features, and cultural content you would like to include.

Step 2. Decide which skill areas you would like to emphasize. Choose some formats from among the samples given in this chapter or in Chapters 5, 6, and 7.

Step 3. Divide the content listed in Step 1 among the item types you have chosen. Be sure to place appropriate emphasis on each aspect of the language you wish to test across skill areas. To do this, construct a testing grid such as the one in Illustration 9.10.

Step 4. Create a simple story, dialogue, or paragraph that includes the features you've identified for each part of your exam. You may find that you can create your own context from models in your text, being sure to keep the themes and cultural content of the lesson in mind. For inspiration, you might want to look at reading passages, cultural commentaries, or passages from a supplementary reader at the same level of difficulty as the material you are testing. Some teachers may want to use authentic texts and design reading or mixed-skills items or item sets based upon them. Before using authentic materials on tests, teachers should make certain that students have had multiple opportunities to deal with such materials in the course

Grammar/Vocabulary To Be Sampled on Test 2	Listening/ Writing	Reading/ Writing	Writing
Avere and *avere* expressions	X	X	
Fare and *fare* expressions			X
Piacere expressions			X
Interrogative words and expressions; word order	X	X	X
Regular -*are* verbs	X	X	X
Irregular -*ere* verb: *dovere*			X
Irregular -*ire* verb: *preferire*	X		
Adjective agreement and placement	X		X
Use of *c'è* and *non c'è*			X
Possessive adjectives		X	X
Vocabulary for lodging	X		X
Descriptive adjectives	X		X
Family vocabulary			X
Part of Test	A. (Dictation with answers)	B. (Question writing)	C. (Room description) D. (Partial translation)
Point values:	15	25	60

Illustration 9.10
Testing grid*

*used to create the sample Italian test in the appendix to this chapter.

of instruction. Classroom tests should not present students with tasks that are significantly different from those with which they are familiar, and questions or activities designed around authentic materials should elicit the same kinds of performance that students have practiced in class.

In creating tests, consider including some global and divergent-production items as well as items that are more discrete-point in nature. If you are not a native speaker of the language you are teaching, have a colleague who is native check the test for the authenticity and accuracy of the language.

Evaluating the Test

Once a preliminary version of a test has been drafted, it is important to look at the way the test as a whole samples the students' use of the language, and how credit is awarded for the various tasks that have been created. A form such as the one presented in Illustration 9.11 can be useful in evaluating tests for authenticity of language use, balance of discrete-point

Illustration 9.11
Criteria for test
evaluation

---

1. **The Parts of the Test.** For each section of the test, place the letter of the part (A, B, C, D, etc.) on the continua below.

   a. How would you rank the task on a continuum ranging from artificial to authentic language use?

D	A B	C

   Artificial   Authentic

   b. How would you rank the task on a continuum ranging from discrete-point to open-ended?

   D   B   AC

   Discrete-point   Open-ended

   c. How would you rank the task in terms of the focus of the activity, ranging from a focus on minor points to a focus on major points in the chapter or unit?

   B   D   A   C

   Minor points   Major points

   d. How would you characterize the task in terms of the components of language use being tested? (Place the letter of the section on the line above the main component(s) tested.)

ABCD	ACD		B
Grammar	Vocabulary	Culture	Reading Comprehension

A			
Listening Comprehension		Pragmatics	Other (specify)

---

versus more global or integrative formats, balance of skills being tested, clarity of directions, and general interest level. In using this particular form, teachers who are preparing a test evaluate it first on a section-by-section basis and then rate it overall using a five-point scale. The first part of the evaluation is done by placing the letter or numeral designating each test section on each of the continua provided on the form. For the test evaluation depicted in Illustration 9.11, the four parts of the sample Italian test in the Appendix to this chapter have been charted, using the letters A, B, C, and D to designate the test sections.

At the University of Illinois, teaching assistants in multi-section courses share in the preparation and evaluation of tests with the help of their course coordinator as well as the Director of Basic Language Instruction. In the French department, several course meetings are planned per semester for review of proposed tests that have been prepared by teams of teaching assistants, usually with two individuals assigned to each exam. As each exam is prepared, a grid, similar to the one provided in Illustration 9.10 is completed to accompany the test draft. The draft is then circulated among

Illustration 9.11
Continued

---

e. How would you rank the clarity of the task and of the directions?

ABCD

Confusing   Clear

f. How would you characterize the general level of interest of the task for your students?

BD   *A*   *C*

Boring   Fun/Interesting

2. **The Test as a Whole.** Based on your analysis of the sections of the test, how would you rate the test overall (on a scale of 1 to 5, with 5 being the best score) on the following criteria?

1. Authenticity of language use?	1	2	③ 4	5
2. Relevance to language proficiency development?	1	2	3 ④	5
3. Clarity of tasks and directions?	1	2	3 4	⑤
4. Interest level of test?	1	2	③ 4	5
5. Balance of skills/components?	1	2	③ 4	5

What would you do to improve this test?

1. Put less emphasis on grammar and more on open-ended creative writing.

2. Include more on culture and pragmatics.

---

the teachers who will be administering the test, the course coordinator, and the Director of Basic Language Instruction. Comments are made on the draft, and the test is revised for the course meeting. At the course meeting, the tests that have been prepared are timed and final changes that may be deemed necessary are made. A team approach to test design such as this encourages every member of the teaching staff to take responsibility for the testing program while allowing for an efficient division of labor in order to save staff time. Typically, members of the teaching staff for a given course need only prepare one exam per semester, but attend all of the course meetings in order to provide continuous input into the test creation process.

Testing Oral Skills

Many classroom teachers feel that oral exams are among the most difficult types of exams to create, schedule, administer, and grade, especially when they have large classes or many classes in the course of a day. For these reasons, some classroom teachers consider oral tests impractical and do not attempt to test oral skills in any regular or consistent fashion. Yet it is clear that one of the priorities in the language teaching profession in recent years has been the development of oral proficiency. If we hope to convince learners via our testing program that communicative language use is a major goal of instruction, we will need to administer some type of oral test, if only once or twice in a semester.

Harlow and Caminero (1990) conducted a study that examined the problems and practices associated with oral testing in Spanish, French, and German at 67 large universities in the United States. Responses were obtained from 106 language program directors and coordinators, representing all three language groups. The results indicated that 57% of the language programs surveyed did administer at least one oral test per term/semester to beginning students, with slightly more than half of the respondents indicating that more than one such test was typically given. There were some differences in oral testing practices by language: 67% of the French respondents reported giving oral tests, while 61% of the Spanish and 50% of the German respondents said that they tested oral skills. Overall, 43% of the language programs represented in the sample did no oral testing of their beginning students, stating that such testing was problematic because of lack of time, large classes, and heavy teaching loads. Among the programs that reported administering oral tests, approximately one-half assigned 10 to 19% of the final grade for this purpose, while another 27% of the respondents assigned between 20 and 50% of the grade on the basis of oral test results. The authors note that this is an encouraging indication that oral skills are considered important in most large institutions, even though they can be difficult to test.

Perhaps one solution to the practical difficulties of oral testing lies in using such tests at different times during the school year with different groups or classes, so that teachers responsible for large numbers of students can reduce their testing load at any one point in time to a manageable level. Tests lasting ten to fifteen minutes might be administered outside of class in the instructor's office, or students can be tested individually or in small groups during class while other class members work on small-group activities. Teachers might also consider administering taped exams in a language laboratory, although this format is the least flexible and has limited potential for testing interactive communication skills.

A variety of ideas for oral testing are presented in the following pages, some of which are based on the principles of the ACTFL Oral Proficiency Interview (OPI). A brief description of the structure of the ACTFL Oral Interview precedes the adaptations. This description is intended to introduce the reader to the *nature* of the procedure, but it is not sufficient for training in the administration of such a test. The teacher interested in oral proficiency interviewing should attend a full-day familiarization workshop first, and follow that with a four-day intensive workshop sponsored either by ACTFL or by an organization working under its auspices. Only after an intensive training period, including several months of monitored testing and rating, is one certifiable as a tester. For more information on familiarization and tester workshops, write to ACTFL, whose address is provided in the notes at the end of the chapter.

It is important to distinguish, at this point, between the administration of an oral proficiency interview and an oral achievement test. As was pointed out at the beginning of this chapter, oral proficiency testing should be reserved for summative evaluation purposes rather than for testing midcourse or end-of-course achievement. As we have already mentioned, oral proficiency interviews, in order to be valid and reliable, must be administered by trained testers and raters. Normally, a teacher should not test his own students when giving "official" oral interviews. In addition, a rating is not considered official until a second, trained rater has verified the results. For these reasons, most teachers will probably not be using the procedure per se to test their students. However, an understanding of the structure of the oral interview should help teachers design valid and reliable *achievement* tests for oral skills to use with their classes.

The Structure of the ACTFL Oral Proficiency Interview

The ACTFL Oral Proficiency Interview is a face-to-face conversation lasting anywhere between 10 and 25 minutes, depending on the level of the person being tested. An untrained observer might think that this "conversation" does not differ markedly from one a teacher might have with a student taking an oral achievement test, or even from an ordinary conversation one might have with a native speaker. However, the structure of the interview is quite complex and purposeful. The tester needs to know at every point in the process what should be elicited from the interviewee and why it should be elicited. If the interview is not structured properly, a ratable sample may not be obtained, and the interview will have to be repeated at some later date.

All oral interviews must be taped for future verification, both by the tester and by a second tester. The interview consists of four phases, all of which fulfill three functions: (1) psychological, (2) linguistic, and (3) evaluative. Illustration 9.12 presents the structure of the interview in graphic form.

The following description of the conduct of the Oral Proficiency Interview (OPI) is synthesized from *The ILR Handbook on Oral Interview Testing* (Lowe 1982), *The ETS Oral Proficiency Testing Manual* (Liskin-Gasparro 1982), and *The ACTFL Oral Proficiency Interview Tester Training Manual* (Buck, Byrnes, and Thompson 1989).

Phase 1: Warm-up. The warm-up portion of the interview is very brief and consists of greeting the interviewee, making him or her feel comfortable, and exchanging the social amenities that are normally used in everyday conversations. Typically, the warm-up lasts less than three minutes, but it serves a variety of purposes. First, on the psychological plane, it allows the interviewee to begin thinking in the language and sets him or her at ease. On the linguistic plane, it reorients the person being tested to

FOUR PHASES: THREE PLANES:	WARM-UP ⟶	LEVEL CHECKS ⟵⟶	PROBES ⟶	WIND-DOWN
		Iterative Process		
PSYCHOLOGICAL	Puts interviewee at ease	Shows interviewee what s/he can do	Shows interviewee what s/h cannot do	Returns interviewee to level at which s/he functions most accurately; gives interviewee feeling of accomplishment
LINGUISTIC	Reacquaints interviewee with language, if necessary	Checks for functions and content handled with greatest accuracy	Checks for functions and content handled with least accuracy	Gives interviewer chance to check that iterative process is complete
EVALUATIVE	Gives tester preliminary indication of skill level	Finds highest level of sustained performance (floor)	Finds first level at which performance can no longer be sustained (ceiling)	

Illustration 9.12
General OPI Structure:
Phases and Planes of
the OPI

Source: K. Buck, H. Byrnes, and I. Thompson, eds. 1989.

hearing and using the language while giving the tester an opportunity to determine where the next phase of the interview should begin. This relates to the evaluative function of the warm-up, which is to allow the tester to get a preliminary idea of the rating that will eventually be assigned. Once the warm-up is completed, the tester moves on to Phase 2.

Phase 2: Level Check. This phase consists of establishing the highest level of proficiency at which the interviewee can sustain speaking performance—that is, the level at which he or she can perform the functions and speak about the content areas designated by the ACTFL Guidelines with the greatest degree of accuracy. On the psychological plane, this phase of the interview allows the person being tested to demonstrate his or her strengths and converse at the level that is most comfortable for him or her. Linguistically, the level check is designed to elicit a speech sample that is adequate to prove that the person can indeed function accurately at the level hypothesized by the interviewer during the warm-up phase. If during the level check, the interviewer can see that his or her hypothesis was incorrect, the level of questions is adjusted upward or downward accordingly. On the evaluative plane, the level check allows the interviewer to get a better idea of the actual proficiency level of the interviewee, establishing the floor of his or her performance beyond a reasonable doubt. This phase of the interview is repeated several times throughout the entire testing process and alternates with the probe phase, described next.

Phase 3: Probes. Probes are questions or tasks designed to elicit a language sample at one level of proficiency higher than the hypothesized level in order to establish a ceiling on the interviewee's performance. Psychologically, this allows the tester to show the person being tested what he or she is not yet able to do with the language, verifying the rating that will eventually be assigned to the speech sample. On the linguistic plane, the probes may result in *linguistic breakdown*—the point at which the interviewee ceases to function accurately or cogently because the task is too difficult. If a probe is successfully carried out, the interviewer may begin level checking at this higher level to see if his or her hypothesis about the true proficiency level is wrong. If the interviewee does demonstrate during the probe phase that he or she does not have the language to carry out the task, then the probe can be considered a valid indicator that the hypothesized level is correct. Several probes should be used during the interview, alternated with level checks, to establish beyond any question the appropriate rating.

Phase 4: Wind-down. When a ratable sample has been obtained, the tester brings the interviewee back to the level at which he or she functions most comfortably for the last few minutes of the interview. This serves to make individuals feel successful and allows them to leave the test with the echo of their own voice still in their ears, reminding them that they functioned well in the language. Linguistically, the wind-down portion of the interview represents the most accurate use of the language of which the person is capable. On the evaluative plane, this last phase gives the tester one more opportunity to verify that his or her rating is indeed correct. The tester may end the interview by thanking the person who was interviewed, saying what a pleasure it has been talking with him or her, and wishing the person a pleasant day. Again, the termination of the conversation should resemble as much as possible the way in which conversations normally end in authentic language-use situations.

Formats and Elicitation Techniques for the Novice through Superior Levels

Novice. The test at the Novice level will last for about ten minutes and will consist of attempts at conversation of a simple nature. Often, test candidates at this level cannot sustain a natural conversation because they cannot yet create with the language they have and are unable to produce much beyond isolated words, short memorized phrases, or simple sentences on a limited number of topics. If conversation fails, the interviewer can use props and ask interviewees to name various objects they see in a picture or in the test room. Among the content areas that Novice-level speakers might be able to handle are such things as colors, names of basic objects, names of family members, articles of clothing, days of the week, dates, and telling time. Essentially, the Novice-level interview is like an oral achievement test, since the learner can produce little more than what he or she has learned in the course of his exposure to the target language, either in a natural setting or in class, if there has been some formal learning involved in the acquisition of the language.

Intermediate. Ideally, the test at this level consists of a conversation, usually quite simple in nature, in which the person being tested also asks some questions and demonstrates some ability to "survive" in a common situation likely to be encountered in visiting the target culture. The tester will probe for narration and description in past and future time (i.e., Advanced-level functions) and will be able to show during the course of the interview that the interviewee is still not able to sustain performance at this level. Intermediate-level speakers can create with the language simply to express their own point of view. Generally, they can speak in short sentences rather than in isolated words or phrases. The Intermediate-level interview must elicit questions from the person being tested, since getting information and sustaining one's own half of the conversation are hallmarks of speech at this level. The interviewee must also be considered intelligible to native speakers used to dealing with foreigners in order to obtain a rating of Intermediate.

Advanced. The interviewer will check to see how the person being tested can handle routine social demands, survival situations with a complication, and narration and description in past, present, and future time. In addition, the tester will probe to see how the interviewee can support an opinion, talk about abstract topics, and hypothesize (Superior-level functions). Speakers on this level will typically speak in paragraphs, rather than in short sentences, and will demonstrate a high degree of accuracy in handling basic structures and vocabulary. They would be able to live on the economy of the target culture and carry out schoolwork or basic job requirements with little difficulty. Speakers at the Advanced level are able to participate fully in casual conversations and are understandable to native speakers *not* used to dealing with foreigners.

Superior. The conversation at the Superior level is geared toward abstract topics and discussions about issues of current interest. Interviewees need to show that they can hypothesize and support an opinion, defending their point of view on some controversial issue. In addition, the person being interviewed is asked to handle an unfamiliar situation (such as explaining that he's just lost his contact lens in the trap of the sink in the bathroom of his hotel room and needs a plumber, or that he's locked himself out of his apartment and the doorknob has just dropped off into the shrubbery). This last activity is used to demonstrate that the interviewee is capable of circumlocution in the absence of specialized or unfamiliar vocabulary and can work his way out of a difficulty. The Superior-level speaker can describe and narrate in detail, and uses most structures of the language accurately and with facility.

A few sample questions that might be appropriate for the Novice through Advanced proficiency levels are given in Illustration 9.13. These

Illustration 9.13

Sample question types for an oral interview

Warm-up Questions

Comment allez-vous? *(How are you?)*
Ça va bien aujourd'hui? *(Are things OK today?)*
Etes-vous fatigué aujourd'hui? *(Are you tired today?)*
Que pensez-vous du temps qu'il fait? *(What do you think of the weather?)*
D'où venez-vous? *(Where are you from?)*
Où habitez-vous? *(Where do you live?)*

Novice

Comment vous appelez-vous? *(What's your name?)*
Où habite votre famille? *(Where does your family live?)*
Parlez-moi un peu de votre famille. *(Tell me a little about your family.)*
Parlez moi un peu de vos cours ce semestre. *(Tell me a little about your courses this semester.)*
Aimez-vous la vie à l'université? *(Do you like it at the university?)*
Décrivez votre chambre pour moi. *(Describe your room for me.)*

When conversation fails... Use the "10 desperate questions," such as asking the student to name objects, colors, days of the week, months of the year, family members, clothing, dates, numbers, tell time, and talk simply about the weather, or any other vocabulary items that may be in his/her repertoire.

Intermediate

Est-ce que vous travaillez? Que faites-vous? *(Do you work? What do you do?)*
Que pensez-vous de vos professeurs? *(What do you think of your teachers?)*
Avez-vous un(e) camarade de chambre? *(Do you have a roommate?)* Décrivez cette personne. *(Describe this person.)*
Que faites-vous le week-end? *(What do you do on weekends?)*
Décrivez pour moi une journée typique. *(Describe for me a typical day.)*
Où mangez-vous d'habitude? Quels plats aimez-vous? *(Where do you usually eat? What dishes do you like?)*
Regardez-vous la télé? Quelles émissions aimez-vous? *(Do you watch television? What programs do you like?)*
Qu'est-ce que vous aimez faire le soir? *(What do you like to do in the evening?)*
Décrivez pour moi votre maison idéale. *(Describe your ideal house.)*

---

examples are meant to demonstrate the *type* of questions that might be used in an interview and are not meant to constitute any type of official list. In fact, every interview is unique, since the person being interviewed often leads the discussion by his or her answers. The art of interviewing consists of eliciting a ratable sample in a way that seems natural conversationally and that is flexible enough to conform to the needs and abilities of each interviewee. The course of the interview is negotiated by both the interviewee and the tester, but it is the tester, ultimately, who must structure the conversation properly in order to obtain a speech sample that can be rated.

Illustration 9.13
Continued

Advanced

Qu'avez-vous fait ce matin avant de venir ici? *(What did you do this morning before coming here?)*

Qu'allez-vous faire après cet examen? *(What are you going to after this exam?)*

Où irez-vous après avoir fini vos études ici? *(Where will you go after finishing your studies here?)*

Avez-vous lu le journal ce matin? Qu'est-ce qui s'est passé? Que pensez-vous de cette situation? [probe for Superior level] *(Did you read the paper this morning? What happened? What do you think of this situation?)*

Etes-vous sorti le week-end passé? Qu'avez-vous fait? Vous êtes-vous bien amusé? *(Did you go out last weekend? What did you do? Did you have fun?)*

Comparez votre ville natale à _____ [name of your city, or of a large city in the U.S. or the French-speaking world]. *(Compare the city where you were born to _____.)*

Que faisiez-vous d'habitude quand vous étiez petit? *(What did you used to do when you were little?)*

Note: Questions for the four phases of the interview should be linked together as naturally as possible to make the conversation realistic and authentic. These sample questions are meant only as illustrations of the types of questions that might be asked to get the conversation going at any particular level. Follow-up questions would also be appropriate, as would questions touching on other subject areas.

Recent Adaptations of the OPI

Because the Oral Proficiency Interview requires a face-to-face interview on an individual basis, it can be impractical to administer, especially in settings where large numbers of people need to be tested in a relatively short time period. In order to accommodate diverse needs for oral testing, various alternative testing methods that can be correlated with the OPI have been developed or are currently being explored. Stansfield and Kenyon (1992) report on the development at the Center for Applied Linguistics of a tape-mediated procedure called the simulated oral proficiency interview, or SOPI. This procedure differs from earlier tape-mediated procedures, including the *Recorded Oral Proficiency Exam* (ROPE) described by Lowe and Clifford (1980), by combining the following characteristics: (1) a format similar to the OPI, including a warm-up and a variety of tasks at different proficiency levels; (2) the use of both aural and visual (print) stimuli in the elicitation of speech; and (3) the use of a scoring system based on the ACTFL Guidelines (Stansfield and Kenyon 1992, p. 129). The SOPI, which can be administered to groups in language lab facilities, is most appropriate for interviewees whose proficiency falls within the range of Intermediate-Low to Superior on the ACTFL scale. First developed to accommodate oral assessment needs in uncommonly taught languages like Chinese, where trained oral interviewers were scarce, the test is now available in Portuguese, Hebrew, Hausa, Indonesian, French, and Spanish (p. 129). The SOPI includes a Master Tape with test directions and questions, a printed booklet with pictures and other materials used in responding, and a cassette for recording the examinee's responses. Stansfield and Kenyon (1992) describe the Indonesian version of the test, which includes five parts: (1) personalized questions; (2) giving directions using a map in the test booklet; (3) narration, using a picture sequence; (4) discussion of various practical and abstract topics; and (5) situational discourse, which asks the examinee to carry out communicative tasks, much like those used in the role-plays of the OPI. The authors report high correlations between the ratings given to samples elicited by the SOPI and the OPI (an average of .95 using the Indonesian version), supporting the use of this type of test as a valid alternative to the face-to-face interview format.

Higgs (1992) describes a pilot project under development at the Language Acquisition Resource Center at San Diego State University called the VOCI (The Visual-Oral Communications Instrument), which uses video stimuli instead of a face-to-face interview to test oral proficiency. This test, like the SOPI, is designed to accommodate the assessment needs associated with large-scale testing. While the OPI is administered to individuals, the VOCI is designed to be used with groups of students in a laboratory setting.

Higgs explains that the VOCI, like the SOPI, is limited in several ways as compared to the OPI. First, it is not interactive in nature: students respond to a fixed set of questions posed by a videotaped interviewer by recording their answers onto a cassette tape. A second limitation of the VOCI is that it can only establish the learners' proficiency with respect to pre-defined levels (such as those established by an exit requirement for graduation) and cannot interact with the learner to establish his or her "floor" or "ceiling" as a live interviewer can. A third limitation is in the recording obtained from the test: the VOCI allows only the students' answers to be recorded, whereas a taped OPI interview contains the entire conversation.

There are certain advantages, however, that make the VOCI an interesting possibility for large-scale oral proficiency testing. First, the test can be administered in a lab and does not require the enormous time commitment of face-to-face individual interviews. Generally, teachers can listen to and evaluate the students' recorded answers in about 10 to 12 minutes. One advantage for students being tested via the VOCI is that they can answer the interviewer's questions at their own pace. Examinees watch the video on their own monitor and then push a button to respond. After they have recorded their response, they push a button to resume the videotape. Thus, they can control the rate at which the test is administered, which may relieve some students of the test anxiety that can be experienced in an interviewer-controlled testing situation.

Higgs reports that preliminary research with Spanish speakers shows that the comparability of ratings using the VOCI and the OPI are quite good. If these results are supported by further research, this kind of video testing may be a viable alternative for universities with appropriate facilities for large-scale testing of this kind.

Adaptations for Classroom Testing: Some Possible Formats for Oral Achievement Tests

Taped Exams. Oral test formats can vary from those in which students respond to taped materials in a laboratory setting to those in which face-to-face interviews are used. Valdman (1981) describes a taped oral exam called the Indiana University French Communicative Ability Test (IUF-CAT) designed for first-semester French students. The test includes three tasks: (1) pictorially cued responses; (2) personal questions; and (3) situational responses. Responses are scored using three criteria: (1) semantic and pragmatic appropriateness; (2) grammaticality and correct form of lexical items; and (3) fluency and accuracy, with greater weight given to the first two categories. Although there are opportunities for students to give open-ended, creative answers on some parts of the IUFCAT, it seems that some of the other options available for achievement testing of oral skills are somewhat more integrative and interactive in nature. However, such alternatives require individual or paired interviews, which can be very time-consuming.

Monologues and Conversational Exchanges. Boylan (1982) has developed several ideas for oral testing at the beginning and intermediate levels in Spanish that merit careful consideration. For students at the fourth-semester level, for example, she suggests using a two-part oral test in which monologues and conversational exchanges are featured. Students, interviewed individually, randomly draw two or three choices from a set of topic cards prepared by the teacher, based on recent course material. Each topic card has a set of opinion questions as a guide for the monologue portion of the exam. For example, a topic card relating to a unit on television and the press includes the following information:

Los métodos de communicación: la televisión y la prensa

You may wish to include the following in your monologue:

1. As forms of communication, what are the advantages/disadvantages of television and newspapers?
2. What, if any, are the various effects of television on children?
3. Should TV and the press always reflect reality?
4. What are your feelings with regard to advertising in newspapers and on TV?

Students study the topic card for a few minutes and then speak briefly about the theme. After their impromptu monologue, the teacher asks follow-up questions based on the information the student has provided. Boylan suggests various questions that teaching assistants might ask for each topic to ensure some consistency across classes.

A second part of the oral test consists of an interview in which students ask questions of the instructor, based either on one of the other topic cards or on a role-play situation. Boylan provides students with question cues, such as the following ones based on the theme of technology:

Your instructor is a door-to-door salesperson, trying to sell the revolutionary new household product, "Plastitex." He or she has already described the product to you, but you want to obtain some more information before making a decision. You may want to find out the following:

1. How much the product costs
2. If it has a guarantee
3. If it could cause any dangerous effects
4. How long the product has been on the market
5. How it was tested before going on sale
6. If he/she has sold many in your neighborhood

The rating scales used by Boylan in both parts of the oral test, as well as the definitions of the scale intervals depicted on the instrument, are presented in Illustration 9.14.

Conversation Cards and Interviews. One type of oral achievement test that has been administered after the first eight weeks of instruction in French 101 at the University of Illinois (approximately midsemester) consists of a set of conversation cards that serve as a focal point for the exam. Students may be interviewed individually or in pairs, depending on (1) time constraints; (2) the desire to provide native or near-native input to the interview (when done with one student) versus the desire to provide students with the security and comfort of working with a partner; and (3) the teacher's individual preference for a one-on-one interview format versus a format in which he or she can be observer and note-taker without active participation. Individual instructors should choose a format that meets their own needs as well as those of their students, but the sample test provided here will serve just as well for individual or paired interviews.

Individual Interviews. The teacher sets up an appointment with each student (or sets aside in-class time while others are doing group work) for about 10 to 15 minutes. A set of situationally based conversation cards (see Bonin and Birckbichler 1975) serve as a stimulus for the student/teacher interview. Illustration 9.15 presents four sample cards created for the exam. The interview begins with the teacher selecting one of these cards at random and using it to interview the student. Then the student selects another card at random and uses it to ask questions of the teacher.

Illustration 9.14
Rating scales and
definitions for Boylan's
oral tests using
monologues and
conversational
exchanges

SPANISH 124	**ORAL FINAL EXAM**	STUDENT _____

Part I: Monologue (34%)

Fluency	1 2 3 4 5 6	_____
Vocabulary	1 2 3 4 5 6 7 8	_____
Structure	1 2 3 4 5 6	_____
Comprehensibility	1 2 3 4 5 6 7 8 9 10 11 12 13 14	_____
	Section total	_____ /34

Part II: Answering Questions on Monologue (26%)

Fluency	1 2 3 4 5	_____
Vocabulary	1 2 3	_____
Structure	1 2 3 4	_____
Comprehensibility	1 2 3 4 5 6 7 8	_____
Listening Comp.	1 2 3 4 5 6	_____
	Section total	_____ /26

Part III: Interview (Asking Questions) (40%)

Fluency	1 2 3 4 5 6	_____
Vocabulary	1 2 3 4 5 6 7 8	_____
Structure	1 2 3 4 5 6	_____
Comprehensibility	1 2 3 4 5 6 7 8 9 10 11 12	_____
Listening Comp.	1 2 3 4 5 6 7 8	_____
	Section total	_____ /40
	Test total	_____ /100

Weighting of Scales

Vocabulary—19%
Fluency—17%
Structure—16%
Comprehensibility—34%
Listening Comprehension—14%

Illustration 9.14
Continued

DEFINITIONS FOR SCALE INTERVALS

Part I: Monologue (34%)

Fluency

1   Speech halting and fragmentary; long, unnatural pauses, or utterances left unfinished

2   Speech very slow and uneven except for short or routine sentences

3   Speech frequently hesitant and jerky; sentences may be left uncompleted

4   Some definite stumbling, but manages to rephrase or continue

5   Speech generally natural and continuous; only slight stumbling or unnatural pauses

6   Speech natural and continuous; no unnatural pauses

Vocabulary (breadth and precision of usage)

1–2   Lacks basic words; inadequate; inaccurate usage

3–4   Often lacks needed words; somewhat inaccurate usage

5–6   Occasionally lacks basic words; generally accurate usage

7–8   Rich and extensive vocabulary; very accurate usage

Structure

1   No utterances structurally correct

2   Very few utterances structurally correct

3   Some utterances rendered correctly, but major structural problems remain

4   Many correct utterances, but with definite structural problems

5   Most utterances rendered correctly, with some minor structural errors

6   Utterances almost always correct

Comprehensibility

1–3   Almost entirely/entirely incomprehensible to native speaker of Spanish

4–6   Mostly incomprehensible; occasional phrases comprehensible

7–9   Many errors, about half incomprehensible

10–12   Many errors, but still mostly comprehensible

13–14   Almost entirely/entirely comprehensible to native speaker of Spanish; only an occasional word not comprehensible/no words incomprehensible

Illustration 9.14
Continued

Part II: Answering Questions on Monologue (26%)

Fluency

1   Speech halting and fragmentary; long, unnatural pauses or utterances

2   Speech frequently hesitant and jerky; sentences may be left uncompleted

3   Some definite stumbling, but manages to rephrase or continue

4   Speech generally natural and continuous; only slight stumbling or unnatural pauses

5   Speech natural and continuous; no unnatural pauses

Vocabulary (breadth and precision of usage)

1   Lacks basic words; inadequate; inaccurate usage

2   Occasionally lacks basic words; generally accurate usage

3   Extensive vocabulary; accurate usage

Structure

1   Few/no utterances structurally correct

2   Some utterances correct, but major structural problems remain

3   Many correct utterances, but definite structural problems remain

4   Utterances almost always correct

Comprehensibility

1–2   Incomprehensible/almost incomprehensible to native speaker of Spanish

3–4   Many errors that impede comprehensibility, less than half understandable

5–6   Some/few errors, but still mostly comprehensible

7–8   Almost or totally comprehensible to native speaker of Spanish

Listening Comprehension

1–2   Student comprehends nothing/little of what instructor says

3–4   Student comprehends some/a lot of what instructor says

5–6   Student comprehends most/all of what instructor says

Illustration 9.14
Continued

Part III: Interview (Asking Questions) (40%)

Fluency

1	Speech halting and fragmentary; long, unnatural pauses or utterances
2	Speech very slow and uneven, except for short or routine sentences
3	Speech frequently hesitant and jerky; sentences may be left uncompleted
4	Some definite stumbling, but manages to rephrase or continue
5	Speech generally natural and continuous; only slight stumbling or unnatural pauses
6	Speech natural and continuous; no unnatural pauses

Vocabulary (breadth and precision of usage)

1–2	Lacks basic words; inadequate, inaccurate usage
3–4	Often lacks needed words; somewhat inaccurate usage
5–6	Occasionally lacks basic words; generally accurate usage
7–8	Rich and extensive vocabulary; very accurate usage

Structure

1	No utterances rendered correctly
2	Very few utterances rendered correctly
3	Some utterances rendered correctly, but major structural problems remain
4	Many correct utterances, but with definite structural problems
5	Most utterances rendered correctly, with some minor structural errors
6	Utterances almost always correct

Comprehensibility

1–2	Entirely/almost entirely incomprehensible to native speaker of Spanish
3–4	Mostly incomprehensible; occasional phrases comprehensible
5–6	Many errors, about half incomprehensible
7–8	Many errors; but still mostly comprehensible
9–10	Almost entirely comprehensible to native speaker of Spanish; only an occasional word not comprehensible
11–12	Entirely comprehensible to native speaker of Spanish; no words incomprehensible

Listening Comprehension

2	Student comprehends one instructor answer
4	Student comprehends two instructor answers
6	Student comprehends three instructor answers
8	Student comprehends four instructor answers

Source: Boylan 1982.

Illustration 9.15
Oral Test Interview
Cards

French 101
Oral Test I

Situation A

Vous parlez de votre chambre à l'université. Posez les questions suivantes. Posez d'autres questions aussi, avec des mots comme *comment?, combien?, pourquoi?, où?, quand?,* etc.

Ask your partner . . .
- how s/he is today
- whom s/he lives with at the university
- if there is a telephone in his/her room
- if his friends like to visit his/her room
- how old his/her roommate is

Situation B

Vous êtes propriétaire et vous avez une chambre d'étudiant à louer. Vous parlez à un(e) étudiant(e). Posez les questions suivantes. Posez d'autres questions aussi, avec des mots comme *comment?, combien?, pourquoi?, où?, quand?,* etc.

Ask your partner . . .
- how s/he is today
- where s/he is a student
- if s/he has any animals
- if s/he has a television, radio, or stereo
- if s/he is a good, serious student

Situation C

Vous êtes étudiant(e) et vous cherchez une chambre à louer. Posez les questions suivantes à la propriétaire. Posez d'autres questions aussi, avec des mots comme *comment?, combien?, pourquoi?, où?, quand?,* etc.

Ask your partner . . .
- how s/he is today
- if s/he has a room to rent
- if there is a shower or sink in the room
- if there is a telephone or TV
- if the room has curtains and a rug
- if the room is expensive

Situation D

Vous parlez avec un(e) ami(e) de vos activités préférées. Posez les questions suivantes à votre ami(e). Posez d'autres questions aussi, avec des mots comme *comment?, combien?, pourquoi?, où?, quand?,* etc.

Ask your partner . . .
- how s/he is today
- if s/he plays tennis a lot
- if s/he likes to go to the movies
- if s/he watches TV sometimes
- if s/he needs a new stereo (use an expression with *avoir*)

The conversation cards should serve as a stimulus for conversation and should not be used as a translation task. Teachers should feel free to expand the interview, asking additional questions that are based on the course material and taking care not to push students far beyond their current level of competence. Students should also be encouraged to expand the interview by asking any follow-up questions that come to mind. Note that ideas for expanding the interview are provided on the cards themselves.

The whole interview process is taped so that the speech sample can be analyzed and scored at a later time. To enable students to keep a record of their speech, they may be asked to provide their own tape. Over the course of several semesters, the oral tests can be recorded on the same tape so that students can hear their progress over time. Often, the progress is quite dramatic, even when the actual proficiency level of the sample has not changed markedly.

When listening to the taped interview later, the teacher can take notes on a score sheet such as the one in Illustration 9.16. This score sheet will be explained in more detail in the next section.

Paired Interviews. In this variant of the oral achievement test, the teacher sets up a 30-minute time slot for each pair of students. Each student chooses a conversation card at random, and one student is asked to begin the exam. The student reads the situation aloud to his or her partner and starts to ask questions based on the cues. As the second student answers, the teacher records the conversation on the score sheet by noting questions on the left and answers on the right (see Illustration 9.16). The students then change roles, with the second student using his or her conversation card to ask questions of the first student. The teacher uses the reverse side of the score sheet, which is lined in the same manner, to take notes again: this time, the second student's questions are recorded on the left and the first student's answers are recorded on the right. When the exam is finished, the teacher can cut the score sheet in half and hand it back to the students individually.

During the conversation the teacher does not intervene, unless the speech of one student is incomprehensible to the other. If this should happen, the teacher can ask the student to repeat the question or answer, or can provide some help, noting down on the score sheet that help was needed. When students have had regular, in-class practice on such conversational activities, they often understand one another quite well and seek little help from the instructor during the interview.

Scoring the Interview Test. On the basis of the speech protocol of each student, the instructor assigns a global grade of A through E for each of the four categories on the lower portion of the score sheet: pronunciation, vocabulary, grammar, and fluency. The score sheet also includes a conversion table that allows for some variability in the letter-grade categories. For example, a very good performance might be given an A or 5.0 grade, whereas a slightly less impressive performance, though still meriting an A

Illustration 9.16
Score sheet for
oral tests

FRENCH 101 & 102 SPEAKING TEST: STUDENT SCORE SHEET

Name _____   Name _____

NOTES: NOTES:

Pronunciation
E   D   C   B   A
[| | | |] __ x4 = __

Vocabulary
E   D   C   B   A
[| | | |] __ x7 = __

Grammar
E   D   C   B   A
[| | | |] __ x6 = __

Fluency
E   D   C   B   A
[| | | |] __ x3 = __

A = 4.5 - 5.0   Total = __
B = 4.0 - 4.4
C = 3.5 - 3.9
D = 3.0 - 3.4
E = 2.0 - 2.9

Pronunciation
E   D   C   B   A
[| | | |] __ x4 = __

Vocabulary
E   D   C   B   A
[| | | |] __ x7 = __

Grammar
E   D   C   B   A
[| | | |] __ x6 = __

Fluency
E   D   C   B   A
[| | | |] __ x3 = __

A = 4.5 - 5.0   Total = __
B = 4.0 - 4.4
C = 3.5 - 3.9
D = 3.0 - 3.4
E = 2.0 - 2.9

Source: Omaggio 1983.

in the instructor's judgment, might be given a 4.5, or A– grade. The instructor can check one box for each category and then convert each letter grade into a number. The number obtained is entered in the first space to the right of the box and multiplied by the weight provided: pronunciation, 4; vocabulary, 7; grammaticality, 6; and fluency, 3. The sum of the weighted scores will add up to 100 if all categories receive a grade of 5.0.

The weighting scheme depicted on this scoresheet is appropriate for Novice and Intermediate students, based on research done by Higgs and Clifford (1981) which shows that speech profiles of learners in this range reflect primarily knowledge of vocabulary and grammar. Pronunciation and fluency, as well as sociolinguistic factors, contribute much less to the overall rating at these levels of competence. The score sheet can also be adjusted to reflect weightings that are more suitable for Advanced-level learners: more weight will then be assigned to grammatical accuracy and fluency, as well as to sociolinguistic features, especially when these goals are emphasized in the program.

At the end of the semester at the University of Illinois, French students come in individually for a final oral achievement test, consisting of an interview much like the ACTFL Oral Proficiency Interview, but limited to topics and structures covered in the course. The interview for first-semester students consists of four parts: (1) a *warm-up*, in which students respond to greetings, questions about the weather, questions about how they are feeling, or about how their day is going; (2) a brief section involving *simple description and information-sharing in the present*, in which students are asked to talk about their families, studies at the university, and/or favorite pastimes; (3) a *description of a familiar drawing or picture*, derived from the textbook or ancillary materials; and (4) a brief *interview* of the instructor, prompted by a situation card that asks students, for example, to create their own questions for a fictitious interview for the school newspaper. All of these topics are related directly to material studied in the course. In second, third, and fourth-semester courses, interview materials are adjusted to allow for other types of tasks that reflect the topics studied in those courses. In all of the oral interview materials, instructors are given ideas for possible starter questions for each section of the test, as well as potential follow-up questions that would allow them to expand the interview if the student is able to elaborate somewhat on the initial topic. Oral tests are recorded, and instructors use the score sheet in Illustration 9.16 to assign a grade to the sample elicited.

Oral quizzes and exams can be structured in many different ways: not all need to be modeled on the OPI. Some instructors prefer to have students describe pictures, engage in role plays, or perform skits for a grade. Others give oral grades based on the evaluation of a selection of interactive tasks that take place in the classroom over a period of several weeks. McPherson (1992) describes an oral assessment procedure that involves in-class interviews with native speakers, after which students provide an oral summary of what they learned on audiotape for a grade. Haggstrom (1992) gives students an interactive task, such as making dates and appointments with others in the classroom, and videotapes each student several times during the activity. She then assesses the samples collected and assigns grades based on the students' performance.

The research referred to earlier in this chapter by Harlow and Caminero (1990) reveals that a variety of oral testing formats are used in the large universities they surveyed. Eighty-seven percent of the respondents reported that oral tests involved answering questions, 55% reported using role-play, 28% had students describe a picture or something they do, 25% had students read a passage for the purpose of grading pronunciation, 23% reported having students ask the instructor questions, and one department asked students to interpret into English an instructor's responses (pp. 492–493). According to the survey results, most oral tests lasted from 10 to 15 minutes, and for 45% of the programs, all testing was done outside of class, usually in the instructor's office. Fifty-five percent of the respondents indicated that they used class time to administer at least some of their oral tests, and several departments indicated that they set aside a day or more of the course syllabus just for oral testing.

It is clear from the Harlow and Caminero study that many instructors consider oral testing to be an important part of an overall assessment program, especially when communicative language proficiency is the stated goal of instruction. As is the case for the other skill areas, tests of oral performance need to resemble authentic language use as much as possible. Formal exams can, of course, be supplemented with informal assessment throughout the semester to allow for the evaluation of student performance in a variety of language-use situations.

Summary: Classroom Testing

The suggestions for classroom testing presented in this chapter are offered as an alternative to achievement tests based mainly on discrete points of grammar and isolated-sentence formats. As our knowledge and expertise in the field of testing increases over the next years, new ideas for classroom testing will be discovered and disseminated that will help us bridge the gap between our statement of course goals in communicative terms and their measurement. A list of professional priorities that should be addressed in the coming years might include the following points:

1. Professional conferences and workshops should be organized to help teachers devise model testing techniques that incorporate natural language as much as possible into their course exams.
2. Local and regional in-service training workshops should be encouraged to disseminate these models to classroom teachers and to stimulate discussion and idea sharing.

3. Computerized item banks should be used to make the development of new or parallel tests less time consuming. When model test items are stored for a given unit, it should be a relatively simple matter to retrieve old items, change the contexts slightly, and thus create new tests for a subsequent semester.
4. Teacher education programs should include a course on test development among the requirements for certification.
5. Textbook publishers should consider using contextualized formats for any test instruments provided with their programs.

These recommendations parallel some of those made by Woodford (1980) in his "plan for action" for foreign language testing. We cannot afford to continue to ignore the problems inherent in conserving our more traditional methods of achievement testing. The means by which we evaluate our students' skills in the classroom today will determine, in large part, the success of our programs in the future.

Notes

1. This chapter is based, in part, on *Proficiency-Oriented Classroom Testing* by Alice C. Omaggio.
2. For readers interested in obtaining information about the training opportunities in oral proficiency testing, write to ACTFL, 6 Executive Boulevard, Upper Level, Yonkers, NY 10701.

• • • • • • • • • • • • *Appendix*

Sample Test: First-year hourly achievement test in Italian

This sample test is given to illustrate how some of the formats described in this chapter might be used to create an hourly exam. The sample is not offered as an "ideal" test, but rather is provided for purposes of discussion (see Question 1 in the "Activities for Review and Discussion" section, on page 477). The construction of this test is described in Illustration 9.10, and a sample evaluation of its strengths and weaknesses is provided in Illustration 9.11.

Italian 101
Unit Test 2
Instructor's Copy

A. *Dettato con risposte.* Read each question twice. Students are to take down the questions as a dictation and then go back and answer them in complete sentences in Italian. (15 points; 3 points per question, 2 points per answer)

1. Preferisce un bel appartamento moderno o una casa piccola?
2. Cerca sempre di avere ragione?
3. Cucina spesso o mangia al ristorante?

B. *Un'intervista.* A reporter for *Epoca* is interviewing an American exchange student in Rome. You are transcribing the interview, but the reporter didn't tell you his questions! For each statement that Eddie makes, write an appropriate question in the blank provided. (25 points; 5 points each)

C. *La camera di Daniela.* Shown below is Daniela's dormitory room. Using the vocabulary you know, answer the questions below the picture. (30 points; Part 1, 24 points, Part 2, 6 points)

D. *Una soluzione semplice.* Daniela and Laura, her roommate, do not like their apartment. One day they decide to look for another place. Complete their conversation. The conversation in English is next to the one in Italian. (30 points)

Italian 101   Nome _____
Unit Test 2
Student Copy

A. *Dettato con risposte.* Each question will be read twice. Take down the questions as a dictation and then go back and answer them in complete sentences in Italian. (15 points; 3 points per question, 2 points per answer)

1. _____ ?
   _____ .
2. _____ ?
   _____ .
3. _____ ?
   _____ .

B. *Un'intervista.* A reporter for *Epoca* is interviewing an American exchange student in Rome. You are transcribing the interview, but the reporter didn't tell you his questions! For each statement that Eddie makes, write an appropriate question in the blank provided. (25 points; 5 points each)

1. Il giornalista: _____ ?
   Eddie: Perchè desidero studiare l'italiano!
2. Il giornalista: _____ ?
   Eddie: Ho ventiquattro anni.
3. Il giornalista: _____ ?
   Eddie: Ci sono quattro americani nella mia classe.
4. Il giornalista: _____ ?
   Eddie: Abito a Frederick, Maryland.
5. Il giornalista: _____ ?
   Eddie: Ritorno negli Stati Uniti il 12 aprile.

C. *La camera di Daniela.* Shown below is Daniela's dormitory room. Using the vocabulary you know, answer the questions below the picture. (30 points)

Source: Omaggio 1983. Illustration by Sonia Kundert.

1. Describe Daniela's room by completing the sentence below. Name eight objects in the room and use a different adjective to describe each object. Choose the adjectives from the following list: antico, bello, grande, comodo, piccolo, nero, verde, vecchio. Be sure to make the adjective agree and to place it appropriately. (24 points)

Nella camera di Daniela c'è un(a) _____, _____, _____, _____, _____, _____, _____, e _____.

2. Write two complete sentences in Italian telling what Daniela does NOT have in her room. (6 points)

_____

_____

D. *Una soluzione semplice.* Daniela and Laura, her roommate, do not like their apartment. One day they decide to look for another place. Complete their conversation. The conversation in English is next to the one in Italian. (30 points)

Laura: Non mi piace _____ appartamento. La cucina è troppo _____ e _____. Inoltre è troppo caro!

I don't like our apartment. The kitchen is too small and there's no garden. Besides, it's too expensive.

Daniela: _____ un appartamento da affittare vicino all'università?

Doesn't your aunt have an apartment for rent near the university?

Laura: Oh sí! _____! Voglio telefonarle prorio adesso!

Ah yes! That's true! I'm going to phone her right away!

Al telefono
Laura: Pronto, Stefano? C'è ____? ...Oh, capisco, lei _____. Possiamo vedere il _____ appartamento in via Garibaldi questo pomeriggio? Noi _____ di trovare un _____ appartamento. ...Va bene, d'accordo. Ciao.

On the phone
Hello, Stephen? Is your mother there? ...Oh, I see, she's doing errands. Can we see her apartment on Garibaldi Street this afternoon? We're hoping to find another apartment.... OK, good. See you soon.

Nell'appartamento
Daniela: È meraviglioso! Ci sono _____, un _____, un _____ ...c'è tutto!

At the apartment
This is great! There are three large bedrooms, a terrace, a pretty living room ...everything!

Laura: _____ pagare l'affitto ora?

Do we need to pay the rent now?

Stefano: No, non adesso.... Incredible! Le donne _____ subito _____ appartamento!

No, not now.... It's incredible! Women choose their apartments fast!

Laura: _____ di trovare un _____ posto come questo.

We're lucky to find a nice place like this.

Daniela: Mi piace sopratutto il lavastoviglie in cucina. _____!

I especially like the dishwasher in the kitchen. I hate to do the dishes.

Source: Adapted from Omaggio 1983, pp. 91–94.

Activities for Review and Discussion

1. Examine the sample Italian test given in the Appendix to this chapter. Using the form in Illustration 9.11, discuss the characteristics of the test with others in a small group. Do you agree with the assessment given on the form in Illustration 9.11? What are the strengths and weaknesses of this exam, in your opinion? How would you

change the exam to improve it? (Keep in mind that this exam was designed for a first-semester course.)

2. Obtain copies of classroom quizzes and tests that (a) you have taken as a language student yourself or (b) are being given in a language program with which you are familiar. Examine these tests using the schema for assessing characteristics of test items presented in Illustration 9.11. How would you characterize the various items on each of the tests? Discuss how well these tests seem to match course goals. What, if anything, would you do to improve the tests you have analyzed?

3. Using one of the suggested format types in this chapter, design an original listening comprehension test item or item set for a particular chapter or unit in an appropriate textbook (either one that you are using or one that your instructor provides). Be sure to write clear directions and explain how the item is to be scored.

4. Find an authentic text appropriate for students reading at the Intermediate level of proficiency (see Appendix A for the ACTFL Guidelines in reading). Design a reading comprehension test item or item set based on this text. You may want to use a fairly simple prose passage or choose an advertisement, brochure, or other appropriate text from an authentic source.

5. Based on a particular chapter or unit in an appropriate language textbook, design two original test items or item sets that involve mixed skills. Feel free to use formats described in this chapter, or design your own formats based on the examples presented here.

6. Develop a testing grid, such as the one presented in Illustration 9.10, for a chapter or unit in the language textbook you are using or in a textbook provided by your instructor. Be sure to include skill emphases, item format types, and point values for your exam.

7. Discuss various options for oral testing that you might use in your own language program. How might oral testing be done efficiently in a teaching situation where you have several classes, each with 30 students or more?

References

Bacon, Susan M. and Michael D. Finneman. "A Study of the Attitudes, Motives, and Strategies of University Foreign-Language Students and Their Disposition to Authentic Oral and Written Input." *The Modern Language Journal* 74 (1990): 459–73.

Barnes, Betsy K., Carol A. Klee, and Ray M. Wakefield. "Reconsidering the FL Requirement: From Seat-Time to Proficiency in the Minnesota Experience." Pp. 55–69 In S. Magnan, ed., *Challenges in the 1990s for College Foreign Language Programs. Issues in Language Program Direction.* Boston: Heinle & Heinle Publishers, 1991.

Bernhardt, Elizabeth B. "Testing Foreign Language Reading Comprehension: The Immediate Recall Protocol." *Die Unterrichtspraxis* 16 (1983): 27–33.

Bernhardt, Elizabeth B. and Charles J. James. "The Teaching and Testing of Comprehension in Foreign Language Learning." Chapter 5 (pp. 65–81) in D. W. Birckbichler, ed., *Proficiency, Policy, and Professionalism in Foreign Language Education.* Report of the Central States Conference on the Teaching of Foreign Languages. Lincolnwood, IL: National Textbook Company, 1987.

Bonin, Thérèse and Diane W. Birckbichler. "Real Communication through Conversation Cards." *The Modern Language Journal* 59 (1975): 22–25.

Boylan, Patricia C. Personal communication, 1982.

Buck, Kathryn, Heidi Byrnes, and Irene Thompson, eds. *The ACTFL Oral Proficiency Interview Tester Training Manual.* Yonkers, NY: ACTFL, 1989.

Clark, John L. D. *Foreign Language Testing: Theory and Practice.* Philadelphia: Center for Curriculum Development, 1972.

Coulont-Henderson, Françoise. Personal communication, 1992.

Dandonoli, Patricia. "ACTFL's Current Research in Proficiency Testing." Chapter 3 (pp. 75–96) in H. Byrnes and M. Canale, eds., *Defining and Developing Proficiency: Guidelines, Implementations and Concepts.* The ACTFL Foreign Language Education Series. Lincolnwood, IL: National Textbook Company, 1987.

Ellis, Rod. *Understanding Second Language Acquisition.* Oxford: Oxford University Press, 1985.

_____. *Instructed Second Language Acquisition.* Oxford: Basil Blackwell, 1990.

Freed, Barbara. "Proficiency in Context: The Pennsylvania Experience." Chapter 14 (pp. 211–40) in S. J. Savignon and M. S. Berns, eds., *Initiatives in Communicative Language Teaching.* Reading, MA: Addison-Wesley Publishing Company, 1984.

_____. "Preliminary Impressions of the Effects of a Proficiency-Based Language Requirement." *Foreign Language Annals* 20 (1987): 139–46.

Grellet, Françoise. *Developing Reading Skills.* Cambridge: Cambridge University Press, 1981.

Gutiérrez, John R. and Harry Rosser. *Ya verás! Segundo nivel.* Boston: Heinle & Heinle Publishers, 1992.

Haggstrom, Margaret. "Using a Videocamera and Task-Based Activities to Make Classroom Oral Testing a More Realistic Communicative Experience." Presentation at the 1992 ACTFL Annual Meeting, Rosemont, IL, November 20, 1992.

Harlow, Linda and Rosario Caminero. "Oral Testing of Beginning Language Students at Large Universities: Is It Worth the Trouble?" *Foreign Language Annals* 23, vi (1990): 489–501.

Higgs, Theodore V. "Group Oral Proficiency Testing Using the VOCI (Visual/Oral Communication Instrument)." Presentation at the 1992 ACTFL Annual Meeting, Rosemont, IL, November 21, 1992.

Higgs, Theodore V. and Ray Clifford. "The Push Toward Communication." In Theodore V. Higgs, ed., *Curriculum, Competence, and the Foreign Language Teacher.* ACTFL Foreign Language Education Series, vol. 13. Lincolnwood, IL: National Textbook Company, 1982.

Hosenfeld, Carol. "Learning about Learning: Discovering Our Students' Strategies." *Foreign Language Annals* 9 (1976): 117–29.

Liskin-Gasparro, Judith. *The ETS Oral Proficiency Testing Manual.* Princeton, NJ: Educational Testing Service, 1982.

Lowe, Pardee. *The ILR Handbook on Oral Interview Testing.* Washington, DC: Defense Language Institute/Language School Interview Transfer Project, 1982.

Lowe, Pardee and Ray T. Clifford. "Developing an Indirect Measure of Overall Oral Proficiency." Pp. 31–39 in James R. Frith, ed., *Measuring Spoken Language Proficiency.* Washington, DC: Georgetown University Press, 1980.

Magnan, Sally S. "Just Do It: Directing TAs toward Task-Based and Process-Oriented Testing." Pp. 135–161 in Richard V. Teschner, ed., *Assessing Foreign Language Proficiency of Undergraduates.* Issues in Language Program Direction. Boston: Heinle & Heinle Publishers, 1991.

McMillen Villar, Susan and Fran Meuser Blincow. Personal communication, 1993.

McPherson, Elina. "Enhancing Linguistic Spontaneity through Interviews with Native Speakers." Presentation at the 1992 ACTFL Annual Meeting, Rosemont, IL, November 20, 1992.

Muyskens, Judith A., Linda L. Harlow, and Michèle Vialet. *Bravo! Communication et grammaire.* Boston: Heinle & Heinle Publishers, 1989.

Omaggio, Alice C. *Proficiency-Oriented Classroom Testing.* Washington, DC: Center for Applied Linguistics, 1983.

Shohamy, Elana. "Affective Considerations in Language Teaching." *The Modern Language Journal* 66 (1982): 13–17.

_____. "Connecting Testing and Learning in the Classroom and on the Program Level." Pp. 154–78 in June K. Phillips, ed., *Building Bridges and Making Connections.* Reports of the Northeast Conference on the Teaching of Foreign Languages. Middlebury, VT: Northeast Conference, 1991.

Slager, William R. "Creating Contexts for Language Practice." In E. Joiner and P. Westphal, eds., *Developing Communication Skills.* Rowley, MA: Newbury House, 1978.

Stansfield, Charles W. and Dorry M. Kenyon. "The Development and Validation of a Simulated Oral Proficiency Interview." *The Modern Language Journal* 76, ii (1992): 129–41.

Tarone, Elaine. "On the Variability of Interlanguage Systems." *Applied Linguistics* 4 (1983): 143–63.

Terry, Robert. Personal communication, 1985.

_____. "Improving Inter-rater Reliability in Scoring Tests in Multisection Courses." Pp. 229–62 in J. C. Walz, ed., *Development and Supervision of Teaching Assistants in Foreign Languages.* Issues in Language Program Direction. Boston: Heinle & Heinle Publishers, 1992.

Valdman, Albert. "Testing Communicative Ability at the University Level." *ADFL Bulletin*13 (1981): 1–5.

Valette, Rebecca M. "Developing and Evaluating Communication Skills in the Classroom." In E. Joiner and P. Westphal, eds., *Developing Communication Skills.* Rowley, MA: Newbury House, 1978.

Wesche, Marjorie B. "Communicative Testing in a Second Language." *Canadian Modern Language Review* 37 (1981): 551–71.

Woodford, Protase E. "Foreign Language Testing." *The Modern Language Journal* 64 (1980): 97–102.

10

Planning Instruction for the Proficiency-Oriented Classroom: Some Practical Guidelines

In Chapters 1 through 9, a variety of methodological approaches and theories of language learning and acquisition were considered using proficiency as the organizing principle. A rationale was given for teaching language in a culturally authentic context and for personalizing language practice as much as possible. Sample formats for proficiency-oriented classroom activities were illustrated, as were ideas for infusing cultural materials into the curriculum.

If the accumulation of a repertoire of teaching strategies were enough to ensure effective instruction in the classroom, it might seem reasonable to end the discussion of methodology here. But planning and delivering effective instruction involves much more than understanding language acquisition theories and knowing some appropriate techniques. Just what makes instruction or a given teacher "effective" is still open to some debate. And characterizing the "perfect" teacher is like trying to develop the "perfect" method: just as there is no "one true way" to teach, there is no one definitive profile of the effective teacher.

Yet there are certain elements that are common to good teaching, even when individual personalities and styles vary considerably. First, effective teachers *plan* instruction carefully and efficiently. They have a clear idea of what the programmatic and course goals are, and they try to reach those goals by actively involving students in their own learning and appealing to their interests and needs. Obviously, daily planning must be related to an overall curricular plan if it is to be effective. Therefore, teachers need to be concerned with long-range curricular goals, and, ideally, should be involved in both the planning and the evaluation of the curriculum in their own institutions.

Because curriculum planning involves such things as the setting of goals (for both the whole sequence of instruction and each individual course), the selection of materials and teaching approaches, the design of the testing program, and the appropriate use of program-evaluation procedures, effective teachers need to be familiar with all aspects of program design. To evaluate outcomes of instruction, teachers need efficient strategies for record keeping and clearly delineated criteria for assigning grades. On a regular basis, they should solicit student input in course evaluations, using that input to alter and improve instruction.

In this chapter, some of the skills necessary in the planning and administration of successful second-language programs are outlined and discussed. Guidelines for goal setting, text selection, syllabus design, lesson planning, record keeping, and course evaluation are suggested.

Setting Goals for a Proficiency-Oriented Program

Medley (1985) has outlined various approaches one might use for designing a proficiency-based curriculum, in both high school and college settings. One approach, developed by Galloway and presented in a workshop co-directed by Medley and Galloway at the University of South Carolina in August 1984, suggests that goal-controlled planning begin with the ACTFL guidelines at each instructional level, from high school through college. Galloway emphasizes that one must not consider the guidelines to be goal statements. However, she does feel that they can be used as an articulation device between holistic proficiency assessment and goal-oriented curriculum design (Galloway, cited in Medley 1985.) Medley describes the development process as follows:

> The task of the curriculum developer is to somehow translate these broad level descriptions [i.e., the ACTFL Guidelines] first into general goal statements, and then into much more specific performance outcome statements for each year or semester of instruction (Medley 1985, p. 25).

The descriptions of functions and content areas typically handled by learners at a given level of proficiency can be translated in various ways into goal statements and performance outcomes. For instance, one might generate goal statements for a four-year high school sequence as follows:

> Upon completion of the prescribed four-year sequence of study, the student will be able to:
> 1. ask and answer questions related to personal needs, familiar topics and current events, as well as work, family and autobiographical information;
> 2. narrate and describe in past, present, and future time; and
> 3. initiate and sustain a conversation, observing basic courtesy requirements and social demands of the culture (Medley 1985, p. 27).

This set of statements relates to the attainment of goals derived from (but not identical to) the Intermediate and Advanced level descriptions of the ACTFL Guidelines. More specific performance outcome statements can be generated from these overall goal statements, with specific course goals outlined in greater detail for all the skill areas.

Medley explains that there are two possible approaches that can be taken in the goal-setting process. One might be to look first at the total curriculum and establish some optimum desired performance level as an ultimate goal, and then plan the individual course outlines for each year so that this ultimate goal can be reached. Medley points out, however, that this type of procedure often results in courses that are "unrealistically cluttered with items that have to be taught before next year" (p. 25). He cites Strasheim (1984), who believed that we need to rethink each instructional level in the sequence of courses that make up a total curriculum, reconciling what we know about language learning with both student needs and realistic expectations.

Rather than trying to achieve some kind of "curricular fit" within an idealized master plan for the entire curriculum, a second approach that Medley describes would begin by setting goals for the first course and continuing course by course until realistic goals have been established for the whole sequence. For example, a college course coordinator for the first two years of instruction in Language X may, after several semesters of testing and observation, in cooperation with colleagues and/or teaching assistants, determine that a realistic expectation for oral proficiency at the end of the first semester course is Intermediate-Low. Some students might be better in oral skills than that, while others who complete the course may still be in the Novice-High range. Knowing, however, that most students are able to attain the Intermediate level of proficiency in oral skills enables the coordinator to set realistic goals for the second semester, and so on. Similar goals can be set for each of the skill areas until the overall expected outcome of the four-semester sequence can be described in a satisfactory manner (Medley 1985, p. 27). Such a procedure facilitates articulation between courses and levels of instruction—including the high school to college transition—a problem that has challenged the language teaching profession for years.

Guidelines for Text Selection

Once a set of goal statements is generated for a given course, instructional materials that are congruent with the specified goals can be selected. Not all classroom teachers have the opportunity to choose their textbook for a given course, but for those who do have a say in the selection, some of the guidelines that follow may be helpful. It is important to bear in mind that the textbook does not, in and of itself, constitute the curriculum, for curriculum includes much more than the set of materials used to deliver instruction. In addition, the text cannot guarantee successful language learning. Only the students and the teacher can determine how effective the course will be in enhancing language proficiency. An excellent teacher working with unmotivated learners and mediocre materials may be able to generate some enthusiasm for learning in spite of the text. On the other hand, a mediocre teacher working with an excellent text may fail to do so. It seems evident, however, that it is much easier for teachers and students to attain proficiency goals when text materials are designed to reflect those goals directly.

Just as there is no one "proficiency method," there are no "proficiency textbooks" per se. However, some textbooks can be more proficiency-oriented than others in terms of their design and general approach to language learning. If the hypothesized principles of proficiency-oriented instruction that were listed in Chapter 3 were applied to textbook selection, a list of optimal features could be generated. For example, a good textbook should include:

1. Contextualized language-practice activities, affording abundant practice in a range of contexts likely to be encountered in the target culture
2. Personalized and creative practice activities that encourage students to express their own meaning in their own words as early in the program as possible
3. Suggestions for group work and active communicative interaction among students
4. Authentic language in exercises, readings, and dialogues, as well as abundant realia throughout the text, integrated with language-practice activities
5. Functional/notional concepts, together with ample opportunities to practice a range of tasks using these concepts
6. Clear and concise grammatical explanations that enable students to work toward accuracy goals from the beginning of instruction
7. Appealing topics, themes, readings, and activities that respond to the needs and interests of students
8. Cultural material integrated with language-practice activities, selected to reflect both deep and surface culture phenomena, and incorporating both "hearthstone" and "Olympian" culture in a balanced fashion that will appeal to students' interests

Bragger (1985) suggests that teachers look at textbooks with questions such as the following in mind. Her inventory of questions is summarized and presented in a somewhat modified form below:

1. To what extent are the exercises, including the simple transformational variety, contextualized and personalized?
2. To what extent are the exercises organized to move from structured pattern practice to open-ended activities? Are the creative practice activities optional, or are they an important part of the text?
3. Are the communicative activities designed to help students accomplish specific functional tasks in a variety of contexts?

4. Are students made responsible for their own learning?

5. Are dialogues in the book and tape program contrived, or do they reflect authentic language use?

6. How varied is the vocabulary? Are students given the opportunity to express likes and dislikes, or is the vocabulary "generic?" Is the vocabulary recycled throughout the text? Is it functional, high-frequency, and current?

7. Are structures presented within a functional orientation and integrated with the themes of the chapter in which they occur?

8. Are the communicative situations simulations of what is likely to happen in a target-culture setting? (Based on pp. 61–62.)

Bragger's set of questions, like the set of features presented earlier, is not meant to be exhaustive, but provides some guidance for the teacher seeking a text that will support proficiency goals and enable students to learn language in context. It is important, when selecting a textbook program, to examine the ancillary materials (workbooks, tapes, computer software, etc.) with these same criteria in mind. If a testing program is included, the tests should be examined and compared to the testing principles suggested in Chapter 9. Obviously, no perfect program exists, but textbook publishers are anxious to satisfy the demands of classroom teachers, and it is important to let them know, on a regular basis, what our needs and expectations are.

Designing the Course Syllabus

A well-designed course syllabus is a necessary component of a successful language program, from both the teacher's and the students' points of view. For teachers, the course syllabus provides direction and guidance in the scope, sequence, and pacing of classroom activities; for students, the syllabus provides at a glance the profile of the semester's work and the expectations for successful completion of that work. It is strongly recommended that teachers distribute course syllabi and any accompanying information sheets on the first day of class so that students will know what is expected of them. A sample course information sheet for a first-semester university-level French course is shown in Illustration 10.1.

The syllabus itself should include information about daily reading and homework assignments, as well as quizzes and tests. Syllabi can range from very simple ones in which page numbers indicate reading assignments to be completed for each class day, to more complex formats in which the content of each class day is more completely described.

Bragger (1985) suggests, for example, that the components of the *ACTFL Guidelines* be used as a basis for syllabus design. She would include function, content/context and accuracy objectives under each daily syllabus entry. For example, a given day on the syllabus might be described as

Illustration 10.1

Course information
sheet

French 101

Instructor ＿＿＿＿＿＿＿＿＿＿
Office No. ＿＿＿＿＿＿＿＿＿＿
Office Hours ＿＿＿＿＿＿＿＿＿

Placement Test

You are reminded that if you have ever taken any high school French and no subsequent coursework in French at the college or university level, you must take the placement exam in order to receive credit for French courses here. You can arrange to take the exam by asking for an authorization form in the French Department office.

Textbooks: (Course text and ancillaries are listed here.)

Evaluation:		
Exams (3)	30%	
Quizzes (4)	15%	
Oral Exams (2)	15%	
Compositions (7)	10%	
Daily Preparation	10%	
Final Exam	20%	

Classwork

Although class attendance is not a formal component of your grade, you should understand that frequent or extended absences will not allow you to develop your oral skills and will therefore influence the instructor's evaluation of your in-class oral performance. The instructor is also under no obligation to accept overdue homework assignments. If you miss a class, it is your responsibility to find out what material was covered during your absence.

Tests and Quizzes

The dates of all tests and quizzes are included on the syllabus. Absence from tests will be excused only if you provide written proof of the reason for your absence. Instructors are not required to give make-up tests.

If you know ahead of time that you will have to miss a test, it is to your advantage to notify your instructor and make appropriate alternative arrangements. The arrangements are at the discretion of your instructor.

There will be two oral tests in the course of the semester. They are given by appointment in your instructor's office. If you are unable to keep your appointment, it is your responsibility to notify your instructor in advance to reschedule the interview.

Illustration 10.1
Continued

Homework and Compositions

Your written assignments are given in the course syllabus and are due on the dates indicated. Assignments in the workbook should be self-corrected, in a contrasting ink color, using the key in the back of the workbook. All assignments that are corrected carefully and turned in on time will be acceptable. Assignments that are not corrected or are incomplete will not be accepted and will receive a grade of 0. You will receive 100 points if all 7 assignments are turned in. You will recieve 90 points for 6 completed assignments, 80 points for 5, 70 points for 4, and 60 points for 3. Less than 3 completed assignments will result in a failing grade for homework.

Laboratory

You should plan to attend lab regularly. Classroom activities and tests are based on the assumption that you are getting the speaking and listening practice provided by the tapes that accompany each lesson in your text.

Communication

Because a very important course goal in French 101 is the development of speaking and listening skills, 25% of your grade will be based on your achievement in these areas. Oral tests and oral participation in class will serve as the basis for evaluation of these goals, as will listening sections on quizzes and unit tests. It is to your advantage to listen to the lab tapes, practice with conversation cards, interviews, and other small-group work in class, and attend all class sessions. If you work on these goals regularly, you should find that your listening and speaking proficiency develops fairly rapidly within the first year of instruction.

Summary of Course Goals

French 101 is designed to help you learn enough about French to enable you to handle your needs adequately if you travel to France or a French-speaking country. You will be able to talk about yourself and your preferences, needs, and interests simply in present and future time. You will learn to greet others, introduce yourself, handle basic social situations, handle routine travel needs, obtain food and lodging, use the phone, carry out simple transactions at the bank and post office, and talk about a variety of topics of common interest. In addition, you will learn how to read and write simply in present and future time and how to understand French well enough to carry out routine tasks and engage in simple conversations. You will also learn about some aspects of everyday culture in France. In short, the goal of this course is to help you learn to cope on your own in French and meet your basic travel needs should you go to a French-speaking country.

follows: Day 17 (or date)—Function: Asking questions; Context: Purchasing clothing; Accuracy: Use of interrogative pronouns, their placement, accurate intonation in interrogative sentences, precision in vocabulary (p. 63). The advantage of such an approach is that students can glance through the course syllabus and know more about what they will be able to do at the end of the course than the mere number of textbook pages they will cover. Such a topical syllabus would be relatively easy to design, although it might become somewhat cumbersome to use, especially when goals relate to reading, writing, listening, and cultural understanding as well as oral proficiency. Teachers using textbooks that clearly outline chapter objectives in terms of contextual, cultural, grammatical, and functional goals may be more comfortable with an abbreviated syllabus. Such a syllabus might be accompanied by a brief prose description of the course goals, following Bragger's suggestion, that will enable students to see clearly what they can hope to accomplish during the semester.

• • • • • • • • • • • *Guidelines for Planning Lessons*

Many of the same principles that apply to the selection of materials can be used in designing daily lesson plans: that is, lessons should be planned to include contextualized and personalized practice, small-group interaction, creative language use, culturally authentic listening and reading practice, and functional tasks similar to those that might be encountered in the target culture.

Teachers may find that the following guidelines will help them plan more effective lessons:

1. *Consider the content that is to be taught for a given class day.* Think in terms of themes, cultural contexts, and functional tasks to be mastered, as well as grammar and vocabulary. Plan a lesson that flows within the contexts you have identified, integrating the grammatical concepts, functions, vocabulary, and cultural information into the chapter themes. Avoid exercises that consist of nonsequiturs or unrelated sentence-length frames. Choose, instead, to embed the practice activity in larger discourse units: minidialogues, paragraphs, roleplays, and the like. For example, if you plan to teach interrogative words and expressions, consider how students can use questioning strategies to accomplish a real-world task that is coordinated with the theme of the unit or chapter. In a unit on travel, students can use the new interrogative structures to ask about train or plane schedules, obtain directions, or request hotel accommodations. In a unit relating to foods, students can practice asking about items on a restaurant menu, requesting prices in making purchases, or finding out about the culinary preferences of their classmates.

2. *Plan activities that will help students reach functional objectives.* Make activities student-centered rather than teacher-centered; that is, plan practice activities that involve *all* students actively during the class hour. Try to avoid lengthy explanations or one-to-one exchanges that leave most students unoccupied and bored. Students need to use the skills they are learning if they are to become more proficient; watching the teacher use the language is not nearly so beneficial to them. Small-group work, board work, dictation, paired interviews, and active listening practice are a few of the strategies that require all students to participate simultaneously and actively.

3. *Prepare an outline of what you intend to do during the class period.* It is helpful to write down an estimated time for each activity so that the lesson flows at a reasonable pace. (See, for example, the sample lesson plans in Chapter 3 for possible formats to use.) Beginning teachers may want to include detailed notes on their lesson plans, while more experienced teachers may function well with just a brief outline. Using index cards or small slips of paper enables teachers to consult their plans easily and unobtrusively during the lesson.

4. *Check for flow and integration of classroom activities.* Plan transitions that either make each activity a logical continuation of the one before it or make it clear that there will be a shift in focus. Sometimes it helps to explain briefly *why* students are doing certain activities; that is, let them see what benefits you hope they will derive from the practice you have planned. For example, a dictation exercise may be introduced by saying, "Now let's practice writing some of the things we've been learning to say. This will help reinforce the new material in your mind."

5. *Provide variety in classroom tasks.* Fifty minutes of the same thing—even if it's an interesting type of exercise—is not varied from the students' perspective. If course goals encompass the four skills, students should have opportunities to listen, write, read, and speak during the hour, both in whole-class and small-group activities. Having students work at the board, move around in a social-interaction game, pair up for interviews, or do role-plays for the rest of the class lends variety to the class hour. Variety gives the impression of a faster pace, which tends to enliven instruction for most learners.

6. *Evaluate your plan after the class is over.* Decide whether you would do the same things if you were to reteach the lesson, or if you would want to make some changes. Ask yourself how well students responded to the activities you planned and try to diagnose the causes of problems you encountered.

In addition to these suggestions for things to do in planning lessons, there are a few things that teachers should avoid doing:

1. *Don't expect students to carry out tasks for which they do not have the requisite knowledge or skill.* Keep in mind their current range of proficiency when planning language-practice activities. For listening and reading tasks, plan to use advance organizers and/or prelistening and prereading practice. For small-group work, plan guidelines for stdents to use as they practice together, as well as clear directions for the activity.

2. *Don't assume that students' performance will be error-free.* Remember that students in the lower ranges of proficiency will make many mistakes, especially when creating with the language. Use student errors as a means of diagnosing what they need in terms of feedback and instruction.

3. *Don't get bogged down in detailed discussions about the language.* If a student expresses interest in some minor detail, ask him or her to talk to you about it after class. Avoid lengthy and detailed grammar explanations or commentaries in English that take up valuable class time that could be used for practice *in the target language.*

4 *Don't assume all learners are alike or learn the same way.* Proficiency-oriented instruction needs to be flexible to accommodate different learner styles, personalities, and strategies.

• • • • • • • • • • • • *The Place of Formal Grammatical Instruction in a Proficiency-Oriented Lesson Plan*

In earlier chapters, a case was made for fostering the development of linguistic accuracy from the beginning of instruction when using a proficiency-oriented approach. Suggestions were made for providing corrective feedback to students so that their hypotheses about the way the new language operates could be shaped in the direction of the target-language norm. But how should students be introduced to the grammatical features of the language in the first place? What is the place of formal grammatical instruction in the proficiency-oriented curriculum?

Traditionally, two approaches to the teaching of grammar have been advocated by various methodologists and learning theorists: (1) an *inductive* approach, which encourages learners to draw conclusions about the underlying rules of the language from the many examples they see and practice, and (2) a *deductive* approach, which moves from the explicit statement of a rule to its application in many examples. Although practitioners and methodologists have, across the years, argued in favor of one approach or the other, it seems that a blend of the two might make the most sense. First, some learners respond best to inductive approaches, while others learn more quickly from deductive presentations. To respond to the needs and cognitive styles of all of our students, we need to be flexible in our instructional approach. Secondly, some grammatical points are more complex than others, and might best be taught deductively, at least to adult learners. Simpler structures, on the other hand, might be grasped more quickly through an inductive presentation.

Whatever type of presentation is chosen for a given class day, the "formal grammar lesson" should be kept as brief and as uncomplicated as possible, at least in lower-level language courses, to ensure that most of the class hour can be spent on active, creative language practice. Teachers who engage in lengthy explanations quite often monopolize class time, bore the students who already understand the concept, and confuse the rest. In addition, such behavior sends a clear message that the focus of the lesson is on talking *about* the language rather than talking *in* the language, an approach that is not congruent with communicative goals.

One approach that allows the teacher to focus on particular structures in a lesson, while encouraging active communication, is to place responsibility for learning about the structures primarily on the student. This procedure may work best with college-level students, who are developing in maturity and responsibility for their own learning. In this approach, students are asked to read grammatical explanations and other lesson content before coming to class. The teacher then uses class time for verifying, through active practice, that the material has been understood. The following description of a lesson in a beginning college-level French class illustrates how this approach might work. In this sample lesson, students are working on a chapter of their beginning text,[1] the context for which is the theme of student housing. Students are practicing the function of description, using simple structures and vocabulary. The grammatical feature to be practiced for this particular class hour is the use of the indefinite article in negative sentences.

9:00–9:05 **Warmup activity.** The teacher reviews the previous day's work by asking students to describe their rooms in a simple question-answer exchange. The teacher asks various people in the class if they have certain objects in their rooms, what color their rooms are, and what sorts of things they like to do in their rooms. The teacher follows up each initial question to a given student with two or three related questions, creating the feeling of a conversation rather than an interrogation.

9:05–9:10 **Introduction of the grammatical structure.** The teacher asks students to turn to a page in their text, where a short description of a student's dorm room is given. A drawing shows a student looking in a bewildered fashion around his new living quarters near the university. In this description, students are introduced to negative sentences as follows:

Il y a une lampe, mais pas d'électricité. (There is a lamp, but no electricity.)

Il y a un lavabo, mais pas d'eau chaude. (There is a sink, but no water.)

etc. (p. 85)

Students are asked to complete similar sentences about the room, looking at another illustration. For example, they can see that there is a table, but no chair, a bookcase, but no books, etc. In this way, they show that they understand the negative construction through their active use of it in a simple exercise.

9:10–9:15   **Student explanation of the grammatical principle.** The teacher then asks students to explain how the negative sentences they have just created are different from the affirmative ones. As students attempt to give a rule, the teacher can see if they have understood the concept. (Because students formulate the rule after seeing various examples of the structure in use, this type of presentation represents an inductive approach to the teaching of grammar.) If students seem to have understood the concept, the rest of the class time is spent in active practice, both oral and written. If they have not understood, the teacher gives a concise explanation, using the sentences just practiced as an illustration. (This second phase of the explanation, if necessary, represents a deductive approach, since the teacher first explains the rule and then illustrates it with examples.)

9:15–9:35   **Active practice: oral.** Students work through a variety of contextualized exercises in the text, practicing the new negative construction while describing various scenes in the dorm, in the classroom, on campus, and in the town. Some of these exercises are done in a whole-class format, while others are done with students working together in pairs. The teacher circulates to help and explain, based on individual needs. It is during this phase of the lesson that students who are still unsure about how the concept works can ask specific questions. The teacher can also listen carefully to see if students are using the new structure appropriately, thereby verifying that they have understood the concept. If many students seem to be confused about the same exercise or are making similar mistakes, the teacher may want to interrupt the practice briefly to explain the concept further. Or the teacher may provide a correct model of the exercise in question and have the students repeat accordingly.

9:35–9:42   **Active practice: written.** The teacher uses a dictation passage in which affirmative and negative sentences are used to describe a new setting—this time, a student room in a private home. Students write the description verbatim and then check their own text against a model text distributed by the teacher.

An alternative to this "seat dictation" is a board exercise in which as many students as possible are sent to the board and asked to write the dictated material while the remaining students write at their seats. This exercise might consist of a series of questions that students write and then answer in the negative or some other type of manipulative practice. As students write at the board, the teacher can see at a glance whether the class has understood the concept underlying the exercise and can point out appropriate responses for all to see and check against their own. If necessary, the teacher can briefly explain why a given answer is appropriate or inappropriate, reinforcing the new concept once more.

9:42–9:50 **Conversational practice.** Students use conversation cards (see Chapter 6) to ask and answer personalized questions, many of which will require negative responses. In this manner, they finish the hour in group practice, actively engaged in using the new grammatical concept in an open-ended exchange.

In this lesson, the teacher spends a minimum of class time on an exposition of rules and makes students responsible for the majority of the talking that takes place. Students are asked to provide the rules themselves, and all then actively engage in contextualized practice. Very few students will have an opportunity to sit quietly while other students answer questions, because virtually all of the class time requires active participation by all class members. Yet the concern for developing accuracy is clearly a cornerstone of this particular lesson, since the practice centers on understanding and using a new structure correctly to convey a variety of messages relating to the chapter theme. Thus, grammar is "taught," but in a way that avoids making it the most obtrusive aspect of the lesson or focusing on structure at the expense of meaning.

In the lesson for the following day, the teacher will incorporate some cultural information into the lesson, using slides of student housing taken in France and talking briefly about how student living arrangements in France might differ from those in the United States. Students will then comment on the slides in the target language, using the new negative construction in their description when appropriate.

Increasing Focus on Students' Interests

To plan lessons that will appeal to students' interests and needs, teachers need to ask students for their input and involve them in shaping instruction. This can be accomplished on the first day of class by having students fill out an information sheet that inquires into their backgrounds and interests in second-language learning.

Another way to create a student-centered atmosphere early in instruction is to use a get-acquainted activity the first day of class. If this is the first course in the language, students can begin by learning how to greet one another and introduce themselves and then practice in small groups. The teacher, in introducing and drilling phrases like "What is your name?" or "Where are you from?", can then ask students to recall information about their classmates as a follow-up activity. In the first few weeks of instruction, much can be learned about students' preferences and interests in paired interviews and report-back activities.

For students who have had previous courses in the language, a good first-day activity is an interview in the target language with a classmate, followed by a report-back phase. The pairs can then introduce each other to the rest of the class.

A third way to get to know students is through short individual interviews, either when students come in for extra help or when they take oral tests. Many teachers find that students are much more motivated and cooperative after an informal visit, especially if the teacher and student both share information about themselves and their interests.

Another essential way in which teachers can obtain student input is through course evaluation. Most course evaluations are solicited at the end of the term and filled out anonymously so that students feel free to express their true opinions. Sometimes, however, it is a good idea to ask students for an informal evaluation earlier in the term, especially when the course or the materials are new. A brief survey instrument can be designed, for example, asking students which classroom activities they consider most helpful, most interesting, least helpful, and least interesting, with room for open-ended commentary. A sample survey instrument of this type is provided in Appendix C (see Form 1).

An example of an end-of-course evaluation form is also provided in Appendix C (see Form 2). Teachers may wish to use other formats, such as open-ended questions, or include other aspects of the course for comment. In any course evaluation, it is a good idea to allow students to comment freely by including at least one or two open-ended questions.

Record Keeping: Setting up the Grade Book

There are many ways in which teachers can record grades, homework assignments completed, attendance, and class participation. The format is far less important than the fact that careful records are kept. Students have a right to know why they receive the grades they do, and the teacher needs to be ready to support those grades in the event that questions arise.

One way to set up a grade book is shown in Illustration 10.2.

This sample grading system is based on the French 101 course described in Illustration 10.1. Grades are assigned according to the percentages, or weightings, illustrated on that sheet. Thus, the three major exams comprise 30% of the course grade; the four quizzes count 15%; the two oral exams, 15%; the compositions, 10%; and the daily homework and class participation grade, 10%. The final exam makes up the remaining 20% of the grade.

The teacher keeps a record of daily participation by recording absences as well as brief notes about in-class oral work (such as a "+" for active participation or a "–" for lack of participation) on the perforated half-pages represented on the left-hand portion of page 1 of the grade book. From these notes, twice a term (at midterm and at term's end), he or she then assigns a daily participation grade. These grades, with the semester average computed from them, are found in the column marked "Classwork" in Illustration 10.2. This daily participation grade is relatively subjective, but a numerical score can be calculated by taking the subjective rating of a student's classwork in terms of A+, A, A–, B+, B, B–, etc., and converting it to a grade of 100, 95, 92, 88, 85, 82, etc.

Homework that has been turned in is recorded next. In this particular course, students have a self-correcting workbook. They receive credit for a homework assignment if it has been done carefully and completely and has been self-corrected using a contrasting ink color. This procedure is used to encourage students to monitor their own work and take responsibility for careful completion of written assignments. Students handing in all seven homework assignments receive a final homework grade of 100. One missing assignment receives a grade of 90, two missing assignments receive a grade of 80, and so on.

Four quiz grades, averaged together at the end of the term, represent another component of the course. Seven compositions, graded with numerical equivalents for A+, A, A–, B+, B, B–, etc., comprise the next section of the record book. Three unit tests are recorded and averaged in the next set of columns, and two oral tests are recorded last. The final set of columns are reserved for the end-of-course calculation of grades. In this system, each component of the course receives a separate weight (e.g., 10% for daily class work, 10% for compositions, 15% for quizzes, 20% for the final exam, etc.). Grades are calculated by multiplying the weight times the average grade (based on 100 points) for each component. Scores are rounded off to the nearest whole number. The total of these component scores, including the final exam score in the last column, is then calculated, and a grade of A, B, C, etc., is assigned.

One advantage of such a grading system is that it allows the teacher to balance a number of factors in calculating a given student's grade, allowing strengths the student has in certain skill areas to compensate for weaknesses in others. In addition, the weightings can be manipulated to reflect course goals and expectations, given the general proficiency level of the students. For example, written work may receive a lower weighting in an elementary course than in a course on advanced grammar and composition. Similarly, spoken skills may be weighted more heavily in a fourth-semester "track" course that emphasizes conversation than in a parallel course emphasizing all four skills. In any course, a defensible plan for assigning grades and careful records of work received are essential. Above all, students appreciate knowing how they are being evaluated, and they will perceive the teacher as being more effective and fair if careful records are kept of their progress.

FALL 199___
FRENCH 101

NAME		DEC 2-5 M T W T F S	DEC 9-13 M T W T F S	CLASSWORK — WEEKS 1-8	WEEKS 9-14	AVERAGE	HOMEWORK ASSIGNMENT — CHAP 1	CHAP 2	CHAP 3	CHAP 4	CHAP 5	CHAP 6	CHAP 7	GRADE	QUIZZES — QUIZ 1	QUIZ 2	QUIZ 3	QUIZ 4
BROWN, L.	1	Ab —	Ab Ab	75	70	72.5	✓	✓	✓	0	0	✓	0	70	80	75	72	70
	2																	
CLARK, R.	3	+ +	+ ++	85	90	87.5	✓	✓	✓	✓	0	✓		90	90	88	88	85
	4																	
EVANS, M.	5	+	+	85	85	85	✓	✓	✓	✓	✓	✓	✓	100	95	90	92	88
	6																	
LEE, S.	7	Ab Ab	—	90	70	80	✓	✓	✓	0	0	✓	✓	80	90	85	70	72
	8																	
(ETC)	9																	
.	10																	
.	11																	
.	12																	

CONVERSION:

7 COMPLETED	= 100 PTS.
6 "	= 90 PTS.
5 "	= 80 PTS.
4 "	= 70 PTS.
3 "	= 60 PTS.
0-2 "	= 0-50 PTS.

Illustration 10.2
Sample format for
grade book

SUMMARY

	COMPOSITIONS									EXAMS					ORAL TESTS			FINAL EXAM		DAILY	COMPOS.	QUIZZES	EXAMS	ORAL	FINAL	AVERAGE	FINAL GRADE
	CHAP 1	CHAP 2	CHAP 3	CHAP 4	CHAP 5	CHAP 6	CHAP 7	AVERAGE		EXAM I	EXAM II	EXAM III	AVG.		EXAM I	EXAM II	AVG		%	10	10	15	30	15	20		
1	75	80	75	75	70	75	75	75		83	73	78	78		85	75	80	82	1	7	7	11	23	12	16	76	C
2																			2								
3	85	90	90	80	85	90	90	87		80	79	90	83		90	86	98	90	3	9	9	13	25	13	18	87	B
4																			4								
5	95	90	95	95	85	90	95	92		96	90	92	93		95	91	93	92	5	9	9	14	28	14	18	92	A
6																			6								
7	95	95	90	80	75	75	80	84		95	80	75	83		90	80	85	84	7	8	8	12	25	13	17	83	B
8																			8								
9																			9								
10																			10								
11																			11								
12																			12								
13																			13								
14																			14								
15																			15								
16																			16								
17																			17								
18																			18								
19																			19								
20																			20								
21																			21								
22																			22								
23																			23								
24																			24								
25																			25								
26																			26								
27																			27								
28																			28								
29																			29								
30																			30								
31																			31								
32																			32								
33																			33								
34																			34								
35																			35								
36																			36								
37																			37								
38																			38								
39																			39								
40																			40								
41																			41								
42																			42								
43																			43								
44																			44								
45																			45								
46																			46								

• • • • • • • • • • • • **In Conclusion**

There is no doubt that the recent focus on proficiency as an organizing principle has stimulated a great deal of interest among theorists and practitioners in the language teaching profession in the last several years. As we saw in Chapter 1, the *ACTFL Guidelines* and associated assessment procedures such as the OPI have been enthusiastically received by some, and challenged by others.

It is through responsible discussion and debate, as well as through data-based research studies, that inadequacies in the present guidelines can be brought to light and improvements can be made. Some possible directions for research in the coming years include further studies to validate the oral proficiency interview procedure and obtain additional reliability data, research projects using this instrumentation to investigate outcomes of various programs—including study-abroad experiences—and further research into language acquisition and learning processes, all of which should shed additional light on appropriate ways to assess language proficiency.

It is our hope, as language teaching professionals, that each successive stage in this process will bring us closer to our goal of developing a common metric for measuring student progress, thereby allowing us to communicate more clearly with one another and with the public about what our programs offer. As we learn more about language proficiency through concentrated research and development efforts, we will undoubtedly discover better ways to teach and test language skills. Our work on developing more effective ways to infuse significant cultural content into the curriculum must also continue, so that American students leave their language learning experience with a greater understanding of other peoples and cultures. In recent years, when accountability and excellence in education have received so much public attention, foreign language teachers are regaining greater visibility, respect, and support in the eyes of the nation. We must continue to strive for excellence as we refine and interpret our approaches to language teaching in the decades ahead.

Notes
1. The text on which the sample lesson plan is based is Muyskens et al. 1982.

• • • • • • • • • • • • **Activities for Review and Discussion**

1. Discuss how instructors might go about setting goals for a language program at either the secondary or postsecondary level.
2. What are some of the instructional factors that need to be considered in curriculum planning? How might these factors be articulated from course to course, both horizontally (i.e., among courses at the same level) and vertically (among courses at different levels)?

3. Using the guidelines for text selection presented in this chapter (see pp. 484–85), or using guidelines you have developed yourself, evaluate one or several foreign language textbooks that you might consider using in a course you teach or will be teaching soon.

4. If possible, obtain a course syllabus for a beginning- or intermediate-level language course with which you are familiar. Based on your understanding of the concepts presented in this book, would you design the syllabus differently? If so, how would you change it? Give a rationale for your answer.

5. Using a textbook with which you are familiar, write out a lesson plan for a given day. Begin with a statement of objectives that you want your students to accomplish by the end of the hour. Then design activities that you feel will best accomplish these goals. Be sure to indicate how much time each activity would take, in your estimation. Check for flow and integration of activities, as well as for thematic and/or contextual unity in your lesson. Be sure to include a variety of activities to ensure a good pace and a high level of interest. You may want to compare your lesson plan with the ones other members of your class have prepared for the same material.

6. Make a list of characteristics you think are typical of effective language teachers. Base your list on your own personal experience, as well as on principles of good teaching you have learned in this book. Compare your list of characteristics with those of others in your class.

• • • • • • • • • • • *References*

Bragger, Jeannette D. "The Development of Oral Proficiency." In A. Omaggio, ed., *Proficiency, Curriculum, Articulation: The Ties That Bind.* Middlebury, VT: Northeast Conference, 1985.

Galloway, Vicki. Personal communication. [cited in Medley 1985.]

Medley, Frank W., Jr. "Designing the Proficiency-Based Curriculum." In A. Omaggio, ed., *Proficiency, Curriculum, Articulation: The Ties That Bind.* Middlebury, VT: Northeast Conference, 1985.

Muyskens, Judith A., Alice C. Omaggio, Claudine Chalmers, Claudette Imberton, and Philippe Almeras. *Rendez-vous: An Invitation to French.* New York: Random House, 1982.

Strasheim, Lorraine A. "Achieving Curriculum Fit for that 'Horrible' Second year." In P. Westphal, ed., *Strategies for Foreign Language Teaching.* Report of the Central States Conference on the Teaching of Foreign Languages. Lincolnwood, IL: National Textbook Company, 1984.

A

ACTFL Proficiency Guidelines

The 1986 proficiency guidelines represent a hierarchy of global characterizations of integrated performance in speaking, listening, reading and writing. Each description is a representative, not an exhaustive, sample of a particular range of ability, and each level subsumes all previous levels, moving from simple to complex in an "all-before-and-more" fashion.

Because these guidelines identify stages of proficiency, as opposed to achievement, they are not intended to measure what an individual has achieved through specific classroom instruction but rather to allow assessment of what an individual can and cannot do, regardless of where, when, or how the language has been learned or acquired; thus, the words "learned" and "acquired" are used in the broadest sense. These guidelines are not based on a particular linguistic theory or pedagogical method, since the guidelines are proficiency-based, as opposed to achievement-based, and are intended to be used for global assessment.

The 1986 guidelines should not be considered the definitive version, since the construction and utilization of language proficiency guidelines is a dynamic, interactive process. The academic sector, like the government sector, will continue to refine and update the criteria periodically to reflect the needs of the users and the advances of the profession. In this vein, ACTFL owes a continuing debt to the creators of the 1982 provisional proficiency guidelines and, of course, to the members of the Interagency Language Roundtable Testing Committee, the creators of the government's Language Skill Level Descriptions.

ACTFL would like to thank the following individuals for their contributions on this current guidelines project: Heidi Byrnes, James Child, Nina Levinson, Pardee Lowe, Jr., Seiichi Makino, Irene Thompson, and A. Ronald Walton.

These proficiency guidelines are the product of grants from the U.S. Department of Education.

Generic Descriptions—Speaking

Novice The Novice level is characterized by the ability to communicate minimally with learned material.

Novice-Low Oral production consists of isolated words and perhaps a few high-frequency phrases. Essentially no functional communicative ability.

Novice-Mid Oral production continues to consist of isolated words and learned phrases within very predictable areas of need, although quantity is increased. Vocabulary is sufficient only for handling simple, elementary needs and expressing basic courtesies. Utterances rarely consist of more than two or three words and show frequent long pauses and repetition of interlocutor's words. Speaker may have some difficulty producing even the simplest utterances. Some Novice-Mid speakers will be understood only with great difficulty.

Novice-High Able to satisfy partially the requirements of basic communicative exchanges by relying heavily on learned utterances but occasionally expanding these through simple recombinations of their elements. Can ask questions or make statements involving learned material. Shows signs of spontaneity although this falls short of real autonomy of expression. Speech continues to consist of learned utterances rather than of personalized, situationally adapted ones. Vocabulary centers on areas such as basic objects, places, and most common kinship terms. Pronunciation may still be strongly influenced by first language. Errors are frequent and, in spite of repetition, some Novice-High speakers will have difficulty being understood even by sympathetic interlocutors.

Intermediate The Intermediate level is characterized by the speaker's ability to:
—create with the language by combining and recombining learned elements, though primarily in a reactive mode;
—initiate, minimally sustain, and close in a simple way basic communicative tasks; and
—ask and answer questions.

Intermediate-Low Able to handle successfully a limited number of interactive, task-oriented and social situations. Can ask and answer questions, initiate and respond to simple statements and maintain face-to-face conversation, although in a highly restricted manner and with much linguistic inaccuracy. Within these limitations, can perform such tasks as introducing self, ordering a meal, asking directions, and making purchases. Vocabulary is adequate to express only the most elementary needs. Strong interference from native language may occur. Misunderstandings frequently arise, but with repetition, the Intermediate-Low speaker can generally be understood by sympathetic interlocutors.

Intermediate-Mid Able to handle successfully a variety of uncomplicated, basic and communicative tasks and social situations. Can talk simply about self and family members. Can ask and answer questions and participate in simple conversations on topics beyond the most immediate needs; e.g., personal history and leisure time activities. Utterance length increases slightly, but speech may continue to be characterized by frequent long pauses, since the smooth incorporation of even basic conversational strategies is often hindered as the speaker struggles to create appropriate language forms. Pronunciation may continue to be strongly influenced by first language and fluency may still be strained. Although misunderstandings still arise, the Intermediate-Mid speaker can generally be understood by sympathetic interlocutors.

Intermediate-High Able to handle successfully most uncomplicated communicative tasks and social situations. Can initiate, sustain, and close a general conversation with a number of strategies appropriate to a range of circumstances and topics, but errors are evident. Limited vocabulary still necessitates hesitation and may bring about slightly unexpected circumlocution. There is emerging evidence of connected discourse, particularly for simple narration and/or description. The Intermediate-High speaker can generally be understood even by interlocutors not accustomed to dealing with speakers at this level, but repetition may still be required.

Advanced The Advanced level is characterized by the speaker's ability to:
—converse in a clearly participatory fashion;
—initiate, sustain, and bring to closure a wide variety of communicative tasks, including those that require an increased ability to convey meaning with diverse language strategies due to a complication or an unforeseen turn of events;
—satisfy the requirements of school and work situations; and
—narrate and describe with paragraph-length connected discourse.

Advanced Able to satisfy the requirements of everyday situations and routine school and work requirements. Can handle with confidence but not with facility complicated tasks and social situations, such as elaborating, complaining, and apologizing. Can narrate and describe with some details, linking sentences together smoothly. Can communicate facts and talk casually about topics of current public and personal interest, using general vocabulary. Shortcomings can often be smoothed over by communicative strategies, such as pause fillers, stalling devices, and different rates of speech. Circumlocution which arises from vocabulary or syntactic limitations very often is quite successful, though some groping for words may still be evident. The Advanced-level speaker can be understood without difficulty by native interlocutors.

Advanced-Plus   Able to satisfy the requirements of a broad variety of everyday, school, and work situations. Can discuss concrete topics relating to particular interests and special fields of competence. There is emerging evidence of ability to support opinions, explain in detail, and hypothesize. The Advanced-Plus speaker often shows a well developed ability to compensate for an imperfect grasp of some forms with confident use of communicative strategies, such as paraphrasing and circumlocution. Differentiated vocabulary and intonation are effectively used to communicate fine shades of meaning. The Advanced-Plus speaker often shows remarkable fluency and ease of speech but under the demands of Superior-level, complex tasks, language may break down or prove inadequate.

Superior   The Superior level is characterized by the speaker's ability to:
—participate effectively in most formal and informal conversations on practical, social, professional, and abstract topics; and
—support opinions and hypothesize using native-like discourse strategies.

Superior   Able to speak the language with sufficient accuracy to participate effectively in most formal and informal conversations on practical, social, professional, and abstract topics. Can discuss special fields of competence and interest with ease. Can support opinions and hypothesize, but may not be able to tailor language to audience or discuss in depth highly abstract or unfamiliar topics. Usually the Superior level speaker is only partially familiar with regional or other dialectical variants. The Superior level speaker commands a wide variety of interactive strategies and shows good awareness of discourse strategies. The latter involves the ability to distinguish main ideas from supporting information through syntactic, lexical and suprasegmental features (pitch, stress, intonation). Sporadic errors may occur, particularly in low-frequency structures and some complex high-frequency structures more common to formal writing, but no patterns of error are evident. Errors do not disturb the native speaker or interfere with communication.

Generic Descriptions—Listening

These guidelines assume that all listening tasks take place in an authentic environment at a normal rate of speech using standard or near-standard norms.

Novice-Low | Understanding is limited to occasional isolated words, such as cognates, borrowed words, and high-frequency social conventions. Essentially no ability to comprehend even short utterances.

Novice-Mid | Able to understand some short, learned utterances, particularly where context strongly supports understanding and speech is clearly audible. Comprehends some words and phrases from simple questions, statements, high-frequency commands and courtesy formulae about topics that refer to basic personal information or the immediate physical setting. The listener requires long pauses for assimilation and periodically requests repetition and/or a slower rate of speech.

Novice-High | Able to understand short, learned utterances and some sentence-length utterances, particularly where context strongly supports understanding and speech is clearly audible. Comprehends words and phrases from simple questions, statements, high-frequency commands and courtesy formulae. May require repetition, rephrasing and/or a slowed rate of speech for comprehension.

Intermediate-Low | Able to understand sentence-length utterances which consist of recombinations of learned elements in a limited number of content areas, particularly if strongly supported by the situational context. Content refers to basic personal background and needs, social conventions and routine tasks, such as getting meals and receiving simple instructions and directions. Listening tasks pertain primarily to spontaneous face-to-face conversations. Understanding is often uneven; repetition and rewording may be necessary. Misunderstandings in both main ideas and details arise frequently.

Intermediate-Mid | Able to understand sentence-length utterances which consist of recombinations of learned utterances on a variety of topics. Content continues to refer primarily to basic personal background and needs, social conventions and somewhat more complex tasks, such as lodging, transportation, and shopping. Additional content areas include some personal interests and activities, and a greater diversity of instructions and directions. Listening tasks not only pertain to spontaneous face-to-face conversations but also to short routine telephone conversations and some deliberate speech, such as simple announcements and reports over the media. Understanding continues to be uneven.

Intermediate-High | Able to sustain understanding over longer stretches of connected discourse on a number of topics pertaining to different times and places; however, understanding is inconsistent due to failure to grasp main ideas and/or details. Thus, while topics do not differ significantly from those of an Advanced level listener, comprehension is less in quantity and poorer in quality.

Advanced   Able to understand main ideas and most details of connected discourse on a variety of topics beyond the immediacy of the situation. Comprehension may be uneven due to a variety of linguistic and extralinguistic factors, among which topic familiarity is very prominent. These texts frequently involve description and narration in different time frames or aspects, such as present, nonpast, habitual, or imperfective. Texts may include interviews, short lectures on familiar topics, and news items and reports primarily dealing with factual information. Listener is aware of cohesive devices but may not be able to use them to follow the sequence of thought in an oral text.

Advanced-Plus   Able to understand the main ideas of most speech in a standard dialect; however, the listener may not be able to sustain comprehension in extended discourse which is propositionally and linguistically complex. Listener shows an emerging awareness of culturally implied meanings beyond the surface meanings of the text but may fail to grasp sociocultural nuances of the message.

Superior   Able to understand the main ideas of all speech in a standard dialect, including technical discussion in a field of specialization. Can follow the essentials of extended discourse which is propositionally and linguistically complex, as in academic/professional settings, in lectures, speeches, and reports. Listener shows some appreciation of aesthetic norms of target language, of idioms, colloquialisms, and register shifting. Able to make inferences within the cultural framework of the target language. Understanding is aided by an awareness of the underlying organizational structure of the oral text and includes sensitivity for its social and cultural references and its effective overtones. Rarely misunderstands but may not understand excessively rapid, highly colloquial speech or speech that has strong cultural references.

Distinguished   Able to understand all forms and styles of speech pertinent to personal, social and professional needs tailored to different audiences. Shows strong sensitivity to social and cultural references and aesthetic norms by processing language from within the cultural framework. Texts include theater plays, screen productions, editorials, symposia, academic debates, public policy statements, literary readings, and most jokes and puns. May have difficulty with some dialects and slang.

Generic Descriptions—Reading

These guidelines assume all reading texts to be authentic and legible.

Novice-Low   Able occasionally to identify isolated words and/or major phrases when strongly supported by context.

Novice-Mid   Able to recognize the symbols of an alphabetic and/or syllabic writing system and/or a limited number of characters in a system that uses characters. The reader can identify an increasing number of highly contextualized words and/or phrases including cognates and borrowed words, where appropriate. Material understood rarely exceeds a single phrase at a time, and rereading may be required.

Novice-High   Has sufficient control of the writing system to interpret written language in areas of practical need. Where vocabulary has been learned, can read for instructional and directional purposes standardized messages, phrases or expressions, such as some items on menus, schedules, timetables, maps, and signs. At times, but not on a consistent basis, the Novice-High level reader may be able to derive meaning from material at a slightly higher level where context and/or extralinguistic background knowledge are supportive.

Intermediate-Low   Able to understand main ideas and/or some facts from the simplest connected texts dealing with basic personal and social needs. Such texts are linguistically noncomplex and have a clear underlying internal structure, for example chronological sequencing. They impart basic information about which the reader has to make only minimal suppositions or to which the reader brings personal interest and/or knowledge. Examples include messages with social purposes or information for the widest possible audience, such as public announcements and short, straightforward instructions dealing with public life. Some misunderstandings will occur.

Intermediate-Mid   Able to read consistently with increased understanding simple connected texts dealing with a variety of basic and social needs. Such texts are still linguistically noncomplex and have a clear underlying internal structure. They impart basic information about which the reader has to make minimal suppositions and to which the reader brings personal interest and/or knowledge. Examples may include short, straightforward descriptions of persons, places, and things written for a wide audience.

Intermediate-High   Able to read consistently with full understanding simple connected texts dealing with basic personal and social needs about which the reader has personal interest and/or knowledge. Can get some main ideas and information from texts at the next higher level featuring description and narration. Structural complexity may interfere with comprehension; for example, basic grammatical relations may be misinterpreted and temporal references may rely primarily on lexical items. Has some difficulty with the cohesive factors in discourse, such as matching pronouns with referents. While texts do not differ significantly from those at the Advanced level, comprehension is less consistent. May have to read material several times for understanding.

Advanced   Able to read somewhat longer prose of several paragraphs in length, particularly if presented with a clear underlying structure. The prose is predominantly in familiar sentence patterns. Reader gets the main ideas and facts and misses some details. Comprehension derives not only from situational and subject matter knowledge but from increasing control of the language. Texts at this level include descriptions and narrations such as simple short stories, news items, bibliographical information, social notices, personal correspondence, routinized business letters and simple technical material written for the general reader.

Advanced-Plus   Able to follow essential points of written discourse at the Superior level in areas of special interest or knowledge. Able to understand parts of texts which are conceptually abstract and linguistically complex, and/or texts which treat unfamiliar topics and situations, as well as some texts which involve aspects of target-language culture. Able to comprehend the facts to make appropriate inferences. An emerging awareness of the aesthetic properties of language and of its literary styles permits comprehension of a wider variety of texts, including literary. Misunderstandings may occur.

Superior   Able to read with almost complete comprehension and at normal speed expository prose on unfamiliar subjects and a variety of literary texts. Reading ability is not dependent on subject matter knowledge, although the reader is not expected to comprehend thoroughly texts which are highly dependent on knowledge of the target culture. Reads easily for pleasure. Superior-level texts feature hypotheses, argumentation and supported opinions and include grammatical patterns and vocabulary ordinarily encountered in academic/professional reading. At this level, due to the control of general vocabulary and structure, the reader is almost always able to match the meanings derived from extralinguistic knowledge with meanings derived from knowledge of the language, allowing for smooth and efficient reading of diverse texts. Occasional misunderstandings may still occur; for example, the reader may experience some difficulty with unusually complex structures and low-frequency idioms. At the Superior level the reader can match strategies, top-down or bottom-up, which are most appropriate to the text. (Top-down strategies rely on real-world knowledge and prediction based on genre and organizational scheme of the text. Bottom-up strategies rely on actual linguistic knowledge.) Material at this level will include a variety of literary texts, editorials, correspondence, general reports and technical material in professional fields. Rereading is rarely necessary, and misreading is rare.

Distinguished   Able to read fluently and accurately most styles and forms of the language pertinent to academic and professional needs. Able to relate inferences in the text to real-world knowledge and understand almost all sociolinguistic and cultural references by processing language from within the cultural framework. Able to understand a writer's use of nuance and subtlety. Can readily follow unpredictable turns of thoughts and author intent in such materials as sophisticated editorials, specialized journal articles, and literary texts such as novels, plays, poems, as well as in any subject matter area directed to the general reader.

Generic Descriptions—Writing

Novice-Low
: Able to form some letters in an alphabetic system. In languages whose writing systems use syllabaries or characters, writer is able to both copy and produce the basic strokes. Can produce romanization of isolated characters, where applicable.

Novice-Mid
: Able to copy or transcribe familiar words or phrases and reproduce some from memory. No practical communicative writing skills.

Novice-High
: Able to write simple fixed expressions and limited memorized material and some recombinations thereof. Can supply information on simple forms and documents. Can write names, numbers, dates, own nationality, and other simple autobiographical information as well as some short phrases and simple lists. Can write all the symbols in an alphabetic or syllable system or 50-100 characters or compounds in a character writing system. Spelling and representation of symbols (letters, syllables, characters) may be partially correct.

Intermediate-Low
: Able to meet limited practical writing needs. Can write short messages, postcards, and take down simple notes, such as telephone messages. Can create statements or questions within the scope of limited language experience. Material produced consists of recombinations of learned vocabulary and structures into simple sentences on very familiar topics. Language is inadequate to express in writing anything but elementary needs. Frequent errors in grammar, vocabulary, punctuation, spelling and information of nonalphabetic symbols, but writing can be understood by natives used to the writing of nonnatives.

Intermediate-Mid
: Able to meet a number of practical writing needs. Can write short, simple letters. Content involves personal preferences, daily routine, everyday events, and other topics grounded in personal experience. Can express present time or at least one other time frame or aspect consistently, e.g., non-past, habitual, imperfect. Evidence of control of the syntax of noncomplex sentences and basic inflectional morphology, such as declensions and conjugation. Writing tends to be a loose collection of sentences or sentence fragments on a given topic and provides little evidence of conscious organization. Can be understood by natives used to the writing of nonnatives.

Intermediate-High   Able to meet most practical writing needs and limited social demands. Can take notes in some detail on familiar topics and respond in writing to personal questions. Can write simple letters, brief synopses and paraphrases, summaries of biographical data, work and school experience. In those languages relying primarily on content words and time expressions to express time, tense, or aspect, some precision is displayed; where tense and/or aspect is expressed through verbal inflections, forms are produced rather consistently, but not always accurately. An ability to describe and narrate in paragraphs is emerging. Rarely uses basic cohesive elements, such as pronominal substitutions or synonyms in written discourse. Writing, though faulty, is generally comprehensible to natives used to the writing of nonnatives.

Advanced   Able to write routine social correspondence and join sentences in simple discourse of at least several paragraphs in length on familiar topics. Can write simple social correspondence, take notes, write cohesive summaries and resumes, as well as narratives and descriptions of a factual nature. Has sufficient writing vocabulary to express self simply with some circumlocution. May still make errors in punctuation, spelling, or the formation of nonalphabetic symbols. Good control of the morphology and the most frequently used syntactic structures, e.g., common word order patterns, coordination, subordination, but makes frequent errors in producing complex sentences. Uses a limited number of cohesive devices, such as pronouns, accurately. Writing may resemble literal translations from the native language, but a sense of organization (rhetorical structure) is emerging. Writing is understandable to natives not used to the writing of nonnatives.

Advanced-Plus   Able to write about a variety of topics with significant precision and in detail. Can write most social and informal business correspondence. Can describe and narrate personal experiences fully but has difficulty supporting points of view in written discourse. Can write about the concrete aspects of topics relating to particular interests and special fields of competence. Often shows remarkable fluency and ease of expression, but under time constraints and pressure writing may be inaccurate. Generally strong in either grammar or vocabulary, but not in both. Weakness and unevenness in one of the foregoing or in spelling or character writing formation may result in occasional miscommunication. Some misuse of vocabulary may still be evident. Style may still be obviously foreign.

Superior   Able to express self effectively in most formal and informal writing on practical, social and professional topics. Can write most types of correspondence, such as memos as well as social and business letters, and short research papers and statements of position in areas of special interest or in special fields. Good control of a full range of structures, spelling or nonalphabetic symbol production, and wide general vocabulary allow the writer to hypothesize and present arguments or points of view accurately and effectively. An underlying organization, such as chronological ordering, logical ordering, cause and effect, comparison, and thematic development is strongly evident, although not thoroughly executed and/or not totally reflecting target language patterns. Although sensitive to differences in formal and informal style, still may not tailor writing precisely to a variety of purposes and/or readers. Errors in writing rarely disturb natives or cause miscommunication.

Note: The *ACTFL Proficiency Guidelines,* developed by the American Council on the Teaching of Foreign Languages, are an academic analog to the government language proficiency level descriptions, originally developed by the Foreign Service Institute and currently revised and used by the various language schools participating in the Interagency Language Roundtable (ILR). The government level descriptions differ from the *ACTFL Guidelines* in that a number system is used to designate eleven levels of proficiency, ranging from 0 to 5 (0, 0+, 1, 1+, 2, 2+, 3, 3+, 4, 4+, and 5), whereas the *ACTFL Guidelines* use the terms Novice, Intermediate, Advanced, and Superior to designate proficiency levels. In addition, the categories of Novice and Intermediate are further subdivided into three categories: Low, Mid, and High; the Advanced level is subdivided into Advanced and Advanced Plus (corresponding to 2 and 2+ on the government scale); the Superior level comprises the government levels 3, 3+, 4, 4+ and 5. Further discussion of the correspondence between the government and academic scales can be found in Chapter 1.

B

Samples of Error Coding Procedures for Written Work

Studies by Kulhavey (1977), Higgs (1979), and Lalande (1982) tend to support the use of discovery procedures and coding devices in the correction of written work. Hendrickson (1980), in reviewing numerous studies on feedback, concludes that error correction of some type is valuable for adult learners in that it increases their awareness of the exact environment for applying grammatical rules and for discovering the precise semantic range of lexical items. However, more research on the correction of written work has to be done to clarify the role of various feedback mechanisms in this domain.

There is general agreement among researchers and practitioners that having the teacher straightforwardly correct every error on students' written work is not the most useful way of providing corrective feedback. This approach is time consuming and resembles editing more than it does correcting. Students may feel extremely discouraged if papers are continually returned to them with as many red marks as there are words on a page. There is also good reason to believe that by supplying the corrections themselves, teachers might actually be hindering the learners' progress in building proficiency in writing.

An alternative to overt correction of all errors is a selective approach, and the use of discovery techniques, such as those discussed in Chapter 7. Hendrickson (1980) believes that the students' proficiency level should be considered when choosing error-correction strategies: lower-level students may not be able to find their own errors and correct them, whereas students at higher levels of proficiency may be better able to do so. As Lalande's (1982) study shows, students whose proficiency in writing is intermediate or advanced may profit best from a cuing system whereby their errors are located for them but they are held responsible for finding solutions.

In using Lalande's system of cuing (the Error Awareness Sheet (EASE), to be used with the Essay Correction Code (ECCO)), teachers tally and record students' errors on successive writing assignments, thereby providing them with an individualized profile of their progress over time.

Error Awareness Sheet (EASE)
Name _____
Course/Section _____

	Essay #1	Essay #2		Essay #3	Essay #4	Essay #5
SV 2–3						
PP 3						
UN 3						
M 1–3						
WO 1–3						
NS 1–5						
? 1–5						
Aux 2						
G 1–2						
T 1–2						
X 1–2						
C 1						
L 1						
N 1						
Nag 1						
Ref 1						
Sp 1						
// 0–1						
+ 1–5						
Points Off						
Grade/R						
Total Errors						

	Time #1	Time #2	Time #3
Which *three* types of errors have you probably made the most on your last two essays?	a) _____ b) _____ c) _____	a) _____ b) _____ c) _____	a) _____ b) _____ c) _____

A student who frequently commits numerous errors in verb form, subject-verb agreement, and tense usage, for example, can see this trend clearly on such a chart and can thus be encouraged to watch particularly for this error type in subsequent work. If teachers wish to use a point system, they may deduct a variable number of points for each error, depending on the gravity they attach to it. For example, a student who has made two errors involving the principle parts of the verb (such as the stem) will receive two tally marks in the second large box in the first column and will

Essay Correction Code (ECCO)

Aux Use of an improper *auxiliary* verb, e.g., *haben* in place of *sein;* also included may be constructions involving *werden* or a modal verb (+ infinitive).

C A part of speech has been assigned the wrong *case.*

G Wrong *gender* assignment to a noun or pronoun, e.g., **Die Mädchen sieht schön aus.*

L A *lexical* or dictionary error, e.g., *wohnen* for *leben;* includes cognates.

M The verb has been placed into the wrong *mood;* usually subjunctive will need to be replaced by the indicative or vice versa.

N Incorrect *number* assignment to a noun or pronoun, e.g., **Er trägt zwei Buch.*

Nag *Noun-adjective-agreements* are faulty in some way, e.g., **Meiner guter Vater.*

NS A completely *new structure* is needed to convey the proper meaning, e.g., in the sentence **Paul hatte einen Vetter hieß Eduard*—the sentence may be corrected by using any one of several structural alternatives. The structure in need of replacement could be underlined.

PP *Principal part* of the verb is incorrect (usually the stem).

R *Rewrite* successfully completed.

Ref If written as a *reflexive* construction, change to non-reflexive or vice versa. The code may also indicate use of an incorrect reflexive pronoun.

Sp *Spelling* error, e.g., **Gestern kame er mit,* or **Ich kenne deisen Mann.*

SV *Subject-verb* agreement is faulty in some way, e.g., **Er kommen morgen.*

T *Tense* selection is in some way inappropriate; usually the student has not been consistent, e.g., **Er setzte sich an den Tisch, grüßt und bestellt ein Bier.*

UN *UNMÖGLICH!* No such word or construction exists in German; includes the use of English words where German versions are not known, e.g., **Ich studierte im Library.*

WO Any error involving *word order.*

X One or more words are missing and must be inserted (exception = reflexive pronouns).

+ Any especially nice touch for which the student may be awarded extra points, e.g., use of the subjunctive or passive.

// Double lines through a word indicate that it is not necessary and must be deleted, e.g., **Ich möchte nach Hause ~~zu~~ gehen.*

? A question mark adjacent to a word, clause, or sentence that is *underlined* indicates that the reviewer could make no sense of the passage whatsoever. The student should consult a teacher, native speaker, etc.

Please note: If the student commits the exact same error more than two times (e.g., he misspells *Fräulein* as *Fraulein*), then he shall not lose additional points and there shall be no additional tallies entered onto the EASE.

Source: Lalande 1982, pp. 148–149.

have 6 points deducted and recorded in the smaller box in the right-hand corner, since this type of error has a valence of 3. Other errors, such as WO (word order), have a variable valence of 1 to 3 points, depending on the comprehensibility of the faulty structure. The total number of points off can then be calculated at the base of the chart and a grade assigned based on the number, type, and gravity of errors recorded. The box designated "Grade/R" is used to record the grade on the original composition and to note whether or not the work was resubmitted with corrections (R = rewrite successfully completed).

The system for French depicted on the following page is somewhat less complex than the system used by Lalande. It is adapted from a charting

Error Tracking System: French

Nom _____

Assign-ment # →	Comp. #1	Comp. #2	Comp. #3	(etc.)											
AC	7	6	6												
E	8	4	1												
SP	12	9	6												
GN	4	2	0												
NB	0	1	0												
NEG	7	4	2												
VC	3	2	2												
ART	6	4	4												
SVA	9	7	5												
VF	1	3	1												
TN	/	/	/												
MD	/	/	/												
PP	/	/	/												
AA	7	7	5												
POS	/	3	3												
DOP	/	/	/												
IOP	/	/	/												
RP	/	/	/												
PRO	/	/	/												
ADV	2	/	1												
PR	4	5	5												
CONJ	2	/	1												
WO	5	4	4												
INC	2	1	1												

Key to Abbreviations

AC   Accent missing or wrong
E   Elision, failure to elide or inappropriate elision
SP   Spelling error
GN   Gender wrong
NB   Number wrong—singular/plural
NEG   Negative wrong, misplaced, missing
VC   Vocabulary wrong, word choice, missing words
ART   Article missing, wrong form used, wrong after negative, expression of quantity
SVA   Subject/verb agreement lacking
VF   Verb form-stem incorrect
TN   Tense incorrect
MD   Mood incorrect (indicative, imperative, or subjunctive)

PP   Past participle wrong—form or agreement
AA   Adjective agreement wrong
POS   Possessive adjective wrong or missing, lacks agreement
DOP   Direct object pronoun wrong or missing
IOP   Indirect object pronoun wrong/missing
RP   Reflexive pronoun wrong or missing
PRO   Other Pronoun—y or en
ADV   Adverb wrong or misplaced
PR   Preposition wrong or missing
CONJ   Conjunction wrong or missing
WO   Word order wrong
INC   Incomprehensible, due to structure of vocabulary choice that makes it difficult to pinpoint the error

Source: Omaggio 1981 (Adapted from Brown 1979).

system described by Brown (1979) to help students analyze and track their composition errors in English. Students record their own performance by counting up the number of errors in each category on a given written assignment and entering the numbers in the appropriate boxes. Teachers correct students' work using the error codes, underlining the error, and placing the code in the margin. In the sample below, the student has done three compositions thus far and has recorded the number of errors in each category for each assignment. For example, on Composition 1, the student made 7 accent errors, 8 elision errors, 12 spelling errors, and so forth. In subsequent compositions, the number of errors is slowly decreasing as the student begins to monitor the work more closely. Teachers can collect error charts periodically and, by glancing through them, identify common trends within a class. Using this information, the teacher can then design more targeted language-practice activities and review those concepts that seem to present the most difficulty.

References

Brown, Cheri. "Individualizing Error Analysis in the Composition Class." Paper presented at the Rocky Mountain Modern Language Association meeting, Albuquerque, NM, 1979.

Hendrickson, James M. "The Treatment of Error in Written Work." *The Modern Language Journal* 64 (1980): 216–21.

Higgs, T.V. "Coping with Composition." *Hispania* 62 (1979): 673–78

Kulhavey, R.W. "Feedback in Written Instruction." *Review of Educational Research* 47 (1977): 214.

Lalande, John F. "Reducing Composition Errors: An Experiment." *The Modern Language Journal* 66 (1982): 140–49.

Omaggio, Alice C. *Helping Learners Succeed: Activities for the Foreign Language Classroom.* Language in Education: Theory and Practice, no. 36. Washington, DC: Center for Applied Linguistics, 1981.

C

Forms Useful in Course Evaluation

Form 1 *Activities Evaluation Form*

We would like to have your input into the classroom activities we have been using in this course. Please indicate your reaction to the following:

1. Dictations
   Very useful _____
   Moderately useful __
   Not useful _____

   Comments _____
   _____
   _____

2. Conversation cards
   Very useful _____   Very Interesting _____
   Moderately useful __   Moderately interesting __
   Not useful _____   Not interesting _____

   Comments _____
   _____
   _____

3. Games/Group Activities
   Very useful _____   Very Interesting _____
   Moderately useful __   Moderately interesting __
   Not useful _____   Not interesting _____

   Comments _____
   _____
   _____

4. Paired Work on Exercises
   Very useful _____
   Moderately useful __
   Not useful _____

   Comments _____
   _____
   _____

What would you like to see us do in class that we are not presently doing? Please give details on the reverse side of this sheet.

What activity or activities would you like to see eliminated? Please explain on the reverse side of this sheet.

Form 2 *Course Evaluation Form*

1. Organization of class meeting

```
/_____/_____/_____/
```
|Noticeable lack of organization | Satisfactory organization | Exceptionally well organized |

2. Instructor's interest in subject

```
/_____/_____/_____/
```
| Interest seemed mild | Strongly interested | Intensely interested |

3. Knowledge of subject matter

```
/_____/_____/_____/
```
| Inadequate | Adequate for routine matters | Broad and thorough |

4. Quality of Instructor's French

```
/_____/_____/_____/
```
| Inadequate | Adequate skill | Excellent model for students |

5. Clarity of explanations

```
/_____/_____/_____/
```
| Usually not very clear | Usually clear | Always clear and complete |

6. How interesting were class sessions?

```
/_____/_____/_____/
```
| Usually dull | Mildly interesting | High level of interest |

7. Freshness of instructor's presentation

```
/_____/_____/_____/
```
| Follows a stale routine | Attempts to bring freshness to presentation | Uses a wide variety of techniques |

8. Tolerance and helpfulness

/_____/_____/_____/
Unconcerned about   Respects student opin- Encourages students/
student needs/opinions ion/available for help   eager to help

9. Classroom activities

/_____/_____/_____/
Usually a   Often of value   Usually very valuable
waste of time

10. Promptness of returning homework, quizzes, etc.

/_____/_____/_____/
Never prompt   Usually prompt   Always prompt

11. Feedback on homework and quizzes

/_____/_____/_____/
Left me uncertain   Usually explains Carefully goes over and
about mistakes   helps improve

GENERAL COMMENTS

1. What did you like best about your instructor?

2. What did you like least about your instructor?

3. What aspects of this course did you most enjoy?

4. What aspects do you think need improvement?

5. What are your impressions of the textbook? tapes? workbooks?

6. Do you think this course met the goals as stated at the outset? Please explain.

Source: Form 2 was developed by Prof. Constance K. Knop, Dept. of French and Italian, University of Wisconsin-Madison.

Text Permissions

Bransford, J.D., and Johnson, M.K., "Contextual Prerequisites for Understanding . . .," *Journal of Verbal Learning and Verbal Behavior.* (1972), courtesy of Academic Press.

Application of Oral Proficiency Testing to Foreign Language Instruction ;
Bacon, S. "Listening for Real in the Foreign Language Classroom." *Foreign Language Annals* 22, 6 (1989);
Buck, Byrnes, & Thompson, *The ACTFL Oral Proficiency Interview Tester Manual.* (1989);
Hague, Sally, Vocabulary Instruction: What L2 can Learn from L1, *Foreign Language Annals* 20, iii (1987);
Lund, R., "A Taxonomy for Teaching Second Language Listening." *Foreign Language Annals* 23, ii (1990);
Richmond, Edmun B. "Utilizing Proverbs as a Focal Point to Cultural Awareness and Communicative Competence: Illustrations from Africa". *Foreign Language Annals* 20, iii (1987), all courtesy of ACTFL.

Omaggio, Alice C., "Using Games and Simulations", courtesy of *Canadian Modern Language Review* 38 (1982)

Omaggio, Alice C., *Proficiency-oriented Classroom Testing.* (1983);
Gaudiani, C., *Teaching Composition in the Foreign Language Curriculum. Language in Education* vol. 43, (1981), courtesy of Center for Applied Linguistics.

Smith, M., *Vacances et week-ends à la ferme 1987,* Paris, Balland: (1988), courtesy of Editions Balland, Paris.

Liskin-Gasparro, J., *ETS Oral Proficiency Testing Manual.* (1982), courtesy of Educational Testing Service.

Barnett, Marva. " Writing as Process", courtesy of *French Review* 63, i (1989).

"Communicating in a Cultural Context: The Global Perspective". *Proceedings of the 1981 summer cross-cultural workshop for FL Teachers.* South Carolina State Department of Education;
"Communicating in a Cultural Context". ACTFL Master Lecture Series, Monterey, CA, Defense Language Institute (1984), courtesy of Vicki B. Galloway.

Tylène Transports Tourisme, Brochure: "Excursions au départ d'Aix-en-Provence", courtesy of Gérante Société, Tylène Transports Tourisme, Paris.

Muyskens, J., Omaggio, A., et. al. Exercise material from *Rendez-vous,* Random House, (1984);
Chung, Ulric. "Qu'est qu'on attend pour faire la fête?" (Excerpts from computer-adaptive video project), courtesy of Language Learning Lab, University of Illinois, Urbana, IL.

L'office de tourisme (Limousin), Brochure: "Séjours en campagne.", courtesy of Comité régional de tourisme du Limousin, France.

Coulont-Henderson, F., McKee, E., & Omaggio, A., *Kaléidoscope: Cahier d'exercises oraux et écrits.* McGraw Hill (1988);
Muyskens, J., Omaggio, A., et. al. Exercise material from *Rendez-vous,* Random House, (1982); McGraw-Hill (1990);
Omaggio, A., Chamberlain, J., et. al. Exercise material from *Kaléidoscope* (1984);
Rochester et al. *Bonjour, ça va?* Random House (1983);

Valdés et al. *Composición: Proceso y síntesis,* (l984), all courtesy of McGraw-Hill, New York.

Sample culture activities in German, courtesy of John Lalande.
Sample activities in Spanish, courtesy of Gail Guntermann.
Sample lesson plan, courtesy of Earl Stevick.
Sample course evaluation form, courtesy of Constance K. Knop.
Sample test items in Spanish, courtesy of Susan McMillen Villar and Fran Meuser Blincow.

Omaggio, Alice, *The Proficiency-Oriented Classroom,* in T. Higgs, Ed. *Teaching for Proficiency, The Organizing Principle,* NTC (1984), courtesy of National Textbook Company, Lincolnwood, IL.

Bachman, L., *Fundamental Considerations in Language Testing.* (1990);
Ellis, R. *Understanding Second Language Acquisition* (1985), courtesy of Oxford University Press, England.

Tarone, Elaine, *Conscious Communication Strategies in Interlanguage* (appeared in ON TESOL '77), courtesy of Teachers of English to Speakers of Other Languages.

Lalande, John. "Reducing Composition Errors: An Experiment", *Modern Language Journal* 66, ii (1982), courtesy of The University of Wisconsin Press, Madison, WI.
Weissenrieder, M., "Listening to the News in Spanish", courtesy of *Modern Language Journal* 71, i (1987)

Index